AF361436

THE HUMANITIES AND
THE DYNAMICS OF INCLUSION
SINCE WORLD WAR II

The Humanities and the Dynamics of Inclusion since World War II

Edited by David A. Hollinger

The Johns Hopkins University Press

BALTIMORE

The Johns Hopkins University Press
2715 North Charles Street
Baltimore, Maryland 21218-4363
www.press.jhu.edu

Library of Congress Cataloging-in-Publication Data
The humanities and the dynamics of inclusion since World War II / edited by David A. Hollinger.
 p. cm.
 Includes bibliographical references and index.
 ISBN 0-8018-8390-3 (hardcover : alk. paper)
 1. Humanities—Study and teaching (Higher)—United States.   2. Humanities—United States—History—20th century.   3. Learned institutions and societies—United States—History—20th century.   4. Learning and scholarship—United States—History—20th century.   5. Multicultural education—United States—History—20th century.   6. Education—Demographic aspects—United States—History—20th century.   7. Demography—United States—History—20th century. I. Hollinger, David A.
 AZ183.U5H839 2006
 001.3071'173—dc22   2005026651

A catalog record for this book is available from the British Library.

CONTENTS

THE HUMANITIES AND
THE DYNAMICS OF INCLUSION
SINCE WORLD WAR II

INTRODUCTION

DAVID A. HOLLINGER

THE ACADEMIC HUMANITIES in the United States after World War II were a major institutional apparatus for bringing evidence and reasoning to domains where the rules of evidence are strongly contested and the power of reason often doubted. These domains, on the periphery of an increasingly science-centered academic enterprise, embraced the messy, risk-intensive issues left aside by the more methodologically confident, rigor-displaying social sciences. These domains constituted the borderlands between *Wissenschaft* and opinion, between scholarship and ideology. Here in these borderlands, the demographic and cognitive boundaries of the entire academic enterprise were the least certain.

This book explores that ill-defined intellectual and social territory. At issue was not only the incorporation of what today are called underrepresented demographic groups. At issue, too, were the specific fields and subfields that would be included at the expense of others, the directions taken in expanding the study of foreign cultures in relation to the study of the United States itself, and the role of the academic humanities in American public discourse. Who was included in or excluded from the community of inquirers? What was within or beyond that community's subject matter? On what basis was this or that idea, text, project, or social group included or excluded? To what extent was scholarship expected to reflect the ethnoracial, religious, or gender group of which a scholar was a member?

These questions were presented to academic humanists after World War II by unprecedented opportunities to expand their ranks and to extend the scope of their operations. The sciences had their own "frontiers," justly if romantically celebrated in 1945 by Vannevar Bush's epic brief for the federal funding of research, *Science—The Endless Frontier*.[1] But many of the least clearly mapped cognitive and demographic frontiers of the larger, shared academic program of bringing evidence and reasoning to inquiry were confronted by humanists.

Before I indicate what this volume tells us about these borderlands and about the process by which humanists mapped, colonized, and organized them, I want to emphasize that the humanities experience after 1945 is a distinctive historical episode, not just another instantiation, under slightly different circumstances, of a virtually timeless set of behaviors and relationships. Questions about cognitive and demographic borders were not new in 1945, and it is too easy, in the wake of that insight, to assume that the boundary disputes and clarifications analyzed in this volume are merely repeats of old quarrels. Professors of humanities had not been obliged to deal with these questions so directly and persistently. Historically unique ideological and geopolitical conditions did much to create this obligation and to give it period-specific shape.

Ideologically, World War II itself, simply by being directed against overtly racist enemies, discredited the complacent practice of excluding from humanities faculties those individuals who were not of Anglo-Protestant background. The same prejudices operated also in the sciences and the professional schools during the 1920s and 1930s, but not as severely as in the humanities, where the strategic foundations of the culture were understood to be at stake. Geopolitically, the postwar engagement with the non-European world, significantly propelled by cold war concerns, greatly enlarged beyond the venerated Mediterranean and European pasts the inventory of cultures that humanists were invited to study and to teach. Asia, especially, but also Africa and Latin America were less easily ignored with a clear conscience.

These basic ideological and geopolitical transformations of the 1940s and 1950s forced new and sustained attention to questions of inclusion and exclusion. Later these same questions were underscored yet more vividly by domestic social movements on behalf of women and nonwhites and by quarrels about the impact of American power on populations in "developing" countries. These successive ideological and geopolitical challenges to traditional disciplinary agendas and constituencies helped make the period after World War II a distinctive episode. But there is more to it.

Academic humanists found themselves expected to serve a much larger segment of society. We all know that the humanities shared with the sciences and social sciences in the prodigious growth attendant on the increase of public funding provided by the G.I. Bill and later by the perceived imperatives of the cold war.[2] A much greater percentage of the population was attending college, which brought academic humanists into the leadership of designing and providing educational programs not simply for the elites, but for masses of Americans, for the "democratic society" heralded by leading educators of the period.[3] The founding of the National Endowment for the Humanities in 1965 helped consolidate the place of humanists in this "Academic Revolution," as the new prominence of a relatively autonomous teaching-and-research establishment in the American social, political, and economic order was termed by Christopher Jenks and David Riesman in a landmark book of 1968.[4] Much more was at stake than before in what humanists did. The social composition of communities of inquiry mattered more, as did the subject matter of research programs and the specific content of curricula.

And there was a yet more deeply qualitative dimension to the altered mission of academic humanists after World War II and to the specific setting in which they engaged issues of inclusion and exclusion. Professors in the disciplines that came by the early twentieth century to be called "the humanities"— a residual category that gained currency when administrators grouped fields that were not "sciences" or "social sciences" or even "arts"— had once known that their job was mainly to preserve culture, understood in its Arnoldian rather than its anthropological sense.[5] "Culture," as one of the most subtle historians of early twentieth-century America has explained, was then an idea of how people "ought to behave but did not."[6] Put more flatly: scholarship and teaching in the humanities disciplines were to facilitate the appreciation and emulation of cultural treasures, which embraced not only the finest works of literature and the arts, but the soundest of philosophical ideas and the great accomplishments in the public affairs of the past. Rigorous philological and archival work was consistent with this broadly ethical purpose. This traditional understanding of the mission of academic humanists still has its champions in the early twenty-first century, especially among Americans inclined to give money to humanities programs. But when this vision was more widely taken for granted, its credibility was based in part on a division of labor that was in effect through the 1930s but then diminished.

That division of labor distinguished between academic scholarship and "letters," which included the writing in a variety of genres for a broader public. In the pre–World War II decades there were many careers beyond the academy devoted to the analysis of literature, history, politics, philosophy, and the arts. To inhabit one of these careers was understood to practice a more frankly opinionated, more "critical," and markedly less *wissenschaftliche* calling than professors were expected to follow. From this nonacademic realm of letters came the histories written by Henry Adams and most of those written by Charles Beard,[7] the literary criticism of William Dean Howells and Edmund Wilson, the political theory of Randolph Bourne and Walter Lippmann, and most of the cultural argumentation published in the *Partisan Review* of the 1930s and in a host of other little magazines. Countless books and articles from this extra-academic discourse would later be counted in peer-reviewed discourses as canonical contributions to their respective fields. By the end of the 1950s, however, the overwhelming majority of men and women who made a career of such writing were employed as professors. In 1967 Harold Cruse, who never even obtained a college degree, became a professor of history at the

University of Michigan on the strength of his writings about African American history.

More and more writers ended up with teaching jobs as the opportunities for steady employment in the expanding educational institutions increased and the chances of making a living from book sales diminished. Intellectuals still flourished outside academia, including some of the most creative and influential, but those who were not primarily writers of fiction were increasingly rare by the 1970s. When cross-disciplinary journals proliferated in that decade and after, their contents were written (and presumably read) almost entirely by people who were on salary at an institution of higher education.[8] Among today's most respected and popular writers on culture are Louis Menand and Henry Louis Gates Jr., whose writings appear regularly in the *New Yorker* and in other nonacademic venues; yet both of these leading intellectuals are career academics currently teaching at Harvard.

The absorption into the academic humanities of more and more of the nation's learned conversation about topics outside the scope of the sciences has sometimes been lamented. Did intellectuals become less independent and less responsive to the needs and interests of the public once they were based on campuses and more caught up in specialized scholarship? No doubt some of them did, especially during and immediately after the intimidations of the era now named for Senator Joseph McCarthy.[9] Before and after McCarthy, moreover, academic humanists had plenty of incentives to downplay the critical side of their work and to emphasize instead its more sciencelike, formally correct, methodologically austere side. The "rigorism" that Carl Schorske and others have identified as a major impulse in the humanities intensified exactly when the humanities were taking over from letters more and more of the critical responsibilities of the "intellectual."[10]

But the commercial market that sustained Lippmann and Wilson, and that today affects which books are reviewed in the *New York Times Book Review* and who writes for the *New York Review of Books,* is not without its own pressures, constraints, and connection-dependent gates of entry. These limiting conditions are rarely acknowledged by those who praise "public intellectuals" and call on academic humanists to get out of their cloisters.[11] If freelance writing has its liberations, it also has its own constraints. The return since the 1990s of a substantial, visible population of nonacademic intellectuals owes much to the financial support of several foundations and institutes defined by political agendas eager to establish a support system for intellectuals who will advance those agendas. Moreover, the diminution of free-market, nonacademic discursive space for serious talk about literature, history, philosophy, politics, and the arts had its important obverse: the increase of peer-reviewed space for the same kind of talk, subject to at least some influence of academia's classical, institutionalized commitments to evidence and reasoning. That is where the demands of "rigorism" and of "critique" met, where the borderlands of the humanities were defined.

As the old division of labor between professorial and nonprofessorial intellectuals diminished, then, the academy became all the more important a site for critical engagement with potentially contentious issues, as well as for the practice of specialized scholarship. The literature professors Lionel Trilling in the 1940s and 1950s and Edward Said in the 1970s and 1980s were moralists as well as close readers of literary texts. The historians C. Vann Woodward, Richard Hofstadter, and John Higham were frequently judgmental in their assessments of the United States. Max Weber's adamant distinction between the vocations of science and politics, often cited by contemporary social scientists as a justification for aloofness from normative questions, did not resonate quite so widely and deeply among humanists.[12]

Hence, the academic humanities after World War II found themselves with greatly enlarged responsibilities. Never before had so great a proportion of the intellectual history of the United States played itself out within the academic humanities. That is why they demand the historical understanding to which this volume seeks to contribute.

ALL THE ESSAYS in this volume address their topics across the chronological divide between two phases in the academic history of the United States since World War II. Stunning growth in size, economic support, and social prestige characterized what is now often called the Golden Age of American universities between 1945 and about 1970. This quarter century is also commonly remembered as a time of robust confidence within virtually all fields, including the humanities.[13] But the next several decades were less golden. Diminished resources, sharper internal contention in response to the political conflicts of the Vietnam era, and a leveling off of institutional growth rendered the years 1970–75 transitional. The proliferation of research and teaching subspecialties commonly accepted as "specialization" in the first phase was more often characterized in the second as "fragmentation."

Yet humanists in the second phase, from the mid-1970s to the present, inherited both the enlarged cognitive ambitions of the Golden Age and the ideological commitment to demographic inclusion that mark off the entire post-1945 period so sharply from the decades before the war. These inherited ambitions and commitments came into play in relation to affirmative action policies generated by the civil rights movement of the 1960s, the feminist movement that accelerated in the 1970s, and the demographic transformation of American society that eventually followed the Immigration and Nationality Act of 1965, which created large numbers of non-European applicants for student admissions and faculty appointments. In the meantime, American political, economic, military, and cultural engagement with the Third World continued through and beyond the end of the Vietnam War and of the cold war. Moreover, the expectations for what the humanities were supposed to do for society did not contract to prewar dimensions. There was no going back. Indeed, in the "multiculturalist" ethos of the 1980s and 1990s, cultural programs led by canon-changing academic humanists were sometimes assigned extravagant power to make society more egalitarian and democratic. The second phase of the post–World War II experience of the academic humanities in the United States differed importantly from the first, but the diversification that Louis Menand describes as the defining feature of the second renders it a continuation, rather than a reversal, of the dynamics of inclusion played out in the first.[14]

This volume examines the humanities more across the disciplines than within them. This approach follows partly from the fact that most of the best scholarship we already have on the humanities since 1945 is discipline-focused.[15] Some of the disciplines, especially English and history, are the subject of many excellent books and articles. To be sure, we still have more to learn from studies of the individual disciplines. Had this volume been organized by discipline it would have given much more attention to art history, classics, musicology, and the languages and literatures of Europe and Asia. But histories of the disciplines, even at their best, give us only indirect or partial access to several vital parts of the history of the humanities that this volume seeks to confront head-on.

One is the demography of the humanities professoriate. What matters here is the categories of persons that came to be included that once were largely excluded. The most obvious of these categories are women, Jews, African Americans, and Catholics. This demographic transformation differed from discipline to discipline in ways that become apparent only within a transdisciplinary perspective. A second discipline-transcending development was the inclusion on a much greater scale than before of the study of non-European history, literature, and art. Increased attention to the literature of the United States—long felt unworthy of the scrutiny of English professors —is one example, but of even greater importance were the foreign "area studies" programs that are usually addressed chiefly in relation to the social sciences and to political imperatives of the cold war. The social sciences important to area studies in the early postwar years became, as the decades passed, less and less engaged with the history, culture, and language of any particular society, which rendered the humanistic element in area studies all the more striking a feature of American academic life in the entire period since World War II.

A third comparable but less institutionally defined development was the incorporation from contemporary European intellectual life of a variety of theoretical orientations perceived to run strongly "against the American grain." A convenient example is the outlook of the political theorist Leo Strauss. Now one of the most widely discussed of the émigré intellectuals of the World War II era, Strauss was long considered too antidemocratic to claim a prominent place in the conversations of American humanists beyond a tiny cult within departments of political science. Furthermore, a disciplinary focus provides only limited access to the efforts to make undergraduate education more inclusive and to bring the results of academic inquiry to a popular audience. Yet humanists were always at the center of these endeavors, from the Harvard Red Book through the reforms of the late 1960s to today's renewed debates about "core curriculum," and from the great books programs of the 1940s through today's quarrels over "public intellectuals." Most of what this volume tells us about the disciplines is told within one or another of these several discipline-transcending frames of analysis.

Yet two discipline-specific articles punctuate this volume on account of the special pertinence of two particular disciplines to the themes of this volume. American studies and philosophy were special, extreme instances of two diametrically opposed impulses felt by many humanists during the period. One impulse was to welcome new ideas and new people and to err on the side of novelty and breadth; the other was to hold the line against pretenders and to concentrate all the more intently on what one most had to offer the world and thereby risk coming across as "too narrow." American studies, one of the newest of the degree-granting formations and one whose practitioners were not even sure it was a discipline, proved to be one of the most omnivorously inclusive of all departmentally institutionalized academic practices. More individuals of the long-excluded population groups were welcomed, and earlier, and even into leadership positions, than was the case in other humanistic callings. The cognitive borders of American studies were porous, too, quickly accommodating anthropological perspectives and popular culture. Religious studies displayed some of the same characteristics but did not achieve the institutional or intellectual prominence in the humanities that American studies did. Why religious studies did not find a larger place in the humanities is a highly interesting question, and one that this volume, for all its breadth, leaves unexplored.

By contrast to religious studies and American studies, philosophy, the oldest and ostensibly the most general of the disciplines, proved to be exceedingly strict in maintaining its intellectual boundaries. Surrounded by discourses that might be construed by outsiders as "philosophical," given the breadth of this term, the leaders of this disciplinary community were strikingly successful in convincing the rest of the learned world that they knew exactly what philosophy was and was not. Even in thus keeping their discipline tightly focused, however, the philosophers incorporated two European intellectual movements, logical positivism from the 1930s and ordinary language analysis from the 1950s. Here we have a splendid illustration of how inclusion (new ideas brought into the discipline) and exclusion (so much for metaphysics and normative ethics) form a syndrome and are best studied together. Philosophy also proved to be one of the slowest disciplinary communities to incorporate women and African Americans, even while males of Jewish origin attained intellectual leadership with striking rapidity during the twenty years following the post–World War II collapse of anti-Semitic barriers. The discipline of classics displayed some of the same tendencies seen in the philosophers; it invites more attention than it receives in this volume, but its text-defined disciplinary charter—classics was understood to be a fixed canon of ancient Greek and Latin works—confined its decisions in ways that philosophy's exceptionally commodious charter did not. Philosophy and American studies, then, illustrate more compellingly than classics and religious studies how differently disciplinary paths could proceed amid the pressures, challenges, and opportunities to which this volume attends.

All thirteen authors are accomplished scholars, and for that reason I have encouraged them to follow their own well-informed instincts rather than to confine their inquiry by a too-literal conception of the theme of inclusion. Hence, these essays range widely and include a multitude of observations and insights beyond the questions the authors were asked to address. Several authors point to policy issues in our own day concerning the teaching and research missions of the humanities; they suggest ways in which we can sharpen our own debates by attending to the historical analyses they present. Yet I want here to call attention to how these essays connect to one another and explore the dynamics of inclusion.

PART 1, "ACADEMIA and the Question of a Common Culture," explores the efforts of humanistic scholars to provide cultural cohesion to the larger public, toward which so many post-1945 academics felt an acute obligation. Millions more Americans were to be included in the constituency of humanistic learning, but on what terms? A whole volume could easily be devoted to the story of how American humanists dealt with this question. The ways in which literature departments, especially English, justified their curricular decisions from decade to decade and from college to college form a phase of this story that this volume addresses only indirectly because that phase is already the subject of a formidable list of books and articles, to which more are being added with impressive regularity. Rather than review the "canon wars," our authors were asked to address the question of a common culture from three other angles: the movement for "general education," the demography of student bodies, and the efforts to develop "popular" humanities through mass media.

John Guillory analyzes the movements for "general education" and charts their destiny from the mid-1940s to the present. The humanities were not the only component in the "education for democracy" programs for which the Harvard Red Book was the leading manifesto. But if the bourgeoning expanse of American undergraduates of middle- and working-class backgrounds needed a broad, common culture, apart from the discipline of their major and their subsequent professional career, the humanities were obviously central to it even in the mind of James B. Conant, the chemist who as president of Harvard commissioned the Red Book. Guillory grounds the post–World War II story of general education in the assumptions, inherited from smaller, more class-bound, prewar programs of the same basic type, that the nation's civic and commercial elites needed at least a rudimentary knowledge of European "high culture." Guillory calls attention to the gap between the increasingly specialized, discipline-specific scholarship that humanists of the 1940s, 1950s, and 1960s were producing and the deeply antispecialist ethos of the general education programs that academia as a whole expected humanists to design and operate. Guillory shows, moreover, that consensus on what the core content of general education should be was so thin that, when challenged in the 1960s, almost all these programs devolved into "distribution requirements," which could be satisfied by the relatively specialized courses that were of more interest to the faculty and more immediately useful to students eager to be credentialed professionally. The "canon wars" within the literature departments of the later twentieth century, Guillory argues, actually made the humanities seem more relevant to the demographically changing undergraduate student bodies otherwise more interested in skills and credentials. These disputes between traditionalist defenders of old classics and reformists demanding that students be taught new texts by new kinds of people reenacted at the level of curriculum the larger social drama of access to American life for previously excluded groups. Yet Guillory cautions that heavy breathing about what to include on an English department's reading list remains caught up in a narrow understanding of what education should be for masses of undergraduates. Without pretending to have figured out what a truly "democratic" educational program might look like, Guillory concludes that the tension between the interests of academic humanists and the interests of the students whose cultural welfare they have been asked to address for the last sixty years has been, and remains, rather more severe than most academic leaders are eager to admit.

What undergraduates do in their last two years of college is at issue in Roger Geiger's study of the ups and downs of humanities majors. Geiger reminds us that veterans who crowded into American colleges and universities under the G.I. Bill were more eager for business and vocational degrees than for the study of the liberal arts. Only about 6 percent of students who took degrees funded by the G.I. Bill majored in the core humanities disciplines of literature and history. But after the veterans had departed, the humanities departments took in an increasing portion of the growing student bodies of the 1950s and 1960s. In a statistical analysis that takes careful account of differences between institutions designed to serve different student constituencies, Geiger finds a striking across-the-board increase of humanities majors in the 1960s and very early 1970s followed by an equally striking decline beginning in the mid-1970s and lasting well into the 1980s. In 1970, 7.6 percent of all bachelor's degrees awarded in the United States went to English majors alone, but this had declined by 1997 to 4.2 percent. And this reflected a difference in absolute numbers, a decline from 63,342 to 49,345. This pattern holds for both men and women. Why did majoring in the humanities become so much less popular beginning about 1975? Geiger explores several possible explanations, including the sharp economic downturn in the early 1970s, the end of the Vietnam War, and transformations in the social composition of student bodies. Yet he concludes that the specific content and style of humanities instruction probably explain much of the decline of student interest. By the early 1970s, he observes, the confident, overarching narratives of the historians, especially as displayed in the Western Civilization surveys by which lower division students had come to appreciate what history departments had to offer, had been largely replaced by more specialized courses that were less determined to "bring it all together." Literature departments, Geiger further observes, increasingly "promoted an agenda of anti-capitalism, confrontation, and fixation on the latent social biases of literature." But if these changes in the predilections of the humanities professoriate played poorly at many of the state colleges, and thereby contributed to the overall statistical decline of the humanities, students in the elite sectors of higher education had adjusted well enough by the 1990s to sustain a slight increase in humanities majors. Geiger concludes that as the humanities disciplines experienced more specialization, contention, and even fragmentation during the later decades of the twentieth century, they continued to play the exploratory, risk-taking role with which leading research universities and liberal arts colleges are more comfortable.

The volume begins with these two essays focusing on undergraduate education because the teaching services of humanists remain central to the terms on which academic humanists relate to institutions of higher education and to American society at large. But a number of leading humanists sought to bring directly to the public what they believed humanists most had to offer Americans at large. Joan Shelley Rubin studies these cultural missionaries. Rubin briefly analyzes the careers of Clifton Fadiman and John Ciardi, two who began in academia but then left it, but she concentrates on the careers of the historian Jacques Barzun and the classicist Gilbert Highet of Columbia and the literary critic Howard Mumford Jones of Harvard. For all of them, "the dynamics of inclusion," Rubin explains, "entailed not so much the incorporation of diverse students into the university as the extension of instruction outward from the classroom lecture to the best seller and the broadcast." These "public professors" were not quite as elitist in sensibility as were the prewar advocates of high culture, or as frankly reactionary as the great books champions, Robert Hutchins and Mortimer Adler. But they did want to instruct rather than mirror or cater to public tastes. Rubin's group saw themselves as custodians of cultural riches that the rapidly growing, imperfectly educated society of the 1940s, 1950s, and 1960s needed to maintain its own coherence and stability, especially in the context of the cold war. Rubin shows how Barzun, Highet, and Jones all rejected the "alienation" from the contemporary bourgeoisie espoused by Irving Howe, Dwight Macdonald, and other contemporaries, resisted modernist trends in the arts and literature, and opposed "the cult of specialization and its badge, the Ph.D." Jones was also a leader in American studies and was one of the key figures in the incorporation of American texts into what was taught as English literature. Barzun managed better than the others to develop a combination that brought him a huge audience beyond the academy as well as within: he "assailed materialism and Marxism alike, scorned and supported the middlebrow, upheld standards and downgraded expertise." But if all this did amount to an expansion of the arena for the academic humanities after World War II, it worked only on the basis of a very traditional consensus about the substance of humanistic learning that was being undercut in the disciplines even as these figures lectured on the radio and supervised their book clubs. Rubin explains the breakdown of this style of public humanities in the 1970s, when its parochial Eurocentrism and its largely affirmative take on American culture were widely discredited. By the 1980s the closest thing to a successor to Barzun, Highet, and Jones was the astronomer Carl Sagan, whose television programs and books made him the most famous American professor of his generation. And in the 1980s and after, when there was a new push for "public intellectuals," the call was usually for a measure of critical, political engagement foreign to Rubin's cast of characters.

Part 2, "European Movements against the American Grain?" analyzes a series of episodes in which American humanists came to grips with ideas that were at once appealing for their apparent depth and suspect for their apparent lack of fit with what was often assumed to be the ethical framework of American public culture. How could these ideas, the products of contemporary European movements, be included in mainstream American humanities scholarship and teaching without excluding cultural elements that a healthy, democratic society might need? This topic, too, could easily be the basis for an entire volume of interesting studies. How intellectual movements of contemporary Europe were absorbed, rejected, critically transformed, and otherwise engaged is one of the chief themes in U.S. intellectual history. Studies of existentialism, structuralism, British Marxism, post-structuralism, and a variety of other initiatives with trans-Atlantic consequences continue to enrich the field. This volume contributes selectively to this literature by addressing several of the movements most at odds with one or another disposition prominently displayed in American academic life.

Martin Jay explores the ways in which émigré intellectuals from Hitler's Europe challenged a traditional faith in the virtues of "linguistic purification and unvarnished truth-telling" in the realm of politics. Lying in public affairs was not always a bad thing, according to Jay's three very different cases, Theodor Adorno, Leo Strauss, and Hannah Arendt. Jay treats these three political theorists of the intellectual migration as early and persisting examples of one of the major themes in the influence of continental thinkers on the academic humanities in the United States through "the linguistic turn" of the 1950s and 1960s and the post-structuralist enthusiasms of the 1970s and 1980s. This theme is a dual emphasis on the difficulty of assigning true meanings to things and on the function of language as a tool of artifice rather than as a tool for referencing a "real" world. Jay does not claim that American humanists were oblivious to these insights before the immigrants of the 1930s and 1940s bore witness to them on American soil, but he does show that it was the Europeans who called sharply into question the ideal, often invoked through the name of George Orwell, that there were plain truths out there, waiting to be told in plain language, if only men and women had the political will to do it. The tension between Strauss and the democratic politics of American liberals was especially acute. Jay points to the increased popularity in our own time of Strauss's writings, despite his "explicitly hierarchical politics based on an allegedly natural order" and his vindication of an elite's reluctance to share what it takes to be true with "the uncomprehending masses."

In an essay that runs parallel to Jay's by examining the tension between the ideas of three European thinkers and prevailing patterns of American thought, James Kloppenberg focuses on a series of challenges to the styles of empiricism emulated in the United States by mainstream social scientists and defended by most philosophers. Kloppenberg briefly analyzes the German gestalt psychologist Wolfgang Kohler and the French Catholic philosopher Etienne Gilson, whose value-centered approaches to perception and metaphysics, respectively, led to their being shunted aside in the 1930s and after. Kloppenberg's third and most extensively examined case is again Strauss, whose rejection of virtually the entirety of the humanities and social sciences as practiced in the United States rendered him distinctly a thing apart, even during his twenty years at the University of Chicago. Although Kloppenberg's purpose is partly to show the limits of inclusion—just what kinds of ideas were rejected by the American academic humanists even as they were expanding their intellectual boundaries —he also demonstrates that many of the political theorists, philosophers, and other humanists who rejected Strauss's assertion of natural law did so on the basis of a system of values of their own, rather than from the parochial hyper-factualism of which they are often accused. Scholars who expected colleagues to participate in give-and-take argumentation and display tolerance for evidence-based disagreement soon were fed up with Strauss's arrogant refusal to engage. Kloppenberg thus tells an ironic story of the intolerance of intolerance, of the marginalization of Strauss right up until his death in 1973 by a humanities establishment increasingly committed to a discourse that could accommodate a variety of perspectives. Yet Kloppenberg generously allows Strauss, in his capacity as a prophet of timeless truths as discerned by Plato and Aristotle, to be the symbol for questions he believes too many humanists dodge: just what answer should humanists offer to students and a public that often yearn for something definite? "If all knowledge has become suspect, if all our inquiries now seek to unmask power and empower the dispossessed, then it is understandable that students wonder why they should bother with the humanities and discursive social sciences instead of simply learning how to wield power themselves once they leave school," Kloppenberg ruminates. Strauss's answers to questions of the order of William James's "What Makes Life Significant?" are obviously inadequate for a democratic society and for an academy devoted to honest collegial exchange, but it will not do, Kloppenberg insists, to shy away from such questions. Strauss's popularity beyond the academy at the dawn of the twenty-first century, he concludes, can serve as a reminder of how strong are the pressures in this society for answers rather than simply a sequence of questions.

Bruce Kuklick takes up potentially problematic European intellectual movements in the distinctive context of the disciplinary community of philosophy, which is possessed of the broadest of all disciplinary charters and indeed is the historic parent of the social sciences and even of modern physical science (commonly called "natural philosophy" into the nineteenth century). The institutionalized leaders of philosophy in the United States began as early as the 1930s the project of strict boundary maintenance that their successors carried out with stunning success through the 1960s and to a large extent thereafter. In one of the most striking intellectual transformations of the midcentury decades, metaphysics and normative ethics, so long vital parts of the discipline, were marginalized. This was effected first by the logical empiricism emanating largely from prewar continental Europe, and second by the linguistic analysis first developed in England. Kuklick traces these developments and the "pluralist" revolt of the 1970s, which pitted the marginalized metaphysicians against a variety of largely younger philosophers attracted to German and French traditions and to a resurrection of American pragmatism, exactly the styles of philosophy that were then being written about and taught increasingly in departments of literature and elsewhere in the humanities and humanistically oriented social sciences. By the 1990s, Kuklick shows, the discipline, while enormously larger in numbers than it had been fifty years before, was increasingly divided between a core group dominant in the leading research universities, devoted largely to the "analytical philosophy" that by then had defined the discipline for several decades, and an imposing diversity of feminist theorists, practitioners of "Continental philosophy," classical metaphysicians, applied ethicists, and cultural theorists who had achieved considerable control over the professional associations. The latter group by 1994 had organized against the very notion of ranking philosophy departments, a practice that served to reinforce the standing of the former group. In the meantime, the analytic philosophers at the leading departments tended to present the recent history of their discipline as if the others did not count, a practice exemplified by the tendency of the core group to devalue the writings of Richard Rorty, the philosopher most widely appreciated during the last quarter century in academia as a whole, especially among literary scholars, historians, and anthropologists.

By way of transition to Part 3 of this volume, I want to add that amid all these struggles over cognitive boundary maintenance, the analytic philosophers themselves after World War II swiftly incorporated large numbers of Jews into their ranks—and Catholics as well. The universalist ethos of analytic philosophy promoted the incorporation of any and all persons who did precisely this kind of science-sympathizing philosophy, including women and ethnoracial minorities. Yet there were relatively few female and minority analytic philosophers, even at the end of the twentieth century. When members of these demographic groups pursued a philosophical career at all, they were drawn to the "pluralist" rather than the "analytic" side of this disciplinary community.

Part 3, "Social Inclusion," addresses the weakening of traditional religious, ethnoracial, and gender barriers to full participation in the humanities. A humanities professorate that in 1945 was overwhelmingly male and Anglo-Protestant eventually became one of the most demographically diverse of all professional communities in the United States. This transformation, like the topics of Parts 1 and 2, could easily be the focus of a substantial volume. The most dramatic case is the sudden absorption in the two decades after 1945 of scholars of Jewish origin. A widely discussed study by the Carnegie Commission found that by 1969 Jews were demographically overrepresented by about 700 percent in the nation's leading departments of history and philosophy. We have a growing and increasingly sophisticated literature on the ways in which Jewish intellectuals turned many humanistic and social scientific discourses in more cosmopolitan directions, challenging the Anglo-Protestant cultural hegemony so unmistakable in the pre–World War II era. The Asian American and Hispanic American cases are also highly relevant but come into play only late in the twentieth century, especially in the wake of the Immigration and Nationality Act of 1965, which revolutionized the demographic base of the population of the United States. This volume addresses the dynamics of social inclusion through three other cases, Catholics, African Americans, and women.

That Catholic scholars made greater contributions in some areas than in others, and were more likely to favor some ideas than others, is a major theme of John McGreevey's study of one of the most important yet rarely addressed stories of inclusion in American academic life. McGreevy shows that Catholics were the most likely to distinguish themselves in the specific subfields of history, anthropology, philosophy, and literary studies, in which they could draw upon the exposure to Latin, religious ritual, and ethical teachings they had experienced growing up in a Catholic atmosphere. Though McGreevy establishes the great range of humanistic endeavors in which Catholics became full participants, he identifies several patterns in basic outlook common among Catholic thinkers. Prominent among these is the communitarian social and ethnic theory that Charles Taylor and Alasdair MacIntyre have developed in opposition to individualist theories more popular among Protestant, secular, and to some extent Jewish intellectuals. McGreevy attends to the differences as well as the similarities between the Catholic case of inclusion and the more widely discussed Jewish case. He emphasizes the role played by the extensive network of Catholic colleges and universities, nearly all of which were greatly strengthened after World War II as a result of the U.S. government's decision to allow federal money to go to Catholic institutions. The Catholic path into the academic humanities began, and long remained, channeled through sectarian campuses. Hence, Catholics had been subject not only to discrimination on the part of empowered Protestant and secular academics, but also to internal pressures that encouraged Catholic scholars to remain somewhat apart. Although both these barriers had begun to weaken before the early 1960s, after Vatican II the entry of Catholic historians, philosophers, and literary scholars into the mainstream journals and faculties proceeded with great rapidity.

But neither in the Jewish case nor in the Catholic case were members of a sometimes stigmatized group expected to confine their studies to things Jewish or Catholic. Yet this is exactly the kind of expectation that African Americans encountered. The expectation that blacks will work on "black topics" is the central theme of Jonathan Holloway's overview of the process by which black scholars gained what acceptance they did find within the institutions and discourses of the humanities. In demographic fact, most of the black Americans who have found stable employment in the academic humanities in the United States until now have done so in relation to the specific study of the history, literature, political movements, or popular culture of black people. This connection between black topics and black scholars was reinforced by a consideration that did not apply to Jews and to Catholics: there had been no generalized movement to bring the history and culture of Catholicism or Judaism into the academy, yet there was a determined effort to correct the demonstrable neglect by mainstream academia of African American history and culture. Hence, Holloway's essay is largely organized around the development of black studies programs and departments and the controversies attendant on them from the 1960s through the present. Holloway shows that the blacks-write-about-blacks expectation, while far from universal, was common among black as well as nonblack colleagues. Holloway traces the tensions this informal principle created in several individual careers, including that of the critic and writer J. Saunders Redding, one of the earliest African Americans to teach in a humanities program in a major university. Holloway observes that the doors have recently become more open, formally, at least, for black people to work in areas that have nothing to do with their ancestral community. One does now and then encounter a professor of medieval European history or of modern English literature who is black, but these instances remain rare. The legacy of the past remains formidable. The inclusion of African Americans in the humanities remains not only small in numbers in proportion to the African American share of the national population, but much more sharply segmented by field than is the case with any other large population group.

Even women, who were often expected by males and females alike to take the lead in developing programs in women's studies, were not as confined as were African Americans by an expectation of this kind. This is among the findings of Rosalind Rosenberg, who traces the eventual integration of women into most humanistic callings, even to the point of becoming by 2000 in the majority of new humanities Ph.D.'s. Rosenberg shows that the situation of women differed from that of other groups that had been systematically excluded. The legendary G.I. Bill, she observes, had a negative impact on women as students simply because 98 percent of the returning soldiers were male. Women actually lost ground in humanities faculties. And only with the National Defense Education Act (NDEA) of 1958 did the federal support of higher education positively affect aspiring women humanists. Rosenberg identifies two different theoretical orientations that accompanied the entry of women into the humanities. One view insisted on uniform intellectual standards across the gender line, while a second defended versions of "standpoint epistemology," according to which the very idea of a uniform standard was a covertly particularist, male construct to be overcome by a greater recognition of the distinctive standpoints brought to knowing and interpreting by gender, ethnicity, sexual orientation, and class position. Rosenberg calls attention to the fact that the decline since the 1970s in funding and in undergraduate enrollments in the humanities has taken place simultaneously with "feminization." Without claiming that some larger, conscious system has acted to devalue the humanities by assigning more and more of its labor to females, Rosenberg points out that fewer and fewer males seek and obtain doctorates in literary studies especially. But the speed and extent of women's entry varied considerably by discipline. Rosenberg finds that philosophy was one of the slowest to absorb women, and American studies one of the fastest.

Part 4, "Area Studies at Home and Abroad," juxtaposes the humanistic study of the United States with that of the non-Western world. The rapid expansion of American studies took place simultaneously with the growth of "foreign area studies" and in the context of some of the same cold war priorities, and the two invite analysis in the same frame of reference. The two initiatives were quite different in tone and style as well as subject matter, yet both were, in their fashion, revolts against Eurocentrism. American studies programs were heavily humanistic from the start and dealt with a society that was assumed to be fully developed, and thus susceptible to study as a synchronic whole. The cross-disciplinary centers and institutes established on the campuses of many of the leading research universities for the study of Japan, China, Africa, and other parts of what came to be called the developing world were more inclined to diachronic perspectives, and they were not presented as primarily humanities endeavors. Hence, area studies is rarely addressed in histories of the humanities and is more often taken up in relation to histories of "modernization theory" and considered an episode in the history of social science and foreign policy. Yet professors of literature and history, and to a lesser extent of other humanities disciplines, were prominent in the leadership of foreign area studies from the start and gained resources and influence after the NDEA injected massive federal funding into foreign-language-related programs. The cultures of the non-European world, once a tiny appendage to the humanities in the United States, had been extensively included by the 1960s and would attract increased attention in the succeeding decades. Just how the growth of federally supported area studies facilitated humanistic scholarship and teaching about the non-Western parts of the globe, and how the enlarged cohorts of humanists specializing in those regions responded to or circumvented the agendas of the cold war, has been a subject more of speculation and anecdotal memoir than of extensive research. The subject matter of Part 4, even more than that of the other three parts of this volume, cries out for an entire volume devoted exclusively to its concerns. A comprehensive, comparative investigation of foreign area studies would deal with African studies, Middle Eastern studies, Chinese studies, South Asian studies, and Southeast Asian studies as well as those covered here. But in a volume of this scope, of which area studies can be merely a part, there is room for only a selection of the relevant foreign cases. The three essays here cover this terrain: Russian studies, Japanese studies, and Latin American studies.

Leila Zenderland shows that American studies has been the poster child for both the demographic and the cognitive dimensions of inclusion. Here all the issues entailed in the expansion of the humanities were confronted in the rawest form because no clearly defined disciplinary charter framed the questions. American studies was not quite history and not quite literature; it was somehow both—and also anthropological in outlook while not forsaking the study of the artifacts of "high culture." Simultaneously a haven for leftists and a pillar of cold war affirmations of the integrity and value of "American culture," American studies of the late 1940s and 1950s drew a variety of young scholars represented for Zenderland by Leo Marx. She quotes Marx's recent recollections of the atmosphere of the early years, when the new collectivity's "democratic standards of equality" helped "open the doors of the sacred patriarchal grove" first to "Jewish, Irish, German, Polish, and other non-WASP white males" and then to women and nonwhites, too. Yet Zenderland is sensitive, as are so many of our authors, to how inclusion and exclusion form a logical syndrome. She shows how the propensity of early American studies scholars to study America "whole" prevented them from focusing on its parts, even while, ironically, these scholars were incorporating representatives of those parts into their social body. And later on, in the 1980s and after, when American studies scholars moved far in the direction of what critics called "identity politics," what became less visible in the journals and curricula of American studies was what rendered the United States a single entity. The multicultural America presented in many journals and programs of American studies after a half century of practice was largely, and perhaps ironically, a canopy for particular cultural segments whose origin was in the parts of the world studied by scholars in foreign area studies.

David Engerman finds that World War II, more than the cold war, shaped the agendas of Russianists and Sovietologists for many decades. Against the claims of a number of critics that cold war–era scholars were predictable ideologues—right from the start, then, we are reminded of the tension between "rigorism" and "critique" so widely evident in the stories told in this volume—Engerman shows that these scholars came out of a great variety of political backgrounds and advanced diverse perspectives in their books and articles. The presence within the scholarly community of exiles from Bolshevism contributed to the anti-Stalinism of the field, but beyond that the exiles were far from unified in their views. Moreover, Engerman argues that humanists, especially historians but also scholars of Russian literature, were central to Russian area studies and not a sideshow to an operation dominated by political scientists and economists. Engerman also finds that the relation of humanistic scholarship to the aims of the funders is elusive. "Though the financial supporters of Soviet studies—including both foundations and government agencies—had created the field to learn more about the Politburo," Engerman summarizes, "they ended up creating experts on Pushkin," and while "they sought insights into Lenin, they also boosted the study of Lermontov."

Andrew Barshay also finds that historians were at the center of things, and that literary scholars took advantage of the area studies boom to advance their own agendas. Barshay provides an account of the vividly contrasting careers and perspectives of two leading historians, both children of missionaries, Edwin Reischauer and E. H. Norman. Barshay gives special attention to the debate over Japanese "modernization" in the late 1950s and 1960s. This phase of the story, Barshay insists on the basis of a fresh reading of conference transcripts and of major works published by the field's leading historians, sociologists, and political scientists, was considerably more nuanced and conflicted than later denunciations of the enthusiasm for modernization theory within Japanese studies have allowed. Barshay explains that students of Japanese literature, even as they flourished within the scholarly boom promoted by area studies initiatives, continued through the 1970s to concentrate on translations and philological studies, moving only in the 1980s in the theoretically self-conscious directions by then popular among scholars of European and American literature. Historians and especially anthropologists provided more broadly interpretive analyses of Japanese culture. Ruth Benedict's best-selling *Chrysanthemum and the Sword* (1946) exemplified the holistic approach to Japan pursued during the war by anthropologists commissioned by the U.S. military. Barshay's scholars of Japan, unlike Engerman's Russianists, included at the start almost no exiles from the country under study. Yet interaction between American scholars and those based in Japan gradually increased and eventually influenced debates within the United States. Barshay cites the case of the Japanese intellectual historian Maruyama Masao as an example of a Japanese humanist whose writings came, through these interactions, to be widely appreciated in the West well beyond Japanese studies.

Rolena Adorno's specialists in Latin America were more intimately involved with contemporary Latin American intellectuals themselves than Engerman's Russianists or Barshay's Japanologists were involved with their counterparts abroad. Hence, her title, "Havana and Macondo," invokes not only the Cuban Revolution and its impact on Latin American studies, but also the village made world famous by the fiction of the great Colombian writer Gabriel García Márquez. Adorno shows how the handful of scholar-teachers devoted to the literary classics of Spain had their discourses and their institutions transformed by the Latin American priorities of the cold war after Castro's success in Cuba. Once attention was focused on Latin America, the Spanish language canon in American universities was suddenly and decisively expanded by the texts not only of Márquez but of Jorge Luis Borges, Pablo Neruda, Octavio Paz, and the other authors who created the "Boom" in Latin American fiction and poetry. Adorno attends carefully to disputes within the community of humanists about just how Latin American literature should be interpreted and to differences between social scientific and humanistic approaches to Latin American experience as a whole. Latin American intellectuals themselves, especially Paz, played a major role in most of these disputes. Adorno's story, even more than Barshay's and Engerman's, is one of a multitude of purposes and impulses extending well beyond the cold war doctrinal outlook and funding priorities that facilitated this striking instance of the expansion of the humanities.

Yet an issue raised by all three of these inquiries into area studies, especially when read together, is just how narrowly we should construe the cold war aims of the federal government and the private foundations that supported the growth of area studies. Did the humanists really subvert the aims of their funding sources, or manage to ignore them, or actually fulfill an enlightened construction of those aims? The results of area studies were of many different sorts, especially when the work of all the social scientists is carefully considered, but one could argue that the bulk of the humanities projects carried out under the protection of area studies programs did serve the best interests of the United States, and even of "democracy," however narrowly the funding agencies responding to Stalin, Sputnik, and Castro had originally understood their mission.

It is not only in relation to area studies that one can ask how well the humanities have served the interests of democracy and the American nation during the six decades since World War II. The question does not admit of a clear and simple answer, but the studies commissioned for this volume under the auspices of the American Academy of Arts and Sciences do show academic humanists striving in a great variety of modes to make their own culture more cosmopolitan than they found it. A Europe-preoccupied humanities professoriate composed largely of Anglo-Protestant males was gradually—although far from steadily, and sometimes amid real resistance—replaced by successor cohorts who engaged more of the world intellectually and incorporated more of the varieties of humankind demographically. Perhaps these expansions constitute no more than a modest service to the nation and to its democratic aspirations. Our contributors are neither uncritical of the actions of their various casts of characters nor complacent about where the humanities have ended up in the early years of the twenty-first century. Moreover, the inability or unwillingness of so many Americans today to distinguish between theories of "intelligent design" and theories warranted by evidence and reasoning can remind us how far from complete is the larger mission of academic humanists to illuminate domains where the rules of evidence are contested and the power of reason doubted.

Notes

1. Vannevar Bush, *Science—The Endless Frontier* (Washington, 1945). A new edition with a helpful preface by the historian of science Daniel J. Kevles (ix–xxxiii) was published by the National Science Foundation in 1990 as part of the NSF's fortieth anniversary observance.

2. An excellent overview of the history of American higher education in relation to the boom of the postwar years is Thomas Bender, "Politics, Intellect, and the American University, 1945–1995," in *American Academic Culture in Transformation: Fifty Years, Four Disciplines*, ed. Thomas Bender and Carl E. Schorske (Princeton, 1998), 17–54.

3. The two most influential articulations of this aspiration were the Harvard Red Book of 1945, so called because of its crimson dust jacket, *General Education in a Free Society* (Cambridge, Mass., 1945), and the 1947 report of President Truman's Commission on Higher Education, *Higher Education for American Democracy*, 6 vols. (Washington, D.C., 1947).

4. Christopher Jenks and David Riesman, *The Academic Revolution* (New York, 1968).

5. For the story of how a variety of disciplinary practices became "the humanities" in the context of the organizational structure of American universities, see the classic study by Laurence Veysey, "The Plural Organized Worlds of the Humanities," in *The Organization of Knowledge in Modern America, 1860–1920*, ed. Alexandra Oleson and John Voss (Baltimore, 1979), 51–106.

6. Henry F. May, *The End of American Innocence: A Study of the First Years of Our Time* (New York, 1959), 30.

7. Beard did begin his career as an academic, but he resigned from Columbia University in 1917 in protest of the summary dismissal by President Nicholas Murray Butler of a colleague critical of American entry into World War I; until his death in 1948 he never held a regular academic post again.

8. For an account of this proliferation, see David A. Hollinger, "The Disciplines and the Identity Debates, 1970–1995," in Bender and Schorske, *American Academic Culture*, 353–371.

9. Of the many studies of this episode, the most comprehensive and reliable is Ellen Schrecker, *No Ivory Tower* (New York, 1986).

10. Carl Schorske, "The New Rigorism in the Human Sciences, 1940–1960," in Bender and Schorske, *American Academic Culture*, 309–329.

11. The question of finding a viable market for serious, nonspecialized work is at least recognized by one important book on this topic: Richard A. Posner, *Public Intellectuals: A Study of Decline* (Cambridge, Mass., 2001).

12. An English translation of Weber's essays of 1919, "Science as a Vocation" and "Politics as a Vocation," became widely available in 1946 in C. Wright Mills and Hans Gerth, eds., *From Max Weber* (New York, 1946). One group of humanists attracted to the sharpness of Weber's distinction was the analytic philosophers associated with logical positivism, unique among humanists in their sympathy for the methodological self-conception of contemporary scientists.

13. A revealing period piece from the climactic years of this era, rarely cited today, is *The Princeton Studies: Humanistic Scholarship in America*. This series of fifteen commissioned volumes presented "a critical account of American humanistic scholarship in recent decades," as described on the dust jackets. The books were edited by Richard Schlatter through Princeton University's Council on Humanities and supported with a grant from the Ford Foundation. Nearly all these books appeared between 1963 and 1965. Although a few of them enjoyed a longer shelf life (notably the two devoted to the disciplines of history and musicology, which were reprinted in the 1970s), most were so outdated after a single decade that they played only a marginal role in the critical discussions of the disciplines to which they were addressed.

14. Louis Menand, "College: The End of the Golden Age," *New York Review of Books*, October 18, 2001, 44. Menand's essay is a cogent rendition of the now-standard narrative of the history of the humanities in the United States since World War II as divided into two phases, which Menand characterizes as the phase of "expansion" and the phase of "diversification."

15. A prominent example is Bender and Schorske, *American Academic Culture*, which examines two humanities disciplines—English and philosophy—alongside two social science disciplines, political science and economics. Another example is the spring 2006 edition of *Daedalus*, guest edited by Patricia Spacks.

I

Academia and the Question of a Common Culture

1

WHO'S AFRAID OF MARCEL PROUST?

The Failure of General Education in the American University

JOHN GUILLORY

I heard thee speak me a speech once, but it was never acted,
or if it was, not above once—for the play, I remember,
pleased not the million, 'twas caviare to the general.
—SHAKESPEARE, HAMLET 2.2.430

IN HIS CONTROVERSIAL *Partisan Review* essay of 1960, "Masscult and Midcult," Dwight Macdonald delivered one of the last unqualified denunciations of American mass culture, reserving special scorn for the deformation called "middlebrow," which Macdonald renamed "midcult." Since the time of Macdonald's essay, perhaps the high-water mark in the old tradition of *Kulturkritik*, many humanist intellectuals have urged a rapprochement with mass culture, though many remain uneasy with its middlebrow emanation. The massification of high culture Macdonald saw as the very worst expression of masscult was also, as he diagnosed it, a peculiarly American development. In England, by contrast, he argued that the survival of the class system ensured the survival of high culture as a genuine concern of the upper classes: "An American living in London is delighted by the wide interest in arts and letters. . . . It is, of course, general only to perhaps 5 percent of the population, but in America it isn't even this much general; it is something shared only with friends and professional acquaintances. But in London one meets stockbrokers who go to concerts, politicians who have read Proust."[1] Despite Macdonald's confidence in his observation, there would appear to be a contradiction between his assertion that British interest in arts and letters is "wide," and yet confined to a mere 5 percent of the populace. How "general," to use Macdonald's term, is 5 percent? More problematically for his argument, it would be hard to deny that museum attendance and concertgoing in the United States are also fairly widespread by the arithmetical measure Macdonald proposes. Still, his main point is that the mode of consumption in the United States is definitively middlebrow. The reference to Proust implicitly makes this distinction, since Proust's readership is undoubtedly very small by comparison to most authors, and even smaller were we to count Americans who read him in French.

The name of Proust functions in Macdonald's essay as the signifier of a genuine high culture for several reasons. In addition to the barrier posed by the French language, which is only partially overcome by translation, *A la recherches du temps perdu* is intrinsically difficult and forbiddingly long. It resists massification in a way that Shakespeare and Austen, for example, have not. Other names might have played this fearful role, but for my purposes the name of Proust will do (especially as we no longer have as much to fear from Virginia Woolf, who has been done up recently in the most respectable middlebrow fashion in the novel and film *The Hours*).[2] Proust's resistance to midcult appropriation is confirmed by his role in an anecdote that Barbara Ehrenreich passed on in her 1989 study of middle-class anxiety, *Fear of Falling*, which among other critical agendas took to task what we used to call "yuppie" culture for its faux sophistication, consisting largely of higher-end consumables such as brie and Chardonnay (it was the 1980s, after all). The anecdote was borrowed from a personal essay by a hospital administrator, Peter Baida, who recounted a dinner party he gave at which he announced to his guests, all highly credentialed professionals, that his wife had recently finished reading Proust. "'Who is Proust?' one of our guests asked. I thought someone else would answer, but all eyes turned toward me. Suddenly I realized that not one of our guests knew who Proust was."[3] Although the first book of Proust's great work *Swann's Way* has been made into a movie (not nearly as successful apparently as *The Hours*), the blank response to Proust's name suggests that some artifacts of high culture have drifted into a cultural stratosphere where they have been lost to sight altogether.

Macdonald was convinced that the triumph of the middlebrow could be attributed in part to the explosive postwar growth of the American university system and to the imperfect dissemination of high culture that occurs there: "This enormous college population . . . is the most important fact about our cultural situation today. It is far bigger, absolutely and relatively, than that of any other country" (58). The very massification of the educational system is responsible for the failure to draw a "line between Masscult and High Culture which the rise of Midcult has blurred." Consequently, "there is something damnably American about Midcult" (59). Although Macdonald's conception of high culture is unlikely to find many adherents today, the connection he made between the American university and midcult raises a question that cannot be so easily dismissed as amateur sociology or elitist posturing. The existence of middlebrow culture as an earnest yet lazy tribute to the residual status of a traditional high culture does have a relation, both positive and negative, to the development of the university system: a negative relation because the American university ceased to be dedicated primarily to nurturing or disseminating high culture since at least the late nineteenth century; and a positive relation because the same system has repeatedly attempted to reincorporate traditional high cultural works into the curriculum by way of programs known as "general education." These programs have been diverse in concept and substance, but all of them have in some fashion attempted to expose students to works of high culture that the American university is perceived otherwise to slight.

General education alone surely does not account for the phenomenon of midcult, but its curricular aim of giving Americans a crash course in the classics is the institutional analogue of the guilty cultural conscience that finds its expressive realization in the artifacts of middlebrow culture. In another essay in which Macdonald wittily debunked Mortimer Adler's great books project as "The Book-of-the-Millennium Club," he had no difficulty in connecting the dots between the middlebrow and the "religion of culture" enshrined in academic great books programs (257).[4] From the vantage of a living high culture, which for Macdonald meant a living avant-garde culture, the piety directed toward the monuments of traditional high culture is the most obvious symptom of bad faith and spoils every massified redaction of a genuine high cultural work with its unctuous stain. Though I would be inclined to allow that these middlebrow works are often interesting and successful in their own right — consider the films of George Cukor, for example, based on great English novels, and yes, even the films of Merchant and Ivory—I would also concede that middlebrow works are often suffused with the cultural anxiety of a professional elite, perennially insecure about its level of sophistication.[5] Similarly, the history of general education is marked by a recurrent failure to produce in its subjects the level of culture for which it reaches — if no longer for an elite fluent in Greek and Latin, then at least for one that would not shift uncomfortably at the mention of Marcel Proust, a name perhaps relegated for many to an unremembered past.

The institution of general education, as historians of the American university remind us, is indeed uniquely American.[6] Its emergence is related to the rapid growth in the twentieth century of the university system and equally to the new "elective" curriculum inaugurated in the later nineteenth century, which retired the classical curriculum and redirected the aims of the university toward the credentialing of students in myriad new professional, technical, business, and managerial fields. General education was a response to the recommitment of the university to the aim of credentialing in specialized fields of knowledge. But if it advanced the contrary aim of reconnecting students to a cultural tradition that would function as minimally "common" for them, the meaning of this aim was not and could not be the same for all the evolving constituencies of the university system. It is not my purpose here either to defend general education or to propose an alternative to it but, first, to survey briefly the social and institutional conditions that burdened it with a seemingly impossible task and, second, to give a more realistic account of its effects in the larger society from which emanates multiple and perhaps inconsistent demands upon the uniquely American version of that ancient institution, the college or university.

Reading through the diverse rationales for general education penned over the last century, I am struck by the consistent expression in these documents of a desire to redress a perceived social ill—a great deficit in "general" knowledge, in the most important knowledge a human being or citizen needs in life. And here we encounter a version of the arithmetical paradox over which we stumbled in Macdonald's essay: although the idea of general education became the basis in a handful of institutions for reconstructing the entire undergraduate curriculum (most famously at the University of Chicago), this program was elsewhere almost always scaled back to occupy a much smaller niche in the curriculum. Most curricular time and space are now dedicated, as they have been for more than a century, to the task of preparing students for entry into professional, managerial, or technical fields or providing them with the credentials necessary for further study in these fields. The disparity between the great social aims of general education and the curricular turf it now occupies in most institutions is a measure of its "failure," an initial sounding of its historical predicament.

THE OCCASION for the emergence of general education is so well known that I will rehearse it here with extreme brevity. Its precondition was resistance to the new elective curriculum pioneered by Harvard in the late nineteenth century, resistance that generally followed the line laid down by the culture critics of the time.[7] The new curriculum serving the professions and sciences was denounced as further dividing the head from the heart while reducing knowledge to sterile specialization. The terms of this critique thus oriented subsequent proposals for reform of the elective system toward a concern for the "whole man" (*sic*) and for "general" as opposed to "special" knowledge. These two premises resound with monotonous regularity in rationales for general education even today and even though they were already rather stale by the time they were invoked in the famous Harvard document published in 1945, *General Education in a Free Society*, commonly known as the Red Book. The authors of the Red

Book enthusiastically endorsed the principle that "education must look to the whole man," always a desideratum in some vague and innocuous sense but immediately complicated whenever translated into an actual curriculum.[8]

The difficulty of translating "culture" into a curriculum was already evident when Matthew Arnold and his contemporaries borrowed the concept of *Kultur* from German philosophy in order to defend the classical curriculum in English schools against encroachment by the sciences. Arnold lost the debate on this subject against Huxley and Spencer because his claim for Latin and Greek as the best vehicle for imparting culture was manifestly unconvincing. In the United States the abandonment of the classical curriculum was a condition for later general education programs (Britain did not follow this path), but the break with language study also undermined subsequent attempts to impose a curriculum of great books upon the university as the necessary vehicle for the attainment of "culture." The profundity of that aim was belied by the very fact of vernacularization, which transformed Homer, Virgil, Dante, and Goethe into great works of *English* literature.

The early history of general education never resolved the question of what content such a curriculum was to have, except that it must be general as opposed to specialist and that it must support norms such as the "whole man" and cultural commonality. Programs based on a great books curriculum ventured to define explicitly what that content was to be, but less rigidly defined programs were no less interested in realizing the basic aim of general education, understood in the terms inherited from the tradition of cultural criticism.[9] Even distribution requirements gesture, if somewhat feebly, to the basic notion underlying the project of general education, that is, to "counterpoise" the effects of specialization (Red Book, 14), although distribution requirements also break with the early emphasis of general education on the literary and philosophical tradition, the so-called Western Tradition. A brief enumeration of the difficulties confronting the aims of general education up to 1945 will lay the basis for some hypotheses about the failure of the program in postwar America.

The first point to be made before considering the postwar situation is that the idea of general education in prewar America was often simply revanchist, by which I mean that it was an attempt to smuggle back in as much as possible of the old liberal arts curriculum displaced by the new system of electives and majors (the major system was instituted by Harvard in 1909, in part to formalize specialized courses of study). The revanchist motive had the effect of confusing general education with liberal education, a much older ideal based on an avowedly elite conception of intellectual inquiry as the pursuit of those freed from labor, who had time to devote to the "liberal arts." The various attempts to reinstate the idea of a "liberal education" in the twentieth century have usually run along a parallel track with general education; but since the latter often borrows its rationale from the former, it is easy to see how general education could become the inevitable curricular expression of that liberal ideal.[10]

Still more problematically, with the recession of liberal education as the governing ideal of the university, general education came to be elided with the humanities disciplines, understood as the fields concerned chiefly with the preservation of traditional high cultural works of literature and philosophy (with allowances in most programs for courses in the other arts). It has been much more difficult to integrate the natural and social sciences into general education for this reason, although an attempt at such integration is the major innovation of the postwar period, as evidenced in the Red Book's program. Nonetheless, that integration has seldom been smooth, and more often than not it has been abandoned for distribution requirements, a point to which we will return. In fact, the humanities faculty has borne the major burden of sustaining the general education project; but even this default delegation has not resolved the problem of the relation between general education courses and the disciplines, which are modern institutional structures very unlike the seven liberal arts of the premodern university. The fact that the humanities in the twentieth century were themselves evolving rapidly into modern disciplines, organized along thoroughly professional lines and with modern research agendas, vitiated the conservative construction of their purpose in general education. Yet the humanities continue to be charged with some general education functions, especially in schools *without* general education programs, with consequent tensions around the responsibility for teaching universitywide courses in the lower division.

The inability of humanities disciplines during the interwar period to step easily into the general education role accounts for the fact that at least thirty independent general education programs were established in the 1920s and 1930s, a remarkable paroxysm that swept through the postsecondary system.[11] Although the rationales and curricula among these programs varied considerably, it does appear that at base they were driven by the perception that students did not know, and had insufficient opportunity to learn, the literature, art, music, philosophy, and history deemed necessary for an educated elite, for the leaders of the nation—or more pointedly, for the dominant class, however shifting the economic and political bases of this domination.[12] The rationale for general education thus drew upon a conception of higher education as desirably and necessarily elite, even within the structure of democratic society. The fact of an electoral process in no way contradicted, in the view of many, the need for a hierarchical educational system whose product would be an elite from which leaders would be chosen. A typical statement of this earlier viewpoint can be found in the work of Irving Babbitt, who in his many polemics expressed open contempt for a democratized educational system and argued instead for the necessity of installing sophisticated cultural credentials in the educated elite as the qualification of its right to rule.[13]

Later commentators on the university continued to express dismay at the educated elite's cultural ignorance, a complaint exemplified in Abraham Flexner's 1930 blast at the contemporary university for its utter helplessness when confronted with a population of entering students "devoid of cultural interests."[14] Granted the usual exaggeration in such polemic, the point to be underscored is that the original impetus behind the first wave of general education programs was unabashedly elitist. This motive obtained even when it was defended on democratic grounds, as in the work of Robert Maynard Hutchins, who saw the curriculum he established at the University of Chicago, based largely on the Western tradition, as serving a progressive critique of industrial and professional society. Hutchins no doubt believed that what Daniel Bell in his 1966 study of general education called the "aristocratic flavor" of the Chicago curriculum (*Reforming*, 15) was a necessary corollary of its legitimate task of providing democratic society with a truly humane and critical corps of intellectuals from which to select its leaders.[15] But the elitism of the impetus behind general education could just as easily be seen as reinforcing the cultural homogeneity of that elite, once universities after World War I began to exercise selective admissions.

This was no doubt not Hutchins's intention at all, but as it happens the general education movement coincides historically with rising anxiety about the cultural and ethnic heterogeneity of the student body—specifically anxiety about the admission of Jews to elite institutions.[16] Columbia University, for example, had no set policy for excluding Jews during the prewar period of the university's growth, as a result of which their numbers increased greatly by 1915; but in the immediate postwar period new, selective admissions procedures were introduced that involved the use of photographs and personal interviews to weed out, none too subtly, otherwise qualified Jewish applicants. Similarly at Harvard, where the Jewish population was growing equally rapidly, President Abbot Lawrence Lowell instituted preliminary measures for "quota" admissions, designed to reduce the Jewish population to 15 percent.[17] In defense of the policy he wrote that "this limitation would work to the benefit of Harvard by enabling it to retain its character as a 'democratic, national university,' drawing from all classes of the community and promoting a sympathetic understanding among them" (Weschler, 161). In his account of this episode, from which I have been paraphrasing, Harold Weschler notes that Lowell's critics remarked upon the "ironic" sense of the word "democratic" in his statement. The point of revisiting this history of anti-Semitism is not only to recall that it spurred the system of selective admissions that has since dominated our university system, counterbalancing its powerful drive to democratization of access. It is much more to recollect the structural selectivity that *always* contradicted the democratizing aims of general education. We need only remember that, whatever the situation with respect to Jewish students, the American university was closed for other reasons to large sectors of the population: women, working-class students, African Americans. The structural impediments to the admission of these groups to postsecondary education (impediments that, let us admit, were only partially and very ineffectively redressed by the institution of apartheid colleges and universities) often survived into the 1960s and beyond, long after President Lowell contemplated his quotas for Jewish students.[18]

What are we to make of the fact, then, that general education, which seems by definition to embrace the generality, was so often instituted in just those institutions that were increasingly selective in their admissions?[19] Here again we confront the arithmetical paradox of Macdonald's observation that in England, unlike America, familiarity with the works of high culture was both "general" and confined to 5 percent of the population. If general education was indeed what every human being, every citizen of a democratic nation, was supposed to know and needed to know, then why was it sufficient that this knowledge be disseminated only to the university population, as though it mattered only whether *this* generality, *this* demos, was possessed of general knowledge? It is no surprise, then, that for some suspicious critics of Hutchins's prodemocratic rhetoric, the agenda of preserving Western culture in general education programs looked more like an alibi for preserving the ethnic or racial homogeneity of Western culture's heirs, a point that Daniel Bell made in his study of general education, and which has been echoed frequently in recent years.[20]

Nevertheless, if the program of general education could fall into line, whatever the intentions of its advocates, with the agenda of resisting "social diversity," a euphemism for Jews, according to Bell, it might also function as a mechanism of assimilation, which it seems eventually to have done at Columbia, as Bell also noted. Hence, a further question can be raised, upon which I will insist throughout this chapter, about how effectively the curriculum of general education produced effects of cultural homogenization and whether these effects can be compared in intensity or scope with the effects of class or ethnic upbringing or with those of mass culture. Let us hypothesize, then, that the coincidence of selective admissions and the structural exclusion of so many groups from the university system would tend to confirm the inevitably homogenizing cultural effect of general education, if by that we mean that the university population was now to be given a *common* curriculum of study, based on a *common* cultural inheritance, before advancing to the level of specialization. But was this program really strong enough and sufficiently widespread in the university system to have such socially homogenizing effects? There is good reason to conclude that in fact it was not.

This brings me to my second large point about the emergence of general education programs, which is that they could not have been instituted were it not for the perceived and probably actual failure of the secondary school system to develop a curriculum that was truly substantive, with the exception, of course, of a handful of elite college preparatory schools. The massification (or democratization) of secondary education in the nineteenth century was, as Sheldon Rothblatt has noted, something more like the development of an underdeveloped pedagogy.[21] For whatever reasons—and they are too complex to enter into here—the secondary schools nearly universally failed to immerse students in a curriculum of mature literary, philosophical, and historical writing. As a result, a constitutive gap opened up between the knowledge *acquired* at the top of the secondary level and the knowledge *demanded* at the bottom of the postsecondary level, a gap that became critical when the rapid growth of the university system started to catch up with the extent of secondary education.[22] The result of this gap was to compel the lower division in most colleges and universities to be given over to a considerable amount of remedial work (Rothblatt, 16). This situation contrasts sharply with that of European secondary schools, such as those in France, where the *baccalauréat* was and probably still is a credential of much greater substance than the American high school diploma. The failure of the secondary system was a condition not only for the emergence of general education, but also for the tacit subsumption of general education to remedial aims, a confusion that came to pervade the curriculum at the lower division, that is, during the years before the major is declared. The task of remediation also confuses, both pedagogically and theoretically, the inculcation of cognitive skills with the transmission of a knowledge base, the latter usually conceived in the context of general education as the Western tradition, but increasingly after World War II as basic knowledge about the social and natural sciences too.

The difficulty of remediation, or catching students up to a level of cultural (or other) knowledge deemed necessary for the grander cultural and ideological aims of general education, tended in practice to impede the realization of those grander aims, at the same time that pressure increased on the "general" sector of the curriculum to produce cultural effects far beyond what could reasonably be expected to result from a small number of college courses, usually organized around the rubric of the Western tradition.[23] In addition to the limitations imposed by the remedial goal, we can also cite in this context the pressure emanating from another quite different "culture," one more directly connected with the *primary* function of the American university system, to credentialize the professional classes. This is the third large point I would like to make about the historical conditions for the emergence of general education. As Burton Bledstein argued in his seminal work, *The Culture of Professionalism*, the middle classes in America were very successful in turning the university into an instrument of cultural formation, but not of the sort that the critics in the *Kulturkritik* tradition were disposed to approve. Instead of that polyglot critical intellectual, widely and deeply immersed in the great works of the Western tradition, the "culture of professionalism" produced a person who "committed himself to an ethic of service, was trained in scientific knowledge, and moved his career relentlessly upward."[24] It was not until some years after this culture was firmly established, enabled in part by the curricular reformation of the late nineteenth century, that the professional-managerial class became uneasy with its neglect of traditional culture, and so it was disposed to endorse the partial reinstatement of that culture in general education programs in the 1920s.[25]

When these programs were inaugurated, the result, I would argue, was a very weak homogenization effect. By this I mean that although it was no longer necessary for the educated elite as a whole to be exclusively or deeply immersed in traditional high culture, it did become desirable after the First World War for many professionals to acquire some familiarity with this culture, which was then incorporated as a new aspect of the "culture of professionalism." Henceforth I will call traditional or high culture *culture*$_1$, and Burton's "culture of professionalism" *culture*$_2$. The incorporation of what we might call a "lite" version of culture$_1$ into culture$_2$ produced a very different cultivating effect from what was intended by the program of general education, one that might be dismissed as superficial but that nevertheless has a real if indirect social function by virtue of its weak homogenization effect.[26] The appearance of the "middlebrow" in the general field of cultural production is a symptom of the incorporation of the lite version of culture$_1$ into the culture of professionalism. This weak acculturation effect also accounts for the fierce reaction of the high modernist artists and critics against the middlebrow, which they saw as confirming the emergence of a poorly educated elite and the failure of the colleges in their historical mission. The appearance of the middlebrow was thus correlated with the emergent class fraction of professionals and managers, as a symptom of both its cultural insecurity and its consequent misplaced piety.

The social effect of general education has been described in terms similar to those I have adopted here by Alain Touraine in his virtuoso study, *The*

Academic System in American Society, as "the consolidation of the social hierarchy."[27] By this he means the consolidation near the top of this hierarchy of a *new* social elite being formed in the new university. Though the attainment of easy familiarity with Western high culture might be strictly unnecessary from the point of view of culture$_2$, some familiarity with traditional culture would shortly become a requisite for achieving certain levels of advancement within the society of the highly credentialed populace. In a university system that was constantly restratifying, universities and colleges that offered some curricular options for studying traditional culture were able to maintain a higher status than those that failed to offer this option. This is why the traditionally elite schools—the expensive liberal arts colleges and most prestigious research institutions—were quick to embrace versions of general education, however dubious the largest claims made for such programs. The relation to high culture provided by these elite institutions might for any individual graduate range from the very deep to the very shallow; but the depth or authenticity of that relation would likely be irrelevant in most professional contexts. Only at the uppermost stratum of the professional elite might the *cultural* capital offered by general education courses be translated into *social* capital: career professionals find it necessary to demonstrate credentials in culture$_1$; they must interest themselves in literary events, opera, or museum exhibitions as a requisite to further advancement in their careers. This engagement is not necessarily shallow, any more than it is necessarily deep. It is only, in some contexts, necessary. A basic knowledge of opera might be desirable, for example, but perhaps not Schoenberg (or in the literary domain, perhaps not Proust!). The interaction of cultural and social capital is no doubt far more complex than this sketch implies, which glances only at the top of the professional hierarchy. There is good reason to think that this interaction is for most members of the professional-managerial class relatively slight. The limitations imposed on the cultural engagement of the professional classes are also likely to stand in a somewhat tense or even antagonistic relation to academic versions of cultural capital, which are sustained, of course, by full-time scholarship.

The effect produced by this lite version of culture$_1$, whatever its value, points to an aspect of the American university system that Touraine's study nicely brings out, namely that the American university is *underdetermining* with respect to American national culture. Insofar as there is a "national culture," it is largely formed elsewhere, as I think we would all now acknowledge, by the mass media—or more accurately, in the complex interaction between mass media and regional or ethnic cultures. This domain of interaction and cultural formation comes into contact only slightly with the culture of the university, the site of general education. Although general education constitutes the curriculum that students supposedly have in *common*, the effects of that curriculum tend to be exaggerated or misidentified by taking at face value the grand rationales that support these programs, the claims for educating the "whole man," or for equipping students with the most essential knowledge they will need for their cultural lives, or for educating citizens for participation in democracy. In fact, students who study electrical engineering, dental hygiene, or urban planning have much more in common *culturally* as a result of their "specialized" disciplines than they have with each other as a result of whatever general education courses they might take. The effects of the pedagogy that the professional disciplines have in common are cultural effects, even if they are not always recognized as such.[28] This much we should have learned long ago from Burton Bledstein. The very vehemence with which the claims of general education have been asserted betrays the dominance of that other culture, the culture of professionalism.

General education programs are also, let us remember, always "lower" with respect to the preprofessional curriculum. Often their exalted claims are undercut by the tacitly remedial function they are forced to serve. For this reason too the "nationalist" or ideological aims of general education have never been as effective as they might seem, judging from the explicit intentions expressed in these rationales.[29] Critics of these programs have been altogether too impressed by the most obvious and clumsy ideological moves, such as the deliberate annexing of the American to the Western tradition, a motive expressed early on in John Erskine's great books curriculum at Columbia, and subsequently ensconced in the rationales for most general education programs. But the need for these programs to annex claims for American democracy to the tradition of Western culture is an obvious sign of their innate weakness as ideological instruments.[30] So the authors of the Harvard Red Book, like the canting William Bennetts of our day, thematize "democracy" as the leitmotif of the Western tradition, a misconstruction both egregious and desperate, as though one could draw a line of inevitable development from Plato to Jefferson.[31]

Although it may appear that such overtly political thematization betrays the real social motives of general education, and therefore its real social effects, Touraine's argument suggests on the contrary that general education served a narrower function in the interwar period; it is described in his discussion of the Columbia University program as "consolidating the power and superiority of a social elite that is threatened by the rise of immigrants, especially in New York, where Jewish families spur their children on to an intellectual success that might make up for the difficulty of crossing certain social barriers" (67). No doubt this effect will seem bad enough, but it could hardly have been accomplished by general education alone, especially given the explicit contradiction between the professed concern for disseminating the Western tradition more widely, at least as far as the student body, formerly free to ignore it altogether under the elective system, and the emergence of highly selective admissions policies. Yet whatever consolidating effects the general education curriculum might have had were far weaker than those of the "old college," where everyone did indeed study the same works, from beginning to end, and far weaker than the consolidating effects produced by assimilation into professional-managerial fields, or the new culture of professionalism. The very fact that Touraine offers this explanation for the institution of general education at Columbia University compels us to explain not the enduring success of the exclusionary agenda but its eventual (postwar) failure. Even if it can be argued (and in this I would agree with Touraine) that general education sustained a residual culturally elitist ethos (much reduced in size) within the American university, as a counterweight to the democratization its advocates supposedly also endorsed, it must be admitted that the cultural bar represented by general education (or the Western tradition) was not raised very high. Was it really knowledge of Plato and Company that granted one access to the cultural elite? And was that knowledge so very difficult to acquire, given the fact that it no longer required that Plato be read in Greek? In the postwar era it was increasingly easy for some of those who might be regarded as permanently outside the traditional elite, or incapable of entering fully into the ancient culture that supposedly was the basis of this elite, simply to leap over the low barrier of general education, or more accurately to absorb its message all too well, and to use it as an instrument of assimilation. The irony of this strategy, however, was that for these outsiders the embrace of the Western tradition, and of the aims of general education, exceeded from the beginning the engagement of most professionally educated persons in traditional culture. Most professionals could make only a weak proprietary claim upon this cultural tradition, because most of them invested their time and energy elsewhere, in the disciplines that ensured their credentialization and their membership in the real cultural elite of the twentieth century, the professional-managerial class.

This analysis suggests that the vast expansion of the university system that took place after World War II was certain to undermine whatever actual elitist or exclusionary effects the program of general education might have had. My point is that these effects were always greatly overestimated. As we know, in the postwar period the postsecondary system became increasingly accessible to nonelite or formerly excluded populations, such as Jews, women, blacks, and other ethnic and racial minorities. And, indeed, it does seem that the impetus driving the formation of general education programs before the war diminished in strength during the 1950s, and that as a consequence new rationales for general education began to appear (such as that proposed by Daniel Bell for Columbia but never instituted).[32] General education did not disappear altogether, so much as it was commuted, reduced to distribution requirements that have the residual purpose of "counterpoising" the emphasis on specialization but attempt very little more. Because courses taken within the framework of the distribution requirements were not usually, if ever, coherently organized with an acculturative function in mind, the point of the old *Kulturkritik* opposition to specialization was simply lost.[33] It is not clear what is accomplished by distribution requirements today other than imposing upon students the obligation to familiarize themselves with several other disciplines—by no means an objectionable aim, but the absence of an articulated rationale for these requirements is more than evident when both students and their advisers casually describe these courses as something to "get out of the way."

Perhaps the most obvious evidence of this failure is the nearly universal distributionalization of social and natural science requirements and the return of general education to its base in the humanities. The most foresighted and promising aspect of the Red Book, as well as of Daniel Bell's thoughtful study of general education, was the recommendation that general education comprehend all the disciplines, and that would liberate it once and for all from its culturalist bias. But this proposal seems to have failed utterly, as general education courses in the natural and social sciences have nearly everywhere been replaced by distribution requirements. Even at Harvard, where the Red Book reigned, the science requirement was distributionalized by 1959 (Miller, 138).

The failure of the strong form of the general education movement in the postwar period coincided both with the intensification and expansion of the modern university's new (or accelerated) function of producing knowledge and with an enormous influx of government money for research occasioned in part by the cold war.[34] The acculturative function ($culture_1$) could then be safely redistributed to the top tier of the university or college hierarchy, with the tacit aim of consolidating an elite fraction *within* the larger corps of the professional-managerial class. Schools that offer students the option and time to study Plato or Bernini or Woolf or Wittgenstein, as opposed to molecular biochemistry or dental hygiene, are almost always the most selective, the most expensive, the most elite. This is not to say, however, that even in these schools a programmatic form of general education triumphed anew over the specialized curriculum. On the contrary, $culture_1$ would continue to be propagated for most students in this fraction of the dominant fraction in its lite version; but the more important point, which marks the difference between the prewar and postwar periods, is that the restratification of the university system, its fracturing into a vast hierarchy extending from the summit of the ivies to the most underfunded of the community colleges, freed the majority of graduates —the credentialed population—from having to incorporate culture$_1$ into the culture of professionalism at all. I will call this population of credentialed graduates a *mass elite*, by which I mean that their credentials set them off economically, and to some extent culturally, from those without credentials. This is, as so much recent theory has been telling us, the new class structure of our society. In calling the credentialed many a mass elite, I mean to signal the fact that this sector of the populace is indeed an elite—it possesses cultural capital in the form of credentials—at the same time that it is enormously larger in number and as a percentage of the populace than any elite that preceded it. Finally, the mass elite is not defined or discernible by its *level of culture*, in the old sense in which cultural knowledge defined the aristocrat, the gentleman, or the bourgeois who aspired to gentility. This mass elite is defined by a much looser common culture, tenuously connected to its technical and professional credentials. For the mass elite there is no longer any need to fear Proust. Cultural anxiety about the level of taste has been displaced largely to the domain of consumables, where niche marketing has established new and complex hierarchies. With the development of this new cultural formation, anxiety about traditional culture would have to be induced by strenuous shaming efforts, such as those undertaken by the two Blooms, Allan and Harold.

The fractioning of the college-educated population into niche cultures of consumption, united more by the artifacts of mass culture and by the credentials that constitute the mass elite, is a paradoxical effect of what we rather innocently call "democratization." As the demand for personnel to occupy professional-managerial fields rose over the twentieth century—and escalated geometrically after World War II—there was no longer any possibility that these fields could be supplied by the children of a prewar-type elite. Democratization of access was inevitable; it absorbed large numbers of nonelite students into the university system for the purpose of turning out the professionals, managers, scientists, and technicians needed in the new postindustrial economy. At the same time, as Touraine points out, the demand for credentials escalated for a host of occupations, which forced larger numbers into the postsecondary system in order to keep up as well as to advance. A high school degree might have been sufficient for a career in hotel management in the prewar period, but after the war it was necessary to have a *degree* in hotel management.

Touraine fairly asks whether this effect should be more accurately called "massification" than "democratization." Massification drove restratification within the university system, as the difference between a high school degree and a college degree reappeared within the system as the difference between degrees from an elite and a nonelite institution. In the prewar period those with a college education were *less* consolidated than the upper class of the nineteenth century but much *more* consolidated than their postwar successors. In the postwar period a difference in size resulted in a transformation of the basic social character of college education and a much greater weakening of its power to produce desired cultural effects by means of a traditional high culture curriculum in the lower division. To these incoming students, the works of the Western tradition would come to seem increasingly unmoored, decontextualized. What appeared before them was, rather, the subject of a discipline like any other, to be approached with the same focus and preprofessional investment as any other. Those students who most enjoyed doing their major in a humanities discipline were more likely to want a professional career in that field than to regard their major as simply a good way to become *generally* educated. Specialization in humanities disciplines no longer had any necessary connection to general education, as a career in a humanities discipline followed a career track much like any other specialized discipline or professional field.[35] In practice this has made staffing general education courses increasingly difficult; many humanities faculty are no more prepared to teach such courses than their colleagues in the natural or social sciences.

Already in 1945 James Bryant Conant, in his introduction to the Red Book, recognized that the function of general education would be irrevocably altered by the expansion of the university system. On the contrast between past and present he wrote: "The restricted nature of the circle possessing certain linguistic and historical knowledge greatly enhances the prestige of this knowledge. 'Good taste' could be standardized in each generation for those who knew. But, today, we are concerned with a general education—a liberal education—not for the relatively few, but for a multitude" (ix). Even in 1945 higher education was becoming a form of mass education. If the tacit assumption of general education before the war was that even though the university system was expanding, it would remain small enough to define a social elite, after the war that assumption was no longer tenable. Responding to this changed landscape, the authors of the Red Book adopted a distinction between two motives for general education—the Jeffersonian and the Jacksonian—which corresponded roughly to the distinction between elite and mass education. The former is concerned with "discovering and giving opportunity to the gifted student," and the latter with "raising the level of the average student" (27). The distinction shows that the Harvard authors were thinking seriously, if worriedly, about the effects of massification, and that they were willing to admit at least by implication that general education in the prewar period was Jeffersonian or elitist. We might want to say now that this elite was "gifted" more by virtue of its upbringing and privileged early education than by innate genius. In any case, let us admit that the democratization of the educational system, which had long since transformed primary and secondary schooling, was really also a process of massification. The question that remains to be addressed is whether the massified system could sponsor a "Jacksonian" version of general education.

The authors of the Red Book, though they were committed to a conception of the ideal educational system as a balance of Jeffersonian and Jacksonian agendas, also admitted that they were more concerned in their discussion of general education with sustaining the vitality of the Jeffersonian ideal—not surprisingly, since they were writing from their perch at Harvard. If this distinction implies different programs of general education, one for the top tier of the university system, another for the middle and lower tiers, its seems evident that the Jacksonian project has been carried on, if at all, as a tacit project of remediation, and not a very successful one at that. We are left with a system in which culture$_1$ continues to define the general education programs of the most elite institutions, while the Jacksonian project has languished in an underdeveloped state.

The persistence of general education in an uneasy, attenuated form, at the same time that the university system was compelled to open its doors to an ever more diverse population, meant that two quite different relations to culture$_1$ emerged among those who were formerly excluded from access to this system. The first relation, which was of course most likely to be found in the elite institutions, expressed a powerful *overinvestment* in traditional high culture, a virtual identification with that culture. These new cultural conservatives took up the cause of the culture critics like Erskine who had once hoped to save high culture by means of general education, but without endorsing or perpetuating the covert identification of an ethnic or racial elite with a cultural elite. While it may be difficult to find a way to put this point with the delicacy it deserves, it is worth making the attempt in order to appreciate the historical irony in the *succession* of cultural critics. It is undeniable, for example, that the Jews who entered the university system in humanities fields in the postwar period became some of its greatest scholars. But it is also the case that some of these figures were spun off, as it were, from the scholarly to the "middlebrow" domain, as a result of what I would call an overidentification with traditional high culture. This overidentification meant that the Anglophile originators of general education such as Erskine and Hutchins would be succeeded ultimately by figures such as Mortimer Adler, Allan Bloom, and Harold Bloom, who started out as specialist scholars but who ended up defending the standard of high culture by forming an alliance with the middlebrow against academic specialists.[36]

Ultimately the figures associated with the cultural project of the "generally" educated person—that is, the person who is widely cultivated in the literature, philosophy, and art of the West—were responsible in part for the transformation of high culture *into a middlebrow concept.* The appearance of Russell Lynes's famous article on levels of taste, "Highbrow, Lowbrow, Middlebrow," in *Harper's Magazine* in 1949, already betrays how thoroughly high cultural taste in the arts had become indistinguishable from styles of consumption in clothing and food. Lynes's notorious diagram of these levels of taste offered these categories: clothes, furniture, useful objects, entertainment, salads, drinks, games, and causes, *along with* reading, sculpture, and records, the last three the only elements of culture that would have belonged to the prewar domain of the high-low distinction. Lynes's article suggests that cultural anxiety about where one stood in a status hierarchy was being steadily displaced from the domain of the "great works" to the domain of consumption or lifestyle. The mixing of consumer goods with high cultural artifacts (which is not quite the same thing as the commodification of high culture, though it proceeds in parallel with that development) suggests that among what I have called the mass elite there was less and less anxiety about traditional high culture, and that this anxiety was being transferred to the domain of consumption generally. In other words, one can describe as a condition for the decline of general education programs in most universities and colleges an *underinvestment* in traditional high culture by the mass elite, which was using the university system primarily to stabilize or increase its income; only later did it explore its "level of taste" by means of its buying power.

The mass elite was characterized by features of internal diversity—gender, ethnicity, race—that were unprecedented before the war and after it could play out in two quite different scenarios, overinvestment and underinvestment in high culture. In the former, the standard-bearers of high culture took on the project of *inducing* the cultural anxiety that was evidently absent from the greater part of the mass elite. For the guests at Peter Baida's dinner party, for example, it would be necessary first to induce shame at not knowing who Proust was as the motive for reading Proust—perhaps not the best motive! At any rate, in the absence of a universal program of general education, it is unlikely that a vehement defense of high culture such as the two Blooms have mounted in recent years can circulate within the mass elite as anything other than another version of the middlebrow, even more attenuated than its prewar version. I suggest, then, that the experience of cultural anxiety about the great works of Western high culture is much less widespread among the mass elite in the postwar period, or much less intense, than it was among the college population of the prewar period. The interesting further effect of this relaxation of cultural anxiety is that the traffic between high culture and its middlebrow appropriations has been considerably easier and less guilt ridden, to the extent that the distinction between the middlebrow artifact, as an appropriated version of high culture, and the high cultural artifact itself is of concern only to the specialist. The mass elite is relatively indifferent to the difference between *Romeo and Juliet* on the stage and *Shakespeare in Love*. It is not that the mass elite mistakes the latter for the equal of the former, but rather that it cannot muster even the smallest portion of the indignation a Dwight Macdonald would have heaped upon a film such as *Shakespeare in Love*.

None of this is to deny that elite institutions (the most selective colleges and universities) continue to propagate through general education a stratum (now culturally quite diverse in some respects) with access to traditional high culture, so defined, along with some of the effects of exclusion accompanying the stratification of mass education at the tertiary level. Who gets admitted to the most prestigious institutions, as we know, is often a matter of chance and circumstance. In conclusion, I point to one other effect of the two opposed relations to high culture I have called overinvestment and underinvestment, an effect that bears on the canon debate of the 1970s and 1980s. Without venturing to reengage this debate in any polemical way, I suggest that its vehemence revealed in the critics of the canon an overinvestment in high culture that corresponded to the overinvestment of those who, like the Blooms, identified with that culture. This complementary overestimation was localized among those minority populations, gender and racial, who leapt easily over the low barrier of general education and established careers in the humanities disciplines. For these scholars overinvestment in the Western tradition was expressed not by identification but by its opposite, by disidentification or, alternatively, identification with the canon of the excluded, the noncanonical. It was only by making an initial investment in the tradition, then, that the antagonists of the cultural conservatives could make their appearance on the scene and make a paradoxical contribution to reinvigorating the frozen monuments of the tradition. The mixed effects of this struggle are very much present to us now in the sense we often have that without an initial investment in the canon, it is not possible to recover the excitement of canon critique, of rediscovering the noncanonical. Can we now describe this peculiar scenario as something that could have taken place only after the decline of general education?

The intuition that traditional high culture functioned to consolidate an elite against encroachment from minority groups was of course absolutely correct, but for the nineteenth century! It was already out of date when President Eliot retired the classical curriculum. After the war it would be possible for some members of marginal social groups, the formerly excluded, to enter into the humanities and to be at once engaged and troubled by their former role in consolidating the cultural identity of historical elites. More puzzling still, their nominal centrality was belied by their actually precarious and marginal position among the disciplines. For a much larger fraction of the mass elite, the situation was understood quite differently. For this group it was evident that economic success and social mobility were less assured in fields relating to high culture than in virtually any other professional, scientific, or technical field. So far as the members of most formerly excluded groups were concerned, democratization and upward mobility could be achieved far more effectively in law, medicine, science, and the host of other moneymaking technical and business fields than in English or classics.

In retrospect, we might say that the canon debates replayed the drama of democratization—exclusion and inclusion—as a narrative about the curriculum itself. The humanities disciplines, as the residual site of a "general education," recovered a value in the very restaging of the drama of access. This restaging, to be sure, confused access to the *university* with entrance into the *canon;* but another way to think of this misunderstanding is as an attempt to revalue upward the cultural value of the canon (along, of course, with the complementary noncanonical works, which were bound indissolubly to that canon). In this sense the critique of the canon was contingent on an overinvestment in high culture that was indeed analogous to the overinvestment of the cultural conservatives, who were just as eager as their left antagonists to *interest* the mass elite in the high cultural tradition.

At this date I am disinclined to dismiss the canon debate as nugatory in its effects, since both the left and right positions in the debate valued cultural works, not always the same works, but the same category of objects—the cultural. Anything that gets people interested! And yet I do wonder whether the entire debate can be located in the line of the Jeffersonian rather than the Jacksonian project, since both positions take for granted the institutional privilege of humanities education, which is still rather a luxury for the larger fraction of the mass elite. This is to say that the Jacksonian project, which the authors of the Harvard Red Book implied is the more urgent, though they failed to take it up, has *never* been taken up, and so general education has languished in the postwar academy. Another way to put this point is yet again to contest the derogation of the humanities disciplines to a residual form of general education, the surest evidence that this project was a historical failure.

I remain doubtful that the project of general education can ever succeed if it is located solely at the university level, which is surely too late for its inauguration. But that fact is no excuse for any of us in the university. If the

Jeffersonian project, in the Red Book's terms, of "raising the level of culture" for the university population (and why not for everyone?) suggests anything desirable, as opposed to something insulting or tacitly elitist, it must first direct our attention to the essential paradox of the American educational system, which sets before us the splendor of the research university surrounded by the intellectual squalor of a nation that seems to celebrate ignorance and superstition.[37] In the United States what Marx called "rural idiocy"— or, to update his term, "suburban idiocy"— has miraculously survived what ought to have been the happier effect of capitalism, at least according to his famous manifesto. But if this means that there is a Jacksonian project for the educational system, it cannot simply be a diluted version of an already diluted Jeffersonian curriculum, which is sure to be some version of the humanities, beefed up and watered down at the same time. Let us remain troubled, then, by the question of what every human being or citizen needs to know. And let us also admit, being troubled by this question, that we are long past the point of returning to a notion of general education as nothing other than what we already teach in the humanities disciplines. I am in truth more disturbed by the tragic grip of creationism on the American populace than I am by its lack of a nodding acquaintance with Plato or Proust, even though I would of course want every student and citizen to know that Plato is worth reading and Proust is worth reading. Knowing this, however, does not tell me what general education is. It only tells me that one experiment failed, and another remains to be imagined.

Notes

1. Dwight Macdonald, *Against the American Grain* (New York, 1962), 64.

2. Woolf herself would have been most distressed to be associated with the category of the middlebrow, which she treats with amiable contempt in a letter to the *New Statesman;* she never sent the letter, but it was later published. See Virginia Woolf, "Middlebrow," in *The Death of the Moth and Other Essays* (New York, 1942).

3. Barbara Ehrenreich, *Fear of Falling: The Inner Life of the Middle Class* (New York, 1989), 241. The passage quoted by Ehrenreich is from Peter Baida, "Confessions of a Reluctant Yuppie," *American Scholar* (Winter 1985–86): 45.

4. Joan Shelley Rubin, in the best recent discussion of the great books phenomenon, *The Making of Middlebrow Culture* (Chapel Hill, N.C., 1992), argues for the underlying ambivalence with which Americans viewed the great works of Western culture, an ambivalence both sides of which John Erskine fully exploited in his career. See also the interesting study by Janice A. Radway, *A Feeling for Books: The Book-of-the-Month Club, Literary Taste, and Middle-Class Desire* (Chapel Hill, N.C., 1997).

5. For reasons I will address later, this anxiety seems to have peaked in the immediate postwar period and to have evolved into quite a different form after the 1960s. The terms *highbrow, middlebrow,* and *mass* are in my view useful in indicating the context of a work's production or reception, but quite useless as a measure of value. If the notion that works produced within

the context of high culture or avant-garde are intrinsically more valuable than those produced as middlebrow or mass cultural is no longer credible, however, neither is it credible simply to ignore the contexts of production and consumption and the cultural markers that are attached to works in circulation. For a contrary argument on this question, the reader may consult Michael Kammen, *American Culture, American Tastes: Social Change in the 20th Century* (New York, 1999).

6. See Alan C. Purves, "General Education and the Search for a Common Culture," in *Cultural Literacy and the Idea of General Education,* ed. Ian Westbury and Alan C. Purves (Chicago, 1988), 1.

7. Gary Miller, *The Meaning of General Education: The Emergence of a Curriculum Paradigm* (New York, 1988), 134, notes that in 1940 Harvard offered four hundred undergraduate courses, not one of them required. For an interesting retrospect and critique of the tradition of cultural criticism, see Francis Mulhern, *Culture/Metaculture* (London, 2000).

8. *General Education in a Free Society: Report of the Harvard Committee* (Cambridge, 1945), 74.

9. Without venturing into the general muddle evoked by the concept of culture, I do want to consider here a kind of cultural anxiety that takes the form of anxiety *about culture*. Obviously the two uses of culture in this sentence do not refer to the same object, as the first characterizes the anxiety of a group in sociological terms, and the second says that the specific anxiety is about an abstracted entity called "culture." I am trying to think, then, about what it meant when Andrew White, writing in 1908 and having retired from the presidency of Cornell, said that "in our eagerness for . . . new things we have too much lost sight of certain valuable old things, the things in university education which used to be summed up under the word 'culture.'" Quoted in Christopher Lucas, *American Higher Education: A History* (New York, 1994), 211.

10. Defenses of liberal education are so easy to come by there is no point in listing them here. For a recent example, see Francis Oakley, *Community of Learning: The American College and the Liberal Arts Tradition* (New York, 1992).

11. See Frederick Rudolph, *Curriculum: A History of the American Undergraduate Course of Study since 1636* (San Francisco, 1937), 256.

12. For an interesting account of the rationales for general education, see Daniel Bell, *The Reforming of General Education: The Columbia Experience in Its National Setting* (New York, 1966). Bell himself cannot quite settle on a definitive list of rationales, and he gives different ones on pp. 13, 51, and 282. Putting these lists together, one comes up with: (1) resistance to specialization; (2) supersession of classical curriculum; (3) response to the changing character of the student body, spurring the need for acculturation or integration through a common curriculum, i.e., works of "Western culture"; and (4) ideological, having to do with national or "American" identity.

13. For a typical statement see Irving Babbitt, *Literature and the American College* (1908, rpt. Washington, D.C., 1986), 112: "In general, the humanitarian inclines to see in the college a means not so much for the thorough training of the few as of uplift for the many; his aim, in short, is extensive, not intensive. He is always likely to favor any scheme that will bring the bachelor's degree within reach of a greater number, even at the imminent risk of cheapening the degree itself."

14. From Abraham Flexner, *Universities: American, English, German* (New York, 1930); rpt. in *American Higher Education: A Documentary History*, ed. Richard Hofstadter and Wilson Smith, 2 vols. (Chicago, 1961), 2: 907. The passage is worth quoting in full: "In the main the student body lacks intellectual background or outlook; that again they cannot help. Their students are in the mass devoid of cultural interests and develop little, for the most part, during their four years at college."

15. For Hutchins's major statement, see *The Higher Learning in America* (New Haven, 1936). Hutchins's hostility to professional education is strongly expressed in this volume and programmatically expressed in his desire to sever the professional schools from the university.

The tendency was of course in the other direction, and the influence of the professional schools on the undergraduate curriculum has only increased. Programs such as "premed," for example, are so extensive as to usurp virtually the entire course of study for premed students.

16. In the following paragraphs I draw upon the work of Harold Weschler, *The Qualified Student: A History of Selective College Admission in America* (New York, 1977), especially chap. 7, "Repelling the Invasion: Columbia and the Jewish Student." See also Marcia Synnott, *The Half-Opened Door: Discrimination and Admissions at Harvard, Yale, and Princeton, 1900–1970* (Westport, Conn., 1979).

17. Nitza Rosovsky, *The Jewish Experience at Harvard and Radcliffe* (Cambridge, Mass., 1986), puts the percentage of Jews at Harvard in 1925 at 27.1.

18. I am indebted here to Anne H. Stevens, "The Philosophy of General Education and Its Contradictions: The Influence of Hutchins," *JGE: The Journal of General Education* 50 (2001): 165–191. Stevens puts the larger point I am making here succinctly: "The general education movement promoted democratic values within exclusionary institutions" (175).

19. See Weschler, *Qualified Student*, 163: "During the late nineteenth and early twentieth century, the demand for expertise occasioned by a rapidly industrializing economy necessitated a widening of elite circles, and the university had undertaken the task of training new recruits in the social and professional skills demanded of their new members in a complex society. But, by the onset of World War I, some university authorities concluded that any further increase in enrollments would reduce the effectiveness of their programs." Obviously, enrollments would continue to increase, despite the founding of many new universities and colleges, but for the more elite institutions the emergence of a finely graded hierarchy of institutions meant that selective admissions could become a real possibility, so they could reinforce their elite status but also provide a means of narrowing the cultural diversity that the open elective system of admissions had actually fostered. In this context the democratizing rationale for general education was sure to be curtailed in realization by the increasing selectivity of elite institutions, with what effect we shall see below.

20. See, e.g., James W. Hall with Barbara L. Kevles, *In Opposition to the Core Curriculum: Alternative Models for Undergraduate Education* (Westport, Conn., 1982), for this position.

21. Sheldon Rothblatt, "General Education on the American Campus: A Historical Introduction Brief," in Westbury and Purves, *Cultural Literacy and the Idea of General Education*, 15–16. Rothblatt notes that "general education" is what happened in the European secondary school, and that "the student who went on to university was expected to have mastered the skills and general knowledge essential for acquiring education at an advanced level" (17). The American university by contrast gave over the lower division to this task, which was further confused by the similarity of this curriculum to that of the liberal arts college. The American university might be said then to have reproduced a truncated version of the college at the lower division; but this only confirms the confusion that elides the difference between liberal education and general education.

22. See Rudolph, *Curriculum*, 207, on the growing realization of the secondary system's failure, which occasioned already in the 1890s the first of many commissions, Harvard's Committee of Ten, to look into the reasons for this failure. See also Charles W. Eliot's contemporary statement, "The Gap between the Elementary Schools and the Colleges," *National Educational Association Journal of Proceedings and Addresses* (1890), 522–533. In the year 2000, 35.5 percent of those eighteen to twenty-four years old were enrolled in college, as opposed to about 2 percent during the nineteenth century. For statistics on the college-age population in the twenty-first century, see the *Chronicle of Higher Education*, Almanac Issue, 1 (August 29, 2003).

23. Rudolph, *Curriculum*, 236–237, puts this point strongly: "The general education movement, as the effort to define and enforce a common curriculum has been called, began as a response to the sense of bewilderment with which many young students faced the freedom of the elective course of study. It received clarification during and after World War I, when a

consciousness of Western values and national problems found expression in courses designed to orient students to their cultural inheritance and their responsibilities as citizens. And, like all impossible dreams, the general education idea was carried along from decade to decade receiving new encouragement in one institution or another, the product of a quixotic conviction that the limits of essential knowledge could be defined."

24. Burton J. Bledstein, *The Culture of Professionalism: The Middle Class and the Development of Higher Education in America* (New York, 1978), 333. This professional culture has some analogy to Durkheim's notion of "professional ethics," based as it is on values of truth and service extrapolated largely though not exclusively from the enterprise of science.

25. This tendency was already evident in the great avatar of the professional-managerial class, Charles William Eliot, chemist and Harvard president. Having done so much to transform the university into the vehicle of professionalization, Eliot both predicted and hoped to remedy cultural insecurity by means of his publication project, the Harvard Classics, the famous "five-foot shelf." Keeping busy professionals in mind, Eliot promised that fifteen minutes of reading in the classics a day would be sufficient to rectify the effects of a narrow professional education. His advice rhymes nicely with the advertising pitches that go with various exercise machines today, which seek to remedy the neglect of the body entailed by sedentary labor. With the right machine, one can even do the reading at the same time. Eliot's project looked forward to general education, in both its curricular and its extracurricular forms of the interwar period.

26. Of course, one might also raise the question, already implied in my comments on Arnold, about how deeply "cultured" the graduates of the old liberal arts institutions really were. By 1918 Thorstein Veblen wrote dismissively of this culture in *The Higher Learning in America:* "By force of conventional propriety, a college course—the due term of residence at some reputable university, with the collegiate degree certifying honorable discharge—has become the requisite of gentility." The notion of "gentility" already announces a culture lite; but the American university continued to produce this effect, alongside the effects of the new professional and disciplinary curriculum, by virtue of all the residual cultural practices that connected members of the upper classes with each other—for example, fraternities and sports. This kind of extracurricular acculturation continues to the present.

27. Alain Touraine, *The Academic System in American Society* (1974; rpt. New Brunswick, N.J., 1997).

28. These cultural effects have been teased out in an important work by Michèle Lamont, *Money, Morals, and Manners: The Culture of the French and the American Upper-Middle Class* (Chicago, 1992). Also interesting in this context is the skeptical account of general education in Christopher Jencks and David Riesman, *The Academic Revolution* (New York, 1968), 492–504.

29. On the connection between general education and the transmission of "democratic values," see W. Hugh Stickler et al., *General Education: A University Program in Action* (Dubuque, Iowa, 1950). On the nurturing of a sense of responsibility toward democracy, see Miller, *Meaning of General Education.*

30. Alvin C. Eurich, "A Renewed Emphasis upon General Education," in *General Education in the American College. The Thirty Eighth Yearbook of the National Society for the Study of Education,* ed. Guy Montrose Whipple (Bloomington, Ind., 1939), 4–5, offers an interesting observation about the correlation of the moment of greatest interest in general education programs with the Great Depression. Interest in traditional culture, or the humanities in general, often coincides with economic downturns, as we have come to recognize over the years. This point confirms from a different perspective the unequal contest between the versions of culture defining general education and defining the professional-managerial fields.

31. See *General Education in a Free Society:* "We are part of an organic process, which is the American and, more broadly, the Western evolution" (45).

32. Bell argues in *The Reforming of General Education* against great books programs and for a notion of general education as an inquiry into "how one knows" rather than what one knows.

Thus, general education would be propaedeutic to the disciplines; it would treat the humanities, the sciences, and the social sciences equally. While Bell's proposals were impractical (he wanted to give both the freshman and senior years over to general education), they do overcome the tacit elision of general education with the humanities, and presumably with culture$_1$.

33. Barry O'Connell complains typically in a multiauthored volume, *The Great Core Curriculum Debate: Education as a Mirror of Culture* (New Rochelle, N.Y., 1979), 28, that core curricula and general education programs are at best today only a watered-down version of what was envisioned at Columbia and Chicago before the war. Jerry G. Graff, *General Education Today: A Critical Analysis of Controversies, Practices, and Reforms* (San Francisco, 1983), 8, notes the decline in the number of general education courses as a percentage of courses in the curriculum. Proposals for course curricula these days, once put into action, seem to have a short half-life, to satisfy no one, and to stir up increasing resentment from faculty who are deported to the lower division for service. Jerry C. Graff, Ernest L. Boyer, and John C. Sawhill go further in "New Models for General Education," *Current Issues in Higher Education* 2, no. 4 (1980), declaring general education a "disaster area." And this from the scholars who have a strong interest in reviving its mission in some form.

34. For an excellent discussion of the emergence of the postwar research university, see Richard Lewinton, "The Cold War and the Transformation of the Academy," in *The Cold War and the University*, ed. André Schiffrin (New York, 1997), 1–34.

35. On this point I diverge from the analysis of general education offered by Gerald Graff in *Professing Literature: An Institutional History* (Chicago, 1987). Graff tends to see general education as compatible with the aims of the New Criticism, on the basis of their similarly shallow historical grounding and emphasis on a decontextualized reading technique. But the New Critics tended to be quite critical of general education, not only because translated texts were an impediment to close reading, but because their sympathies were on the side of the "specialist" and "modernist" and against the middlebrow. On this point, see Reuben Brower's critique of great books–type courses in his important essay "Reading in Slow Motion," in *In Defense of Reading: A Reader's Approach to Literary Criticism*, ed. Reuben Brower and Richard Poirier (New York, 1963), 18.

36. I have attempted to make sense of this peculiar alliance of highbrow and middlebrow against the academy in a review-essay on Harold Bloom's *The Western Canon*, "The Ordeal of Middlebrow Culture," *Transition* 67 (1995): 82–92. This conjunction in itself was anticipated in the career of John Erskine, as Joan Shelley Rubin observes in *The Making of Middlebrow Culture*; the difference is the historical irony of succession, from Erskine the Episcopal insider to Bloom the Jewish outsider.

37. I offer as an emblem of this paradoxical condition Johns Hopkins Medical Hospital, which rises from the slums of East Baltimore, as if to say to the surrounding population that the great advances in medical knowledge taking place within its walls are actually contingent upon denying *them* access to health care. So it is with our supposedly democratized university system, which racks up Nobel Prizes while vast numbers look to the stars for their fates and know next to nothing about the world beyond the borders of the nation.

2

DEMOGRAPHY AND CURRICULUM

The Humanities in American Higher Education from the 1950s through the 1980s

ROGER L. GEIGER

THE MODERN American university is a cognitive omnivore, feasting on all legitimate fields of knowledge. Different forms of knowledge, in fact, are more readily distinguished by their locus and organization outside universities than within. The humanities, however, find their principal home in university departments. This is not to say that the production and enjoyment of literature, history, and the arts are confined to academic precincts, but rather that the organized study of such subjects, compared with other fields, is concentrated in institutions of higher learning. For most of the twentieth century this has been advantageous. In particular, the great postwar expansion of American higher education provided employment for the world's largest collection of professional humanists. And their teaching brought a fairly high level of exposure to humanistic subjects to the world's largest population of postsecondary students. This chapter will examine the dynamics of the humanities during the great postwar demographic expansion of higher education and try to explain the shifting relationships among student enrollments, institutions of higher education, and the content of the humanities subjects that were taught there.

On the surface the outline of these developments is fairly clear. After the postwar G.I. enrollment bulge dissipated, the educational system began a prolonged natural expansion that was based on population growth and rising participation. The number of seventeen-year-olds doubled from 1950 to the early 1970s, and high school graduation rates rose from 60 to 75 percent. At the same time the propensity to go to college rose from 42 to 53 percent. When these multiples are multiplied, the result is a more than threefold increase in the number of students entering college. Total undergraduate enrollments increased far more—by a factor of five—from under 2 million to over 9 million. States and localities could not build colleges, nor graduate schools train college teachers, fast enough to accommodate these burgeoning numbers. But then the expansion ground to a halt. In the mid-1970s American higher education ceased to grow for the first time in its history—a condition dubbed the "steady state." The steady state caused painful adjustments throughout higher education, but nowhere was the pain more acute than in the humanities. (See Figures 2.1 and 2.2.)

When the last of the G.I.s graduated in 1950, bachelor's degrees in the core humanities disciplines of languages and history constituted just over 8 percent. Their share rose another 2 percentage points during the 1950s, but then shot up to 16 percent in the mid-1960s. For that entire decade the annual number of humanities graduates tripled. In the mid-1970s, however, this category commenced a precipitous drop. A decade later humanities majors represented barely 6 percent of college graduates. This same roller-coaster pattern was repeated for humanities doctorates. These aspiring professionals saw demand for their services evaporate almost overnight. Not only was there an impossible surplus of credentialed humanists, but intellectual shifts also left many of them trained to teach in now-unfashionable fields.

This striking record of unsuccess was accompanied by turmoil within humanities fields. In strategic discussions of the postwar shape of higher education, the humanities were accorded pride of place as fundamental components of a liberal education. They clearly built upon this stature in the years of rapid expansion. At the height of their popularity, however, the humanities were wracked by controversy over relevance and political bias. In some ways the crisis of the curriculum in the humanities paralleled the crisis in its enrollments, but a relationship between the two, if one exists, is far from clear.

Nor are the causes clear behind the boom and bust pattern traced by the humanities from the 1950s to the 1980s. Several factors seemed to play a role, and they will be explored below. Clearly the trend toward vocationalism had an impact, whether as cause or effect.[1] The changing composition of college students and the types of institutions in which they studied both seem relevant. Gender has also been identified as a factor, since male and female students had different study preferences, and the gender balance shifted markedly during these years.[2] Perhaps most challenging is the question of how the changing content of the humanities curriculum influenced this pattern of development.

The Humanities in the Academic Enterprise

The basic concern of this chapter is the vitality of the humanities in American higher education. Accordingly, the kinds of data just referred to are relevant as vital signs of the organism or enterprise. Healthy vital signs do not in themselves assure intellectual vitality, but in a soundly structured enterprise growing

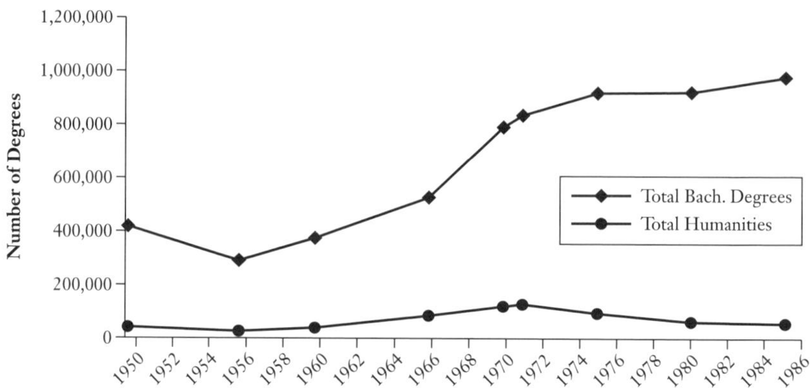

FIGURE 2.1. Bachelor's degrees in the humanities relative to all bachelor's degrees, 1950–1985.

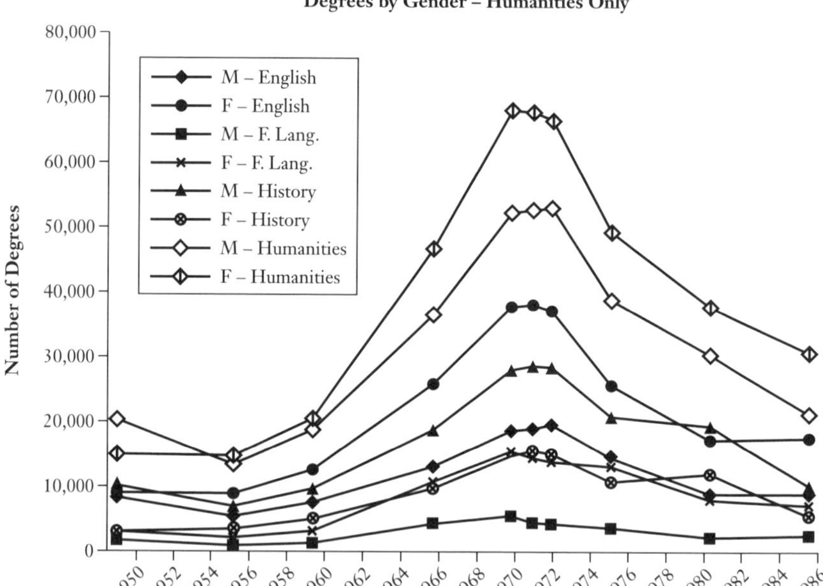

FIGURE 2.2. Bachelor's degrees in the humanities by gender, 1950–1985.

numbers of clients and professionals ought to be conducive to an expanding and relevant knowledge base. In any case, this chapter can deal only obliquely with this issue. The other contributions to this volume in fact speak directly to the intellectual content and achievements of humanistic fields. Furthermore, there is no reason to prejudge the importance of vital signs at this point. The aim of this inquiry is to determine the dynamics of the academic humanities and then to draw inferences about causation and significance.

The vitality of the humanities in the academic enterprise is expressed in the fulfillment of three roles. First, the humanities were considered to be an integral part of a liberal education. Hence, the number of students entering regular academic programs in colleges and universities largely determined the demand for the required components of a liberal or general education. This relationship, however, depended on some ideological assumptions. In particular, each requirement had to possess a "warrant"—an assumption or premise that made the connection between a goal of liberal education and the content of a humanistic course.[3] Such warrants thus constitute one nexus between enrollment and curriculum. This chapter will give particular attention to the course on the history of Western civilization that was required or taught almost universally in the 1950s and 1960s.

Second, the humanities are constituted from subjects that are studied in their own right. Here the obvious measure is the number of bachelor's degrees awarded to majors in the humanities disciplines. Other students naturally took advanced courses in the humanities, but there is no reason to think that these consumers would not fluctuate much like the number of majors. Here the major trends within the humanistic disciplines would determine course content. The major battles over paradigms may occur at the graduate and professional level, but the victors' spoils include the determination of what is taught in undergraduate classes. Undergraduate majors are the most numerous consumers of what humanist scholars produce.

Third, the training of doctoral students constitutes a crucial activity for humanistic and other disciplines. In the humanities nearly 90 percent of doctorates entered academic employment, so their numbers represent fairly directly the supply of new teacher-scholars.[4] Doctoral training also reflects the fine structure of specialization within disciplines. Ph.D. candidates vote with their dissertation topics on the future shape of their fields. Hence, both their numbers and the approaches they take to their subjects are relevant to this inquiry.

Being able to count and analyze these outputs would seem to presume a definition of the humanities.[5] The actual situation is almost the reverse— what can be counted tends to define the domain of analysis. In this case the National Center for Education Statistics has maintained continuous records for degrees in three core areas of the humanities: English language and literature, modern ("foreign") languages and literature, and history (although grouped with the social sciences).[6] These fields will be used here to measure the humanities' vital signs. Philosophy would be included except for missing data, but it accounted for just 1 percent of bachelor's degrees at its relative peak. The fine and performing arts accounted for about 4 percent of graduates, but these heterogeneous majors form a category of their own. Graduates of the various "studies" might fit the working definition of humanities of this volume, but they constitute small numbers of undergraduate degrees, and almost none before 1980.[7]

The Boom and the Bust, 1955–1985

The United States was the first society in the world to attain a system of mass secondary education.[8] By 1940 more than one-half of relevant age cohorts were graduating from high school. Mass secondary education was the foundation for a system of mass higher education after 1945. Most immediately, it paved the way for a surge of enrollments by ex-servicemen under the provisions of the G.I. Bill. This was a phenomenon that could occur only in the United States, where so many soldiers were high school graduates. Even as colleges and universities struggled to cope with the sudden overpopulation, visions of a more permanent expansion were in the air. The President's Commission on Higher Education in 1947 confidently announced that one-half of American youth were intellectually fit for college study, one-third of them in community colleges and the rest capable of earning bachelor's degrees.[9]

The number of college graduates who had studied under the G.I. Bill peaked in 1949–50. Just over 6 percent of them studied the core humanities fields of languages, literature, or history. This figure may be close to a baseline. For example, in 1967 the census reported that 6 percent of male college graduates held their highest degree in those fields.[10] During the 1950s, when college demographics returned to normal, the share of humanities majors among male graduates crept up to 8 percent. Among women graduates, humanities majors represented a fairly steady 15 percent. In 1960, however, women received only 37 percent of bachelor's degrees, fewer than before the war. To complicate this picture further, languages and literature were the feminine humanities by a ratio of better than 2 to 1, while history and philosophy were masculine humanities to roughly the same degree.

On the whole the 1950s deserves its reputation for social conservatism. College-going rates rose slowly for men and women. Steadily growing enrollments were largely fueled by a 50 percent rise in high school graduates. Male students continued to choose the same pattern of majors. Perhaps the most distinctive feature of enrollments was the low participation of women. Before the war slightly more than two women enrolled for every three men, but during the 1950s the proportion fell below that figure. The 1950s was a nadir for female careers. For women who did attend college, 40 percent of economic returns resulted from marrying college-educated men—the earlier the better. Hence, choice of major was not critical. Teaching was an ideal backstop for a limited career, if necessary. Education majors (predominately elementary) increased during the decade, and most humanities majors undoubtedly acquired credentials for secondary school teaching. Overall, women's choices of majors were less like men's in the 1950s than previously or anytime since.[11]

The 1950s pattern changed markedly after 1960. Two stages are evident. From 1960 to 1966 humanities graduates increased from 8 to 12 percent for men, and from 15 to 21 percent for women. This jump occurred during years when the undergraduate population was demographically quite stable; that is, before the front edge of the baby boom generation arrived in 1964. Between 1956 and 1962, when those respective cohorts entered college, the college-going rate grew from 40 to 43 percent for men and from 25 to 31 percent for women. The rise in humanities preferences for men is the more remarkable. For women, the proportion choosing either education or humanities remained stable for these years (61%). Thus, the drift toward humanities may represent a preference for secondary rather than elementary teaching. Still, the clear jump in the popularity of the humanities in these years has never been explained.

Also puzzling is the fact that this pattern persisted through the front wave of the baby boom generation. In 1970 the proportion of humanities graduates had attenuated only slightly for both men and women, and the number of these degrees was a third higher. Two years later, the numbers of degrees had changed little (only foreign languages decreased, for both sexes), although the percentages were now shrinking as the total number of graduates rose. The first baby boom cohorts to enter college, between 1964 and 1968, largely sustained the popularity of the humanities established by their predecessors. But after them the bottom fell out. The year 1975 saw precipitous drops in humanities graduates, male and female, that accelerated through the remainder of the decade. Students entering college in the 1970s, the largest cohorts in the nation's history, were increasingly alienated from the humanities. The decade, in fact, seemed to be cursed. The decline reached its nadir in the early 1980s, as the last students who had entered in the 1970s graduated.

Thus, there are two striking developments to explain in the academic evolution of the humanities: the first might be tagged the boom of the 1960s, and the second the bust of the 1970s. The demographic factors just outlined are helpful in defining the question, but they offer few answers. The underlying pattern of increasing participation should have brought more students into expanding second-tier public institutions, which graduate relatively few humanities majors. Furthermore, first-generation college-goers should have been more likely to select vocational majors. Both these factors would operate counter to the boom of the 1960s, particularly its second stage.[12] One could argue that both these factors might have exerted greater influence for cohorts entering after 1970, but such an argument could not account for the acceleration of the decline in that decade. Nor does the increasing participation of women exert a determinative effect. The rise and decline of each humanities discipline occurred with remarkably consistent gender balance.[13] Demography does not seem to be destiny for the humanities. It is more likely that developments within the humanities played some role in this evolution.

The Rise of the Humanities, 1945–1965

The humanities in postwar American higher education were initially linked closely with the notion of general education. This concept was publicized in 1945 by the Harvard study *General Education in a Free Society*. This articulation of a theory of general education was commissioned and written not just for Harvard, but for American education, secondary and higher. Accordingly, it reflected not Harvard's traditional exclusiveness, but rather the goals of democratic citizenship and social usefulness held by Harvard's President James B. Conant.[14] The Harvard report was widely read and discussed, most likely because it spoke to a pervasive dissatisfaction with prewar practices and curricula. For example, it seems to have influenced the Commission on Higher Education appointed by President Harry S. Truman. Its report, *Higher Education for American Democracy*, also embraced the concept of general education.[15] These influential interpretations of postwar educational purpose both looked to the humanities to play a crucial role.

Conant saw general education as perpetuating the "liberal and humane tradition," particularly fostering understanding of those areas where "man's emotional experience" and "value judgments are of prime importance." The Truman report included virtually everything that might contribute toward living in a free society, but it also stressed cultural heritage and the formation of values. Both reports aimed above all at instilling a common body of knowledge to provide the cultural foundation for democratic citizenship. Both reports also elevated general over liberal education. Conant stressed that general education was inclusive and shared, while liberal education might be claimed by particular subjects (as Latin and Greek once did). The Truman report found liberal education to be somewhat aristocratic and thus inconsistent with its goal of wider access. Finally, general education included an implicit condemnation of the academic disciplines. In its quest for unity, it specifically aimed to overcome the fragmentation of knowledge that academic specialization had produced. For the humanities, this task seemed necessary to recover the core values that disciplinary specialization had obscured.[16]

The Harvard report opened its discussion of the humanities by explicitly disassociating the understanding of literature from the types of scholarship prevailing in English departments. It proposed a course in the great texts of literature that would deliberately eschew information about authors, periods, textual analysis, literary traditions, "or anything else." These concerns were for the specialized training of literary scholars. General education would focus instead on "the greatest, most universal, most essential human preoccupations." The Truman report more briefly endorsed this same approach toward "great" literature without distracting "details."[17]

History's entrée to general education in the Harvard report was the course Western Thought and Institutions, which was proposed as the central offering in the social sciences. This too was accompanied by remarks on the inadequacy of "narrowly specialized courses," and it was intended to displace the European survey course (History 1 at Harvard). Instead of offering a continuous historical narrative, Western Thought would focus on "significant movements and changes in Western society," along with classical writings associated with them. As envisioned, it would be a combination of history and political thought. Although never implemented at Harvard, this proposal crystallized a number of contemporary trends and thus helped to inspire the widespread adoption of courses in the history of Western civilization. An ideal medium for pursuing the ideological goals of general education, Western Civ also posited a spiritual unity among the Atlantic powers that had defeated the fascist foes. It furthermore gave purpose and unity to the widely taught but rather amorphous survey of European history, which prior to the war, ironically, had purveyed a decidedly pessimistic view of world history.[18]

In Western Civ history received a more specific warrant for its role in general education than did literature, but the value of literature was also affirmed. It mattered little, however, that the stated goals of general education, although possessing a strong ideological appeal, were vague and unachievable in any practical sense. General education was a necessity for colleges and universities committed to teaching cultural heritage as well as professional and specialized knowledge. In practice, general education was largely consigned to the freshman and sophomore years, a curricular no-man's-land between high school and the major. Western Civ served these purposes well even if, as Peter Novick has suggested, "with the passage of time few involved in the courses were conscious of their ideological roots."[19] Hence, the sharp dichotomy between general education and the disciplines posited in the original texts was, with few exceptions, greatly attenuated in practice. Given a warrant to teach in their field, humanists followed the proclivities of their disciplines.

After the war virtually all academic disciplines experienced a surge of intellectual vitality, impelled by some combination of postwar confidence, expanding positions, growing graduate enrollments, increasing numbers of newly trained scholars, and an influx in some fields of European scholars. In the sciences new discoveries helped to drive these developments. In the humanities the "scientific revolutions" occurred more slowly but were just as surely led by paradigmatic change.

In literature the revolutionary movement marched under the banner of the New Criticism, which insisted that each piece of literature be interpreted as a work of art in itself and thus be judged solely by intrinsic criteria. As an insurgent movement before the war, the New Criticism had been fastidious about literary standards and truculent toward its supposed enemies. In the postwar environment, however, it received more tolerant formulations. As it conquered graduate English departments, it became an inclusive and compelling key to the study of literature, an approach that seemed to fit the needs of a burgeoning discipline.[20] Superficially, the New Criticism fit with general education. By rejecting as irrelevant all extrinsic aspects of a literary work, it eschewed those features of time, place, or author that general education sought to avoid. When interpreting texts, however, the New Critics pursued their own professionalizing agenda. But as was the case with Western Civ, compromise in the classroom prevailed. Pedagogically, New Critical approaches were easy to teach, malleable in practice, and compatible with the professional ambitions of the teachers. The New Criticism also indirectly helped bring modern authors into the orbit of literary studies, where they soon dominated in terms of student popularity. The New Criticism, once firmly in control of English departments, implied an immense project for the profession: to reread and reinterpret the corpus of English literature.

Although the New Criticism, with its inherent aestheticism and subjectivity, carried the seeds of its own destruction, the fresh perspective it brought to literary studies stimulated a prolonged outpouring of scholarly energy. Alvin Kernan in his memoir of graduate study and teaching at Yale in the 1950s, the center of the revolution, recounted the enthusiasm among the disciples who were about to carry forth the new doctrine. Kernan found the New Criticism "too attractive to resist, offering so many new, sprightly things to do." At the same time literary historians and biographers, who practiced a more painstaking craft, were dismissed as mere "reconstructionists." "We thought we were building up an accurate reading of literature, and that our formalist methodology concentrated unbiased attention on the objective literary text in the same way that the scientist looks closely and without bias at nature."[21] From such conviction movements are born. The élan of growing cadres of New Critics produced an efflorescence of literary scholarship by the mid-1960s.

Historians would seem to be less easily herded into movements, but the postwar profession nevertheless exhibited some definite proclivities. The most conspicuous tendency, according to Peter Novick, was "counterprogressive." That is, postwar historians rejected the centrality of class conflict in progressive history as well as the insinuation that history ought to engage social causes. American historians, in particular, increasingly found consensus and cultural unity underlying our country's tempestuous historical record. But historians of all stripes drifted toward a professional consensus over what Novick calls an "objectivist posture."[22] Like the New Critics, historians believed that, purged of relativism, their science could approach as close to objective truth as sources would allow.

History may have lacked any central, unifying theory, but the corpus of significant studies nevertheless grew slowly but surely. Novick's most frequent characterization of the postwar profession is "self-confident." Acutely aware of the heresy of "presentism," historians immersed themselves in their respective periods and increasing professional autonomy.[23] This stance was not congenial to the warrant for Western Civ, whose very conception was presentist through and through. But here too professionalism prevailed in the classroom. The harmonizing of these divergent aims can be seen in the influential work of Robert R. Palmer. His study *The Age of Democratic Revolutions* imposed an overarching unity on Atlantic civilization, but the many teachers who used his classic *History of the Modern World* as a text for Western Civ were essentially teaching European history.

Although the humanities showed evidence of increasing vitality, it seems that the full development of these intellectual trends did not occur until well into the 1960s. The first half of the 1950s endured the Korean War and the pall of McCarthyism. Only in the second half of the decade did the academic world shed its defensiveness. At that juncture the condition of the humanities looked anything but bright to contemporaries. In light of the federal support for the natural sciences and foundation patronage of the social sciences, the humanities were indeed the neglected branch of the tree of learning.

Reacting to this situation, the Carnegie Corporation in 1955 supported the American Council of Learned Societies to establish a Commission on the

Humanities. Two years of deliberations and two years of writing yielded an authoritative document by its chairman, Howard Mumford Jones: *One Great Society: Humane Learning in the United States.* This airy overview is almost entirely devoted to establishing the rightful place of the humanities in the world of learning—interpreting the development and predicament of modern man. Only the last pages deliver the mundane message that this will cost a lot of money—an additional $50 million for starters. In other words, since humanists made legitimate and important contributions to knowledge, they should receive funding for the kinds of appurtenances that academics in other fields were now getting—for fellowships, publications, conferences, research grants, and "permanent institutes."[24] Thus, at the end of the 1950s, humanists by their own reckoning had not yet been fully incorporated into the academic revolution. But they would not wait for long. The intellectual seedbed of the postwar years would bear fruit in the 1960s, with a large assist from demographics.

Writing in the late 1960s, Christopher Jencks and David Riesman found the essence of the "academic revolution" in the ascendancy of the graduate schools of arts and sciences to a position of dominance over the undergraduate curriculum and the corresponding outlook of faculty: "The academic graduate schools are the primary force for growth within the modern university. Their enrollments have been rising at a fantastic rate. . . . Their status is also rising. . . . They occupy a position somewhat comparable to that of theology in the medieval university. . . . The graduate academic departments are for the most part autotelic. They resent even being asked whether they produce significant benefits to society beyond the edification of their own members, and mark down the questioner as an anti-intellectual."[25]

Despite the last sour note, the authors recognized substantial benefits from the revolution. Students in American higher education were better prepared and more serious than ever before, and so were their teachers. The graduate schools, in particular, had spearheaded the institutionalization of meritocratic values that now permeated higher education. Moreover, these developments are pertinent to the subject at hand: the timing of the academic revolution—as distinct from the long prelude described by Jencks and Riesman—was coterminous with the boom in the humanities and the arts and sciences generally.

The intellectual awakening in the humanities that gathered momentum in the 1950s exerted its full impact on universities by the early 1960s. Timing is crucial to this argument. It depends on an intricate relationship among undergraduate majors, enrollments in doctoral programs, and the hiring of new faculty. This relationship has been modeled for more or less normal conditions, but the 1960s were far from normal. In fact, contemporaries badly misread these developments.[26] One complicating factor was that in 1960 only half of teaching faculty possessed a Ph.D. Until the end of the 1960s it was common practice to hire new faculty out of graduate school when they were A.B.D. So, while the number of Ph.D.'s rose, many were awarded to employed faculty. This practice helps to explain the remarkable fact that during the most rapid expansion of American higher education, the quality of the educational inputs actually rose. That is, student-faculty ratios declined slightly as new faculty increased faster than enrollments; the percentage of faculty with Ph.D.'s rose as well; and the ratio of full-time to part-time faculty increased too. What this meant in practical terms was an enormous influx of new faculty trained in the latest doctrines and techniques in university graduate schools. During the first few years of the 1960s faculty numbers grew at a respectable 6 percent annual rate. Full-time faculty then shot upward from 184,000 in 1963 to 331,000 in 1968. When attrition is factored in, perhaps 58 percent of faculty had been hired in the previous five years. Nearly half of active faculty were age forty or younger.[27] New blood was the rule throughout higher education, and the humanities were no exception.

Explaining the Boom

There are four types of variables that might explain fluctuations in the number of students studying the humanities: the structure of educational opportunities, the content of the curriculum, the relative prestige of humanistic studies, and career prospects in the labor market.[28] The first of these, the number of places available, is a supply-side variable; the other three affect student demand. Although conceptually distinct, these factors obviously interact. Supply and demand have a reciprocal relationship, and student preferences can be influenced by multiple considerations. The relative dynamism of these factors is also relevant. Although the structure of higher education is normally quite stable, this was anything but the case during the frantic expansion from the 1950s to the 1970s. Much the same could be said of the curriculum, which, as we just saw, experienced rejuvenation during the postwar era. The social prestige of different studies ought to be quite stable, but rising family incomes might induce larger numbers of students to pursue more ambitious educational strategies. Finally, conditions in the labor market for college graduates are probably the most volatile element in this mix, although they seem to have changed little during most of the great expansion.

Growing enrollments in the humanities are one component of the well-documented growth in degrees in the liberal arts and sciences. This growth can be distinguished in three types of settings, which may have occurred for somewhat different reasons. First, the number of arts and sciences majors grew at large, multipurpose universities. These institutions tended to expand rapidly until they reached their physical limits. They offered an abundance of curricular choices, however. Thus, increases in these settings should be attributed predominately to changing student demand. Second, Liberal Arts 1 colleges (LA1 in the Carnegie Classification) grew during these years at a slower rate than total enrollments, but most of their graduates majored in arts and sciences. A sample of LA1 colleges, for example, increased enrollments by 62 percent from 1955 to 1970. In that last year all LA1 colleges produced 4.5 percent of graduates, which should have accounted for 7 percent of arts and sciences graduates.[29] The expansion of these institutions occurred for largely internal reasons, and it was accompanied by the initiation or enhancement of student recruitment. In this sense, the contribution of the LA1 colleges was a structural factor.

Nevertheless, the most significant structural changes occurred at institutions that had previously offered few or no arts and sciences degrees. The chief components of this third category were teachers colleges that made the transition to regional universities. Similar changes also occurred at unselective Liberal Arts 2 (LA2) colleges and large technical universities. Ball State University is prototypical of the first kind of institution. Despite a strong teacher-training ethos, it began to widen its curricular offerings as it doubled its enrollment between 1957 and 1964. Some new majors were vocational, but the path of least resistance was to create arts and sciences majors. The greater prestige of pure arts and sciences disciplines was an undeniable influence. Ball State had been denied a Phi Beta Kappa chapter, for example, because of a lack of liberal arts majors. The path to university status encouraged creation of disciplinary bachelor's and master's degrees, a joint doctoral program, and an honors program with a year-long humanities sequence. Qualified faculty were more easily found for arts and science subjects than for vocational ones. Colleges of business, in particular, were constrained by a dearth of competent instructors. Ball State was still frustrated in the mid-1970s in searching for business faculty with doctorates—a must for accreditation.[30] Throughout much of the country, former teachers colleges were following this same path and multiplying enrollments in the process.

Dedicated land-grant universities like Michigan State and Purdue experienced a similar evolution in these years. At the latter institution President Frederick Hovde wished to restrict the humanities to a service role, but he faced mounting opposition from new faculty, epigones of the academic revolution, who sought provisions for research and doctoral programs.[31] Pressure for the expansion of humanities (and arts and science subjects) had been building since the late 1950s and had become virtually irresistible by the 1960s at institutions where they had not previously been offered.[32] This development probably accounts for the most consequential structural change. Large numbers of students attended regional universities because of low cost and proximity. Many of these students, like past students going back to their normal school days, essentially sought an advanced education with only hazy notions about a major or career. The creation of degree programs in the humanities for a time provided a congenial route to their goal and undoubtedly helped to inflate the number of humanities graduates.

On the demand side, it is scarcely possible to disentangle the influence of curriculum, prestige, and career considerations, but all signs pointed in the same positive direction. The rejuvenation of the curriculum in English and history, described above, soon reached and enlivened the undergraduate classroom. English majors could now read Faulkner and Hemingway for credit, while enduring only perfunctory acquaintance with *Paradise Lost* or *The Faery Queene*. History too presented a richer palate of studies, portraying more intellectually compelling accounts of historical change. Students in both types of classrooms were likely to encounter youthful instructors, brimming with the learning and enthusiasm of their own recent or current studies. Students not only enrolled in such courses in growing numbers but also registered their satisfaction by majoring in these subjects—and then enrolling in graduate school for more.

Since the Yale Reports of 1828, the liberal arts have possessed the cachet of providing both a superior education and a foundation for further professional studies. Although often challenged, this belief has persisted in residual form, no doubt bolstered by the strength of the liberal arts at the nation's most prestigious colleges and universities. Within institutions, such values may have been buoyed in the 1960s by the relative weakness of alternative courses. The sad state of business education, for example, was the object of two national studies in the late 1950s. Students in universities no doubt had to balance these factors against signals from the marketplace. From roughly 1960 to 1970, however, students faced a benign labor market in which graduation from college was highly rewarded for students with all degrees. As Steven Brint has noted, where "opportunities are relatively plentiful" and "average incomes are growing," students will be less mindful of the market and more likely to feel they can afford to major in arts and sciences.[33] More subtle cultural trends no doubt reinforced such choices. Many students of the 1960s rejected their parents' overbearing emphasis on education for employment. And by the late 1960s they were becoming more negative as well toward the prospect of working in government or industry.

To summarize, from the late 1950s places for the study of arts and sciences, including humanities, were greatly expanded, especially at new institutions serving first-generation students. For their part, students found the traditional respectability of these subjects made all the more attractive by interesting subject material taught with youthful enthusiasm. Nor did employment prospects discourage such behavior. Thus, the demand side and supply side factors seem consistent with the enrollment pattern of the boom years. Note that they are not specific to the baby boom generation, but rather are likely to have been operating by 1960 and to have exerted increasing influence until late in the decade. What, then, terminated the boom of the 1960s for the humanities and triggered the bust of the 1970s?

The Bust of the 1970s

A taste for the humanities began to wane with the freshmen entering in 1970. Bachelor's degrees started to plummet in 1974 and reached their nadir in the mid-1980s. Entering students then apparently began a slow rediscovery of the humanities, so that the number of graduates turned up by the end of the decade. Still, little of the demographic loss was recouped. Two broad explanations have been offered for the bust. One looks primarily to the changing job market for college graduates and the consequent attraction of vocational subjects. The other points to the cultural crisis within the humanities and its possible ramifications for student choice.

Some glimmer of insight into the minds of first-year students can be gained from the annual surveys of freshman attitudes and characteristics.[34] Indeed, these data document a seismic shift in student attitudes occurring around 1970. The value that comes closest to signifying identification with the humanities or liberal arts is the desire to "develop a meaningful philosophy of life." The percentage of first-year students considering that to be "very important" fell from 82 percent in 1969 to 61 percent in 1974, and then down to 43 percent in 1985. A subtler indicator is the percentage of incoming students who wanted to become college teachers. For men a figure of 2.1 percent in 1966 declined to 0.6 percent in 1975 and just 0.3 percent in the mid-1980s. For women the percentage fell from 1.5 to 0.6 to 0.2. These figures suggest a turnabout from some degree of identification with academe to outright alienation. This alienation was not confined to the humanities, since a 75 percent drop occurred in men's intention to become research scientists as well.

The declining career and earning prospects for college graduates were widely reported in the early 1970s. Particularly relevant was the collapse of the market for schoolteachers. Shortages of teachers were reported as late as 1969, but excess applicants were evident just two years later. For college graduates in general the earnings premium over less-educated workers fell after 1969, and it fell steeply from 1972 to 1974. These developments were accompanied by anecdotal accounts of the difficulties faced by liberal arts majors.[35] Interestingly, students did not react immediately by pursuing vocational courses. The initial choice of a business major—the litmus test for vocationalism—actually declined for men from the late 1960s to 1972, and began to climb only in 1975. Women showed little inclination for business before 1972, but then, perhaps fleeing education, doubled their numbers from 5 to 10 percent in 1975. These numbers seem to suggest that vocationalism followed rather than led to disillusionment with the liberal arts, and undoubtedly with the humanities.

In fact, the rise of vocationalism occurred well after distinctive intellectual crises had developed in literature and history during the late 1960s. These crises affected all three levels of academic work—the paradigms of professional practice for scholars and doctoral students, advanced classes in the major, and general education.

Perhaps the first casualty was general education. Despite heroic efforts at resuscitation by Daniel Bell, among others, general education had become a lifeless corpse by the late 1960s.[36] Many blamed the relentless specialization of the disciplines, even though that had been the problem general education was supposed to resolve. The deeper issue was the collapse of any consensus over content—over what general knowledge an educated person ought to possess. Western Civilization was not yet castigated as a scourge of mankind, but the relevance of European history, which is what it had become, was evaporating in two senses. The Europe of the Common Market and NATO was no longer in the center of global events. More important, few historians believed in or wished to make the link between European history, Western heritage, and the fundamental values and institutions that inform our civilization. The most prestigious colleges and universities abandoned Western Civ as a required course in the late 1960s, supplementing it with elective surveys of world civilizations, usually structured to fulfill distribution requirements.

Historians themselves led this abandonment. Motivated primarily by their own specialties, they no longer believed in quaint notions of heritage or civilization. But when they rejected a meaningful narrative of a common past, they did great disservice to students and ultimately to the profession. Without this narrative, history programs became "a superstructure of advanced courses without the supporting foundation of an introductory class where students could be prepared and recruited."[37] More damaging, the absence of a narrative that historians themselves could endorse robbed the field of validation that historical knowledge was an essential component of liberal learning—something worth studying as a college major.

While historians retreated from battle into increasingly esoteric specialties, literary scholars battled one another with such ferocity that they redefined the discipline itself in ways that were alien to general education and what had formerly been considered humanistic learning. The enormous literature on this conflict, polemical and otherwise, lies beyond the scope of this study. The dominant tendencies are germane, however, if inevitably contested. One commentator places the tipping point of this revolution in 1969, when self-proclaimed radicals gained ascendancy in the Modern Language Association and promoted an agenda of anticapitalism, confrontation, and fixation on the latent social biases in literature.[38] Indeed, "humanistic" became a term of derision to those on the radical side of the now-polarized profession.

In the euphoria of confrontation, liberal tolerance substantially eroded in the decade after 1965. In its place the predominant outlook among literary scholars became what David Bromwich has called "disidentification":[39] a pervasive hostility to Western or European heritage—political, economic, and intellectual. Disidentification evolved from the confrontations of that period over the war in Vietnam, civil rights, and women's liberation, but after 1975 (when those issues had been more or less resolved much as radicals had originally wished) it hardened into a residual repudiation of most mainstream elements of American life.[40]

In the humanities boom of the 1960s, it has been argued, undergraduate students identified to some degree with young, newly trained instructors, who presented fresh and relevant material. By the mid-1970s, in contrast, just the opposite situation prevailed. Humanities faculty members in this era frequently complained of the "apathy" and lack of political commitment among students. But students were now chronologically removed from the heroic struggles of the student rebellion (or had already rehearsed such postures in high school). Students identifying themselves as liberal fell by almost one-half (35 to 18%) from 1971 to 1981; but, rather than becoming conservative, students tended toward a nonideological, "middle-of-the-road" position.[41] The growing incompatibility between a new generation of students and their radical (or cynical), no-longer-youthful teachers in the humanities seems likely to have contributed to the declining popularity of the humanities after 1975.

Student attitudes evolved throughout the 1970s. Early in the decade incoming students may have been alienated somewhat from the humanities, but they were alienated as well from American society. Antimaterialistic outlooks seemed to predominate until middecade. Freshmen considering it "very important" to become "very well off financially" registered in the low 40 percent range from the late 1960s until 1973. Their numbers then shot upward to 50 percent in 1975 and to 71 percent in 1985. Once again, the tipping point for undergraduates appears to be around 1975. Nevertheless, predominantly non-materialistic students entering in the early 1970s increasingly gravitated toward vocational or professional majors.[42] Apparently, their outlooks changed while they were in college, influenced most likely by ideological incompatibility and abundant publicity about a deteriorating market for college graduates. After 1975, however, an unequivocal trend, dubbed the "new vocationalism," was in full swing.[43] Most likely this represented the reciprocal interaction of supply and demand rather than a direct response to labor market signals.

At this juncture, near the midpoint of the bust in humanities enrollments, I was struck by the rapid erosion of interest in the arts and sciences and attempted to interpret contemporary developments for an explanation.[44] Sidestepping the question of liberal education, my analysis focused on the decline of degrees in the academic disciplines and the rise in graduates in "instrumental" fields. I further adopted from the economist Lester Thurow a model of job competition, wherein education functioned chiefly to earn priority in the labor queue for training opportunities (i.e., jobs) in which productive skills were actually acquired. I concluded that the disciplinary specialization encouraged by the academic revolution had little to offer average college students in middling institutions, and that this was particularly true for the humanities and social sciences. Rather, "the lasting benefits of disciplinary study seem[ed] to depend upon ability, motivation, and institutional setting." Specifically, disciplinary studies were most valuable in research universities and true liberal arts colleges, where they prepared academically able students for graduate or professional school or other intellectually challenging pursuits. I was skeptical, perhaps overly so, that instrumental programs taught useful knowledge (created human capital). Nevertheless, "the competitive environment of the late 1970s in higher education—students desperate for jobs and colleges desperate for students—has been highly conducive to the creation of instrumental programs quite irrespective of their economic justification." In other words, colleges and universities, in efforts to combat declining enrollments, supplied increasing numbers of vocational programs.

Subsequent research has on balance supported and elaborated this general picture. When Joan Gilbert examined the decline in arts and sciences degrees by type of institution, using the old Carnegie Classification, she found little erosion in Liberal Arts 1 (LA1) colleges. Moreover, LA1 and Research 1 universities, institutions enrolling the strongest students, registered the highest percentage of liberal arts degrees. Research 1 universities, Comprehensive colleges, and Liberal Arts 2 colleges all experienced a parallel trajectory of declining liberal arts majors from the early 1970s to the early 1980s. At that point research universities alone began a marked recovery, whereas LA2 colleges

continued their slide into the 1990s.[45] Many of these institutions had been relentlessly restructuring into small professional schools.[46] By adding programs
in growth areas such as business and health sciences, they were adapting to a
clientele of middling abilities and aspirations. At comprehensive or doctoral
universities like Ball State, vocational programs not only expanded but were
considerably strengthened as well. Nevertheless, the supply of vocational programs, and possibly their quality as well, was greatly enlarged within the nonselective sector of higher education. Indeed, the propensity to major in liberal
arts was correlated with academic ability, as measured by SAT scores, both
across sectors and within sectors.[47]

Steven Brint and his associates also concluded that social and intellectual
stratification was the most important trend underlying the differentiation of
disciplinary and practical degrees: "[They] found a particularly strong occupational emphasis in institutions enrolling high proportions of students with
low test scores and, by extension, from lower socio-economic backgrounds."
These institutions, in their words, "were becoming mass terminal institutions."[48] In contrast, the authors found arts and sciences degrees now concentrated in "the elite segments of the system"—the LA1 colleges and the more
selective Research 1 universities: "this suggests that what was once largely a
functional divide—different kinds of institutions emphasizing different curricula—has become largely a status divide."

Indeed, this finding sheds light on an additional puzzle: given the forces
just described, what accounts for the modest recovery in degrees in the arts
and sciences and, somewhat later, the humanities? This recovery may well
be linked with the growing prestige and influence of the selective sector of
higher education.[49] The recovery became perceptible toward the end of the
1980s and peaked in the early 1990s. About the same time the growing prestige and difficulty of entry to the strongest of these institutions, combined
with their traditional cultivation of the humanities, provided much-needed
validation for humanistic study. In addition, a chief attraction to such places
was preparation for postgraduate studies. Further, adjustments internal to the
humanities have undoubtedly encouraged enrollments. Humanities majors
have been linked with instrumental subjects, especially business, to provide
presumably marketable combined degrees. And, in a tendency sometimes
deplored, special topics courses have been shamelessly designed for internal
marketability to prospective students.[50]

Such small steps may signify a much larger internal transformation of the
humanities. In the 1970s the academic environment changed but the humanities in large measure did not. Alienation sold well during the cultural mael-
strom at the end of the 1960s, but it had a short shelf life. Too many teachers

lost commitment to their subjects and were consequently unable to instill commitments in students. In a context of anomie, students of the early 1970s first drifted away from the humanities and then migrated in ever-increasing numbers to the newly supplied vocational and professional possibilities. The fact that the humanities preserved their position best at the most academically prestigious institutions was a source of strength. It meant that demographic decline was not translated into intellectual stagnation. Quite the contrary, as the other chapters of this volume illustrate.

In the 1990s, for whatever reasons, the academic humanities manifested more solicitude for the interests and the career prospects of their students, an approach consistent with the consumerism now pervading undergraduate education in the United States. That solicitude in itself might account in part for the modest demographic expansion. But I would speculate that here as earlier content is also important, and perhaps the dynamics of inclusion is most important of all. The humanities may have sustained their intellectual vitality not by resolving the deep and debilitating internal fissures of the bust years, but rather by expanding to encompass a greater range of subjects and a more diverse array of potential humanists. In other words, specialization and fragmentation, so often portrayed as the bugbear of the humanities, may well have proved to be its salvation. From this perspective, the relative number of humanities students in the population of American colleges and universities is a misleading measure. The boom of the 1960s was a bubble (see Figure 2.2), inflated by understandable but fundamental misperceptions of reality; and its bursting, like that of other bubbles, was inevitable. The contemporary humanities may be smaller demographically than a generation ago, but the intellectual ferment of its multiple fields suggests continuing vitality, not decadence.

Notes

1. Roger L. Geiger, "The College Curriculum and the Marketplace: What Place for Disciplines in the Trend toward Vocationalism?" *Change* (November–December 1980): 17–23, 53–54; Arthur Levine, *When Dreams and Heroes Die* (San Francisco: Jossey-Bass, 1980).

2. Sarah E. Turner and William G. Bowen, "The Flight from the Arts and Sciences: Trends in Degrees Conferred," *Science* 250 (October 26, 1990): 517–521.

3. Wayne C. Booth, Gregory G. Colomb, and Joseph M. Williams, *The Craft of Research* (Chicago: University of Chicago Press, 1995), 90–92.

4. National Research Council, *A Century of Doctorates: Data Analyses of Growth and Change* (Washington, D.C.: National Academy of Sciences, 1978), 79. Master's degrees are also an output of the humanities, but their dynamics mirror those of other degrees.

5. Definitions of the humanities are elusive: J. Sperna Weiland, "Humanities: Introduction," *The Encyclopedia of Higher Education*, ed. Burton R. Clark and Guy Neave, 4 vols. (Oxford: Pergamon Press, 1992), 1981–1989.

6. All data on enrollments and degrees, unless otherwise noted, are from various volumes of the National Center for Educational Statistics, *Digest of Education Statistics* (Washington, D.C.: GPO, annual publication).

7. E.g., in 1996–97 area, ethnic, and cultural studies accounted for about 0.5 percent of all bachelor's degrees. African American studies and women's studies each claimed one-tenth of that total.

8. Claudia Goldin, "The Human Capital Century and American Leadership: Virtues of the Past," *Journal of Economic History* 61 (June 2001): 263–291.

9. President's Commission on Higher Education, *Higher Education for American Democracy*, 6 vols. (Washington, D.C.: GPO, 1947). The proportion of twenty-five- to twenty-nine-year-olds who have graduated from college has risen as follows: 8 percent in 1950; 11 percent in 1960; 16 percent in 1970; 22.5 percent in 1980; 23 percent in 1990; and 29 percent in 2000; NCES, *Digest of Education Statistics, 2002 Edition*, table 8.

10. *Digest of Education Statistics, 1975 Edition*, table 112. Bachelor's degrees were not tabulated by major before 1945; however, arts and sciences degrees before the war constituted fewer than 40 percent of the total, making it unlikely that humanities degrees could have exceeded 6–8 percent.

11. Claudia Goldin, "The Meaning of College in the Lives of American Women: The Past One-Hundred Years" (Working Paper 4099, National Bureau of Economic Research, June 1992).

12. Turner and Bowen, "Flight from the Arts and Sciences."

13. Turner and Bowen find that "in the humanities alone, the changing curricular choices of women have dominated the other determinants of changes in shares" (ibid., 520). Their definition of the humanities, however, excludes history—the masculine wing—which accounted for 6 percent of male bachelor's degrees from 1966 to 1972 and 2 percent fifteen years later.

14. See James B. Conant, Introduction to *General Education in a Free Society: Report of the Harvard Committee*, by Harvard University (Cambridge: Harvard University Press, 1945), v–x; Morton Keller and Phyllis Keller, *Making Harvard Modern: The Rise of America's University* (New York: Oxford University Press, 2001), 42–45.

15. President's Commission, *Higher Education for American Democracy* (Washington, 1947).

16. Harvard University, *General Education*, viii–ix, 205–207; President's Commission, *Higher Education*, 1: 47–48, 54–55.

17. Harvard University, *General Education*, 205; President's Commission, *Higher Education*, 1: 55.

18. Harvard University, *General Education*, 213–217. On this proposed course and circumstances at Harvard, see Gilbert Allardyce, "The Rise and Fall of the Western Civilization Course," *American Historical Review* 87 (1982): 695–725; Allardyce notes (714) the growing pessimism in the 1930s of Carlton J. H. Hayes, the author of *A Political and Cultural History of Modern Europe*; indeed, by 1939 Hayes was blaming liberalism and democracy for the wretched state of the world; Peter Novick, *That Noble Dream: The "Objectivity Question" and the American Historical Profession* (New York: Cambridge University Press, 1988), 244–245.

19. Novick, *That Noble Dream*, 314. This statement certainly describes my experience when I began college teaching as a Western Civ instructor.

20. Gerald Graff, *Professing Literature: An Institutional History* (Chicago: University of Chicago Press, 1987).

21. Alvin Kernan, *In Plato's Cave* (New Haven: Yale University Press, 1999), 64, 109. For similar testimony from a different perspective, see Richard Ohmann, *English in America: A Radical View of the Profession* (1976; rpt. Hanover, N.H.: Wesleyan University Press, 1996), 69–79.

22. Novick, *That Noble Dream*, 332, 415.

23. Ibid., 362–377. The popular guide by E. H. Carr, *What Is History?* (London: Macmillan, 1961), illustrated the perils of presentism. In John Higham's overview of the discipline,

confidence in current historical work is nearly obscured by a backward-looking reference to "classic" studies. This self-referential perspective no doubt emphasized the autonomy of the discipline; John Higham with Leonard Krieger and Felix Gilbert, *History* (Englewood Cliffs, N.J.: Prentice-Hall, 1965).

24. Howard Mumford Jones, *One Great Society: Humane Learning in the United States* (New York: Harcourt, Brace, 1959), 235–241.

25. Christopher Jencks and David Riesman, *The Academic Revolution* (Chicago: University of Chicago Press, 1968), 250.

26. The exception was Allan M. Cartter, whose analysis informs this discussion: *Ph.D.'s and the Academic Labor Market* (New York: McGraw-Hill, 1976).

27. Ibid., 109, 165. Non-Ph.D.'s had a far higher rate of attrition than doctoral degree holders (7.1% vs. 3.1%); my estimate is based on a 3.5 percent attrition for these years.

28. Steven Brint et al. provide a model to explain the rise of practical-vocational majors that emphasizes, in somewhat different terms, structure and status; "From the Liberal to the Practical Arts in American Colleges and Universities: Organizational Analysis and Curricular Change," *Journal of Higher Education* 76 (March–April 2005): 151–180.

29. Elizabeth A. Duffy and Idana Goldberg, *Crafting a Class: College Admissions and Financial Aid, 1955–1994* (Princeton: Princeton University Press, 1998), 7; Joan Gilbert, "The Liberal Arts College—Is It Really an Endangered Species?" *Change* (September–October 1995): 37–43.

30. Anthony O. Edmonds and E. Bruce Geelhoed, *Ball State University: An Interpretive History* (Bloomington: Indiana University Press, 2001), 157–167, 219.

31. Robert W. Topping, *The Hovde Years: A Biography of Frederick L. Hovde* (West Lafayette, Ind.: Purdue University, 1980).

32. This expansion included new branch campuses; Fred Beuttler, "Envisioning an Urban University: President David Henry and the Chicago Circle Campus of the University of Illinois, 1955–1975," *History of Higher Education Annual* 23 (2003–4): 107–142. Gilbert provides evidence of substantial increases in arts and sciences majors at a sample of LA2 colleges, which (if the 50-plus % of graduates can be generalized) would account for another 7 percent of all these graduates in 1970.

33. Brint et al., "From the Liberal to the Practical Arts."

34. Alexander Astin, Kenneth C. Green, and William S. Korn, *The American Freshman: Twenty Year Trends* (Los Angeles: Higher Education Research Institute, UCLA, 1987). All data are from this aggregation of the annual reports.

35. Richard B. Freeman, *The Over-educated American* (New York: Academic Press, 1976), 85, 14; Carnegie Commission on Higher Education, *College Graduates and Jobs* (New York: McGraw-Hill, 1973), 163–167.

36. Daniel Bell, *The Reforming of General Education: The Columbia College Experience in Its National Setting* (New York: Columbia University Press, 1966).

37. Allardyce, "Rise and Fall," 696.

38. Margery Sabin, "Evolution and Revolution: Change in the Literary Humanities, 1968–1995," in Alvin Kernan, *What's Happened to the Humanities?* (Princeton: Princeton University Press, 1997), 84–103.

39. David Bromwich, "Scholarship as Social Action," in Kernan, *What's Happened to the Humanities?* 220–243, 230.

40. For example, Richard Ohmann concludes that "socialist revolution" is the only "cure" for the ills of English and the humanities: "teach politically with revolution as the end"; *English in America*, 256, 335. A contemporary critique of conditions in the humanities charged that "tendentious, ideological" teaching, such as that Ohmann advocated, was driving students from the humanities; William J. Bennett, *To Reclaim a Legacy: A Report on the Humanities in Higher Education* (Washington, D.C.: National Endowment for the Humanities, 1984). Reviled then

and since for advocating curricula based on the Western heritage, this report incorporated the judgments of a study group of humanists convened by Bennett.

41. Astin et al., *American Freshman*, 97.

42. Earl F. Cheit, *The Useful Arts and the Liberal Tradition* (New York: McGraw-Hill, 1975). Steven Brint calls these subjects the "practical arts"; in an earlier paper I called them "instrumental" subjects. Here I use the term "vocational" to align these different fields with the trend toward vocationalism. For specific subjects, see Geiger, "College Curriculum and the Marketplace," 18.

43. Lewis B. Mayhew, *Legacy of the Seventies* (San Francisco: Jossey-Bass, 1977), 131–133.

44. Geiger, "College Curriculum and the Marketplace."

45. Gilbert, "Liberal Arts Colleges," 39, 43. The decline of liberal arts at nonselective institutions is also emphasized by Francis Oakley, *Community of Learning: The American College and the Liberal Arts Tradition* (New York: Oxford University Press, 1992).

46. David W. Breneman, *Liberal Arts College: Thriving, Surviving, or Endangered?* (Washington, D.C.: Brookings Institution, 1994), 11–12, 139–141. Gilbert, "Liberal Arts Colleges," 42, notes that many colleges classified as LA2 were not originally liberal arts colleges at all, but they participated in the increased "supply" of liberal arts places during the boom years.

47. The top quartile of students was 50 percent more likely to enroll in liberal arts at LA1, RU1, LA2, and Comprehensive institutions: Gilbert, "Liberal Arts Colleges," 43.

48. Brint et al., "From the Liberal to the Practical Arts," 173–174.

49. Roger L. Geiger, *Knowledge and Money: Research Universities and the Paradox of the Marketplace* (Stanford: Stanford University Press, 1994), chap. 3.

50. Sabin, "Evolution and Revolution," 89–90, 94–96; Francis Oakley, "Ignorant Armies and Nighttime Clashes: Changes in the Humanities Classroom, 1970–1995," in Kernan, *What's Happened to the Humanities?* 63–82.

3

THE SCHOLAR AND THE WORLD

Academic Humanists and General Readers in Postwar America

JOAN SHELLEY RUBIN

TWO SCENARIOS currently dominate historical accounts of American literary and cultural criticism in the decades immediately following the Second World War. Taking off from the position Irving Howe articulated in his 1954 essay "This Age of Conformity," the first depicts intellectuals abandoning the adversarial politics and aesthetic experimentation of the prewar period for the shelter and safety of the nation's expanding universities. In their comfortable circumstances, literary scholars increasingly become devoted practitioners of text-bound New Criticism, a method of analysis that suits their desire to back away from social issues and enables them to serve more easily the large numbers of students flocking to their classrooms. The second story line (running somewhat counter to the first) casts the intellectual as battler against the pernicious influences of mass and middlebrow culture. That familiar tale places in starring roles figures situated both outside and within the academy: for instance, in the former category, Dwight Macdonald and Howe himself; in the latter, the sociologists Paul Lazarsfeld and Ernest Van den Haag. What the two scenarios share is the distance they each postulate between the scholar or critic and the "average intelligent reader." Academics, relinquishing their concern, to use Howe's phrase, for "the problem of the quality of our culture," restrict their discourse to other specialists in their "subject," while disaffected observers of popular taste follow Howe's directive to assume a stance of "alienation" from the mainstream.[1]

Both narratives have been powerful for the scholarly generations that, since the 1960s, have sought to define themselves against their predecessors by affirming their commitment to social change and by embracing artifacts such as movies and romance novels as texts. And both portrayals are right. At the same time the picture of the critic in retreat from the public (one way or another) does not consider the various ways in which certain proponents of the humanities in the United States between 1945 and 1960 actively sought a

73

wide constituency for their expertise. In particular, it ignores the challenge some figures within the university mounted to the assumption that conveying general knowledge to popular audiences was incompatible with the role of the academic professional.

Before exploring that challenge, it is important to recall the individuals who, in the postwar years, continued to station themselves outside academia as interpreters of the humanities. Such individuals included Lewis Mumford, still an exemplar of the unaffiliated "man of letters," who commanded a hearing from fellow intellectuals, academics, and sophisticated readers drawn to his trenchant social criticism and his columns in the *New Yorker*. Despite his aloofness from the university, Mumford engaged in a certain amount of "crossover" activity that signaled his endorsement of academic ventures. From 1955 to 1958, for instance, he was on the editorial board of *American Quarterly*, the journal of the American Studies Association. His willingness to serve the needs of a scholarly publication intersected with currents in the other direction: a group within the early ASA that wanted to extend the association's reach by shedding academic professionalism.

Other nonacademic proponents of the humanities sustained their prewar reputations by ministering to a wider swath of the reading public, the middle-brow audience of "average intelligent readers" (overlapping but not coextensive with the middle class) that looked for guidance to institutions that had burgeoned in the two decades before the war. A prime example was Clifton Fadiman. Born in New York City in 1902, Fadiman entered Columbia University in 1920, the year the faculty implemented its General Honors version of the great books curriculum English professor John Erskine had devised before World War I. Under the tutelage of Erskine's students Mortimer Adler and Mark Van Doren, Fadiman soaked up the "classics" of Western civilization that the General Honors course comprised. Apparently thwarted in his ambition to become a teacher and scholar because Lionel Trilling had secured the one position the Columbia English Department had allocated to a Jew, Fadiman turned to publishing, journalism, and radio instead. In 1944 he joined the Book-of-the-Month Club board, a post he held into the 1990s.

Fadiman's ventures in the immediate postwar era continued to enhance his stature as a guide to the humanities for an audience comprising, in Carolyn Heilbrun's words, "the intelligent, the curious, the serious, the unponderous." One of the most visible of these activities was his involvement in a radio program called *Conversation*. Like *Invitation to Learning*, another offshoot of the Erskine great books tradition on the air from the late 1930s into the 1960s, *Conversation* attempted to expose listeners to "civilized, noncontroversial, discursive, nonpatronizing talk" instead of gossip or unremitting facts. In addition, Fadiman wrote or edited dozens of introductions, anthologies, and essays on literary and contemporary themes.[2]

In everything he undertook, Fadiman was militantly and self-consciously a nonacademic generalist. As he explained in 1955: "I have been a kind of pitchman-professor, selling ideas, often other men's, at marked-down figures, which are easier to pay than the full price of complete intellectual concentration. I do not apologize for this. . . . At the moment we are producing a large class . . . of highly educated citizens, and a much larger class of formally instructed but under-educated citizens. . . . High-level literary criticism becomes more and more learned . . . and moves further and further away from the mass of moderately educated Americans who . . . feel cut off from first-class intellectual leadership. The same thing is happening in poetry, in philosophy, and in other areas of thought." His purpose, he declared, was to try "closing the gap" by enlisting in the ranks of America's "middlemen of thought and opinion." Fadiman's decision to do so outside the university—as "perhaps only a hemi-demi-semi-quasi-professor"—furnished him a role as viable after 1945 as before the war, although his relationship with his audience depended on and buttressed an invidious distinction between his activities and what "real" professors did.[3]

A second model of the humanist as mediator to the reading public—the sometime academic—may be found in the career of the poet and critic John Ciardi. Ciardi, who was born in 1916, discovered his poetic vocation as an undergraduate in the late 1930s and published his first volume of verse in 1940. That same year, however, he gravitated to college teaching, taking a job at the University of Kansas City. Following wartime military service, Ciardi returned to higher education, this time accepting an appointment as an instructor in English at Harvard. After failing to secure a permanent post there, he moved to Rutgers University in 1953.

Yet Ciardi's pursuits included poetry and literary journalism as well. In 1956 he took over the poetry department of the *Saturday Review of Literature*, widely regarded by its friends and foes alike as the epitome of the middlebrow periodical. In agreeing to the assignment, Ciardi acted on the same impulse to "raise the whole level" of literary taste in the United States that animated Fadiman. Ciardi's academic affiliation both strengthened and impeded his efforts in that regard. When controversy erupted the next year over his devastating evaluation of Anne Morrow Lindbergh's poetry, readers at odds with his views attributed them partly to his academic standing and implicitly to his affirmation of the New Criticism. Ciardi's insistence that Lindbergh had perpetrated "a violence against language" through her "slovenliness" and "counterfeit sentimentality" prompted the *New York Times Book Review* editor J. Donald Adams, for example, to deplore the "holier-than-thou attitudes of so many of our academic critics." Ciardi's beleaguered situation is worth noting because it undercuts the stereotype of the university appointment in the 1950s as sinecure and refuge: for some intellectuals, academic affiliation brought more turmoil than escape. Ironically, Ciardi had his own misgivings about the "near-total absorption of our poets in the universities," and he resigned from Rutgers in 1961 to join Fadiman outside campus walls.[4]

The nonacademic and the erstwhile professor exemplified by Fadiman and Ciardi, respectively, coexisted in the postwar years with a third career pattern among disseminators of the humanities: that of scholars or literary critics who held academic positions throughout their professional lives while simultaneously addressing a wide audience. That group is even easier to overlook than the first two, if only because commentators who, since the 1950s, have dismissed Fadiman and Ciardi as middlebrow have given them a certain measure of negative attention in categorizing them. The remainder of this chapter deals with three of these neglected but influential academics: Gilbert Highet, Jacques Barzun, and Howard Mumford Jones. For those figures the dynamics of inclusion entailed not so much the incorporation of diverse students into the university as the extension of instruction outward from the classroom lecture to the best seller and the broadcast.

Such outreach was not unprecedented. In the prewar period, for example, the Yale English professor William Lyon Phelps had wielded enormous influence over American taste by compiling anthologies, writing literary essays in periodicals, and reviewing books on the radio while continuing to teach university students. At Harvard, Phelps's counterpart (minus the broadcasting) was the beloved "Copey"—Charles Townsend Copeland. More important, because of its New York City location, Columbia University had a long record of engagement with ordinary readers. Apart from its history of promulgating the great books curriculum to community groups, Columbia facilitated faculty involvement with the public by offering the greatest access to the social networks of the publishing world. Especially since the 1920s, when, for example, two alumni, Richard Simon and M. Lincoln Schuster, had started their own firm, its graduates had been well-placed within the book business and other communications industries. Furthermore, as Irwin Edman (another faculty member who achieved a large readership before World War II) observed in 1954, the metropolitan environment encouraged an awareness of the connections between classic texts and current preoccupations: "A student of the Greek drama has before his eyes what is happening to the theater of our own day. No one can read Thucydides without the kind of reflections on war and peace induced by being next-door neighbor to the UN." Edman added that the Columbia community made it impossible to "treat the humanities simply as a smugly appreciative study" by virtue of an "atmosphere" on campus that was "ever alive to the changing place and part of the unchanging values of a humanistic education."[5]

As Edman's remarks imply, however, after 1945 some of the prewar factors that had shaped Phelps's or Copey's popularity and Columbia's external relationships intensified, combining with the pressures of the cold war to create a changed cultural context for the academic humanities. The rise in college enrollments during the late 1940s and 1950s was even more dramatic than in the interwar years, heightening the demand among graduates and nongraduates alike for figures who could summarize what the successful person should know. The fresh memories of the threat World War II had posed to the survival of Western civilization intersected with fears of nuclear annihilation and totalitarianism, which lent greater urgency, in some quarters, to the task of preserving the values enshrined in classical and European literature and philosophy. Those who welcomed atomic energy for the abundant leisure it promised nevertheless stressed the importance of spending that extra time on worthwhile humanistic pursuits.

Moreover, the war and its aftermath stimulated widespread debate over America's priorities at every level of the educational system. In part the controversy merely brought to the surface reactions to intellectual and social forces that had been transforming the United States since the early twentieth century. One contribution to the debate over schooling, the Harvard University committee report *General Education in a Free Society* (1945), began by identifying three such factors: the specialization of knowledge, the "staggering growth" of the nation's schools, and the increased complexity of American life. But wartime exigencies produced other sources of consternation. A teacher shortage, which worsened following the war into the "most acute" in the nation's history, was one. Another was the perception that college students had been slow to respond when "told that democracy was in danger," and that postwar national security required greater stress on civics and American history. To Robert M. Hutchins, who, as president of the University of Chicago, had instituted a rigid variant of Erskine's program before the war, the only course of study that could meet the challenges of the nuclear age was one consisting entirely of readings from great books; after 1945 he and Mortimer Adler promoted that view to adult learners as well as undergraduates. By contrast, for some observers the training involved in mobilizing America's youth for military service and industrial production demonstrated the limitations of the liberal arts. In the words of Robert G. Sproul, president of the University of California, "Catastrophe lies ahead unless we . . . return to fundamentals, to the disciplined education of our students, first, as citizens, and second, as vocational specialists." That lesson seemed especially clear on campuses that had undergone the "sudden substitution of war subjects for academic studies and service men for regulation students." As the reviewer of two sociological approaches to the issue stated in 1944, "The war has put the whole emphasis of higher education on technical and scientific training." The influx, under G.I. Bills, of veterans seeking immediately useful skills promised to prolong that trend. Still other commentators, however, worried that the imposition of any single curriculum would be inappropriate to a nation that had just defended freedom and choice.[6]

Perhaps not surprisingly, given the institution's history, two of the most prominent academic humanists who responded to these new conditions came from the Columbia faculty. One was the classicist Gilbert Highet. His advocacy of the humanities displayed three salient characteristics: it involved the dissemination of his discipline; it was built on preexisting agencies of middlebrow culture; and it won him the disparagement of some of his specialist colleagues.

Born in Glasgow, Scotland, in 1906, Highet learned Latin and Greek with ease as a child. After compiling a stellar record at Glasgow University, he studied at Balliol College, Oxford, from 1929 to 1932, where he continued to distinguish himself academically. Subsequently he stayed at Oxford to obtain a master's degree and to teach. In 1937 he accepted a one-year visiting appointment at Columbia. The next year Columbia gave him a post as full professor, and he settled permanently in New York with his wife, Helen MacInnes, a novelist who wrote best-selling spy thrillers. Drawn into the latter-day version of Erskine's great books curriculum, Highet became a spellbinding instructor in the required humanities course for first-year students. During World War II he went on leave to serve with British Intelligence. He returned to the Columbia faculty in 1946 and was named Anthon Professor of the Latin Language and Literature in 1950, occupying the position until his retirement in 1972.[7]

In 1949 and 1950 Highet also brought out two books that demonstrated his facility for captivating general readers as well as undergraduates. The first was *The Classical Tradition.* More than seven hundred pages long (including notes), the volume traced the influence of Greek and Roman writers on subsequent European literature. Highet's overarching theme was the resilience and vitality of ancient culture, which made it "an essential and active part" of contemporary civilization. Despite that persistence, Highet nonetheless took pains to identify the factors responsible for the decline of classical studies in Britain and the United States since the nineteenth century. The archaeological exploration of ancient sites and the predominance of the scientific method, he argued, had resulted in a veneration of precision and detail. Academically based classicists in the United States, dedicated to abstruse research, had grown increasingly out of touch with the average student in the relatively democratic setting of the large American university. The scientific method, the fragmentation and narrowing of subject matter, and the fetish of the Ph.D. had produced in turn classroom practices that disconnected Greek and Latin literature from feeling, insight, and pleasure. Highet's analysis contained the blueprint for his own career. Rather than contribute to the death of his field, he resolved to repudiate the emphasis on linguistic technicality, bridge the gulf between professor and student, and fulfill the scholar's "responsibility" to spread as well as to amass knowledge.[8]

Highet's volume of 1950, and his most famous work, extended his diagnosis of poor pedagogy beyond his discipline. Entitled *The Art of Teaching*, the book was inspired by the Abbé Ernest Dimnet's best seller *The Art of Thinking*, which had appeared in 1928. His intention, Highet later explained, was "to encourage mature teachers, and even more, to advise and cheer on young men and women who are beginning the career." Originally published by Alfred A. Knopf, Highet's volume achieved wide circulation in a Vintage paperback still in print at this writing. It was distributed in Greece by the United States Information Service, purchased by the military, and eventually translated into sixteen languages.[9]

In the preface Highet distanced himself from educational theorists; his goal, he announced, was to convey "suggestions" based on his classroom experience. Moreover, he distinguished between science, which depended on a system, and teaching, which rested on "human values" and feelings that could not be measured. Specifically, he urged instructors in the humanities to avoid prepackaging lessons at the expense of spontaneous give-and-take and to spend more time on explaining texts as a whole than on minutely analyzing them. In contrast to the great books movement, which came to favor seminars, Highet assigned equal merit to lectures, tutorials, and recitations in which teachers asserted their authority by varied means. With the British boys' school apparently in mind, he recommended that educators harness the force of tradition to make students aware of their intellectual potential and their moral obligations. Highet illustrated his pedagogical principles with sketches of "great teachers" from antiquity through the early twentieth century. The work concluded with a section on "teaching in everyday life," which classified the communications of parents, artists, and even advertisers as educational transactions.[10]

The most notable aspect of *The Art of Teaching* was Highet's assumption that his pedagogical principles transcended subject matter; as he used it, "teaching" denoted a generic process. As such, Highet sidestepped what Howard Mumford

Jones, reviewing one of Highet's later books, called "the real question," namely, "How much, and what parts of practicable knowledge are both possible and desirable towards the training of citizens in this republic in the year 1954?" Furthermore, Highet stressed that learning arose not so much from the curriculum as from the effects of the human relationship between instructor and pupil. At its best, he asserted, teaching stopped being "the mere transmission of information" and became "the joint enterprise of a group of friendly human beings who like using their brains." That view, as well as Highet's emphasis in the last pages of his book on the undeniable virtues of patience, restraint, and selflessness, gave his work an aura of timeless truth.[11]

Nonetheless, Highet's inclusion of two sections—a discussion of the good and bad practices of the fathers of "great men" and the concluding one on parents as teachers—directly addressed a concern of Americans in 1950: to use the language of the period, the role of the weak father in the social maladjustment of boys. "Juvenile courts and mental homes," Highet remarked, are "full of youngsters" whose view of life came from the movies: "Their fathers never told the boys how to control their powers and arrange their lives." Here, as throughout *The Art of Teaching*, Highet's own persona as a teacher—at once "friendly" and authoritative, forceful and calm—reassured readers that they could master the educational principles that would redress such social ills. The book's final chapter was similarly timely in explicating "Communist" techniques of political indoctrination so that proponents of American democracy could harness them for their own cold war agenda.[12]

The Classical Tradition and *The Art of Teaching* launched Highet on his project of breathing "new life and meaning" into Greek and Roman literature and on the trajectory that would make him what one eulogist called "the most recognized and most talked-about classical scholar in American history since Thomas Jefferson." In 1952 Highet augmented his fame by embracing the medium that middlebrow commentators such as Phelps had used before him: the radio. He agreed to do a weekly program called *People, Places, and Books*, sponsored by Oxford University Press and broadcast on WQXR, the radio station of the *New York Times*. The arrangement allowed him to discuss books by any publisher. Over the next seven years, Highet built an audience that ultimately involved listeners to more than three hundred stations in the United States and Canada, as well as those who heard him over the BBC and the Voice of America. The program was "unbelievably popular." Some observers likened him to Alexander Woollcott, whose radio book reviews had earned him a loyal following in the 1930s, but Highet's academic credentials gave the role greater weight than Woollcott's verbal playfulness had lent it. At intervals Oxford issued the talks as collections of essays. The first, which came out in 1953 and shared the title of the show, had sold more than fifteen thousand copies by 1958 and "made the best-seller lists." Later volumes included *A Clerk of Oxenford* (1954) and *Talents and Geniuses* (1957).[13]

On the air Highet typically used recent publications as starting points for reflections on many facets of the humanities. These often consisted of anecdotes about authors with eccentric habits or unusual backgrounds. Alternatively, Highet tied new books to accounts of locations he knew well or to his avocations, such as mountain climbing and playing the piano. He also considered older writings with which he assumed his audience was at least partially familiar, offering listeners a pithy description of a literary question (was Hamlet mad?) and furnishing a definitive answer (yes, sometimes). In particular, thanks to listener responses after the first season, Highet turned the radio programs into occasions for him to draw on his training in Greek and Latin; for instance, he traced the adaptations by Pierre de Ronsard, Abraham Cowley, and Shelley of a drinking song attributed to Anacreon. Among his most well-received talks were those on the sound, structure, and purposes of poetry and on the works of individual poets. (The one called "Seventeen Syllables" may well have launched the fascination with the haiku among "creative writing" teachers in postwar high schools.) In 1960 Oxford published these talks as *The Power of Poetry*.[14]

Yet the most noteworthy aspect of Highet's broadcasts was not their theme but their style and tone. Highet's prose, one reviewer testified, captivated readers so fully that it became almost "hypnotic," drawing attention away from his ideas. Highet achieved that result by imparting to his analysis of literature the warmth and directness he exhibited in *The Art of Teaching*. One essay, "The Pleasures of Satire," was characteristically personal: evoking immediacy by means of the present tense, Highet began: "My old friend, the Roman satirist Juvenal, says . . ." (One correspondent reported that, as a result of that reference, the reading experience very much resembled "meeting an old acquaintance.") His other trademarks included direct address of the listener to create intimacy and informality, as in the phrases "Have you ever read?" and "You know them." On occasion he employed the same tactic that Woollcott had used so effectively to grab listeners' attention: turning his subject into a mystery man by concealing an author's identity until the conclusion of his remarks. At the same time Highet demystified the topic of rhythm in verse by introducing no term more technical than "iambic pentameter." His accent marked him as a cultivated European gentleman, but his frequent allusions to Manhattan locales bespoke his affection for the United States. (On becoming an American citizen, he praised the nation's energy and humor.) Such references also allowed listeners and readers access to his cosmopolitan milieu.[15]

Together those devices and traits amounted to a formula sufficiently recognizable that it was susceptible to parody. Reviewing in the *New York Times* a book Highet produced for Columbia's bicentennial in 1954, Orville Prescott illustrated that fact in his opening lines: "Yes. Thought is difficult, but it is exciting, tremendously exciting. Plato wrote one of the first books about thought. There have been many since, hundreds of thousands, no doubt. And now I propose to discuss with you still another. It is a little book published by the Columbia University Press." Prescott called his first paragraph "a tribute (of sorts)"—a label that captures the mixed responses Highet incurred from other critics over time. Many noted—both positively and negatively—his intermediate location between the academy and the general public. At a time when "universities like to retain experts instead of scholars," the *Buffalo Evening News* asserted in a review of *The Clerk of Oxenford*, "and when the genus, gentleman, is almost as extinct as the great auk, the only possible descriptive term for the Highet speciality is conversation at its most civilized." Corroborating the prevalence of the impulse to retreat into specialization, another newspaper writer pronounced Highet a professor who found it "not beneath his dignity to write or broadcast pleasant little essays"; the same reviewer assured readers that while Highet was "sometimes professorial," in that mode he could be "very enlightening." The most favorable summary of Highet's departure from academic discourse appeared in a *Commonweal* review entitled "Humanist's Report." Writing in 1954, John Sisk declared: "There is a great need for such books as this, wherein the university teacher addresses himself to the literate public, but does so with dignity and integrity, out of a sense of responsibility that cannot be satisfied with an audience made up exclusively of his colleagues." By the same token, Highet's ambivalent or disaffected critics regarded his simplicity and enthusiasm as an accommodation of general readers that contravened the scholar's obligations. "If his judgments are conventional and his criticism superficial," one asserted, "remember he was writing for a radio audience, not for a seminar in English literature." Bergen Evans, the Northwestern University English professor and popular author who was also prominent on radio and television, averred in the *Saturday Review* that "the clerk of Oxenford is trying a little too hard to identify himself with the laity." He added, "Sometimes the friendly guide lapses into the grade-school teacher and the charm chills to a briskness perilously near to fatuity." A Memphis writer traced Highet's appeal to his knack for slightly disagreeing with his audience in a way that confirmed the readers' prejudices.[16]

Although Highet's ability to be "erudite yet winning" usually prevented him from giving "offense to the extremes who may variously suspect him of smuggling in the contraband of 'culture' or charge him with huckstering it," the compromise he struck seemed to his greatest detractors merely a "safe, useless middle ground" on which literature could be "smelled, touched, quoted, and chatted about over the radio with neither risk nor originality, but with perfect ease, sincerity, and assurance." In its allusions to safety and pre-packaging, and in affiliating Highet with marketable commodities, that verdict resembled attacks on middlebrow mediators in the pre–World War II era. As if to confirm his status as a latter-day middlebrow authority, Highet replaced Henry Seidel Canby on the Book-of-the-Month Club Board of Judges in 1954, where he served along with Fadiman until 1978.[17]

Yet though Highet's affinities to Phelps, Woollcott, and Canby made him look like something of a holdover from an earlier time, in two respects he was actually more in tune with the future than with his middlebrow antecedents. The first lay in his openness to modernist literature and his willingness to assist his audience in understanding it. In *The Clerk of Oxenford* Highet created an avenue of approach to *Finnegans Wake* by comparing it to more familiar instances of nonsense and double-talk, such as "Jabberwocky" in *Alice in Wonderland.* Elsewhere he issued his readers a calm invitation to consider the poetry of T. S. Eliot, assuring them that they did not have to grasp every word to appreciate it. Around the same time that the poet Randall Jarrell interrogated the widespread assumption that the public bridled against "obscurity" in verse, Highet provided grounds for reconciling modernist poets and ordinary readers by arguing that "obscurity" was necessary for some types of verse to be effective. Not all Highet's followers could tolerate that conclusion, but Highet mitigated their discomfort by coupling his defense of Joyce and Eliot with attacks on Faulkner's *A Fable* and on Pound's misuse of Homer. Thus, he staked out a middle way between the contempt for the modernist aesthetic and total allegiance to it. Second, Highet made a tentative move toward the late twentieth-century critic's celebration of popular culture. In 1954, fifteen years after Clement Greenberg publicized the word to American intellectuals in his essay "Avant-Garde and Kitsch," Highet brought his audience up to speed by defining "kitsch" as "junky art"— of which he was unabashedly fond. Bad poetry, he explained (using Pound as an example here as well), was as much an "extension of experience" as the good. At the same time Highet consistently tempered his affection by withholding any presumption that "kitsch" could ever come close to classical literature's cultural preeminence.[18]

Highet's larger accomplishment was nevertheless his representation of continuity with the past, not his acceptance of change. In the face of troubling postwar circumstances—the prospect of nuclear war, the Soviet menace, the challenge young people posed to their parents' moral values, the decline of the nonspecialist—Highet in effect declared: the ancient Greeks have survived, modern Europeans have survived, and so will Americans. (By implication,

Communists, whom, John Chamberlain wrote in 1953, Highet thought "as bad as Nazis," would not.) As one correspondent told Highet about *The Classic Tradition*, she had read it with her housemate in the fall of 1950, at a time "when people were conscious of peril and perplexity but carefully avoided admitting it"; the two women found the book "a veritable 'shadow of a rock in a weary land.'" Highet's most explicit statement of his hopeful message appeared in the Columbia bicentennial book, significantly entitled *Man's Unconquerable Mind.* There he announced that "those who are most easily depressed about the precarious future of Western civilization are usually people who do not know the full history of its past." Highet acknowledged that Communism and fascism had triggered a "war for the enslavement or liberation of the mind of humanity"; he saw dangers as well in the pursuit of pleasure and in "thought control." Yet he believed that Western culture—"the most intellectual of all cultures"—furnished precedents for human progress through knowledge.[19]

In a 1954 review of *A Clerk of Oxenford*, Richard Armour declared that Highet could be "understood by the middlebrows and yet admired by the highbrows." But the admiration was only partial: as his popular reputation grew, Highet had difficulty maintaining his academic stature. After publication of *Juvenal the Satirist* (1954), his scholarship foundered. One reason it did so was that his critics found him inadequate as a translator of Latin. As M. L. Rosenthal wrote in assessing *Poets in a Landscape* (1957), "Why Gilbert Highet should offer his own pitiful verse-translations . . . when so many more accomplished versions were available, is one of the great mysteries." Highet's decision to reproduce in English the structure and meters of Latin texts seemed especially questionable. "Of course he fails; he was bound to fail, the job cannot be done," the poet and classicist Dudley Fitts remarked. "Even if his ear were extraordinarily sensitive (which, in a creative sense, it certainly is not) he must still trip over his assumption" that replicating cadence and other textual attributes would yield the best results. Those judgments were accompanied by some classicists' derogation of him as a "popularizer"—meaning that he was neither competent as a specialist nor intellectually serious.[20]

The assaults on Highet's professional standing at least partially explain why Highet did not finish a work in progress on oratory: "I became disgusted and discouraged by malicious attacks on me and my work, both printed and verbal," he told one correspondent in 1970, "and instead of pushing on with my writing I gave up much time and energy to advising Ph.D's." That revelation assays the personal cost to some academic humanists who tried to juggle disciplinary expectations and public demands. Yet, earlier, writing of *The Classical Tradition*, Fitts had accurately placed Highet in more positive terms—ones that can apply to his entire career. The book, Fitts stated, was not "primarily for classical scholars.

The scope is general; and it is the general, thoughtful reader, aware of and worried about the predicament of contemporary civilization, who will find here the greatest rewards."[21]

The second highly visible emissary of the humanities from Columbia between 1945 and 1960, Jacques Barzun, did not pay the price that Highet did because his career was more compartmentalized: although always an accessible stylist, he self-consciously staked the greater part of his identity on his original scholarship in European cultural history. ("I feel I run the risk of becoming a professional Educator," he declared in 1945, "and that is not really my métier. I prefer to think of myself as an historian and critic.") Born in Paris in 1907, Barzun spent much of his early childhood in the company of the French modernists—Marcel Duchamp, Jean Cocteau, and Guillaume Apollinaire, among others—who were friends of his father, a writer. In 1919 he came to the United States; in 1923 he entered Columbia College. His activities as a student foreshadowed his stance later on. As his colleague Lionel Trilling recalled, "Jacques's relationship to the undergraduate establishment was the exact opposite of mine. Where I began in passivity and deference and ended in contempt, he took the measure of every organization which might bear upon his interests. . . . By the time he graduated (at age nineteen), he was the dramatic critic of *Spectator*, editor of *Varsity*, president of Philolexian, and author of the 1927 Varsity Show." He was also at the top of his class. Immediately appointed a lecturer in the first-year great books course Contemporary Civilization, he subsequently undertook graduate study at Columbia and received a Ph.D. in history in 1932.[22]

In the 1930s, while rising through the ranks of the Columbia faculty, Barzun published two volumes related to his dissertation on the concept of race. His next ventures into cultural biography were *Darwin, Marx, Wagner* (1941) and *Berlioz and the Romantic Century* (1950). In between, he also brought out three books of criticism. He became a full professor in 1945. Along with a number of translations, Barzun produced several essay collections in the 1950s, including *The Energies of Art: Studies of Authors Classic and Modern* (1956). He became Columbia's dean of the graduate faculties in 1955. Three years later he was named dean of faculties and provost, a post he held until 1967. Barzun's extraordinary productivity as a scholar (in 2005 he was still writing and publishing), his prominence in the Columbia administration, and his association with Trilling in the famous Trilling-Barzun humanities seminar (another permutation of the great books curriculum) safeguarded his academic stature and immunized him against the dismissal as a popularizer that Highet experienced.

Yet Barzun was leading a double life—functioning not only as a professional historian but also as an authority on the centrality of the humanities to education and culture. His mode of fulfilling the latter role was less dependent on middlebrow precedents and even more attuned to the particular anxieties of the times than Highet's was. That approach is most visible in the two best sellers Barzun wrote in the immediate postwar period.

The first, *Teacher in America*, appeared in 1945. Responding to many of the same concerns that impelled Highet to focus on the figure of the teacher five years later, the book also resembled *The Art of Teaching* in its longevity and its appeal to ordinary readers. Excerpted in general circulation magazines before its publication by Little, Brown, *Teacher in America* sold more than ten thousand copies in its first six months and was reissued three times in its second edition (1954, 1971, and 1981).[23]

In contrast to Highet's soothing demeanor and avoidance of the curricular issues, however, Barzun weighed in on the educational controversies of the 1940s directly and contentiously: he offered a resounding defense of liberal learning and a brief for mandated great books courses. In the volume's opening sections Barzun opposed his ideal of good teaching—the creation of an independent student—to the prevalent emphasis on transmitting "meaningless formula," bare fact, empty moralism, and cliché. Barzun denominated all those features of poor instruction "hokum," a word that cast him as exposer of illusion and defender of the real. Later chapters surveyed the degree of hokum infiltrating several subjects and suggested alternatives. For example, citing the misguided attempt to legislate more "date-and-fact history" to foster "Americanism," Barzun countered that history should impart knowledge of the continuities between past and present. A "sense of the past," he concluded, was "the humanizing faculty par excellence."[24]

Predictably, in Barzun's view that recommendation—along with his stipulations for the study of science, mathematics, foreign language, classics, and the arts—materialized in the Columbia College curriculum, which Barzun lovingly described in the second half of *Teacher in America.* He followed that discussion with reflections on such matters as objective tests, gender-based schooling, and university extension programs. In stronger terms than Highet, he objected to requiring humanities professors to hold doctorates: borrowing the phrase "The Ph.D. Octopus" from William James, he claimed that the practice encouraged dissertations on unimportant topics and consigned undergraduates to the classrooms of halfhearted "section men." Better teaching and learning went on in the evening courses of extension schools, which Barzun lauded as civic-minded—as long as institutions held the line between "real academic work for full academic credit" and its night-school diplomas. Barzun saved his last word for the "young man" who aspired to be a scholar, advising him to return to canonized works in the humanities in order to nurture unity, insight, and truth.[25]

Barzun's case rested on several underlying premises that related both to the controversies astir in 1945 and to the positions Barzun would sustain over the next fifteen years. The first of these was his predilection for the "harder way," as against what he called (also appropriating James) the "softer pedagogy" and emotional coddling of the progressive classroom. No less than Sproul, he valued rigor, structure, and discipline, which he counterposed to "the desire to be kind, to sound new, to foster useful attitudes, to appear 'scientific,'" and to accommodate individual choice. As this remark suggests, however, Barzun reversed the customary association of science with tough-mindedness, equating it instead with vocational preparation, jargon (or "hokum"), and technique—all of which he judged inimical to the proper, humanizing aims of education and to genuine understanding. His most interesting move in *Teacher in America* was his proposition that the sciences, instead of remaining the province of the "single-track expert," belonged in the undergraduate program *"as humanities"*: "The point is that science is made by man, in the light of interests, errors, and hopes, just like poetry, philosophy, and human history itself." Accordingly, he urged the creation of compulsory courses that involved a modicum of laboratory work but substituted the history of science for "mere voodoo formulas." That proposal manifested the "dynamics of inclusion" in the sense that Barzun imagined the humanities engulfing and recasting the competition threatening their curricular preeminence.[26]

Barzun's attitude toward inclusion with respect to the American student population was a different story, one that relied on a third assumption: his conviction that there was "nothing undemocratic or iniquitous about selecting the best for the highest training." The "best" meant, first of all, mostly men. Barzun deserves some credit for writing about women's education at all; as Carolyn Heilbrun recalled, he was the only one of her mentors at Columbia who took seriously the accomplishments of women intellectuals and her own aspirations. Yet *Teacher in America* mirrors the reality of academia in the 1940s by its relentless references to the "senior man," the "younger man," the men on campus. Furthermore, Barzun thought women's colleges should abandon "scholar-making" in favor of recognizing that "most young women are likely to lose touch with books, ideas, and current events on the far side of the altar." For them he advocated a Columbia plan modified to acknowledge gender difference. Second, Barzun's "best" was implicitly white and middle- or upper-class: although he insisted that a "democratic university" should welcome workers to its campus, he saw the extension school as the most likely place for them, while race made no appearance in his analysis except obliquely, as in his presumption that men shared a "common descent" from historical actors such as the Pilgrim Fathers. Third, democracy as Barzun understood it did not preclude hierarchies of taste and authority. With respect to educational radio programs, he asserted, "Why not frankly face the fact of a limited appeal comprising three million highbrows and satisfy *them* instead of trying to cater for all and disappointing the fraction of actual devotees?" He likewise assumed that his own outlook as an intellectual should take precedence over that of most people. His claim that "vocational training has nothing to do with education," one observer noted, would mean "for 90 per cent of the students and returning veterans" that "college has nothing to do with them." Yet, conceding that majority opinion was against him, Barzun queried: "But are the directing members of the university world to follow other people's untutored impulses or to guide and redirect them?"[27]

Barzun's beliefs about the humanities, science, and democracy informed his second best-selling volume on education and American culture, *The House of Intellect* (1959). The book reiterated the purpose of the "academic humanities": to "serve the arts, philosophy, and religion by bringing order into the heritage of civilization." By the late 1950s, however, the drive for specialized, preprofessional curricula had proved unstoppable: at colleges throughout the United States, Barzun lamented, "'real life'" had "crept in and ousted academic subjects." In addition, the Soviets' launch of the Sputnik satellite had intensified American anxieties about the adequacy of instruction in technical fields. The prestige an "overawed" citizenry accorded science at the expense of the humanities was, in Barzun's view, one of the "enemies" assaulting "intellect"— defined as the life of the mind and the social institutions supporting it. Nonscientist scholars had made matters worse by reconceiving their research as an exercise of scientific method. Barzun was similarly dismayed by two other current phenomena: the adulation of art and the surrender to philanthropy. Both tendencies, he argued, reflected democratic ideals gone awry.[28]

Barzun indicted American concepts of art on two charges. First, embellishing his earlier remarks on progressive education, he debunked the focus on "creativity" within the nation's elementary and secondary schools. To reward students for self-expression, Barzun contended, was to succumb to the egalitarian but wrongheaded idea that education should advance "individual goals." His diatribe against the preoccupation with creativity was closely allied with his attacks on several other facets of educational theory in the late 1950s: the infamous adjustment curriculum that sought to help students fit into adult behavioral norms; the assumption that lessons should involve "excitement" and "challenge" rather than work; the devaluation of subject matter so that students graduated with "no knowledge that is precise and firm." Second, Barzun made art an enemy of intellect because, unlike Highet, he had no patience with mid-twentieth-century modernism. As Trilling reminded readers in a memoir written just before his death, Barzun's happy childhood in Europe and the traumatic experience of war impelled him to demarcate the affirmative experimentation of the modernist movement before 1914 from the "impoverished version" that came later. Before World War I artists and writers reached new heights of originality; afterward—up to the present day—things went from bad to worse. Barzun particularly objected to the later modernists' valorization of what he called "love of confusion," irrationality, meaninglessness, and despair, which critics promoted by favoring such qualities as ambiguity, imagination, and irony. The result was that art undermined the "articulate precision" of a cultivated mind. On this point Barzun's cultural criticism intersected not only with his autobiography but also with his interests as a historian: he traced the current state of affairs to the triumph of Romanticism in the nineteenth and twentieth centuries, the primary effect of which was "to raise art and confound in a common ruin Intellect and Philistinism."[29]

Barzun quirkily defined philanthropy, his third enemy of intellect, as "the liberal doctrine of free and equal opportunity as applied to things of the mind." In part his analysis of the philanthropic impulse anticipated the critique of the therapeutic ethos that Christopher Lasch would offer subsequently: for example, he blamed the influence of psychology on education for the accepted view that "the school is not to teach but to cure; body and mind are not to use for self-forgetful ends but to dwell on with Narcissus' adoring anxiety." Furthermore, the philanthropists' rhetoric of "helping," Barzun maintained, eventuated in the imperative to make print journalism, broadcasting, and scholarship palatable by simplifying, overselling, or "enlivening" them at the cost of intellectual integrity. More concretely, philanthropic donors also damaged intellect by awarding grants to "projects" described in pseudoscientific jargon, whereas "humanities gave rise to no projects properly so called, were not expensive enough, and promised few social benefits." The conferences they sponsored (in contrast, of course, to the one occasioning this essay) were merely "a substitute for work" and a "form of intellectual togetherness."[30]

Barzun's protests against the vogue of science, art, and philanthropy registered again his long-standing distress at the deterioration of language and his rejection of ease—positions he conveyed in a tone even more strident and urgent than the one governing *Teacher in America*. At the same time *The House of Intellect* moved beyond the concerns framing Barzun's earlier volume by participating in the self-conscious appraisals of the intellectual's place in American consumer culture from the late 1940s through the 1960s. In the first paragraph of his text, Barzun alluded to—and separated himself from—the posture of alienation that Irving Howe had prescribed five years earlier as an antidote to complacency. Barzun had implicitly rejected that posture in *God's Country and Mine* (1954), a semifanciful rebuttal of European smugness toward American practicality and materialism. He had also permitted his photograph to appear on the cover of *Time* in 1956 as part of a story on the new, unalienated American intellectual. In *The House of Intellect*, however, Barzun explicitly derided alienation as a form of self-delusion and a species of solipsism. "The real disaster haunting the intellectual today," Barzun commented, "is that the alienation, the disinheriting, the loss of authority have occurred, not between the intellectuals and the rest—the commercial rump—of society, but among the intellectuals themselves and as a result of their own acts."[31]

Barzun was hardly alone among artists and writers in spurning the role of outcast. As Richard Hofstadter (still another Columbia professor) pointed out in *Anti-Intellectualism in American Life* (1964), a study that contributed to the same discourse by locating it historically, the "overwhelming majority" of the respondents—including Barzun—in the famous *Partisan Review* symposium of 1952, "Our Country and Our Culture," largely welcomed the "growing *rapprochement* between the intellectuals and their society." Furthermore, as Hofstadter noted, tensions attended the remarks of almost everyone who examined the American intellectual's circumstances. What was unusual about Barzun's outlook, however, was the way it managed to discredit the stance of alienation while simultaneously assenting to key elements of the disaffected intellectual's viewpoint. Barzun rebuked contemporary thinkers for decrying conformity to the point that they relished defeat, yet in his remarks about the debasement of language he labeled the simplistic "thought-cliché" the essence of a conformist mentality. He opposed the science worship that elevated technical skill over unfettered play of mind—in effect asking the same question that worried observers of the growing partnership between universities and government: whether, in assuming the function of an expert, the intellectual was actually a "mere technician." After condemning Americans' reluctance to voice their opinions without self-protective disclaimers ("You'll correct me if I'm wrong"), he announced, "The native critics of Western culture blame commercialism for this mind-destroying habit, as if trade by itself produced the wormlike stance." The real cause, Barzun said, was democracy, "which has made accountability universal and thus caused everybody to be forever 'selling himself' to everybody else." Yet as the phrase "selling himself" suggests, Barzun himself criticized the way in which intellectuals became "infected" by the "spirit of trade" insofar as they collaborated in the reduction of knowledge to skill and sought greater "material reward" for art and thought. Never a fan of Marxism (he saw it as preying on a need for "system"), he acknowledged the liabilities of capitalism for the life of the mind.[32]

Barzun struck a similar balance in his perspective on middlebrow culture. As if reacting directly to Fadiman's description of himself, he devoted considerable space in *The House of Intellect* to denouncing the "middleman" as a figure who "professes devotion to the highest standards" but who routinely sacrifices them for the sake of attracting large numbers of readers. Echoing Dwight Macdonald and other critics of "midcult," Barzun laid most of the blame for the transformation of "mind-stuff" into products on such "caterers" to the "public mind." Editors and other middlemen reduced thought to commodities "answering exactly to specifications" so as to make them easy to sell and to consume. Science abetted that process by valuing error-free outcomes, philanthropy by seeking to alleviate difficulty and promote agreeableness. By the same token, Barzun sardonically reported on the popularity of the television series *Sunrise Semester* in 1957, pointing out that viewers created a market for a repackaged edition of Stendhal's *The Red and the Black* "in utter ignorance of its contents."[33]

Nevertheless, Barzun, who had called at the end of *Teacher in America* for a "dissemination of intelligence" in order to improve American public life, repeatedly acted as a middleman himself. To be fair, Barzun distinguished manipulative "caterers," who recognized "no mediation possible" between their knowledge and their audience's ignorance, from his own efforts to provide such mediation. Yet the latter were not always consistent with his critique of commodification. Indeed, his complaints seem often to have resulted from personal experience: he appeared on the *Invitation to Learning* and *Conversation*, as well as a television series on twentieth-century thought underwritten by the Ford Foundation. He endured (albeit unhappily) the excision of "humanities" from the title of his article in a popular magazine because an editor thought the term too intimidating; he lectured at the 1951 Aspen Festival, where organizers requested that speakers "use words containing no more than three syllables." In 1951 he joined W. H. Auden and Lionel Trilling in launching the Readers' Subscription Book Club, envisioned as a more serious endeavor than the Book-of-the-Month Club. While the Readers' Subscription did offer more demanding titles than its competitors sent out, however, the venture involved Barzun in the same accommodations to consumerism that the BOMC epitomized. Here is Louis Menand's comment on a recently published collection of essays from the Readers' Subscription newsletter: "The pieces are not criticism; they are blurbs, blurbs of rare discernment perhaps, but blurbs. Their purpose, after all, was to persuade subscribers to buy the selections. . . . What the essays advertised was not just the books; it was a sense of intellectual ease and familiarity that readers might, through a steady consumption of such books, hope to acquire themselves. 'Read this,' the editors seem to say, 'and sound like us.'" In that regard they were simply reenacting Fadiman's role a notch or two up the cultural hierarchy.[34]

The tensions marking *The House of Intellect* suggest its multiple appeals to the fifty thousand readers who had purchased the book by 1960. Those tensions also argue that Barzun's cultural role involved more than the complicity between intellectuals and cold war policy makers that historians have lately emphasized. It is true that Barzun (with Auden and Trilling) was a member of the American Committee for Cultural Freedom and turned to its former executive director to help it find funding when the Readers' Subscription regrouped as the Mid-Century Book Society in 1959. Because he was French by birth and therefore presumably civilized, his appearance on the cover of *Time* suited perfectly the interests of the U.S. government in wooing western Europeans away from the temptations of Communism. (Highet was good for the same purpose.) One might counter that those facts were offset by Barzun's vocal opposition to certain other cold war initiatives: for one thing, he believed that the cultural exchange programs of the period were sentimental and misconceived; for another, he thought area studies not a way to prepare Americans for global leadership but, rather, a blow to language instruction that promoted superficial knowledge and the illusion of employability. He also asked the War Department to ensure that foreign readers to whom it distributed *Teacher in America* would know that it was "not written as ad hoc propaganda for their present consumption." In the mid-1950s he participated in selecting books for the Carnegie Corporation's "American Shelf" project, which strove to portray the United States accurately to foreigners by unblinking inclusion of such themes as race and class prejudice, feminism, and conformism.[35]

But in any event the full power of Barzun's public image—his cultural usefulness—derived not just from his Frenchness but from his Frenchness and his Americanness yoked together, as well as from the equipoise he exhibited in other respects. In joining the roles of academic historian and social critic, he offered cosmopolitanism without disaffection, sophistication without incomprehensibility. He assailed materialism and Marxism alike, scorned and supported the middlebrow, upheld standards and downgraded expertise.

Barzun's appeals become clearer if we compare him with Ciardi, who in the struggle over Lindbergh incurred readers' anger for seeming to symbolize not only academia but also the modernist's predilection for arcane form and language and the New Critics' substitution of technique for feeling. Barzun's antipathy to modernism and New Criticism alike protected him against such a fate. More than that, in contrast to Ciardi's vituperative outbursts, Barzun joined Highet in mastering an alluring prose style that carried readers along until they found themselves thinking hard. But Barzun's version of this "relaxed erudition" went beyond seduction. "He cuts deep and draws blood," one journalist observed, "but he makes you like it even when it's your blood. He always operates gracefully and urbanely; at his very wittiest, he hurts most, but helps most too." A reader agreed: "Each time I read one of the passages directed at such people as I represented," he wrote, "I would grimace, stop reading, and rationalize, justifying my insulted ego. . . . [I am] a butt of many of your criticisms, but I blame myself for [my] shortcomings." All these balances contributed to what Hofstadter bemoaned as the "absorptive tolerance" afflicting intellectuals by 1964; they enabled Barzun's readers to side with him even though he had "just eviscerated their way of life" and, in agreeing with him, to conclude that they were acting to redress the ills he catalogued.[36]

Alongside Highet's dissemination of his discipline and Barzun's Europe-oriented social criticism, the career of the literary and cultural historian Howard Mumford Jones furnishes a third, homegrown mode in which academic humanists addressed the reading public during the 1940s and 1950s. Jones was born in Michigan in 1892 and grew up in Wisconsin. After receiving a master's degree in 1915 from the University of Chicago, he held a series of teaching posts at state universities in the West, Midwest and South. In the early 1930s he also tried his hand at reaching ordinary readers by writing a weekly column on books of interest to southerners. Those experiences influenced Jones's decision to shift from a concentration on European literature to a scholarly identity as an Americanist (albeit one with a well-developed comparative perspective). In 1936 he joined the English Department at Harvard University. He served multiple terms as president of the American Academy of Arts and Sciences in the 1940s and was chair of the American Council of Learned Societies (ACLS) between 1955 and 1959. The author of *The Theory of American Literature* (1948), he produced his most famous works on the culture of the United States following his retirement in 1962: *O Strange New World* (1964), *The Age of Energy* (1971), and *Revolution and Romanticism* (1974). Jones also embodied American (or at least non–New England) traits: in place of Highet and Barzun's aura of European cultivation, he was energetic and volatile. At the time of his death in 1980 he was at work on a study of the American cowboy, with whom he sympathized by temperament and background.[37]

Although his cultural histories won him recognition outside academia, Jones was not as familiar a public figure as Highet or Barzun; he was not a media celebrity and wrote no best-selling polemics. Nevertheless, he addressed the lay reader in more limited ways. Apart from the occasional magazine article on educational issues, he frequently contributed to popular periodicals as a book reviewer. Between 1929 and 1960 he published roughly 125 reviews in the *Saturday Review of Literature*. He wrote even more often for the *New York Times Book Review*, at least twice a month in the late 1940s. In the 1960s he made several radio appearances, including a spot on *Invitation to Learning* with Perry Miller as his fellow panelist. More important, Jones published four books (two originating as lectures) for nonspecialists on education and the nature of the humanities. If Jones's activities as mediator between the university and the public were more circumscribed than those of his Columbia counterparts, they were nonetheless a significant variant of Highet's and Barzun's undertakings because in their performance Jones self-consciously delineated a distinctively American attitude toward humanistic study in the postwar period.

The first of Jones's four volumes directly pertinent to the humanities was *Education and World Tragedy*, the Rushton Lectures for 1946. There Jones sounded three themes that would reappear in his subsequent works: the humanists' complicity in the veneration of science; the ideal model of graduate training; and the inadequacy of the great books version of the college curriculum. Scientists, Jones argued, were not responsible for the subordinate position of the humanities in American higher education. Neither were the proponents of professional or vocational study, which Jones himself endorsed. The real problem was the failure of faculty members outside the sciences to insist on the equal merits of their subject matter. Scholars in literature, history, and the social sciences, Jones declared, "have inevitably tended to believe that their own 'disciplines' approach perfection" insofar as "they can be subjected to technical and even technological manipulation." Nonscientists had thus become committed to research—"innocently thought of as paralleling research in 'science'— and hence to the specialization and aloofness from individual and societal needs that was its inevitable result. Because doctoral programs perpetuated that tendency, Jones proposed the establishment of a separate institution (a graduate college rather than a research training institute) to prepare future professors as humanistic generalists capable of meeting the "social, political, and intellectual responsibilities" of a world transformed by the threat of nuclear annihilation.[38]

Although his criticism of specialization and the worship of the Ph.D. closely resembled Barzun's stands, Jones was unalterably opposed to Barzun's remedy for those perceived defects. The idea that American education required the infusion of a prescribed reading list drawn from the products of the European past seemed to Jones wrong on several counts. Especially in its hardened form at the University of Chicago, the great books curriculum had a dictatorial tone that Jones rejected as inappropriate to a "victorious democratic society organized as a technological culture of great complexity and richness." More than that, he found the Western tradition itself inadequate, because it was, "to a surprising degree, a tradition of scepticism, authoritarianism, and despair of ordinary humanity." Instead of seeking refuge in the past, universities needed to devise curricula based on a "dynamic for democratic culture." Equally dubious about the virtues of an eclectic general education program confined to the first two years of college, Jones urged as a first step toward reform a set of requirements that included courses on science, psychology, Russia, and Asia to offset the sole emphasis on the past and the West.[39]

As Jones developed as an Americanist, his provisional proposals of the mid-1940s gave way to a more specific understanding that young people in the United States could prepare for adulthood only by grasping the differences as well as the similarities between American and European culture. He articulated that view in second volume for the general public, *American Humanism: Its Meaning for World Survival* (1957). The book appeared in a series entitled World Perspectives, under the editorship of the philosopher Ruth Nanda Anshen. (Barzun had discussed publishing *The House of Intellect* under the same auspices, but found the constraints of the prescribed format too restrictive.) Anshen's introduction yoked Jones to her desire to "point to a reality of which scientific theory has revealed only one aspect"—the unity between "spirit" and "nature." Once illuminated, that principle and its corollary, the unity between individual and collectivity, promised "world unity on the basis of the sacredness of each human person and respect for the plurality of cultures." Implicitly, Anshen counterposed her project to the cold war antagonisms dividing nations at the time she was writing; her dream of one world in which human beings experienced "dignity, integrity and self-realization" was an alternative to the "totalitarianism of both left and right."[40]

In the text of *American Humanism*, Jones assented in a general way to Anshen's outlook (although not to her mysticism), endorsing humanistic knowledge because it assumed and enhanced the "dignity of man." Instead of her notion of an apolitical future, however, Jones matter-of-factly asserted the likelihood that the West (led by the United States) would triumph over Communism. (For Jones, a strong civil libertarian and advocate of academic freedom, this was simply a reading of reality, not militant anti-Communism.) With the American Century at hand, the issue for Jones was not who would rule the globe but, rather, which aspects of American culture would dominate it. His purpose in the book was thus to indicate how Americans had modified European humanism and to weigh the costs and benefits of those adaptations. Elaborating on his earlier doubts about staking education on the Western classics, Jones noted how Old World reverence for antiquity had eroded in the New World setting, with the result that Latin and Greek were gradually erased from the American conception of liberal education. In contrast to Highet, Jones did not seek to keep classical ideals alive by reinterpreting them but, instead, accepted their demise. At the same time he reiterated that American humanists, susceptible to the national "passion for *expertise*," had cooperated in their own marginalization by putting their energies into such technical exercises as the New Criticism and by writing unintelligibly. If that argument had some affinity with the impatience of Ciardi's readers, so did Jones's assertion that the quintessentially modernist pose of "despair" and flirtation with irrationality did not advance a "humane point of view." As disaffected from modernism as Barzun, Jones instead contended that the "American version of humanism"—the democratic, affirmative tradition of Jefferson and Emerson—held the best hope for repelling the specters of totalitarianism and global destruction.[41]

Jones's fullest treatment of his vision for the academic humanities appeared in *One Great Society: Humane Learning in the United States* (1959), the report of an ACLS commission convened in 1955 and 1956 to explore "the relation of humane learning to the national culture." Published for a general readership by Harcourt, Brace, the book originated in the realization that America's corporate leaders had little appreciation for the goals of humanistic scholarship. The commission, consisting of representatives from business and the arts as well as the university, strove to "explain to a generous-minded but puzzled organization chief what the ACLS was all about and what it intended to do." Thus, it saw itself answering for the businessman such questions as "What can the humanities do for me, for my family, for my business, for my community?" and "What would be the best way for the business world to assist the humanities?"[42]

The circumstances under which Jones produced his report in 1957 and 1958 were somewhat different from those that had colored his earlier role as interpreter to the public: in the background was not only the ongoing prestige of science but also the recent appropriation of massive federal funds for science education. (Jones examined the latter topic at length in lectures published as a fourth volume on the humanities, *Reflections on Learning* [1958].) With experts so firmly entrenched, he modified his attack on specialization by making a place for humanistic specialists who, he insisted, were as entitled as their scientific colleagues to pursue scholarship for an audience restricted to their peers. By the late 1950s, moreover, Jones had witnessed the failure of the United States to compete successfully for power with the Soviets when Americans remained ignorant of "the traditions, the art, the philosophy, the religion, the moral system, and the history of the peoples" whose allegiance it was trying to win. Thus, *One Great Society* touted the ACLS and Rockefeller Foundation's wartime Intensive Language Program as an illustration of the benefits that could accrue to diplomacy and business from the study of Asian and other foreign languages. Jones was likewise cognizant of the critique of conformity American intellectuals had leveled by this time. With David Riesman in mind, he therefore argued for the humanities as the agent by which the "human heritage" becomes "meaningful and available as individual experience rather than as mass and generalization." Like Highet, however, he also made a place for popular culture: "It is as wrongheaded for the humanist to scorn the popular arts," he averred, "as for the ignorant to scorn the humanities." What mattered was knowing the difference between entertainment and the "greater world of humane art," replete with richer resources for achieving "personal integrity."[43]

Yet ultimately Jones sustained his previous case for redressing the "cultural imbalance" between science and the humanities on social terms. (Elsewhere he echoed Barzun by deploring the preoccupation with self-expression, but he staked his objections on the attendant loss of community.) To his putative businessman Jones replied that if humane learning disappeared, the ability to understand American ideals of equality and justice would also vanish, along with the basis for apprehending beauty. He argued that the humanities were essential in a democracy because collective decisions were good ones "only in proportion as they come from a decider whose life has been enhanced by an experience of what the best and happiest minds can tell him." Reaffirming the "civic responsibility" of the scholar, he charged humanists with drawing from tradition "wisdom and beauty appropriate to the present," in the service of the "housewife" and "citizen" as well as the "thinker" and "scientist." To that end, he distinguished between the monograph and the treatise: that is, between the necessary but narrow contribution to a discipline and the exploration of a broadly significant subject for both specialists and "a cultivated and intelligent general public." Such a work—exemplified, in Jones's view, by Highet's *The Classical Tradition*—was the "crown of a scholarly career."[44]

In *Reflections on Learning*, Jones had distinguished between "knowledge *of* and knowledge *about* the humanities"— between immersion in the materials of history or philosophy and acquaintance with the purposes of such fields. Although Jones regarded the last two decades of his life as the time when he deepened his "dedication to the task of fusing humanism and history" through his writing, up to the 1960s his contributions to increasing public support for humanistic scholarship fell into the *about* category. So did Barzun's more polemical efforts on behalf of the Western canon. Highet was more properly a disseminator *of* his subject. The three departed from each other on both stylistic and intellectual grounds, the two Columbia colleagues personifying, in very different fashions, a continuity with the European past (and a cold war utility) that Jones could not have supplied even if he had wanted to. Yet Highet, Barzun, and Jones resembled each other as much as they differed. All rejected alienation as a response to American society. To some extent, each was wary of modernism. All three resisted the cult of specialization and its badge, the Ph.D. All addressed the needs of postwar readers in search of stability and access to education by charging scholars with making cultural traditions available to people outside academia. And all thought the diffusion of the humanities essential to the survival of civilization.[45]

In the years after Highet, Barzun, and Jones established themselves as academic mediators, other humanists followed their example of looking outward from the campus. Their efforts, however, took somewhat different forms. In 1964 another ACLS commission swept aside qualms about government entanglement in humanistic scholarship, arguing that federal funds should underwrite the humanities as well as science. The creation the next year of the National Endowment for the Humanities furnished the nation's college and university faculties with countless opportunities to collaborate on exhibitions, films, and other projects designed to "transmit the achievement and values of civilization . . . and make widely available the greatest achievements of art." A representative example is the book discussion program, begun in the early 1980s and cosponsored by the American Library Association, that supported the participation of academic experts in conversations with members of local book clubs.[46]

As Barzun's foray into television indicates, the advent of public broadcasting similarly augmented the available mechanisms for the extension of the humanist's classroom. As early as the mid-1950s, while the television industry was struggling to define its educational role, Frank Baxter, an English professor—he was always identified as "Doctor"—from the University of Southern California, had demonstrated the medium's potential to inform as well as to entertain. Dubbed the "Liberace of the Library," Baxter, one industry pioneer recalled, "aroused educational television's audience in a wholly different way, drawing viewers away from *Dragnet* and *Father Knows Best* with an unlikely hook entitled *Shakespeare on TV.*" Initially aired locally in Los Angeles by CBS, Baxter's show went national under the auspices of PBS's precursor, the Educational Television and Radio Center. Baxter also starred in a second series, *The Written Word.* The creation of the Corporation for Public Broadcasting in the wake of a 1967 Carnegie Commission report on television institutionalized a distinction between programs for classroom instruction and informally educational shows of "human interest and importance," a decision that gave priority to scholars like Baxter who were "gifted with the power of popularization."[47]

The establishment of both the NEH and PBS has nurtured and sustained up to the present day the middlebrow audience receptive to the academic humanist. Yet those agencies could not offset (and in some respects contributed to) the countervailing pressures that, after the mid-1960s, increasingly militated against the emergence of younger figures in the mold of Highet, Barzun, or Jones. The premium on specialization within the discipline of history, for example, widened the gulf between academic and public authority. Arthur Schlesinger Jr., Gerda Lerner, and Christopher Lasch were among those who still sought to bridge the gap. Yet as early as 1966 the self-trained historian Barbara W. Tuchman was remarking that the narrative form she favored was "rather looked down on" by the "advanced academics"; although she won an enormous popular following for her meticulous scholarship, she was not an academic except on an intermittent, temporary basis and saw herself as an "independent" rather than a "professional" historian.[48]

In addition, it seems likely that the accelerating growth of the college-educated population, hand in hand with the continuing specialization and prestige of science, shifted the public demand for expert interpretation from humanistic to scientific subjects. That is, college graduates might conclude that they could grasp the Greek view of the heavens on their own but that they needed help comprehending the physicist's view. In any event, while academic historians played minor roles in such public broadcasting ventures as Ken Burns's *The Civil War* and have an ongoing presence (like their colleagues in the Modern Language Association) on public radio, none became the latter-day equivalent of Baxter; instead, the scientist Carl Sagan was the most prominent American university-based television star. Humanistic programs such as *Masterpiece Theatre* and *Civilisation* featured British-born hosts (Alistair Cooke, Kenneth Clark) or down-to-earth ones (Bill Moyers) who lent either an aura of European high culture or a homey touch to drama, art, and literature without superfluous professorial intervention. Along the same lines, of the individuals honored by the NEH for "outstanding contributions to the public's understanding of the humanities" between 1989 and 2000, only about one quarter were affiliated with institutions of higher education.[49]

Finally, the very trends toward the inclusion of African Americans, Catholics, Jews, and women in the university, however salutary, undermined one of the premises that made Highet, Barzun, or Jones's stance tenable. As Menand has argued, up to about 1975 "most educators subscribed to the ideas that the great works of the Western tradition are accessible to all students in more or less the same way, that those works constitute a more or less coherent body of thought." As diversity and difference achieved sway over a coherent canon, any pronouncements about the universality of the humanities—Highet's insistence on the viability of the classic tradition as an agent of progress, or even his and Barzun's prescriptions for effective pedagogy—became suspect. Very few academic humanists were willing to expend their energies, as Jones had, defending the value of their disciplines for "one great society," let alone invoke "greatness" as a critical category.[50]

Given that situation, it is easy to tick off the ways in which Highet, Barzun, and Jones's versions of inclusion failed, beginning with Highet's battered reputation and ending, in 2006, with the entrenchment of splintered disciplines, modernist despair, opaque language, self-expression, a distinctly inhumane foreign policy, and the ubiquitous Ph.D. The most pessimistic conclusion about the academic popularizers of the immediate postwar period is that, for all their efforts, they merely substantiated the lines from Henry Wadsworth Longfellow's "Morituri Salutamus" that Jones interpolated at the end of his autobiography: "The scholar and the world! The endless strife,/The discord in the harmonies of life!" Longfellow's verse went on to counterpose the "sweet serenity of books" to the marketplace. Yet the lesson of Jones's own career, like that of Highet's and Barzun's, was that such discord could be minimized, that it was possible—indeed, necessary—to straddle the boundary between scholarship and commerce, between "sequestered nooks" and public forums. If that possibility seems remote at present, a more constructive view of the academic humanists' achievements would involve drawing inspiration from their determination (in contrast to the posture of the alienated intellectual) to make clear the social value of their scholarly endeavor. For all the shortcomings of their particular proposals, the conceit of the scholar *in* the world that certain academic humanists approximated fifty years ago still embodies worthwhile hopes, even if the dynamic required to realize those hopes remains elusive.[51]

Notes

I am grateful to Jacques Barzun for permission to quote from the Barzun Papers and to Ian Highet for permission to quote from the Gilbert Highet Papers. Both collections are in the Butler Rare Book Manuscript Library, Columbia University, New York, New York. The materials in both the Barzun and Highet Papers are also used by permission of Columbia University.

1. See, e.g., Irving Howe, "This Age of Conformity," *Partisan Review* 21, no. 1 (1954): 26, 30; Richard Chase, "The Fate of the Avant-Garde," *Partisan Review* 24, no. 3 (1957): 363–375; Richard H. Pells, *The Liberal Mind in a Conservative Age: American Intellectuals in the 1940s and 1950s* (New York: Harper and Row, 1985); Gerald Graff, *Professing Literature: An Institutional History* (Chicago: University of Chicago Press, 1987), 145–208; George Cotkin, "The Tragic Predicament: Post-war American Intellectuals, Acceptance, and Mass Culture," in *Intellectuals in Politics*, ed. Jeremy Jennings and Anthony Kemp-Welch (London: Routledge, 1997), 248–270; Harvey M. Teres, *Renewing the Left: Politics, Imagination, and the New York Intellectuals* (New York: Oxford University Press, 1996).

2. Clifton Fadiman, *Any Number Can Play* (New York: Avon, 1957), 45–46, and *Party of One* (Cleveland: World Publishing, 1955), 25–26; Carolyn G. Heilbrun, *When Men Were the Only Models We Had* (Philadelphia: University of Pennsylvania Press, 2002), 43; Timothy P. Cross, "Clifton Fadiman '25: An Erudite Guide to the Wisdom of Others," *Columbia College Today*, September 1999 (www.college.columbia.edu/cc/Sep99/40a.html); Joan Shelley Rubin, *The Making of Middlebrow Culture* (Chapel Hill: University of North Carolina Press, 1992), 320–326.

3. Fadiman, *Party of One*, 23–25.

4. Edward M. Cifelli, *John Ciardi: A Biography* (Fayetteville: University of Arkansas Press, 1957); John Ciardi, *Dialogue with an Audience* (Philadelphia: J. B. Lippincott, 1963), 90–92, 119. For an extended account of the Ciardi-Lindbergh episode, see Joan Shelley Rubin, "The Genteel Tradition at Large," *Raritan* (Winter 2006): 70–91.

5. Rubin, *Middlebrow Culture*, 281–290; Irwin Edman, "A Liberal Arts College in a Metropolitan University," in *A History of Columbia College on Morningside* (New York: Columbia University Press, 1954), 268–269.

6. Paul Boyer, *By the Bomb's Early Light: American Thought and Culture at the Dawn of the Atomic Age* (New York: Pantheon, 1985), 154, 160–161; Harvard University, *General Education in a Free Society* (Cambridge: Harvard University Press, 1945), 5; Benjamin Fine, "Teacher Shortage Imperils Our Public School System," *New York Times*, February 10, 1947, 1; William Allan Neilson, "Challenge to Our Colleges," *New York Times Magazine*, June 7, 1942, 12, 34; Lawrence E. Davies, "Dr. Sproul Assails 'Progressive' Craze," *New York Times*, March 24, 1944, 21; Edmund C. Richards, "Problems of Post-War Education," *New York Times Book Review*, November 26, 1944, 32; Benjamin Fine, "Education in Review," *New York Times*, October 29, 1944, E9.

7. Robert J. Ball, "Living Legacies," *Columbia University Alumni Magazine*, Fall 2001 (www.columbia.edu/cu/alumni/Magazine/DeBaryIntro.html).

8. Gilbert Highet, *The Classical Tradition* (New York: Oxford University Press, 1949), 3, 468–469, 494–500.

9. In 1951 the editors of *Vogue*, impressed by the response to *The Art of Teaching*, hired Dimnet, Highet, and eighteen others to contribute to a monthly feature they called *The Arts of Living*; after a three-year run, Simon and Schuster published the pieces in a book of that title, with a preface by Highet. The quotation about Highet's intention is in Gilbert Highet to L. James, November 7, 1951, box 7, Gilbert Highet Papers, Butler Rare Book and Manuscript Library, Columbia University Libraries, New York City. See also Ball, "Living Legacies."

10. Gilbert Highet, *The Art of Teaching* (New York: Vintage, 1954), vii, 73, 135–142, 234–250.

11. Howard Mumford Jones, "The Precincts of Knowing," *Saturday Review of Literature*, March 6, 1954, 14; Highet, *Art of Teaching*, 153, 248–250.

12. Highet, *Art of Teaching*, 222–233.

13. Ball, "Living Legacies"; Lon Tinkle, "Our Own Citations for This and That," *Dallas Morning News*, December 26, 1954, in box 12, Highet Papers; Mr. Boardman to Mr. Brett-Smith, Oxford University Press, memorandum, November 12, 1958, box 17, Highet Papers.

14. Gilbert Highet, *A Clerk of Oxenford: Essays on Literature and Life* (New York: Oxford University Press, 1954), 146, 156–164, 176, 205.

15. Samuel F. Morse, "Polished Prose," *Hartford Courant*, November 28, 1954, in box 12, Highet Papers; Evelyn Ross Robinson to Gilbert Highet, May 8, 1955, box 12, Highet Papers; Highet, *Clerk of Oxenford*, 47, 79, 235, 236; Gilbert Highet, *People, Places, and Books* (New York: Oxford University Press, 1953), 117; Gilbert Highet, *The Powers of Poetry* (New York: Oxford University Press, 1960), 68–74.

16. Orville Prescott, "Books of the Times," *New York Times*, March 10, 1954, 23; "Wit, Candor Characterize Highest [*sic*] Tart Criticisms," *Buffalo Evening News*, December 11, 1954,

box 12, Highet Papers; I.N.S., "An Essayist Rather of the Old School Muses on Life," *Ottawa Evening Journal*, January 8, 1955, box 12, Highet Papers; John Sisk, "Humanist's Report," *Commonweal*, March 12, 1954, box 16, Highet Papers; Gerald W. Johnson, "More Than Meets the Ear," *New York Herald Tribune*, December 5, 1954, box 12, Highet Papers; Bergen Evans, "Lover of Books," *Saturday Review of Literature*, October 30, 1954, 18–19, 42; Sarah Thesmar, "Gilbert Highet Recaptures All the Delights of Reading," *Memphis Appeal*, November 7, 1954, box 12, Highet Papers.

17. "'U' to Broadcast Highet's Talks," *Minneapolis Tribune*, March 29, 1952, box 6, Highet Papers; Adrienne Foulke, "Ranging at Large through Literature," *New Leader*, December 6, 1954, box 12, Highet Papers; Robert Phelps, "Ticket to the World of Books," *San Diego Union*, November 14, 1954, box 12, Highet Papers.

18. Highet, *Clerk of Oxenford*, 74, 210–229, 245–247; Highet, *Powers of Poetry*, 27–35, 136–137; Randall Jarrell, "The Obscurity of the Poet," in *Poetry and the Age* (New York: Knopf, 1953), 3–27; Clement Greenberg, "Avant-Garde and Kitsch," *Partisan Review* 6, no. 5 (1939): 34–49.

19. John Chamberlain, "A Critic's Critic," typescript, May 3, 1953, box 13, Highet Papers; Grace Goodale to Gilbert Highet, April 8, 1952, box 9, Highet Papers; Gilbert Highet, *Man's Unconquerable Mind* (New York: Columbia University Press, 1954), 14–15, 57–60.

20. Richard Armour, "Highet Makes Learning Painless," *Los Angeles News*, November 7, 1954, box 12, Highet Papers; M. L. Rosenthal, "The Virtue of Translation," *Nation*, November 16, 1957, 371–372; Dudley Fitts, "Visits with Some Romans," *New York Times Book Review*, March 17, 1957, 17; Ball, "Living Legacies."

21. Gilbert Highet to Arthur E. Gordon, July 13, 1970, box 12, Highet Papers; Dudley Fitts, "The Classical World: A Living Tradition," *New York Times Book Review*, January 29, 1950, 18.

22. Jacques Barzun to Thomas H. Johnson, October 2, 1945, box 2, folder 10, Jacques Barzun Papers, Butler Rare Book and Manuscript Library, Columbia University Libraries, New York City. Lionel Trilling, "A Personal Memoir," in *From Parnassus: Essays in Honor of Jacques Barzun*, ed. Dora B. Weiner and William R. Keylor (New York: Harper and Row, 1976), xvii–xxii.

23. Michael Murray, Introduction to *A Jacques Barzun Reader* (New York: HarperCollins, 2001), xvi.

24. Jacques Barzun, *Teacher in America* (Boston: Little, Brown, 1945), 21–24, 107, 114.

25. Ibid., 199, 266, 315–319.

26. Ibid., 34, 56, 90–91, 101.

27. Ibid., 96, 107, 249–250, 255, 262, 266–268; Heilbrun, *When Men Were the Only Models*, 126, 138–139.

28. Jacques Barzun, *The House of Intellect* (New York: Harper, 1959), 20–21, 27, 117, 212. See also Jacques Barzun, "Science vs. the Humanities," *Saturday Evening Post*, May 3, 1958, 26, 58, 60, 62–63.

29. Barzun, *House of Intellect*, 17–18, 98, 103, 124, 133, 166; Trilling, "A Personal Memoir," xxi; Heilbrun, *When Men Were the Only Models*, 130–133; Jacques Barzun to Richard K. Manoff, February 17, 1960, box 51, Barzun Papers.

30. Barzun, *House of Intellect*, 21, 23, 56, 182, 188; Christopher Lasch, *The Culture of Narcissism: American Life in an Age of Diminishing Expectations* (New York: W. W. Norton, 1978).

31. Barzun, *House of Intellect*, 9.

32. Richard Hofstadter, *Anti-Intellectualism in American Life* (New York: Vintage, 1966), 394; Barzun, *House of Intellect*, 13, 15, 35, 51, 69–71, 157.

33. Barzun, *House of Intellect*, 13, 35, 37–38, 64; Dwight Macdonald, "Masscult and Midcult: I," *Partisan Review* 27, no. 2 (1960): 203–233; Dwight Macdonald, "Masscult and Midcult: II," *Partisan Review* 27, no. 4 (1960): 589–631.

34. Barzun, *Teacher in America*, 309; Barzun, *House of Intellect*, 35, 36; Marshall Sprague, "Changes at Aspen," *New York Times*, June 17, 1951, X19; Louis Menand, "Culture Club," *New Yorker*, October 15, 2001, 202.

35. Menand, "Culture Club," 210; Francis Stonor Saunders, *The Cultural Cold War* (New York: New Press, 1999); Barzun, *House of Intellect*, 194–195; Barzun, *Teacher in America*, 144–145; Jacques Barzun to Stan [Salmen], June 5, 1947, box 4, folder 1, Barzun Papers. The material on the "American Shelf" project is in box 74, Barzun Papers.

36. Menand, "Culture Club," 202; Wendell Taylor to Barzun, February 4, 1945, box 2, folder 2, Barzun Papers; W. G. Rogers, AP features review of *Teacher in America*, box 2, folder 2, Barzun Papers; John P. Comaromi to Barzun, July 2, 1961, box 51, folder 2, Barzun Papers; Hofstadter, *Anti-Intellectualism in American Life*, 418–419.

37. Howard Mumford Jones, *Howard Mumford Jones: An Autobiography* (Madison: University of Wisconsin Press, 1979); Peter Brier, *Howard Mumford Jones and the Dynamics of Liberal Humanism* (Columbia: University of Missouri Press, 1994), 160.

38. Howard Mumford Jones, *Education and World Tragedy* (Cambridge: Harvard University Press, 1946), 50, 166.

39. Ibid., 59, 61.

40. Ruth Nanda Anshen, "World Perspectives," in *American Humanism: Its Meaning for World Survival*, by Howard Mumford Jones (New York: Harper, 1957), ix, xi–xiv.

41. Jones, *American Humanism*, 37, 54, 102–108.

42. Howard Mumford Jones, *One Great Society: Humane Learning in the United States* (New York: Harcourt, Brace, 1959), vii, 3–4; Jones, *Autobiography*, 255.

43. Jones, *One Great Society*, 9, 32–33, 36–39, 53, 57, 59–60, 100; Howard Mumford Jones, *Reflections on Learning* (New Brunswick: Rutgers University Press, 1958).

44. Jones, *One Great Society*, 71–72, 77–79, 92, 116–117; Jones, *Reflections on Learning*, 61.

45. Jones, *Reflections on Learning*, 6–7; Jones, *Autobiography*, 263.

46. National Foundation on the Arts and the Humanities Act of 1965 (P.L. 89–209), www.neh.fed.us/whoweare/legislation.html; NEH, *Rediscovering America: Thirty-five Years of the National Endowment for the Humanities* (Washington, D.C.: GPO, 2000), 57.

47. James Day, *The Vanishing Vision: The Inside Story of Public Television* (Berkeley: University of California Press, 1995), 67, 118.

48. Barbara W. Tuchman, *Practicing History* (New York: Knopf, 1981), 48, 57.

49. NEH, *Rediscovering America*, 83–85.

50. Louis Menand, *The Marketplace of Ideas* (New York: American Council of Learned Societies, 2001), 7; Menand, "Culture Club," 204.

51. Jones, *Autobiography*, 263.

II

EUROPEAN MOVEMENTS AGAINST THE AMERICAN GRAIN?

4

THE AMBIVALENT VIRTUES OF MENDACITY

*How Europeans Taught (Some of) Us to
Learn to Love the Lies of Politics*

MARTIN JAY

Toute vérité n'est pas bonne à dire.
—FRENCH PROVERB

"UNTRUTH AND CONSEQUENCES" screamed the headline on the cover of the
July 21, 2003, issue of *Time* magazine, which dealt extensively with the then-
burning question "How flawed was the case for going to war against Saddam?"
Once again it seemed that an American president was in danger of losing his
credibility and being excoriated for the sin of telling lies to the American people. Only a short time after his predecessor had been impeached for perjuring
himself about his sex life, leaving, as the title of Christopher Hitchens's nasty
philippic put it, "no one left to lie to,"[1] George W. Bush was struggling to parse
his way out of the discrepancies between his statements about the imminent
threat of Iraqi weapons of mass destruction and what the evidence now seemed
to show. Once again outrage against political mendacity coursed, albeit vari-
ably depending on whose ox had been caught fibbing, through the American
public sphere. Liberals like Al Franken could hit the best-seller lists by calling
their polemics *Lies and the Lying Liars Who Tell Them: A Fair and Balanced Look
at the Right*, in response to conservative rants like Ann Coulter's *Slander: Liberal
Lies about the American Right*.[2] And critics of Bush's war on Iraq could name
their books, with easy cleverness, *Weapons of Mass Deception*.[3]

Not surprisingly, a political culture that takes as one of its founding myths
the refusal of its chief Founding Father to lie about the felling of a cherry tree
and fondly calls its most revered leader "Honest Abe" has been especially keen
on rooting out mendacity from the political sphere. In fact, American culture
in general, as Michael T. Gilmore has recently reminded us, has been on a
dogged quest for perfect legibility, fueled by a yearning for full disclosure that
stretches from the Puritans' antimonastic insistence on "holy watching" and

107

distrust of Catholic casuistry to the widespread acceptance of psychoanalysis as a therapy of unconstrained candor.[4] Although Americans admired "the arts of deception" in the popular culture of what has been called the "age of Barnum,"[5] when it came to extending them to political discourse, strict limits were set. Not for us, Americans have prided themselves on believing, are the Machiavellian machinations of Old World politics, with their haughty disdain for the transparency of democratic decision making.[6] Not for us are the even more dangerous deceptions of totalitarian ideology based on the imposition of an audacious Big Lie on a supine populace no longer able to tell the difference between truth and falsehood.[7] We are determined, as the reigning cliché now has it, "to speak truth to power."[8]

In the academy, ever since Harvard picked its familiar motto, a comparable assumption has ruled that truth, or at least the quest for it, is an unimpeachable value.[9] Interestingly, that motto was originally "Veritas pro Christo et ecclesia" ("Truth for Christ and his Church"), but it was shortened to allow other, more profane purposes to be served by that quest. When the secularization of intellectual life undermined appeals to divinely revealed truth, this often came to mean a surrogate faith in the scientific method, however that might be defined, as a viable alternative. Even when American pragmatists questioned traditional notions of certainty and referential correspondence in favor of a more consequentialist alternative, they did not abandon the search for truth as the telos of inquiry and action. With the growth of departments of political science, which often adopted the approach that came to be called behavioralist, the appeal to honesty in political practice could be reinforced by a comparable attempt to study politics in a neutral way. At times, in fact, some came to believe that technocrats with the tools of political science at their command would be the best leaders of a polity that wanted to avoid the untidiness of ill-informed opinion and untested prejudice. During the Progressive Era in particular, advocates of scientific administration such as Walter Lippmann and L. L. Bernard advocated organization, efficiency, and enlightened management.[10] Truth in politics, it was argued, would be achieved by transcending the cacophony of competing voices and allowing those with the skills and knowledge to cut through to the core of problems and deal with them effectively. Only they might avoid confusing the news with the truth, as Lippmann contended in *Public Opinion* in 1922.[11] Only they might avoid being duped by deliberate propaganda, a concept that came into its own during World War I but was derived from an earlier religious notion of propagating the true faith (traceable to the Catholic Church's *Sacra Congregatio de Propaganda Fide* of 1622).[12]

At the heart of this project is a desire to strip political language of its irrational, emotive, and ornamental excrescences and find a way to express ideas, arguments, and motivations with full clarity and univocal meaning. Formal eloquence and elevated diction were stigmatized by being identified with a gentlemanly code of stuffy decorum that seemed outdated in the era of plain speech and colloquial idiom.[13] If common men and women looked up to anyone now, it was the technical expert rather than the literary stylist. Even if this goal did not entail imposing a neutral scientific language on the messiness of everyday speech, it was still widely held to be a powerful tool in the campaign against mendacity in the public realm.

No more rhetorically powerful expression of this distrust of the dangers of unchecked rhetoric can be found than the celebrated essay by George Orwell that quickly established itself as a touchstone of political truth telling on both sides of the Atlantic, "Politics and the English Language" of 1946. Widely anthologized, incessantly taught in schools, and cited with numbing frequency, Orwell's essay claimed that a debased, impure, inflated, euphemistic, pretentious, cliché-ridden language was more than a symptom of political decline; it was one of its main causes. "In our time," he lamented, "political speech and writing are largely the defense of the indefensible. . . . Political language— and with variations this is true of all political parties, from Conservatives to Anarchists—is designed to make lies sound truthful and murder respectable, and to give an appearance of solidity to pure wind."[14] Avoid stale figures of speech, unnecessarily long words, the passive voice, foreign phrases, and abstruse jargon, he urged, and perhaps the wind would die down.

When *Nineteen Eighty-Four* added a brilliant exposition of the ways in which totalitarianism depended on the deliberate lies of Newspeak and Doublethink, Orwell's reputation as the saint of liberal democratic honesty was augmented. By 1955 commentators such as Lionel Trilling could describe him in worshipful terms: "He told the truth, and told it in an exemplary way, quietly, simply, with due warning to the reader that it was only one man's truth. He used no political jargon, and he made no recriminations. He made no effort to show that his heart was in the right place, or the left place. He was not interested in where his heart might be thought to be, since he knew where it was. He was interested only in telling the truth. . . . And what matters most of all is our sense of the man who tells the truth."[15]

Although since Trilling's time Orwell has been subjected to considerable scrutiny, not all of it flattering, which has uncovered some of his own less attractive biases, his critique of linguistic obfuscation and its political consequences has become itself a standard trope in political rhetoric. For both the right and the left his legacy has been a ready source of epithets against their allegedly deceitful opponents. In the words of Hannah Pitkin, he stood for the "truth of witness,"[16] in which it was incumbent on the reporter to tell the facts of the story as they are. It is thus not surprising to find that Orwell remains a heroic model for self-proclaimed scourges of mendacity in the public realm who, like Christopher Hitchens, have bounced from one camp to another.[17]

But what has also occurred, and this is the main point of this chapter, is a growing undercurrent of uncertainty about the wholesale embrace of the values of linguistic purification and unvarnished truth telling, or more precisely, their embrace in the political arena defined as a relatively autonomous realm. Much of that uncertainty, I want to argue, has been fueled by receptiveness to ideas from Europe, which have permeated at least a portion of the American consciousness in the latter decades of the twentieth century and which remain potent into our own. Broadly speaking, these involve what has been called "the linguistic turn," which includes, inter alia, a new respect for rhetoric, an acceptance of the necessity of hermeneutic interpretation, and a willingness to tolerate the inconclusive deconstruction of univocal meaning.[18] Because truth itself seems so difficult to attain, the value of truth telling — subjective truthfulness or veracity—is implicitly called into question as inherently aesthetic notions of language as more a tool of imaginative fabulation than a means of referencing the real world come to the fore. Although many of these ideas have been associated with the so-called post-structuralist thought that emanated from France in the 1970s, variations on them can be discerned still earlier among that generation of Central European émigrés who so enriched American intellectual life during the Nazi era and who have continued to exert considerable influence well after they passed from the scene.[19] As survivors of the pervasive cynicism that pervaded the Weimar Republic, "the German Republic of Imposters,"[20] as it has been called, they understood what might ensue once politics became thoroughly discredited, but they also had learned that the antidote was not self-righteous moralizing. In what follows, I want to concentrate on three in particular who in very different ways have helped us reach a more complex understanding of the relationship between political life and mendacity: Leo Strauss, Theodor W. Adorno, and Hannah Arendt.

Their inclusion in the canon of political theorists has, in fact, had an impact beyond the halls of the academy, narrowly construed. This effect is now most self-evident in the case of Strauss, a number of whose neoconservative followers have gained considerable influence in the highest reaches of American government during the presidency of George W. Bush.[21] Perhaps most widely remarked of these is Assistant Secretary of Defense Paul Wolfowitz, who did his doctoral work under Straussians at the University of Chicago and is a major architect of the new recklessness in American foreign policy. One of its chief cheerleaders is William Kristol, the editor of the *Weekly Standard*, who served in the administration of Bush's father as adviser to Vice President Quayle.

Wolfowitz in particular is relevant to our theme because of his now notorious admission that the Bush administration's hype of Saddam Hussein's weapons of mass destruction was designed to elicit the strongest possible popular support for a cause whose real motivations, still not very clear, lay elsewhere.[22] For in this moment of candor, he betrayed one of Strauss's most salient assumptions: that the masses need to be manipulated into following their best interests by an elite who are privy to the deeper truths of reality. Strauss, that is, was a believer in the possibility of knowing the truth, including the truth about the type of government that is objectively the best. He insisted that the modern age had lost its bearings because of its descent into relativist historicism; it has forgotten the truths, grounded in a proper understanding of nature, that the ancient philosophers had once possessed. But he also believed that the only way to regain them was to maintain a meaningful distinction between the esoteric knowledge of the few and the exoteric knowledge of the many.

Implicitly drawing on his experience of exile, Strauss argued that persecution had forced ancient thinkers to mask their true intentions in ways that required deciphering by disciples with the skills to read between the lines.[23] What was a necessity became a virtue when it led to independent thinking, at least for the minority with the talents and tenacity to attempt it. It was for them, as he put it in his 1939 essay "The Spirit of Sparta or the Taste of Xenophon," "a matter of duty to hide the truth from the majority of mankind."[24] The tradition of esoteric teaching had withered, Strauss claimed, in the Enlightenment, although its decline was already under way when Machiavelli made explicit the techniques of statecraft that the ancients had known must be kept as the private knowledge of rulers alone. The disappearance of the tradition, he lamented, roughly coincided with the "victory of higher criticism and of systems of philosophy which claimed to be sincere but which certainly lacked moderation."[25] Liberal notions of an egalitarian public sphere in which transparency and sincerity were the premises of enlightened political opinion were the sorry outcome of this betrayal.

Strauss, as might be expected, has been an easy target for defenders of rationalist liberalism as well as egalitarian democracy.[26] And I am certainly not inclined to offer a defense of his explicitly hierarchical politics based on an allegedly natural order whose self-evidence neither he nor his disciples have satisfactorily demonstrated. But what has to be acknowledged is that his animadversions on the dangers of sharing truths with the uncomprehending masses have given legitimacy to the old Platonic idea of the "noble lie," the *gennian pseudos*,[27] to an important segment of the conservative intellectuals of our day. They, of course, would be disinclined to express their scorn for egalitarian democracy explicitly, but it takes no great exegetical skill to read between the lines of their texts—and observe their political actions—to come to this conclusion.

A very different, and much more oblique, defense or at least understanding of mendacity in politics, however, emerges if we turn to the next figure in our triumvirate, whose political agenda was very far from Strauss's. Adorno, to be sure, also held on to a strong, "emphatic" notion of truth, often arguing, for example, for the "truth-content" of works of art against those who see the aesthetic as mere illusion or fabulation. Likewise, he refused to privilege opinion, public or otherwise, over truth.[28] As a result, he cannot be rightly aligned with the Nietzschean post-structuralists, who take the linguistic turn to the extreme of questioning the capacity of words to refer without mediation to what exists outside the prison house of language. Nor, for all Adorno's putative elitism and disdain for mass culture, would it be correct to identify his position with a cynical defense of philosopher-kings who can tell noble lies to the herd unable to see through them. Underlying his radical politics was always a firm belief in the ultimate value of an enlightened democracy with citizens able to cast off the spell of ideological mystification.

If Adorno can be said to have contributed to the critique of traditional American notions of political honesty, it would be only indirectly, through his questioning of the premises of the conventional wisdom about unequivocal language and truth telling. Adorno, to be sure, never developed a sustained analysis of language, although it has been possible to piece together his thoughts from disparate sources in his vast oeuvre.[29] What stands out is his distrust of easy notions of communicability, which assume the transparency of the current universe of discourse and the ability of individuals to judge freely for themselves what is fed them by the mass media. In the words of a recent student of the history of the idea of communication, "There was no more formidable critic of the commercialized culture of sincerity."[30] As a result, he has come to be positioned in accounts of current debates about obscure academic writing on the left as the anti-Orwell, the champion of the difficult, dense prose—stigmatized as "bad writing"—associated with such figures as Judith Butler and Homi Bhaba.[31]

Typical of Adorno's skepticism about transparent communicability were the bitter observations in one of the aphorisms in *Minima Moralia*, composed around the same time that Orwell wrote his celebrated essay: "Regard for the object, rather than for communication, is suspect in any expression: anything, not taken from pre-existent patterns, appears inconsiderate, a symptom of eccentricity, almost of confusion. The logic of the day, which makes so much of its clarity, has naively adopted this perverted notion of everyday speech. . . . Few things contribute so much to the demoralization of intellectuals. Those who would escape it must recognize the advocates of communicability as traitors to what they communicate."[32]

Although agreeing with Orwell that stale clichés are the enemy of clear thought, Adorno differed from him in stressing the value of difficulty and complexity, which defeated the effortless absorption of prepackaged ideas. He also questioned Orwell's desire to purify language of its ornamental excrescences, in particular foreign words. With a somber awareness of what a similar campaign had meant in the context of the country from which he had escaped, Adorno wryly noted that "German words of foreign derivation are the Jews of language."[33] That is, linguistic purification went along with cleansing of a far more sinister kind.

Adorno's suspicion of the agenda behind purifying language of alien intrusions was of a piece with his critique of what he called "the jargon of authenticity" in a book of that name published in 1964.[34] Adorno's ire was directed at the German existentialists, most notably Heidegger and Jaspers, who elevated the values of genuineness, authenticity, and original meaning to normative status above the content of what was believed or meant. Aiming to overcome the abstractions of reified life, they preached a pseudoconcreteness that denied the historical reasons for the depredations of modern culture. In their hands mere commitment, speaking from the heart, becomes an antidote to nihilism, no matter the cause to which the commitment is dedicated.[35] The individual who makes that commitment is understood in possessive terms as entirely owned by the speaker, whose integrity and sincerity are favored over his mimetic relationship with others in the world. Likewise, language, purified of its historical accretions, should return to its archaic roots to regain its true meaning (a bit like Orwell's preference for good old Anglo-Saxon words against their effete Latinate surrogates, although Adorno didn't make the comparison).

Already in *Minima Moralia*, written in his exile years, Adorno had seen the political implications of the jargon, which were frighteningly regressive and xenophobic. The supremacy of the original over the derived, he warned, "is always linked with social legitimism. All ruling strata claim to be the oldest settlers, autochthonous."[36] Along with the striving for ultimate, original meaning went a suspicion of ambiguity and rhetoric, which meant a denigration of sophistry in both philosophy and politics. "With the assertion of meaning at all costs," Adorno wrote, "the old antisophistic emotion seeps into the so-called mass society." Ancient Sophistry, to be sure, had failed to fight against injustice in the name of truth, preferring to ratify whatever was the status quo. But when it is one-sidedly combated in the name of original, univocal meanings, sophistry's important insight, that language is never fully adequate to objects or concepts either because it can't express their full complexity or because it says more than it means, is sacrificed.[37]

The same loss is suffered when clarity becomes a fetish, either in philosophy or politics. In an essay entitled "Skoteinos, or How to Read Hegel," published in 1963, Adorno defended the notorious difficulty and opacity of that most obscure philosopher's style.[38] "Someone who cannot state what he means without ambiguity is not worth wasting time on," wrote Adorno, contemptuously characterizing the current orthodoxy. "Like the desire for explicit definitions, to which it is related, this concept of clarity has survived the [Cartesian] philosophy in which it originated and has become autonomous."[39] Its survival has led to a preference for stability over flux, as objects are able to be clearly designated only when they stop moving and make themselves available to the scrutiny of the enlightened gaze. Absolute clarity also presupposes a nondynamic subject whose use of language is no less reified. Philosophy like Hegel's, which incorporates movement into its own thought processes, at least offers some resistance to this condition, which is inherent in language itself. "The very form of the copula, the 'is,' pursues the aim of pinpointing its object, an aim to which philosophy ought to provide a corrective; in this sense all philosophical language is language in opposition to language, marked with the stigma of its own impossibility."[40]

Adorno's critique of straightforward clarity of expression based on the putative identity of word and thing is aimed at philosophical discourse, at least in this essay. But it is not hard to see its applicability in the realm of politics as well, where rhetoric, uncertainty, and constant change play even more central roles. Indeed, Bill Clinton's notorious defense of his deception that it all depends on "what the meaning of 'is' is" resonates with Adorno's reading of Hegel's refusal to be restricted by the identitarian implications of the copula. Adorno, to be sure, never praised mendacity as an actual virtue in politics or abandoned his hope in an emphatic concept of truth that would survive all ideological attempts to assume its mantle in the present. But by alerting us to the ways in which those attempts often hid other agendas, he made us aware that simple appeals to clarity, communicability, authenticity, and integrity could become obstacles to precisely what they purported to defend. Truth, he followed Walter Benjamin in arguing, was best understood as intentionless, rather than the product of subjective positing; *Wahrheit* (truth), in short, was not reducible to *Wahrhaftigkeit* (truthfulness).[41]

The third figure in our triumvirate, Hannah Arendt, is also the one who most explicitly addressed the role of lying in politics. Personally hostile to both Strauss and Adorno,[42] she also disdained their belief that philosophers like Plato or Hegel had anything to teach those who were active in the realm of politics. The idea of the "noble lie," she argued, was not only wrong, but also a misreading of the text in *The Republic*.[43] Whereas Strauss was concerned primarily with the lies rulers tell the ruled, Arendt was more interested in the ways in which competitors in the political arena shade the truth in their interactions with each other. Although learning much from the Heidegger and Jaspers excoriated by Adorno as adepts of the jargon of authenticity,[44] she steadfastly resisted their emphasis on the primacy of philosophy. Instead, she attempted to build a firewall between politics and philosophy, at least if the latter was understood as the search for eternal, universal essences rather than contingent, plural appearances.

In two essays in particular, "Truth and Politics" of 1967 and "Lying in Politics" of 1971, Arendt drew radical conclusions from her idiosyncratic political theory for the issue of mendacity in the public realm. Occasioned by two controversies over lying, the first involving her own work on Adolf Eichmann's trial, the second resulting from the leaking of the Pentagon Papers, these two essays provide a more fundamental challenge to the American quest for full disclosure in the public realm than anything written by Strauss and Adorno. Ironically, the first essay was stimulated by the charge that Arendt had unwisely told the truth about the Jewish role in enabling the Holocaust—or more precisely, that of the Jewish Councils—to the detriment of current political causes. She had, in other words, foolishly followed the dangerous principle of "*fiat veritas, et pereat mundus.*" Without denying that she was dedicated as a scholar to truth telling, Arendt was moved to ponder the problematic effects of that practice in the political arena.

"Truth in Politics" opens with a direct and unequivocal challenge to the critical evaluation of those effects, which we have seen was so powerful a part of American conventional wisdom: "No one has ever doubted that truth and politics are on rather bad terms with each other, and no one, as far as I know, has ever counted truthfulness among the political virtues. Lies have always been regarded as necessary and justifiable tools not only of the politician's and the demagogue's but also of the statesman's trade."[45]

Indeed, lying itself was not considered a cardinal sin until modern times; Plato, for example, thought ignorance and error worse than deliberate mendacity. "Only with the rise of Puritan morality, coinciding with the rise of organized science, whose progress had to be assured on the firm ground of the absolute veracity and reliability of every scientist, were lies considered serious offenses."[46]

Still, for ancient philosophy the quest for truth was paramount, a truth that was understood in the Platonic tradition in terms of rational oneness.

The realm of politics was far more messy and divisive, ruled by sophistic rhetoric and contingent *doxa* rather than dialogic ratiocination: "To the citizens' ever-changing opinions about human affairs, which themselves were in a state of constant flux, the philosopher opposed the truth about those things which in their very nature were everlasting and from which, therefore, principles could be derived to stabilize human affairs. Hence the opposite to truth was opinion, which was equated with illusion."[47]

Rational notions of truth, Arendt argued, no longer hold much sway in the modern world, but they have been replaced by belief in the truth of facts, which is much more of a challenge to the political realm. For factual truth is dependent on intersubjective agreement and therefore is closer to political opinion than to deductive reason. But they are not the same, for all truth claims differ from mere opinion by the way in which they assert their validity, which has a moment of coercion in it. "Factual truth, like all other truth, peremptorily claims to be acknowledged and precludes debate, and debate constitutes the very essence of political life. The modes of thought and communication that deal with truth, if seen from the political perspective, are necessarily domineering; they don't take into account other people's opinions, and taking these into account is the hallmark of all strictly political thinking."[48] Political judgment is the ability to incorporate other opinions, producing what Kant called an "enlarged mentality," not the search for the one true opinion. Philosophy is an exercise in searching for a singular truth; politics is the interplay of plural opinions. Even the self-evident truths Jefferson pronounced to be the justification for declaring American independence were, after all, prefaced by the concession that "we hold these truths to be self-evident"; the implication was that contingent consent and agreement—the holding of the beliefs—rather than the coercion of the ideas themselves were the basis of the claim.

There is another consideration, Arendt continued, that makes lying itself a central dimension of political life. A lie "is clearly an attempt to change the record, and as such, it is a form of *action*. . . . [The liar] is an actor by nature; he says what is not so because he wants things to be different from what they are—that is, he wants to change the world."[49] One of the main reasons truthfulness is not a genuine political virtue is that it doesn't produce a desire for change, although, of course, it can contribute to undermining a status quo built entirely of lies. There is, Arendt went on to argue, a tendency in the modern world toward the systematic, organized mobilization of lying to create wholly fictitious political worlds—thus the adoption of the Big Lie in totalitarianism.

There is, however, a limit to the capacity of those who organize mendacity to keep truth entirely at bay. Thus, facts, as past events that cannot be entirely effaced, stubbornly resist the construction of a world of total untruth. And there are ways in which institutions like the judiciary, which are inside the political arena, and the academy, which are outside, do provide a check on the capacity of political mendacity to build a world entirely out of thin air. Politics is a limited realm, circumscribed by truths that it cannot undo, insofar as they involve a past that cannot be changed.

But to the extent that politics deals with the possible future, depends on opinions rather than hard facts, traffics in contingencies instead of eternal verities, mobilizes rhetoric rather than deductive logic, and is based on plurality rather than singularity, lying cannot be entirely expunged from its precincts. Thus, when it came to responding to the outcry against the mendacity revealed in the Pentagon Papers, Arendt, who had doubts about our intervention in Vietnam, was in a bit of a dilemma. "Lying in Politics" begins by rehearsing the argument of her earlier essay: "Truthfulness has never been counted among the political virtues, and lies have always been regarded as justifiable tools in political dealings. . . . The deliberate denial of factual truth—the ability to lie—and the capacity to change facts—the ability to act—are interconnected: they owe their existence to the same source: imagination."[50] Thus, moralizing about mendacity in politics is fruitless, as is the hope the contingent facts can ever achieve indubitable status.

But the Pentagon Papers, Arendt then conceded, introduce something new into the debate about lying in politics. In addition to lying for the sake of their country's image, those responsible for American intervention were also active problem solvers who prided themselves on the rational, unsentimental nature of their actions. For this reason, they attempted to import scientific reasoning into politics, substituting calculation for political judgment. "What these problem-solvers have in common with down-to-earth liars is the attempt to get rid of facts and the confidence that this should be possible because of the inherent contingency of facts."[51] But to impose their new reality entirely required the wholesale destruction of stubborn facts, which not even totalitarian leaders like Stalin and Hitler could accomplish, despite their will to do so. Ultimately, the architects of American foreign policy had to face the consequences of their deceptions.

But ironically, the reason for their downfall was less their reliance on mendacious image making than their mistaken attempt to apply reason to politics rather than learn from experience. "The problem-solvers did not *judge*; they calculated," Arendt explained. "Their self-confidence did not even need self-deception to be sustained in the midst of so many misjudgments, for it relied on the evidence of mathematical, purely rational truth. Except, of course, that this 'truth' was entirely irrelevant to the 'problem' at hand."[52] Here instead of being on the opposite side of the fence dividing politics from science, lying and rational theorizing worked hand in hand: "defactualization and problem-solving were welcomed because disregard of reality were inherent in the policies and goals themselves."[53]

In the end Arendt's attempt to distinguish radically between politics and truth-telling rationalism was thus thwarted by the complexities of the case before her, just as her other categorical distinctions between the political and the social or the moral were also perpetually in danger of coming undone. Still, despite the difficulties she had in making a watertight argument for them, her insights into the fatal affinity between politics and mendacity, if added to those we have already encountered in Strauss and Adorno, make a suggestive case against any simpleminded critique of lying in the public realm.

For even if one rejects the idea of the Platonic "noble lie" as the elitist contempt for the idea of an enlightened public that it is, it is hard to dismiss the insights that Adorno and Arendt both supply into the ways in which language necessarily defeats any attempt to be utterly transparent and univocal in the messy realm of politics. Moreover, if we acknowledge that plural opinion rather than singular truth means that there will always be different interpretations of what is and what should be, we can relax our expectation that the conventional norm of political speech is limpid truthfulness and that lying is an aberrant deviation. It is perhaps better to say that spin, exaggeration, evasion, half-truths, and the like are as much the stuff of political discourse and the struggle for power as straightforward speaking from the heart.

As ethical theorists understood before the onset of Puritanism, subtle distinctions can be made between, on the one hand, secrecy or closedness, dissimulation or withholding of the truth, and simulation or the positive fabrication of stories to hide the truth and, on the other, outright lies pretending to be the truth.[54] The last of these was particularly insupportable when the parties involved were engaged in face-to-face relations. But any watertight opposition between deliberately affirming known falsehoods and producing erroneous impressions by the cunning suppression of relevant facts or the feigning of diversionary stories is hard to maintain in the modern political arena, where intimate personal relations are rare.[55] As we have come to know from experience, primary election opponents defaming their rivals miraculously unite around the victor and sing his praises, memoirs of statesmen acknowledge the duplicity of their negotiations, politicians give coyly evasive answers to probing journalists, laws are deliberately written with ambiguities that only lawyers can love, campaign promises are given with fingers crossed, treaties are written in deliberately vague language allowing each side to claim advantage, and so forth. Although it is certainly the case that the balance between truth telling and fabrication, with all the gray area in between, is historically variable, historians would be hard pressed to identify any polity of whatever kind in which perfect veracity was the norm.

The fear that images have replaced substance or that the aestheticization of politics is a new departure ignores the extent to which politics, rhetoric, and theatricality have always been intimate bedfellows.[56] It also underestimates the extent to which the logic of politics is modal rather than propositional, that is, dealing with promises and plans about the future rather than statements about what is currently the case, with what should or ought to be rather than simple matters of fact. In addition, it fails to see that persuasion often works in politics through the power of narratives, which, as Hayden White has made clear in the case of history in general, are always as much emplotted via figural tropes as referentially true.[57] And insofar as such narratives always find their end point in a putative future, either to be realized or avoided, they contain an even stronger imaginative moment, a moment of fabulation, than is the case with those dealing only with the past.

Still another consideration is the role played by myth, or at least conceptual fabrication, in underlying even the most seemingly transparent of politics. One need not go all the way with Georges Sorel to acknowledge that even non-redemptive politics is based on certain notions that would not easily bear close epistemological scrutiny. Take, for example, the idea of "national interest," which is so often mobilized as a cover for partial interests masking as general. Or even more fundamentally, consider the idea of "the people," an enormously elastic term whose boundaries are never very precise and whose exclusions are rarely acknowledged.[58] Those who claim to speak in the name of the national interest or the people are not necessarily lying—they may intend to represent the common interest these terms purport to embody—but a politics that is based on this kind of legitimation necessarily introduces a mythic moment into its discourse.

All this is not to say, of course, that valuing truth telling and wariness about falsehoods should simply be banished from the political realm, which is nothing but a contest of competing lies. Strauss and Adorno, as we have seen, hold on to an emphatic notion of truth, which stands apart from normal political life, while Arendt admits that at least factual truth is an inherent part of any political discourse. It would indeed be dangerous to allow cynicism to undermine entirely the indignation that should accompany any disclosure of outright deception. There should be some consequences for an excessive pattern of untruth, to return to the issue of concocted weapons of mass destruction and our point of departure.

What it does suggest, however, is that rather than seeing the Big Lie of totalitarian polities as met by the perfect truth sought in liberal democratic ones, a truth based on that quest for transparency and clarity in language we have seen endorsed by Orwell and his earnest followers, we would be better advised to see politics as the endless struggle between lots of half-truths, cunning omissions, and competing narratives, which may offset each other but never entirely produce a single consensus. Although it is certainly the case that veridical discourses, such as the judicial where participants are sworn to "tell the truth, the whole truth, and nothing but the truth," do intersect with politics at crucial moments—as Bill Clinton can well attest—they never entirely subsume it. In fact, the great irony of the goal of absolute truth and truthfulness is that it mirrors the Big Lie and total mendacity of the totalitarianism it is designed to thwart. Both endanger the plurality of opinions and interminability in the fallible process of agonistic human interaction that has come to be called politics. Both enforce orthodoxy, the "making straight" of heterogeneous and unruly *doxa.* Lots of little competing dissimulations and contestable half-truths, ironically, may ward off that enforcement more effectively than any attempt to establish and defend a single, universally shared truth.

It is often argued that the basis of trust in any civil society is the assumption of veracity on the part of those with whom we deal, whether personally and face-to-face or in the impersonal public sphere or marketplace. Indeed, as Bernard Williams has argued, in English there are etymological links between "trust" and "truth."[59] But it may well be that in politics the shared assumption is rather that the endless struggle for power and advantage necessitates or at least tolerates a less rigorous calculus of transparency and sincerity. That is, we trust our opponents to be shading the truth to their advantage, as they surely trust us to do the same. Although attempts are made to judge claims by more neutral observers—for example, the *New York Times* has taken to printing the texts of political ads on television and commenting on their plausibility—the participants are not disqualified from playing the game if they fail the test. We even will defend a certain duplicity on the part of those who claim to represent us, accepting the necessity of "secrets of state" or "classified" information as the price to be paid for protecting our interests, although here too, of course, abuses inevitably arouse protests for fuller disclosures. But the "public's right to know" has its tacit limits even in a democracy, at least a representative one. And when it comes to those representatives lying on our behalf in international affairs, especially with our foes but often with our friends as well, we tend to be even more forgiving.

These lessons have begun to permeate our political consciousness. Although it would be wrong to exaggerate the effect of the three foreign-born theorists I have discussed—in what is perhaps the most influential general study of mendacity in recent years, Sissela Bok's *Lying: Moral Choice in Public and Private Life*, Strauss and Adorno are utterly ignored, while Arendt's essay "Truth and Politics" is cited in passing and with total disregard for its main argument[60]—it is at least arguable that they have provided us the tools to think more deeply than before about the issue. But let the last word go to another defender of the virtues of mendacity from abroad, Oscar Wilde. In his famous essay of 1889, the imagined dialogue called "The Decay of Lying," Wilde has one of his interlocutors denounce with mock horror the effects on American culture of our exemplary founding anecdote: "It is not too much to say that the story of George Washington and the cherry-tree has done more harm, and in a shorter span of time, than any other moral tale in the whole of literature." And then he added with the brilliant irony for which Wilde was justly celebrated, "And the amusing thing is that the story of the cherry-tree is an absolute myth."[61]

Notes

1. Christopher Hitchens, *No One Left to Lie To: The Triangulations of William Jefferson Clinton* (London, 1999). See my review of this book and of George Stephanopolous, *All Too Human*, in *London Review of Books*, July 29, 1999, where some of the issues of this essay are first addressed.

2. Al Franken, *Lies and the Lying Liars Who Tell Them: A Fair and Balanced Look at the Right* (New York, 2003); Ann Coulter, *Slander: Liberal Lies about the American Right* (New York, 2002).

3. Sheldon Rampton and John C. Stauber, *Weapons of Mass Deception: The Uses of Propaganda in Bush's War on Iraq* (New York, 2003). See also Joe Conason, *Big Lies: The Right-Wing Propaganda Machine and How It Distorts the Truth* (New York, 2003).

4. Michael T. Gilmore, *Surface and Depth: The Quest for Legibility in American Culture* (New York, 2003). It would, of course, be wrong to ignore the canonical discussions of lying in other cultures, ranging from Socrates' *Hippias Minor* to Rousseau's *The Reveries of the Solitary Walker* and Kant's "On a Supposed Right to Lie Because of Philanthropic Concerns."

5. James W. Cook, *The Arts of Deception: Playing with Fraud in the Age of Barnum* (Cambridge, Mass., 2001).

6. As Bernard Williams has noted, "In the British Parliament, there is a convention that ministers may not lie when answering questions or making statements, but they can certainly omit, select, give answers that reveal less than the whole relevant truth, and generally give a misleading impression." Williams, *Truth and Truthfulness: An Essay in Genealogy* (Princeton, 2002), 108.

7. The term comes from *Mein Kampf*, whose author infamously asserted that "the great masses of the people . . . will more easily fall victims to a big lie than to a small one."

8. This formula implies that only those outside power can be truth tellers, a tacit admission that once you have the political clout to achieve anything, truth is harder to speak so unequivocally. The link between impotence and truthfulness was already apparent in C. Wright Mills, "The Powerless People: The Role of the Intellectual in Society," *Politics* 1 (April 1944), where the "politics of truth" is assigned to intellectuals as a kind of compensation for their powerlessness. I am indebted to Daniel Geary's "The Power and the Intellect: C. Wright Mills, the Left and American Social Science" (Ph.D. diss., University of California at Berkeley, 2004) for drawing this essay to my attention.

9. The official use of the motto did not begin, in fact, until 1843, some time after Yale had adopted "Lux et Veritas" for its motto. See the discussion in www.yalealumnimagazine.com/issues/01_03/seal.html.

10. See David A. Hollinger, "Science and Anarchy: Walter Lippmann's *Drift and Mastery*," in his *In the American Province: Studies in the History and Historiography of Ideas* (Bloomington, Ind., 1985). He argues that Lippmann's version was less technocratic and more democratic than Bernard's. See also Dorothy Ross, "Modernist Social Science in the Land of the New/Old," in *Modernist Impulses in the Human Sciences, 1870–1930*, ed. Dorothy Ross (Baltimore, 1994), which argues that "mainstream sociologists developed a technocratic conception of science aimed at prediction and control" (187).

11. Walter Lippmann, *Public Opinion* (New York, 1922), 358.

12. See the discussion in Garett S. Jowett and Victoria O'Donnell, *Propaganda and Persuasion* (Thousand Oaks, Calif., 1999), 2. Lippmann argued that propaganda had been used by both sides in the First World War (*Public Opinion*, 42).

13. Kenneth Cmiel, *Democratic Eloquence: The Fight over Popular Speech in Nineteenth-Century America* (New York, 1990). He shows that the transition took place between 1885 and 1900.

14. George Orwell, "Politics and the English Language," in *A Collection of Essays* (Garden City, N.Y., 1953), 166, 171.

15. Lionel Trilling, "George Orwell and the Politics of Truth" (1955), reprinted in George Orwell, *Nineteen Eighty-four: Text, Sources, Criticism*, ed. Irving Howe (New York, 1963), 226.

16. Cited from an unpublished talk in David Lloyd and Paul Thomas, *Culture and the State* (New York, 1998), 175.

17. Christopher Hitchens, *Why Orwell Matters* (New York, 2002).

18. See, e.g., the essays in John S. Nelson, Allan Megill, and Donald N. McClosky, eds., *The Rhetoric of the Human Sciences: Language and Argument in Scholarship and Public Affairs* (Madison, Wisc., 1987).

19. In fact, one of the most extensive explorations of lying by a post-structuralist thinker, Jacques Derrida, draws heavily on the earlier work of Hannah Arendt to be discussed below. See Derrida, "History of the Lie: Prolegomena," in *Without Alibi*, ed. and trans. Peggy Kamuf (Stanford, Calif., 2002).

20. Peter Sloterdijk, *Critique of Cynical Reason*, trans. Michael Elred (Minneapolis, 1987), chap. 23. See also Helmut Lethen, *Cool Conduct: The Culture of Distance in Weimar Germany*, trans. Don Reneau (Berkeley, Calif., 2002).

21. The public appreciation of the influence of Straussians on actual policy really emerged only with the Iraq War. The extent of the discussion is apparent in Web sites like www.straussian.net, which has a section on Straussians in the news.

22. Wolfowitz's admission was that "the truth is that for reasons that have a lot to do with the U.S. government bureaucracy we settled on the one issue that everyone could agree on which was weapons of mass destruction as the core reason." Cited in the interview he gave *Vanity Fair*, where he also talks about his debts to Strauss and Straussians such as Alan Bloom. See the text at_www.scoop.co.nz/mason/stories/WO0305/S00308.htm. For an exploration of Strauss's influence on the mendacity of the Bush administration, see Danny Postel's interview with the Strauss scholar Shadia Drury in *Open Democracy* at www.opendemocracy.net/entry_points/Noble_lies_and_perpetual_war.jsp. One of Wolfowitz's own protégés, it should be noted, was I. Louis "Scooter" Libby.

23. See in particular Leo Strauss, *Persecution and the Art of Writing* (Glencoe, Ill., 1952). For a detailed account of the role of exile on Strauss's thought, see Eugene R. Sheppard, *Leo Strauss and the Politics of Exile* (forthcoming).

24. Leo Strauss, "The Spirit of Sparta or the Taste of Xenophon," *Social Research* 6 (November 1939): 535.

25. Ibid.

26. See, e.g., the chapter devoted to him in Stephen Holmes, *The Anatomy of Illiberalism* (Cambridge, Mass., 1993).

27. The precise translation of this phrase from *The Republic* has been much disputed, being rendered variously as "pious fraud," "royal lie," and "bold flight of the imagination." For a discussion, see Sissela Bok, *Lying: Moral Choice in Public and Private Life* (New York, 1999), 306. She insists on the standard translation, arguing that it fits well with Plato's defense of a natural hierarchy in which nobility of breeding excuses lying to those lower on the social scale. Derrida, however, notes that "pseudos" in Greek could mean lie, cunning, mistake, deception, fraud, as well as poetic invention. See Derrida, "History of the Lie," 30.

28. See his complicated analysis of the relationship between opinion and truth in Theodor W. Adorno, "Opinion Delusion Society," in *Critical Models: Interventions and Catchwords*, trans. Henry W. Pickford (New York, 1998).

29. For a very helpful overview, see Peter Uwe Hohendahl, *Prismatic Thought: Theodor W. Adorno* (Lincoln, Neb., 1995), chap. 9.

30. John Durham Peters, *Speaking into the Air: A History of the Idea of Communication* (Chicago, 1999), 221.

31. James Miller, "Is Bad Writing Necessary? George Orwell, Theodor Adorno, and the Politics of Language," *Lingua Franca* (December–January, 2000). Interestingly, both men were born in 1903, but into very different worlds.

32. Theodor W. Adorno, *Minima Moralia: Reflections from Damaged Life*, trans. E. F. N. Jephcott (London, 1974), 101.

33. Ibid., p. 110.

34. Theodor W. Adorno, *The Jargon of Authenticity*, trans. Knut Tarnowski and Frederic Will (London, 1973).

35. In the empirical study he made in 1943 of the American radio demagogue Martin Luther Thomas, Adorno saw the evidence for this danger: "His confessions, actual or faked, serve to satisfy the listener's curiosity. This is a universal feature of present-day mass culture. It is catered to by the gossip columns of certain newspapers, the inside stories told to innumerable listeners over the radio, or the magazines that promise 'true stories.'" Theodor Adorno, *The Psychological Technique of Martin Luther Thomas' Radio Addresses* (Stanford, Calif., 2000), 2.

36. Adorno, *Minima Moralia*, 155. I have tried to develop the implications of the aphorism from which this citation comes, "Gold Assay," at greater length in my essay "Taking on the Stigma of Inauthenticity: Adorno's Critique of Genuineness," *New German Critique* 97 (Winter 2006).

37. Adorno would continue to stress the value of rhetoric against attempts to denigrate it as misleading ornamentation. In a section called "Rhetoric" in *Negative Dialectics*, trans. E. B. Ashton (New York, 1973), 56, he would write, "In dialectics, contrary to popular opinion, the rhetorical element is on the side of content."

38. Theodor W. Adorno, *Hegel: Three Studies*, trans. Shierry Weber Nicholsen (Cambridge, Mass., 1993). "Skoteinos" refers to the work of Heraclitus, who is opposed as the avatar of obscurity to Descartes, the modern defender of clarity.

39. Ibid., 96.

40. Ibid., 100.

41. In the celebrated "Epistemo-critical Prologue" to *The Origin of German Tragic Drama*, trans. John Osborne (London, 1977), Benjamin had written: "Truth is an intentionless state of being, made up of ideas. The proper approach to it is not therefore one of intention and knowledge, but rather a total immersion and absorption in it. Truth is the death of intention" (36). In his inaugural lecture of 1931, "The Actuality of Philosophy," Adorno echoed this claim: "The task of philosophy is not to search for concealed and manifest intentions of reality, but to interpret unintentional reality." *The Adorno Reader*, ed. Brian O'Connor (Oxford, 2000), 32.

42. Elisabeth Young-Bruehl, *Hannah Arendt: For Love of the World* (New Haven, Conn.,

1982), 80, 98. For comparisons of their work, see Peter Graf Kielmansegg, Horst Mewes, and Elisabeth Glaser-Schmidt, eds., *Hannah Arendt and Leo Strauss: German Emigrés and American Political Thought after World War II* (Cambridge, Mass., 1995), and Dirk Auer, Lars Rensmann, and Julia Schulze, eds., *Das Unmögliche Denken: Vergleichende Studien zu Theodor W. Adorno und Hannah Arendt* (Frankfurt, 2003).

43. Hannah Arendt, "Truth in Politics," in *The Portable Hannah Arendt*, ed. Peter Baehr (New York, 2000), 574–575.

44. Precisely what she learned and how valuable were the lessons have been the source of considerable controversy, especially after the disclosure of her romantic attachment to Heidegger. For two opposing accounts, see Dana R. Villa, *Arendt and Heidegger: The Fate of the Political* (Princeton, 1996), and Richard Wolin, *Heidegger's Children: Hannah Arendt, Karl Löwith, Han Jonas, and Herbert Marcuse* (Princeton, 2001). For her debt to Jaspers, see Lewis P. Hinchman and Sandra K. Hinchman, "Existentialism Politicized: Arendt's Debt to Jaspers," in *Hannah Arendt: Critical Essays*, ed. Lewis P. Hinchman and Sandra K. Hinchman (Albany, N.Y., 1994).

45. Arendt, "Truth in Politics," 545.

46. Ibid., 549.

47. Ibid. As Habermas has shown, however, the absolute distinction between truth and opinion began to waver in complicated ways with the rise of the bourgeois public sphere and the idea of "public opinion." See Jürgen Habermas, *The Structural Transformation of the Public Sphere: An Inquiry into a Category of Bourgeois Society*, trans. Thomas Berger and Frederick Lawrence (Cambridge, Mass., 1991), chap. 12.

48. Arendt, "Truth in Politics," 556.

49. Ibid., 563.

50. Hannah Arendt, "Lying in Politics," in *Crises of the Republic* (New York, 1972), 4–5.

51. Ibid., 12.

52. Ibid., 37.

53. Ibid., 42.

54. See the discussion in Steven Shapin, *A Social History of Truth: Civility and Science in Seventeenth-Century England* (Chicago, 1994), 103–107. He shows that only the fourth of these, outright lies, was condemned unequivocally until the Puritans. For a general consideration of lying in early modern Europe, see Perez Zagorin, *Ways of Lying: Dissimulation, Persecution, and Conformity in Early Modern Europe* (Cambridge, Mass., 1990).

55. For a distinction between the "direct lie method" and the "blank page method," see Andrus Pork, "History and Moral Responsibility," *History and Theory* 29, no. 3 (1990).

56. For a recent discussion of their entanglement at the birth of modern politics, see Paul Friedland, *Political Actors: Representative Bodies and Theatricality in the Age of the French Revolution* (Ithaca, N.Y., 2002).

57. Hayden White, *Metahistory: The Historical Imagination in Nineteenth-Century Europe* (Baltimore, 1973). This work has, to be sure, generated an extraordinary response, much of it dedicated to qualifying the radical constructivism of White's argument. His central point about the ways in which rhetorical tropes inevitably inflect our telling of narratives about the past still stands. For an alternative view of the importance of maintaining the quest for truth in historical writing and its relation to politics, see Alan B. Spitzer, *Historical Truth and Lies about the Past* (Chapel Hill, N.C., 1996).

58. See George Boas, *The History of Ideas* (New York, 1969), chap. 8, for an excellent overview of the history and variable meaning of this term.

59. Williams, *Truth and Truthfulness*, 93.

60. Bok, *Lying*, 142, cites Arendt's critique of the "consistent and total substitution of lies for factual truth" as causing the destruction of the capacity to tell the difference between lies and truth. This argument was aimed, as we have seen, against the totalitarian "Big Lie," not the normal give-and-take of small lies in the political realm. Bok also claims that lying, not

truth telling, is ultimately more coercive, though she does not engage Arendt's arguments to the contrary. But see Jeremy Campbell, *The Liar's Tale: A History of Falsehood* (New York, 2001), for a defense of deception in ways that indicate Bok's position may no longer be unchallenged in mainstream considerations of the issues. Even more directly relevant to the issue of lying in politics is Ruth W. Grant, *Hypocrisy and Integrity: Machiavelli, Rousseau, and the Ethics of Politics* (Chicago, 1997), which makes a powerful case for the inevitability of hypocrisy whenever dependency is a part of political life, including democratic dependency on voters and allies.

61. Oscar Wilde, "The Decay of Lying," in *Aesthetes and Decadents of the 1890's*, ed. Karl Beckson (Chicago, 1981), 183.

5

THE PLACE OF VALUE IN A CULTURE OF FACTS

Truth and Historicism

JAMES T. KLOPPENBERG

CARVED IN STONE on the Social Science Research Building at the University of Chicago are the following words: "When you cannot measure, your knowledge is meager and unsatisfactory." That bold proclamation, attributed to Lord Kelvin, reflected the convictions of the sociologist William F. Ogburn, chair of the Committee on Symbolism, which was charged with ensuring that the exterior of the building accurately projected the aspirations of the social scientists it would house. Like natural scientists in their laboratories, some social scientists at the University of Chicago, such as Ogburn, the first sociologist ever named president of the American Statistical Association, envisioned themselves engaged in a quest for truth. From reliable measurements of empirical data they intended to generate significant and satisfactory results that would enable their contemporaries to solve pressing social problems. Not all Ogburn's colleagues agreed with him, or with Kelvin. Some preferred Aristotle's more open-ended dictum "man is a political animal." At least one denied that any words could capture the rich diversity of the work to be done by scholars who would follow different methodological paths toward diverse, and changing, conceptions of truth. Another of Ogburn's foes, the political scientist Charles E. Merriam, never accepted the claim emblazoned on his workplace; he wanted the misleading words removed.[1] The terms and the stridency of these scholars' debates have echoed ever since within the humanities as well as the discursive social sciences.

The same year that building opened, 1929, a new president, Robert Maynard Hutchins, arrived at the University of Chicago. The thirty-year-old Hutchins presided over the dedication ceremonies of the Social Science Research Building, and he almost immediately locked horns with its faculty. As a breathtakingly young professor and then dean of the Yale Law School, Hutchins had established himself as a champion of Legal Realism, which challenged the timelessness of legal principles and the usefulness of abstract reasoning. But when he arrived in Chicago, Hutchins made it clear immediately that he did not share Kelvin's faith in measurement or Ogburn's commitment to empirical investigation. In his first address at the university he told the class of 1929 that "the purpose of higher education is to unsettle the minds of young men." The goal of education "is not to teach men facts, theories, or laws; it is not to reform them, or amuse them, or make them expert technicians in any field; it is to teach them to think, to think straight, if possible, but to think always for themselves."[2]

To that end Hutchins endeavored to transform the undergraduate curriculum at the University of Chicago. He wanted students to develop their ability to think not by learning to measure but by confronting the timeless wisdom contained in the great books of the Western tradition. Hutchins sought to appoint scholars who shared his enthusiasm for ancient philosophers such as Aristotle and medieval theologians such as Thomas Aquinas, scholars wary of Kelvin's confidence in natural science and equally skeptical about American pragmatism. Even though John Dewey had left Hyde Park for Columbia almost twenty years before Hutchins arrived, the sensibility associated with Dewey and with his fellow pragmatists Charles Sanders Peirce and William James remained influential at the University of Chicago. Two of Dewey's allies and champions, James H. Tufts and George Herbert Mead, bristled at Hutchins's attempt to appoint Mortimer Adler, Richard McKeon, and Scott Buchanan to the faculty. When the Chicago philosophers first met Adler and explained that they introduced first-year students to the discipline by assigning Will Durant's popular, accessible, and pragmatist-leaning *Story of Philosophy*, Adler is said to have fumed, "But—but—but that's a very bad book." Adler had first burst on the academic scene when, as a student at Columbia, he had enraged Dewey at a meeting of the undergraduate philosophy club by denouncing Dewey's account of "the religious" in *A Common Faith*. The usually equable Dewey, protesting that "nobody is going to tell *me* how to love God," walked out. Now Adler was turning his ire on the Chicago philosophers, and Hutchins was urging them to make room for scholars who would teach classical and medieval philosophy instead of instrumentalism. They responded much as Dewey had: Tufts resigned, and Mead made plans to move to Columbia. The philosophers who stayed eventually accepted McKeon but not Adler or Buchanan. Hutchins persisted; Adler joined the faculty of the Law School. Every Tuesday, for two decades, Adler and Hutchins together taught an honors course for freshmen, History of Ideas, in which undergraduates sat around a seminar table discussing the great books with two men committed to unsettling their minds.[3]

Although the battle between the sciences—both natural and social—and the humanities was seldom as pronounced as it was at Hutchins's Chicago, more muted versions of the same struggle erupted elsewhere in the years after 1929. Equally spirited conflicts emerged within individual disciplines during the interwar years. Philosophers inspired by Dewey's conception of a pragmatist community of inquiry were challenged by analytic philosophers who focused on rigorous studies of ordinary language. Both had to face the challenge of the even harder-edged positivists who shared Rudolf Carnap's conviction that the "only proper task of *Philosophy* is *Logical Analysis*." When the exiled Carnap began teaching in the gothic buildings at Hutchins's University of Chicago, he admitted that being surrounded by Aristotelians and Thomists gave him the distinctly "weird feeling" of having fled Vienna only to find himself "sitting among a group of medieval learned men with long beards and solemn robes."[4] Scholars of literature likewise divided into (at least) three different camps. Those who conceived of themselves as scientists sought to generate reliable bodies of knowledge about linguistics and historical philology. New Critics sought to discover and elucidate principles of literary form and expression through close readings that banished intent and context. Traditionalists continued to think of education as the cultivation of judgment along the lines of German *Bildung* and believed that such cultivation was best achieved by placing students in a situation in which they could read and reflect on challenging books of enduring value.[5] A few natural scientists (Albert Einstein and Jacques Monod come to mind) continued to muse about the philosophical and even theological implications of their findings; others did not hesitate to declare such speculations a waste of time.

This chapter examines briefly two particular moments at which thinkers outside emerging scholarly orthodoxies tried—without great success—to defend the legitimacy of their forms of value-oriented humanistic inquiry against hostile critics; it then discusses in somewhat greater detail a more enduring effort in political philosophy that persists at the heart of American universities into the twenty-first century. The first two incidents, involving the German Gestalt psychologist Wolfgang Köhler and the French neo-Thomist philosopher Etienne Gilson, occurred in Cambridge, Massachusetts. The third, involving the German Jewish political philosopher Leo Strauss, is international in scope. I argue that all three are connected, albeit in paradoxical ways, and that they are important for our contemporary understanding of the humanities and discursive social sciences in liberal education.[6]

The American Academy of Arts and Sciences stands across Irving Street from the home of William James, a gray clapboard house perfectly attuned to its neighborhood, and in the shadow of fifteen-story-high William James Hall, an imposing white modernist monolith that dominates the Cambridge skyline.

Unlike the Social Science Research Building at Chicago, William James Hall does not bear an inscription, but its towering form and its arrogant disregard for its surroundings suggest the imperious claims made for the work done by the social scientists it houses. In the decades before 1963, when Harvard built this temple to the behavioral sciences, the university paid homage in a different, more appropriate way to the maverick genius who studied both mind and truth: it sponsored the William James Lectures.

In 1934 the Harvard Department of Philosophy extended an invitation to deliver those lectures to Wolfgang Köhler, a renowned German scholar whose research was generating widespread interest on both sides of the Atlantic. Until later in the 1930s the Department of Philosophy included both philosophers such as James's biographer Ralph Barton Perry and experimental psychologists such as Edwin G. Boring; both disciplines were still proud to claim James's heritage in ways neither would do today.

Along with his colleagues Max Wertheimer and Kurt Koffka, Köhler was among the founders of the Gestalt school of psychology. As James himself had done, the Gestalt psychologists criticized the two traditions that dominated their discipline in its early years, associationism and intuitionism. They were equally critical of the newest development in psychology, behaviorism. Indeed, as Perry wrote in an appreciative review of books by Köhler and Koffka published in the *Saturday Review of Literature* in 1925, their work showed "the *esprit* of an armed revolution." Their "freshness of treatment" and "inventiveness and fertility of method" produced "an effect very much like the opening of a window."[7]

The Gestaltists argued, as James had done in *The Principles of Psychology*, that standard atomistic interpretations of experience as the combination of discrete simple elements mangled a more complex reality. They emphasized the importance of Gestalten, or configurations, in perception, and they argued that patterns of stimuli must be correlated with structures and relations within the perceptual field. Only thereby can we explain the human capacity to recognize the same tune played in different keys, or our ability to interpret sequences of blinking lights that the mind combines to read as signs or words. Our environment, according to *Gestaltists*, does not merely consist of physical objects near us, but must be understood instead as the result of the interaction between our perceptual field and those physical objects. All organisms impose on their environment certain configurations that filter and transform stimuli so that the organisms can deal with their environment. In 1929 Boring reported to Koffka, after Köhler had delivered a lecture in Cambridge sponsored by the Harvard Philosophical Club, that he was impressed with the new science. Boring's students had begun to characterize him as a Gestaltist, and he did not deny the charge. By that time Köhler held a prestigious chair at the University of Berlin. As a reflection of his prominence, he was invited in 1929 to deliver one of the two plenary addresses at the Ninth International Congress of Psychology held at Yale. Ivan Pavlov delivered the other.[8]

That early consensus on the value of Gestalt psychology as an alternative to behaviorism did not endure. When Boring published his *History of Experimental Psychology* late in 1929, he was already beginning to worry that the Gestalt psychologists would never develop their ideas beyond their critiques of prevailing views. When Köhler's *Gestalt Psychology* appeared that same year, behaviorists began a counterattack. Frederick Lund, in "The Phantom of the Gestalt," charged that the notion of configurations "has no assignable value in psychological description nor any real existence within the experimental sequence." If it had no value for experimental psychologists, it could safely be ignored.[9]

The philosophers, however, remained intrigued, and with Perry taking the lead they selected Köhler to deliver the third series of William James Lectures in 1934. The book that resulted, *The Place of Value in a World of Facts*, the title of which inspired the title of this chapter, was greeted with greater enthusiasm by philosophers than by psychologists.[10] Köhler observed that the natural sciences had difficulty addressing the question of valuation. Whereas many philosophers were urging their colleagues to banish the study of ethics and aesthetics from philosophy—or to characterize value statements as descriptions of emotions and nothing more—as part of their program to become scientific, Köhler recommended instead that science must acknowledge that values are irreducible dimensions of human experience: "Certain facts do not only happen or exist, but, issuing as vectors in parts of contexts, extend toward others with a quality of acceptance or rejection." All our experience, Köhler reasoned, is imbued with valuings. If we ignore that dimension of human life simply because we cannot conduct experiments on it, then our science might appear to rest on a more sturdy foundation of experimentation but will fail to address what it is and what it feels like to be human. He urged psychologists and philosophers to adopt a revised phenomenological conception of experience more consistent with the Gestalt psychologists' outlook than with Husserl's philosophy. Far from contending that his view of experience was inconsistent with the natural sciences, Köhler insisted that the natural sciences must be expanded to take into account the pervasive human experience of valuing. If we cannot yet see how we can build such concepts as "requiredness" into our experimental programs, then the challenge is to rethink our procedures rather than to truncate experience so that it corresponds to what we can now measure with confidence. In the history of psychology, perhaps no writer had developed such ideas with greater insight, or defended them with more energy, than William James.[11]

Whereas the community of social scientists was being urged to measure lest its results be meager, and logical positivists and emotivists were advising philosophers not to confuse value judgments with meaningful statements of fact or logic, Köhler was urging scholars instead to widen their concepts of measurement and logic. Perry and some other members of Harvard's Philosophy Department greeted that message with enthusiasm. They urged Harvard's new president, James Conant, to make Köhler a tenured member of the faculty. Perry, one of several highly regarded scholars who contributed to a volume entitled *The Meaning of the Humanities*, which was reviewed in *Ethics* together with Köhler's *The Place of Value in a World of Facts*, still thought it possible to combine empirical studies with traditional humanistic inquiries into human values. But neither Perry's discipline nor Boring's was heading in that direction. Instead, the scholarly community of mainstream analytic philosophers and behavioral psychologists has echoed the judgment Boring expressed in a letter after Köhler's lectures: "I can say only that I heard the whole series and am terribly disappointed, and a little humiliated at the knowledge that I took the time to go to them. The content was not informed nor related to current knowledge. The ideas were not important or clear."[12] Boring and his fellow experimentalists succeeded in blocking Köhler's appointment, and none of the leading Gestaltists would end up teaching in a major American research university. The ideas of Gestalt psychology and phenomenology all but vanished from Harvard. The university only ratified institutionally what had already happened intellectually when it divided its increasingly behavioral psychologists into a department distinct from that of its increasingly analytic philosophers. Today, seventy years after Köhler's lectures, with the exception of issues in cognitive science, Harvard's Department of Psychology and its Department of Philosophy have little contact and little in common.

Two YEARS after Köhler's William James Lectures, in 1936, Harvard celebrated its tercentennial. In a special issue of the *New York Times Magazine* commemorating the event, the historian Samuel Eliot Morison wrote, "The world is not going very well for learning, or for universities. The heavy hand of the State has quenched the flame of academic freedom in Germany, where in modern times it was rekindled. Pressure groups in America, copying the technique of Fascist Italy, are demanding oaths by teacher and professor to the Constitution and the flag, and tagging every sign of independent thinking in the social sciences as treason. Universities must serve the people, but they can only serve the people in the future, as in the past, by remaining constant in their search for the truth and true to their function of teaching it."[13] During these years of crisis many Americans, including many prominent American scholars in addition to Morison, worried that the principal danger facing the nation came from within. Many located that threat in the relativism they associated with Dewey and other pragmatists, who were understood by many to have inspired Mussolini's fascism. Others worried instead about the absolutist dogmatism of American Catholics, who were feared to be dupes of the pope and probably inclined toward Il Duce themselves. Still others pointed accusing fingers in a different direction, at value-neutral philosophers such as those of the Vienna Circle, who turned their backs on the great traditions of ethics and metaphysics. Given those anxieties, it came as something of a surprise when Harvard announced the names of those to whom it would award honorary degrees at its tercentennial celebration. They included prominent members from all those groups of suspects: the arch-empiricist from Chicago, Robert MacIver; the logical empiricist Rudolf Carnap; the cognitive psychologist Jean Piaget; and the neo-Thomist philosopher Etienne Gilson, among others. The university made a point of indicating that Dewey was not included only because he had already been awarded an honorary Harvard degree. In his remarks Gilson saluted his hosts by confirming their own inflated sense of their importance. He observed that the presence of so many eminent Europeans at the Harvard celebration demonstrated "that the fate of European culture and Western civilization ultimately rests with what the United States will make of it in the next 100 years."[14]

The following year, coincidentally, Harvard selected Gilson to deliver the William James Lectures—perhaps to signal its commitment to entertaining ideas considered repugnant by many Americans, perhaps to persuade wealthy Catholic donors to adopt Harvard, or perhaps to reward his perspicacity at the tercentennial.[15] In the book that resulted, *The Unity of Philosophical Experience*, Gilson listed first among those to whom he was grateful Ralph Barton Perry. Gently needling his hosts, Gilson noted that his invitation testified to the continuing spirit of tolerating diversity that James had noted in 1901 as the hallmark of the Harvard Philosophy Department. "I think the delightful thing about us" philosophers, James had written to G. H. Palmer, "is our deep appreciation of one another, and our on the whole harmonious co-operation toward the infusion of what probably is objective truth into the minds of our students. At any rate it's genuine liberalism, and non-dogmatism." As James's puckish qualifiers "on the whole," "probably," and "at any rate" suggested, he had no illusion that he and his colleagues were dispensing "objective truth." Gilson sustained the same ironic tone when he applauded the persistence of James's broad-mindedness in "the Harvard of Perry, Whitehead, Hocking, Lewis, and Sheffer." Gilson did not acknowledge the presence of W. V. O. Quine, who had recently joined the Philosophy Department after completing his Ph.D. in two years, an oversight one imagines Quine was happy to reciprocate. "When non-dogmatism shows itself generous enough to welcome even dogmatism," Gilson concluded mischievously, "it has obviously reached the point of its perfection."[16]

Gilson's compliment was as double-edged as James's. His lectures made abundantly clear how little he prized the nondogmatism with which he credited his hosts. He traced the path of modern philosophy from Descartes through Kant to Hegel and Comte, and then to James, Bergson, and contemporary irrationalism and agnosticism. Although Gilson had no doubt that such abominations would pass—"Philosophy always buries its undertakers"—he worried that the current mania for science might do some damage while it lasted. Gilson urged the community of philosophers to return to the urgent task of metaphysics, which had occupied all the great classical and medieval philosophers and without which they could not hope to escape the trap of historicism. In the absence of metaphysics "what is now called philosophy is either collective mental slavery or scepticism." The servile inclined toward Marxism, which satisfied "a fundamentally sound craving" "for positive and dogmatic truth" even though it was otherwise entirely wrongheaded. The skeptics, inspired by Hume, now turned toward varieties of behaviorism, or James's pragmatism, or Perry's neorealism, or Hans Vaihinger's philosophy of "As If." But none of those could meet the urgent demands of the age: "The time of the 'As If' is over," Gilson predicted. "What we now need is a 'This is so,' and we shall not find it, unless we first recover our lost confidence in the rational validity of metaphysics and our long-forgotten knowledge of its object." A renewed commitment to metaphysics, undertaken within the proper Roman Catholic framework, might enable us "to free ourselves from historical relativism" and open "a new era of constructive philosophical thinking."

Overall, however, notwithstanding his clear confidence in his creed, Gilson avoided the pugnacious tone of Köhler and Koffka. He concluded with these words: "Were it in my power to do so, I would rather leave you with a gift. Not wisdom, which I have not and no man can give, but the next best thing; the love of wisdom, for which philosophy is but another word. For to love wisdom is also to love science, and prudence; it is to seek peace in the inner accord of each mind with itself and in the mutual accord of all minds."[17] In the aftermath of Gilson's William James Lectures, though, the Harvard Department of Philosophy not surprisingly returned to its own professionalized version of that quest, seeking not wisdom as Gilson understood it but the precision of a discipline that viewed scholastic metaphysics with a distaste bordering on contempt.

WHEREAS GILSON, like his revered Thomas Aquinas, considered philosophy to be consistent with (indeed, in the service of) scholastic theology, it was common in the 1930s to observe that at the University of Chicago Jews taught Catholicism to atheists. Hutchins and Adler revered Aquinas as much as they did Plato and Aristotle. Appalled by recent developments in American academic philosophy, they welcomed to the faculty a Jewish émigré who appeared to share their scorn for analytic philosophy and logical positivism and their enthusiasm for ancient and medieval thought and for the careful study of great books. In Leo Strauss, however, they got more than they bargained for. Strauss fancied himself an authentic philosopher and dismissed Hutchins and Adler just as Adler had dismissed Durant, as dabblers who enjoyed posing as scholars while they engaged in entrepreneurial adventures inconsistent with the life of a university.[18] Strauss was an atheist; his own attitude toward Judaism was complex, even murky. But Christianity he held in little-disguised contempt. Like Nietzsche, he considered it a slave religion utterly inconsistent with the life of a philosopher.

If Strauss proved a surprise and a disappointment to his patrons after he finally joined the faculty of the University of Chicago in 1948, it was only the last of several ironic twists in the long road that took him to Hyde Park. When Strauss first lectured at Chicago in 1936, the English historian Conyers Read, writing to a colleague, described Strauss unenthusiastically as "a little mouse kind of a man without much in the way of stimulating personality. I think with more experience he will develop into a fair teacher."[19] The recipient of that letter, the economist John U. Nef, was a Hutchins ally who later founded the Committee on Social Thought and proved instrumental in Strauss's appointment. Nef admired the work and the Christian socialist principles of the English scholar R. H. Tawney, whom he and Hutchins wanted very much to lure to Chicago. Tawney and Strauss became acquainted when Strauss arrived in London in 1936, and the young German, at work on the medieval Jewish philosopher Moses Maimonides, made a lasting impression. In one of his letters replying to Nef's overtures, Tawney described Strauss as "certainly the best scholar among the refugees whom I have had to deal with."[20] Tawney, like Strauss and Nef, distrusted historicism. Tawney longed for a world radically unlike the bourgeois liberal capitalism of his day, a return, in Tawneys words, to "the true nature of man," or, as Nef put it, "to the ideals of classical and medieval philosophy, softened and enriched by the best traditions of the nineteenth-century English humanitarians."[21] Hutchins and Nef found such ideas attractive, which explains their interest in Tawney. But the romantic, Ruskin-scented sentiments of his English champion repelled Strauss as much as did the ersatz neo-Thomism of the philistines Hutchins and Adler. He had encountered such ideas before.

Leo Strauss was born into an orthodox Jewish family in 1899, served in the German army during World War I, then completed his doctoral studies at the University of Hamburg. Although the neo-Kantian Ernst Cassirer directed his dissertation, a study of the counter-Enlightenment philosopher Friedrich Jacobi, Strauss's sensibility took shape in response to the deeper impact of several other thinkers, notably Edmund Husserl, Franz Rosensweig, and especially Martin Heidegger. Already in his study of Jacobi, Strauss expressed his dissatisfaction with the Enlightenment's confidence in reason and his respect for Jacobi's attempt to unearth an authentic, ancient Jewish faith that refused to compromise with secular modernity or make peace with Christian persecutors. While working at the Academy of Jewish Research in Berlin, Strauss embarked on studies of Spinoza, Hobbes, and the birth of what he would call for the rest of his life "the modern." Whereas the ancients had understood that we have lost contact with nature, a condition captured by Plato in his image of the cave, Strauss argued that modern man, without realizing his condition, was in a far worse predicament, stuck in a second cave buried far beneath the first. So far had man fallen from the light of reason, from awareness of natural right, that he believed he would need altogether new tools to escape that deeper cave. Although Strauss began ruminating on this condition as early as 1932, he elaborated his argument about "the natural obstacles to philosophy" only in *Persecution and the Art of Writing*, a book published twenty years later. There he contended that science and history, more potent even than the passion and superstition that troubled Spinoza, conspired to blind modern man to nature. New tools such as hermeneutics and social science only further obscured what man needed to know, the nature of the eternal, unchanging problems probed by ancient philosophers such as Socrates, Plato, Aristotle, and Xenophon.[22]

From 1932 at least until 1938, when he arrived in the United States and began teaching at the New School for Social Research in New York City, Strauss worked on developing the ideas that would make him a heroic champion to some and an evil genius to others. Strauss is perhaps best known today for having developed several sets of dichotomies, each of which has been examined in loving detail by Strauss's many admirers and scrutinized by his even more numerous critics with degrees of disapproval ranging from bitter disagreement to unmitigated fury. The first is the esoteric versus the apparent meaning of texts; the second is the classical versus the modern; the third is natural right versus historicism; and the fourth—the most complex and thus the most intriguing—is Athens versus Jerusalem. Although these dichotomies may seem at first difficult to comprehend, even intimidating, with the exception of the last they are fairly straightforward.

First, Strauss contended that great thinkers, including philosophers such as the ancients and a few medieval giants such as Maimonides, Averroës,

Alfarabius, and, notoriously, Machiavelli, masked their deeper insights by writing so as to conceal their explosive message from ordinary readers. This technique of esoteric writing requires readers to penetrate layers of apparent meanings before arriving at the hidden truths accessible only to those with the necessary intelligence, patience, and skill. Whereas in some traditions interpreters of texts win admiration for their ability to read creatively, Strauss insisted that the most careful readers always end up with the same interpretation of the problems addressed in the greatest texts, an interpretation he laid out—albeit through his own version of bivalent writing—in his own books and articles.

Second, Strauss distinguished between the classical philosophers, whose writings give us true accounts of virtue, beauty, reason, nature, and truth, and modern writers, who are stuck in the muck of relativism because they think science can provide knowledge when it really just gets in the way. Strauss called himself a friend of liberal democracy, but he savaged its failings and its excesses with venom equal to that of Friedrich Nietzsche or Herbert Marcuse at their most scornful. Whereas classical philosophers valued the genuine individualism of Socrates, the wise seeker of truth, liberal individualists inflate the unreflective desires of the most degraded persons into natural rights. Whereas classical philosophers understood that only the truly exceptional can discern truth and live the life of virtue, democracies pretend that all people are equal, a manifest lie that flatters the worst and robs the best of the opportunity to strive for excellence.

Strauss's third dichotomy, natural right versus historicism, flows from the second. Whereas classical philosophers understood that natural right, the one thing "truly needful," is the same always and everywhere, modern scientists deny the existence of eternal truth and offer instead only value-free empiricism, which cannot provide access to man's nature and inevitably culminates in the dead ends of historicism and relativism. Developed in its bluntest form in the book based on the Walgreen Lectures Strauss delivered at the University of Chicago in 1949, *Natural Right and History*, this is the distinction for which Strauss is probably best known. Strauss opened by quoting the Declaration of Independence: "We hold these truths to be self-evident, that all men are created equal, that they are endowed by their Creator with certain unalienable Rights, that among these are Life, Liberty, and the pursuit of Happiness." Strauss then contrasted this noble creed to the pernicious historicism that had enveloped his own native Germany and plunged the world into the most devastating war in history. Our "contemporary rejection of natural right leads to nihilism—nay, it is identical with nihilism." Moderns seek to escape the irrationality of nihilism, but "the more we cultivate reason, the more we cultivate nihilism."

As Strauss saw it, only two armies contest the field of modern philosophy, "liberals of various descriptions" and the "Catholic and non-Catholic disciples of Thomas Aquinas." Unfortunately, both armies are misled by their belief in modern science, which blinds them to the light of Aristotelian teleology and prevents them from seeing that "all natural beings have a natural end, a natural destiny, which determines what kind of operation is good for them." The ancients understood eternal natural right. Moderns have abandoned it and instead embraced "conventionalism," another term for the historicism that emerged in the horrified reaction of Europeans to the French Revolution and ended by destroying all "objective norms." Thus, modern man finds himself facing, together with Nietzsche, a stark choice: "According to Nietzsche, the theoretical analysis of human life that realizes the relativity of all comprehensive views and thus deprecates them would make human life itself impossible, for it would destroy the protecting atmosphere within which life or culture or action is alone possible." To avert that danger, Strauss continued, "Nietzsche could choose one of two ways: he could insist on the strictly esoteric character of the theoretical analysis of life—that is, restore the Platonic notion of the noble delusion—or else he could deny the possibility of theory proper and so conceive of thought as essentially subservient to, or dependent on, life or fate."[23] Nietzsche himself might have known better, but all other moderns made the latter, wrong choice, opting for history, science, or even scholastic theology—unsatisfactory and unsatisfying alternatives inferior to the dangerous, harrowing, lonely, difficult, but ultimately rewarding life of genuine philosophy, the search for the eternal, unchanging truth.[24]

The fourth and final distinction, between Athens and Jerusalem, is more subtle. Much as Strauss claimed to prefer Jacobi to Spinoza, and Maimonides to later moderate Jews who tried to assimilate to modernity, and much as he embraced Jewish communities that would always be inassimilable and persecuted, he never renounced his own atheism. Strauss could not believe in God, but he appreciated the reasons why fellow atheists such as Plato tolerated, or even prized, religious faith: it stabilized society for unthinking nonphilosophers. Strauss particularly admired those Jewish philosophers such as Maimonides who embedded their ideas in esoteric writing to keep from unsettling the authority of the rabbis and the simpleminded religious faith of ordinary people. The tension between the lure of reason in classical philosophy (Athens) and the power of genuine belief (Jerusalem) remained the single acknowledged unreconciled problem in Strauss's writing. If we cannot find the answers to our questions in science or modern philosophy, can we find them in biblical religion? Strauss was ambivalent. The craze for scholasticism cannot help; neo-Thomism offers only the false comfort of dogma. But in the deeper mysteries of theology, somewhere beyond the consolation of familiar rabbinic teachings and the deeper mysteries of Kabbalah, might lie a genuine and perhaps even compelling alternative not only to modernity but to classical rationalism. The ancients too had puzzled over the problem of piety, and all the most profound thinkers, from Socrates and Plato to Maimonides and Alfarabius (and, at least by implication, to Strauss himself), pondered the question of embracing religious faith. Strauss's invocation of "return" in his lectures in the 1950s at the University of Chicago's Hillel House seems to point less toward a renewed classical natural right than toward what Thomas Pangle, one of Strauss's most avid followers and among his most perceptive interpreters, calls "the precondition for true progress, human reverence and humility," which may in turn be the "precondition for the discovery of true human dignity; a certain sense of homelessness may be the precondition for true homecoming."[25] I will return to this problem in my conclusion.

Those four distinctions not only convey Strauss's central ideas, but also indicate the most prominent of the targets on which his critics have concentrated their fire. From the first reviews to the most recent denunciations, Strauss has attracted spirited attacks, a feature of his writings that his defenders interpret—much as Strauss himself did—as irrefutable evidence of his wisdom and his critics' wrongheadedness. Strauss never bothered to situate his interpretations in the scholarly literature or to locate the texts he studied in their historical contexts. He did not care much about his contemporaries in the community of scholars or about what meanings earlier readers might have taken from the writers he studied. His concept of esoteric writing—applied initially to those he studied and eventually to his own production as well—provided him an all-purpose escape hatch from any criticism. From Strauss's perspective, those who disagreed with him simply lacked the intelligence, the integrity, the insight, the erudition, or the persistence to read with sufficient care. According to his critics, Strauss's method showed his monumental arrogance and authorized his virtuoso performances of willful misreading.

Finally, and most maddening of all, Strauss never felt compelled to advance arguments on behalf of the idea of natural right he found in the ancient philosophers he most admired. He considered their superiority self-evident and their meaning accessible enough for those inclined and equipped to study them as he did.[26] "I *really* believe," he wrote in a letter to the German historian of ideas Karl Löwith in 1946, "that the perfect political order, as Plato and Aristotle have sketched it, *is* the perfect political order."[27] Or as Strauss expressed his animating conviction in 1963: "Philosophy in the strict and classical sense is [the] quest for the eternal order or for the eternal cause or causes of all things. It presupposes then that there is an eternal and unchangeable order within which

History takes place and which is not in any way affected by History."[28] If we are to take these statements of his convictions not as examples of esoteric writing to be decoded but at face value, as his students and followers urge us to do, they signal clearly Strauss's unshakable attachment to his understanding of the ideals of Plato and Aristotle and to his understanding of their conceptions of philosophy, politics, and the world. But it is striking—and bewildering—that Strauss never deigned to explain either how to reconcile the obvious disagreements among the ancients he revered or the reasons why anyone else should agree with him about the enduring value of their ideas.

Strauss brought his extraordinary self-confidence with him when he arrived in New York City to teach at the New School for Social Research. In two lectures that he delivered there in 1941, he excoriated the methodological approaches of Marx, Weber, Dewey, Heidegger, Karl Mannheim, and Lenin—practically all the thinkers to whom his fellow faculty members had expressed their debts. Moreover, he faulted scholars on the left and right alike for failing to provide through sufficiently charismatic teaching the leadership that might have prevented German youth from falling under Hitler's spell. In short, not only were academics guilty of corrupting philosophy by succumbing to the lure of historicism; Strauss also charged them with facilitating Nazism.[29]

When Strauss arrived at the University of Chicago, he had done nothing to mask his contempt for most of the work being done there. His critiques of empirical social science, pragmatism, individualism, and neo-Thomism were well known. Whereas many mainstream social scientists interpreted Kelvin's command to "measure" as a warrant for value-free empirical research, Strauss offered an alternative to that approach: "Political things are by their nature subject to approval or disapproval, to choice and rejection, to praise and blame." Their "essence" is "not to be neutral but to raise a claim to men's obedience, allegiance, decision, or judgment." One cannot understand "political things," Strauss insisted, "if one does not measure them by some standard of goodness or justice. To judge soundly one must know the true standards. If political philosophy wishes to do justice to its subject matter, it must strive for genuine knowledge of these standards."[30] From Strauss's vantage point, meager and unsatisfactory indeed were the measurements generated by scholarship not grounded on the bedrock of classical philosophy.

The "ritual" that social scientists called "methodology" or "logic" blinded them to their responsibilities. "While the new political science becomes ever less able to see democracy or to hold a mirror to democracy," Strauss warned, "it ever more reflects the most dangerous proclivities of democracy," its tendency toward the least common denominator of the herd. "By teaching in effect the equality of literally all desires," empirical political science "teaches in effect that there is nothing of which a man ought to be ashamed." By thus "destroying the possibility of self-contempt, it destroys" even "the possibility of self-respect." By leveling all values, "by denying that there are things which are intrinsically high and others which are intrinsically low," political science "unwittingly contributes to the victory of the gutter."[31] Such charges echoed the worries of Tocqueville, Mill, and Arnold in the nineteenth century and paralleled other anxieties being expressed in the 1940s and 1950s by critics of mass culture on the left and the right. But both his shrill tone and his unapologetic declaration of indebtedness to the truths of ancient wisdom differentiated Strauss's arguments from those issued by other critics of democracy.

During the eighteen years Strauss was at Chicago, American culture changed in ways he either did not recognize or refused to acknowledge in his writing. By 1967, when Strauss reached age sixty-five, his relentless denunciations of his scholarly colleagues, academic culture, and liberal democracy had worn down the forbearance of the administration of the university. As was the case at Brandeis University, where the equally tireless German émigré Herbert Marcuse was continuing to launch from the left his own denunciations of American democracy, spirited efforts by the old men's allies did not save them from being forced to retire. Marcuse headed west, to the lotusland of La Jolla, California, where he briefly became the darling of leftist rebels. Strauss continued teaching the ancient texts he revered, within the rigorous curriculum of St. John's, Annapolis, until his death in 1973. From the left and from the right, drawing on insights from early Marx and Freud, and from Aristotle and Maimonides, these two lonely voices kept calling on social scientists and political philosophers to return to the questions of value bracketed by mainstream social science. Outside the academy Marcuse and Strauss were sometimes heralded as prophets. Most scholars working within their own disciplines dismissed them as embarrassing cranks and got on with the serious work of measuring empirical data.

WHAT HAS HAPPENED to the distinct challenges that Köhler, Gilson, and Strauss presented in the middle decades of the twentieth century? Although certain insights from the Gestaltists were to resurface later on the fringes of cognitive psychology, in the developmental psychology of Jean Piaget and his followers, and in the "humanistic psychology" of the 1960s, the discipline as a whole has continued to move in the direction of behaviorism. Finding funds for behavioral studies is easier, in part because their results can be measured and thus characterized more plausibly as science, and in part because such research is prestructured according to the instruments of control sought by an expert society.[32] For a variety of reasons, psychology as a discipline rarely examines the issues of consciousness or values central to the inquiries of the Gestaltists. The questions that once brought together philosophers and psychologists are rarely asked outside the fields of developmental or educational psychology. When they are, the answers tend to come from cognitive scientists such as Daniel Dennett or Arthur Zeman, who think in terms of parallel processors or electroencephalographic measurements of neural activities rather than the experience of awareness or the phenomenology of volition.[33] Reflective undergraduates intrigued by such issues are gently steered from psychology toward philosophy. There they encounter courses in logic and linguistic analysis often taught by technicians who shrug that value statements describe emotional states outside the purview of serious philosophy.[34] Not surprisingly, such students sometimes wind up in cultural studies, where their passionate engagement is "validated" (if not always heightened or deepened), or, more often, they leave the world of scholarship altogether. Paradoxically, in recent decades the concern of Gestalt psychology with meanings and frameworks has reentered academic life through a series of side doors, largely as a result of work done by scholars outside the disciplines of psychology and philosophy. This broader development has attracted considerable scholarly attention.[35]

Scholasticism too is not what it used to be. But if the Gestalt psychologists would be demoralized by the evaporation of their profession's interest in the questions that drove their investigations, Gilson might be even more surprised by what has happened to Catholic thought. The shift away from unquestioning allegiance to Thomas Aquinas was already apparent in the later work of Gilson's fellow French émigré Jacques Maritain, some of whose ruminations had carried him in the direction of Vatican II by the mid-1950s. The spirited exchange between Robert MacIver and John Courtney Murray, reported by John McGreevy in chapter 7 in this volume, indicates that the divide separating many Catholic thinkers from secular social scientists remained as wide in the early 1950s as it had been when Hutchins imported Aristotelians to save the University of Chicago from Kelvin's measuring sticks. Were Gilson's heirs, with their yearning for universal truth, then to be Strauss's allies? Not immediately, and certainly not all of them, for several reasons that merit consideration. First, when Strauss was passing through Paris on his way to England and eventually to the United States, the neo-Thomist Maritain was, with Alexandre Kojève, among the French intellectuals whom he encountered. At the time Maritain was already experimenting with the idea of a "Judeo-Christian tradition." He used the phrase in lectures delivered in Spain in 1934; in his book *Humanisme intégral* (1936) he was among the first scholars to identify the close relation between "Judeo-Christian values" and the concept of alienation advanced by Marx in the 1840s. The fact that Maritain had converted to

Catholicism from Protestantism and his beloved wife Raissa to Catholicism from Judaism no doubt played a part in broadening his sensibility. So too did the political convictions that led Maritain to admire Dorothy Day and the Catholic Worker movement, a progressive sensibility that prompted some observers to dub Maritain "the Catholic Marx" or, more aptly, "the Catholic Jaurès."[36]

But none of that ecumenical spirit impressed Strauss, for whom Judaism remained distinct from all forms of Christianity, and for whom philosophy, not theology, remained fundamental. From Strauss's perspective reason could provide no foundation for religious faith. For him scholasticism represented a retreat from philosophy into dogmatism. Using the concept of the "Judeo-Christian tradition," he observed, served only "to blur and to conceal grave differences. Cultural pluralism can only be had, it seems, at the price of blunting all edges."[37] Strauss preferred to keep his edges sharp.

So too did those on both sides of another divide that widened in the late 1930s, the divide between pragmatism, allied with science, and religion, which despite Strauss's grumbling came increasingly to mean just such an undifferentiated "Judeo-Christian tradition." Maritain was widely admired in Catholic circles as a neo-Thomist scholar, but unlike Gilson he wrote as much about contemporary issues as he did about medieval culture. His prominence drew the attention of Hutchins, who tried three times to recruit him to Chicago. Hutchins wanted Maritain as a counterbalance to the university's prevailing tendencies toward either Dewey's pragmatism or Carnap's logical positivism. For precisely that reason Chicago's philosophers objected to appointing a man they considered an "absolutist" and a "propagandist" rather than a scholar.[38]

Similar mutual antagonism marred the efforts of Adler, the conservative rabbi Amos Finkelstein, and the Harvard astronomer Harlow Shapley to convene a national conference to air, and perhaps resolve, the tensions among science, philosophy, and religion. The conference organizers, following the architecture suggested in Maritain's *The Degree of Knowledge* (1922), conceived of knowledge ascending from a solid base of empirical science to the intermediate stage of metaphysics and finally culminating at the pinnacle of religious faith. The conference they had in mind would ratify Maritain's conception of science as subservient to philosophy, and both as subservient to religion. But Adler, typically, poisoned the proceedings even before they could begin. He demanded that the conference "repudiate the scientism or positivism which dominates every aspect of modern culture." Lest there be any misunderstanding, he insisted that "religious knowledge, because supernaturally generated, must be superior to philosophy and science as merely natural knowledge." MacIver replied that Adler's demands would end inquiry before it began and thus prevent the "exploration" that Shapley offered as the purpose of the gathering. When the conference convened at New York's Jewish Theological Seminary in September 1940, Adler's paper "God and the Professors" picked up where Adler had left off when he was an undergraduate at Columbia. "Democracy has much more to fear from the mentality of its teachers," Adler wrote, "than from the nihilism of Hitler." Without firm religious foundations, he warned, American culture would crumble. Adler's listeners had no trouble identifying Dewey, America's premier teacher, and his naturalist allies as Adler's chief targets. Maritain, striking a more moderate tone, spoke in support of the idea that "experimental science" should not be taken as "the supreme standard of thought."

The philosophers Sidney Hook and Horace Kallen, Dewey's and James's bulldogs, returned fire immediately. Both Hook and Kallen remained engaged for the next three years as successive conferences debated the relative merits of pragmatism and religion and their affinities with democracy, which champions of both camps claimed as their own. Dewey himself, although invited by Finkelstein to participate in the discussions, refused on the grounds that naturalists should not be forced to subordinate their own worldview to that of religious apologists—as had happened in the opening session of the conference in 1940. Kallen's public presentations and his correspondence revealed his deep-seated distrust of Catholicism: ever since Al Smith's 1928 presidential campaign, the "totalitarian intent of the church has been extraordinarily aggressive and activist."[39] Kallen, usually heralded as one of the leading champions of cultural pluralism, had come a long way from James's celebration of the varieties of religious experience. That distance testified to the ways in which the international and cultural tensions of the late 1930s and early 1940s widened the rift between naturalists—including most pragmatists, empirical social scientists, and professional philosophers—and defenders of the new triple alliance of Protestant, Catholic, and Jewish leaders grouped beneath the rubric of the "Judeo-Christian tradition." Despite the depth and significance of that gap, however, another divide was beginning to emerge that would cut across and partially obscure it.

Evidence of that new rift appears in the different trajectories of Strauss and Maritain in the 1950s. Strauss, although as impatient with Catholic dogmatism as he was with value-free social science, nevertheless lamented the consequences of the decline of religious observance. Much as Strauss loathed the notion that philosophy should bow to religion, as Adler and Maritain both believed it should, he admitted that faith could keep ordinary people from interfering in matters beyond their understanding. When religion declined, culture suffered. As he put it, since we now read the morning paper instead of saying the morning prayer, we face a crisis: "Not every day the same thing, the same reminder of man's absolute duty and exalted destiny"—the stuff of religious practice—"but everyday something new with no reminder of duty and exalted destiny." Modern man has lost his moorings. He is drowning in "specialization, knowing more and more about less and less; the practical impossibility of concentration upon the very few essential things upon which man's wholeness entirely depends." He tries to compensate for that specialization with "sham universality, by the stimulation of all kinds of interests and curiosities without true passion." In short, although Strauss did not draw this connection, we moderns face precisely the threat that Tocqueville and Weber as well as Nietzsche feared, "the danger of universal philistinism and creeping conformism."[40]

Maritain, by contrast, was moving in the direction that the Catholic Church as a whole would take in the aftermath of Vatican II. Rather than insisting on the distance between faith and knowledge, or between the afterlife and this life, Maritain became increasingly adamant about applying the principles of Christianity to the problems of society and politics. He conceded that "supernatural faith does not provide us with any particular social or political system," but he insisted that the fundamental Christian doctrine of the equality of all of God's children provided the strongest foundation for the democratic ideals to which the United States was committed as a nation.[41] In a nod to Dewey's conception of a "common faith," he conceded that people could share the same commitment to justice even though they grounded it on different philosophical premises: "The point we are again stressing is that this faith and inspiration, and the concept of itself which democracy needs—all these do not belong to the order of religious creed and eternal life, but to the temporal or secular order of earthly life, of culture or civilization. The *faith* in question is a *civic* or *secular* faith." Although religious believers would continue to base their political thinking on their religious faith, they should be able to ally with secular people who share their commitment to "truth and intelligence, human dignity, freedom, brotherly love, and the absolute value of moral good." Such allies should be able to reach agreement, Maritain wrote, on a "democratic charter" that would include a long list of ideals, a list that might seem banal to most readers today but was hardly that among Catholics in 1951. Maritain included, among many other ideals, "political rights and liberties, social rights and liberties, corresponding responsibilities," "mutual rights and duties of groups and the State; government of the people, by the people, and for the people; functions of authority in a political and social democracy," "human equality, justice between persons and the body politic," and, finally, "civil friendship and an ideal of fraternity, religious freedom, mutual tolerance and mutual respect between various spiritual communities and schools of thought."[42] Few French Catholics endorsed such ideas so enthusiastically a decade before Vatican II.

Not only did Maritain commit himself to the ideals of democracy, equality, and pluralism, but he also argued that just as those who challenged social hierarchy were considered heretics in the Middle Ages, so "in a lay society of free men the heretic is the breaker of the 'common democratic beliefs and practices,' the one who takes a stand against freedom, or against the basic equality of men."[43] He singled out and explicitly renounced Aristotle's conception of static social orders and his exclusion of ordinary people from participation in public life as antithetical to the democratic creed. The mid-twentieth-century heretic, in other words, was an unrepentant Aristotelian such as Leo Strauss.

In stark contrast to Dewey and to Maritain, Strauss did believe in hierarchy. In equally stark contrast, he denied that his classical political ideal could ever be realized in practice. For that reason he advised those committed to the pursuit of truth that they should separate themselves from the affairs of the polis. All the great philosophers of the past had learned a hard lesson from the death of Socrates: the masses will neither understand nor appreciate your quest for truth. If you persist, and if you let the common people know what you are doing, you will be persecuted. Philosophers should instead withdraw into esoteric writing. They should take refuge behind a veil that masks their dangerous ideas from all but those few brave souls with the intelligence and courage to become disciples.[44] Philosophers, Strauss insisted, should devote themselves to the heroic quest for unchanging truth, which is to be found, as Strauss put it in the letter to Löwith already quoted, in the proper understanding of Plato and Aristotle. Strauss proclaimed himself friendly to liberal democracy—although his admission that he could not flatter it might be taken as a hint to his deeper readers—yet his concept of eternal natural right was essentially inconsistent with the principles of equality, toleration, mutual respect, and popular sovereignty that Maritain and Dewey both offered as the heart of an open-ended and experimental culture of democracy.

When American Catholic culture left its seclusion and wholeheartedly embraced the civic ideals of American democracy after World War II, the most virulent forms of American anti-Catholicism began to wane. When the vision of Catholicism that emerged from Vatican II began to attract increasing numbers of Catholics, and when their commitment to transforming their church began to antagonize those who remained committed to its older traditions of isolation, hierarchy, and obedience, the American Catholic Church, previously divided along ethnic lines but more or less united on doctrine and practice, ruptured. Millions of ecumenically inclined post–Vatican II Catholics made common cause with Reform Judaism and the denominations of liberal Protestantism, while more conservative Catholics went looking in other directions for the stability and serenity they missed. Many such disgruntled Catholics turned toward the idea of natural law, and some believed that Strauss's classical political rationalism could offer them a philosophical home.

Some of Strauss's own writings about religion seem to suggest grounds for such an alliance. From the time of his early critique of Spinoza's naturalism and his appreciation of Maimonides' rationalism, Strauss portrayed the rabbinical and Christian traditions of biblical hermeneutics as the opposite of genuine religion just as he portrayed positivist science as the opposite of genuine philosophy. Strauss thought that revelation must provide believers with bedrock truths as unchanging as the truth of natural law. But like his account of philosophy, his account of religion provoked spirited criticism. As Strauss's contemporary Simon Rawidowicz argued in his essay "On Interpretation," the rabbinic tradition put at the center of Judaism a series of intersubjectively established understandings of scripture. Rather than a unitary truth revealed once and for all, a truth grasped immediately by reason, Rawidowicz identified an unstable and unfolding tradition of interpretations. Just as Strauss rejected the practice of empirical philosophy, which he saw as a pathetic and futile denial of ancient wisdom, so he rejected the practice of biblical hermeneutics. But in both cases his uneasiness with doubt exposed him as a captive of the post-Cartesian obsession with certainty that he excoriated when he saw it in the modern philosophers of science and naturalism. Strauss rejected the alternative that his bêtes noires, Rousseau, Weber, James, and Dewey, embraced, the possibility that uncertainty might prove fruitful rather than sterile. If truths are discursively generated and admittedly provisional, they lack the grandeur Strauss sought in philosophy. But in light of Strauss's late admission of his own uncertainties about the relation between religion and philosophy, an admission I will discuss in my conclusion, and in light of his final denial that there was a rational basis for choosing between the claims of faith as he understood it and the claims of reason, the confidence of many of his followers that they could make common cause with conservative Christians—and vice versa—seems misplaced.[45]

AT THEIR LEAST convincing, Strauss and his students sometimes resemble the pre–Vatican II Catholic Church: inward-looking, cultish, ritualistic, dogmatic, authoritarian, and convinced they have access to a truth known to them alone. And at our most intemperate, we critics of Strauss and his followers can resemble the conspiracy-mongering anti-Catholics of the 1930s and 1940s (mea culpa). If the dynamic of inclusion drew Catholics out of their parochialism and into the broader culture and drove the most fanatical of their foes to control their paranoia, might a similar dynamic lead more Straussians and anti-Straussians, and perhaps other scholarly antagonists, to moderate their claims and counterclaims?[46] Does it matter?

The stakes for the twenty-first century remain high. Nationally, enrollments in nonrequired courses in the humanities and the discursive social sciences are shrinking. Students today have urgent questions. Do humanists and social theorists have any answers? A look back to the middle third of the twentieth century suggests that international tensions can poison academic discourse, and the implications of the recent return to prominence of Straussian ways of thinking and talking can hardly encourage those of us still stuck in the second cave. As the resurgence of interest in Strauss should remind us, in times of perceived crisis Americans have frequently turned to the rock-hard principles of patriotism and xenophobia. Strauss is back in vogue in part because he claimed to know the eternal and unchanging truth. Do we in the academy who criticize Strauss have any convincing alternatives to offer students who ask why they should believe us and not him? Many observers have noted that the dynamic of inclusion in American academic life has operated in such a way that the very ideals that drove it, tolerance of diversity and the celebration of pluralism, the ideals that Gilson accurately attributed to William James and Ralph Barton Perry, have undercut our confidence in the ideas of universal reason and human dignity. If all knowledge has become suspect, if all our inquiries now seek to unmask power and empower the dispossessed, then it is understandable that students wonder why they should bother with the humanities and discursive social sciences instead of simply learning how to wield power themselves once they leave school.

In 1945, when Harvard rethought its curriculum at the behest of President James Conant and issued *General Education in a Free Society*, the Red Book, which sold more than forty thousand copies and helped shape secondary and higher education for a generation, its authors invoked the idea of a "coherent national culture" that was "not wholly of the new world since it came from the old," and "not wholly given to innovation since it acknowledges certain fixed beliefs." Nor was this national sensibility "wholly a law unto itself," since Americans concede "there are principles above the state." Among the "intangibles of the American spirit" the report sought to incorporate were "the ideal of co-operation on the level of action irrespective of agreement on ultimates—which is to say, belief in the worth and meaning of the human spirit, however one may understand it." Harvard committed itself to teaching "the place of human aspirations and ideals in the total scheme of things."[47]

Reading language of that sort today makes many scholars cringe. We distrust coherence, fixed beliefs, principles, ideals, ultimates, aspirations, and loose talk about "the human spirit." Yet the culture outside our universities is saturated with such talk, and many of our best students hunger for it. Meanwhile, we busy ourselves making our humanistic studies ever more particularist and historicist, and our philosophical and social scientific studies ever more bloodless and abstract. Professional pressures can be difficult to resist.

Despite the best efforts of analytic philosophers and value-free social scientists, however, and against the odds, all three of the unconventional challenges to mainstream academic culture discussed in this chapter have survived. First, interpretive or hermeneutical strands of inquiry descended from or reminiscent of Gestalt psychology persist in anthropology, history, and sociology, and even on the fringes of some first-rate departments of economics, psychology, and political science.[48] Second, Christian moral theologians, although less likely to invoke Gilson or Maritain then Curran or Küng, have created a thriving field, with contributions coming from women as well as men, and from the southern as well as the northern hemisphere. Amid the cacophony of world Christianity some believers perceive reasons for hope concerning the future of their faith, despite the gloomy prospects facing the state churches of northern Europe.[49] Third, and finally, Strauss's brand of Aristotelianism continues to attract ardent adherents uncowed by the persistent ridicule they face in scholarly circles. The appeal of the idea of eternal truth appears to have considerable staying power.[50] None of these rival discourses occupies a place in the academic mainstream; none has routed its foes. Yet all three persist, and I think they are here to stay. Why?

Strauss's most arresting and surprising ideas, I believe, appeared in a series of talks he gave for Jewish audiences in the Hillel House at the University of Chicago in the late 1950s. Consideration of those talks will lead to my conclusion. "Philosophy in its original and full sense," he contended, "is certainly incompatible with the Biblical way of life. Philosophy and the Bible are the alternatives, or the antagonists in the drama of the human soul. Each of the two antagonists claims to know or to hold the truth, the decisive truth, the truth regarding the right way of life." Although Strauss did not frame the inquiry in this way, from our perspective fifty years later I think we could add to his account of this struggle between Aristotle and the Bible two further contenders, the philosophy profession dominated by descendents of Carnap and Quine and the social and behavioral sciences pursued under the aegis of Kelvin and within William James Hall. Imagine then, in place of Strauss's battle between religion and philosophy, a four-way tussle. Yet, in Strauss's words, "there can be only one truth: hence, conflict between these claims, and necessarily conflict among thinking beings; and that means, inevitably, argument."

No independent, objective way to resolve this central disagreement exists, according to Strauss, because believers and nonbelievers alike invoke their own experience as irrefutable evidence to validate their claims. Since both sides must concede at least the possibility that the other might be right, even "the choice of philosophy," just as much as the choice of religion, "is based on faith. In other words, the quest for evident knowledge rests itself on an unevident premise. And it seems to me that this difficulty underlies all present-day philosophizing, and that it is this difficulty which is at the bottom of what in the social sciences is called the value problem: that philosophy or science, however you call it, is incapable of giving an account of its own necessity." Neither William James nor Max Weber could have put it better. Indeed, it was precisely the problem they identified at the heart of modernity, although Strauss conveniently neglected to acknowledge the perceptiveness of their analysis when addressing his audience at Hillel House.

Strauss resisted the impulse to decide such matters according to any consensus reached by the appropriate communities of inquiry, or according to consequences, as pragmatists or utilitarians might do, because he judged the consequences of both natural science and social science ambiguous at best and disastrous—"in the age of the hydrogen bomb"—at worst. He did concede, however, that this inescapable "antagonism" must be worked out "by us in action. That is to say: it seems to me that the core, the nerve, of Western intellectual history, Western spiritual history, one could almost say, is the conflict between the Biblical and the philosophic notions of the good life"—and, I would add, also between the visions offered by their competitors from twentieth-century logic and empirical social science. Acknowledging the inescapability of this conflict, Strauss admitted in a rare understatement, is "at first, a very disconcerting observation," especially within the framework of Strauss's own ambitious claims for classical rationalism. But there is nevertheless "something reassuring and comforting about it," he continued, because the "very life of Western civilization is the life between two codes, a fundamental tension."

Strauss's closing words strike a chord that should reverberate as we reflect on the status of the humanities today, on the dynamic of inclusion in the humanities, and on the consequences of that dynamic for ourselves and our students: "This comforting thought is justified only if we live that life, if we live that conflict. No one can be both a philosopher and a theologian, nor, for that matter, some possibility which transcends the conflict between philosophy and theology, or pretends to be a synthesis of both." There will be no via media here. "But every one of us can be and ought to be one or the other, the philosopher open to the challenge of theology or the theologian open to the challenge of philosophy."[51]

In the end even Strauss, among the most vociferous proponents of the idea of unchanging natural right in the twentieth century, was forced to face the stark choice imposed by the world's disenchantment. He had to concede that his choice—every individual's choice—is ultimately a leap of faith. After all the abuse Strauss had heaped on James and Weber, there is something uncanny about his own return to the existential dilemma that sparked their best writing in such essays as James's brilliant "On a Certain Blindness in Human Beings" and Weber's haunting "Politics as a Vocation." There is also something bracing, and perhaps even inspiring, about Strauss's advice to leave ourselves open to the challenges posed by the options we decide not to choose. Whether one leaps in the direction of Kelvin's measurements or Carnap's logic, or in response to Köhler's *Gestaltist* valuings or Gilson's scholasticism or Maritain's ecumenism, in the direction of Strauss's own concept of unchanging natural right, or in the direction of any other ideas or ideals, it is not possible to avoid choosing any more than James, or Weber, or Strauss himself could avoid it. Kelvin to the contrary notwithstanding, every measurement we make in the *Geisteswissenschaften* depends on qualitative judgments that we should face directly rather than trying to evade. All the chapters in this volume show how the *Geisteswissenschaften* and the range of people involved in such studies have broadened in recent decades. Were the scope of the questions we ask to shrink at the conclusion of those processes of expansion and inclusion, that result would be not only ironic but tragic. Studying the questions of value at the heart of the humanities and discursive social sciences remains worth the effort because it can help us, and because it can help our students, see more clearly and judge more perceptively the nature of the problems and the cultural rewards and the collective costs of the choices we make among the options we face. If we can persuade those we teach—and if we ourselves concede—that the unchanging truth that Ogburn tried to derive from Kelvin and that Strauss sought in Plato will elude us forever, we might enable our students to find through rigorous humanistic inquiry the resources they will need to answer for themselves James's urgent, perennial question: "What Makes a Life Significant?"[52]

Notes

1. The quotation attributed to Kelvin actually appears on the Social Science Research Building with elegant rosettes situated where ellipses belong. The full passage reads: "When you can measure what you are speaking about and express it in numbers, you know something about it; but when you cannot measure it, when you cannot express it in numbers your knowledge of it is of a meager and unsatisfactory kind." A more accurate rendering here would therefore be "When you cannot measure . . . your knowledge is . . . meager . . . and . . . unsatisfactory." In that form, however,

the words not only lack the force they communicate when seen on the building itself, they mock the message it conveys. Thus, "When you cannot measure*your knowledge is*meager*and*unsatisfactory" comes closer to reproducing the effect Ogburn and the architects sought. Jacob Viner spoke for several dissenters on the Chicago faculty when he quipped, "And if you can measure . . . your knowledge will still be meager and unsatisfactory." For information on the Social Science Research Building I am grateful to conversations and correspondence with Professor William Novak of the University of Chicago Department of History and to current faculty members of the Committee on Social Thought, who discussed these issues with me when I visited Chicago in February 2004, to deliver the John U. Nef lecture. Further information on Ogburn's role in designing the building and the controversy surrounding its decoration is available in the Ogburn Papers at the University of Chicago; Barry Karl, *Charles E. Merriam and the Study of Politics* (Chicago: University of Chicago Press, 1974); Mark C. Smith, *Social Science in the Crucible: The American Debate over Objectivity and Purpose, 1918–1941* (Durham: Duke University Press, 1994); and Mark C. Smith, "A Tale of Two Charlies: Political Science, History, and Civic Reform," in *Historicizing Politics: Anglo-American Approaches to Political Science since 1900*, ed. Robert Adcock, Mark Bevir, and Shannon Stimson (Princeton: Princeton University Press, forthcoming).

2. Hutchins quoted in Milton Mayer, *Robert Maynard Hutchins: A Memoir*, ed. John H. Hicks (Berkeley: University of California Press, 1993), 90.

3. On Hutchins's attempt to appoint Adler and the response of Tufts and Mead, see Irene Tufts Mead's interview with Lloyd E. Stein, reported in "Hutchins of Chicago: Philosopher-Administrator" (Ph.D. diss., University of Massachusetts, 1971), 99–101; and Mayer, *Robert Maynard Hutchins*, 120–126. For Adler's account of his run-in with Dewey, see Mortimer Adler, *Philosopher at Large* (New York: Macmillan, 1977), 49.

4. Rudolf Carnap, *Philosophy and Logical Syntax* (London: Kegan Paul, 1935), reprinted in *The American Intellectual Tradition*, vol. 2, *1865 to the Present*, ed. David A. Hollinger and Charles Capper, 2nd ed. (New York; Oxford University Press, 1993), 253; see also Carnap, "Intellectual Biography," in *The Philosophy of Rudolf Carnap*, ed. Paul A. Schilpp (LaSalle, Ill.: Open Court, 1963), 36. For overviews, see Bruce Kuklick, *Philosophy in America: A Cultural and Intellectual History* (New York: Oxford University Press, 2001); and his essay in this volume, "Philosophy and Inclusion in the United States, 1929–2001" (chap. 6).

5. On divisions within literature, a good place to begin is M. H. Abrams, "The Transformation of English Studies, 1930–1995," in "American Academic Culture in Transformation: Fifty Years, Four Disciplines," ed. Thomas Bender, *Daedalus* 126 (Winter 1997): 105–131.

6. A great deal has been written about the role of European émigrés in twentieth-century American thought. Since several of the contributors to this volume have done distinguished work on many of these thinkers—particularly Martin Jay on the Frankfurt School—it would be pointless for me to focus on those who have already been subjected to close scrutiny. My reasons for choosing instead the less familiar Köhler and Gilson, and the all-too-familiar Strauss, will, I hope, become apparent.

7. Perry's review of Koffka, *The Growth of the Mind: An Introduction to Child-Psychology*, trans. Robert M. Ogden (New York: Harcourt, Brace, 1924), and of Köhler, *The Mentality of Apes*, trans. Ella Winter (New York: Harcourt, Brace, 1925), is quoted in Michael E. Sokal, "The Gestalt Psychologists in Behaviorist America," *American Historical Review* 89 (1984): 1240–1263; the quotation is on pp. 1245–1246. More comprehensive accounts of the Gestaltists in Germany and the reception of their ideas in the United States include Mitchell G. Ash, *Gestalt Psychology in German Culture, 1890–1967: Holism and the Quest for Objectivity* (Cambridge: Cambridge University Press, 1995); Anne Harrington, *Reenchanted Science: Holism and German Science from Wilhelm II to Hitler* (Princeton: Princeton University Press, 1996); Mitchell G. Ash, "Emigré Psychologists after 1933: The Cultural Coding of Scientific and Professional Practices," in *Forced Migration and Scientific Change: Emigré German-Speaking Scientists and Scholars after 1933*, ed. Mitchell G. Ash and Alfons Söllner (Cambridge: Cambridge University Press,

1996), 117–138; and Katherine Pandora, *Rebels within the Ranks: Psychologists' Critique of Scientific Authority and Democratic Realities in New Deal America* (Cambridge: Cambridge University Press, 1997).

8. Edward Boring to Kurt Koffka, April 20, 1925, quoted in Sokal, "The Gestalt Psychologists in Behaviorist America," 1246.

9. Frederick Lund, "The Phantom of the Gestalt," *Journal of General Psychology* 2 (1929): 307–323. See also F. M. Greeg, "Materializing the Ghost of Köhler's Gestalt Psychology," *Psychological Review* 39 (1932): 257–270.

10. Arthur Liebert, writing in the *Philosophical Review* 44 (1935): 24–45, concluded a survey of recent German work in the fields of epistemology, value, and ontology, an article paying respectful attention to thinkers ranging from Heidegger to the neo-Kantians, with the following sentences: "It should be observed, however, that in these works the concept of *Gestalt* is no longer taken in a merely critical sense as a methodological or heuristic principle but is accepted as a genuine form of reality. . . . Of this development we have offered here merely a few noteworthy examples. The account might be, indeed should be, extended, especially by enumerating works from the *Gestalt* psychology, so fruitfully developed by Wolfgang Köhler and Max Wertheimer. With justice, this psychology is widely known and highly valued in the United States" (45).

11. Wolfgang Köhler, *The Place of Value in a World of Facts* (New York: Liveright, 1938), 100.

12. Edwin Boring to Leonard Carmichael, December 20, 1934, quoted in Sokal, "The Gestalt Psychologists in Behaviorist America," 1261.

13. Samuel Eliot Morison, "Harvard Celebrates, 1636–1936," *New York Times Magazine*, September 13, 1936, section 7, pp. 1, 2, 24.

14. Gilson's remarks, reported in *Time*, September 28, 1936, 22–26, are quoted in Morton Keller and Phyllis Keller, *Making Harvard Modern* (New York: Oxford University Press, 2001), 9.

15. On the efforts made to persuade Catholic donors that Harvard was receptive to scholasticism, see Bruce Kuklick, *The Rise of American Philosophy: Cambridge, Massachusetts, 1860–1930* (New Haven: Yale University Press, 1977), 455. On anti-Catholicism, see John McGreevy, *Catholicism and American Freedom: A History* (New York: W. W. Norton, 2003); and McGreevy's contribution to this volume, "Catholics, Catholicism, and the Humanities since World War II" (chap. 7).

16. Etienne Gilson, *The Unity of Philosophical Experience* (New York: Charles Scribner's Sons, 1941), viii–ix. On the crucial role played by Quine in reorienting American philosophy toward a conception attuned to natural science and averse to questions of metaphysics and ethics, see Joel Isaac, "W. V. Quine and the Origins of Analytic Philosophy in the United States," *Modern Intellectual History* 2, no. 2 (2005): 205–234.

17. Gilson, *The Unity of Philosophical Experience*, 293–296, 306–307, 319–320.

18. For Strauss's withering critique of "general education" and the great books conceived as "a machine, or an industry," see his *Liberalism Ancient and Modern* (Chicago: University of Chicago Press, 1968), 23–25.

19. Conyers Read to John U. Nef, October 29, 1936, John U. Nef Papers, University of Chicago Regenstein Library, cited in Eugene Sheppard, "Leo Strauss and the Politics of Exile" (Ph.D. diss., University of California at Los Angeles, 2001), 111.

20. Tawney to Nef, March 17, 1942, Nef Papers, quoted in S. J. D. Green, "The Tawney-Strauss Connection: On Historicism and Values in the History of Political Ideas," *Journal of Modern History* 67 (1995): 264.

21. Nef to W. V. Morgenstern, March 21, 1939, quoted in Green, "The Tawney-Strauss Connection," 275; and Tawney, *Religion and the Rise of Capitalism* (London: J. Murray, 1926), 285. To compound the irony, two of Strauss's other patrons were the British political theorist Ernst Barker and the socialist Harold Laski. See Gunnell, *The Descent of Political Theory*, 176.

22. Leo Strauss, *Persecution and the Art of Writing* (Glencoe, Ill.: Free Press, 1952), 155–156. My understanding of Strauss's ideas derives from reading his work and from a number of intel-

ligent critical commentaries, the most lucid of which, in my view, is Robert B. Pippin, "The Modern World of Leo Strauss," originally published in *Political Theory* 20 (1992): 448–472, and reprinted in *Hannah Arendt and Leo Strauss: German Emigrés and American Political Thought after World War II*, ed. Peter Graf Kielmansegg, Horst Mewes, and Elisabeth Glaser-Schmidt (Cambridge: Cambridge University Press, 1995), 139–160. Another particularly clear account, unfortunately marred by its tendentiousness, is Thomas Pangle's introduction to Leo Strauss, *The Rebirth of Classical Rationalism: An Introduction to the Thought of Leo Strauss* (Chicago: University of Chicago Press, 1989), vii–xxxviii. Most scholarly treatments of Strauss, pro and con, require readers to penetrate a fog of polemical excesses that obscures his already murky ideas.

23. Leo Strauss, *Natural Right and History* (Chicago: University of Chicago Press, 1950), 1–26.

24. I will indicate only a few of the ways in which recent scholarship challenges the interpretations of modern theorists that Strauss advanced in *Natural Right and History*. Strauss indicted all social science for its simpleminded, unreflective empiricism, a characterization offered with greater sophistication (and no less invective) by several members of the Frankfurt School. His account depended on his characterization of the thought of Max Weber, "the greatest social scientist of our century," in which he flattened Weber's complex and subtle writings concerning the relation between ethical commitment and scholarly objectivity into a simple statement of ethical neutrality. See Strauss, *Natural Right and History*, 35–80; the quotation is from p. 36. I have discussed Weber's ideas on these issues in my *Uncertain Victory: Social Democracy and Progressivism in European and American Thought, 1870–1920* (New York: Oxford University Press, 1986), 331–346, and "Democracy and Disenchantment: From Weber and Dewey to Habermas and Rorty," in *The Virtues of Liberalism* (Oxford: Oxford University Press, 1998), 100–198.

Strauss conceded that his wildly unbalanced account of Locke as the theorist responsible for justifying unlimited property accumulation was shared only by the Marxist C. B. Macpherson; it is a view that few students of Locke since Peter Laslett and John Dunn in the mid-1960s have taken seriously. See Strauss, *Natural Right and History*, 202–251, and contrast his reading with two recent overviews of the literature on Locke and his significance in shaping American liberal democracy, Joshua Foa Dienstag, "Serving God and Mammon: The Lockean Sympathy in Early American Thought," *American Political Science Review* 90 (1996): 497–511, and Dienstag, "Between History and Nature: Social Contract Theory in Locke and the Founders, *Journal of Politics* 58 (1996): 985–1009; and with the recent study by Jeremy Waldron, *God, Locke, and Equality: Christian Foundations in Locke's Political Thought* (Cambridge: Cambridge University Press, 2002).

Strauss's readings of Rousseau, Kant, Hegel, and Marx, when viewed from the perspective of more thorough, less polemical, and more historically contextualized accounts, are no more convincing. See Strauss, *Natural Right and History*, 252–295, and compare the splendid survey of these issues, and the convincing demonstration of the inadequacy of Strauss's interpretations, in Pippin, "The Modern World of Leo Strauss." Multiplying such observations would be easy—and pointless. Strauss did not care what mere historians, or mere historians of philosophy or political theory, thought of his ideas, nor do his followers care now. His readings, attuned as they were to the eternal truth, allowed no room for dissent.

Given Strauss's own dogmatic self-assurance, there is something either comic or pathetic about his followers' inevitable squabbles (inevitable at least from the perspective of an intellectual historian committed to Dilthey's hermeneutics and a moderate historicism) about the proper way to understand his ideas and honor his achievements. For clear evidence of their disagreements, which demonstrate eloquently if unwittingly the folly of insisting on the possibility of providing interpretations true for all readers and all time, see the essays by his followers collected in John L. Deutsch and John A. Murley, eds., *Leo Strauss, the Straussians, and the American Regime* (Oxford: Rowman and Littlefield, 1999).

25. Pangle's Introduction to Strauss, *The Rebirth of Classical Political Rationalism*, xxxvii.

26. Samples of the critiques Strauss has attracted over several decades include the following. Strauss's fellow émigré Carl J. Friedrich, "Thomas Hobbes: Myth Builder of the Modern

State," *Journal of Social Philosophy* 3 (1938): 251–256, puzzled by Strauss's idiosyncratic reading of Hobbes, suggested that Strauss might turn out to be a "historical relativist" himself. The renowned classicist Gregory Vlastos, reviewing *On Tyranny* in the *Philosophical Review* 60 (1951): 592–594, observed that Strauss managed to misinterpret Socrates, Plato, and Xenophon, perhaps as a result of "his addiction to the strange notion that a historical understanding of a historical thinker is somehow a philosophical liability." The historian of political thought George H. Sabine, reviewing *Persecution and the Art of Writing* in *Ethics* 63 (1953): 220–222, observed that Strauss's reliance on an alleged distinction between exoteric writing for the vulgar and esoteric writing for the elite holds little attraction for historians, challenged the accuracy and coherence of Strauss's interpretation of Spinoza, and worried that Strauss's method provides a warrant for the cultivation and display of "perverse ingenuity." John Schaar and Sheldon Wolin, reviewing Herbert Storing, ed., *Essays on the Scientific Study of Politics*, a book that contains an epilogue in which Strauss advanced a stinging indictment of empirical social science, in the *American Political Science Review* 57 (1963): 125–150, detailed the problems raised by Strauss's "intemperate," "dogmatic" "polemic" and concluded by wondering what would happen if the profession of political science were to produce scholars actually forced to choose between the "two stark alternatives" Strauss laid out: "either a morally corrupt and intellectually sterile scientism or a version of political philosophy distinguished by moral fervor and an intellectual certainty that the essential nature of all political situations has been revealed long ago" (150).

Versions of most of the critiques directed against Strauss over the past fifty years are conveniently available in the relentless indictment by Shadia Drury, *The Political Ideas of Leo Strauss* (New York: St. Martin's Press, 1988), and in capsule form in Stephen Holmes's chapter "Strauss: Truths for Philosophers Alone," in his *The Anatomy of Antiliberalism* (Cambridge: Harvard University Press, 1993), 61–87. Two collections of inconsistent quality are Deutsch and Murley, *Leo Strauss, the Straussians, and the American Regime*, and Kielmansegg et al., *Hannah Arendt and Leo Strauss*. For an example of the restraint usually shown by Strauss's critics, consider this careful judgment by Drury, *Leo Strauss and the American Right*, 49: "Whenever Strauss examines the work of a great thinker, he invariably uncovers himself. Strauss's interpretations of Plato, Aristotle, Xenophon, Alfarabi, Averroes, Maimonides, and the other greats, tells us more about Strauss than about the thinkers in question. The point that Strauss wishes to impress upon us is that there can never be any disagreements among the wise on any matters of substance. And since his own teaching accords perfectly with ancient wisdom, its truth cannot be questioned, and anyone who dares to question it must be a fool. One thing for which Strauss deserves credit is his masterful use of the old argument from authority—something is true because the divine Plato says so. This is the subtle process of intimidation that is integral to a Straussian education." Thomas Pangle responds to Drury and some of Strauss's many other critics with similar equanimity in his Introduction to *The Rebirth of Classical Political Rationalism*, ix–xv.

27. Strauss to Karl Löwith, August 20, 1946, quoted in Sheppard, "Leo Strauss and the Politics of Exile," 177.

28. Strauss, "Restatement," a segment of his reply to Alexandre Kojève missing from the British version of *On Tyranny*, quoted by Laurence Berns with Eva Brann, "Leo Strauss at St. John's College (Annapolis)," in Deutsch and Murley, *Leo Strauss, the Straussians, and the American Regime*, 31–32.

29. On these lectures, entitled "Philosophy and Sociology of Knowledge" and "German Nihilism," see Sheppard, "Leo Strauss and the Politics of Exile," 164–166. Strauss elaborated his critique of Dewey's naturalism in a review of Dewey's *German Philosophy and Politics* published in *Social Research* in 1942; it is reprinted in Strauss, *What Is Political Philosophy?* (Chicago: University of Chicago Press, 1959), 279–281. Strauss chided Dewey for failing to recognize that the United States stands on the "absolute" rather than "experimental" foundation of unchanging, God-given, "unalienable rights." Strauss's charges concerning the dangers of relativism

resembled those that some American scholars were beginning to sling at Dewey—and at each other—at about the same time. See Edward Purcell, *The Crisis of Democratic Theory: Scientific Naturalism and the Problem of Value* (Lexington: University Press of Kentucky, 1973), 115–232. Two illuminating essays that contextualize Strauss's project by locating it between the competing styles of "epic" political theory (practiced principally by other German émigrés such as Hannah Arendt), on the one hand, and the behavioral theory of American political scientists such as David Easton, on the other, are Robert Adcock, "Historical Political Science in the Behavioral Era," and Robert Adcock and Mark Bevir, "The Remaking of Political Theory," both in Adcock, Bevir, and Stimson, *Historicizing Politics*.

30. Strauss, *What Is Political Philosophy?* 12.

31. Strauss, *Liberalism Ancient and Modern*, 222–223.

32. See James H. Capshew, *Psychologists on the March: Science, Practice and Professional Identity in America, 1929–1969* (Cambridge: Cambridge University Press, 1999); and Ellen Herman, *The Romance of American Psychology: Political Culture in the Age of Experts* (Berkeley: University of California Press, 1995). In his fine historical survey "Psychology," in *The Cambridge History of Science*, vol. 7, *The Modern Social Sciences*, ed. Theodore M. Porter and Dorothy Ross (Cambridge: Cambridge University Press, 2003), 251–274, Mitchell G. Ash concludes that the predominance of behaviorism in the middle third of the twentieth century should be understood as merely "an episode in a much larger story" and that the discipline of psychology has since become more open to diverse ideas and methodologies (274).

33. See Daniel Dennett, *Consciousness Explained* (Boston: Little, Brown, 1991), which, as a number of critics have noted, should be entitled *Consciousness Described*, because Dennett considers the attempt to explain the experience of awareness an unfortunate holdover of the old-fashioned "Cartesian theater," and the somewhat more eclectic but nevertheless physiologically (rather than "philosophically," in the preanalytic sense of the word) oriented Arthur Zeman, *Consciousness: A User's Guide* (New Haven: Yale University Press, 2003). Although Zeman's own explanations concentrate on neurophysiology, some of his observations recall James and Köhler at their most ambitious: "Our knowledge of the world pervades perception; we are always seeking after meaning. Try *not* deciphering a road sign, or erasing the face of the man in the moon. What we see resonates in the memory of what we have seen; new experience always percolates through old, leaving a hint of its flavor as it passes. We live, in this sense, in a 'remembered present'" (181).

Consider a second example. Scholars engaged in "affective forecasting," an informal categorization of social scientists who study how people respond to happiness and cope with unhappiness, aim less to understand felt experience than to predict future behavior based on the analysis of empirical data. See Jon Gertner, "The Futile Pursuit of Happiness," *New York Times Magazine*, September 7, 2003, 44–91.

Finally, some medical schools now expose physicians-in-training to courses in "narrative medicine," which are designed to equip them with a radical new diagnostic tool: listening. Some renegade psychiatrists contend that patients themselves might be the best judges of whether "talking through" trauma has greater therapeutic value than repressing memories of pain and loss. Making sense of medical conditions by understanding patients' lives and listening carefully to their stories before turning them over to the machines that will yield the measurements on which diagnoses will be based are approaches that descend directly (although probably unconsciously) from the insights of Gestalt psychology. Whether such techniques will meet the rigorous standards of insurance companies that determine medical practice by measuring costs against benefits remains to be seen.

34. In his chapter in this volume Bruce Kuklick quotes W. V. O. Quine's dismissive characterization of such a seeker as "misguided" and probably just "not a very good student." Kuklick's account of the abdication by most professional philosophers of any responsibility for addressing questions of value (an account that makes clear why John Cleese is the ideal choice as the offi-

cial voice for the outreach efforts of the American Philosophical Association) might also help to explain why courses in intellectual history, in some of which at least such issues remain central, continue to attract student interest.

35. See the concluding pages of Kuklick's chapter in this volume, and cf. David A. Hollinger, "How Wide the Circle of the 'We'? American Intellectuals and the Problem of the Ethnos since World War II," originally published in *American Historical Review* 98 (1993), and incorporated in Hollinger, *Postethnic America*, rev. ed. (New York: Basic Books, 2000). I have addressed these issues in two articles: "Why History Matters to Political Theory," in *Scientific Authority in Twentieth-Century America*, ed. Ronald Walters (Baltimore: Johns Hopkins University Press, 1997), 185–204, reprinted in James T. Kloppenberg, *The Virtues of Liberalism* (New York: Oxford University Press, 1998), 155–178; and "Pragmatism: An Old Name for Some New Ways of Thinking?" *Journal of American History* 83 (1996): 100–138, reprinted in Morris Dickstein, ed., *The Revival of Pragmatism* (Durham: Duke University Press, 1998), 83–127. See also Richard J. Bernstein, *The Restructuring of Social and Political Theory* (New York: Harcourt Brace Jovanovich, 1976), and Bernstein, *Beyond Objectivism and Relativism: Science, Hermeneutics, and Praxis* (Philadelphia: University of Pennsylvania Press, 1983), two brilliant studies that remain the best accounts of the complex dynamics that restored the rich traditions of critical theory, phenomenology, pragmatism, and hermeneutics to (at least the margins of) American academic discourse. A more recent overview of such work is Joan W. Scott and Debra Keates, eds., *Schools of Thought: Twenty-five Years of Interpretive Social Science* (Princeton: Princeton University Press, 2001).

36. Jacques Maritain, *Humanism intégrale* (Paris: Aubier, 1936), 55. See also John Hellman, "The Opening to the Left in French Catholicism: The Role of the Personalists," *Journal of the History of Ideas* 34 (1973): 381–390; Mark Silk, "Notes on the Judeo-Christian Tradition in America," *American Quarterly* 36 (1984): 65–85; and James Terence Fisher, *The Catholic Counter-culture in America, 1933–1962* (Chapel Hill: University of North Carolina Press, 1989), 71–99.

37. Strauss, "An Introduction to Heideggerian Existentialism," in *The Rebirth of Political Rationalism*, 31. On Strauss in Paris, see Sheppard, "Leo Strauss and the Politics of Exile," 80–90.

38. On the campaign to hire Maritain, see Mayer, *Robert Maynard Hutchins*, 118–119.

39. My account of these conferences and the disputes they engendered follows the excellent account in James Gilbert, *Redeeming Culture: American Religion in an Age of Science* (Chicago: University of Chicago Press, 1997). All quotations are taken from pp. 62–93.

40. Strauss, "An Introduction to Heideggerian Existentialism," 31.

41. Two excellent compilations of Maritain's writings have been edited by Joseph W. Evans and Leo R. Ward, *The Social and Political Philosophy of Jacques Maritain* (New York: Charles Scribner's Sons, 1955), and *Challenges and Renewals* (Notre Dame, Ind.: University of Notre Dame Press, 1966). The quotation is from the former volume, p. 122.

42. Maritain, *Social and Political Philosophy*, 136–140.

43. Ibid., 140–141, 328–329. See also 264–265, in which Maritain emphasizes the duty of Christians to put their ideals into practice rather than remain aloof from politics. I do not want to exaggerate the progressivism of Maritain's social thought. His embrace of democracy is noteworthy only in contrast to the prevailing Catholic scholasticism of the nineteenth and early twentieth centuries. In the years following Vatican II his reputation waned among those Catholics eager for more rapid change than he was willing to countenance. See Bernard E. Doering, *Jacques Maritain and the French Catholic Intellectuals* (Notre Dame, Ind.: Notre Dame University Press, 1983).

44. Those in contemporary American politics (including some in the administration of President George W. Bush) who declare their allegiance to Strauss seem to have missed this important point, although Strauss himself emphasized it often enough. For one recent example of this curious blindness to the master's explicit warnings, see Steven Lenzner and William Kristol, "What Was Leo Strauss Up To?" *Public Interest* 153 (Fall 2003): 19–39. After acknowledging the danger of persecution that philosophers face and the consequent significance of

Strauss's reliance on esoteric writing, Lenzner and Kristol nevertheless opine that Strauss's preferred "classical writers" are "for almost all practical purposes what now are called conservatives" and conclude that "President Bush's advocacy of regime change—which avoids the pitfalls of a wishful global universalism on the one hand, and a fatalistic cultural determinism on the other—is a not altogether unworthy product of Straussian rehabilitation of the notion of regime." The distance separating such partisan polemics from Strauss's own conception of philosophical writing seems self-evident.

45. For the argument in this paragraph I am indebted to my colleague Peter Gordon, who directed my attention to the essay by Simon Rawidowicz, "On Interpretation," originally published in 1957 and reprinted in Rawidowicz, *Studies in Jewish Thought*, ed. Nahum Glatzner (Philadelphia: Jewish Publication Society, 1974). As Gordon put it in an e-mail message to me dated March 3, 2004: "What makes Rawidowicz so appealing is that he cuts against [Strauss's] authoritarian notion of an incorrigible religious knowledge with the suggestion that, contra the Spinozistic phantasm of revelation, the rabbis and the greatest philosophers of the Jewish tradition understood that all revelation is interpretive, i.e., intersubjectively established. This possibility—the promising possibility of an ongoing intersubjective discussion as to what 'revelation' is, or as to what 'values' have a grip on us—is just what Strauss misses, since he seems to fear that any concession to the intersubjective and historical constitution of values is a concession to the mob, to history, and a betrayal of what he thinks values are supposed to be: incorrigible and beyond intersubjective revision, just like hard-and-fast naturalistic facts." Strauss appealed, Gordon concludes, "to a model of values that is not the *alternative* to a culture of facts, but seems to be modeled *after* the culture of facts." I return to this problem in my conclusion.

46. In other words, might William Kristol learn to sound more like William Galston?

47. *General Education in a Free Society* (Cambridge: Harvard University Press, 1945). See the discussions of this book in Keller and Keller, *Making Harvard Modern*, and Richard Norton Smith, *The Harvard Century: The Making of a University to the Nation* (Cambridge: Harvard University Press, 1986).

48. Even among champions of rational choice, change may be stirring. Following the pioneering efforts of founders such as William Riker and Mancur Olson, a later generation of rational choice theorists has begun taking its cues from political scientists such as Robert Bates. In his studies that apply rational choice models to developing countries, Bates recommends an eclectic approach that takes into account cultural meanings, social structures, and institutions. In his words, "Anyone working in other cultures knows that people's beliefs and values matter, so too do the distinctive characteristics of their institutions." See Bates, "Macropolitical Economy in the Field of Development," in *Perspectives on Positive Political Economy*, ed. J. Alt and Ken Shepsle (Cambridge: Cambridge University Press, 1990), 87. For broader discussions of this phenomenon, see Gabriel Almond, "Political Science: The History of the Discipline," in *A New Handbook of Political Science*, ed. Robert E. Goodin and Hans-Dieter Klingemann (New York: Oxford University Press, 1996), and S. M. Amadae, *Rationalizing Capitalist Democracy: The Cold War Origins of Rational Choice Liberalism* (Chicago: University of Chicago Press, 2003). On the more general topic of hermeneutics in the social sciences, see Bernstein, *The Restructuring of Social and Political Theory*; Bernstein, *Beyond Objectivism and Relativism*; and Scott and Keates, *Schools of Thought*.

49. On these developments see Alister E. McGrath, *The Future of Christianity* (Oxford: Blackwell, 2001); Lamin Sanneh, *Whose Religion Is Christianity? The Gospel beyond the West* (Grand Rapids, Mich.: Eerdmans, 2003); and Philip Jenkins, *The Next Christendom: The Coming of Global Christianity* (Oxford: Oxford University Press, 2003).

50. Straussians' access to the generosity of wealthy foundations makes it difficult to portray them convincingly as marginalized outsiders, the image they cherish.

51. Strauss, "Progress or Return?" in *The Rebirth of Classical Rationalism*, 260–261, 269–270.

52. Are any of us prepared, as historians of the humanities and the discursive social sci-

ences, to make a case for what contribution these disciplines should make to American culture in the twenty-first century, or for what colleges and universities should offer their students as a liberal education? We are master unmaskers, superb debunkers, but what constructive ideas can we offer? I believe there are resources within the American tradition of pragmatism that remain attractive to us as inheritors and participants in a democratic culture descended from the classical and Judeo-Christian traditions. I have advanced that argument and discussed James's essays "On a Certain Blindness in Human Beings" and "What Makes a Life Significant?" in the introductory and concluding sections of my contribution to *Education and Democracy: Reimagining Liberal Learning in America*, ed. Robert Orrill (New York: College Board, 1997), 69–75, 100–104. James delivered several versions of these two essays in the mid-1890s; they were published in his book *Talks to Teachers on Psychology and to Students on Some of Life's Ideals* (1899; rpt. Cambridge: Harvard University Press, 1983). Weber's speech "Politik als Beruf," first delivered and published in 1919 and translated as "Politics as a Vocation," is available in *From Max Weber: Essays in Sociology*, trans. and ed. Hans Gerth and C. Wright Mills (1919; rpt. New York: Oxford University Press, 1948), and in a different and, from my perspective, superior translation in *Max Weber: Selections in Translation*, ed. W. G. Runciman, trans. E. Matthews (1919; Cambridge: Cambridge University Press, 1978).

6

PHILOSOPHY AND INCLUSION IN THE UNITED STATES, 1929–2001

BRUCE KUKLICK

IN WRITING about "philosophy in the United States," I mean to write about an academic discipline whose substance spilled over into other academic disciplines in the second half of the twentieth century, but whose perennial concerns—fundamental questions about the human place in the universe—engaged thoughtful members of the culture long before departments of philosophy existed. Understanding philosophy's recent history requires that we look at variables not usually treated in the history of ideas—demography, ideology, professionalization, and management, as well as what may be a unique factor, what I call the tension between vision and technique. Philosophy, moreover, has struggled with questions about diversity among practitioners in the discipline, and with its ability to reach out to other disciplines, to a wide variety of students, and to a public beyond the academy. All these factors, of course, play out in a realm of human endeavor that thrives on the intellectual quality of its attainments.

This chapter focuses on two chronologically linked stories, the consolidation of analytic philosophy in the two decades after World War II and its decline in the era of Vietnam and after. I have also taken a running start in an earlier time to set the stage for the era after World War II; and I have surveyed developments up through the turn of the century.[1]

The Postwar System

The system of higher education in which most philosophers operated in the mid-twentieth century had grown only slowly after the "founding" of 1870–1910. Then, after World War II, there was a boom, in part to meet the needs of tens of thousands of returning servicemen, in part to respond to the federal government, which began to fund education deemed essential to the nation's defense in the period of the cold war with the old Soviet Union. Despite this growth, the earlier structure of prestige, in the academic world in general and in philosophy in particular, remained intact and indeed became more rigid. As one historian has pointed out, the "Harvard model" became standard: even schools that served regional needs or catered to specialized groups of students downgraded service and teaching and hired and promoted faculty on the basis of credentials beginning with the doctoral degree and eventuating in productivity evidenced by writing.[2] In philosophy Harvard itself maintained its distinctive, easily commanding rank, and leadership flowed to its fellow Ivy League universities; to other fortunate private institutions on the East Coast, such as Johns Hopkins; to the great public institutions of the Midwest and the University of Chicago; to select liberal arts colleges; and to a few large schools on the West Coast—Stanford, Berkeley, and UCLA.

Long before the postwar period, by the 1920s, a young man who realistically thought of himself as becoming a philosopher was not thinking about a life of contemplation in the cloister or in the ministry or as a sage; he was, rather, going to apply to graduate school in philosophy at one of these institutions.

Harvard was *the* place to obtain advanced training. C. I. Lewis made his early mark as a logician, and *Mind and the World-Order* (1929) and *The Analysis of Knowledge and Valuation* (1946) established him as the most influential philosopher and a thinker of originality and merit. Lewis and the philosophers who followed him at Harvard underscored the role of human choice in the construction of knowledge. But Lewis concentrated on the hard sciences and mathematics as the model for knowledge, disregarded religion, and had a constrained view of the public role of philosophy. His "conceptual pragmatism" was a later version of John Dewey's instrumentalism without passion or reformism. On the other hand, Alfred North Whitehead, who had come to Cambridge as a philosopher of science, proved to be an audacious metaphysician when he published *Process and Reality* (1929), and he popularized his ideas in books such as *Science and the Modern World* (1925) and *Adventures of Ideas* (1933). Harvard had philosophers of international stature, and students could choose between empirical, scientific emphases and a more speculative set of concerns.

Although Berkeley in California was a clone of Harvard, several other institutions remained credibly independent in their approaches. At Columbia mediocre leadership had produced, after the retirement of Dewey in 1930, a nondescript department. Nonetheless, it purveyed a version of his ideas—"naturalism"—that attracted students. On the basis of Dewey's ecumenical leadership of a secular group of thinkers, many of Jewish background had gotten a foothold in the philosophy departments of the schools of New York City—NYU, City and Brooklyn Colleges, and the New School for Social Research.

At Chicago Dewey's onetime colleague George Herbert Mead carried on in the classroom the exposition of Deweyan ideas, but this point of view was more faintly expressed after his death in 1931. The administration of Chicago had passed into the hands of the educational innovator Robert Hutchins in 1929, and his elevation altered philosophical instruction at Chicago. Hutchins disdained professionalism in the academy and emphasized "great books" and the otherworldly nature of speculation. In this endeavor Hutchins relied on a philosopher he hired from Columbia, Mortimer Adler, who had rebelled against everything for which Dewey stood. A weakened group of the followers of Mead and Dewey in the Department of Philosophy became permanently embattled with an educational leadership committed to more traditional, even anti-empirical philosophy.[3] A joke of the era had it that Chicago was a place where Jews (Adler) taught Catholicism (the value-absolute neo-Thomism favored by Hutchins) to atheists (Chicago's secular and radical students).

Nonetheless, Chicago and Columbia—and Yale and Princeton—remained pivotal institutions. After Whitehead retired in 1937, broad-gauged speculative thought came to have a smaller role at Harvard. While it maintained its overwhelming authority, these departments outside Cambridge now carried the banner of philosophies not limited to scientific understanding, despite their collective drift toward the modern. Younger men such as Richard McKeon and Charles Hartshorne at Chicago often pitted "empiricism" against "metaphysics," and even Justus Buchler at naturalistic Columbia scorned the cramped thinking of philosophers who made science their only focus.

Perhaps more important than the parting of ways between empiricists and metaphysicians was that no professionally respected thinker claimed the public mantle of Dewey, who in his seventies and eighties still embodied philosophy for the most contemplative of the college-educated elite and spoke to its urge for guidance in a corporate world. To the extent that this role was filled, it was taken up by figures of the second-rank, such as T. V. Smith of Chicago and Irvin Edman of Columbia, while Will Durant, who had no academic affiliation, valiantly presented the history of thought to a wide audience of nonacademics.[4]

Catholic schools of higher learning had at the end of the nineteenth century come out of a period of somnolence and developed a commitment to a modern version of the philosophy of St. Thomas Aquinas. The neo-Thomists were about as intellectually prepossessing as the American naturalists or metaphysicians, but they were enthusiastic about vanquishing the secular modernism embodied in philosophy in the United States. In 1926 the Thomists formed the American Catholic Philosophical Association, which they hoped would be the spearhead of their advance. But their leaders could not even convince Thomist troops to read the enemy, nor did they engage in a dialogue. On the other side, a joint session of the American Philosophical Association and the ACPA in 1937 resulted in the Catholics being charged with fascism. The meeting, which left bitter feelings in the ACPA, symbolized the isolation of Catholic institutions and the closed anti-Catholic professionalism of non-Catholic philosophers, Christian and not, who found their primary foes not in Berlin or Rome, but at Notre Dame or Catholic University of America.[5]

Nonetheless, the collapse of the international system in the late 1930s and the spiral toward war did not go unnoticed by professorial philosophy. During World War I philosophers had—famously or notoriously—supported Woodrow Wilson's declaration of war against Germany and his commitment to internationalism. Now, in 1937, 1938, and 1939, philosophers were tangential to the dialogue about the growth of German power between interventionists and isolationists. Philosophers agonized over the impotence of their ancient calling, which they blamed on specialization within the profession and occasionally on an empiricism that downgraded moral and religious thinking. The thinkers worried about how the scientific and democratic society for which Dewey spoke could justify its commitments and maintain an intellectual coherence that, they thought, religion had traditionally imparted. Two examples of this pervasive malaise are worth noting.

In 1940, soon after the beginning of World War II, a wide academic community of humanists, social science theorists, and philosophers, as well as some independent intellectuals, convened the continuing annual Conference on Science, Philosophy, and Religion in Their Relation to the Democratic Way of Life. Heavily weighted to the "metaphysicians" in professional philosophy, the meetings nonetheless included a visible group of "empiricists," and the center of gravity was the position Dewey had expressed in *A Common Faith* (1934): that it was legitimate to term "religious" that ideal way of life promoting democracy and science. The upright leadership of this group never made an impact, and a major legacy was to provide a forum for a young Willard Quine of Harvard to complain about the strategy of liberal religious thinkers who allied themselves with Dewey. Conservatives, said Quine, had tried to make "the rest of us" religious through conversion; "the cardinal method . . . [of] their liberal brethren [was] definition."[6]

The second example occurred in the middle of World War II, when the American Philosophical Association (APA) decided to survey its ranks on the role of philosophy in contributing to liberal education after the war. A committee of philosophers questioned APA members, as well as a host of interested laymen, and conducted seven conferences around the country on the state of philosophy. In 1945 *Philosophy in American Education* summed up their efforts and most significantly expressed the dissatisfaction apparent from the late 1930s to the early 1950s. The philosophers most involved were not entirely on the side of the metaphysicians, or against the secular group, but they were high-minded and looked back to the turn of the twentieth century, when, they claimed, philosophy had a more sturdy cultural influence. They lamented professionalization and specialization but only halfheartedly embraced more speculative philosophies as the solution to what they perceived as the discipline's problems. In the end they hoped that after the war philosophy might again thrive as a core study clarifying conceptual and methodological matters for other scholars and as a teaching area central to new "general education" requirements that might come into effect after the war.[7]

In the postwar period these men and even the older generation of thinkers at Harvard (like Lewis and his colleague Ralph Barton Perry), as well as philosophers at colleges like Amherst and Williams, continued to promote what from the time of World War I may be called *the responsibilities of departmental philosophy* in the United States.

The philosophers adapted a conception of the thinker in higher education from nineteenth-century Germany. Each major school had its own local professorial hero who embodied the philosophical essence, and these schools hired their own graduate students, forming a bonded group of acolytes. They perceived themselves as the bearers of the tradition of Western thought that began with the Greeks, progressed through the medieval period, and culminated in modern philosophy: Descartes, Spinoza, and Leibniz; Locke, Berkeley, and Hume; Kant; and then Hegel and those who came after him. The task of the men in this pantheon had been to reason about the human niche in the universe and present the accumulated insights to an elite. Now philosophers in American higher education advanced this elevated enterprise. The study of philosophy was not only the best way for (usually male) undergraduates to understand man in the cosmos but also essential to the growth of moral integrity. Moreover, the philosopher had a prudent social function: to offer aids to reflection about the soul's anxieties but to warn against untoward political expression.

Acting on these ideals expanded the range of undergraduate teaching. In addition to conventional courses in ancient and modern philosophy (through Kant or Hegel), by the 1950s students could study a "continental" tradition of the nineteenth century that included Kierkegaard and Nietzsche and ended in the twentieth century with the existentialism of Jean-Paul Sartre. Despite the fact that faculty slanted new classes in social thought toward welfare capitalism, they also introduced their charges to socialism and Marxism.

Although university philosophers easily justified themselves as conservators of learning, essential to the civilizing mission of the university, they were also hard put to consider themselves genuine thinkers. With the exception of Harvard, the pedestrian was the rule. At Princeton after the war an adviser to its president described the philosophy department as "a group of men . . .

mediocre in mental capacity and in scholarly achievement,"[8] and its department was not just typical but also highly ranked in various studies. In this sense philosophy in America from the 1920s to 1950s was a dreary enterprise. Original or even capable thinkers were rare. Perhaps it is fairer to say that there was a gap between the aspirations expressed about undergraduate education and the reality of professional training. There, in graduate school, professorial worldviews—idealism, realism, instrumentalism, pragmatism, naturalism—vied for clients, and mentors formed an inward-looking organization that seldom reached out to the wider culture.

The Rise of Analytic Philosophy

The 1950s brought a dramatic change as two currents from abroad reshaped professional life. The logical positivism of the Vienna Circle, which had migrated to the United States after the Nazis came to power in Germany, matured as a potent philosophical force; and the philosophical analysis of Oxford, England, gained adherents.

Lewis's work was indebted to the "classic" pragmatists, and symbolic logic gave him and those he influenced a new resource to do philosophy. The empiricism of logical positivism was stricter, and the Vienna Circle made logic central; indeed, the positivists emphasized the *exclusive* claim of science to knowledge, downgrading any philosophical pursuits that did not acknowledge such exclusivity and espousing arguments that ruled out constructive work in ethics, aesthetics, and metaphysics. As thinkers fled Hitler's Europe in the 1930s, American universities gave posts to several formidable positivists. While numerically a small number, the Europeans and their advocates in the United States became potent after World War II because of their ability and their cogently stated doctrines. Among those who had high-profile jobs were Hans Reichenbach of UCLA; Rudolph Carnap at Chicago and UCLA; Herbert Feigl at Minnesota; Carl Hempel at Princeton; and Ernest Nagel at Columbia.

Positivism added to the spell of the secular empiricism of people like Lewis, and to its opponents it represented the wickedness of the spell. Many of those who stressed science were equated by their adversaries, even if incorrectly, with the positivists. Men like Quine at Harvard were often so categorized not because of the intellectual connection, which existed, but because of a commitment that made more capacious understandings of philosophy nugatory.

Oxford's philosophical analysis was originally associated with Cambridge, England, and its dons, G. E. Moore, Bertrand Russell, and Russell's student Ludwig Wittgenstein. Hostile to metaphysics and to the claim that philosophy was a guide to wisdom, analysis considered philosophy an activity that clarified ordinary talk and the structure of science. The analysts taught not how to live the good life but how to find out how we use a word like "good" or "ought"; they defined concepts that might have their own existence but were always expressed in language. We might use these concepts, but it was a more difficult task to spell out what they implied and what were the criteria for their employment.[9]

In Oxford philosophers who had come to maturity and institutional importance after the war promulgated these views—Gilbert Ryle, Paul Grice, Peter Strawson, and J. L. Austin. Through an extraordinary international exchange Harvard, followed by Princeton, which was remaking itself in a generous image of Harvard, brought Oxford analysts to the United States in the 1950s and 1960s and sent Americans to Oxford.

At Oxford "analysis" was more a manner than a program, perhaps stuffy and arid in its concerns. In the United States it joined with the empiricism of Lewis and his students and with positivism to produce the commanding orientation of American philosophers in the third quarter of the century—analytic philosophy. A peculiar version of it—pragmatic analysis—was linked to Harvard, which maintained its dominance in the United States through the efforts of Quine, Nelson Goodman, Hilary Putnam, and John Rawls. There philosophers taught "naturalized epistemology"—an exploration that looked to the practice of scientists to find whatever we might learn of the ultimate structure of things.

The movement was diffuse. Some analysts modeled their work on an idealized view of science; others were more interested in unpacking the meaning of concepts. All believed symbolic logic was necessary for philosophic reasoning. Although suspicious of any absolutistic comprehension of science and frequently skeptical in their leanings, analytic philosophers often elevated scientific understanding as the only kind and made "the philosophy of science" a subfield almost coterminous with epistemology. But Oxford was less formal than Vienna, and while reinforcing the clubby ethos of American philosophy, the English may have directed American analytic philosophy away from an even greater logical and scientific focus than it otherwise might have had. In focusing on the actual use of language, its possible clarification, or its restructuring, analytic philosophers indebted to Oxford invented "the philosophy of language," another subfield to go along with the philosophy of science.

In part this "linguistic turn" echoed a denigration of the status of the philosopher. Dewey had thought that philosophy might change the world; the interwar generation had worried that it was not changing the world; by the 1950s philosophers had stopped agonizing about their shrunken role and even embraced it. In emphasizing that philosophy was about language, philosophers were noting a new impotence. A dimension of this impotence was the trivializing of other fields of philosophy. Although analysts did not dismiss some philosophies as meaningless as logical positivism had, by not attending to them they implied that they did not need attention. In general, an apolitical, secular temper that saw philosophy as a professional field of study joined analysts together.

Among important institutions only Yale chose a different course. Its traditionalist leader, Brand Blanshard, called it "a bastion of metaphysics," and its department was even willing to forgo an entrenched anti-Semitism to advance its ideology. After World War II Yale determined to build on its speculative strengths by hiring Paul Weiss from Bryn Mawr College, a student of Whitehead's and a wide-ranging philosopher who had grand, creative interests. The problem for philosophy at Yale was that Weiss was, culturally at least, a Jew: in addition to having taught women, he had bad manners that reflected the impoverishment of his background. Weiss prevailed, however, and at Yale in 1950 founded the Metaphysical Society of America.[10] This appointment signaled the basic acceptance of Jews into philosophy, though Weiss himself was far more spiritual in orientation than many of his cultural background: non-Christian secularism and scientific empiricism were cousins, as the Jewish role in philosophy in New York City manifested most clearly.

Yale and the schools most drawn to its ideas were earnest in their dislike of a confined philosophical mode and their view of the importance of philosophy to conduct. Just as Socrates could not take his debates with the Sophists as a mere argumentative game, so in New Haven abstract principles meant something in the world. Yale had a minor tragic dilemma. From a long perspective, its own principles, which privileged a faux-Christian theism, look limited, illiberal, and racist. But it is unclear that that posture was worse than tolerance of "private" political, moral, and religious beliefs and the evolving secular professionalism, both of which underscored the fact that philosophy did not cut much ice in the world.

The public philosophy that Dewey had promoted almost vanished. In the 1920s and 1930s he had engaged with nonphilosophers of the likes of Reinhold Niebuhr, Walter Lippmann, and Harold Lasswell (a policy scientist) in conversations that professionals deemed an essential aspect of philosophy. By the 1950s professional thinkers rarely thought of such conversations as part of philosophy at all. From 1940 to 1970 Dewey's most prominent follower, Sidney Hook, was an active participant in many intellectual debates outside the academy, and he spoke to issues that involved Niebuhr and Lippmann, as well as Hannah Arendt (a German émigré political theorist), John Courtney Murray (a Roman Catholic thinker), Paul Blanshard (a social commentator), Milton Friedman (an economist), and Arthur Schlesinger Jr. (a prominent historian). But these debates did not count for promotion in the profession of philosophy, and few people who were known as philosophers participated in them. Just as political options shrank for the United States during the cold war from 1945 through the early 1960s, so did options that could be construed as "real" philosophy. Analysis narrowly defined the boundaries of philosophy, demarcating the questions constitutive of university thinking and marginalizing many others. Analysis was the philosophy of the democratic imperial West, with Great Britain in a junior partnership with the United States. Not only the politically active but also the metaphysicians were shunted to the sidelines, as soul-searching about the nature of philosophy disappeared. The institutional clout of Harvard, its pragmatic analysis, and Quine's prestige especially promised the extermination of rival schools of thought.

The Transformation of the 1960s

In the late 1960s analytic philosophy and the university system in which it flourished came under attack, critically undermined by the sheer growth in higher education. Sustained prosperity and an American desire to open up university learning to anyone who wanted to attend school multiplied the number of institutions and thus eventually the number of "thinkers" in departments of philosophy. Especially noteworthy were the increases in schools that individual states funded. For example, New York, Ohio, Wisconsin, and California enlarged the number of public universities under their purview. Many states—Michigan and California being two outstanding examples—also added another tier of institutions, state colleges.

When these establishments created philosophy departments, older schools trained more philosophers, and the new ones themselves opened graduate programs. One observer has noted that in the first half of the twentieth century the United States, Britain, and Canada founded 30 philosophy journals. Between 1950 and 1960, 15 more were added, and 44 in the 1960s—as many as in the previous sixty years—and then about 120 in the next twenty years![11] By 2000 close to ninety institutions in the United States awarded students the doctoral degree in philosophy. The membership of the American Philosophical Associations was about 260 in 1920; 1,500 in 1960; and well over 8,000 in the 1990s. While the American population grew by 70 percent from 1920 to 1960, the APA thus jumped by 475 percent. By the 1990s the population had grown by 135 percent, and the philosophical population by 2,970 percent. To put these numbers in another context: in 1920 there was one member of the APA for every 407,000 Americans; in the 1990s one for every 31,000.[12]

From 1900 to 1915 the Great Department at Harvard, at the height of its fame, produced an average of six doctorates of philosophy a year. At the end of the twentieth century Harvard produced five a year and Yale produced four. The following exemplary schools, some of which did not exist in 1900 and none of which then had a doctoral program in philosophy, had a greater production: University of Colorado and Fordham, six; Vanderbilt, seven; Stony Brook, Buffalo, and the University of Massachusetts at Amherst, eight; University of Texas at Austin, ten.[13]

What do these figures tell us? When Yale College was the premier place to learn philosophical theology in the eighteenth and nineteenth centuries, the theologian or philosopher had a lofty role in society, and he may have been a repository of special truths. Of course, there was continual change as the collegiate and university system expanded from 1830 to 1960. But the quantum leap of the 1960s was distinctive. Those called to a philosophical vocation in 1800 may have had a distinctive mental prowess. It is hard to make the same argument for most of the thousands who taught in graduate programs in philosophy in the late twentieth century. It is difficult to see, for example, how a historian of ancient philosophy at a branch of a state college or a logician at a major university might be regarded as a moral compass. It is a nice question, which the intellectual historian cannot discount, of how a social practice that comes into being via a few exceptional minds is altered when enlarged by several thousand more ordinary minds. I call the transformation *mass professionalization.*

By the late 1960s the great number of people in philosophy was changing the activity and making it impossible even for practitioners to monitor what was going on. Moreover, other changes complicated the demographic shifts. More money in the system meant that many universities could offer enormous salaries and perquisites to philosophers they wanted on their faculties. Research budgets, reduced teaching loads, helpful assistants, frequent leaves of absence, and subventions for travel became available. Universities created research centers to make their schools attractive to outsiders, and entrepreneurially minded philosophers might find it desirable to run such centers or to hire more people in their fields. Philosophers, like most others academics, became caught up with the many perquisites their profession offered, and— protests to the contrary—gave public engagement a low priority.

Far greater mobility resulted. Before the 1960s philosophers of originality might be "called" to professorships in institutions more desirable than the ones from which they came. By the 1960s philosophers were more peripatetic. The common use of the jet plane made geographic locus less a factor than it previously was. The California schools, for example, benefited from coast-to-coast air travel. Philosophers might also relocate because of climate or a promised lifestyle—in addition to schools in California, for example, those in Florida and Arizona were more sought-after than they had previously been.

Schools that previously would not have been imagined to be of the first rank intruded into the old hierarchical system in philosophy. State universities themselves outside the Midwest and California—Florida, Texas, New York—challenged wealthy eastern institutions. For the first time in American history southern colleges became nationally prominent in philosophy—Virginia, Duke, the University of North Carolina. Sectarian institutions, which had refused the secular revolution of the late nineteenth century and had been written off the map of higher education since that time, made a modest comeback as places like Calvin College of Michigan and Wheaton College of Illinois attracted capable scholars. More important, Roman Catholic universities were at last recognized as part of the philosophical scene. For years such schools pursued the study of medieval or Thomistic thought and commented on American thought as if from a foreign country. Now Fordham, Catholic University, and Notre Dame drew noteworthy philosophers with a Catholic perspective and placed their doctoral students in non-Catholic institutions. They made inroads into the system in the same way that philosophers of Jewish origin had some thirty years before.

Although general education was diluted in the 1960s and thereafter, philosophy maintained a foothold of mandated courses, as did other established disciplines. These requirements and the willingness of newly minted philosophers to teach almost anything in their courses—to expand the realm of what constituted philosophy for undergraduates—meant that the discipline prospered in its institutional setting.[14] It also reflected the growing heterogeneity of the academic world, as women, people of color, and those of alternative sexual persuasion achieved places in philosophy, although even late in the century they were denied the legitimacy accorded to Jewish and Catholic interests.

In the 1960s and 1970s these structural changes accentuated three coincident struggles about the substance of philosophy itself. First, analytic philosophy fragmented. Second, assorted nonanalytic philosophers challenged analysts. Third, other disciplines opposed philosophy's exclusive right as the discipline to "do" philosophy. In the background to all these struggles—and sometimes in the foreground—were the political upheavals of the 1960s, precipitated by the drama of the civil rights movement, the war in Vietnam, and their cultural residue.

The Proliferation of Analytic Philosophies

Analytic philosophy was premised on a secular vision of the world. Physics was the science that told us what the world was "really" like, although it shared its primacy with biology. Since materialism underlay the position, it was necessary to examine not only how physical science and evolution were compatible but also how knowledge and culture were possible—how natural creatures could so develop as to be conscious of and reflective about the environment in which they were located. In its most systematic variants analytic philosophy undertook to connect these realms—the physical, the biological, and the social—without reducing one to the other. Wilfrid Sellars, an influential philosopher at the University of Pittsburgh, wrote from the late 1940s through the 1970s, and his stock has remained high subsequent to his *fluorit*. Sellars best expressed this comprehensive agenda, but his work was often programmatic and only barely comprehensible; and it was unclear—at least no compelling treatise made the point—that one could proclaim materialist ideas and not fall into skepticism. Thinkers could not show how knowledge could come about if they embraced a scientific outlook. More important, most analytic philosophers were not interested in an architectonic exposition of their vision.

Graduate training in analytic philosophy solved small problems, which contributed to filling in the big picture. Philosophers were technicians. Graduate students participated in an arcane conversation about nuances in the theory of knowledge. They were not interested in large questions about the meaning of life that, in any event, their premises would probably not allow them to answer in a happy fashion.

The first intrasystematic confrontation with Harvard and the schools in its orbit, such as Princeton and Berkeley, occurred in these circumstances. A number of institutions gathered together academics leaning to common research projects of high profile. The Massachusetts Institute of Technology, the University of California at Irvine, New York University, and Rutgers, for example, became distinctive centers of analytic philosophy that altered the old network of prestige. Each pursued a strategy of inquiry that reflected one of many straitened conceptions of how to treat issues. Analytic philosophy splintered, and Harvard lost its more-than-a-century-long hold as the premier place to study.

Analysts versus Pluralists

A more serious sort of test came from institutions that taught a different brand of philosophy. In the 1960s analytic philosophers could not head off accusations of irrelevance. The Vietnam era unleashed rage against all ruling orders.

In part the strength of the rebellion derived from the support of undergraduates. The leaders of the student armies that rocked the academy had studied existentialism. They rejected an apolitical positivism, which they identified with conventional American philosophy. Sartre's issues of autonomy, responsibility, and integrity were just those of students defining their identities in the clamor about American racism, at home and abroad. The

"Port Huron Statement" of 1962, credited with formulating the dream of the New Left, adopted an existentialist idiom.

The undergraduates had also come across Herbert Marcuse, who briefly made twentieth-century Marxist theory prominent in the United States. In 1964 he had written *One Dimensional Man* and in 1965 a crucial essay, "Repressive Tolerance." *One Dimensional Man* analyzed American life and argued that the social system smothered dissent. "Repressive Tolerance" claimed that the intellectual pluralism in the United States guaranteed the triumphs of the capitalists, because it downgraded claims of any social theory to be *the true* analysis of the poverty of spirit; tolerance of various opposing ideas assured the victory of conservative ones. Marcuse advocated intolerance of conservative ideas and a climate of erudition that would stifle antirevolutionary life. He excoriated Quine's writing as exemplary of the aridity of conventional philosophy, of its distance from social concern, and of its complicity in a "manipulative-technological" life.[15]

Marcuse's more philosophical prose was well nigh unintelligible, and even his work of 1964 and 1965 was not easy reading. And Marcuse himself, at Brandeis and later in the 1960s when he left Brandeis for the University of California at San Diego, was hardly a zealous activist—he was seventy in 1968. But readers got the apocalyptic side of the message, and suddenly he became the theoretician of the student left, not just in the United States but in Europe as well. In the late 1960s and early 1970s his books were academic best sellers exploring "the system" that undergraduates were rejecting. The phrase *"drugstorisation* of Marcuse" captured his celebrity status in France, and he engendered nationwide controversy in the United States.[16] Indeed, Ronald Reagan, then the governor of California, was involved in Marcuse's struggles in the system of higher education until the university did not renew his contract after 1970—he was seventy-two.

Analytic philosophers spoke to wider issues during this period. A new magazine, *Philosophy and Public Affairs*, founded in 1969, signaled the efforts of some analysts to escape the stereotypical view of the American philosopher as unconnected to philosophy's perennial interests. More important, John Rawls published *A Theory of Justice* in 1971.

Rawls taught at Cornell when he published his pathbreaking essay, "Justice as Fairness," in the *Philosophical Review* of 1958. He first argued that examining concepts embedded in the language was not "normative"; he uncovered what we would *call* justice, to reach "a higher order of abstraction." To unpack this concept Rawls conducted a thought experiment for his readers. Imagine a group of rational intelligences founding a society; they could not be actual people, for they had no idea in advance what role they themselves would play—young or old, rich or poor, male or female, white or black. This was "the original position" in which creatures acted from "a veil of ignorance." The philosopher had to figure out what rules they would draw up. Rawls argued that members of this putative society would behave so that a modicum of benefits might accrue to the least advantaged. A rational mind would always be open to the thought: under the veil of ignorance, I could be one of the least advantaged. Justice *meant* being fair.

By the time *A Theory of Justice* had fleshed out Rawls's ideas and made him famous for reinvigorating political philosophy, Harvard had attracted him, and he was associated not merely with the analytic philosophy practiced there, but also with the substantive commitments of political liberalism. A wide audience took up Rawls because his conclusions were consonant with a belief in compensatory justice that was a heritage of the 1960s. He gave an academic and non-Marxist imprimatur to egalitarian proposals acceptable on other grounds. Yet despite Rawls's influence as the most prominent practical philosopher of the second half of the century, he also shared the disregard for the study of practices that were often supposed to dominate the "naturalized epistemology" of philosophy at Harvard. Rawls was uninterested in the history of political economy and the attempts of politicians in critical periods to build a just state. The American Fathers of the 1780s, the French Revolutionaries of a decade later, and the Bolshevik leaders of the early twentieth century meant little to Rawls. To talk about justice, he created a scenario that could not possibly involve human beings; he was investigating rationality, not politics. Just as other philosophers regularly eschewed practices when they wrote about the world, so Rawls ignored the collective experience of attempts to construct a just society. In real life ignorance of cultural locus—our sex, age, social status, and race—would disqualify us from political participation, if not from claims to be human; Rawls made such ignorance the sine qua non of acceptable, truly human participation.[17]

Rawls failed to satisfy the growing enemies of analytic philosophy. Analytic moral and political philosophers, even at the top of the hierarchy of the "old" university system, found themselves derided. Proud of their rarefied intelligence and commitments to formalist research, they were attacked as much for their pride as for the substance of their work. By the end of the Vietnam War (1975) analysts were opposed by many scholars who may have been less intellectually gifted but who were convinced of the parochialism of analytic philosophy. These scholars commanded hiring at many colleges with no tradition of analytic philosophy—or indeed no tradition of philosophizing at all—but with resources that could make them viable trainers of graduate students and pleasant places of employment often on a par with more settled schools.

As the conflict escalated in the 1970s, commentators described it as that between the successors to the empiricists—the analysts—and a wide group including the older metaphysicians—the "pluralists." As one commentator put it, the pluralists accentuated "immediate grievances, the general theme being the arrogance of the philosophical establishment"; this establishment perceived the pluralists as "second-rate philosophers who seek to gain politically what they have been denied on the basis of merit considerations."[18]

The tension between what I call vision and technique, endemic in the history of Western thought, now became crucial, mixed up with mass professionalization. Thinkers like Plato or, closer to home, William James, who have commanded both the sustained notice of their peers and a wider audience, have been rare. It is far more common for vision and technique to be distinct, and students of philosophy more usually honor thinkers for their expertise than their ability to convey their ideas to thoughtful nonprofessionals—Kant is an outstanding example, as is Charles Peirce in the United States. In America in the second half of the twentieth century, as Yale was prone to observe, most philosophers did not demonstrate vision. In the profession as a whole a remarkable division emerged. Philosophy still exerted a pull on exceptional minds, but they were more than ever drawn to techniques far more rigid than those Kant and Peirce contemplated. It was not that most mid-twentieth-century technicians had a vision too complex to become popular but, rather, that in their focus on technique they might just as well have been lawyers or neurosurgeons or computer programmers.

Those whom Yale called empiricists, positivists, or analysts controlled technique, and New Haven became the premier locus for rebelling against technique in the name of vision. As a bastion of *ressentiment*, Yale and a few other older institutions linked to it—Emory and Northwestern—led the attack on analytic philosophy, which climaxed at a critical APA meeting at the end of 1979, when the pluralists reordered the structure of the association.[19] Hiring and tenure decisions, the biases of journals, and election to positions in the APA's three divisions all reflected this dispute, which continued until the end of the century. The fight was made more complex by the struggle to attract faculty, which turned not just on doctrine and personality, as it had when white males were the only figures in the academy, but also on sex, race, and sexual preference.

Pluralists did not merely resist analysis. They represented minor, competing voices before the 1960s; social upheaval gave them an identity and common enemy. Although metaphysicians formed the base of opposition, more important were expounders of "Continental philosophy," which along with metaphysics found a headquarters at Yale. Continental speculation epitomized the maturation of the impulse that had claimed Sartre for an American audience after World War II.[20] Its adherents studied the European precursors of the existentialists, Edmund Husserl and Martin Heidegger, and wrote academic treatises about topics that these thinkers had made popular. Americans also commented on more recent French and German thought (although none of them emerged as independent interpreters of this tradition as had, say, the Europeans Hans Georg Gadamer and Jürgen Habermas).

Unremarked on was the remarkable impact not of continental Europe but of Catholic Europe. The existential tradition in Sartre had been atheistic, but many of his European peers were straining to find a basis for faith as intellectual Christianity declined. In the United States, Continental philosophy often had a religious blush: only a commitment to the spiritual could save us from life-denying science, logic, and analysis. Although the rumor of angels was more widespread, Roman Catholic institutions of higher learning, or strategically placed Catholic believers at non-Catholic institutions, also attacked secular philosophy.

In addition to Continental philosophers, feminist, Marxist, and African American thinkers, among others, swelled the ranks of the pluralists, arguing that gender, class, and color determined certain aspects of the supposedly neutral study of epistemology. Examining the cultural stance of the knower challenged standard claims of the theory of knowledge. Finally, the pluralists revived interest in "classic" American philosophy. According to them, the tradition of thought that had seemingly ended with Dewey and extended back to Peirce, James, and Josiah Royce—and by some accounts to Ralph Waldo Emerson—was far more involved with the world beyond the academy than was analysis, and it had a far less parochial conception of philosophy. Professors who evaluated the American canon believed that analytic philosophy had betrayed the tradition from which it sprang, and they leagued themselves with the pluralists.

One publishing venture reflected this state of affairs. The Library of Living Philosophers was the lifetime project of Paul A. Schilpp, a professor of philosophy at Southern Illinois University. In the late 1930s Schilpp determined to honor great thinkers while they were still alive, and he contracted with them and many critics to produce a bibliography of writings, an autobiography, a collection of essays, and a response to them by the selected philosopher. The orientation was not American but displayed the way Schilpp saw the philosophic world refracted in the United States. He began with John Dewey (1939); George Santayana (1940), who had left the United States permanently in 1912; and Alfred North Whitehead (1941).

Over the next sixty years Schilpp and his successor from 1981, Lewis Hahn, produced handsome volumes commemorating the living ideas of some thirty thinkers. Schilpp and Hahn made selections representing the competing factions in American philosophy and the European resources on which they drew. Thus, the Library of Living Philosophers printed volumes on Lewis, Carnap, Quine, and Donald Davidson; and their interlocutors G. E. Moore, A. J. Ayer, and P. F. Strawson; but also on Hartshorne, Weiss, and Marjorie Grene; and their interlocutors Sartre, Gadamer, and Paul Ricoeur, among many others. The volumes of the Library of Living Philosophers often lived in different universes and displayed the many nonoverlapping professional conversations in the United States. One historian of twentieth-century analytic philosophy, when puzzling over the importance of his subdiscipline, admitted that he had *never heard of* one of the nonanalysts selected for commemoration.[21]

The APA abetted the chaos. In 1994 its Board of Officers deplored all attempts at ranking departments of philosophy. On the one hand, the APA conceded that departmental esteem and reputation were not "utterly undeserved." On the other hand, in reasoning that imbibed the relativism of the 1960s and obvious disagreements on what constituted quality, the organization questioned the "justice" of "impressions" of esteem and reputation. The APA argued that no polling of philosophers could generate a reasonable ranking; that quantitative measures based on survey data were untrustworthy; and that the very idea of rankings might be "fundamentally unreliable." All this flew in the face of the fact that everyone knew that some departments were better than others, and that national rankings, while always contestable, did accurately portray the academic landscape. In officially denouncing rankings, the APA was throwing up its hands at the disorder in its own house. If it could not advise students where to look for philosophical instruction, who could?[22]

A flood of books ruminated on the crisis in "the profession" and proposed various nostrums for revitalizing thought. Two of these books illustrated the split. In *Post-Analytic Philosophy* (1985) the editors selected essays by thirteen thinkers who, they suggested, might take analytic philosophy into greener pastures. The institutions represented by these philosophers were Berkeley, Columbia, Harvard (four), MIT, New School for Social Research, NYU, Princeton, Stanford (two), and Yale. Another volume, *Portraits of American Continental Philosophers* (1999), contained autobiographical statements of twenty-two thinkers. Their institutions: Boston College (two), DePaul, Duquesne, Emory, Empire State College, George Mason, Georgetown, Hunter College, Northwestern, Penn State (four), Purdue, Rice, SUNY–Stony Brook (two), University of California at Riverside, University of Memphis, University of Texas at Austin, and Villanova.[23]

At the same time a comprehensive survey by the APA in the mid-1990s showed that 40 percent of all schools of higher education did not teach courses in either twentieth-century analytic or Continental philosophy, and another

40 percent offered such courses only every two years or "occasionally." The demand for such courses I would best estimate as "low moderate." The report by the Committee on the Status and Future of the Profession ranked twentieth-century analytic philosophy as one of two courses whose demand was reported as "low" by at least 30 percent of responding departments. The other such course was medieval philosophy. But the preparer of this report was identified with the pluralists and, in truth, their flagship courses did not fare much better.[24] The fracas absorbing the profession seemed to have little impact on the students who took philosophy courses.

Yet some conclusions about the discipline would be mistaken. White men still dominated it, and their undergraduate students were disproportionately male—more so than any other major in the humanities. Women who did train to be philosophers were far less likely to find jobs than male counterparts, and a black presence was minuscule. Various minority voices *did* add to a professional cacophony and confusion.[25]

"Theory" outside Philosophy

A third and final challenge to philosophy complicated the intraprofessional fights. In the first half of the twentieth century American philosophers had lived off the social capital created by the thinkers at Harvard, on the one hand, and Dewey at Chicago and Columbia, on the other. These men had positioned philosophy as a central scholarly discipline: it schooled undergraduates in the Western tradition; spoke to educated disquiet about the human condition; and provided, to other disciplines, expert counsel on how warranted investigation might be carried out. Philosophers in the 1940s and 1950s effectively purveyed versions of Dewey's instrumentalism and positivism as the premises out of which legitimate inquiry grew.

Later analytic philosophers, however, did not aspire to be public figures, or even cross-disciplinary advisers. They began to write themselves out of such advisory positions or out of careers as "public intellectuals."

The dominance in this period of the emotive theory of ethics, which undercut a reasoned account of moral, social, and political decisions, strikingly confirms this fact. The public culture of the United States was obsessively caught up first with the rise of fascism and Communism, then with World War II, and then with the cold war, McCarthyism, and the nuclear arms race. Yet philosophers were saying, in all sorts of complicated ways, that these commitments had no rational basis and that they might indeed even be meaningless. These philosophical affirmations testified to the "internalist" dynamics of the profession. As Quine put it in a striking piece in *Newsday* in 1979, the student who "major[ed] in philosophy primarily for spiritual consolation is misguided and is probably not a very good student"; philosophy did not offer wisdom, nor did philosophers "have any peculiar fitness for helping . . . society."[26]

By the 1960s the conversations in analytic philosophy were baffling and their application to other disciplines uncertain. This was true for both analytic philosophers and their opponents. While analytic philosophy was unintelligible to many because of its often forbidding use of mathematical symbolism, nonanalytic philosophy was not known for its clarity; Heidegger was as incomprehensible as Sellars. Except for the public standing of Marcuse, notable nonanalytic philosophers sank into the same relative obscurity as, say, Ernest Nagel and Nelson Goodman.

In these circumstances scholars in other fields philosophized for themselves, doing philosophy out of whole cloth, or teaching themselves in philosophy. The result was that the harder social sciences often retained positions for theorists or methodologists who may or may not have had any philosophical training but were "the philosophers" in these departments. Departments of history, other humanities departments such as religion, and the softer social sciences departments such as anthropology established similar roles for philosophically inclined scholars who were not philosophers. While the ideas expounded in these disciplines varied, departments of social science took a standard line: long after even the most committed of scientific philosophers rejected logical empiricism, this philosophy gained a new lease on life when scholars in other disciplines defended it. The followers of the sociologist Paul Lazarsfeld at Columbia; many economists who developed "rational choice"; political scientists at universities such as MIT, Michigan, and Berkeley; proponents of the new "processual" archaeology and anthropology of the 1960s of Lewis Binford and his associates; and influential historical methodologists like Lee Benson and Alan Bogue: all championed a positivistic philosophy of science.

Another development of this sort was the invention of "applied philosophy." Professional schools of business, law, and medicine favored courses in "business ethics," "legal ethics," or "medical ethics," and budding professionals in those areas, which often developed their own expert faculty who were not professional philosophers, taught them. The philosophers themselves were confused. Sometimes they refused to have anything to do with the interlopers, but just as frequently—lured by the prospect of increasing enrollments—philosophers of "meta-ethics" tried to dominate these courses while distancing themselves from the tainted practicality of the professional schools.

By the 1980s departments of English were doing the most significant philosophy outside philosophy departments. English department philosophers took up any one of a number of versions of cultural relativism, or the relativism of meaning and interpretation more generally, all positions often connected to the pragmatists. These departments frequently looked not just to pragmatism but to Europe for inspiration, and they sometimes found allies in American Continental philosophers. But the latter group differed from the literary theorists who read contemporary French thinkers for guidance, for example Michel Foucault and Jacques Derrida, and who themselves became part of a tradition outside the discipline of philosophy. Edward Said of Columbia, Frederic Jameson of Duke, and "the Yale Critics," Harold Bloom, Paul DeMan, Geoffrey Hartman, and J. Hillis Miller, were not merely scholarly commentators on a European tradition but themselves figures in that tradition. They were more prestigious than American Continental philosophers.[27] By the 1990s, when academics thought of acquainting themselves with "theory," they turned to departments of literature.

In 2000 the *Concise Routledge Encyclopedia of Philosophy* announced that it had contributions from more than twelve hundred of the world's contemporary leading thinkers. Whom was one to believe? To whom should one listen? Was Richard McKeon "one of the most profound and brilliant philosophers of the twentieth century"? Were Paul and Patricia Churchland "towering figures" in philosophy? Was Hector-Neri Castañeda "one of the most important philosophers of the late twentieth century"? Was Edward Said "among the truly important intellects of our century?" Was John Kekes's *Against Liberalism* a book that "deserves a place on the same shelf with Burke, Tocqueville, and Hayek"?[28] The historian sorting through hard questions about the quality of thought that plague the history of philosophy had an impossible time. Analytic philosophy itself had split. But pursued by talented if abstract thinkers, it had to be judged not only by whatever common standards it had but by the standards of many antagonists who might disagree among themselves but who accurately saw a lack of breadth in analytic philosophy. Quine himself wrote that it was hard to separate philosophers into "sages and cranks" and that philosophical writing was often "incompetent."[29]

In grasping these issues, I have discerned the wide authority, in all the competing camps, of the new philosophy of science of Thomas Kuhn and a consensus on materialism that prompted the work of Richard Rorty.

Harvard had educated Kuhn as a physicist, but Quine in the Philosophy Department had also influenced him. After Kuhn taught in the sciences in Cambridge, Berkeley recruited him in 1956; there he held a joint appointment in philosophy and history. In 1957 he published a book on astronomy, *The Copernican Revolution*, which, along with other writing, exhibited the blend of philosophy and history that he brought to his work on scientific thought. In 1961

Ernest Nagel published his masterwork, *The Structure of Science*. Carl Hempel's collection of his most formidable essays, *Aspects of Scientific Explanation*, followed in 1965. Kuhn's second book, *The Structure of Scientific Revolutions*, a slim volume of 1962, was thus sandwiched between what later appeared to be two positivist dinosaurs. It was the most influential philosophical volume of the last third of the century, and Kuhn himself became, as one historian put it, "one of the most widely discussed academic intellectuals of the century."[30]

Focusing on the actual practice of science, the book depicted two kinds of changes in scientific belief. The first was part of "normal" research within a "paradigm." The second occurred when a "scientific revolution" took place in which scientists perceived counterexamples calling into question the paradigm itself. Dramatic "paradigm shifts"—like Einstein's replacement of Newtonian physics—implied different views of the world and premised "progress" that was not in any simple sense cumulative.[31]

Kuhn favorably contrasted a thick analysis of scientific practice to the abstract scientific studies of Hempel and Nagel. His style, common in the 1960s, was like that of the iconoclastic thinker Paul Feyerabend and of such works as Norwood Russell Hanson's *Patterns of Discovery* and Michael Polanyi's *Personal Knowledge*, both of 1958; Peter Berger and Thomas Luckmann's book of 1966, *The Social Construction of Reality*; and Clifford Geertz's *Interpretation of Cultures* of 1973. Their popularity through the 1960s and beyond must, I think, be attributed in part to the same fevered social scene in the United States in which Sartre and Marcuse flourished. The 1960s not only put the positivists at risk but also valorized romantic and subjective views. Many philosophers who knew little about the hard sciences, including the burgeoning American Continental philosophers, found comfort in Kuhn's willingness to dislodge science from its privileged claim to objectivity. Religious thinkers also relished Kuhn's attack, since if science was an acceptable belief system even if it did not progress, theological "paradigms" might come back; and social scientists rallied around Kuhn by explaining that they *would become* scientific by building "paradigms" in their own fields.

In 1960–61, when Kuhn was putting the finishing touches on *The Structure of Scientific Revolutions*, Berkeley took up his elevation to a full professorship. Influenced by positivism, the senior philosophers there agreed to Kuhn's promotion only if it was made in the history department. Although the philosophers did not inform Kuhn, they argued that he had few pretensions to being a philosopher, and that his history of science had little connection to philosophy. The History Department at Berkeley embraced Kuhn, but two years after what was termed his "eviction" from Philosophy, and a year after the publication of "the book," he left for a position in the history of science at Princeton.[32] The Berkeley decision—arguably the worst in the American academy in the twentieth century—underscored the constraints of analytic philosophy and its suspicion of the practices of real groups of knowers.

Rorty did an undergraduate degree at Chicago and his doctorate at Yale with Paul Weiss in 1956, early on hearing complaints about analytic philosophy. He became one of only a few of its prominent figures without a Harvard connection, making his reputation with a 1979 volume, *Philosophy and the Mirror of Nature.* Rorty focused simultaneously on Kuhn's ideas and on the materialism consensual among those in the tradition of Wilfrid Sellars. Going further than Kuhn, Rorty urged that we cannot honor the scientific community. Essential to human life is a series of sometimes competing, sometimes cooperative dialogues, which enable human beings to cope more or less effectively with the problems and troubles of existence. But to speak of any statements in these dialogues as being true about the world—as scientists did—is illegitimate. At the same time Rorty regularly allowed that he was a materialist; that mind is no more than behavior; that everything falls into a causal nexus about which science is our only guide; and that God does not exist.[33] Were these assertions true?

To these tension-laden approaches, Rorty added a bit of Sartre, and he lambasted the university setting of analytic philosophy, which, said Rorty, had often lost its audience. He entertained the view of a layperson who might ridicule philosophers unable to agree on how many angels could dance on the head of a pin: what was the point of all the argument? Yet using the resources of Anglo-American thought, Rorty articulated existentialist ideas. In a world bereft of meaning, human beings have to make themselves, and they do so through their conversational gambits, which shape whatever purposes they have. In a compromising American style Rorty melded the scientific, antireligious views of positivists, on the one hand, and ruminations about human life characteristic of Continental philosophy, on the other.

Some analytic philosophers thought the resulting combination of materialism and pragmatism contradictory, and Rorty's perceived lack of seriousness in confronting the contradiction infuriated them. He responded to them first by joining "the pluralists" and then by leaving the discipline of philosophy, as had Kuhn. Rorty forsook the Princeton Department of Philosophy for a position in the humanities at Virginia and, later in his career, for one in comparative literature at Stanford.

Nonetheless, a part of the analytic community responded positively to Rorty's critique, and Continental philosophers, although dismayed at his interpretation of several members of their tradition, acknowledged his concern. When classic American pragmatism was reassessed in the 1980s and 1990s—

partly through Rorty's efforts—other "pluralists" in the history of American thought recognized his input to their historical assessment. Drawing assorted scholars into a dialogue, Rorty influenced all intellectuals who denominated themselves theorists, whether or not in the discipline of philosophy. The secret to his appeal was the respect he received from some members of all the warring factions. He became the best-known American thinker, and he even attracted attention as a public intellectual. Rorty's historical significance is undeniable.

At the end of the twentieth century, philosophers of all stripes surveying their field regularly worried over their role in the university and their withdrawal from the civic realm, but their attempts to explain their situation showed how professional training had actually disabled them from understanding their place in the world.[34] After Kuhn arrived at Princeton and his book had made him famous, he restricted his teaching to graduate students, took no part in general university business, and cultivated an inability in departmental affairs to avoid administrative duties. Despite the fact that over the next thirty years he never produced anything remotely as important as *Structure*, Princeton officials were only too glad to give him a commanding salary.[35] The same pattern was at work in Quine's career.[36]

Rorty was the exception who proved the rule: he took the unabashedly secular orientation of many American philosophers and went out in the open with it, while they remained in the cloister. The result was ambiguous, certainly so when he declaimed against religion as "a conversation stopper" and consciously positioned himself outside what was acceptable even for the educated upper middle class. Also ambiguous were his various appeals to the best instincts of a democratic polity, for he simultaneously proclaimed his relativism and the certainty of the moral and political opinions that he had acquired in the seminar room and not in the "public square." And finally ambiguous was his self-conscious role as a sage who rejected philosophy.

In 1982 the APA proclaimed that philosophy was constantly useful to realize wisdom and to benefit American citizens, and it professed such beliefs through the end of the century. But to celebrate the one hundredth anniversary of the APA in 2001, the association formed a Centennial Committee "for the purpose of reaching a broader audience for philosophy." In its report to the membership the committee acknowledged that "philosophers have no experience with this sort of work; as a result we are not very good at it." The report left it unclear if this "work" was publicizing philosophy's "social usefulness" or actually being socially useful, or some combination of the two. In any event, the committee's good works included symposia at the yearly professional conventions; cash prizes for the best op-ed pieces written by a member of the APA; obtaining "a letter from President Bush indicating an appreciation of the contribution of philosophy"; a four-dollar CD with a series of thirty-second radio spots recorded by John Cleese and available as "appetizer-size philosophical ideas"; and an endowment to allow the APA to continue its "outreach activities."[37]

In the middle of the committee's deliberations Al-Qaeda attacked the United States, and the executive director of the APA told the membership that philosophers were "in a prime position to serve as a resource for reflective public discourse on the moral and social dimensions of the 21st-century dilemmas created by these acts of terror." But the only follow-through was to send philosophers a letter to the president and Congress for them to sign; a Canadian psychologist had written the letter.[38]

THE POST–WORLD WAR II expansion of the academy that propelled "inclusion" had certainly contributed to the nondescript nature of philosophy and to its genuine befuddlement about its place in collegiate and noncollegiate life. Yet after the Golden Age of American speculation, philosophy in the interwar period had been pretty nondescript also. Although philosophy in that era was not confused about its role, it served up an ordinary blend of consolation and edification to a small group of white men. After World War II more ethnically and intellectually diverse students were able to get a wider comprehension of what the philosophical traditions were about, even though spiritual understanding continued to have less and less a grip on philosophical educators. Greater secularization and professionalization—from pragmatism, to positivism, to analysis—meant that philosophy in the late twentieth century was more isolated than it had been before 1945. But secularism was not all bad, and pluralism hindered the crablike movement away from religion. While most disciplinary philosophers stumbled about in trying to connect to other areas of inquiry or the world outside their doors, bastardized forms of their ideas—known as "theory"—were a common scholarly currency; and two of their number, Kuhn and Rorty, despite the profession's ambivalence about them, were usually identified as philosophers and as two of the leading intellectual personages of the age. Nonetheless, times had changed. Philosophy used to be a core area of inquiry; it no longer is. Do we ignore it at our peril?

Notes

1. The alert reader will note that while specific points are footnoted, many of my interpretative remarks are not. They are, however, based on wide examination of material. I have depended on four journals: *Journal of Philosophy, Philosophical Review* (hereafter *PR*), *Philosophy and Phenomenological Research*, and *Review of Metaphysics*. Also important are the various publications of the American Philosophical Association (hereafter APA). I have also used reputational studies. Allan

M. Cartter, *An Assessment of Quality in Graduate Education* (Washington, D.C.: American Council on Education, 1966), cites the results of previous studies in 1925, 1957, and 1964. It was followed by Kenneth D. Roose and Charles J. Andersen, *A Rating of Graduate Programs* (Washington, D.C.: American Council on Education, 1970); L. V. Jones, G. Lindzey, and P. E. Coggeshall, *An Assessment of Research-Doctorate Programs in the United States: Humanities* (Washington, D.C.: National Academy Press, 1982); Marvin L. Goldberger et al., eds., *Research-Doctorate Programs in the United States: Continuity and Change* (Washington, D.C.: National Academy Press, 1995). I have used the available records on philosophy, of very varying quality, at Chicago, Harvard, Hopkins, MIT, Pennsylvania, Princeton, UCLA, and Yale. The reader is also referred to my own *Churchmen and Philosophers: From Jonathan Edwards to John Dewey* (New Haven: Yale University Press, 1985), *The Rise of American Philosophy: Cambridge, Massachusetts, 1860–1930* (New Haven: Yale University Press, 1976), and *Philosophy in America: A Cultural and Intellectual History* (Oxford: Oxford University Press, 2001) for background. I have also drawn on my essay "Philosophy at Yale in the Century after Darwin," *History of Philosophy Quarterly* 21 (2004): 313–336. Finally, Nicholas Rescher, "American Philosophy Today," *Review of Metaphysics* 46 (1992–93): 717–747, presents statistical and demographic data that amplify and corroborate many of the points that I make.

2. See Richard Freeland, *Academia's Golden Age* (New York: Oxford University Press, 1992).

3. Harry S. Ashmore, *Unseasonable Truth: The Life of Robert Maynard Hutchins* (Boston: Little, Brown, 1989), 88–105, 153–164.

4. George Cotkin, "Middle-Ground Pragmatists: The Popularization of Philosophy in American Culture," *Journal of the History of Ideas* 55 (1994): 283–302; Joan Shelley Rubin, *The Making of Middlebrow Culture* (Chapel Hill: University of North Carolina Press, 1992).

5. William M. Halsey, *The Survival of American Innocence* (Notre Dame, Ind.: University of Notre Dame Press, 1980), 145, 207–208n31.

6. Van Wyck Brooks, "Conference on Science, Philosophy, and Religion," in *Science, Philosophy, and Religion: A Symposium* (New York: Harper and Brothers, 1941), 1–10; and Quine's comment in *Science, Philosophy, and Religion, Second Symposium*, ed. Lyman Bryson and Louis Finkelstein (New York: Harper and Brothers, 1942), 238–239.

7. Brand Blanshard et al., *Philosophy in American Education* (New York: Harper and Brothers, 1945), vii–xii, 3–65.

8. Henry Van Deusen to Harold Dodds March 27, 1947, Philosophy folders, Dodds Papers, Mudd Library, Princeton University.

9. Morton White gives this description from the 1950s in his autobiography, *A Philosopher's Story* (University Park: Penn State University Press, 1999), 189–252.

10. For Blanshard, see his Epilogue in Arthur Pap, *An Introduction to the Philosophy of Science* (New York: Free Press, 1962), 429; on Weiss, see Charles Hendel to Brand Blanshard, October 2, 1945, and Yale News Bureau release, April 15, 1950, both in Charles Seymour Papers, Series I, box 127, folder 1077, Yale University Archives.

11. Susan Haack, *Manifesto of a Passionate Moderate* (Chicago: University of Chicago Press, 1998), 197.

12. *PR* 29 (1920), 158–164; APA, *Proceedings and Addresses*, 1960, 1991–2001, membership lists. The population of the United States: 106 million in 1920, 180 million in 1960, and 250 million in the 1990s.

13. Data from *Guide to Graduate Programs in Philosophy* (Newark, Del.: APA, 1998, 2002).

14. This is a main point of Rescher, "American Philosophy Today."

15. See Herbert Marcuse, *One Dimensional Man* (Boston: Beacon, 1964), esp. 149, 216–217; Marcuse, "Repressive Tolerance," in *A Critique of Pure Tolerance*, by Robert P. Wolff, Barrington Moore Jr., and Herbert Marcuse (Boston: Beacon, 1965), 81–117.

16. Alain Martineau, *Herbert Marcuse's Utopia*, trans. Jane Brierley (Montreal: Harvest House, 1986), 7–26.

17. For Rawls's original formulation see his *A Theory of Justice* (Cambridge: Harvard University

Press, 1971), viii. For his popularity, see Lenn Goodman, "Political Philosophy," in *The Future of Philosophy*, ed. Oliver Leaman (New York: Routledge, 1998), 63–66, and Rawls's own comments in *Philosophers in Conversation: Interviews from the Harvard Review of Philosophy*, ed. S. Phineas Upham (New York: Routledge, 2002), 8.

18. A. J. Mandt, "The Inevitability of Pluralism," in *The Institution of Philosophy*, ed. Avner Cohen and Marcelo Dascal (La Salle, Ill.: Open Court, 1989), 79.

19. See Bruce Wilshire, *Fashionable Nihilism: A Critique of Analytic Philosophy* (Albany: SUNY Press, 2002), 50–64.

20. There are two outstanding sources on Sartre in America: Ann Fulton, *Apostles of Sartre* (Evanston, Ill.: Northwestern University Press, 1999), and George Cotkin, *Existential America* (Baltimore: Johns Hopkins University Press, 2003).

21. Avrum Stroll, *Twentieth-Century Analytic Philosophy* (New York: Columbia University Press, 2000), 250, on Seyyed Hossein Nasr. Some of the contributors to C. P. Ragland and Sarah Heidt, eds., *What Is Philosophy?* (New Haven: Yale University Press, 2001), exhibit the same problem; see the contributions of Allen Wood and Martha Nussbaum.

22. The answer to this rhetorical question is "The Philosophical Gourmet Report," www .blackwellpublishers.co.uk.gourmet, run by a University of Texas philosopher, which shows an obsession with rankings. For the official statement see "Ranking of Departments and Programs" (1994) in APA, *Statements on the Profession* (1997), 33–34.

23. John Rajchman and Cornel West, eds., *Post-Analytic Philosophy* (New York: Columbia University Press, 1985); James R. Watson, ed., *Portraits of American Continental Philosophers* (Bloomington: Indiana University Press, 1999). A companion to the latter book is Walter Brogan and James Risser, eds., *American Continental Philosophy: A Reader* (Bloomington: Indiana University Press, 2000).

24. Report prepared by Richard Schacht, in APA, *Philosophy in America 1994: Summary and Data* (1997), 28, 41.

25. See Brook Sadler, "Women in Philosophy," *APA Newsletter* 2 (Spring 2003): 118; the Newsletter on Philosophy and the Black Experience, ibid., 41–90; and, in fact, the entire issue relates to this point.

26. Willard Quine, "Has Philosophy Lost Contact with People?" reprinted in *Theories and Things* (Cambridge: Harvard University Press, 1981), 193; an earlier statement of similar views appeared in 1964 in the *National Observer* and was reprinted as "A Letter to Mr. Osterman," in *The Owl of Minerva: Philosophers on Philosophy*, ed. Charles J. Bontempo and S. Jack Odell (New York: McGraw-Hill, 1975), 227–230.

27. For philosophy in English departments see Gerald Graff, *Professing Literature: An Institutional History* (Chicago: University of Chicago Press, 1987); Robert Scholes, *The Rise and Fall of English* (New Haven: Yale University Press, 1998).

28. Ads for the *Concise Routledge Encyclopedia of Philosophy* in *New York Review of Books*, April 13, 2000, 2; Churchlands mentioned ibid., 39 ; the McKeon quote comes from the Vanderbilt University Press catalogue, Spring 2000; Castañeda is mentioned in *New York Review of Books*, July 15, 1999, 25; the Said reference is in *New York Times Book Review*, November 7, 1999, 34; the Kekes quote is from *Against Liberalism*'s dust jacket.

29. Quine, "Has Philosophy Lost Contact with People?" 192.

30. David A. Hollinger, Afterword, in Gene A. Brucker, Henry F. May, and David A. Hollinger, *History at Berkeley* (Berkeley: University of California Press, 1998), 43.

31. Kuhn, *Structure of Scientific Revolutions*, 2nd ed. (Chicago: University of Chicago Press, 1970).

32. Hollinger, Afterword, 43–45, 48–50; "A Discussion with Thomas S. Kuhn," in Kuhn, *The Road since Structure*, ed. James Conant and John Haugeland (Chicago: University of Chicago Press, 2000), 301–302.

33. Richard Rorty, *Philosophy and the Mirror of Nature* (Princeton: Princeton University Press, 1979), 382, 384, 387–390; Rorty, *Contingency, Irony, and Solidarity* (New York: Cambridge University Press, 1989), 5, 17; Rorty, "International Books of the Year and the Millennium," *Times Literary Supplement*, December 3, 1999, 11 (on Darwin); Rorty, "Religion as a Conversation Stopper," in *Philosophy and Social Hope* (New York: Penguin Books, 1999), 169 (as an atheist).

34. Wilshire's *Fashionable Nihilism* and John McCumber's *Time in the Ditch: American Philosophy and the McCarthy Era* (Evanston, Ill.: Northwestern University Press, 2001) exemplify embarrassing statements by nonanalysts on the role of philosophy in American life; an equally off-the-mark view is Robert Audi, "Philosophy in American Life," *Proceedings and Addresses, APA* 72 (1999): 139–148.

35. See the yearly reports from 1967 on in the Thomas Kuhn faculty file, Mudd Library, Princeton University.

36. See Willard Quine, *The Time of My Life* (Cambridge: MIT Press, 1985).

37. APA, *Philosophy: A Brief Guide for Undergraduates* (1982), 8, 12; APA e-mails to membership, October 10, 2000; October 1, 2001; October 21, 2001. APA, e-mail to membership, September 21, 2001.

38. APA, e-mail to membership, September 21, 2001.

III

SOCIAL INCLUSION

7

CATHOLICS, CATHOLICISM, AND THE HUMANITIES SINCE WORLD WAR II

JOHN T. MCGREEVY

"TODAY IN AMERICA," explained the Jesuit John Courtney Murray to the Columbia University sociologist Robert MacIver in 1952, "there is really no such thing as a genuine intellectual community." Instead, "each professor is a law unto himself, entitled to make and present his own synthesis, his own order of truth. And out of all the competing orders the student must be free to make his own choice." Murray regretted, too, that MacIver's soon-to-be published study of academic freedom declined to emphasize the important role the university must play in conserving "the intellectual, social and spiritual heritage of the community."[1]

MacIver demurred. "The kind of truth on which all men agree," he retorted, "is based on inference from data or evidences. It is the quest for truth, so understood, rather than the exposition of it, that is the universal bond of scholarship." The achievements of science, in particular, where "astronomers of Soviet Russia are in essential agreement in their field with the astronomers of the United States," demonstrated that "common devotion to truth seeking" trumped shared beliefs. "What common tradition can there be . . . if the Buddhist and the follower of Confucius and the Jew and the Methodist and the Roman Catholic and the agnostic are equally welcome so long as they are competent seekers of knowledge?"

The "denominational college," MacIver pointedly added, must be distinguished from "the university." Such colleges had their proper function but "in the light of so many historical warnings it would be perilous to identify it with the university. Its creed, whatever it may be, takes certain things as given, not to be questioned, and these things subtly reach into and impinge upon the field of scientifically discovered knowledge."[2]

THE STATUS of the correspondents is noteworthy. Murray was the most important American Catholic intellectual of the twentieth century, a central figure in the Catholic effort to combat what he termed in 1950 "a newly articulate, organized and doctrinal secularism," as well as the guiding influence on the Declaration on Religious Freedom (*Dignitatis humanae*) issued at the conclusion of the

189

Second Vatican Council in 1965.[3] A distinguished sociologist, MacIver directed the era's most comprehensive effort to define and defend academic freedom, an effort spurred by attacks on alleged Communists on university faculties.[4]

The two men exchanged several cordial, even frank, letters. Three themes in the correspondence locate Catholics and Catholicism within our assigned rubric, "The Humanities and the Dynamics of Inclusion since World War II" (although the natural boundaries of the subject require forays into the history of the social sciences as well).

The first is Catholic access: Murray knew that Catholic students (especially) and Catholic faculty (much less so) were increasingly visible within American higher education in the first years after the war. When the exchange with MacIver began, Murray was finishing a year as a visitor at Yale University, "the land of the infidel" as he wryly termed it, where he hoped that "sheer presence" might defuse tensions between Catholics and non-Catholics.[5] (Upon learning of Murray's appointment, one of Yale's most prominent alumni and guardians, the minister Henry Sloane Coffin, privately warned that Murray was "outwardly smooth, but can be poisonous.")[6]

The second is Catholic intellectual life. Murray's dismissal of MacIver's effort to base the secular university on anything but pragmatic grounds— "the university cannot presume to know what to think or to teach anyone to think. Let it be content to teach people how to think"—did not prevent him from despairing at the state of Catholic inquiry.[7] In 1955 Murray applauded as "splendid both in content and in tone" his friend Father John Tracy Ellis's influential attack on "the perpetuation of mediocrity" within Catholic universities.[8] That same year Murray's Jesuit superiors forced him to stop publishing in his area of greatest expertise, church and state, because of pressure from Vatican officials. Nonetheless, Murray's sustained engagement with critics inside and outside the church helped edge Catholics toward the center of contemporary debates over American pluralism.[9]

The third theme is the suspicion with which some American intellectuals in the 1940s and 1950s viewed Catholics and Catholicism. MacIver's own foreboding about any "authoritative faith, the priests of which interpret its doctrines to the faithful" was clear.[10] Just weeks before initiating his correspondence with Murray, MacIver had read William F. Buckley's minor cause célèbre, *God and Man at Yale* (1951), which charged Yale's faculty with condoning socialism and abandoning the university's Christian heritage. Neither the book nor Buckley's Catholicism won him many admirers in Catholic intellectual circles, in part because his zeal for free market economics ran against the then-dominant Catholic grain. ("Too much publicity," Murray thought, had been given that "unfortunately conceived utterance" and the "rather ignorant young man who made it.") MacIver, however, soberly warned Yale's president, A. Whitney Griswold, that Buckley "envisages the university as primarily an indoctrination school" while defending a religion that has "perpetuated utterly false notions respecting the physical universe [and] has persecuted and even destroyed those who dared to extend the range of human knowledge in ways that conflicted with ancient lore."[11]

RELATIVELY FEW Catholics attended college before World War II in large part because Catholics remained an overwhelmingly working-class population. (Catholics, one 1945–1946 survey concluded, paralleled Baptists "almost precisely in stratification.")[12] Irish Catholics were the most affluent Catholic group, but even the Irish had a sizeable working-class population. One study of a largely Irish parish in the northeast in the late 1930s found only two of the parish's students attending college, both at local Catholic schools.[13]

The economic boom of the 1940s and 1950s proved transformative. Disproportionately located in fast-growing metropolitan areas and prime beneficiaries of both higher wages in industrial unions and increasing numbers of lower management positions, Catholics matched or surpassed national income and education averages by the mid-1960s.[14]

In contrast to American Jews, many Catholics entered the academy through a network of sectarian institutions—Catholic colleges and universities. The educational benefits available through the 1944 G.I. Bill benefited these institutions enormously, since Congress, remarkably, permitted veterans to use federal moneys to attend religious colleges and universities.[15] The number of students enrolled in Catholic colleges alone grew from 92,000 in 1944–45 to 220,000 in 1947–48, and by 1963 Catholic colleges awarded 11 percent of all bachelor's degrees.[16] By 1960 Catholic women's colleges educated more women than non-Catholic women's colleges.[17]

Data on Catholics attending non-Catholic colleges is sketchier, but the general trends are clear. By 1966 Catholics numbered 28.2 percent of entering students at all postsecondary institutions (even as they made up only 25% of the general population) and 91.7 percent of entering students at Catholic colleges.[18] Between 60 and 70 percent of Catholic students were enrolled at non-Catholic colleges, a figure that had increased from roughly 50 percent early in the twentieth century, held steady into the 1970s, and then increased in the last generation, as expanding public universities and community colleges took a greater share of the enrollment pie. (The largest "Catholic" university in Illinois, for example, is probably the University of Illinois at Chicago, where half the undergraduate student body is nominally Catholic.) During the same period the percentage of Catholic students at some Catholic colleges decreased. (By fall 2001 only 54% of Georgetown's first-year students identified themselves as Catholic.)[19]

Because Catholics were a largely working-class population into the 1950s, and because one-third of Catholics attended Catholic institutions, Catholics never applied to elite non-Catholic institutions in numbers large enough to raise questions about institutional identity. (In fact, the more common problem was intermittent tension between a largely non-Catholic student body and working-class Catholics in cities such as Cambridge and New Haven.)[20] As early as 1934, 13 percent of Yale's entering class, uncontroversially, was Catholic; in the 1920s 7 percent of Harvard's student body was Catholic (up to 10% in 1944 and 12% by the mid-1950s).[21] In 1947, 13 percent of Stanford's entering class was Catholic.[22] By 1965 Catholics numbered 18 percent of Northwestern's undergraduate student body.[23]

These cohorts attracted little notice even as a national controversy engulfed Harvard after President A. Lawrence Lowell proposed a 25 percent student quota for Jews.[24] At Yale, too, secret societies that uniformly excluded Jews welcomed the occasional Catholic.[25] Any barriers (however slight) faced by Catholic undergraduates ended after the Second World War. In the late 1950s Catholic winners of National Merit Scholarships, likely to gain admission to top universities and able to use the scholarship to allay financial concerns, were slightly more likely to choose non-Catholic schools than Catholic schools.[26]

The situation for Catholic faculty members in the humanities was more complex. Until the 1950s Catholic faculty members at the leading secular universities were barely visible. One query sent to universities across the country in 1938–39, in the last era when "church affiliation" might be tabulated on faculty hiring forms, produced startling results: at Stanford, there were 8 Catholics reported on a faculty of 781, or 1 percent; at Johns Hopkins, 3 of 651, or .005 percent. The percentage of Catholics rose slightly at the great state universities: at Wisconsin, 58 Catholics of 831, or 7 percent, and more consistently at less prestigious teachers colleges, such as the University of Newark (now Rutgers at Newark), where Catholics made up 13 percent of the faculty.[27] These figures almost certainly underestimate the Catholic faculty presence—with forms filled out by harried assistant deans—but survey data taken in 1969 also suggest that Catholics numbered fewer than 10 percent of faculty at elite universities before World War II.[28]

Anecdotal evidence indicates that even as the number of Catholic faculty members increased in the 1950s, Catholics remained disproportionately located in various professional schools, especially medicine, and not in the humanities and social sciences.[29] Within the humanities Catholics clustered in language programs, as professors of French, Spanish, Portuguese, and German.[30] As the number of Catholics attending graduate school and receiving Ph.D.'s soared in the late 1960s, Catholics remained underrepresented on the faculties of elite universities, claiming roughly 13 percent of positions even as Catholics made up 25 percent of the national population.[31]

Far more important than discrimination was the existence of a parallel Catholic career track. Bookish Catholic men and women remained likely candidates for the priesthood or religious life. The most influential of the male Catholic religious orders, the Jesuits, maintained a twelve-year training regimen that piled extensive work in philosophy, languages, and theology onto a disciplinary Ph.D., along with stints teaching high school or mission work. (John Courtney Murray spent one year teaching high school in the Philippines.)[32]

When these men and women became eligible for academic employment, the expanding system of Catholic seminaries, colleges, and universities drafted many of the most capable into administrative positions. A significant number of Catholic laymen and a few laywomen followed a similar arc—undergraduate degree with a Catholic college, a graduate degree at a secular university, and then employment with a Catholic college. Salaries remained low (no Catholic college or university came close to the top salary rating of the American Association of University Professors), and most faculty taught four or five courses a semester.[33] (A frustrated Catholic graduate student complained in 1959 that only secular colleges offered a "living wage" and "frequent sabbaticals.")[34] One 1962 study of colleges and universities enrolling a certain percentage of high scorers on the National Merit Scholarship Qualifying Test listed nineteen Catholic colleges and universities, including Boston College, DePaul University, and St. John's in New York, in the list of the thirty least well endowed (under $326 per student). Not a single Catholic college made the list of the thirty best endowed colleges and universities (above $9,829 per student.)[35]

Self-segregation into impoverished Catholic colleges and universities, however, was not the entire story. Catholics faced nothing comparable to the crude stereotyping endured by Jewish scholars in the 1930s and 1940s. (Father John Tracy Ellis noted his sadness in 1942 at hearing from the Harvard historian Arthur Schlesinger Sr. that "noble" young Jewish scholars struggled to find academic positions.)[36]

But if Jews consistently suffered because of who they were, Catholics occasionally suffered because of what they were understood to believe. The same scholars championing the elimination of anti-Semitic barriers in the universities could express reservations about the intellectual capabilities of practicing Catholics. The Yale philosopher Brand Blanshard, for example, privately termed Catholicism a "stupid creed" and cheered on his brother Paul's widely publicized attacks on the church, even as he used his position as chair of the Philosophy Department in the late 1940s to ensure the appointment of the first Jew to the Yale College faculty.[37]

Accusations of anti-Catholicism on hiring committees produced little evidence. Still, as late as 1959 Jerome Kerwin, a political theorist at the University of Chicago and reputedly the first Catholic faculty member at that university when hired in 1923, complained that "in the Social Sciences and the Humanities, dealing as they do with the affairs, the thinking and the history of men, Catholics are still suspect in many quarters. It is unhappily true that frequently scholars in these fields believe that Catholics have all their ideas and opinions formed for them by that mysterious force called the hierarchy."[38]

What made academics suspicious? Most obviously, some Catholics seemed lukewarm supporters of democracy and positively hostile to religious liberty. The Vatican negotiated concordats with Italy and Germany in the early 1930s, and American Catholic bishops became vocal supporters of Spain's General Franco. President Franklin Roosevelt tapped the most prominent Catholic historian in the United States, Columbia's Carlton Hayes, for service as ambassador to Franco's Spain during World War II. A group of young leaders in the historical profession, including Richard Hofstadter, Frank Friedel, and Kenneth Stampp, thought this service disqualifying, and they almost prevented Hayes from becoming president of the American Historical Association, even as one of Hayes's Catholic supporters wrote to him that the "little cabal" had "made a sorry show of themselves as professional historians whose business it is to divest themselves of prejudice."[39]

Similarly, Father Charles Coughlin's popularity within the United States, and his obvious anti-Semitism after 1936, seemed a domestic counterpart to European and Latin American demagogues. The young Arthur Schlesinger Jr. berated Father John Tracy Ellis in 1942 for his "evasion" on the subject of the Vatican's responsibility to discipline Coughlin.[40]

Finally, Catholic politicians, dominant in almost all the northern cities by the 1940s, seemed dismissive of academic freedom. The removal of the philosopher Bertrand Russell from his post at New York's City College in 1940 became an important cause célèbre. An Episcopalian bishop led the charge against Russell, but most observers attributed the termination of Russell's contract to influential Catholic politicians convinced that Russell's views on sexuality and marriage made him an enemy of "common decency."[41]

Russell privately blamed Catholic influence for his plight, and his friends Horace Kallen and John Dewey quickly put together a volume of essays on the case. "You need have no scruples," Kallen told one contributor, the Yale law professor Walter Hamilton. "You are dealing with a bully [Judge John E. McGeehan, who upheld the revocation of Russell's appointment] who spoke not for himself but for the whole Catholic hierarchy."[42]

At Harvard, President James Bryant Conant apparently made contingency plans to move university offices to its Dumbarton Oaks campus in Washington, D.C., should threats to academic freedom from Boston's Catholic pols become intolerable.[43] The Harvard sociologist Talcott Parsons wondered in 1939 if "it may well be interpreted as an obligation of Harvard Professors to take especial care in what they say publicly about the Catholic church, because of the possible repercussions through political channels on the university."[44]

A cluster of incidents after World War II—two important Supreme Court cases on religion and public education, a dispute over birth control restrictions in Massachusetts, the failed effort to name an ambassador to the Vatican, and a brawl over funding for parochial schools between New York's Cardinal Francis Spellman and the liberal icon Eleanor Roosevelt (who would list John F. Kennedy's Catholicism as reason not to favor his presidential candidacy as late as 1958)—only heightened liberal-Catholic tensions.[45] John Dewey warned liberals against concessions to a "reactionary world organization" in 1947, and the Johns Hopkins University philosopher George Boas described the Church as the "most bitter opponent of the liberal tradition."[46] The warm reception given Senator Joseph McCarthy by some Catholic audiences only cemented the association made between Catholicism and intolerance. Seymour Martin Lipset, in one of the first scholarly analyses of McCarthy, worried about an "extreme moralizing" and "anti–civil libertarian" Catholicism.[47]

This anxiety illuminates a wider scholarly canvas. Recent investigations of the origins of the humanities in the first North Atlantic research universities detail an opposition to "dogmatic" or orthodox religion.[48] Fears about Catholicism's debilitating role, in particular, were widespread in the late nineteenth century, waned during the first decades of the twentieth century, and then resurfaced with greater intensity in the 1930s and 1940s. The triumph of fascism in much of Europe and Latin America, in particular, pushed American intellectuals into sustained reflection on links between personal identity, culture, and political conviction.[49]

The fear was palpable. "Free society," worried Arthur Schlesinger Jr. in 1949, "alienates the lonely and uprooted masses," while totalitarianism provided "a structure of belief, men to worship and men to hate and rites which guarantee salvation."[50] Or as the historian Perry Miller put it, Catholicism's inherent antagonism to a "free and critical education" might threaten the "democratic way of life."[51]

This perceived hostility between Catholicism and modernity—defined as respect for the individual, tolerance of ambiguity, capitalism, civil liberties, and experimental science—intrigued scholars in several disciplines. The most powerful source was Max Weber. Weber famously traced the connection between a Protestant ethic and capitalism, and his experience in late nineteenth-century Germany reinforced his suspicion of Catholic backwardness.[52] Political scientists drew upon Weber for the notion of civic culture and wondered if Catholic authoritarianism might prevent the emergence of European democracies as stable as the United States and Britain.[53]

Sociologists and psychologists found Weber's arguments especially enticing. Talcott Parsons, Weber's English translator, agreed that the Reformation marked a turning point for the modern West, and he concluded that "Anglo-Saxon Protestant traditions" provided the most substantial barrier to an American fascism. By contrast, Parsons noted an "authoritarian element in the basic structure of the Catholic church itself which may weaken individual self-reliance and valuation of freedom."[54]

Parsons also directed attention to the work of Robert Merton, for whom Parsons had served as a thesis reader. In one of the most influential essays ever written by an American on the history of science, Merton claimed to confirm Weber's speculation that the Protestant ethic supported not only capitalism but the emergence of modern, experimental science. Calvinist Protestants in seventeenth-century England were willing to replace "cloistered contemplation" with "active experimentation." Merton counted Catholic and Protestant scientists, satisfying himself that Protestants, even in predominantly Catholic France, were more likely to achieve distinction.[55] Parsons began referring to the "Weber-Merton thesis" and the inability of the medieval "schoolmen" to advance scientific knowledge.[56]

Again, the stakes were considerable. A crucial marker of a democratic culture, liberals agreed, was an enthusiasm for science. Or as Merton argued in a 1942 essay, experimental science rested most comfortably in modern democracies, with their climate of "organized skepticism."[57]

The academic mills began to churn. Two volumes produced by a team of Wesleyan scholars traced the educational background of American academics. In science, especially, "the most distinguished accomplishment of our Western civilization," Catholic colleges proved inadequate. The authors pondered whether "Catholicism has permitted comparatively little secularization of outlook among its constituents and has maintained a firm authoritarian structure." Or alternatively, "Catholicism has been a consistent opponent of physical monism, that philosophical tradition under which science has for the most part advanced." Another analyst offered the view that science depended on a "moral preference for the dictates of individual conscience rather than for those of organized authority." Unfortunately, Catholics seemed to place less emphasis on "critical rationality."[58]

The Harvard social psychologist David McClelland took a different tack, connecting Catholic child-rearing habits to economic growth. McClelland claimed that a particular *n* achievement value measured each person's initiative and self-reliance and, drawing on Weber, that Catholic families and cultures produced few individuals with high achievement potential.[59]

Confirmation came from a variety of sources. Following a series of studies done on Connecticut families, researchers concluded that parents who insisted that a *"child be able to perform certain tasks well by himself"* would produce children with high *n* achievement.[60] Protestant families did this work quite well, but Catholic families, McClelland explained, restrained initiative. In fact, "the view toward authority and control which is consciously promoted by the church, has had what is probably an unintended consequence on the child-rearing practices of Catholic parents." McClelland even traveled to Germany, where he claimed that Catholic parents were less likely to buy walkers for their sons, and thus foster independence, and more content to stick with playpens.[61] Stagnation in such Catholic countries as Spain and Chile became a consequence of not producing high-achievement (male) individuals, a claim McClelland made in testimony before Congress and in research sponsored by the federal government.[62]

Just as Catholic authoritarianism seemed incompatible with intellectual autonomy, Catholic families might crush psychological independence. In their influential 1950 study of the connection between psychological tendencies and political views, *The Authoritarian Personality*, Theodor Adorno and his colleagues clearly included Catholics when they warned of overly restrictive religious families whose children might channel their frustration into fascist politics. (And at least one of Adorno's colleagues had urged a study of links between Catholicism and anti-Semitism as early as 1944.)[63]

Adorno alluded to "official" Communism and Catholicism as two all-encompassing ideologies, and the enormous secondary literature spawned by *The Authoritarian Personality* carried this theme forward. One 1960 study, funded by the Social Science Research Council and the National Institute of Mental Health and one of the most cited books in the psychological literature, forthrightly compared Catholicism and Communism and assumed that adherents of each belief system were "dogmatic" and less capable of tolerant judgments about the world around them.[64]

Historians, too, directed attention to the gap between Catholicism and modernity. One group of leadings historians, in an anti-Catholic aside, insisted in 1946 that colleagues working in the "scientific spirit" must "seek to place absolute systems of thought in their appropriate settings of time and place."[65] Another group of scholars agreed that "it was no accident that democracy should have run half its course in modern history before it invaded a Roman Catholic country."[66]

Henry Steele Commager, in his influential 1950 survey of the "American mind," worried that Catholicism might prove "inconsistent with the American principles of liberty and democracy, complete freedom of expression, separation of church and state, and secular control over public education."[67] More subtly, historians portrayed Catholic belief as an essentially conservative, anti-intellectual force. Oscar Handlin's study of immigration, *The Uprooted*, described European Catholic peasants as not making an "individual choice" about religious belief but instead falling into "conformity." Indeed, "the Church gave no reasons for being; it was."[68]

Philosophy was a special case. The enormous Catholic investment in the discipline, with all undergraduates at Catholic colleges virtually required to take a second major in philosophy, gave it disproportionate influence in the Catholic milieu. (The bull market for philosophy Ph.D.'s in Catholic colleges, for example, meant that Catholic University produced more doctoral degrees in philosophy than any other university in the country in the 1940s and 1950s.) Almost all Catholic philosophers labored on translations and technical problems from within the Thomistic tradition, and they were often casually dismissive of modern philosophy from Descartes onward.[69]

Most American philosophers returned the favor. Although mid-century Thomists in both Europe and the United States made a point, ironically, of separating philosophical from theological claims, they could not shed the impression among non-Catholic philosophers that Thomists labored as an advance guard for Catholic authoritarianism. When Jacques Maritain, the most influential Thomist of the twentieth century, applied for a visiting position at the University of Chicago after the fall of France in 1940, the chairman of the Philosophy Department declined to pursue the matter. "Professor Maritain's reputation in this part of the world," he explained, "is largely that of an apologist or propagandist for Catholic doctrine."[70] Two leading American pragmatists voiced the conventional wisdom. "The only religion appropriate to the democratic faith," the University of Chicago's Charles Morris announced in 1944, "is a non-dogmatic religion."[71] Max Otto at the University of Wisconsin described "authoritarian religion and the democratic way of life" as incompatible.[72]

Medieval philosophy generally was slighted. Scanning a bibliography prepared in the early 1950s by Yale's Philosophy Department for "intensive majors," John Courtney Murray discovered that it skipped from Plato to Descartes.[73] The more austere linguistic analysis or analytical philosophy that became dominant in leading departments in the 1950s softened polemics from the non-Catholic side, although this development further isolated the more adventurous Thomists, now beginning serious work not just on Aquinas but on Husserl and Heidegger. (Only 9% of philosophers teaching in Catholic colleges in 1966 defined themselves as "analytic and empiricist" philosophers.)[74] Even so, as late as 1960 the academic honor society Phi Beta Kappa chose to deny the University of Notre Dame membership, in part because required "philosophy courses are rather too wholly and specifically Thomistic in content and orientation to provide a sufficiently liberal education on the philosophical level."[75]

THIS SITUATION — an open door for Catholic undergraduates, but reservations about Catholicism as an institution and an intellectual tradition, with hints of discrimination against Catholics at elite universities—lasted from the mid-1940s until the early 1960s. The most powerful source of change remained the continued, steady assimilation of Catholics into all sectors of American life, symbolized most powerfully by the election of John F. Kennedy to the presidency in 1960. If Kennedy's politics, or more accurately those of his father, Joseph P. Kennedy, disturbed his Harvard constituents when he first ran for Congress in 1946, the intervening years were a tonic.[76] In the first months of Kennedy's presidential campaign, Arthur Schlesinger Jr. privately described his Democratic opponent Hubert Humphrey's attacks on Kennedy—Humphrey enjoyed playing "Give Me That Old Time Religion" on the stump—as a "disservice to the Democratic Party and to liberalism" and publicly argued that opposition to Kennedy on religious grounds smacked of bigotry.[77]

Change also came from graduate students, the canaries in the university coal mine. As early as 1958 one study claimed that 22 percent of graduate students in the arts and sciences were Catholic, and by the 1960s Catholics entered graduate school at or modestly below the percentage of Catholics in the population.[78] Because graduate programs at Catholic universities remained small (no Catholic university was among the top twenty in Ph.D.'s granted through the 1960s, and Catholic universities produced under 3 percent of the total number of Ph.D.'s in the United States) and because graduate programs at secular universities remained superior, the overwhelming majority of Catholic graduate students attended non-Catholic graduate schools.[79]

They faced few barriers. Precisely because mid-twentieth-century liberals prided themselves on avoiding racial or religious bias (notably against African Americans or Jews), aspiring Catholic chemists and Catholic musicologists, usually white men, after all, comfortably made their way. Students working in psychology and sociology, as well as some branches of history, philosophy, and political theory, may have chosen dissertation topics and advisors with caution (one Catholic historian pleaded with his advisor to suggest to prospective employers that he was *not* a Catholic), but self-conscious groups of Catholic graduate students existed at all the leading research universities by the early 1960s.[80]

At Harvard, for example, Michael Novak (then a left-leaning political and religious commentator, now a leading neoconservative), Sidney Callahan (a psychologist), Daniel Callahan (*Commonweal*'s editor and later the founder of the Hastings Center on bioethics), Robert Kiely (later a professor of English at Harvard), Jana Kiely (a biologist), Jill Ker Conway (a historian and later president of Smith College), and John T. Noonan Jr. (a legal scholar at Notre Dame and Boalt Hall and later a judge on the Ninth Circuit U.S. Court of Appeals) moved in some of the same social and religious circles with an exhilarating sense of being at home in both church and university.[81] Sidney Callahan recalls Catholics as understood to be a bit "low status" but working to "develop ourselves intellectually"; her husband, Daniel Callahan ,wrote in 1959 of the ever "more congenial" world of the secular university.[82] The Harvard historian H. Stuart Hughes commented in 1966 that although Catholic graduate students in the Department of History before World War II had been "few in number, mostly undistinguished, and on the margin of intellectual exchange," Catholic students were now "some of the very best I have, they are right in the center of student life, and they do not hesitate to discuss the most prickly topics frankly and cordially."[83]

As residual hostility toward Catholicism in the secular universities faded, and as the quality and number of Catholic graduate students increased, Catholics complained more frequently about hostility from within the Church. One Catholic student at Amherst in the early 1950s recalled episodic denunciations of "Godless Amherst" from a local monsignor.[84] A Catholic graduate student at the University of Wisconsin privately lambasted "shockingly ignorant" priests holding "stereotyped notions of secular colleges as hot-beds of anti-Catholicism."[85]

But these tensions, too, diminished. The intellectual history of the Second Vatican Council (1962–65) remains only dimly understood, but one clear theme, voiced by influential theologians such as the French Jesuit Henri de Lubac, the French Dominicans Yves Congar and Maire-Dominique Chenu, and John Courtney Murray, was a call for Catholics to engage contemporary society, not simply condemn it.[86] For the Europeans, especially, the political crisis of the 1930s and then the Second World War revealed a church in which many members (and leaders) understood religion as either a pious afterthought to daily life or a reliable bulwark of the social order. In the United States Catholic self-criticism included John Courtney Murray warning coreligionists against a propensity to censorship and younger lay Catholics dissatisfied by Catholic complacency on emerging issues such as African American civil rights. The opening line of the most widely read conciliar document, *Gaudium et spes* (1965), thrilled Catholic intellectuals in both the United States and Europe, urging them to share in the world's "joys and hopes . . . griefs and anxieties."[87]

The surge in interreligious and ecumenical discussions that mark the mid-1960s depended on these sentiments. At Harvard one of the central conciliar figures, the biblical scholar Cardinal Augustin Bea, delivered a set of lectures in 1963, with commentary by leading Protestant and Jewish theologians.[88] At Stanford the Swiss Catholic theologian Hans Küng gave an endowed set of lectures in 1966.[89]

Even more rapid changes occurred at Catholic universities. When Catholic educational leaders referred to "effective witness in a pluralistic society" in the late 1960s, they did not mean bringing a Catholic perspective to bear upon the disciplines, a strategy thought tried and found wanting. Instead, they emphasized the importance of respecting the "internal autonomy" of disciplinary standards and cautioned against "theological and philosophical imperialism."[90] Most important, Catholic university leaders, led by Theodore Hesburgh, C.S.C., of Notre Dame and Paul Reinert, S.J., of St. Louis University, transferred ownership of their institutions to lay-dominated boards of trustees, convinced that religious orders needed greater lay collaboration to chart the future of increasingly complex and ambitious academic institutions.[91]

Fiscal uncertainties pushed this new ideational posture forward. Already in the late 1940s anxiety about Catholic influence in American culture helped push some Supreme Court justices toward advocating a strict separation of church and state, and several state and U.S. Supreme Court rulings during the late 1960s and early 1970s adopted an especially rigorist interpretation, causing Catholic administrators to fear that federal moneys might become unavailable to religious colleges and universities. (In New York State legislators demanded that Catholic colleges not use the word "Catholic" in promotional materials.) Over time new rulings superseded these interpretations, but nervous Catholic college leaders in the late 1960s judged this threatening legal climate a further reason to stress secular competencies.[92]

How DID the first generation of postwar Catholic scholars—formed in a defensive religious subculture during the 1940s and 1950s, come of age in the less constrained intellectual and ecclesiastical world of the 1960s, and now passing from the scene—meld faith and work? Most did not consider the question an interesting one. In contrast to their more combative Catholic predecessors, the founders of the American Catholic Philosophical Association (1926), the American Catholic Sociological Society (1938), and the Catholic Theological

Society of America (1946), Catholic scholars absorbed the pull toward universalism that so marked postwar intellectual life. (The same distaste for special religious or ethnic pleading proved even more attractive to, and in large part was developed by, Jewish scholars.)[93]

The idea of a distinct confessional perspective was unattractive. In 1950 John Tracy Ellis asked a friend studying at Columbia to "try to disabuse them [non-Catholics] of the [idea] that Catholics write history in an essentially different way than those who are not Catholics."[94] A decade later, even as claims to universal standards of knowledge first came under siege, Catholics traded sectarian groupings for the mainstream. The members of the American Catholic Sociological Association changed the name of their journal from the *American Catholic Sociological Review* to the less parochial *Sociological Analysis* just before the founding era for new programs in African American, Latino-Latina, and women's studies.

The lingering influence of the vast Catholic subculture, however, proved more difficult to erase. The sheer number of Catholic scholars in the academy by the 1960s, even the number of Catholic scholars within the humanities, makes any listing idiosyncratic, but certain issues and approaches do seem characteristic. Ironically, given the Catholic tradition, Catholic contributions in the fine arts were minimal. Jacques Maritain's discussion of art and scholasticism inspired some writers, including Flannery O'Connor and Thomas Merton, and Maritain delivered the first A. W. Mellon lectures at the National Gallery in 1952, but this aspect of Maritain's thought never penetrated very deeply into the secular university milieu.[95]

By contrast, a major contribution came in fields with high linguistic barriers. Students at Jesuit high schools, often from the working class, endured mandatory Latin (and often Greek) into the 1960s, and instructors at Jesuit seminaries conducted most classes in Latin. (Boston College dropped the requirement that all students demonstrate Latin competency only in 1958.)[96] This stress on languages fostered the careers of the medievalist David Herlihy, the literary scholar Walter Ong, S.J., and Garry Wills, a onetime Jesuit seminarian and arguably the most versatile American intellectual of the postwar period. Wills began his career as a journalist with *National Review*, did a stint as a classics professor at Johns Hopkins (before being denied tenure), and then became a prominent journalist and historian. Later, in books on topics as varied as the Gettysburg Address, Renaissance Venice, and St. Augustine, Wills repeatedly drew upon his familiarity with Greek and Latin texts.[97] Of the twenty scholars at Catholic institutions to win Guggenheim awards between 1949 and 1959, fifteen worked in classics or medieval and early modern history and literature.[98]

Allied to this facility with languages was a certain cosmopolitanism. Accustomed to thinking of "the West," Catholic historians and political theorists were among the first scholars to describe Europe and the Americas as sharing an "At-lantic community."[99] The very isolation of Catholic scholars, especially Catholic philosophers and theologians, from American currents guaranteed tight links to Catholic Europe. Moral theologians, medievalists, liturgists, and biblical schol-ars in the United States lived in a genuinely North Atlantic scholarly community, publishing in European and American scholarly journals and meeting with Eu-ropean speakers who embarked each summer on the American Catholic college lecture circuit.[100] By the 1930s the majority of nuns teaching in Catholic women's colleges such as College of St. Catherine in St. Paul and Trinity College in Wash-ington, D.C., had studied in Europe, often at Munich, Fribourg, or Louvain. European exiles to American Catholic universities during and after World War II cultivated these ties, as did the many Catholic scholars, primarily priests, who obtained Ph.D. degrees in Louvain, Laval (Quebec), and Rome. As late as 1966, 26 percent of philosophers in Catholic colleges had received their doctorates in Europe, more than triple the number of philosophers in Catholic colleges who had received their doctorates from a secular college in the United States.[101]

A second Catholic contribution came in anthropology. The foremost fig-ure was England's Mary Douglas, who in her fieldwork among the Lele in the Belgian Congo drew upon her prior immersion in the tightly ordered world of the Sacred Heart boarding school in Roehampton. (The same sublima-tion of self that attracted the young Douglas —including injunctions against acting too "brainy"—pushed a near contemporary, the literary critic Helen Vendler, away from a Catholic milieu that she found entirely oppressive. But even Vendler remained grateful for her Latin.)[102] Douglas's defense of Catho-lic tribalisms discarded after the Second Vatican Council, such as the ban on eating meat on Fridays, testifies to a passionate interplay between theological and anthropological concerns, as does her recent interest in (and uneasiness with) women's ordination. Her work on ritual and taboo, and that of Victor and Edith Turner, also Catholic, proved formative for a generation of schol-ars, notably the medievalist Caroline Bynum and Peter Brown, a historian of late antiquity who discovered in his first reading of Douglas's *Natural Symbols* (1970) something akin to a "universal law of gravity."[103]

A third contribution came in ethics. Here the long tradition of Catho-lic casuistry—the discipline of deciding just what actions were or were not permissible, and how priests must handle such queries or sins within the con-fessional—proved decisive.[104] Medical ethics was a favored topic, since not only did Catholic patients, doctors, chaplains, and nurses visit the confessional, but Catholics also ran the nation's largest system of private hospitals. The result by the mid-twentieth century was a literature of unusual sophistication. Even the foremost critic of Catholic views on contraception, abortion, and end-of-life questions, Joseph Fletcher, conceded in 1954 that the "Catholic literature on the morals of medical care is both extensive and painstaking in its technical detail, while Protestant and Jewish literature is practically non-existent."[105] In the late 1960s and early 1970s a disproportionate number of Catholics, seasoned (or shattered) by fierce intramural disputes over the morality of contraception, played leading roles in the emergence of modern bioethics. Leading figures included Daniel Callahan, the founder of the Hastings Center, the first think tank devoted to the subject, and Richard McCormick, S.J., the Rose Kennedy professor of Christian ethics at the Kennedy Institute of Ethics at Georgetown University, also the first such university-based center. (The longtime disability rights activist Eunice Kennedy Shriver and her husband, Sargent Shriver, along with André Hellegers, a Catholic Johns Hopkins scientist immersed in the contraception debate, arranged for the initial endowment of the institute.)[106]

Finally, a focus on intellectual traditions, and their relationship to the religious or political communities that sustain them, also seems characteristic. Obviously, such foci are not unique to Catholic scholars, but the concatenation is noteworthy. John Noonan's influential studies of the twists and turns of Catholic doctrine on contraception and usury, for example, parallel his equally important work on the history of bribes, religious freedom, and federalism. Gliding from court to church and back again, Noonan refused to reflexively equate dogma with control.[107] More recently, Mary Ann Glendon has teased out the individualist underpinnings of statutes and court rulings on human rights, abortion, and divorce law;[108] Eamon Duffy has attempted to check the assumption that more communal forms of religion serve only as prelude to modern, individualistic alternatives;[109] Michael Buckley, S.J., and James Turner have emphasized the ironies of modern unbelief arising from within religious communities,[110] and Nicholas Boyle has located Goethe and German literary culture in the context of liberal Protestantism and the form of the German university.[111]

Interest in intellectual traditions and the communities that supported them is even more obvious in philosophy. The vast Thomistic edifice constructed within the Catholic milieu in the early twentieth century never shaped the world of secular philosophy in the United States to any effect, beyond natural law marriages of convenience between Thomists and disciples of Leo Strauss.[112] By the end of the 1950s leading Catholic scholars bridled at the tendency of Thomists to confuse scholarship with a "prefabricated scheme," and young Jesuits morbidly referred to "ghetto Thomism."[113] The Second Vatican Council further diminished the influence of Thomism within Catholic circles, as the council's architects stressed a more historical approach to theological inquiry and a new reliance upon biblical and patristic sources.[114]

A more diverse Catholic philosophical landscape then became visible, including a Catholic variant on analytical philosophy, most notably in the work of Elizabeth Anscombe and John Finnis.[115] The two most influential Catholic intellectuals since the 1970s, however, the philosophers Charles Taylor and Alasdair MacIntyre, both stressed the importance of grounding philosophical arguments in historical narratives, or, in Taylor's phrasing, understanding that "philosophy and the history of philosophy are one."[116]

Both men also reflected aspects of the postwar North Atlantic Catholic experience. Taylor's childhood in a bilingual, Catholic household in Montreal sparked his initial interest in the relationship between language and culture.[117] At Oxford in the late 1950s he read widely in the theological literature emanating from the Continent. His suspicion of a clericalism that denigrates the "temporal" and creates a "dualism between Church and world" is of the period, as is his sympathy for the worker-priest experiment in France.[118] These themes reappeared in subtle ways in his published work during the next four decades, notably in his magisterial *Sources of the Self* (1989), which emphasized the salutary development of a focus on ordinary life and individual self-expression in the West, even as Taylor worried that a contemporary focus on the individual obscures the necessity of locating "a self only in relation to certain interlocutors."[119] In an important recent essay, Taylor claimed that modern notions of human dignity or individual rights required the collapse of medieval Christendom, even if the sustenance of such notions still depends on religious sources of meaning.[120]

MacIntyre's celebrated *After Virtue* (1981) marked the beginning of an ongoing defense of a historical Thomism that, in his view, had gone off track in the Thomistic revival of the early twentieth century.[121] MacIntyre's rejection of modern liberalism, as a Marxist early in his career and as a Thomist since the late 1970s, predisposed him to view contemporary moral philosophy as not only incoherent but positively destructive in its enthusiasm for a "conceptual mélange" that dissolves particular "communities whose historical ties with their past remain strong."[122] (The contrast with the late 1960s, when Catholic scholars felt compelled to assert the compatibility of Catholicism and modernity, is striking.) MacIntyre's dismissal of the "Enlightenment project" distinguished him from Taylor and other Catholic communitarians; but like Taylor, and like so many Catholic scholars of the postwar period, including John Noonan and Mary Douglass, MacIntyre specialized in locating moral and theological inquiry within particular communities, at particular historical moments. Indeed, in retrospect, he understood his own early intellectual development as a tug-of-war between "a Gaelic oral culture of farmers and fisherman, poets and storytellers" that emphasized "particular loyalties and ties" and a more formal academic culture of "theories."[123]

SHOULD ROBERT MACIVER and John Courtney Murray resume their correspondence today, after a fifty-year silence, what would they say? One effect of
the steady absorption of Catholics into the opinion-making sectors of American
society might surprise both men. MacIver devoted much of his career to the
study of American pluralism, noting the collapse of religious prejudice in the
day-to-day life of most Americans, but he upheld a division between "scientific
knowledge" and "theological truth" that entailed a private understanding of
religious belief. Now Catholics on the Supreme Court and hosting television
talk shows discuss the relationship of religion to public life.[124]

At the same time the Catholic subculture upon which a distinctive intellectual
contribution rests is increasingly fragile. Murray and other Catholics in the 1950s
knew that the price of the Catholic advancement they so desired might be steep.
"It is not so much that religion and moral law are denied or rejected," worried one
Jesuit sociologist in 1956 after surveying families in the new suburbs, "they are
simply judged not pertinent as guiding norms of practical action."[125]

The past two decades, especially, have witnessed sharp declines in weekly
Mass attendance (accelerated by the current sexual abuse crisis), vocations to the
religious life (especially among women), massive, anguished dissent from church
teachings on contraception and homosexuality, and a continued assimilation of
American Catholics to American mores (although here the role of Latino and
Latina Catholics, now one quarter of the Catholic population, remains unpre-
dictable.)[126] Scholars who happen to be Catholic—working on specific problems
with no reference to their religious beliefs—have always and understandably
outnumbered Catholic scholars eager to bring a particular religious tradition to
bear upon common concerns. But forming a new generation of Catholic scholars
now seems an especially daunting challenge.[127] The novelist and Johns Hopkins
professor Alice McDermott's brilliant dissection of the Catholic subculture and
its dissolution reflects a self-consciousness that can only herald transition.[128]

The gains made by many Catholic universities in recent decades are a modest counterweight. Upon these institutions and the initiatives they develop
falls a considerable burden, since other tributaries of Catholic intellectual life
have run dry.[129] Neither Catholic seminaries nor the men's or women's religious orders, for example, now constitute an independent intellectual center.
(Murray, in a marker of the once idiosyncratic contours of American Catholic
intellectual life, spent almost his entire career at a Jesuit seminary in rural
Maryland.)[130]

How Catholic universities balance engagement with the world and the
cultivation of a particular intellectual tradition remains unclear, even if the
fragments of a distinctive curriculum—a focus on philosophy and theology,

a commitment to languages and study abroad—remain.[131] The absence of institutional pluralism at the highest levels of American higher education—hiring practices, curricula, and department structures are virtually identical at Princeton, Duke, and the University of Michigan—means a paucity of models for steering between sectarian isolation and absorption into the wider academic culture, a perennial risk in a depressed (and national) academic job market.

Ironically, the two men might find common ground on academic freedom, the subject of their fiercest exchanges. Murray chided MacIver for defining the university as an institution in "free pursuit of the truth" even as he advocated banning a "present member of the Communist party" from any university faculty. MacIver cautioned against the "perils of the purge" but did think the "subservience" required of a Communist made him or her "not a fit and proper person for an academic position."[132]

Both MacIver and Murray, however, recognized the intricate connections among understandings of truth, academic freedom, and the structure of the university. MacIver's definition of the scholar as "in search of the truth" and the university as placing "its trust in reason" appears quaint to academics enamored of Michel Foucault, as does Murray's worry about the "dissolution of the idea of truth itself, to the point where no assertion may claim more than the status of mere opinion."[133]

Is such complacency warranted? Truth seeking, or an ability to distinguish scholarship from propaganda, lies near the heart of lifetime tenure and the request that taxpayers subsidize professors teaching four courses a year.[134] Given that only 12.7 percent of bachelor's degrees conferred in 1993 were in the humanities (as opposed to 20.7% in 1966),[135] humanists might be especially leery of claims that aesthetic, philosophical, and historical judgments rest upon present politics. Already even the most affluent universities allow market pressures to determine salaries and aspects of their research and teaching missions, with a consequent weakening of faculty solidarity.[136]

Viewed from this angle, a religious tradition claiming that reason is universal and can lead to faith has strategic value. Perhaps MacIver and Murray's most surprising discovery in the year 2006 would be this: that the survival of Catholic intellectual life may be more than a parochial concern.

Notes

1. John Courtney Murray to Robert MacIver, [1952], box 2, folder 142, John Courtney Murray Papers, Georgetown University Special Collections (hereafter cited as JCM).

2. Robert M. MacIver to John Courtney Murray, August 26, 1952, box 2, folder 142, JCM.

3. John Courtney Murray, S.J., "The Crisis in Church-State Relationships in the U.S.A."

(1950), reprinted in *Review of Politics* 61 (Fall 1999): 687–704. On Murray, see John T. Mc-Greevy, *Catholicism and American Freedom: A History* (New York: W. W. Norton, 2003), 189–215; John T. Noonan Jr., *The Lustre of Our Country: The American Experience of Religious Freedom* (Berkeley: University of California Press, 1998), 331–353.

4. Robert M. MacIver, *Academic Freedom in Our Time* (New York: Columbia University Press, 1955); Richard Hofstadter and Walter P. Metzger, *The Development of Academic Freedom in the United States* (New York: Columbia University Press, 1955).

5. John Courtney Murray to Vincent McCormick, [n.d.; 1952?], box 2, folder 151, JCM.

6. Henry Sloane Coffin to A. Whitney Griswold, September 19, 1951, YRG 2-A-16, box 42, file 405, Yale University Archives.

7. Murray to MacIver [1952], box 2, folder 151, JCM.

8. John Courtney Murray to John Tracy Ellis, October 11, 1955, box 5, "M" file, 1954–55, John Tracy Ellis Papers, Archives of the Catholic University of America (hereafter cited as JTE). John Tracy Ellis, "American Catholics and the Intellectual Life," *Thought* 30 (Autumn 1955): 351–388, quote on pp. 375–376. On the essay's influence and Catholic higher education generally, see Philip Gleason, *Contending with Modernity: Catholic Higher Education in the Twentieth Century* (New York: Oxford University Press, 1995), 287–297.

9. Joseph A. Komonchak, "The Silencing of John Courtney Murray," in *Cristianesimo nella storia: Saggi in onore di Giuseppe Alberigo*, ed. Alberto Melloni et al. (Bologna: Mulino, 1996), 657–702.

10. Robert M. MacIver, *The Ramparts We Guard* (New York: Macmillan, 1950), 111.

11. John Courtney Murray to Robert M. MacIver, April 17, 1952, box 2, folder 142, JCM; Robert M. MacIver to A. Whitney Griswold, February 14, 1952, YRG-2-A-16, box 43, file 406, Yale University Archives. On the episode, see George M. Marsden, *The Soul of the American University: From Protestant Establishment to Established Nonbelief* (New York: Oxford University Press, 1994), 10–16.

12. Liston Pope, "Religion and the Class Structure," *Annals of the American Academy of Political and Social Science* 256 (March 1948): 86.

13. Brother Gerald J. Schnepp, *Leakage from a Catholic Parish* (Washington, D.C.: Catholic University of America Press, 1942), 169.

14. Andrew Greeley, *The American Catholic: A Social Portrait* (New York: Basic Books, 1977), 43–47, 53–67. It is striking that Catholics in West Germany moved into the middle and upper classes during exactly these years as well. See David P. Conradt, "Changing German Political Culture," in *The Civic Culture Revisited: An Analytic Study*, ed. Gabriel A. Almond and Sidney Verba (Boston: Little, Brown, 1980), 261–262.

15. Elizabeth A. Edmondson, "Without Comment or Controversy: The G.I. Bill and Catholic Colleges," *Church History* 71 (December 2002), 820–847; Gleason, *Contending with Modernity*, 209–211.

16. William P. Leahy, S.J., *Adapting to America: Catholics, Jesuits, and Higher Education in the Twentieth Century* (Washington, D.C.: Georgetown University Press, 1991), 126; Christopher Jencks and David Riesman, *The Academic Revolution* (New York: Doubleday, 1968), 359. The figure is now roughly 5 percent. See Peter Steinfels, *A People Adrift: The Crisis of the Roman Catholic Church in America* (New York: Simon and Schuster, 2003), 132.

17. I interpolate from the data in Thomas M. Landy, "The Colleges in Context," in *Catholic Women's Colleges in America*, ed. Tracy Schier and Cynthia Russett (Baltimore: Johns Hopkins University Press, 2002), 62, 78.

18. Alexander W. Astin, Robert J. Patnos, and John A. Creager, "National Norms for Entering College Freshmen—Fall 1966," *American Council of Education Research Reports* 2 (1967): 22.

19. On the general trends, see Gleason, *Contending with Modernity*, 168; Astin et al., "National Norms for Entering College Freshmen," 8. On UIC, see www.uic.edu/las/catholic/; on Georgetown, www.communcations.georgetown.edu/fact_sheets/2003/glance.htm.

20. Morton Keller and Phyllis Keller, *Making Harvard Modern: The Rise of America's University* (New York: Oxford University Press, 2001), 60; Alvin Kernan, *In Plato's Cave* (New Haven: Yale University Press, 1999), 134–135.

21. Jeffrey Wills, ed., *The Catholics of Harvard Square* (Petersham, Mass.: St. Bede's Publications, 1994), 89, 54. For more data, see Jerome Karabel, *The Chosen: The Hidden History of Admission and Exclusion at Harvard, Yale, and Princeton* (Boston: Houghton-Mifflin, 2003), 23.

22. Father Armando Trinidade, "Roman Catholic Worship at Stanford University: 1891–1971" (Ph.D. diss., Stanford University, 1971), 153.

23. Harold F. Williamson and Payson S. Wild, *Northwestern University: A History 1850–1975* (Evanston, Ill.: Northwestern University, 1976), 322.

24. Wills, *The Catholics of Harvard Square*, 89. On Yale, see Dan A. Oren, *Joining the Club: A History of Jews at Yale* (New Haven: Yale University Press, 2000), 76–77.

25. Oren, *Joining the Club*, 77.

26. Jencks and Riesman, *Academic Revolution*, 387.

27. Burnett C. Bauer, "Catholic Scholarship and Modern Apologetics" (master's thesis, University of Notre Dame, 1945), 34–56.

28. Greeley, *American Catholic*, 84.

29. Jerome Kerwin, "The Catholic Scholar in the Secular University," in *Roman Catholicism and the American Way of Life*, ed. Thomas T. McAvoy (Notre Dame, Ind.: University of Notre Dame Press, 1960), 58.

30. Wills, *The Catholics of Harvard Square*, 89–90; Keller and Keller, *Making Harvard Modern*, 276; Trinidade, "Roman Catholic Worship at Stanford," 75, 117; Robert H. Knapp, *The Origins of American Humanistic Scholars* (Englewood Cliffs, N.J.: Prentice-Hall, 1964), 105.

31. Stephen Steinberg, *The Academic Melting Pot: Catholics and Jews in American Higher Education* (New York: McGraw-Hill, 1974), 103.

32. On the Jesuits, see Peter McDonough, *Men Astutely Trained: A History of the Jesuits in the American Century* (New York: Free Press, 1994).

33. "The Economic Status of the Profession, 1962–1963: A Report on the Self-Grading Compensation Survey," *AAUP Bulletin* 49 (Summer 1963): 151; Ernan McMullen, "Philosophy in the United States Catholic College," in *New Themes in Christian Philosophy*, ed. Ralph McInerney (Notre Dame, Ind.: University of Notre Dame Press, 1968), 386–388; Andrew Greeley, *From Backwater to Mainstream: A Profile of Catholic Higher Education* (New York: McGraw-Hill, 1969), 52–53.

34. Donald Kommers to Rev. Francis Connell, May 10, 1959, Father Francis Connell Papers, Archives of the Baltimore Province of the Redemptorist Fathers, Brooklyn, N.Y. (hereafter cited as CP).

35. Alexander W. Astin and John L. Holland, "The Distribution of 'Wealth' in Higher Education," *College and University* 37 (Winter 1962): 116.

36. John Tracy Ellis to Edward Cardinal, April 27, 1942, JTE.

37. Brand Blanshard, "Theology and the Value of the Individual," in *The Scientific Spirit and Democratic Faith, 1945* (New York: King's Crown Press, 1945), 74–86; Brand Blanshard to Paul Blanshard, June 15, 1951, box 2, folder 9, Paul Blanshard Papers, Bentley Library, University of Michigan; Oren, *Joining the Club*, 261–266.

38. Kerwin, "Catholic Scholar," 58. Also see Trinidade, "Roman Catholic Worship at Stanford," 140.

39. Ironically, Hayes was a Catholic liberal on most issues and was privately critical of the Spanish Catholic Church for its claim to represent "religious unity" on the Iberian peninsula. Carlton Hayes to John Courtney Murray, March 22, 1943, box 5, M–N Correspondence files, Carlton Hayes Papers, Columbia University Rare Books and Manuscripts (hereafter cited as CH). On the episode, see Peter Novick, *That Nobel Dream: The "Objectivity Question" and the American Historical Profession* (Cambridge: Cambridge University Press, 1988), 321–322. On

support for Hayes, see John Tracy Ellis to Carlton Hayes, February 13, 1946, box 6, Return to U.S. Correspondence file, CH.

40. John Tracy Ellis to Edward Cardinal, March 30 and April 11, 1942, JTE.

41. Bertrand Russell, *Why I Am Not a Christian*, ed. Paul Edwards (London: Allen and Unwin, 1967), 183; Paul Blakely, S.J., "The Teacher and Caesar's Wife," *America* 63 (April 13, 1940): 6; "Comment," *America* 63 (April 13, 1940): 2.

42. Horace Kallen to Walter Hamilton, November 6, 1940, box 71, file 11, Horace Kallen Papers, American Jewish Archives, Cincinnati.

43. Interview with the former Harvard president Nathan Pusey, cited in Richard Norton Smith, *The Harvard Century: The Making of a University to a Nation* (New York: Simon and Schuster, 1986).

44. Talcott Parsons, "Academic Freedom" (1939), in *Talcott Parsons on National Socialism*, ed. Uta Gerhardt (New York: Aldine de Gruyter, 1993), 198.

45. On Roosevelt, see Robert Dallek, *An Unfinished Life: John Fitzgerald Kennedy, 1917–1963* (Boston: Little, Brown, 2003), 233–234.

46. John Dewey, "Implications of S.2499" (1947), in Dewey, *The Later Works, 1925–1953*, vol. 15, *1942–1948*, ed. Jo Ann Boydston (Carbondale: Southern Illinois University Press, 1989), 284–285; George Boas, review of Paul Blanshard, *American Freedom and Catholic Power* in *Philosophical Review* 59 (January 1950): 126–128.

47. Seymour Martin Lipset, "The Sources of the Radical Right," in *The New American Right*, ed. Daniel Bell (New York: Criterion, 1955), 355–356.

48. James Turner, "Secularization and Sacralization: Speculations on Some Religious Origins of the Secular Humanities Curriculum, 1850–1900," in *The Secularization of the Academy*, ed. George M. Marsden and Bradley J. Longfield (New York: Oxford University Press, 1992), 74–106; Turner, *The Liberal Education of Charles Eliot Norton* (Baltimore: Johns Hopkins University Press, 1999); Julie Reuben, *The Making of the Modern University* (Chicago: University of Chicago Press, 1996). For a case study, see Christian Smith, "Secularizing American Higher Education: The Case of Early American Sociology," in *The Secular Revolution: Power, Interests, and Conflict in the Secularization of American Public Life*, ed. Christian Smith (Berkeley: University of California Press, 2003), 97–159. For specific fears about Catholicism, see, e.g., the comments of the leading nineteenth-century political scientist, John Burgess, "The 'Culturconflict' in Prussia," *Political Science Quarterly* 2 (June 1887): 338.

49. Ira Katznelson, *Desolation and Enlightenment: Political Knowledge after Total War, Totalitarianism, and the Holocaust* (New York: Columbia University Press, 2003), 123–124; Philip Gleason, *Speaking of Diversity: Language and Ethnicity in Twentieth-Century America* (Baltimore: Johns Hopkins University Press, 1992), 123–149.

50. Arthur M. Schlesinger Jr., *The Vital Center: The Politics of Freedom* (Boston: Houghton Mifflin, 1949), 244.

51. Perry Miller, review of Paul Blanshard, *Communism, Democracy, and Catholic Power*, in *New York Herald Tribune*, June 10, 1951, sec. VI, 1. On the general subject, see McGreevy, *Catholicism and American Freedom*, 167–188; Gleason, *Speaking of Diversity*, 207–228; David A. Hollinger, *Science, Jews, and Secular Culture: Studies in Mid-Twentieth-Century American Intellectual History* (Princeton: Princeton University Press, 1996), 157–159; Edward A. Purcell, *The Crisis of Democratic Theory: Scientific Naturalism and the Problem of Value* (Lexington: University Press of Kentucky, 1973), 202–204.

52. Thomas Nipperdey, "Max Weber, Protestantism, and the Context of the Debate around 1900," in *Weber's Protestant Ethic: Origins, Evidence, Contexts*, ed. Hartmut Lehmann and Guenther Roth (Cambridge: Cambridge University Press, 1993), 78; Friedrich Wilhelm Graf, "The German Theological Sources and Protestant Church Politics," in *Weber's Protestant Ethic*, 27–28; Guenther Roth, Introduction to *Weber's Protestant Ethic*, 5–7.

53. Gabriel Almond to Talcott Parsons, May 2, 1941, box 17, Weber translation file, HUG 14.20, Talcott Parsons Papers, Harvard University Archives (hereafter TP); Gabriel Almond, "The Christian Parties of Western Europe," *World Politics* 1 (October 1948): 30–58, esp. 58; Gabriel Almond, "The Political Ideas of Christian Democracy," *Journal of Politics* 10 (November 1948), 734–763.

54. Talcott Parsons, "Memorandum: The Development of Groups and Organizations Amenable to Use against American Institutions and Foreign Policy and Possible Measures of Prevention" (1940), in Gerhardt, *Talcott Parsons on National Socialism*, 106–107, 130; Benton Johnson and Miriam M. Johnson, "The Integrating of the Social Sciences: Theoretical and Empirical Research and Training in the Department of Social Relations at Harvard," in *The Nationalization of the Social Sciences*, ed. Samuel Z. Klausner and Victor M. Lidz (Philadelphia: University of Pennsylvania Press, 1986), 138; Talcott Parsons, "Sociology and Social Psychology," in *Religious Perspectives in College Teaching*, by Hoxie N. Fairchild et al. (New York: Ronald Press, 1952), 324, 326.

55. Robert Merton, *Science, Technology, and Society in Seventeenth-Century England* (1938; rpt. New York: Howard Fertig, 1970), 99–136. The explosion of interest in science conducted under Catholic auspices during the seventeenth and eighteenth centuries has complicated Merton's definition of what constitutes science, as well as the theological underpinnings of his argument. For overviews, see Rivka Feldhay, "The Cultural Field of Jesuit Science," in *The Jesuits: Cultures, Sciences and the Arts 1540–1773*, ed. John W. O'Malley, S.J. (Toronto: University of Toronto Press, 1999), 107–130; J. L. Heilbron, "Science in the Church," *Science in Context* 3 (1989): 9–28; Steven J. Harris, "Transposing the Merton Thesis: Apostolic Spirituality and the Establishment of the Jesuit Scientific Tradition," *Science in Context* 3 (1989): 30–66.

56. Talcott Parsons to Eric Voegelin, August 18, 1941, box 17, Voegelin file, HUG 15.2, TP.

57. Robert Merton, *Social Theory and Social Structure* (1942; rpt. Glencoe, Ill.: Free Press, 1957), 550–561. See also Hollinger, *Science, Jews, and Secular Culture*, 80–96.

58. Robert H. Knapp and Joseph J. Greenbaum, *The Younger American Scholar: His Collegiate Origins* (Chicago: University of Chicago Press, 1953), 47; R. H. Knapp and H. B. Goodrich, *Origins of American Scientists* (Chicago: University of Chicago Press, 1952), 24, 288–289; Bernard Barber, *Science and the Social Order* (Glencoe, Ill: Free Press, 1952), 136.

59. Nicholas Lemann, "Is There a Science of Success?" *Atlantic Monthly*, February 1994, 83–98.

60. David C. McClelland et al., *The Achievement Motive* (New York: Appleton-Century-Crofts, 1953), 275. See also David C. McClelland, A. Rindlisbacher, and Richard deCharms, "Religious and Other Sources of Parental Attitudes toward Independence Training," in *Studies in Motivation*, ed. David C. McClelland (New York: Appleton-Century-Crofts, 1955), 389–397.

61. McClelland et al., *Achievement Motive*, 277; David C. McClelland, *The Achieving Society* (Princeton: Van Nostrand, 1961), 361.

62. On McClelland and foreign aid, see Ellen Herman, *The Romance of American Psychology: Political Culture in the Age of Experts, 1940–1970* (Berkeley: University of California Press, 1995), 139–141.

63. Frederick Pollock to Horace Kallen, March 29, 1944, folder 946, Horace Kallen Papers, YIVO Institute for Jewish Research, New York.

64. Theodor Adorno et al., *The Authoritarian Personality* (New York: Harper, 1950), 734, 230; Milton Rokeach, *The Open and Closed Mind: Investigations into the Nature of Belief Systems and Personality Systems* (New York: Basic Books, 1960), 4. These works by Adorno, Rokeach, and McClelland are listed as among the one hundred books most cited by social scientists between 1969 and 1977; Eugene Garfield, "The 100 Books Most Cited by Social Scientists, 1969–1977," in *Essays of an Information Scientist* (Philadelphia: ISI Press, 1980), 3: 621–631.

65. *Theory and Practice in Historical Study: A Report of the Committee on Historiography* (New York: Social Science Research Council, 1946), 136.

66. Henry Sloane Coffin, Foreword to James Hastings Nichols, *Democracy and the Churches* (Philadelphia: Westminster Press, 1951), 7.

67. Henry Steele Commager, *The American Mind* (New Haven: Yale University Press, 1950), 97, 194.

68. Oscar Handlin, *The Uprooted: The Epic Story of the Great Migrations That Made the American People* (Boston: Little, Brown, 1951), 119. Contrast this with a recent important essay, Margaret Lavinia Anderson, "The Limits of Secularization: On the Problem of the Catholic Revival in Nineteenth-Century Germany," *Historical Journal* 38 (1995): 657–691.

69. I rely on the unusually lucid survey by Arthur Madigan, S.J., *Catholic Philosophers in the United States Today: A Prospectus* (Notre Dame, Ind.: Erasmus Institute, 2002), 1–9; Knapp, *Origins of American Humanistic Scholars*, 32.

70. Charner Perry to Richard McKeon, July 30, 1940, box 48, Maritain file, Richard McKeon Papers, Regenstein Library, University of Chicago. For Maritain's own recognition of the challenges faced by Thomism among leading American academic philosophers, see Florian Michel, "Jacques Maritain en Amérique du Nord–I," *Cahiers Jacques Maritain* 45 (December 2002): 234–236. On Thomism in France, see Gary Gutting, *French Philosophy in the Twentieth Century* (Cambridge: Cambridge University Press, 2001), 94–98.

71. Charles Morris, "The Authoritarian Attempt to Capture Education," in *The Scientific Spirit and the Democratic Faith: Papers from the Conference on the Scientific Spirit and Democratic Faith* (New York: King's Crown Press, 1944), 142.

72. Max Otto, "Authoritarianism and Supernaturalism," in *Scientific Spirit and the Democratic Faith*, 19.

73. John Courtney Murray to Richard Taylor, January 28, 1956, box 1, folder 22, JCM.

74. McMullen, "Philosophy in the United States Catholic College," 373; Madigan, *Catholic Philosophers*, 1–9. See also Alexander Nehamas, "Trends in Recent American Philosophy," *Daedalus* 126 (Winter 1997): 209.

75. Carl Billman to Dr. Bernard Kohlbrenner, December 16, 1960, 1961–64 file, Phi Beta Kappa Collection, Manuscripts and Archives, University of Notre Dame.

76. Bernard de Voto to Arthur M. Schlesinger Jr., May 25, 1946, box P-12, de Voto file, Arthur M. Schlesinger Jr. Papers, Kennedy Library, Boston (hereafter cited as AS).

77. Arthur M. Schlesinger Jr. to Joseph Rauh Jr., February 18, 1960, box P-16, Humphrey file, AS; Dallek, *An Unfinished Life*, 253; Arthur M. Schlesinger Jr., "Catholics in America," *New Republic*, March 21, 1960, 13–14.

78. The literature on the subject is large and contested. For 1955 data, see James A. Davis et al., *Stipends and Spouses: The Finances of American Arts and Sciences Graduate Students* (Chicago: University of Chicago Press, 1962), 26–27. A series of studies claimed that the stultifying atmosphere of Catholic colleges did not prepare students for academic careers. (See McClelland et al., *Achievement Motive*, and McClelland, *The Achieving Society*.) For a pioneering essay challenging these studies, see Andrew M. Greeley, "Influence of the 'Religious Factor' on Career Plans and Occupational Values of College Graduates," *American Journal of Sociology* 68 (May 1963): 658–671. For later data that support Greeley, see Steinberg, *Academic Melting Pot*, 115. For a reinterpretation of the data used by Steinberg and a conclusion that Catholics matched non-Catholic achievement less rapidly than Greeley allows, see Robert Wuthnow, "Is There an Academic Melting Pot?" *Sociology of Education* 50 (January 1977): 7–15. Finally, for a solid summary, see Mark S. Massa, S.J., *Anti-Catholicism in America: The Last Acceptable Prejudice* (New York: Crossroad, 2003), 128–148.

79. Jencks and Riesman, *Academic Revolution*, 359.

80. Novick, *That Noble Dream*, 367.

81. See Jill Ker Conway, *True North: A Memoir* (New York: Vintage, 1994); Kevin Starr, "Judge John T. Noonan, Jr., a Brief Biography," *Journal of Law and Religion* 11 (1995): 151–176.

82. Wills, *The Catholics of Harvard Square*, 161; Daniel Callahan, "After the Self-Criticism," *Commonweal* (April 3, 1959): 11.

83. H. Stuart Hughes quoted in John Tracy Ellis, "Fragments from My Autobiography, 1905–1942," *Review of Politics* 6 (October 1974): 582.

84. Robert Kiely, *Still Learning: Spiritual Sketches from a Professor's Life* (Catalina, Ariz.: Medio Media, 1999), xii.

85. Kommers to Connell, May 10, 1959, CP.

86. The basic starting point is now the multivolume series edited by an international team of scholars, *History of Vatican II*, ed. Giuseppe Alberigo and Joseph A. Komonchak (Maryknoll, N.Y.: Orbis Books, 1995): vol. 1, *Announcing and Preparing Vatican Council II: Toward a New Era in Catholicism*; vol. 2, *The Formation of the Council's Identity: First Period and Intersession, October 1962–September 1963*; vol. 3, *The Mature Council: Second Period and Intersession, September 1963–September 1964*. On American Catholic intellectual life generally, see the selections in an important new reader, R. Scott Appleby, Patricia Byrne, C.S.J., and William Portier, eds., *Creative Fidelity: American Catholic Intellectual Identities*, (Maryknoll, N.Y.: Orbis Books, 2004).

87. *Gaudium et spes* in *The Documents of Vatican II*, ed. Walter M. Abbot, S.J. (New York: Guild Press, 1966), 201–203; McGreevy, *Catholicism and American Freedom*, 193–215.

88. Wills, *The Catholics of Harvard Square*, 99.

89. Trinidade, "Roman Catholic Worship at Stanford," 288.

90. James Tunstead Burtchaell, C.S.C., *The Dying of the Light: The Disengagement of Colleges and Universities from the Christian Churches* (Grand Rapids, Mich.: Eerdmans, 1998), 589.

91. "Land o' Lakes Statement: The Nature of the Contemporary Catholic University," (1967), in *American Catholic Higher Education: Essential Documents, 1967–1990*, ed. Alice Gallin, O.S.U. (Notre Dame, Ind.: University of Notre Dame Press, 1992), 8.

92. On the 1940s, see McGreevy, *Catholicism and American Freedom*, 183–186. On the 1960s, see Burtchaell, *Dying of the Light*, 598–602; Alice Gallin, O.S.U., *Negotiating Identity: Catholic Higher Education since 1960* (Notre Dame, Ind.: University of Notre Dame Press, 2000), 35–39.

93. Philip Gleason, *Keeping the Faith: American Catholicism Past and Present* (Notre Dame, Ind.: University of Notre Dame Press, 1987), 141; David A. Hollinger, *Science, Jews and Secular Culture*, 17–41; Hollinger, "How Wide the Circle of the 'We'? American Intellectuals and the Problem of the Ethnos since World War II," *American Historical Review* 98 (April 1993): 317–337.

94. John Tracy Ellis to Rev. Franklin Fitzpatrick, November 5, 1950, box 5, F 1946–52 file, JTE.

95. Jacques Maritain, *Creative Intuition in Art and Poetry* (New York: Pantheon, 1953); Paul Elie, *The Life You Save May Be Your Own: An American Pilgrimage* (New York: Farrar, Straus and Giroux, 2003), 85–87, 151–152.

96. Burtchaell, *Dying of the Light*, 576.

97. David Herlihy, "My Life in the Profession" (1990), in *Women, Family, and Society in Medieval Europe: Historical Essays, 1978–1991*, by David Herlihy, ed. A. Molho (Providence: Berghahn Books, 1995), x; Thomas J. Farrell, "An Overview of Walter J. Ong's Work," in *Media, Consciousness and Culture: Explorations of Walter Ong's Thought*, ed. Bruce E. Gronbeck et al. (Newbury Park, Calif.: Sage Publications, 1991), 25–43; Garry Wills, *Why I Am a Catholic* (Boston: Houghton Mifflin, 2002), 13–52; Patrick Allitt, *Catholic Intellectuals and Conservative Politics in America, 1950–1985* (Ithaca: Cornell University Press, 1993), 243–288.

98. *Reports of the Secretary and Treasurer, John Simon Guggenheim Memorial Foundation* (New York: The Foundation, 1949–59).

99. Bernard Bailyn, "The Idea of Atlantic History," *Itinerario* 14 (1990): 22–23.

100. See, e.g., Monica K. Hellwig, "A Catholic Scholar's Journey," in *Faith and the Intellectual Life: Marianist Award Lectures*, ed. James L. Heft, S.M. (Notre Dame, Ind.: University of Notre Dame Press, 1996), 82.

101. Karen Kennelly, "Faculties and What They Taught," in Schier and Russett, *Catholic Women's Colleges in America*, 105–108; McMullen, "Philosophy in the United States Catholic College," 373.

102. Mary Douglas, *A Feeling for Hierarchy* (Dayton: Marianist Award Lecture, 2002), esp. 14. On Douglas, see Richard Fardon, *Mary Douglas: An Intellectual Biography* (New York: Routledge, 1999), esp. 3–24. Helen Vendler, *A Life of Learning: Charles Homer Haskins Lecture for 2001* (New York: American Council of Learned Societies, 2001), 7–10.

103. Mary Douglas, "Sacraments and Society: An Anthropologist Asks What Women Could Be Doing in the Church," *New Blackfriars* 77 (December 1995): 28–40; Mary Douglas, "The Garden of the Beloved," *Heythrop Journal* 36 (1995): 397–408; Peter Brown, "The Rise and Function of the Holy Man in Late Antiquity, 1971–1997," *Journal of Early Christian Studies* 6 (October 1998): 359–360; Caroline Walker Bynum, "Curriculum Vitae," *Common Knowledge* 9 (Winter 2003): 11. On the Turners, see Victor Turner and Edith Turner, *Image and Pilgrimage in Christian Culture: Anthropological Perspectives* (Oxford: Oxford University Press, 1978); Victor Turner, "Ritual, Tribal and Catholic," *Worship* 50 (November 1976): 504–526.

104. Albert R. Jonsen and Stephen Toulmin, *The Abuse of Casuistry: A History of Moral Reasoning* (Berkeley: University of California Press, 1988).

105. Joseph Fletcher, *Morals and Medicine* (Princeton: Princeton University Press, 1954) 16.

106. Albert R. Jonsen, *The Birth of Bioethics* (New York: Oxford University Press, 1998), esp. 20–24.

107. On Noonan, see Starr, "Judge John T. Noonan," 151–176; John T. McGreevy, "A Case for Doctrinal Development," *Commonweal* (November 17, 2000): 12–17.

108. Mary Ann Glendon, *Abortion and Divorce in Western Law* (Cambridge: Harvard University Press, 1987); Mary Ann Glendon, *Rights Talk: The Impoverishment of Political Discourse* (New York: Free Pres, 1991).

109. Eamon Duffy, *The Stripping of the Altars: Traditional Religion in England, 1400–1580* (New Haven: Yale University Press, 1992).

110. Michael J. Buckley, *At the Origins of Modern Atheism* (New Haven: Yale University Press, 1987); James Turner, *Without God, without Creed: The Origins of Unbelief in America* (Baltimore: Johns Hopkins University Press, 1985); James Turner, *Language, Religion, Knowledge: Past and Present* (Notre Dame, Ind.: University of Notre Dame Press, 2003), 129–142.

111. Broadly, Nicholas Boyle, *Goethe: The Poet and His Age*, vol. 1, *The Poetry of Desire 1749–1790* (New York: Oxford University Press, 1991). More specifically, Boyle, "'Art,' Literature, Theology: Learning from Germany," in *Higher Learning and Catholic Traditions*, ed. Robert E. Sullivan (Notre Dame, Ind.: University of Notre Dame Press, 2001), 87–112.

112. In 1953 Strauss exempted "Roman Catholic social science" from his attack on "present-day American social science," which was incapable of defending natural rights. Leo Strauss, *Natural Rights and History* (Chicago: University of Chicago Press, 1953), 2.

113. Gustave Weigel, S.J., "American Catholic Intellectualism—A Theologian's Reflections," *Review of Politics* 19 (July 1957): 305; Joseph M. Becker, S.J., *The Re-Formed Jesuits*, vol. 1, *A History of Changes in Jesuit Formation during the Decade 1965–1975* (San Francisco: Ignatius Press, 1992), 290.

114. Joseph A. Komonchak, "Thomism and the Second Vatican Council," in *Continuity and Plurality in Catholic Theology: Essays in Honor of Gerald A. McCool, S.J.*, ed. Anthony J. Cernera (Fairfield, Conn.: Sacred Heart University Press, 1998), 53–73.

115. John Finnis, *Natural Law and Natural Rights* (Oxford: Clarendon Press, 1980); G. E. M. Anscombe, *Religion, Ethics and Politics* (Minneapolis: University of Minnesota Press, 1981).

116. Charles Taylor, "Philosophy and Its History," in *Philosophy in History*, ed. Richard Rorty, J. B. Schneewind, and Quentin Skinner (Cambridge: Cambridge University Press, 1984), 17.

117. Ruth Abbey, *Charles Taylor* (Princeton: Princeton University Press, 2000), 6–7; Mark

Redhead, *Charles Taylor: Thinking and Living Deep Diversity* (Lanham, Md.: Rowman and Little-field, 2002), 13–17.

118. Charles Taylor, "Clericalism," *Downside Review* 78 (Summer 1960): 175, 178–179.

119. Charles Taylor, *Sources of the Self: The Making of Modern Identity* (Cambridge: Harvard University Press, 1989), 36.

120. James L. Heft, ed., *A Catholic Modernity? Charles Taylor's Marianist Award Lecture* (New York: Oxford University Press, 1999).

121. Alasdair MacIntyre, *Three Rival Versions of Moral Enquiry: Encyclopaedia, Genealolgy, and Tradition* (Notre Dame, Ind.: University of Notre Dame Press, 1990), 58–81.

122. Alasdair MacIntyre, *After Virtue*, 2nd ed. (Notre Dame, Ind.: University of Notre Dame Press, 1984), 252.

123. "An Interview with Giovanna Boradori" (1991), in *The MacIntyre Reader*, ed. Kelvin Knight (Notre Dame, Ind.: University of Notre Dame Press, 1998), 255–256.

124. Robert M. MacIver, *The More Perfect Union* (New York: Macmillan, 1948), 12; MacIver, *Academic Freedom in Our Time*, 287. Noam Scheiber, "Class Act," *New Republic*, June 25, 2001, 22–25. On Justice Antonin Scalia, Catholicism, and the death penalty, see transcripts available at pewforum.org/deathpenalty/resources/transcript3.php3.

125. John L. Thomas, S.J., *The American Catholic Family* (Englewood Cliffs, N.J.: Prentice-Hall, 1956), 8–9.

126. Steinfels, *A People Adrift* is a superb overview.

127. Mark Roche notes that only 4.11 percent of undergraduates at Notre Dame eventually received Ph.D.'s in the 1980s, compared with 7.05 percent at Duke and 12.22 percent at Princeton. Mark W. Roche, *The Intellectual Appeal of Catholicism and the Idea of a Catholic University* (Notre Dame, Ind.: University of Notre Dame Press, 2003), 47.

128. Alice McDermott, *Charming Billy* (New York: Farrar, Straus and Giroux, 1998); Alice McDermott, *At Weddings and Wakes* (New York: Farrar, Straus and Giroux, 1992).

129. Thomas M. Landy, "Catholic Studies at Catholic Colleges and Universities," *America* 178 (January 3, 1998): 12–17. On the Erasmus Institute at Notre Dame, see Turner, *Language, Religion, Knowledge*, 143–156.

130. On the new institutional location of Catholic theology, see Christopher Ruddy, "Young Theologians," *Commonweal* (April 21, 2000), 17–19.

131. For two especially insightful analyses, see Alasdair MacIntyre, "Catholic Universities: Dangers, Hopes, Choices," in Sullivan, *Higher Learning and Catholic Traditions*, 1–21; Roche, *The Intellectual Appeal of Catholicism*. A higher percentage of Notre Dame and Georgetown students spend some portion of their academic career abroad than do students at any other American university, with the exception, intriguingly, of Yeshiva University. See data from the Institute of International Education at opendoors.iienetwork.org/?p=35946.

132. John Courtney Murray to Robert M. MacIver, April 17, 1952, box 2, folder 142, JCM; MacIver, *Academic Freedom in Our Time*, 172, 161, 169

133. MacIver, *Academic Freedom in Our Time*, 4, 256; John Courtney Murray, *We Hold These Truths: Catholic Reflections on the American Proposition* (New York: Sheed and Ward, 1960), 129.

134. For a brilliant meditation on these themes, see Thomas Haskell, "Justifying the Rights of Academic Freedom in the Era of 'Power/Knowledge,'" in *Legal Rights: Historical and Philosophical Perspectives*, ed. Austin Sarat and Thomas R. Kearns (Ann Arbor: University of Michigan Press, 1996), 113–176. Also see Louis Menand, ed., *The Future of Academic Freedom* (Chicago: University of Chicago Press, 1996).

135. Alvin Kernan, ed., *What's Happened to the Humanities?* (Princeton: Princeton University Press, 1997), 248, table 1.

136. David Hollinger, "Money and Academic Freedom a Half-Century after McCarthyism: Universities amid the Force Fields of Capital," in *Unfettered Expressions: Freedom in American*

Intellectual Life, ed. Peggie J. Hollingworth (Ann Arbor: University of Michigan Press, 2000), 161–184; Derek Bok, *Universities in the Marketplace: The Commercialization of Higher Education* (Princeton: Princeton University Press, 2003). From a slightly different angle is Nicholas Boyle, *Who Are We Now? Christian Humanism and the Global Market from Hegel to Heaney* (Notre Dame, Ind.: University of Notre Dame Press, 1998), 28–29.

8

THE BLACK SCHOLAR, THE HUMANITIES, AND THE POLITICS OF RACIAL KNOWLEDGE SINCE 1945

JONATHAN SCOTT HOLLOWAY

IN 1963 THE eminent historian John Hope Franklin offered his assessment of the cost of racial thinking to the store of knowledge. The assessment was not positive. Likening black scholars' situation in the academy to a dilemma, Franklin angrily lamented the loss that defined black scholars' lives. In the late nineteenth and into the twentieth centuries, Franklin observed, black academics had to fight against a social Darwinist ideology that deemed them incapable of coherent thought in the first place. Though not confined solely to writing in a reactive mode, black intellectuals still had to overcome political, social, economic, and cultural barriers that severely limited their professional opportunities and conspired in such a way that they had to carry a heavy burden of proof that they were capable. Franklin's anger and sorrow were clear: "It must have been a most unrewarding experience for the Negro scholar to answer those who said that he was inferior by declaring: 'I am indeed *not* inferior.'"[1]

Franklin asked readers to put themselves in these scholars' shoes to try to come to grips with the loss they and the larger intellectual community suffered. There had always been a pressure to publish, Franklin told his readers, but black scholars were under a different kind of pressure from the one felt by their white counterparts. Franklin continued:

Imagine, if you can, what it meant to a competent Negro student of Greek literature, W. H. Crogman, to desert his chosen field and write a book entitled *The Progress of a Race.* Think of the frustration of the distinguished Negro physician C. V. Roman, who abandoned his medical research and practice, temporarily at least, to write *The Negro in American Civilization.* What must have been the feeling of the Negro student of English literature Benjamin Brawley, who forsook his field to write *The Negro Genius* and other works that underscored the intellectual powers of the Negro? How much poorer is the

217

field of the biological sciences because an extremely able and well-trained Negro scientist, Julian Lewis, felt compelled to spend years of his productive life writing a book entitled *The Biology of the Negro?*[2]

These observations concerned scholars from the first half of the twentieth century. Given the fact that Franklin published his essay on the cusp of some of the greatest civil rights changes in the nation's history and at a time when blacks were never closer to full citizenship rights and a generalizable social acceptance into the mainstream, one might expect that Franklin's model of black intellectual struggle no longer applied. Sadly, this conclusion would be wrong.

In a fundamental sense not much had changed as far as the professional possibilities for black scholars. Of the relatively few blacks who were teaching at universities in the mid-1960s, the great majority had to live their careers in a highly prescribed fashion. Upon entering the university's front door, they were greeted with an expectation of expertise that was both intense and narrowly conceived. Black scholars were to know "black things" best and little else beyond that.

It is here where most conversations regarding black involvement in the academy start and end. This much is understandable, given the long history of academic segregation. Indeed, read collectively, the literature on black intellectuals is reducible to what I have termed elsewhere "the crisis canon."[3] Owing in large measure to social realities, political expectations, personal senses of duty, and the effects of plain and simple racism, the great majority of the literature on the black scholar is written from the perspective of crisis. Black scholars have been in "crisis," have faced unique "dilemmas," and have "failed."[4]

Speaking in general terms, crises are problems that have escalated to the point where they are given attention in the best and worst ways. Without doubt, the most tradition-bound individuals and institutions in the academy viewed the post–World War II democratization of higher education as a crisis.[5] Would standards perish? Would the campus community as "community" suffer with the push to diversify (first age and income, later gender and race)?

But crises, when taken seriously, do get addressed as people try to ameliorate their root causes. Radical or even modest change, however, has a way of precipitating unintended consequences. In some ways, this may be what is so shocking about the "crisis" of black intellectuals and their inclusion in the academy—the crisis has remained in place even though so many of the variables informing the positions of blacks in society at large and in the university more specifically have changed. Administrators, philanthropic foundations, faculty, and students have tinkered and made more substantial changes, but the black presence in the academy remains highly politicized. Furthermore, the debate about what is worth knowing, particularly as it relates to fields of knowledge in which there are greater numbers of minority scholars, still rages on. For example, it is exciting that increasing numbers of black scholars are not limited by external forces to write on black topics. What is not surprising is the extent to which these same scholars are often ignored (at best) or challenged (at worst) for having the audacity to speak on topics so "foreign" to their supposed native knowledge base.[6]

This chapter analyzes blacks' role and participation in the humanities since World War II by looking at the black presence in the academy on three levels: the individual, the institutional, and the ideological. While the scope of the chapter runs from 1945 to the present, particular attention is paid to the mid-1960s through the mid-1970s. This decade bore greater witness to individual, institutional, and ideological change regarding the status, place, and role of blacks in the academy than any other moment in the history of higher education. What stuns, however, is the fact that despite these changes the presumptions about blacks' place and role in the humanities is fundamentally the same.

THE HISTORY of black scholars in the academy must start on the campuses of black colleges. These schools, almost all quite small and frequently in financial difficulty, were the proving grounds for future generations of black leaders. This much is unsurprising. But there are some interesting aspects to these institutions' structural histories and their place in American society that merit a closer look and bear significantly on the efforts to integrate faculties at traditionally white colleges and universities after 1945. The most important things to understand about the black colleges are how few of them there were, how few of these schools bore any resemblance to "mainstream" four-year institutions of higher learning, and how few of them were staffed by an appreciable number of faculty with advanced degrees.

In the early 1940s there were only seventy four-year colleges for blacks in the country. The campuses were typically small—a median enrollment of 310 resident undergraduates—and only half the schools were accredited.[7] In truth, part of this failing was due to black colleges' southern locations and the long-standing refusal of the Southern Association of Colleges and Secondary Schools to consider accrediting them.[8] But the fact remains that of the thirty-five fully accredited black colleges, only a handful were oriented toward teaching *and* research—a result of racist state legislatures that provided only the bare minimum of education for blacks, philanthropic foundations that envisioned specialized centers of black research in a few southern locations, and a federal government under Franklin Roosevelt that wanted a "national Negro university" in Washington, D.C., and thus poured money into Howard University.[9] Advanced degree programs at black schools were only beginning in the late 1930s, and those schools in this vanguard were the most highly desired by the growing black professoriate. The relevant statistics in this regard are stunning: by 1936 more than 80 percent of all black holders of the doctorate were found at Atlanta, Fisk, and Howard Universities—and Howard was home to the great majority of these individuals.[10] The combination of these factors had personal and professional implications for the scholars who did not enjoy the relative luxury of teaching at the triumvirate or who merely felt overwhelmed in a profession that was still virtually all white.[11] The vast majority of these individuals remained at black colleges and universities for the duration of their careers. A handful of black scholars—the historian Michael Winston counts only three employed at white universities in the mid-1930s—existed outside this box until the 1940s.[12] With the gradual desegregation of white campuses and faculties after World War II, black professors began to leave even the very best black schools.

The numbers of black faculty who departed for white schools were so small at first that it is difficult to envision these individuals—no matter how great their scholarship—as little more than racial tokens. Abram Harris's experiences when he moved to the University of Chicago are a case in point. Harris left Howard in 1946. Although he was already the leading black economist of his generation and was one of the few blacks who met with publishing success in white-controlled scholarly journals, Harris never received an appointment in Chicago's Department of Economics, nor did he teach graduate students. Instead, he was relegated to the Philosophy Department and lived out the rest of his career in relative obscurity.[13] For those professors who remained at black schools, the abiding segregation in the professional and personal worlds cannot be ignored. Michael Winston points out the depth and extent of this racial illogic: "It is easy to forget now just how segregation operated as a powerful deterrent to sustained research or writing. In the South, Negro scholars were almost universally barred from libraries, from white university laboratories, and from meetings of local chapters of learned societies. Farther north, in Washington, D.C., even the meetings and dinners of a national organization like Phi Beta Kappa were closed to Negro members, most of whom were Howard University faculty who had been inducted at New England colleges and universities."[14]

In light of Winston's disquieting general observations it is helpful to turn toward the specific experiences of one individual—in this case, J. Saunders Redding—to contextualize the effect of systemic racism upon the personal and professional lives of black academics. Redding is an effective barometer of the glacial pace of and nuances attendant on the integration of our nation's university faculties. He was among the first blacks to teach at a historically white university and, fortunately, left a gift of autobiographical musings for historians to ponder.

It is important to note that Redding was not the first black scholar to break the race barrier on college faculties. (One of the crueler ironies of this situation is that because black colleges did not offer Ph.D.'s at this time, black graduate students went to schools such as Harvard, Columbia, and Chicago for their doctorates but could not teach in like institutions upon completion of the degree.) In 1941 the Julius Rosenwald Fund, one of a handful of philanthropic foundations that dedicated millions of dollars to all levels of black education in the first half of the twentieth century, discovered that there were only two blacks on the faculties at the nation's white colleges and universities, neither of whom held teaching positions. Determined to change that situation, the Rosenwald Fund arranged for the prominent sociologist Allison P. Davis to be appointed at the University of Chicago. The school was willing to hire Davis because the Rosenwald Fund subsidized his salary. In short, the university paid nothing or close to it and received a leading scholar on the sociology of race and community formation in return. This arrangement spoke volumes about the resistance white schools presented to the integration of their faculties, particularly when it came to the use of scarce resources in service of what many considered a political agenda.[15] Perhaps as a result of the Rosenwald Fund's arrangement with Chicago or perhaps as a manifestation of the pace of a changing tide, within three years fifteen blacks could be found on the rosters at white colleges. Redding was part of this tide.

In some ways it is unsurprising that J. Saunders Redding would live his life at the leading edge of racial change. Born in Wilmington, Delaware, to parents who prized education, civic engagement, and activism (his father was the long-standing secretary of Wilmington's local branch of the NAACP; a sibling, Louis, was the first African American to pass the bar in Delaware), Redding started college at Lincoln University but completed his studies at Brown. He performed with distinction there and earned Phi Beta Kappa honors. Even though he graduated from college in 1928, the honor society or Brown (or both) did not see fit to admit him until 1943, after he had already become a nationally prominent writer and literary critic.[16]

After teaching for a few years at Morehouse College, Redding returned to Brown, where he completed a master's degree in English and American Literature in 1932. He secured positions at a variety of black southern schools over the course of the next three decades. Redding spent two of those three decades at Virginia's Hampton Institute, where in his last nine years he served as James Weldon Johnson Professor of Creative Writing.[17] In 1949, however, he broke this pattern of employment and served as a visiting professor at Brown. There are scarce details about the terms of his appointment or his personal experiences while there, but there is little doubt today how Brown assesses Redding's relationship to the school.

In a special edition celebrating its one hundredth year of publication, in 2000, *Brown Alumni Magazine (BAM)* presented a digest of what its editors and a survey of Brown alumni deemed the one hundred most important and influential people to graduate from the Providence school. Breaking the list down into categories (from biochemistry to graphic design to zoology), the editors of the magazine declared that Redding was one of four alumni who accomplished great things in the field of history. Ignoring the fact that Redding was not actually a historian, his *BAM* entry pointed immediately to his groundbreaking credentials: "He was the first black member of an Ivy League faculty, the first black to serve as a Brown fellow, and the first black to have his portrait hung in Sayles Hall."[18] What is not mentioned here is the brevity of his appointment to Brown: he taught there for only one term.

Of course, by their very nature, alumni magazines are celebratory glossies dedicated to sustaining open connections between a school and its graduates. But given the highly contested pace and nature of change regarding race relations and the present racial diversity on college campuses, it is worth considering *BAM*'s commemoration also as a racial celebration of sorts. As it happens, one of the other four historians honored in this special issue is black: Spencer Crew, Brown class of 1971, in 2000 director of the Smithsonian's National Museum of American History. Post–civil rights celebrations of diversity are not unusual, but their contextualization, understanding the history of struggle behind the celebration, is always important. Redding's history is profoundly revealing, especially in light of the circumstances surrounding his eventual full-time move to a white campus in 1970.

Redding was a prolific writer whose fiction and nonfiction prose appeared in essay and book form. By the time he published his memoir, *On Being Negro in America*, in 1951, he had already produced four other major works: *To Make a Poet Black* (1939), *No Day of Triumph* (1942), *Stranger and Alone* (1950), and *They Came in Chains: Americans from Africa* (1950). It is his memoir, however, that best reflects how the combination of institutional racism and more personal acts of racial antagonism amounted to a daily, low-level psychological battle with which black scholars like Redding found they had little choice but to engage.

Redding opened his memoir with a wild swing at Richard Wright and his 1941 book, *12 Million Black Voices*. Redding spoke with outrage that Wright sought to describe blacks via his analysis of New Deal Farm Security Administration photographs that captured black folklife: "This [memoir] is personal. I would call it a 'document' except that the word has overtones of something official, vested and final. But I have been clothed with no authority to speak for others, and what I have to say can be final only for myself. I hasten to say this at the start, for I remember my anger at the effrontery of one who a few years ago undertook to speak for me and twelve million others. I concurred with practically nothing he said. This was not important in itself, but when one presumes to speak for me he must reflect my mind so accurately that I find no source of disagreement with him. To do this, he must either be a lack-brain parrot or a god."[19]

While Redding did not mention Wright by name and thereby softened the blow—after all, Wright did pen the introduction to Redding's *No Day of Triumph*, in which he heartily praised the book—Redding's opening words here are instructive. They speak to his frustration that whites as well as blacks too quickly reduced the diversity of black America into a single type or form. They also make plain the extent to which race and racial thinking overdetermined the life chances for all black Americans. Redding continued: "Though there are many lack-brains, historic and present circumstances prove that there are no gods dealing with the problem of race—or, as dangerous to the American ideal and exhausting to individual Americans as it has been for three hundred years, it would have been settled long ago. Else the gods are singularly perverse."[20]

Raised in a family of civil rights activists, Redding articulated a sense of self that acknowledged racial differences but insisted upon the fundamental "Americanness" of black culture; that black and white were inextricable. This is an ideology that would become unpopular with the black militants of future decades, but in 1951 Redding's personal ideology, manifested in such a way that the individual was ascendant, was not unusual. This integrationist ethos or call to respect the individual in each person, however, was undermined at every turn by a system of seeing race and imbuing it with constant meaning. Throughout his memoir, Redding insists his "right" to speak on his views of race does not extend beyond his self. Clearly wanting to avoid the trap that he suggested Wright fell into when he claimed to speak for all blacks, Redding also took this stance because he wanted to personalize the psychological trauma that blacks and whites incurred by racial thinking. He saw in his memoir a quest for "a purge, a catharsis, wholeness."[21] By claiming expertise in the personal, Redding then felt comfortable extending beyond himself, drawing connections from his private quest for a god of reason to larger phenomena that frustrated him and other like-minded seekers.

Redding saw his memoir as "the epilogue to whatever contribution I have made to the 'literature of race.'" Although John Hope Franklin did not mention Redding in his 1963 essay on the black scholar, it is clear that Redding experienced the same sense of personal loss and bitterness that Franklin identified: the frustration with the expectation that black scholars spoke for the race or to the race in order to be heard. Redding announced his desire to "get on to other things. I do not know whether I can make this clear, but the obligations imposed by race on the average educated or talented Negro (if this sounds immodest, it must) are vast and become at last onerous. I am tired of giving up my creative initiative to these demands. I think I am not alone."

Redding continued this line of reasoning by citing the experiences of a famous singer who lamented the constant expectation that she sing spirituals in every concert. Although she sang them well, "she was weary of the obligation of finding a place for them in every program, 'as if they were theme music' wholly identifying her." She, like Redding, felt arrested in what he termed "ethnocentric coils." Drawing from his own experiences and that of the unnamed singer, Redding then made a declaration about his memoir's value: "The specialization of the sense and talent and learning . . . that is expected of Negroes by other members of their race and by whites is tragic and vicious and divisive. I am tired of trying, in deference to this expectation, to feel my way into the particularities of response and reaction that are supposed to be exclusively 'Negro.' I am tired of the unnatural obligation of converting such talent and learning as I have into specialized instruments for the promotion of a false concept called 'race.' This extended essay, then, is probably my last public comment on the so-called American race problem."[22]

Although the memoir would not be Redding's final public comment on the race problem, his anger at the forces that inspired such a sentiment run throughout his book. One hears it when he agonizes that his heart is "sickened at the realization of the primal energy that goes undeflected and unrefined into the sheer business of living as a Negro in the United States." One hears it when he points out that "ignorance and willful distortion of the facts of American life and history in regard to the Negro's role have set the Negro scholar what up to now has been a thankless task. In pure self-defense he has had to try to set the record straight." And one hears it when Redding insists that the "psychopathic resistance to self-knowledge that the American mind has developed must be broken down."[23]

It was with great reluctance that Redding so publicly addressed these issues in the first place. This reluctance, however, could not withstand the "daemonic force" that drove him to speak on the race problem with an eye toward eliminating it. This need to address race matters, Redding spat, "has always been a galling affliction to me and the root of my personal grievance with American life."[24] Redding was not alone in this grievance, just as he was not alone in feeling a sense of compulsion to address America's race problem. But although his grievances spoke across generations, the tactics others pursued toward a more just society changed rapidly from the 1950s into the 1960s.

After Redding's short stint at Brown he returned to Hampton, continuing to write weekly book reviews for the *Baltimore Afro-American* in addition to his more scholarly work, which took the form of books and journal articles. It was during these quietly productive years that the scope and tactics of civil rights reform and the kinds of questions being asked of society changed in critical ways. Redding remained true to his integrationist ideology, which fell out of favor with many college-aged youth as the civil rights movement lurched into its black power phase. There is no doubt that his strong adherence to the integrationist ethos made him the object of desire for those university campuses that became serious about diversifying in the wake of early 1960s civil rights triumphs.

Redding's path to a just society must have seemed almost quaint in the wake of student-led occupations of administration buildings that began to sweep the country in 1968. Among other things, the students called for curricular reform that would introduce the black experience to their studies, and they called for an increased diversity of the student body, administration, and faculty. In most places these demands were articulated with relative calm. On a few campuses, however, the result was quite the opposite. In 1969 the protesting students at Cornell University embodied the most extreme manifestation of this phenomenon when they literally took up arms and threatened to use force if their demands were not met. There is no coincidence to be found in the fact that Redding secured his first permanent job at a white campus within months. When he was appointed full professor in Cornell's English Department in 1970 he became the first black at that rank in the school's College of Arts and Sciences as well as the first black to hold an endowed chair. Redding taught at Cornell from 1970 to 1976.[25]

We can be certain that Redding was never the student militants' choice. Redding had maintained his commitment to integrationist policies at the moment when militant separatism was the passionate call of students. (While at Cornell, Redding had no official affiliation to that campus's Africana Studies and Research Center.)[26] Redding's presence, however, was a valve that reduced pressure on the Cornell administration to do something that demonstrated an acknowledgment of the need for some measure of racial diversity on its campus. Redding, of course, was not alone in his newfound role as an object of desire. Beginning in the late 1960s, unprecedented numbers of black scholars began to find their way to teach on historically white campuses. This fact led Rayford Logan, a longtime Howard University professor of history, to express grave concern that "it is likely that more of our best scholars will, in the future, leave permanently or temporarily to teach at other [i.e., white] institutions and that they will be replaced by less mature and less capable teachers and scholars."[27]

This new desire for black faculty followed an upsurge in the numbers of black undergraduates at white universities. In a Ford Foundation report on the development of black studies in the nation's colleges and universities, the historian Nathan Huggins charted the dramatic growth in college enrollment as a result of the G.I. Bill and the postwar baby boom.[28] Black college matriculation approached 10 percent of total student enrollment by the mid-1970s, and with this rise came pressure to address the needs and desires of this relatively new constituency. But Huggins made sure to add an important caveat to this received wisdom: black students were not the only source of pressure to change the appearance and pedagogy of white universities. New visions of universities' ability to shape society and an increasing focus on career training prompted school administrators to rationalize departments' respective utility. Administrators now felt freer to ask, for example, what was the pragmatic value that a department of philosophy brought to a campus community. "Merely" contributing to the store of knowledge was being threatened by a heightened devotion to particular knowledge's market value or its potential for demonstrating social relevance. In this new environment the social sciences and hard sciences along with the professional schools found it relatively easy to rationalize their existence and "value" to a campus and its students. Humanities programs and departments, on the other hand, faced a steeper challenge.[29] Following this line of reasoning, we can discern another motivating factor behind the universities' decisions to create institutional and pedagogical spaces that were relevant to the black experience in the United States.

That the humanities would lean, in part, on their ability to address social problems related to race as a basis to justify their value is ironic since, as a mode of inquiry, so many humanities programs had been criticized as embodying Eurocentric culture, art, and thought. Whether it was true or not, black students criticized humanities courses for failing to speak to the circumstances of their lives and traditions. "Relevance"—real or imagined—was the catchword of the moment and the either/or presumption dictated that one was part of the problem if one was not working toward a solution. The solution at many campuses was to hire one or two black faculty and have them teach one or two courses on topics like "black literature" and "black history." Typically, these courses were fully integrated into the standing curricular offerings.[30] But this was only one solution. One would be remiss to ignore the other path—and the debates that cluttered it—that schools followed to integrate blackness into their curricula: the disciplinary establishment of black studies.

The very real threat of a violent outbreak at Cornell was the most extreme manifestation of student activism in service of a call for racial, pedagogical, and curricular diversity at a university. But the Ithaca school was not the only place where the development and then incorporation of a black studies program exposed serious fault lines between students and administrators. It is worth taking a few moments to explore the different models of black studies programmatic formation and then to ask serious questions about these different models.

The first black studies program in the country was established at San Francisco State in 1968. Before the program was created and in an attempt to demonstrate its commitment to diversifying its faculty and, perhaps more truthfully, have black bodies teach black studies courses, the administration had hired G. M. Murray, a member of the Black Panther Party, as a lecturer. Murray did not have an advanced degree and was open about the fact that he was teaching classes "related to revolution." In late September 1968 word of his classes and their hyperpoliticized nature came to the attention of the Board of Trustees of the California State College System, which then voted, 85–5, to fire Murray. This decision sent shock waves through the campus and resulted in student strikes, violence between police and the community, and the school's closure.[31]

Eventually San Francisco State's new president, S. I. Hayakawa, managed to reopen the campus (with the enforcement assistance of California's Governor Ronald Reagan) and offered to create a permanent black studies department as a means to address black student frustrations. Hayakawa proposed hiring the sociologist Nathan Hare, who, incidentally, had just been fired from Howard for his support of and engagement with striking students there.[32] The Bay Area student-activists had a different agenda in mind, however, which went much further than the mere establishment of a black studies program or department. They issued a ten-point list of demands that called for the establishment of an independent black studies department and, among other things, insisted upon universal acceptance of black applicants, the elimination of the Board of Trustees' ability to dissolve black programs at San Francisco State and elsewhere, and the rehiring of G. M. Murray.[33] The students also demanded that Hare, who was chairing the black studies program, "receive a full professorship and a comparable salary according to his qualifications."[34]

The students' demands fell on deaf ears. This much was made evident when Hare notified the students that President Hayakawa did not renew his contract. Clearly, Hare did little to inspire Hayakawa's trust. Hare recounted that soon after he arrived at San Francisco State his assumption that he had been hired to "'coordinate' the nation's first black studies program" proved incorrect. This assumption "soon dissolved into deception as I discovered that I had been brought there to appease black students. I refused the role of a troubleshooter and tumult was not long in breaking loose. I could not and did not try to stop the student protest."[35] There were very real consequences that appeared in the wake of Hayakawa's and Hare's mutual refusals. Most immediate was the resignation of four of the school's six black administrators, who left publicly claiming that Hayakawa was a racist. A few months after the group resignation and apparently without blinking, Hayakawa threatened to disband the Black Studies Department. Within the year Hayakawa made good on those threats when he ousted the department's faculty.[36]

The point here is not so much the nature of the dispute between Hayakawa, the Board of Trustees, and San Francisco State's black students. Rather, the events at the school make evident that one must pay careful attention to the way that race politics were rife with controversy and that black professors were caught in the vortex of the disputes that generally started in the student body and were directed toward administrations. These late 1960s debates most typically revolved around the establishment of black studies programs or at least a reshaping of the college curriculum in such a way that the black experience would be fairly reflected in the course offerings. That black faculty found themselves caught in this debate reveals a core aspect of the racial expectations driving the creation of these new institutional or at least curricular spaces: "black courses" were to be taught by black faculty. If a university did not have black courses it would hire black faculty to teach them. If a university wanted to find a space where it could point a bright light on the diversity of its hiring practices it might create a black studies program and place black faculty in it. It probably goes without saying that university administrations took so many of these actions because they mitigated black student anger and salved their disaffection.

It was at this juncture and in light of these dynamics that another philanthropic foundation committed financial resources to changing the university landscape. In a move that echoed the Rosenwald Fund's 1941 decision to finance the hiring of black scholars, the Ford Foundation awarded over $1 million to twelve colleges and universities in 1969 and 1970 to help them develop interdisciplinary black studies programs.[37] Yale University was one of the institutions that enjoyed the foundation's largesse and it set about creating its own Afro-American studies program. In no small part because of this institutionally organized and external support, the history of the formation of Yale's program and the politics behind its formation are significantly less turbulent than those at Cornell or San Francisco State.

A breadth of scholars and foundation representatives points to the establishment of the Afro-American Studies Program at Yale—referred to throughout the literature as "the Yale Case"—as the best example of how a process that was committed to maintaining a scholarly approach to black studies (instead of a "therapeutic approach") could survive that era's complicated race politics.[38] As was true at other schools, the movement to start a black studies program at Yale sprang from undergraduate desire. Instead of occupying administration buildings, however, representatives from the school's Black Student Alliance met with Yale's president, Kingman Brewster, in early 1968 and then with various administration and faculty representatives on a weekly basis over the course of the following three months. By the spring of that year, students had organized a two-day conference that revolved around the question of black studies, its value to college curricula, and its anticipated role at Yale. The conference featured white and black speakers who represented the breadth of the political and methodological spectrum.[39]

The debate among Yale and non-Yale faculty resulted in a publication, *Black Studies in the University*, and, a year later, the formation of the Ivy League's first black studies program. In these early days of black studies programs, Yale's was seen as the role model. Other university administrators admired if not envied what transpired in New Haven because it was done without threats of violence or even serious public displays of disaffection. Established scholars like Nathan Huggins praised the Yale model for its inclusiveness, "the constructive attitude of the university's senior faculty and the deft leadership of its administration."[40] But tangled up in this sense of good feeling were some of the same antagonistic or defensive race dynamics that one found in other campus communities.

David Brion Davis, then in the History Department at Cornell but soon to move to Yale, felt compelled to declare in his closing remarks (a summation of the conference proceedings) that black studies, if it was to succeed as a discipline, could not close the door to white scholars. The ability to interpret a racialized past could not logically be limited to a native (might one say "natural"?) insiders' ability to interpret blackness. If blackness could trump training, knowledge, and the freedom to explore complex and even controversial ideas, Davis warned, the university would fail in its role as a "custodian as well as an innovator." Paraphrasing the political theorist Martin Kilson, another conference panelist, Davis concluded, "Oppression conveys no special intellectual or moral virtues."[41] Nathan Hare countered Davis's claims to cross-racial interpretive ability. Elsewhere, he recalled his performance at Yale, "where I had the occasion to ponder the blank and (in a good many cases) open-mouthed stares of ignorance on faces in the predominantly white audience when I related how all white students given a test by a black colleague and me had fundamentally flunked, being unable to identify such commodities as hog maws, fried beans, and butter roll."[42] Hare's point was simple: who better to know and interpret the full complexity of black culture and the black experience than black people? Hare's suggestions were not well received. Huggins, for one, merely dismissed Hare and his fellow presenter at the Yale conference, the cultural nationalist Maulana Ron Karenga, as "deeply anti-intellectual and hostile to the academy."[43]

Huggins or Davis could have added that Hare's and Karenga's nationalist assertions also did violence to the actual history of black studies in the first place. Since at least the late 1930s the anthropologist Melville Herskovits, a student of Franz Boas and a prominent supporter of cultural relativism, had called for a sustained investigation of the retention of African culturalisms among American blacks. Granted, Herskovits was not literally advocating the formation of black studies programs, but his work, particularly his 1941 book, *The Myth of the Negro Past*, became the intellectual bedrock for future black studies advocates. A child of Jewish immigrants, Herskovits was an Africanist by training but became deeply invested in advocating the "Afro-American tradition." A people without an acknowledged history were a people denied their own humanity, and *The Myth of the Negro Past* (the myth being that blacks had no past) set out to correct this conscious oversight. It is unclear if Hare and Karenga would have been dismissive of a white Jew like Herskovits, who dedicated his career to the "espousal of the solidity and authenticity of a distinguishable Afro-American culture," but Nathan Huggins clearly thought they should have known the history of their own field better.[44]

If one did not want to fault Hare and Karenga for failing to acknowledge appropriately Herskovits's influence on the emerging discipline, one would have been absolutely remiss a few years later to ignore the prominent role that white scholars such as Herbert Gutman, Lawrence Levine, Gerda Lerner, and Eugene Genovese played in fostering a deepening awareness of blacks as active agents in the making of their own identity and history.[45] By the mid-1970s an honest and less politically driven assessment of black studies scholarship would have had to confess that some of its most important practitioners were white.

Acknowledging white scholars' growing interest in or even fascination with blackness or Herskovits's foundational role in black studies did not mean that black scholars were late to come to black studies or that they came to the field only in the wake of student protests or administrative or philanthropic fiat. If one took a more liberal approach to the institutional definitions of what constitutes black studies in an academic setting, one would likely share the opinion offered by the black studies scholars James Turner and C. Steven McGann. In their 1980 essay, "Black Studies as an Integral Tradition in African-American Intellectual History," Turner and McGann assert that black studies could trace its roots back to the young W. E. B. DuBois and Carter G. Woodson. DuBois created the Atlanta University Studies Series in 1913 and thus laid the foundation for black studies via the series' working papers on various aspects of the black experience. Woodson, the so-called Father of Negro History, created Negro History Week, established the Association for the Study of Negro Life and History, and founded the *Journal of Negro History* at almost the same time that DuBois's series appeared. Taken together, Woodson's actions demonstrated the humanistic contributions of black Americans to the larger society. For Turner and McGann, DuBois's and Woodson's actions constituted the intellectual structure upon which later black studies programs were built.[46]

Related to the diverse means by which they became institutionalized on college campuses in the late 1960s and into the early 1970s, black studies programs represented a range of political and theoretical approaches to the budding discipline. A few programs were methodologically traditional as far as the disciplinary questions they entertained by linking new black studies programs to established humanistic fields such as English, history, and philosophy. Many more focused large aspects of their curricular agenda on constructing bridges between the campus and community. Still other programs were explicitly race-first in their consciousness, determined to reserve black studies for black people. These programs were disciplinarily traditional, community oriented, and militantly political, and their modes and styles reflected those of the individuals who were hired to run them. But no matter where they happened to find an institutional home, black studies programs and their teaching staff constantly lived on the edge of controversy.

Figures like the ubiquitous Nathan Hare often seemed to do what they could either to seek out or to provoke controversy. More than once Hare declared that he thought black studies, if done right, represented a vanguardist movement that could revolutionize the university and society. This was education in service of a larger political goal. "To solve the problems of the black race," Hare announced, "Afro-American education must produce persons capable of solving the problems of a contagious American society. To solve the problems of American society, Afro-Americans must first blackwash—revamp—the existing educational system, and revolutionize America's youth—black, yellow, brown and white."[47] This "blackwashing," in Hare's opinion, was the work of black studies departments and the black faculty who should staff them.

The theologian Vincent Harding, who attempted through his leadership of the Institute of the Black World (an Atlanta-based think tank established in 1969) to find ways to connect scholarship directly to the needs of the black community, was much more explicit in his declaration that black scholars had a duty to "speak the truth" to black America.[48] While Harding allowed for the white intellectual examination of black life, he spoke about a moral calling that blacks had to heed: "The calling of the black scholar is to move insistently beyond . . . abdication, whatever its cause. Let others study us if they will (although the studies slacken off when they become less profitable), but self-definition is an intrinsic part of self-determination. It is *we* who must understand our families, our churches, our works of art, the schools our children attend, the economic, political, and spiritual structures which uphold—and oppress—the communities in which we live. It is *we* who must understand how all these structures and institutions are related to our oppression and our struggle for liberation. It is *we* who must painfully diagnose our own deepest illnesses and identify with great joy our most soaring aspirations towards new humanity."[49] Taken together, Hare's and Harding's comments created the intellectual space and rationalization for black studies programs that were oriented toward community service or political militancy, if not separatism.

White and black scholars—as would be expected—reacted with great passion to these kinds of sentiments. We have already read David Davis's polite insistence that the pursuit of knowledge be color-blind even when society, subject matter, and the politics informing the knowledge were not. Other white scholars were hardly so polite. Eugene Genovese, for example, raged on about the implications, scholarly, personal, and otherwise, of race-exclusive enclaves within academe:

> Responsible black scholars have been working hard for an end to raiding and to the scattering of the small number of black professors across the country. Among other obstacles, they face the effort of ostensibly nationalist black students who seek to justify their decision to attend predominantly white institutions, often of high prestige, by fighting for a larger black teaching staff. The outcomes of these demands is the obscurantist nonsense that black studies can and should be taught by people without intellectual credentials since these credentials are "white" anyway.
>
> [Few] good universities have ever refused to waive formalities in any field when genuine intellectual credentials of a nonacademic order could be provided. What has to be resisted firmly is the insanity that claims, as in one recent instance, that experience as a SNCC field organizer should be considered more important than a Ph.D. in the hiring of a professor of Afro-American history. This assertion represents a general contempt for all learning and a

particular contempt for black studies as a field of study requiring disciplined, serious intellectual effort—an attitude that reflects the influence of white racism, even when brought forth by a black man.[50]

Using a less strident tone, but one still bristling with rage about racial politics run amok on the college campus, the social psychologist Kenneth B. Clark expressed his dismay over the decision by Antioch College administrators to cave into black student demands for a new black studies program. Clark's anger did not spring from the idea of such a program but from the mode of articulation in Antioch's case. There, campus officials politically and financially supported the establishment of the Afro-American Institute and an undergraduate house that were racially exclusive. For someone who had staked his career on integration, Clark felt his principles violated by Antioch's decision. Clark responded to this violation by resigning from Antioch and issuing a public statement about the proper role of race on college campuses: "The white liberal for his part who concedes black separatism so hastily and benevolently must look to his own reasons, not the least of them perhaps an exquisite relief. To encourage or endorse a separate black program not academically equivalent to the college curriculum generally, indeed to endorse any such program, is to reinforce the Negro's inability to compete with whites for the real power of the real world. It is no excuse to justify the deed by citing the demand." Invoking the same language of caretaking that motivated David Davis's opinion, Clark continued, "Colleges and universities must be the custodians of the rational and intellectual approach to the study and eventual solution of complex human problems. To succumb to any form of dogmatism, to institutionalize the irrational is to fail in fulfilling this important obligation."[51]

This is only a sampling of the angry rhetoric, denunciations, and celebrations that reverberated throughout this era. Critical questions, almost always politically motivated, threw in bold relief precisely how racial knowledge affected the curricular, pedagogical, and institutional landscape on the nation's campuses. Was black studies a legitimate field of inquiry? Was it a discipline? Who should teach black studies courses? Do black studies programs drain black faculty away from black colleges and universities? Do these programs relieve other departments from having to teach topics that relate to race? Are black studies programs solely a pressure valve for student discontent? Are black studies programs conceived as a strategic means to diversify a faculty? Who should major in black studies? And so forth.

These were the questions that dogged those black scholars who may have been reluctant to engage the topic or who even had nothing to do professionally with black studies. These were also the questions that other black scholars addressed eagerly, seeing in the reception and consumption of their own answers recognition of their expertise in at least one topic. The sense among black faculty that they were going to be "allowed" to be expert in only one particular field of inquiry and the fact that there was a major institutional push, for all manner of reasons discussed in this chapter, toward the development of black studies programs combined to create a great opportunity for a series of new scholarly initiatives. These initiatives often came in the form of academic journals.

The most important new journal in this regard was the *Black Scholar* (first edition in 1969), edited by Nathan Hare. Other scholarly efforts include the *Journal of Black Studies* (1970), *Afro-American Studies* (1970), and the *Journal of Afro-American Issues* (1972).[52] Like the individuals who ran them and the institutions that supported them (if, indeed, institutional support was forthcoming), these journals underscored the breadth of opinion on the theory and substance of black studies. Prefatory statements and mission statements in the first issues reflect their sponsors' political orientations.

The *Journal of Afro-American Issues* was the least doctrinaire. Privately published by Educational Community Consultants Associates, an organization run by the education consultant and author Roosevelt Johnson, merely said that it was "devoted to the scientific determination and explication of issues affecting blacks in America." The journal published essays by academics who were mostly concerned with issues regarding professional development and the social sciences. Essays with titles such as "Urban Teachers as Change Agents" and "Teaching Black Studies for Social Change" (an essay on teaching models rather than pedagogical substance) were commonplace.[53]

The *Journal of Black Studies* (*JBS*) and *Afro-American Studies* (*AAS*) were more representative of mainstream humanistic scholarship. Instead of essays that focused on professional development, the *JBS* and *AAS* brought together an interdisciplinary collection of essays written by political scientists, historians, literary critics, linguists, and sociologists. Sponsored by the City University of New York and the University of California at Los Angeles, respectively, these two journals expounded upon the pedagogical thrust and political position of black studies within the academy. At least once an issue readers would encounter such pieces as "In Defense of Black Studies," "Teaching Afro-American History," "Black Studies: Interpretation, Methodology, and the Relationship to Social Movements," "Black Students and the Impossible Revolution," and "The Significance and Challenge of Afro-American Studies."[54]

Both journals were clearly conceived as reflective and critical supplements to the development of black studies programs throughout the country. Indeed, from the very start, *Afro-American Studies* made its purpose plain: "Interdisciplinary in approach and outlooks, *Afro-American Studies* serves educators and professionals in colleges and other educational institutions initiating and developing curricula, programs, institutes, and faculties in Black Studies."[55] Arthur Smith, the director of UCLA's Afro-American Studies Center and the editor of the *Journal of Black Studies*, was more expansive in enunciating his journal's proposed role even though it was not substantively different. Smith opened the first issue with a signed editor's message. He observed: "Seldom in the history of academic disciplines has an area of study been born with so much pain and anguish as Black Studies, also called Afro-American Studies. Discussions initiated, for the most part by university students, produced significant reevaluations of curricula, research, and pedagogy." Later, in the same message, he became more specific about his journal's aspirations: "It is hoped that the founding of the *Journal of Black Studies* will mark an important juncture in the synthesis of the field. Capitalizing on the enormous body of literature, with its concomitant scholars, who are finding new streams and enlarging upon existent ones, the Journal seeks to encourage dynamic, innovative, and creative research. It plans to nurture the expanding community of scholars whose immediate interests are in adding to the factual, analytical, and evaluative bases upon which Black Studies must be established."[56]

Aside from the greater detail in *JBS*'s mission statement, the only thing that substantively distinguishes the two journals' opening statements is tone. Smith's *JBS* statement evinced a style that was suggestive of what one associated with the political militant and racial nationalist. Given the fairly traditional nature of the articles in the journal—beyond their focus on black studies, that is—it would seem that the *Journal of Black Studies* was trying to do two things at once: present itself in the most academically accepted ways and deploy a language that pointed to what Houston Baker calls the "moral panic" associated with the development of black studies programs.[57]

It is this moral panic, this sense of heightened stakes for all concerned, this sense of realizing that one identified a threat too late to stop its advance, that one witnessed in the debates and protests in places like San Francisco State and Cornell and that one heard in the anxious declarations of someone such as Eugene Genovese. But no scholar was more effective than Nathan Hare at addressing and fomenting a moral panic regarding black studies. As we have seen, his work was published widely and he appeared, it seemed, just about everywhere a debate on black studies was being enjoined. It is safe to say that much of his desirability as a speaker or contributor to journals grew out of his willingness, if not tendency, to take controversial stances and out of his role as publisher of the *Black Scholar*, the premiere journal of criticism related to the field of black studies.

Inside the front cover of the first issue, an unsigned statement (by either Hare or the *Black Scholar*'s editor, Robert Chrisman) enunciated the *Black Scholar*'s agenda and made plain that black artists and writers had a moral obligation to embrace this agenda as well. Among other things, black academics had to "shape a culture, a politics, an economics, a sense of our past and future history." The *Black Scholar* would serve as the best space where black intellectuals could present their analyses that would attend to these needs. The authors' words were grave and absolute: "We cannot afford division any longer if our struggle is to bear fruit, whether those divisions be between class, caste or function. Nothing black is alien to us."[58]

Opening up the pages of the *Black Scholar* revealed an unmistakable political agenda that was, if not purely nationalist, certainty militant. Each number of the journal carried a special theme around which that issue's essays were organized. Looking over the themes for the *Black Scholar*'s first year brings the reader immediate clarity about the journal's political orientation. The seven numbers to appear in the *Black Scholar*'s first year were titled "The Culture of Revolution," "Black Politics," "In Memoriam: W. E. B. DuBois," "Black Psychology," "Black Cities: Colonies or City States," "Black Revolution," and "Black Culture." The essays inside each issue were substantively similar in tone.

Taken together, the *Black Scholar*, *Afro-American Studies*, the *Journal of Black Studies*, and the *Journal of Afro-American Issues* accurately reflect the broad scope of possibility that defined black studies and black intellectual production despite attempts to ignore or limit the field's or individuals' development. But what does it mean that the most important of these journals and the longest-lasting as well, the *Black Scholar*, was committed to a line of reasoning that extended the race bar further and possibly exacerbated tensions between black and white groups? What did it matter that black intellectuals were still being called to serve a community or risk being seen as irrelevant? Were the politics of racial knowledge unavoidable? Were the dynamics of inclusion—the means by which blacks became incorporated into the system—too complicated or simply too unforgiving to think that black scholars ever could be fully integrated in meaningful ways?

Answers to these questions, of course, depended on whom one asked. Certainly, the *Black Scholar* and its brethren were not the only sources for these questions or answers. Other scholarship from the 1970s demonstrates that there was no shortage of individuals offering their own opinions in the debate.[59] Two of the most important texts in this regard are Joyce Ladner's anthology *The Death of White Sociology: Essays on Race and Culture* and Gloria Hull, Patricia Bell Scott, and Barbara Smith's collection, *All the Women Are White, All the Blacks Are Men, but Some of Us Are Brave: Black Women's Studies*.[60]

Ladner's and Hull, Scott, and Smith's anthologies are critical to this conversation because they remind us of the political consciousness that drove much of black studies scholarship and call our attention to the relationship of this scholarship to disciplinary boundaries and gendered ideologies.

Ladner's *Death of White Sociology* set out to address the ideological shifts that accompanied the changing face of American universities in the 1960s, the increasingly effective student protests for a racially inclusive pedagogy, and the recognition that the long-standing exclusion of the black experience in scholarly discourses was an injustice. Ladner was not forecasting the end of mainstream sociology, but she wanted to call attention to the fact that the sociological discourse that typically branded blacks as deviants would no longer go unchallenged. *The Death of White Sociology* was a reactive text, spurred on by the rising popularity of black deviance narratives through the 1960s, but it also needs to be seen as a generative text.[61] In her own contribution to the anthology, "Tomorrow's Tomorrow: The Black Woman," Ladner criticized mainstream scholarship for looking at blacks as problems and called for new social science approaches that were significantly more introspective and sensitive to structures of inequality instead of outlier behavior patterns. Ladner argued that there had to be "a strong concern for redefining the problem. Instead of future studies being conducted on *problems* of the Black community as represented by the *deviant perspective*, there must be a redefinition of the *problem as being that of institutional racism*." Ladner continued, "Studies which have as their focal point the alleged deviant *attitudes* and *behavior* of Blacks are grounded within the racist assumptions and principles that only render Blacks open to further exploitation."[62]

Ladner did not invoke black studies scholarship by name, but her critique of the state of current disciplinary practice was absolutely consistent with the collective sense among academics advocating for the establishment of black studies scholarship norms. This was an advocacy that recognized the humanity in blacks and the complexity of their experience. This was also a scholarship that angrily denounced the idea that blacks were a people without a past. But as much as Ladner was in line with the guiding principles of black studies, she was different from the majority of black studies advocates in that she paid serious attention to the role of the black woman in the formation of a modern black identity.[63] Although *The Death of White Sociology* was clearly a reaction to the popularity of social science studies that viewed the matriarchal black family structure as pathological, Ladner's work also appeared at a moment of a rising independent black feminist consciousness. In the world of letters, Hull, Scott, and Smith captured much of this 1970s consciousness in their anthology.

Like *The Death of White Sociology*, *All the Women Are White* is a work that is simultaneously reactive and generative. Hull, Scott, and Smith felt the need to act on behalf of generations of ignored black women scholars and black women's scholarship. Aside from the fact that the book made an important contribution simply from the standpoint of including new voices in scholarly discourses, it sheds valuable light on black studies by the way in which it offers an incisive critique of the formative impulses behind the discipline. Hull, Scott, and Smith enthusiastically embraced the new attention that blacks were receiving in lecture halls, seminars, journals, and books, but theirs was a qualified enthusiasm. Revisiting the lead editorial in the first issue of the *Black Scholar* (1969) reveals the kind of mind-set that had to infuriate black women intellectuals and give feminists pause. In that issue the editors called for a collective black struggle for independence and recognition and highlighted the black intellectual's role in that fight. "A black scholar recognizes this fact," the editors concluded. "He is a man of both thought and action, a whole man who thinks for his people and acts with them, a man who honors the whole community of black experience."[64] Black women scholars also wanted to honor the whole community of the black experience but understood with utterly clarity that racial cohesion meant gendered erasure.[65]

Quite unconsciously, black men's blindness combined with a white feminist racism that ignored or even disparaged black women's feminist consciousness in the early 1970s. As a result, black women's studies scholars were left with few opportunities in which to present work or collaborate with like-minded academics. Hull and her coeditors urged their readers to combine the best aspects of feminist and black studies scholarships in order to fashion a black feminist movement that would, in turn, "lend its political strength to the development of Black women's studies courses, programs, and research, and to the funding they require."[66] This call for a structural shift in the work of the university echoed perfectly the call made just over a decade earlier by black studies advocates like Nathan Hare and restive undergraduates. It also came at a moment of astonishing growth in the amount of attention being paid to black women's place in society and in academia.

In the introduction to their anthology Hull, Scott, and Smith hail the 1970s renaissance in black women's art and literature, pointing to the novelist and poet Alice Walker as one of the critical figures of that moment. While acknowledging Walker's important literary contributions, Hull, Scott, and Smith are more interested in calling attention to the pedagogical and disciplinary change that Walker initiated in 1972, when she taught the first course on black women writers at Wellesley College. More precisely, this was the first course on the topic taught at any college.[67] That this barrier was broken so late in the century is shocking, perhaps, but that fact pales in comparison to the intensity of the literary renaissance that came to full bloom shortly thereafter. Black women's literature—or, at least, some black women's literature—went from a virtual unexplored country in college classrooms to a well-mapped landscape of required reading.

Again, Walker gets credit for much of this transformation because of her efforts to bring Zora Neale Hurston's work to the public's attention. Through Walker's literary archaeology, Hurston, who died in poverty and essentially forgotten, was placed at the center of black women's and black studies' literary discussions, near the center of feminist literary discussions, and in the larger circle of most introductory American literary discussions.[68] Indeed, Hurston's tremendous transracial popularity in the 1980s, an era of a so-called nihilistic crisis in black America, caused the literary scholar Hazel Carby to wonder if Hurston's *Their Eyes Were Watching God* was "the most frequently taught black novel because it acts as a mode of assurance that, really, the black folk are happy and healthy."[69]

We can hear in Carby's question a sense of the dangers that lurk within every success. Black women's literature, for example, may have become tremendously popular and, in its way, transformative within English and black studies courses, but its very popularity could have signaled to some that it was doomed to become a passing fancy, an interesting thought experiment that was largely a reflection of the heightened sense of possibility that accompanied a rising black feminist consciousness. This is clearly something that Carby did not want to see happen, but the fact remains that an increased scrutiny surrounds those disciplinary fields or intellectual projects that emerge out of political and social activism. "Relevance" in the most traditional rooms of the ivory tower might as well be dismissed as "faddism."

THERE IS no debating the fact that since the 1970s black scholars across the disciplines have enjoyed, in principle, much greater potential for professional freedom. Black scholars are free to study what they desire, and there are increasing numbers, though still small, who work in fields ostensibly divorced from "blackness." Black students, without controversy, now attend any graduate school to which they gain admission and, again in principle, can look forward to the possibility of teaching anywhere in the country upon graduation. In so many structural ways, it seems that there is no end to the potential for black scholars to live a full and rich intellectual life, free from so many of the burdens of past ages.

But "potential" always operates in the abstract.

Today, the great majority of black scholars still teach at historically black colleges and universities—schools that remain seriously underfunded, often operating as second-class citizens in the world of higher education. Black faculty representation at the nation's leading universities is pitifully low and, despite the literal freedom to study what one wants, the expectation that black scholars exclusively specialize in black topics remains alive and well.

Black studies programs have a permanent presence on college campuses but still serve as political lightning rods in an age in which prominent combatants in the "culture wars" criticize area studies and cultural relativism as antithetical to the mission of the university. (And when black studies programs are not explicitly named in a struggle over the intellectual integrity of the university, black people often take their place as targets. Speaking to this point directly is the fact that at the turn of the twenty-first century legal challenges to affirmative action in college admissions—and, for many, these challenges are implicitly about the "right" of minority students even to attend certain colleges—have become an annual ritual.) Even among their most ardent supporters, black studies programs and scholarship remain in struggle.

In February 2003 a conference on black studies was held at the Schomburg Center for Research in Black Culture.[70] The purpose of the conference was to assess the state of black studies roughly thirty years after the field's establishment and in light of the 2000 federal census report that showed Latinos had passed black Americans as the nation's largest minority group. Some participants voiced concern that the country's changing demographics suggested a looming crisis for black studies. Others were less worried, citing the centrality of slavery to the country's history and the tortured history of racialized struggles over citizenship since emancipation. Before the conference began, however, Howard Dodson ignited a controversy with his comments concerning the latest generation of black studies scholars. Dodson, the director of the Schomburg and one of the key figures in the history of the creation and institutionalization of black studies programs (he was, for example, the executive director of the Institute of the Black World for much of the 1970s), declared that he was unhappy with the direction of the new black studies scholarship. He could not understand, for example, the "social utility" of scholarship that studied black homosexuality and felt that a "commitment and clear sense of direction seems to be missing" from black studies scholarship in general.[71] For those black studies scholars who work in lesbian, gay, bisexual, and transgender studies and who are convinced that they are working at the cutting edge of black studies scholarship, this comment was a slap in the face. It also amounted to a kind of intellectual policing that black studies scholars could anticipate from certain quarters in academia but were less prepared to accept from within the black studies community.[72]

Black scholars and black studies programs, once so invisible, now exist in a contradictory state: they operate under the lens of a microscope and are simultaneously hypervisible. We can see from the example with Howard Dodson that the field and its practitioners can still be embroiled in political and intellectual controversy for even trying to expand the interpretive boundaries of black studies' focus. In this way, black scholars and black studies still seem to enjoy only minimal operating room. But as much as they may feel over-scrutinized, black scholars and black studies programs also enjoy a kind of exaggerated prominence.[73] Part of this hypervisibility is due to our post–civil rights urge to reward black excellence wherever we find it; much of this hypervisibility is due to the ways in which university administrators still look to black studies programs and their very diverse but typically majority black faculties to stand for something more than mere scholarship. That black scholars are heard best when speaking to blackness has not changed since John Hope Franklin's angry observations in 1963. There is precious little to indicate that this fact will be any different come tomorrow.

Notes

1. John Hope Franklin, "The Dilemma of the American Negro Scholar," in *Race and History: Selected Essays, 1938–1988*, ed. John Hope Franklin (Baton Rouge: Louisiana State University Press, 1989), 299.

2. Ibid.

3. Jonathan Scott Holloway, "The Black Intellectual and the 'Crisis Canon' in the Twentieth Century," *Black Scholar* 31 (Spring 2001): 2–13.

4. The following list of essays and books that discuss black intellectuals throughout the twentieth century is illuminating in this regard: James Weldon Johnson, "The Dilemma of the Negro Author," *American Mercury* 60 (December 1928): 477–481; Sterling Brown, "The American Race Problem as Reflected in American Literature," *Journal of Negro Education* 8 (July 1939): 275–290; L. D. Reddick, "A New Interpretation for Negro History," *Journal of Negro History* 22 (1937): 17–28; John Hope Franklin, "The Dilemma of the Negro Scholar," in *Soon One Morning: New Writing by American Negroes, 1940–1962*, ed. Herbert Hill (New York: Knopf, 1963); E. Franklin Frazier, "The Failure of the Negro Intellectuals," *Negro Digest* (February 1962): 26–36; Martin Kilson, "The New Black Intellectuals," *Dissent* 16 (July–August 1969): 304–310; Vincent Harding, "The Vocation of the Black Scholar and the Struggles of the Black Community," in *Education and Black Struggle: Notes from the Colonized World* (Cambridge: *Harvard Educational Review*, 1974), 3–29; Cornel West, "The Dilemma of the Black Intellectual," *Cultural Critique* 1 (Fall 1985): 109–124; and Harold Cruse, *The Crisis of the Negro Intellectual: A Historical Analysis of the Failure of Black Leadership* (1967; rpt. New York: Quill, 1984).

5. Allan Bloom, *The Closing of the American Mind* (New York: Simon and Schuster, 1987), 93–94.

6. In 2002, to cite one of the more recent and public examples, the philosopher and critic Cornel West found himself at the center of a controversy when a New York University conference in honor of Sidney Hook's hundredth birthday almost disintegrated because of West's announced participation. (West joined the conference late as a replacement for his fellow philosopher Richard Rorty.) Upon learning of this change, four participants, Irving Kristol, Gertrude Himmelfarb, Hilton Kramer, and John Patrick Diggins, withdrew. Kristol, Himmelfarb, and Kramer refused entreaties to rejoin the conference, claiming that West "knew nothing about Hook" and that West "wasn't

a real intellectual." Diggins, who withdrew because West, in his opinion, had left scholarship behind for popular culture, changed his mind and joined West on a panel assessing Hook's evolving politics. West, a black scholar then associated with Harvard University whose work includes such titles as *Prophesy Deliverance! An Afro-American Revolutionary Christianity, The American Evasion of Philosophy: A Genealogy of Pragmatism,* and *Keeping Faith: Philosophy and Race in America,* had recently been ridiculed by conservative writers in such places as the *Wall Street Journal* for releasing a spoken word album, *Sketches of My Culture* (which critics typically referred to as a "rap" album—a highly loaded term of racial identification regardless of the changing demographics of who buys, produces, and consumes such music). The conflict over West's open involvement in progressive and liberal political campaigns and his album exploded when West and Harvard's President Lawrence Summers disagreed over West's scholarly productions. As the dispute worsened, West left Harvard for Princeton, claiming that Summers wanted West to report to him directly on a bimonthly basis about the progress of his latest scholarship. West was bitter over what he considered Summers's condescension. Simmering as a subtext to all these controversies was the specter of race: Summers did not police other (white) Harvard scholars who were similarly engaged in political discourses or who wrote for the lay public. Emily Eakin, "An Invitation Ruffles Philosophical Feathers," *New York Times,* June 29, 2002, 7; Danny Postel, "Despite Boycott by Neoconservatives, Conference on Sidney Hook Pleases Participants," *Chronicle of Higher Education* (web daily) October, 28, 2002, squawk.ca/lbo-talk/0210/2091.html; Sherri Day, "Think Tank: A Professor Who Can Rap," *New York Times,* March 12, 2001, 11; Michael Lerner, "An Interview with Cornel West," *Tikkun,* September–October 2002, www.tikkun.org/magazine/index.cfm/action/tikkun/issue/tiko209/article/020912.html.

7. Florence Murray, *The Negro Handbook, 1944: A Manual of Current Facts, Statistics, and General Information Concerning Negroes in the United States* (New York: Current Reference Publications, 1944), 58.

8. Michael Winston, "Through the Back Door: Academic Racism and the Negro Scholar in Historical Perspective," *Daedalus* 100 (Summer 1971): 694.

9. Ibid., 695; Jonathan Scott Holloway, *Confronting the Veil: Abram Harris Jr., E. Franklin Frazier, and Ralph Bunche, 1919–1941* (Chapel Hill: University of North Carolina Press, 2002), 80–81.

10. Winston, "Through the Back Door," 695.

11. Of the 74,946 people who self-identified as "college president, professor, and instructor" in the 1940 U.S. census, only 2,339 were black—barely over 3 percent. Unfortunately, the census does not break down these employment categories in more specific detail. Murray, *The Negro Handbook,* 195. If one uses the Ph.D. as a predictor of status and professional position within higher education (e.g., professor, not lecturer), the numbers are more arresting. Between 1926 and 1942, 38,765 Ph.D.'s were awarded in the United States. Over a roughly similar period, 316 doctorates went to blacks—or eight-tenths of 1 percent of the grand total. Harry Greene, *Holders of Doctorates among American Negroes: An Educational and Social Study of Negroes Who Have Earned Doctoral Degrees in Course, 1876–1943* (Boston: Meador, 1946), 24.

12. Winston, "Through the Back Door," 695.

13. Holloway, *Confronting the Veil,* 200–202.

14. Winston, "Through the Back Door," 702.

15. Reginald Wilson, "African Americans in Predominantly White Institutions," in *Encyclopedia of African American Education,* ed. Faustine Jones-Wilson et al. (Westport, Conn.: Greenwood Press, 1996), 362.

16. J. Saunders Redding, *On Being Negro in America* (Indianapolis: Bobbs-Merrill, 1951), 34–37; Faith Berry, Introduction to *A Scholar's Conscience: Selected Writings of J. Saunders Redding, 1942–1977,* ed. Faith Berry (Lexington: University Press of Kentucky, 1992), 1–2.

17. Berry, *Scholar's Conscience,* 5.

18. *Brown Alumni Magazine* 101 (November–December 2000), brown.edu/Administration/Brown_Alumni_Magazine/01/11-00/features/history.html.

19. Redding, *On Being Negro in America,* 9.

20. Ibid., 9–10.

21. Ibid., 26.

22. Ibid., 26–27.

23. Ibid., 122, 125, 128.

24. Ibid., 18.

25. Berry, *Scholar's Conscience*, 8.

26. Ibid., 9.

27. As quoted in Kenneth Janken, *Rayford W. Logan and the Dilemma of the African-American Intellectual* (Amherst: University of Massachusetts Press, 1993), 213.

28. Nathan Huggins, *Afro-American Studies: A Report to the Ford Foundation* (New York: Ford Foundation, 1985), 6–7.

29. Ibid., 9–12.

30. James Cass, "Can the University Survive the Black Challenge?" in *Basic Black: A Look at the Black Presence in the University Community*, ed. John Buerk et al. (Melrose, Mass.: Keating and Joyce, 1970), 46.

31. Huggins, *Afro-American Studies*, 22.

32. Nathan Hare, "The Battle for Black Studies," in *Black Scholars on Higher Education in the '70s*, ed. Roosevelt Johnson (Columbus, Ohio: ECCA Publications, 1974), 75.

33. Ibid., 79–80.

34. Ibid., 79.

35. Huggins, *Afro-American Studies*, 23; Hare, "Battle for Black Studies," 75–76.

36. Huggins, *Afro-American Studies*, 23.

37. Jack Bass, *Widening the Mainstream of American Culture: A Ford Foundation Report on Ethnic Studies* (New York: Ford Foundation, 1978), 7.

38. Huggins, *Afro-American Studies*, 26–27; Bass, *Widening the Mainstream*, 7–9; Houston Baker Jr., *Black Studies, Rap, and the Academy* (Chicago: University of Chicago Press, 1993), 22.

39. Some of the scholars who attended this conference include McGeorge Bundy, president of the Ford Foundation; Sidney Mintz, anthropology, Yale; Boniface Obichere, history, UCLA; Harold Cruse, Center for Afroamerican and African Studies, Michigan; Alvin Poussaint, psychiatry, Tufts; and Gerald McWorter, sociology, Spelman College.

40. Huggins, *Afro-American Studies*, 26. Years later the "deft leadership" Huggins praised was analyzed differently by Houston Baker, who observed that in Yale's case a combination of good timing and luck helped that campus to mitigate the more radical impulses in black studies by formalizing the creative process of the program before black radical undergraduates came to campus a year or two later. Baker, *Black Studies, Rap, and the Academy*, 22.

41. David Brion Davis, "Reflections," in *Black Studies in the University: A Symposium*, ed. Armstead Robinson et al. (New Haven: Yale University Press, 1969), 220.

42. Hare, "What Should Be the Role of Afro-American Education in the Undergraduate Curriculum?" in Buerk et al., *Basic Black*, 19.

43. Huggins, *Afro-American Studies*, 26.

44. Sidney Mintz, Introduction to Melville Herskovits, *The Myth of the Negro Past* (1941; rpt. Boston: Beacon Press, 1990), ix, xiv.

45. See, most specifically, Herbert Gutman, *The Black Family in Slavery and Freedom, 1750–1925* (New York: Vintage Books, 1976); Lawrence Levine, *Black Culture and Black Consciousness: Afro-American Folk Thought from Slavery to Freedom* (New York: Oxford University Press, 1977); Gerda Lerner, *Black Women in White America: A Documentary History* (New York: Pantheon, 1972); Eugene Genovese, *Roll, Jordan, Roll: The World the Slaves Made* (New York: Pantheon, 1974).

46. James Turner and C. Steven McGann, "Black Studies as an Integral Tradition in African-American Intellectual History," *Journal of Negro History* 49, no. 1 (1980): 52–53.

47. Hare, "What Should Be the Role of Afro-American Education in the Undergraduate Curriculum?" 15.

48. Stephen Ward, "'Scholarship in the Context of Struggle': Activist Intellectuals, the Institute of the Black World (IBW), and the Contours of Black Power Radicalism," *Black Scholar* 34 (Fall–Winter 2001), 44–45.

49. Vincent Harding, "The Vocation of the Black Scholar and the Struggle of the Black Community," in *Education and Black Struggle: Notes from the Colonized World* (Cambridge: *Harvard Educational Review*, 1974), 12.

50. Eugene Genovese, "Black Studies: Trouble Ahead," in Buerk et al., *Basic Black*, 39–40.

51. Kenneth Clark, "Letter of Resignation from Board of Directors of Antioch College," in *Black Studies: Myths and Realities* (New York: A. Philip Randolph Educational Fund, 1969): 33, 34. Clearly, Clark would have had little patience for James Turner and C. Steven McGann's assertion that "it has long been widely proclaimed among American scholars that their work is independent of political issues. A cardinal axiom in the philosophy of American education is that knowledge and learning—whether science, the humanities, or scholarship in general—are distinct from and should be kept separate from politics and ideology. Black studies scholars condemn this stance of neutrality as a sham." Turner and McGann, "Black Studies as an Integral Tradition," 59.

52. Other journals came into existence before and after these four. Periodicals such as the *Journal of Negro History*, the *Journal of Negro Education*, and *Phylon* had been around for decades. Other noteworthy publications include *Transition, Negro American Literature Forum* (now *African American Review), Callaloo*, and the *Western Journal of Black Studies*. This chapter focuses on the ones named in the text for their very specific attention paid to the question of black studies from disciplinary, political, and pedagogical perspectives.

53. Leroy Keith, "Issues Facing Black Students and Faculty at Predominantly White Institutions," *Journal of Afro-American Issues* 1 (Summer 1972); James Banks, "Teaching Black Studies for Social Change," *Journal of Afro-American Issues* 1 (Fall 1972).

54. James Allen Moss, "In Defense of Black Studies: Some Additional Notes," *Afro-American Studies* 1 (January 1971); Ronald Walters, "Teaching Afro-American History: An Interpretive Essay," *Afro-American Studies* 1 (April 1971); Harold Cruse, "Black Studies: Interpretation, Methodology, and the Relationship to Social Movements," *Afro-American Studies* 2 (June 1971); Vincent Harding, "Black Students and the Impossible Revolution," *Journal of Black Studies* 1 (September 1970); and Boniface Obichere, "The Significance and Challenge of Afro-American Studies," *Journal of Black Studies* 1 (December 1970).

55. Editorial Statement, *Afro-American Studies* 1 (May 1970): inside front cover.

56. Arthur Smith, "Editor's Message," *Journal of Black Studies* 1 (September 1970), 3.

57. Baker, *Black Studies, Rap, and the Academy*, 19.

58. Unsigned statement, *Black Scholar* 1 (November 1969): inside front cover.

59. Even the American Academy of Arts and Sciences entered the fray with a special issue of its journal *Daedalus* dedicated to "The Future of the Black Colleges." While there is a specific focus on black colleges in this issue, many of the essays focus on the role of black scholars within such institutions and the relationship that black colleges should have with the communities in which they are located and from which they draw their students and faculty. See, for example, Henry Allen Bullock, "The Black College and the New Black Awareness," 573–602; C. Eric Lincoln, "The Negro Colleges and Cultural Exchange," 603–629, Michael Winston, "Through the Back Door: Academic Racism and the Negro Scholar in Historical Perspective," 678–719; Mack H. Jones, "The Responsibility of the Black College to the Black Community: Then and Now," 732–744; and St. Clair Drake, "The Black University in the American Social Order," 833–897. All in *Daedalus* 100 (Summer 1971).

60. Joyce Ladner, ed., *The Death of White Sociology: Essays on Race and Culture* (New York: Vintage, 1973); Gloria Hull, Patricia Bell Scott, and Barbara Smith, eds., *All the Women Are White, All the Blacks Are Men, But Some of Us Are Brave: Black Women's Studies* (Old Westbury, N.Y.: Feminist Press, 1982).

61. Becky Thompson, "Reflections on Ethics in Research: *The Death of White Sociology* Twenty-five Years Later," in Ladner, *The Death of White Sociology* (1973; rpt. Baltimore: Black Classic Press, 1998), 477. In her introduction Ladner points to the long history of the deviance scholarship—starting with Robert Park and Ernest Burgess's Chicago School of sociology in the 1920s—and demonstrates how much of the 1960s scholarship relied on these old models. Ladner was speaking most specifically of scholarship like Nathan Glazer and Daniel P. Moynihan's *Beyond the Melting Pot*, which observed, "The Negro is only an American and nothing else. He has no values and culture to guard and protect." Ladner, Introduction to *The Death of White Sociology*, xxiii.

62. Ladner, *The Death of White Sociology*, 419.

63. Ladner studied black female teenagers for four years and concluded that "the total misrepresentation of the Black community and the various myths which surround it can be seen in microcosm in the Black female adolescent. Her growing-up years reflect the basic quality and character of life in this environment, as well as anticipations for the future." Ladner added, "By understanding the nature and processes of her development, we can also comprehend the more intricate elements that characterize the day-to-day lives of the Black masses." Ladner, "Tomorrow's Tomorrow: The Black Woman," in *The Death of White Sociology*, 428.

64. Unsigned statement, *Black Scholar* 1 (November 1969): inside front cover.

65. Even well-meant efforts to call attention to women's abiding second-class status in America could fall flat. In the fifth appendix (of ten) to the massive social science survey *An American Dilemma: The Negro Problem and Modern Democracy*, Gunnar Myrdal addressed "A Parallel to the Negro Problem." In this six-page appendix (of nearly fifteen hundred text pages), Myrdal points out that "in every society there are at least two groups of people, besides the Negroes, who are characterized by high social visibility expressed in physical appearance, dress, and patterns of behavior, and who have been 'suppressed.' We refer," Myrdal concluded, "to women and children." Although Myrdal was certainly making a move toward inclusion, it is telling that he neglected to consider that black women may have experienced a kind of suppression different from what either "Negroes" in general or women in general had experienced. Black women are not mentioned once in this appendix. See Myrdal, *An American Dilemma* (New York: Harper and Row, 1944), 1073–1078.

66. Hull, Scott, and Smith, "Introduction: The Politics of Black Women's Studies," in *All the Women Are White*, xxi.

67. Ibid., xxvii.

68. Hazel Carby, "The Politics of Fiction, Anthropology, and the Folk: Zora Neale Hurston," in *History and Memory in African-American Culture*, ed. Genevieve Fabre and Robert O'Meally (New York: Oxford University Press, 1994), 28–29.

69. Ibid., 41.

70. The conference was cosponsored by Princeton University's Program in African-American Studies, the City University of New York (CUNY) Institute for Research on the African Diaspora in the Americas and the Caribbean, and the Schomburg Research Center. After opening at the Schomburg, the conference moved to CUNY's Graduate School.

71. Felicia Lee, "New Topic for Black Studies Debate, Latinos," *New York Times*, February 1, 2003, A1.

72. Although he offered his thoughts on the topic more than five years before the State of Black Studies Conference, the literary scholar Dwight McBride wrote insightfully about the politics of straight, black authenticity and how it could silence alternative voices. McBride argued: "There are any number of narratives that African American intellectuals employ to qualify themselves in the terms of race discourse to speak for the race. And while one routinely witnesses the use of narratives of racial discrimination, narratives of growing up poor and black and elevating oneself through education and hard work . . . we could scarcely imagine an instance in which narrating or even claiming one's gay or lesbian identity would authenticate or

legitimate oneself as a racial representative." McBride, "Can the Queen Speak? Racial Essentialism, Sexuality, and the Problem of Authority," *Callaloo* 21, no. 2 (1998), 376–377.

73. One can arrive at this conclusion merely by bearing witness to *New York Times* or *Wall Street Journal* reporters' and columnists' heavy breathing over anything Henry Louis Gates Jr. or Cornel West might do or over the latest action taken by Harvard University's program in African and African-American Studies.

9

WOMEN IN THE HUMANITIES
Taking Their Place

ROSALIND ROSENBERG

THE HUMANITIES academy in the 1940s was an overwhelmingly masculine enterprise, more so, indeed, than it had been a generation before, because of the success of "professionalization": women were moved out of jobs in English, history, and philosophy, even at many women's colleges. Mary Calkins, for example, the philosopher and psychologist who trained with William James in the 1890s and spent her career at Wellesley College, was elected president of the American Philosophical Association in 1918, but she, along with women in other fields, enjoyed declining influence in later years, as men who were less "amateur" shoved women aside.[1] Women were not able to reverse this trend until the late 1950s, when government funding and an expanding economy finally helped them begin to increase their share of Ph.D.'s and faculty positions.[2] Women did more than increase their numbers. Inspired by the civil rights and feminist movements, in which they became central actors in the 1970s, they founded journals, created new academic programs, and questioned traditional approaches to scholarship in every discipline, from English to philosophy. They challenged traditional canons, attacked accepted disciplinary distinctions, called for greater diversity, and pioneered new methods. Above all, in an intellectual community that celebrated Olympian detachment, they championed personal engagement. In the beginning the work they chose to pursue contributed further to their marginalization, focusing as it often did on women, but by the end of the century women across the humanities had come to define their projects in more ambitious terms, not simply as a reclamation of lost lives and texts, but also as a reconceptualizing of the world as a place in which gender structured power relations and even perspective.

The Fall and Rise of Women in the Humanities

Women first entered academe in significant numbers in the late nineteenth century, and they steadily increased their share of all faculty positions into the 1930s.[3] But a long-term trend toward professionalization—marked by the

increased production of Ph.D.'s and growing emphasis on scholarly research—
put women in higher education increasingly at risk. Shouldering family responsibilities from which society usually excused men, lacking the services of a
wife who could support their careers, less able to claim the resources necessary
to remain productive as scholars, women gradually lost ground. Women's colleges held out longer than universities, but even they tended to give way by
the 1930s and started to replace women with men.[4] Women continued to find
academic employment in the lower ranks, especially in the labor-intensive language departments, even without a Ph.D., but to become a professor a woman
not only had to be better than any available man, she had to comport herself, as
much as possible, as though she were one. The Smith College English professor Marjorie Hope Nicolson became a leading exemplar of this phenomenon
when she left Smith in 1940 to become Columbia University's first female full
professor. A brilliant lecturer and prolific scholar, Nicolson came quickly to be
known as "the best man at Columbia."[5]

Higher education expanded dramatically after World War II, as universities grew to meet the needs of returning soldiers and as the federal government began to fund education deemed essential to the nation's defense
during the cold war. But women's proportion of academic positions continued
to contract (even as their absolute numbers grew), until it bottomed out at 20
percent in the late 1950s. The principal cause of both the expansion for men
and the contraction for women was the 1944 G.I. Bill of Rights. Since 98
percent of returning soldiers were male, the chief beneficiaries of government
funding through the G.I. Bill were men. It was this cohort that came to define
the intellectual culture of the universities for the next two decades.[6]

Denied the economic benefits so widely available to men, would-be female
academics also suffered from a cultural climate that, after fifteen years of depression and war, celebrated domesticity and maternity. As women's average
age at marriage sank below twenty and the birthrate soared, the challenge of
combining a full-time academic career and family obligations, as then defined,
became increasingly difficult. Not until the 1958 passage of the National Defense Education Act, which made money available for training in languages,
did women begin to reverse their downward slide. As the baby boom generation came of age, the available supply of male professors was inadequate, and
women made further gains. By the late 1960s women were earning as many
Ph.D.'s as men had earned in the early 1940s, and by the early 1970s they had
regained the share of the academic doctorates that women had achieved in the
late 1920s. The rise of the women's movement, with its polemical force and
sense of shared endeavor, accelerated this upward trend dramatically. In 1970
women were earning less than a quarter of all degrees in the humanities. By

the end of the century they would be earning more than half. Women continued to lag behind men in faculty positions, particularly at the senior levels, but no longer were they ignored.[7]

The Outsiders, 1945–1970

The women who entered the humanities in the years immediately after World War II faced not only limited opportunity but also a much less welcoming intellectual climate than the one that had prevailed in the period of women's early twentieth-century success. Indeed, that early success, leading as it did to a widespread fear of feminization, may have played a part in the intellectual shifts of the next generation. In philosophy the pragmatism of Dewey and James, with its emphasis on practice and social reform, had drawn significant numbers of women to the field. But pragmatism lost favor in the face of its alleged inability to respond to the danger of the Nazi assault of the 1930s and 1940s; logical positivism—with its mathematical and scientific emphasis—gained ascendancy in its place. In anthropology the cultural relativism of Franz Boas, Ruth Benedict, Margaret Mead, and Zora Neale Hurston gave way to a scientific materialism concerned more with what peoples ate then with how cultures shaped their beliefs. In literature and in art history, modernism—with its commitment to art for art's sake and its emphasis on canonical works—left little room for women's experience. And in history the study of political life, from which women had been largely excluded, overtook the Progressive Era celebration of the New (social) History. Across the board, the approaches to humanistic learning by which women of the first quarter of the twentieth century had made their mark were supplanted by a more scientific, more mathematical, more male-centered approach to scholarship.

There were some institutional points of resistance. The Seven Sisters women's colleges sent more women on to graduate work, per capita, than other schools of the time, and two of these colleges made special efforts. Radcliffe, under the determined leadership of President Mary Bunting, took steps to lure older women, many of whom had interrupted their education to have children, back into academe. Her work led in 1960 to the founding of the Mary Ingraham Bunting Institute, a multidisciplinary research center for women scholars, scientists, artists, and writers. Barnard, which was the only one of the Seven Sisters to have a faculty with more women than men (as well as the only one to welcome students forced out of other colleges when they married), made a particular point of preparing its students for graduate study. In the three decades following World War II, Barnard sent many more women on to graduate school than any other school of its size.[8]

And yet, even at the women's colleges, most students were careful to chart their careers, as Marjorie Hope Nicolson had done, according to the standards determined by their male mentors. Even many who would eventually make their mark as feminist scholars studiously avoided work on women out of fear that they would not be taken seriously. In the early 1950s, for instance, the future historian Natalie Zemon Davis, a product of Smith College, was assigned a paper on Christine de Pisan in a graduate seminar at the University of Michigan. Worried that her professor had asked her to write about a woman simply because she was female, Davis decided against pursuing the topic further. "I didn't want to be put in a category of a woman doing a woman's thing," Davis later recalled.[9] She decided, instead, to work on male workers in sixteenth-century Lyon. But, even though she avoided the explicit study of women, she found inspiration from a source that would lead her back to them: radical politics.

Born in Detroit, Michigan, in 1928, Natalie Zemon discovered radicalism at Smith, from which she graduated in 1949, before taking an M.A. at Radcliffe in 1950 and a Ph.D. at Michigan in 1959. Before finishing college, she married the Harvard-trained mathematician Chandler Davis, with whom she had three children. In 1954 Chandler Davis, then a lecturer at Michigan, was fired for refusing, on free speech grounds, to tell a faculty committee whether he was or had been a Communist. Declining further to testify before HUAC, he was cited for contempt of Congress and served time in federal prison in 1960. When he was released, the Davises left the country for jobs at the University of Toronto.[10]

Feeling isolated from other scholars in the witch-hunting days of the 1950s, Natalie Davis found inspiration in the work of a group of radical French scholars, including Ferdinand Braudel, who had founded the journal *Annales d'histoire économique* in 1929 in Strasbourg. The *Annales* school urged that scholars study long-term historical forces rather than political crises, peasants rather than kings, and families rather than armies. While the emphasis, even in the study of family history, tended to be on men—on fathers and sons rather than mothers and daughters—the attention that social historians gave to demography meant that women's fertility had to be included as a legitimate historical topic, and the possibility of enlarging history's mission to include even more of the experience of women was clear to increasing numbers of female students.[11]

One of the first women to see this potential was Davis. She became best known to the public for her book *The Return of Martin Guerre* (1982), the story of how an imposter disrupted life in a small French town in the sixteenth century. Her influence in history, however, rested on an earlier series of essays in cultural history in which she drew on the lessons not just of the *Annales* school but also of cultural anthropologists to examine the lives of artisans and peasants who were only partly literate. Her work inspired a generation of female students who followed her example to recover the lives of women, so few of whom, especially in the early modern period, had left any written records. Davis encouraged students not only through her scholarly example, but also through her teaching, which she pursued, following Toronto, at Brown, Berkeley, and Princeton, and through her professional leadership, which culminated in her election to the presidency of the American Historical Association in 1987.[12]

The historian Gerda Lerner, who like Davis found inspiration in radical perspectives on the past, made an even more direct contribution to the recruitment of women into the humanities. Having escaped from Nazi-controlled Austria in 1938 as a teenager, Lerner immigrated to the United States, where she worked at a series of low-skilled jobs in New York City, married, had two children, moved with her film editor husband to the West Coast, joined the Communist Party, became a vocal critic of male chauvinism within the party, and developed into a writer with a passionate interest in the history of women. Like Davis, Lerner experienced the post–World War II Red Scare firsthand when her husband was blacklisted. Moving back to New York, the couple led a financially precarious existence, and Lerner decided that to be taken seriously as a scholar she would have to seek professional credentials. In 1958 she enrolled in the New School for Social Research to complete the credits she needed for a bachelor's degree. She taught a pioneering course in women's history there in the spring of 1963, while writing a biography of two abolitionists from South Carolina, Sarah and Angelina Grimké.[13] Determined to earn a Ph.D., Lerner shopped around to find a program that would allow her to turn her biography into a dissertation. Columbia University, which for years had led the country in the production of female doctorates, was the only place she could find where the department chairman was willing to tailor the institutional regulations to meet the needs, in Lerner's words, "of this eager, somewhat superannuated, and certainly 'different' student." Under the supervision of her Columbia professors, all male, Lerner learned the trade of the professional historian. She completed her Ph.D. in 1966 after only three years. But she never lost her crusading dedication to the proposition that historians had for too long failed to ask a central historical question: "Where are the women?" In seeking an answer, Lerner wrote pathbreaking articles and books, including "New Approaches to the Study of Women in American History" (1969), "The Lady and the Mill Girl" (1969), and "Black Women in the United States" (1973). She went on to create a master's program in women's history at Sarah Lawrence and a Ph.D. program at the University of Wisconsin. She founded Women's History Month and served as president of the Organization of American Historians (1981–82).

In 2002 she was the first woman ever to be awarded the Bruce Catton Lifetime Achievement Award by the OAH.[14]

While Davis and Lerner challenged the traditional ways of doing history, others tested the traditional ways of studying literature. The founders of American studies programs led the way. Established across the country, beginning in the late 1930s, American studies emphasized popular culture and thereby gave space to perspectives not then welcome in either literature or history.[15] Linda Kerber, who graduated from Barnard College (1960) before earning a degree in history at Columbia (1968), later credited the instruction she received as an undergraduate in American studies with her decision to become an academic. At a time when most professors of English were concentrating on high culture, unconnected to social context, American studies faculty pursued a broader, more democratic mission. Those who sought to do so included a Barnard College English professor, John Kouwenhoven, who taught the course American Vernacular Literature and Art, in which he focused on popular culture, dime novels, folktales, and comics with attention to "their relationship to traditional forms and to dominant forces in American life." In Kouwenhoven's vision, what was American about America was the grid plan of cities, jazz, the Constitution, and soap operas. "Grids could be endlessly expanded; jazz admitted infinite varieties and entrances," Kerber recalled learning. "In his vision democracy was composed of components without prescribed limits or closure. And that meant that there was space for us. . . . Somehow we understood that the maverick, the outsider, is what the intellectual is *supposed* to be."[16]

American studies also opened the door to minority scholars before other disciplines did so. Pauli Murray, for example, had sought graduate training in literature at the University of North Carolina at Chapel Hill in 1938, only to be rejected because of her race. Determined to fight the injustice that prevented her from pursuing her dream, Murray became a lawyer and played a critical role in bridging the gap between the civil rights movement and the modern woman's movement in the early 1960s, when she served on President John F. Kennedy's Commission on the Status of Women (1962–63) and formulated the constitutional strategy by which women would win basic rights over the next decade. Not until 1968, however, was she able to achieve her dream of becoming an academic. Having finally earned a Ph.D. (in law) at Yale University, she was recruited to teach American studies and to develop a program in African American studies at Brandeis University. At long last she was able to combine her interests in literature, history, civil rights, and feminism in an academic setting and to open up the questions asked and topics pursued in literature and history.[17]

"Sexual Politics"

Throughout the 1960s, despite the efforts of these and other pioneers, women who worked in the humanities did so, for the most part, on male terms. And then came Kate Millett. Born in 1934, Millett grew up in St. Paul, Minnesota, the daughter of a Catholic family. Her father, an alcoholic, abandoned his wife and children, consigning them to a life of genteel poverty. Despite hardship at home, Millett excelled at parochial school and attended the University of Minnesota. After her graduation in 1956 a wealthy aunt sent her to study at Oxford University, a gesture that had less to do with the aunt's respect for Kate's intellectual gifts than with the family's discovering that Kate was in love with another woman. After winning an exceptional "first-class honors" along with her master's degree in 1958, Millett returned to the United States, worked in the civil rights movement, and taught English for a year in North Carolina. In 1961 she moved to Japan, where she taught English, pursued an interest in sculpture, and met the artist Fumio Yoshimura. She returned to the United States with Yoshimura in 1963, settled in the Bowery on New York City's Lower East Side, and married him to protect him from being deported in 1965. In the meantime, she entered Columbia's graduate program in English and Comparative Literature, taught English at Barnard College, and discovered feminism. In short order she joined the National Organization for Women (NOW), Downtown Radical Women, and Radicalesbians. These very different organizations provided the lessons in defying male authority that enabled Millett, and the legions of women who followed her, to enter the humanities in historically high numbers. Although not all women who entered the academy were feminists, it is difficult to imagine the sudden surge in their numbers in the absence of the women's movement and the ambition that it bred.[18]

Millett's feminist consciousness found extended exposition in her dissertation, "Sexual Politics." An updated version of Simone de Beauvoir's *The Second Sex* (1952), "Sexual Politics" was part cultural criticism (with extended analyses of anthropological, sociological, Marxist, and psychoanalytic theory) and part literary criticism (with biting attacks on some of the leading authors of the twentieth-century sexual revolution). Millett dismissed Norman Mailer as "a prisoner of the virility cult," D. H. Lawrence as a believer in the "mystery of the phallus," and Henry Miller as a writer whose "ideal woman is a whore." To Millett the only major male author who came close to understanding women's position in society was Jean Genet, a homosexual.[19]

In "Sexual Politics," which went from dissertation to best-selling book in a matter of months in 1970, Millett argued that sexism permeated society. It was not simply a function of misguided public policy, as many of NOW's leaders seemed to believe, but rather part of a patriarchal system that affected every aspect of social relations. Sexism was institutionalized in the family, the schools, the church, the economy, the government, and the legal system. It ensured that men and women would develop different personalities and play different social roles. "Male and female are really two cultures, and their life experiences are utterly different," Millett wrote. Sexism guaranteed that men would rule and that women would remain subordinate. Women would depend on men, define themselves in relation to men, and develop contempt for both themselves and other women in the process. Only a social revolution that abolished sex roles could hope to liberate all women.[20]

Millett's most important contribution to the humanities was to insist that women brought a different perspective to literature. As the feminist critic Carolyn Heilbrun noted, "For the first time we have been asked to look at literature as women; we, men, women, and Ph.D.'s, have always read it as men."[21] Heilbrun's point was not that females read differently from males, for, as she indicated, women can read, and have read, as men. She was simply asking that women avoid reading as men have done, that they learn to identify and correct the distortions of which men have so often been guilty.[22] Heilbrun recognized Millett's book as the beginning of a transformation of literary criticism. But hers was a minority view. Most of the graduate faculty in English at Columbia regarded *Sexual Politics* as part of political firestorm that would soon burn itself out.[23]

Affirmative Action

Instead, the firestorm grew hotter, as a woman's movement, inspired by the civil rights struggle of the 1960s, led women to demand greater opportunity. For academic women the 1960s had initially seemed filled with promise. The Soviet Union's launching of Sputnik in 1957 had led both the federal government and private foundations to fund higher education as never before, and in the process unprecedented levels of fellowship support became available. Moreover, the demographic bulge produced by the baby boom guaranteed that student demand would soon outstrip the available supply of male faculty.[24] Even making allowances for the discrimination that women had always faced in seeking jobs, a woman able to secure a Ph.D. stood a fighting chance of winning an academic position somewhere. And then came the crash. In 1969, just as doctoral production hit a historic high, faculty hiring plummeted as universities, which had grown increasingly dependent on federal and foundation funding, watched those funds shrink or be redirected, in the face of the Vietnam War and urban riots, to other, more pressing needs. If ever there was a revolution of rising, and summarily dashed, expectations, it happened among women in academe at the end of the 1960s.[25]

In response, women began forming committees at their universities and in their professional organizations to investigate the status of women in academe. At Columbia, Harvard, Michigan, Chicago, women compiled studies that confirmed what they had long suspected: women had been earning at least one in every ten doctorates for decades, but they occupied fewer than one in every twenty professorships around the country. They did better in art history and languages than they did in history or philosophy. But across the board their professional success lagged seriously behind their educational accomplishments. Women were able to win positions as lecturers, and even as assistant professors, but they simply did not get promoted in significant numbers beyond that. Academic women wrote reports and then descended on Washington, where after intensive lobbying they persuaded the Department of Education to suspend federal contracts at any university that could not produce a credible affirmative action plan for the advancement of women and minorities.[26]

Although many women felt strongly that only the pressure of goals would produce change, many men on the country's faculties decried what they saw as the government's abuse of power. In their view the government's demand for hiring data and affirmative action plans was a blatant assault on academic standards, freedom, and privacy. They were appalled at the idea of having to work with government statisticians who seemed to think, for instance, that all historians were fungible and that a department looking for a specialist in twentieth-century Central European history could just pluck one out of the general pool of Ph.D.'s in history. Concerned faculty were even more resistant to the idea of turning over confidential personnel files to government investigators.[27]

To many Jewish men, the entire project smacked of anti-Semitism. They saw the goals and timetables required by an affirmative action plan as the equivalent of quotas. Having struggled for decades to eradicate the quotas that had limited the admission and hiring of Jews in the Ivy League, they denounced any policy that might lead to quotas being imposed once more, however noble the purpose might be.[28]

Frustrated by their marginalization within academe, determined to make affirmative action work, and inspired by feminist activism outside the academy, female scholars accelerated their organizing efforts. They founded caucuses at the annual meetings of the Modern Language Association (1968), the American Historical Association (1969), and the American Philosophical Association (1970). At these caucuses women demanded change within the academy to meet their needs. At the 1972 meeting of the American Studies Association, for instance, a resolution called for day care, pregnancy and parental leave (for men as well as women), and options in the pace of career tracks.[29] Women academics also founded or expanded scholarly groups dedicated to

women's issues. The Berkshire Conference of Women's Historians, formed in
the 1930s by a handful of women who felt isolated within the historical profession,
flowered in the early 1970s into the major forum for scholars of women's
history to present their work. In 1974 the Barnard College Women's Center,
founded in 1970, launched a yearly conference entitled "The Scholar and the
Feminist," which sought to attract scholars throughout the academy and even
beyond its walls. The very title was provocative. To suggest that scholarship
could, indeed should, be politically engaged was to challenge a core value of
the academy: its declared detachment from ideology. In 1960 the sociologist
Daniel Bell had famously celebrated the post–World War II era as an "End of
Ideology," a period free of both Marxist and fascist repression, an open society
in which the university could flourish as never before. Throughout the academy,
scholars had long argued that intellectual inquiry should be "value-free."
Many male scholars looked on the influx of self-identified feminists as a threat
to this goal.[30]

Feminist scholars had two responses. The first was to agree that the university
should be a more open place and to point to the academy's treatment
of women and women's writing as a violation of its own standards. The second
response was to draw on philosophical critiques of rationality and objectivity
to question the viability of the "value-free" principle. Arguing that all people
act within an ideological framework—that is, on a set of values, beliefs, and
interests—feminist scholars asserted that the very claim of "value-free" inquiry
was itself an ideology. Scholarship, they contended, was inevitably affected
by one's particular situation in life—one's gender, race, religion, geographical
place, and class—and that the good scholar was attuned to the beliefs that
flowed from that situation, not blind to them. Their critical powers heightened
by their near universal participation in consciousness-raising groups, feminist
scholars insisted that they were simply more aware than many traditional scholars
of the values that informed their search. Indeed, they credited their own
gender-born perspective on life with generating the idea that power, wielded
disproportionately by men, structured all of life, from the state on down to
the family. The "Scholar and the Feminist" conferences drew scholars from
across the country who gave such papers as "Feminist Literary Criticism in
the University," "A Feminist Perspective on Art History," "Psychoanalysis and
Feminism in France," and "Towards a Politics of Sexuality."[31]

The Challenge to Disciplinary Boundaries

Because of the sense of isolation women felt within traditional fields, they increasingly
reached across disciplinary boundaries to find support from other

women. An English professor, Florence Howe provided key leadership in this effort. A 1950 graduate of Hunter College, Howe earned an M.A. in English from Smith in 1951 and pursued doctoral work at Wisconsin for the next three years. Leaving before she completed her Ph.D., she taught at Hofstra, Queens, and Goucher in the 1950s and 1960s. In 1968 she was a key organizer of the first woman's caucus at the MLA convention, and two years later she put together two panels at the MLA, one on women's status in the modern languages and the other on male bias in the curriculum. In 1971 Howe left Goucher, where her proposal to teach a course entitled Women and Identity had been rejected as "offensive," and moved to the new SUNY at Old Westbury, a working-class, multiracial campus dedicated to interdisciplinary study. There she founded a women's studies program and, with the help of a small grant from Mariam Chamberlain at the Ford Foundation, began studying the rapidly evolving women's studies movement. She quickly became, in her words, "the historian and record-keeper of the women's studies movement." Building on the model of American studies, faculty across the country began lobbying their schools to create women's studies programs and research centers dedicated to scholarship on women. Organizers sought to found interdisciplinary programs rather than departments both to provide networks of support for isolated women and to improve the prospects of generating curricular change. The idea was to hire scholars interested in women who would have one foot in traditional departments like English and French and a second foot in women's studies. Women scholars created the first women's studies programs on opposite sides of the country, at San Diego State University and at Cornell University in 1970. Within a decade the number of women's studies programs had increased to over 350. By the end of the century there were more than 600 programs across the country, and women's studies was enrolling more students than any other interdisciplinary program. Women's studies spread most quickly through the state universities. Harvard University did not have a program until 1986.[32]

Women scholars also created new means for publishing forgotten texts and new scholarship. Florence Howe founded the Feminist Press in 1972. The same year saw the creation of *Feminist Studies* and *Women's Studies*. The journal *Signs* followed in 1975. By the end of the century there were more than five hundred journals devoted to scholarship on women. The founder of *Signs*, Catharine Stimpson, provides an example of a scholar who made the transition from the margins to the center of the academy through feminism. Born in Willingham, Washington, she felt early an "ambition, not to marry the boy next door." This goal took her to Bryn Mawr College, where she earned a B.A. in 1958, and then on to Newnham College, Cambridge, where she earned a second B.A., with honors, in 1960. Returning to the States, she entered the Department of English at Columbia, from which she earned a Ph.D. with distinction in 1967; her thesis title was "The Early Novels of Iris Murdoch." She began her career at Barnard College in 1963, when she joined the ranks of lecturers in the English Department while working on her doctorate. Her closest friend was Kate Millett, a lecturer then as well, with whom she shared an office and with whom she encountered the world of radical feminism down in the Bowery, where they both lived. Kate "looked more conservative than I, in her long skirts, pumps, and hair drawn back in, yes, a bun. I jumped around the corridors in miniskirts, tights, and unruly, unkeyed, naturally curly locks, " Stimpson later recalled. "I might have looked the more radical," she added, "but I was, intellectually, the more conservative, prudent, and buttoned up."[33] Millett was fired in 1968, then hired briefly by the Barnard Philosophy Department to teach in Barnard's Experimental College, only to be fired for good in 1970. That was the year *Sexual Politics* was published, members of the Radicalesbians outed her at a Columbia forum, and *Time* put her on its cover. The more politically contained Stimpson survived, winning promotion to assistant professor in 1968 upon completion of her doctorate. Stimpson was one of a small group of young academics determined to make academe more receptive to the radical insights of modern feminism. And she did, first through *Signs*, and then as a professor at Rutgers, director of the MacArthur Foundation, president of the Modern Language Association, and dean of the Graduate School of Arts and Sciences at New York University.[34]

Sameness versus Difference

Feminist concerns shaped the research of female scholars in the humanities more than any other factor in the 1970s and 1980s. Some women, following Kate Millett's example, challenged men's long-standing use of sex differences as a justification for discriminating against women. In "The Republican Mother" (1975), Linda Kerber examined the ways in which the Founding Fathers used motherhood to deny basic rights of citizenship to women. In *The Lay of the Land* (1975), Annette Kolodny showed how male writers in America had "feminized" nature and thus combined the goals of territorial and patriarchal domination in writings about the American West. In *The Heroine's Text* (1980), Nancy Miller revealed a persistent tendency in French literature to kill off (or marry off) heroines, rather than permitting them to lead autonomous lives. And in *Women in Western Political Thought* (1979), Susan Miller Okin reviewed classic works of political theory to show the ways in which theorists from Aristotle to Rousseau had denied women political agency. These revelations of misogyny began to have a discernable effect by the early 1980s. As Lawrence Lipking observed in his 1983 essay "Aristotle's Sister," "Something peculiar has been happening lately to the classics. Some of them now seem less heroic, and some of them less funny."[35]

In addition to exposing misogyny, feminist scholars engaged in what Gerda Lerner called "contribution" history: the uncovering of women who had made a contribution to history but had been forgotten. These women included brilliant figures such as the American transcendentalist Margaret Fuller, whose work demonstrated that sex had nothing to do with the operations of the mind, and political leaders like the Grimké sisters, who played critical roles in fomenting the abolitionist movement. Two works in European history, *Becoming Visible* and *Hidden from History*, sought to show that women were makers of history, and in art history Ann Sutherland Harris and Linda Nochlin's *Women Artists, 1550–1950* demonstrated that women had always painted.[36] Other scholars showed that women's assumed differences from men were often a function of male historians projecting their own middle-class, mid-twentieth-century experiences onto the past. Gerda Lerner and Alice Kessler-Harris in American history and Joan Scott and Louise Tilly in European history disputed the widespread portrayal of women as living in a domestic sphere, supported by men. In nineteenth-century Europe and America, poor women had been compelled to join the labor force outside the home by the pressures of capitalism, while a parallel process of professionalization had driven many middle-class women out of the labor force. The underlying message of these early works was that underneath the differences imposed by a patriarchal, capitalist order, women were fundamentally the same as men.[37]

But were they? Even as some feminist critics attacked traditional scholarship for denigrating, excluding, and misrepresenting women, they began to value the ways in which women differed from men. They found that women had a history, art, and literature of their own—work that was worthy of scholarly attention on its own terms. Moreover, feminist scholars began to rethink many of the assumptions about how scholarship should be organized and evaluated. They questioned the belief that men should be the measure of all that was worthy. They asked why women should have to model themselves on men to merit attention. They even began to rethink the meaning of time. The European historian Joan Kelly-Gadol's pioneering essay "Did Women Have a Renaissance?" demanded that scholars challenge the temporal categories that had been adopted in traditional—that is, men's—history. Events and periods important to the development of male ideas and institutions might not be important for women.[38] Indeed, women's experiences, values, and achievements might be better viewed along a completely different temporal line, one created from female experience. Linda Gordon discussed the history of birth control in *Woman's Body, Woman's Right* (1976); Laurel Thatcher Ulrich wrote about seventeenth- and eighteenth-century domesticity in *Good Wives* (1982); and Ruth Schwarz Cowan wrote about housework in the twentieth century in *More Work for Mother* (1983).

In literature, scholars began to define women's writing as a distinctive undertaking. Elaine Showalter provided a pioneering example of this approach in *A Literature of Their Own* (1977). A future president of the Modern Language Association (1998), Showalter began her career, as did many female academics, by following her husband as he moved from job to job. Born in Cambridge, Massachusetts, in 1941, she graduated from Bryn Mawr in 1962, married English Showalter, a Haverford French professor, followed him to California (where she began graduate work in English at the University of California at Davis), and then followed him back to Princeton before her graduate work was done. In 1968 she found herself in New Jersey "with a small child trying to write what seemed to be a hopeless dissertation on the double critical standard applied to Victorian women novelists." Her endeavor was "hopeless" on two scores. Women who wrote on women were still not taken seriously in academe, and two of the three colleges that were within commuting distance told her that they did not hire women. But she got a part-time job at Douglass College, the women's college of Rutgers University, participated in the 1968 protest at the MLA, and through feminism found the courage to complete her thesis and embark on a career. The women's movement enabled her to see her work as valuable, even though the profession she wanted to enter conveyed the clear message that it was "eccentric." Showalter completed her thesis in 1970 and went on to write *A Literature of Their Own*, in which she explored the recurring images, themes, and plots that emerged from women's experience in male-dominated cultures.[39] Showalter was quickly joined by others, not only academics but also feminist writers, artists, and poets—Adrienne Rich, Marge Piercy, Judy Chicago, and Alice Walker—who began to assert the existence of a woman's culture that had been neglected. Women combed library stacks for works by earlier women that had been long forgotten or little valued. Charlotte Perkins Gilman's *The Yellow Wallpaper* (1891) and Kate Chopin's *The Awakening* (1899) are just two examples of the texts that soon appeared on reading lists around the country.[40]

The precise nature of the distinctive female experience that Showalter and others sought to chart was the subject of controversy from the start. Some scholars identified it with lesbian consciousness. In "Toward a Female Aesthetic," published in 1977 in the women's culture journal *Chrysalis*, Julia Penelope Stanley and Susan Wolfe equated the flowing, conjunctive, nonlinear style of the lesbian author Gertrude Stein with "women's style" in general.[41] In history, Carol Smith Rosenberg pointed to a "Female World of Love and Ritual" in nineteenth-century America, before homosexuality came to be demonized, when women could establish romantic bonds with each other without fear of social disapprobation.[42]

To others the concept of a female experience or distinctively female style was linked to the mother-daughter relationship and the broader communities of female relationships connected to it. Adrienne Rich argued in her book *Of Woman Born: Motherhood as Experience and Institution* (1975) that the key relationship in life was with the mother. Drawing on the object-relations theory branch of psychoanalysis, Nancy Chodorow agreed and went on to stress the centrality of the pre-Oedipal mother-infant relationship in producing gender differences in *The Reproduction of Mothering* (1978). The problem of separating from the mother posed a greater challenge to sons than to daughters, Chodorow argued. To become men sons had not only to separate from but also to become unlike their mothers, a task that led men to value detachment, independence, and rationality. Daughters, by contrast, could separate from their mothers without losing the connectedness of a common gender identity, and thus had less reason to distinguish between self and other in their mental and moral lives. Seeing the mother-daughter relationships in a more positive light than had previously been the case became more common throughout the humanities, from work on the Greek myth of Demeter and Persephone to what the historian Nancy Cott called the bonds of womanhood (in her 1977 book of that title) in early nineteenth-century America.[43]

Confronting Race

The celebration of gender difference raised the question of *differences* more generally. How much did gender matter in literature, history, and other humanities? Was it as important as class or race? A number of African American writers argued that the "difference" to which most feminist scholars appealed in their critiques tended to be a white, middle-class difference from white, middle-class men. In 1970, the year in which Kate Millett published *Sexual Politics*, Toni Morrison published *The Bluest Eye*, which opened with a parody of America's ubiquitous grade school reader, with its stereotypically white family of mother, father, Dick, Jane, dog, and cat. In 1975 Alice Walker rekindled an interest in the work of Zora Neale Hurston, a leading member of the Harlem Renaissance whose books had been out of print for decades, with an article in *Ms.* magazine. Hurston's *Their Eyes Were Watching God* (1937), with its lampooning of white, middle-class sensibilities, quickly became one of the favorite texts of English and women's studies courses. The connection between race and gender did not become a central concern in the humanities, however, until the 1980s, when an explosion of writing on women of color appeared. The former slave Sojourner Truth provided inspiration for many scholars of color. In 1981 the feminist literary critic bell hooks (née Gloria Watkins) published *Ain't I a Woman: Black Women and Feminism*. Born in Kentucky and educated at Stanford University (B.A., 1973), the University of Wisconsin (M.A., 1976), and the University of California at Santa Cruz (Ph.D., 1983), hooks argued that race must be an integral part of gender analysis. Also in 1981 Cherríe Moraga and Gloria Anzaldúa published *This Bridge Called My Back*, a collection of essays that set the terms of dissent from the discourse of unity that then characterized feminist criticism. The authors refused to identify themselves as feminists because the whiteness of feminism's universal subject did not include them. Shortly thereafter, four histories of black women appeared almost simultaneously: Paula Giddings (Howard, B.A., 1969), *When and Where I Enter: The Impact of Black Women on Race and Sex in America* (1984), Darlene Clark Hine, *Black Women in the Nursing Profession* (1985), Deborah G. White, *Ar'n't I a Woman? Female Slaves in the Plantation South* (1985), and Jacqueline Jones, *Labor of Love, Labor of Sorrow: Black Women, Work, and the Family from Slavery to the Present* (1985).

This new attention to the black female experience inspired African American students across the country to demand the hiring of more faculty of color, new programs in African American, pan-African, and ethnic studies and greater attention to issues of race throughout the curriculum. Attention to race spread quickly throughout the academy in the years that followed, and the resulting research had a profound effect on the way some traditional topics were understood. The rediscovery of Ida B. Wells Barnett, for example, led scholars to look more closely at the history of lynching and to see the ways in which white men's violence against black men was used to control both black and white women.[44]

The Rise of Theory

For all their internal differences, feminist scholars in the United States generally shared an empirical bent, as illustrated by their efforts to describe women's lives and recover their texts. But by the 1980s theory became a much more central concern as debates over the use and power of language entered the academy from France via feminist scholars in comparative literature. Inspired by the neo-Freudian Jacques Lacan, the deconstructionist philosopher Jacques Derrida, and the structuralist critic Roland Barthes, French feminists pointed to the importance of language in defining, representing, and repressing "the feminine." French feminists celebrated *l'écriture féminine*, a practice of writing that subverted traditional narratives. *L'écriture féminine* need not necessarily be written by women. Broadly speaking, it formed part of the avant-garde style that had been pioneered by James Joyce and Stéphane Mallarmé. But, according to the most radical of the French femininsts, Hélène Cixous, the author of *Laugh of the Medusa*, this writing was connected to the rhythms of the female body, and therefore women presumably had an advantage in producing this radically disruptive form of writing.[45]

Gender as a Category of Scholarly Analysis

Despite the remarkable success of the new feminist scholarship, some feminist academics worried about the tendency to focus too narrowly and separately on the history and writings of women. As Natalie Zemon Davis argued, women could never be understood without reference to men because each was defined in terms of the other. "It seems to me that we should be interested in the history of women and men, that we should not be working only on the subjected sex any more than a history of class can focus entirely on peasants."[46] Davis suggested that scholars examine gender as a way of understanding the social organization of the relationship between the sexes. The historian Joan Scott concurred, pointing to the ways in which gender served not only as an element in social relationships that were based on perceived differences between sexes, but also as a primary way of signifying relationships of power. Scott, who had earned her Ph.D. at Wisconsin in 1969, founded the Pembroke Center for Research on Women at Brown in 1981 and joined the Institute for Advanced Study at Princeton in 1985, worried about the tendency of many feminist scholars to emphasize female difference. Working with the historian Louise Tilly, Scott had argued in *Women, Work, and Family* (1978) that the idea of women's separate sphere was a middle-class concept that did not apply to nineteenth-century peasant families and that historians needed to learn how to look beyond standard assumptions about gender roles to see how they were affected by class. Taking a theoretical turn in the early 1980s, she went a step further by calling for a postmodernist effort to deconstruct sexual differences. She drew in particular on the French philosophers Michel Foucault and Monique Wittig, who brought new attention to the ways in which power has shaped the meaning of sex, and on the work of Jacques Derrida, who provided guidance in deconstructing binary oppositions like male-female in language.[47]

In Foucault's view sexuality must not be seen as a biological given, but rather as "an especially dense transfer point for relations of power: between men and women, young people and old people, parents and offspring, teachers and students, priests and laity, and administration and population."[48] Monique Wittig argued, in turn, that heterosexuality was not a biological given but rather a cultural institution, one that was, in her view, a greater source of oppression for women than the institution of patriarchy. Rather than believing, as some lesbian scholars did, that lesbians represented the true female aesthetic, she argued in stark contrast that lesbians should not be considered "women" at all since they were outside the symbolic order of heterosexual relationships.[49]

Jacques Derrida's yearly trips to the United States to teach at Johns Hopkins, Cornell, and Yale made him a greater influence among feminists in America, greater even than he was in France. Feminists found inspiration in Derrida's work to move beyond the binary division of male-female, to see that each included the other. This insight proved particularly influential to postcolonial critics such as Gayatri Spivak, who found in Derrida's critique "a feminization of the practice of philosophy," which led to an "ultimately political practice."[50]

In seeing gender not as a synonym for women but rather as a concept referring to the social relationships based on perceived differences between the sexes and, more broadly, as a way of signifying relationships of power, feminist scholars believed that they had found an important tool for understanding culture, even where women were absent. Calls to war, for instance, had often been justified by appeals to manhood, while middle-class reformers defended their efforts on behalf of male workers in terms of the workers' allegedly femalelike weakness. By employing the concept of gender, scholars could bring new insights to all sectors of the humanities.[51]

Impact on the Humanities

By the end of the twentieth century women had achieved considerable influence within the humanities. They regularly served as presidents of the nation's professional societies and garnered record numbers of Guggenheim Fellowships, Pulitzer Prizes, and MacArthur Awards. Never had so many women reached the rank of full professor, nor had the pipeline to the professoriate been so full. By the year 2000 women were winning half of all new doctorates in the humanities. Not that female Ph.D.'s had achieved parity in all fields. In literature women earned more than half of all doctorates: 62 percent in foreign languages and 58 percent in English. Elsewhere the figures were lower: 38 percent in history and 28 percent in philosophy.[52]

Women's intellectual influence reflected the share of Ph.D.'s they gained. From departments of English and comparative literature to those of the modern languages, gender figured prominently in scholarly debates.[53] History offered greater resistance. Survey texts remained largely the narrative of past politics, in which men's experience predominated, and even works that emphasized social history tended to include attention to gender by providing sections on women, rather than using gender as a category of analysis. No field of the humanities resisted the insights of feminism more strongly, however, than philosophy, long the discipline with the lowest numbers of female Ph.D.'s and the fewest female full professors. Most women who trained as philosophers and turned to feminism were exiled, if they survived at all, to departments of literature or political science on the grounds that their work did not qualify as philosophy. And yet, even within philosophy feminist criticism was beginning to have an effect, as it insisted that philosophical argument be seen as part of a set of historical, cultural, and institutional practices.[54]

In a few short years women in the humanities made an important difference in expanding the scope and nature of scholarly inquiry. Still, when scholarly associations embarked on a new cycle of surveys of women in academe at the end of the twentieth century, they uncovered some stubborn continuities with the past, as well as some unsettling new trends. A number of studies found that women were continuing to find greater difficulty than men in balancing family and work. Women still shouldered the principal responsibility for the physical and emotional care of kin, whose life cycles often played as large a part in dictating their careers as did their own. Women also reported taking on disproportionate responsibility for the committee work and student advising that maintained the fabric of campus life.[55]

In addition to the difficulties women encountered in trying to balance their professional and private lives, they faced significant problems associated with what an MLA study in 2000 identified as a "drastic gender reversal" in the fields of literature.[56] Women's growing presence within the fields of English and the foreign languages reflected not increasing numbers; in fact, women's numbers remained fairly stable. Instead, the number of men earning doctorates declined sharply. This gender reversal coincided with a severe contraction in the numbers of full-time, tenure-track academic positions and an increasing institutional reliance on part-time, non-tenure-track faculty members. The rise in part-time positions was so pronounced by the end of the 1990s that, for the first time in decades, more women took part-time positions than entered tenure-track jobs.[57]

A similar shift from male to female workers occurred in grade school teaching in the nineteenth century and in office work in the twentieth. As employment opportunities came to be identified primarily with women, working conditions, salaries, and status declined. Were employment opportunities in the study of literature, and the humanities more broadly, declining because of the declining presence of men? Or were men leaving because of declining opportunities?[58]

In a further threat to job opportunities, in the final decades of the twentieth century universities shifted resources away from the humanities and toward the sciences, where the numbers of women had long been relatively lower. As a result, even as women increased their relative presence within the humanities, the humanities came to occupy a more marginal place within the larger academy.[59]

The entry of women into the humanities in the three decades following World War II, in short, greatly expanded realms of inquiry and brought new perspectives to bear on traditional fields. But the consolidation of these changes in the 1980s and 1990s took place in the midst of a sharp decline in the number of men seeking doctorates, as well as a shift of academic resources away from the arts to the sciences. These dramatic changes raised a new concern for men and women alike. Would the humanities remain a vital part of the academic enterprise in the years ahead?

Notes

1. Mary Calkins fulfilled all qualifications for a Ph.D. at Harvard but was denied the degree by the Board of Overseers on account of her gender. She was unusual, however, among female faculty, indeed, all faculty, in the sophistication of her training. Holding a Ph.D. was not essential to holding a faculty position in the humanities in the early twentieth century, but by midcentury it had become increasingly necessary. Jessie Bernard, *Academic Women* (New York: Meridian, 1964), 117–126. For the origins of professionalization in academe, see Mary O. Furner, *Advocacy and Objectivity: A Crisis in the Professionalization of American Social Science, 1865–1905* (Lexington: University Press of Kentucky, 1975).

2. Lindsey R. Harmon and Herbert Soldz, *Doctorate Production in United States Universities, 1920–1962, with Baccalaureate Origins of Doctorates in Sciences, Arts, and Professions* (Washington, D.C.: National Academy of Sciences, 1963), 50–52; Lindsey R. Harmon, ed., *A Century of Doctorates: Data Analysis of Growth and Change* (Washington, D.C.: National Academy of Sciences, 1978), 17.

3. Harmon, *Century of Doctorates*, 17.

4. Bernard, *Academic Women*, 54–55.

5. Interviews with Nicholson's former students and colleagues, including Betty Jemmott, Joseph Ridgley, Chris Royer, and Robert Hanning. For a broader discussion of this phenomenon see Bernard, *Academic Women*, 41–55.

6. Harmon and Soldz, *Doctorate Production*, 50–52; Margaret Wilson, "Report of the Subcommittee on the Status of Women," in *Proceedings and Addresses of the American Philosophical Association* (Clinton, N.Y.: American Philosophical Association, 1971–72), 117–126.

7. W. Vance Grant and et al., *Digest of Educational Statistics* (Washington, D.C.: National Center for Educational Statistics, 1975), 105–113; *Doctorate Recipients from United States Universities: Summary Report 2000* (Washington, D.C.: National Science Foundation, National Institutes for Health, U.S. Department of Education, National Endowment for the Humanities, U.S. Department of Agriculture, and National Aeronautics and Space Administration, 2000), 10–11; MLA Committee on the Status of Women in the Profession, "Women in the Profession, 2000," in *Profession 2000* (New York: Modern Languages Association, 2000), 192–193.

8. Harmon, *Century of Doctorates*, 137.

9. Natalie Zemon Davis, interview by Rob Harding and Judy Coffin, "Natalie Zemon Davis, 1981," in *Visions of History*, ed. Henry Abelove et al. (New York: Pantheon, 1984), 104. See similar accounts by women scholars who went on to specialize in gender: Sandra M. Gilbert, "Life Studies, or, Speech after Long Silence: Feminist Critics Today," *College English* 40, no. 8 (1979): 849–850, and Estelle B. Freedman, *No Turning Back: The History of Feminism and the Future of Women* (New York: Ballantine Books, 2002), x.

10. Harding and Coffin, "Natalie Zemon Davis, 1981," 101–119.

11. Jacques Revel and Lynn Hunt, eds., *Histories: French Constructions of the Past* (New York: New Press, 1995), 1–63; Lynn Hunt, ed., *The New Cultural History* (Berkeley: University of California Press, 1989), 1–22.

12. Natalie Zemon Davis, "Women's History in Transition: The European Case," *Feminist Studies* 3 (1975–76): 83–103; Natalie Zemon Davis, *Society and Culture in Early Modern France: Eight Essays by Natalie Zemon Davis* (Stanford: Stanford University Press, 1975); Suzanne Desan, "Crowds, Community, and Ritual in the Work of E. P. Thompson and Natalie Davis," in Hunt, *The New Cultural History*, 63–71. Clifford Geertz, *Works and Lives: The Anthropologist as Author* (Stanford: Stanford University Press, 1988), 107; *Contemporary Authors*, s.v. "Natalie Zemon Davis."

13. Gerda Lerner, *Fireweed: A Political Autobiography* (Philadelphia: Temple University Press, 2002), 254, 95, 367.

14. Lerner's first articles were later published, with an autobiographical introduction, in Gerda Lerner, *The Majority Finds Its Past: Placing Women in History* (New York: Oxford University Press, 1979), xiii–xxxii.

15. Elaine Tyler May, "The Radical Roots of American Studies: Presidential Address to the American Studies Association, November 9, 1995," *American Quarterly* 48 (1996): 179–200; David Potter, *People of Plenty: Economic Abundance and the American Character* (Chicago: University of Chicago Press, 1954).

16. Columbia University, *Bulletin of Information* (New York: Columbia University, 1952–53); Linda Kerber, "Angles of Vision: What American Studies Has Been; What American Studies Might Be" (paper presented at the Sixty Years of American Studies at Barnard College conference, New York, 1999), 7–8; Linda Kerber, "In Memorium: John Kouwenhoven," *American Quarterly* 44, no. 3 (1992): 463–466; Linda Kerber to author, October 4, 1999 in author's possession.

17. Pauli Murray, *Pauli Murray: The Autobiography of a Black Activist, Feminist, Lawyer, Priest, and Poet* (Knoxville: University of Tennessee Press, 1987), 115, 351, 87.

18. Kate Millett, interview by author, September 11, 2000, New York City; Catharine Stimpson, interview by author, April 14, 2000, New York City; and Ann Prescott, interview by author, September 20, 2000, New York City. Marcia Cohen, *The Sisterhood: The True Story of the Women Who Changed the World* (New York: Simon and Schuster, 1988), 72–80, 143–254.

19. Cohen, *Sisterhood*, 314, 238, 301, 56.

20. Ibid., 31, 23–58, 158, 362–363.

21. Carolyn Heilbrun, "Millett's Sexual Politics: A Year Later," *Aphra* 2 (1971): 38–47.

22. Jonathan Culler, *On Deconstruction: Theory and Criticism after Structuralism* (Ithaca: Cornell University Press, 1982), 55.

23. Professor George Stade, Columbia University, interview by author, February 23, 2003, New York City.

24. According to figures from the Department of Education, university enrollment in 1960 stood at 900,000; by 1970 the figured had doubled to 1,800,000.

25. Robert B. Townsend, "Precedents: The Job Crisis of the 1970s," *Perpsectives* (April 1997).

26. For a fuller discussion of this movement and the way it played out at Columbia University, see Rosalind Rosenberg, *Changing the Subject: How the Women of Columbia Shaped the Way We Think about Sex and Politics* (New York: Columbia University Press, 2004).

27. Walter Goodman, "The Return of the Quota System," *New York Times Magazine*, September 10, 1972; Bart Barnes, "Reverse Bias Alleged in College Hiring," *Washington Post*, March 5, 1973.

28. Carolyn G. Heilbrun, *When Men Were the Only Models We Had: My Teachers Barzun, Fadiman, Trilling* (Philadelphia: University of Pennsylvania Press, 2002), 64–65.

29. American Studies Association, "Resolutions on the Status of Women," *American Quarterly* 24 (October 1972): 550–554.

30. Jane S. Gould, *Juggling: A Memoir of Work, Family, and Feminism* (New York: Feminist Press, 1997), 186–205; Daniel Bell, *The End of Ideology: On the Exhaustion of Political Ideas in the Fifties* (Glencoe, Ill.: Free Press, 1960).

31. Catharine R. Stimpson, "Feminist Criticism," in *Redrawing the Boundaries*, ed. Stephen Greenblatt and Giles Gunn (New York: MLA, 1992), 258–259; Gould, *Juggling*, 186–205; Susan Brownmiller, *In Our Time: Memoir of a Revolution* (New York: Dial Press, 1999), 295–330; Carole S. Vance, ed., *Pleasure and Danger: Exploring Female Sexuality* (Boston: Routledge and Kegan Paul, 1984).

32. Florence Howe, ed., *The Politics of Women's Studies: Testimony from Thirty Founding Mothers* (New York: Feminist Press, 2000), xi–xxvi, 3–38, 229–242; Florence Howe, "Women's Studies and Curricular Change," in *Women in Academe: Progress and Prospects*, ed. Mariam K. Chamberlain (New York: Russell Sage Foundation, 1988), 3, 133–161; Marilyn J. Boxer, *When Women Ask the Questions: Creating Women's Studies in America* (Baltimore: Johns Hopkins University Press, 1998).

33. Stimpson, "Feminist Criticism," 258–259.

34. Stimpson interview.

35. Lawrence Lipking, "Aristotle's Sister: A Poetics of Abandonment," *Critical Inquiry* 10 (1983): 79.

36. Lerner, *The Majority Finds Its Past*, 4; Sheila Rowbotham, *Hidden from History: 300 Years of Women's Oppression and the Fight against It* (London: Pluto Press, 1973); Renate Bridenthal and Claudia Koonz, eds., *Becoming Visible: Women in European History* (Boston: Houghton Mifflin, 1977). Ann Sutherland Harris and Linda Nochlin, *Women Artists, 1550–1950* (New York: Random House, 1976).

37. Alice Kessler-Harris, *Women Have Always Worked: A Historical Overview* (New York: Feminist Press, 1981); Gerda Lerner, "The Lady and the Mill Girl: Changes in the Status of Women in the Age of Jackson," in *The Majority Finds Its Past*, 15–30; Joan W. Scott and Louise A. Tilly, "Women's Work and the Family in Nineteenth Century Europe," *Comparative Studies in Society and History* 17 (1975): 36–64.

38. Joan Kelly-Gadol, "Did Women Have a Renaissance?" in Bridenthal and Koonz, *Becoming Visible*, 137–164.

39. Elaine Showalter, "Women's Time, Women's Space: Writing the History of Feminist Criticism," *Tulsa Studies in Women's Literature* 3, no. 1–2 (1984): 33.

40. See also Patricia Meyer Spacks, *The Female Imagination* (1975), Ellen Moers, *Literary Women* (1976), and Sandra Gilbert and Susan Gubar, *The Madwoman in the Attic* (1979).

41. Elaine Showalter, ed., *The New Feminist Criticism: Essays on Women, Literature, and Theory* (New York: Pantheon, 1985), 7.

42. Carroll Smith-Rosenberg, "The Female World of Love and Ritual: Relations between Women in Nineteenth Century America," *Signs* 1 (1975): 1–29.

43. Celeste Schenck, *Mourning and Panegyric: The Poetics of Pastoral Ceremony* (University Park: Pennsylvania State University, 1988); Mary Lefkowitz and Maureen B. Fant, eds., *Women in Greece and Rome* (1977; rpt. Baltimore: Johns Hopkins University Press, 1982); Nancy F. Cott, *The Bonds of Womanhood: "Woman's Sphere" in New England, 1780–1835* (New Haven: Yale University Press, 1977). It should be noted that Cott's choice of "Bonds" was meant to indicate both the bonds that united women and those that limited their public influence. See also Joyce Antler, "After College What? New Graduates and the Family Claim," *American Quarterly* 32, no. 4 (1980): 409–434.

44. Linda O. McMurry, *To Keep the Waters Troubled: The Life of Ida B. Wells* (New York: Oxford University Press, 1998), 157–161; Jacquelyn Dowd Hall, *Revolt against Chivalry: Jessie Daniel Ames and the Women's Campaign against Lynching* (New York: Columbia University Press, 1979).

45. Showalter, *The New Feminist Criticism*, 9.

46. As quoted in Joan Wallach Scott, "Gender: A Useful Category of Historical Analysis," *American Historical Review* 91, no. 5 (1986): 1054.

47. Ibid.

48. Michel Foucault, *The History of Sexuality*, vol. 1, *An Introduction* (New York: Random House, 1978), 103.

49. Joan Wallach Scott, ed., *Feminism and History* (New York: Oxford University Press, 1996), 6–7.

50. As quoted in Showalter, "Women's Time, Women's Space, " 38.

51. Scott, "Gender," 1073.

52. MLA Committee on the Status of Women in the Profession, "Women in the Profession, 2000" (New York: Modern Language Association, 2000), fig. 1; National Science Foundation et al., *Survey of Earned Doctorates. Doctorate Recipients in the United States: Summary Report* (Washington, D.C.: National Science Foundation, 2000), table 6 and appendix table 1A.

53. Anne Matthews, "Rage in a Tenured Position," *New York Times*, November 8, 1992.

54. Joanne B. Waugh, "Analytic Aesthetics and Feminist Aesthetics: Neither/Nor?" *Journal of Aesthetics and Art Criticism* 48 (1990): 317.

55. Linda Kerber, "Personal Lives and Professional Careers: The Uneasy Balance," in *Report of the Women's Committee of the American Studies Association*, by Lois Banner et al. (Washington, D.C.: American Studies Association, 2002); Mary Ann Mason and Marc Gouldin, "Report: Do Babies Matter? The Effect of Family Formation on the Lifelong Careers of Women" (Berkeley: Graduate Division, University of California at Berkeley, 2002); "Report of the Steering Committee for the Women's Initiative at Duke University" (Durham: Duke University, 2003), available at www.duke.edu/womens_initiative/report_report.htm; "The Report of the Provost's Advisory Committee on the Status of Women Faculty" (Stanford: Stanford University, 2004), available at universitywomen.stanford.edu/reports.html.

56. MLA Committee on the Status of Women in the Profession, "Women in the Profession, 2000," 196.

57. Ibid., 192, 194, fig. 2.

58. Ibid., 192–193.

59. Thomas B. Hoffer et al., *Doctorate Recipients from United States Universities: Summary Report 2000* (Chicago: National Opinion Research Center, 2000), 9.

IV

Area Studies at Home and Abroad

10

CONSTRUCTING AMERICAN STUDIES
Culture, Identity, and the Expansion of the Humanities

LEILA ZENDERLAND

AMONG THE countless international conferences held in the decade following World War II was a UNESCO meeting organized to discuss Article 27 of the Universal Declaration of Human Rights, approved by the U.N. General Assembly in 1948. Article 27 states: "Everyone has the right freely to participate in the cultural life of the community, to enjoy the arts and to share in scientific advancement and its benefits." Invited to Paris in 1954 to consider the educational implications of this article were representatives from twelve countries. Among them was the American educator John Everett, president of Hollins College, whose account of his experiences was published in *American Quarterly*, the journal of the recently founded American Studies Association.[1]

According to Everett, this conference proved frustrating. Attendees could not agree on what "the right freely to participate" in cultural life meant, for they disagreed on the connotations of the words "free" and "participate." Far more problematic were the different meanings associated with the crucial word "culture," for Europeans, Everett told his readers, largely rejected the broad "sociological definition" he associated with this term. "It is not for them the 'complex whole which includes knowledge, belief, art, morals, law, custom and any other capabilities and habits acquired by man as a member of society,'" he reported.[2] Instead, his European counterparts espoused a different understanding, which he summarized: "There is a small group of creators—the term 'creative minority' kept recurring like a base theme throughout the meeting—who do all of the active producing in any given period of time. It is from this group that the rest of the world receives 'masterpieces' at periodic intervals. The next lower rung on the ladder is the 'appreciative minority' who are trained in history, endowed with vision, and possessed of a sufficiently disciplined taste to understand and appreciate the true creators. Below these two lies the general population which finds it difficult to see even the moving shadows let alone the bright sun of the good, the true and the beautiful."

To Everett these differences had profound pedagogical implications. It was a concern for culture as a "complex whole," he argued, that had increasingly led Americans to embrace general education, a type of university curriculum with "no counterpart in Europe." Of course, Everett did acknowledge what he called "the indigenous American concept of culture." "Most American citizens find 'culture' to be an obnoxious word designating activities . . . primarily for women and which should never be allowed to dilute the manly strength of our red-blooded American boys," he conceded. "But at the same time that we sound like such Philistines," he quickly added, Americans were pouring billions of dollars into "schools, colleges, museums, libraries, symphonies, adult education programs, and book publishing."

Still, Everett reported, Europeans invariably asked the same question: "Where are the American masterpieces?" "And here a good many Americans tend to hang their heads and feel ashamed," he admitted, for all the "great names" in art, music, philosophy, law, and science were European. Yet Everett was clearly proud of American cultural success. "A culture should not be judged by its assumed or real masterpieces," he concluded, but by the "opportunities it affords people to rise above the necessary business of getting and spending." Americans saw culture as "accessible to everyone and not something for an assumed elite," he insisted. Most crucial was the commitment to a pluralistic society, for it was "only in such a pluralism that the American emphasis upon the 'complex whole' is even remotely possible."[3]

Everett's 1954 article, with its familiar stereotypes pitting European cultural elitists against American cultural pluralists (as well as culture-loving females against action-oriented males), is intriguing for what it suggests about its intended audience: those involved in the emerging academic field then calling itself "American civilization" or "American studies." Begun in the 1930s but vastly expanded in the postwar decade, this interdisciplinary educational enterprise had declared the study of "American culture" to be its central intellectual endeavor. Yet just what such an endeavor included and how it was to be structured as part of an academic curriculum still remained open questions. In exploring how this field was constructed, particularly in the postwar period, and how it was later "deconstructed" in the decades that followed, we find that three key issues repeatedly emerge. Each of these issues is suggested in the 1954 conversation between John Everett and his European contemporaries.

The first concerns the multiple meanings associated with the word "culture." By the 1950s, the anthropologists A. L. Kroeber and Clyde Kluckhohn reported, culture had become a ubiquitous part of academic discourse, a concept in "explanatory importance and in generality of application" comparable to "gravity in physics, disease in medicine, evolution in biology."[4] Yet as Everett's essay shows, this widespread acceptance actually masked efforts to reconcile two popular, overlapping, and yet different conceptions of what "culture" meant—efforts that mirrored the broader determination of American studies scholars to reconcile the insights of humanists with findings from social scientists. Still powerful within the humanities were the ideas of the British critic Matthew Arnold, who in 1869 had explained culture as "the best which has been thought and said in the world"—in short, as masterpieces—and who had disparaged those failing to appreciate such works as Philistines.[5] Challenging Arnold's understanding was the definition supplied by the British anthropologist E. B.Tylor two years later, also cited by Everett—that is, as the "complex whole . . . acquired by man as a member of society."[6] In the United States Franz Boas had expanded upon this anthropological definition and made it a linchpin of academic social science, and his students Margaret Mead and Ruth Benedict had popularized it by discerning the "patterns of culture" evident in the everyday lives of the peoples they studied. Even so, Arnold's concerns, particularly about protecting aesthetic sensibilities in an age of machinery and materialism, had hardly disappeared; if anything, they intensified in the postwar period as critics increasingly confronted the products of the mass media. And although many American studies scholars would try to reconcile both meanings, tensions between them frequently reemerged. Should the academic study of "American culture" essentially involve a type of aesthetic evaluation—or a kind of social documentation? Was it better done by focusing on the work of this culture's most exceptional artists—or on its most representative?

Second, Everett's comments suggest the ways that both understandings of "American culture" were intertwined with larger debates over what came to be called American national "identity"—a concept embodied in the feelings of both shame and pride that Everett expressed as a self-conscious American discussing "culture" in Europe. If the word "culture" would become a key concept by the 1950s, so too would the word "identity," for it would be popularized through the writings of Erik Erikson.[7] And while these connections between national and cultural self-consciousness had been apparent in American history since the founding of the nation, they took on a new significance in a postwar world dominated not only by American military power but also by American cultural products—a process that one American studies scholar as early as 1952 would call "coca-colonization."[8]

Finally, Everett's discussion raises questions about the complexities embedded in the very idea of a "complex whole." How exactly did such a "whole" function, and how could it best be studied within the university? What did such holism actually include? More important, what was it excluding?

This chapter explores the dynamics of inclusion by following the debates over these three issues among practitioners of American studies. It will focus in particular on what inclusion meant and on how its meaning changed by examining the controversies surrounding the best means of assessing and understanding American cultural products, the intertwining of ideas about American culture and American identity, and the relationship between cultural wholes and parts.

Constructing American Studies: Inclusion as the "Culture of the Whole"

Notwithstanding their prewar precedents, American studies programs within universities can in many ways be considered a product of World War II. Though in the 1930s about seven institutions had begun to offer degrees in American civilization, largely by integrating coursework in American history and American literature, more than a dozen new programs were introduced in the 1945–46 school year alone. Within three years of the war's end, sixty American institutions, both large and small, were offering B.A. degrees in this interdisciplinary field, and about fifteen offered M.A. or Ph.D. degrees.[9]

Many concepts and methods basic to this field were developed during the interwar decades, when the meanings attached to the words "civilization" and "culture" began to be explored in new ways. Especially influential were Charles and Mary Beard's *The Rise of American Civilization* (1927), a sweeping interdisciplinary historical survey written for general readers, and Ruth Benedict's *Patterns of Culture* (1934), one of the most popular anthropological studies ever produced.[10] Important as well, however, were developments outside the university. These included the intense concern with culture among an increasingly educated middle class that "bought books, valued the classics, cared about the opera, liked the theatre as well as the movies, and sought guidance from critics,"[11] as well as the actions of the 1930s Popular Front in bringing the culture of the "common man" to national consciousness. All would affect American studies, as would the growing influence of new media in disseminating American cultural products with a "distinctly plebeian accent."[12]

Equally crucial in shaping American studies was the ideological nature of the war itself. Rising fears that fascism was making inroads with the public, as it had in Europe, led to what the historian Philip Gleason has christened the "democratic revival"—a fiercely argued defense of American democratic ideals that became the subject of literally hundreds of books in the late 1930s and early 1940s, among them John Dewey's *Freedom and Culture* (1939). Influential as well was the man President Roosevelt called his "minister of culture," Archibald MacLeish; appointed Librarian of Congress, this poet used his position to rally intellectuals, academics, artists, and journalists to fight Nazism by explaining and defending democratic, pluralistic, and humanistic values to broad audiences. Thus, whereas Nazi ideology repeatedly stressed the significance of racial, religious, and ethnic differences, the ideology of the democratic revival instead emphasized a common American identity open to anyone who subscribed to the universal ideals of the Enlightenment. By the war's end, both American culture and American identity had become closely linked to a set of ideas variously called "the American creed," "the American dream," the "American way of life," or simply "democracy." It was the "cultural interpretation of democracy," Gleason argues, that "brought the ideological revival into close interaction with American Studies," for American studies took as its task "understanding the national culture holistically."[13]

Many universities explained their new postwar American studies programs in the very language of the democratic revival. "Now that thousands of Americans have laid down their lives in order that the American way of life may go on," a University of Maryland report of 1945 stated, this faculty felt a "plain duty" to make Americans "aware of the values included in our tradition."[14] "The war undoubtedly has influenced the faculty of Augustana College," a professor there reported the same year, for the new American studies program reflected this faculty's belief that "in a democracy it is essential to stress democratic ideals" as well as its broader efforts to discourage "isolationism, the presence of which . . . must to some degree be attributed to the failure of American colleges to create a strong spirit of internationalism."[15] Several older programs were reorganized in the wake of the war. Although Yale had offered graduate work in American "History, the Arts, and Letters" since 1933, its new undergraduate American studies program began in 1946 with an emphasis on the "socio-anthropological approach to culture."[16] Robert Spiller helped reorganize the University of Pennsylvania's program when he joined it in 1946.[17] "We planners . . . may prefer to remain as members of 'regular' departments because we are too old to risk our hard-won academic securities," he conceded, but his students were "grappling with the fundamental questions about the meaning of civilization and culture" while also making "the integrations which to their teachers are little more than paper plans in catalogues."[18]

In his own research on American literary history, begun during the war, Spiller enunciated some of the objectives that would shape this movement. After decades of conflict, he explained, his own era had embraced the goals of "assimilation and synthesis."[19] Equally evident was a postwar commitment to what one historian, in studying the 1940s, labeled the "culture of the whole"—the belief not only that culture, as anthropologists repeatedly insisted, was indeed holistic, but that "it was both possible and good to make one out of many, that a culture of the whole was an appropriate object of humanity's striving."[20]

Such sentiments are most obvious in the writing of Tremaine McDowell, one of the founders of the ambitious new program at the University of Minnesota that began in 1945. In a 1948 monograph McDowell surveyed the state of this field. And while his expansiveness echoed that of Walt Whitman, whom he repeatedly quoted, no words proved more potent than the postwar ideals of "reconciliation" and "unification." Thus, his opening chapter stressed the need to reconcile "past-minded colleges and a present-minded public" by linking past, present, and future—what McDowell called "uniting the tenses" (and would later be called "relevance").[21] Studying different regions would counter the destructive effects of an earlier and more divisive "sectionalism." As for studying the nation, McDowell hoped to see Dewey's term "cultural nationality" replace "nationalism," a word, he declared, that had been discredited by "the crimes committed in its name." At the same time internationalism would counter both imperialism and isolationism. (While McDowell recognized the potential danger of American "economic imperialism," in 1948 he considered this less a "deterrent to the creation of a world community than is our isolationism.") Thus, American studies would foster "the reconciliation of the tenses, the reconciliation of the academic disciplines, and . . . reconciliation of region, nation, and world."[22]

Similar sentiments are evident in *American Quarterly*, the first American studies journal, founded at the University of Minnesota in 1949 and moved to the University of Pennsylvania in 1951. According to its first editor, the literary scholar William Van O'Connor, its goal too would be to bridge all sorts of divisions. "*American Quarterly* will attempt to find the common area of interest," O'Connor's editorial statement began, between "specialists" and "the aware reader." This journal would publish "studies in the culture of America, past and present" written by academics and nonacademics. It would also try to reconcile national and international concerns, for its first issue would focus on "American world influences."[23]

Among the most popular means of bridging differences were interdisciplinary symposia, conferences, and institutes, usually organized around extremely broad themes. Princeton began sponsoring symposia in American civilization in 1942–43; among the publications ensuing from this program were *Foreign Influences in American Life* (1944), *The Constitution and World Organization* (1944), *Evolutionary Thought in America* (1950), and *Socialism and American Life* (1952). Penn's American Studies Club organized the 1948 Benjamin Franklin

Lectures around the theme of "Changing Patterns in American Civilization"; scholars discussed literature, science, religion, philosophy, and the "contemporary scene" in roundtable discussions with students as well as in public lectures.[24] Most striking in its efforts at educational outreach was the University of Minnesota's summer program, a one-week, noncredit institute in American studies for teachers and the nonacademic public. In 1946 this institute included such lectures as "The American Novelist and American Society," taught by the novelist James T. Farrell, "American Folkways," taught by Philip Jordan, "High Culture and Popular Culture," taught by Alfred Kazin, and "The Music of the American Negro," taught by the African American poet Sterling Brown.[25] "The voice of America is indeed the voice of Dewey, Watson, Whitehead, and their colleagues," McDowell noted, "but it is also the voice of folk say and folk song."[26]

Another postwar outcome was the creation of American studies programs abroad, particularly in Europe. While a few academic exchanges had been established in the prewar decades, most European professors had paid scant attention to American subject matter, and many still saw the United States as "a country wholly materialistic in its outlook, without genuine culture."[27] By contrast, the postwar era created new opportunities for a small group of "pioneering" Europeans who specialized in the study of the United States. Among these were Sigmund Skard, who filled the new chair in American literary history established by Norway's parliament at the University of Oslo in 1946, and Arie den Hollander, who began teaching "Americanistics" at the University of Amsterdam in 1947.[28] As the cold war intensified, both the U.S. government and private foundations massively increased their funding for foreign libraries, guest professorships, and American studies activities abroad, thus reinforcing an ever more problematic and suspect relationship between the study of American culture and the promotion of American foreign policy. Yet equally important, Skard insisted, was a "reorientation among the Europeans themselves" in responding to the "simple pressure of events." "Discrepancy between the position of the United States in the world and its place in syllabuses and curricula," Skard explained, "had long been growing; after 1945 it proved intolerable."[29]

Exemplifying these new interactions was the Salzburg Seminar in American Studies, first conceived by Harvard students and begun in 1947 (and held annually thereafter). The first of these drew nearly one hundred students, teachers, artists, writers, journalists, and labor leaders from seventeen European countries. Meeting in Schloss Leopoldskron, an Austrian eighteenth-century rococo palace, they discussed American literature, history, economics, sociology, and fine arts with a faculty that included F. O. Matthiessen, Alfred

Kazin, Margaret Mead, and Walt Rostow. In the wake of the war, Matthiessen declared, he and his colleagues had come to Europe "to enact anew the chief function of culture and humanism: to bring man again into communication with man." Henry Nash Smith, who taught in Salzburg in 1948, concurred, for he saw the very strangeness of the new subject matter as encouraging dialogue among a group of Europeans who would "almost certainly fall into mutually repellent factions if they were invited to discuss abstractions like international good will." Such material was hardly irrelevant, moreover, given "the weight of the United States in the modern world"—and the fact that the American army still occupied Salzburg.[30]

Similar concerns are evident in the establishment of the American Studies Association in 1951, for according to its first president, Carl Bode, it too would work to promote interdisciplinarity while eschewing "intellectual isolationism." In fact, the ASA's first major project was an international conference, "Europe's View of America Today," held at the Library of Congress in 1952. Among those invited were professors who had taught abroad in the incipient Fulbright program.[31]

In these and other ways academics from a variety of backgrounds institutionalized American studies. Their goal, they repeatedly declared, was to construct a new field that would explore the distinctive development of "American civilization" by including materials from a variety of art forms as well as a range of disciplines. More broadly, they hoped to unify the study of literature and history, the humanities and the social sciences, and past and present, thereby explaining the functioning of American culture as a coherent "complex whole."

New Types of Scholarship: Linking Interdisciplinarity and "Americanness"

With its "holistic" emphasis, the early American studies movement proved particularly attractive to academics interested in breaking down traditional disciplinary boundaries. Especially enthusiastic were literary scholars alienated from the reigning ahistorical paradigm then dominating English departments, "New Criticism." Those interested in the serious study of American art and music found an academic home as well. Also attracted were historians and social scientists interested in learning each other's methods, including the historian Richard Hofstadter, the sociologist David Riesman, and the anthropologist Margaret Mead, all of whom wrote articles, reviewed books, and served on the editorial board of *American Quarterly*.

Particularly liberating in opening up new areas for study was the justification of exploring the arts not merely for their aesthetic qualities but for their worth as historical documents illustrating broader cultural changes. As early as 1927 Vernon Parrington had employed this strategy in his influential study, *Main Currents in American Thought*, for this English professor had chosen "to follow the broad path of our political, economic, and social development, rather than the narrower belletristic."[32] Such an approach allowed Parrington to reconsider American colonial literature, a body of writing hardly worth studying if one's criterion was the exemplary use of the English language, but important if used to illuminate the historic development of American democratic ideals. An even better model for interpreting literature in the postwar era was F. O. Matthiessen's *American Renaissance* (1941), a richly textured analysis of five nineteenth-century authors whose "one common denominator," Matthiessen argued, was "their devotion to the possibilities of democracy," and whose writings reflected a striking self-consciousness about their identities as Americans.[33]

The "Americanness" issue allowed scholars to reconsider what were often provincial or marginal works in complex and original ways. For instance, as the art historian Wanda Corn has argued, by emphasizing historical contexts and cultural difference, scholars could explore the visual appeal of American painting "without having to apologize for the fact that it did not measure up to the innovation and originality of its European peers." Thus, the portraits of John Singleton Copley, though clearly inferior to English aristocratic portraits of the same era, could be studied as examples of "middle-class, democratic, American-style portraiture," and scholars could interpret Winslow Homer as a distinctively American "pragmatic realist," rather than as an "Impressionist *manqué*."[34]

Particularly self-conscious in spelling out such an argument was the 1948 study *Made in America* by John Kouwenhoven, who taught American studies at Barnard. "Culture, the theory goes, is brought here from Europe by 'carriers'"—that is, by artists who had migrated or by Americans who had studied abroad. Instead, Kouwenhoven chose to study what he labeled American "vernacular culture," a type of art "developed by people 'who didn't know anything about art.'" Such a strategy allowed Kouwenhoven to analyze design elements and decorative motifs found in useful American artifacts from farm tools to steamships to cast-iron washstands in strikingly new ways.[35]

Similar strategies proved useful in other fields—fields in which American accomplishments might hardly merit a footnote if framed within a traditional European intellectual or aesthetic tradition. For instance, one could talk about the Americanness of American music, or the Americanness of American philosophy, or even the Americanness of American science, and thereby reframe academic debates in ways that challenged traditional canons.

Especially productive was the new approach to Puritanism originated by Perry Miller, who taught in Harvard's American civilization program. Miller was much more than a "historian of ideas," insisted Murray Murphey, a professor in Penn's department, for "the point was to see behind the ideas, to grasp the emotions, the psychic strains and needs, the terrors, the mysteries, and the exaltation of Puritan inner life" in ways that offered new explanations for American distinctiveness and self-consciousness, or that illuminated what the literary scholar Sacvan Bercovitch would later call the "Puritan origins of the American self."[36] According to the cultural historian Michael Denning, within American studies it was Puritan studies that provided an exemplar of the "interdiscipline," for it was precisely the "distance, even marginality, of the Puritans from the canons of orthodox literary criticism, historiography, political science, sociology, and religious studies, combined with their presumed centrality to American culture," that generated "a richness of interdisciplinary work."[37]

American studies proponents often used similar arguments to legitimate the study of contemporary popular materials, for although such works might possess few obvious aesthetic qualities, one could still analyze them for what they suggested about broader cultural patterns. For instance, as Carl Bode argued in 1950, if nearly all anthologies of American literature included the seventeenth-century poem "The Day of Doom" by the Puritan minister Michael Wigglesworth, a work "practically bare—so it has seemed to almost every critic—of literary merit," then why not study the writings of the twentieth-century clergyman Lloyd Douglas, the author of the best-selling religious novels *The Robe* and *The Big Fisherman*? The American studies scholar could "afford to study *The Robe* in the same way that he studies 'The Day of Doom,'" Bode insisted, for "both cast light on the popular mind."[38]

In its first decade, in addition to countless articles on the writers of the American Renaissance, *American Quarterly* published articles on hot-rod culture and football; on the nineteenth-century "scribbling women" who wrote popular stories for *Godey's Lady's Book* and on the sporting journalism published in *Spirit of the Times*; on the ideas of Edward Bellamy, Chauncey Wright, and Thorstein Veblen; on Currier and Ives scenes, the engravings found in nineteenth-century gift books, and camp meeting hymnody; and on numerous other subjects that rarely received scholarly attention. Such studies were, as critics would later claim, overwhelmingly Eurocentric. In fact, quite a few explored the effects of European-American cultural exchange explicitly, in ways that understood culture in one or the other of its two meanings. Thus, they might deal with the influence on American artists of studying in Italy, or the influence on American college students of serving as ambulance drivers in France during the First World War.[39] Despite their disparate subject matter, many authors saw themselves as illuminating pieces of a larger pattern that defined a distinctive American cultural whole. Within this decade American studies scholars also developed a set of paradigms that helped to unify such findings.

Unifying Paradigms: "Myth-and-Symbol" and "National Character" Studies

The potential promise of this new interdisciplinarity seemed evident with the publication of the first postwar American studies classic, Henry Nash Smith's *Virgin Land: The American West as Symbol and Myth.*[40] In 1950 the very word "myth" bridged boundaries—temporal, spatial, and disciplinary. "Myth" and "symbol" were literary concepts used by the New Critics. At the same time anthropologists routinely documented the culturally distinct myths believed by the peoples they studied, and psychoanalytic theories stressed the universality of mythmaking, a meaning popularized in Joseph Campbell's 1949 best seller, *The Hero with a Thousand Faces.* In the context of World War II, "myth" also acquired a new political significance, for many saw the belief in myths (such as the "economic myths about the Jews") as fomenting war, a meaning echoed in the anthropologist Ashley Montagu's influential 1942 study, *Man's Most Dangerous Myth: The Fallacy of Race.*[41]

Smith's uses of the terms "myth" and "symbol," as critics would later point out, were neither precise nor consistent, but they were suggestive and original. As his student Barry Marks explained, Smith "welded together the imagistic concerns of literary critics, the focus on folktales, songs, and mythology of cultural anthropologists, and the emphasis on perception of psychologists and sociologists" and used the concept that emerged to reinterpret American history.[42] Most striking in hindsight is the degree to which Smith's history took what would later be called "the linguistic turn," for in using the close reading techniques employed by the New Critics to reinterpret different types of written materials, his book showed how language, metaphor, and discourse had subtly shaped historical perception and even behavior.

Smith framed his study as a critique of the writings of Frederick Jackson Turner. Whereas historians had analyzed Turner's social and economic arguments, Smith focused on Turner's "poetic account of the influence of free land as a rebirth, a regeneration, a rejuvenation." Such metaphors were mythic rather than economic, Smith argued, and "threaten to become themselves a means of cognition and to supplant discursive reasoning." They resonated so deeply with American audiences (including historians) because they had been invoked so frequently in discussing "the West."[43]

Virgin Land explored these intersections among language, literature, history, politics, and psychology by interpreting a range of writings from the colonial era to Turner's day. These included creative works by Walt Whitman and James Fenimore Cooper, the political rhetoric of Ben Franklin and Thomas Jefferson, folk legends about Daniel Boone and Kit Carson, and prose produced by long-forgotten minor authors, local politicians, economic boosters, railroad promoters, and journalists. Most evocative were Smith's readings of nineteenth-century dime novels. Although these stories about Deadwood Dick and Calamity Jane lacked "every vestige of the interest usually sought in works of the imagination," Smith conceded in analyzing works usually shunned by English departments, they were worth studying for their historical value, for they suggested "an objectified mass dream, like the moving pictures, the soap operas, or the comic books that are the present-day equivalents."[44] Historians of 1950 apparently agreed, for this book by an English professor won the American Historical Association's Dunning Prize and its Beveridge Prize as well as the Bancroft Prize in history.

Several writers soon followed Smith's lead in analyzing long-standing historical patterns of American mythmaking and symbolic discourse. John William Ward's study *Andrew Jackson: Symbol for an Age* (1955) explored the language of nineteenth-century presidential image making, including the words found in political cartoons and in an 1822 popular song praising Jackson's exploits. R. W. B. Lewis, in *The American Adam: Innocence, Tragedy, and Tradition in the Nineteenth Century* (1955), hoped to identify "the first tentative outlines of a native American mythology" by studying the ways that novelists, historians, and clergymen had used the terms "innocence, novelty, experience, sin, time, evil, hope, the present, memory, the past, tradition."[45] By the mid-1950s "myth-and-symbol" studies, with their rich linguistic analyses, psychoanalytic insights, surprising fusions of highbrow, middlebrow, and lowbrow, and sweepingly broad conclusions demonstrating a common pattern of verbal and visual imagery throughout much of American history, had largely come to define American studies scholarship.

If the focus on myth linked the concerns of humanists with those of social scientists, so too did a second concept closely connected with American studies and accentuated by the war, "national character." Although works of this type had a long and dubious history, the 1950s version was loosely based on the "culture-and-personality" studies of the 1930s—studies that tried to connect anthropological and sociological theories of group behavior with theories of individual development proposed by psychologists and psychoanalysts. Part of a broader effort to reject race as an explanatory concept, these studies explained group differences as the result of child-rearing techniques, education, and socialization. And though such studies had seemed largely theoretical in the 1930s, they were apparently put to practical uses during World War II, when Margaret Mead, Ruth Benedict, Erik Erikson, and many others were asked to conduct similar studies for the government.[46]

It was not only Americans who saw such questions as important, however, for foreign scholars too had much to say on this subject; in fact, in the decade following 1942, during which about 3 million American soldiers and civilians passed through Britain, English writers alone produced nearly fifty books analyzing "American character."[47] In the postwar era American studies scholars would try to connect culture-and-personality theories with insights from both contemporary observers and astute visitors of the past, such as Alexis de Tocqueville (whose *Democracy in America* was republished in 1945). In such work democracy itself often became a trait closely associated not only with American culture but also with American character.

The most sophisticated effort to mix social scientific research on culture-and-personality with historical evidence was *The Lonely Crowd*, produced in 1950 by David Riesman and his coauthors, Reuel Denney and Nathan Glazer. Strongly influenced by neo-Freudians like Erich Fromm, Riesman hoped to develop what he called a "socially oriented psychoanalytic characterology" that could be applied to "problems of historical change." Toward this end, he tried to expand the types of evidence usually considered by historians. "Like the anthropologists," he explained, "the psychoanalysts had been insistent on the importance of previously neglected or underprivileged data: fleeting memories, dreams, the games of children, the modes of weaning, the symbolic content of advertisements, popular stories, and films—all had become the stuff of history." They also had "the temerity to tackle whole cultures" in trying to link a "type of character structure in childhood to the adult society's mode of production, love, war, and folklore." The goal of such scholarship was "to see what went with what, what hung together, how a society channeled its drives of sex and aggression."[48] Particularly memorable was Riesman's new language of historical "characterology," with its emphasis on the shift from a formerly "inner-directed" nineteenth-century character type toward an increasingly "other-directed" twentieth-century type. With its suitability for a variety of college classes, its surprising appeal to general audiences, and its haunting title, a shorter 1955 paperback version eventually became the best-selling book ever by an American sociologist.[49]

By the mid-1950s all these theories had blended to produce a recognizable pattern of American studies scholarship. Such studies encouraged the exploration of a wide range of American cultural materials. Many scholars, however, ultimately explained what they found in terms of common patterns of mythmaking, or as illustrating common traits inherent in the American character, or as illuminating the functioning of a common "American mind." And though later scholars would find such interpretations embarrassingly chauvinistic and politically naïve, they did legitimate the academic study of new kinds of data, new types of research questions, and new versions of inter-disciplinary synthesis.

Too Little Inclusion: "Assimilating" Differences

In considering this version of studying American culture "as a whole," most disturbing in hindsight is the way it dealt with—or, rather, failed to deal with—different experiences. Instead, the "consensus" scholarship of the cold war era largely continued the wartime pattern of maximizing national unity while minimizing conflict. In much of this scholarship the most divisive issue of all, racial discrimination, seems invisible. For other scholars, however, the strong emphasis on assimilation itself suggested racial progress, particularly when the very belief in racial difference was labeled "man's most dangerous myth." Several articles published in *American Quarterly* during these years il-lustrate the tensions inherent in these efforts to assimilate racial and ethnic differences.

Among the most intriguing, both for what it suggests about this discipline and for what it reflects about the culture it was describing, is a 1950 article entitled "Hollywood as a Universal Church." In this study the critic Parker Tyler analyzed five postwar films that dealt with what he called "the com-monplace act of 'passing'" by Jews and blacks: *Gentleman's Agreement* (1947), *Crossfire* (1947), *Home of the Brave* (1949), *Lost Boundaries* (1949), and *Pinky* (1949). All ultimately presented Hollywood's "garden variety of success epic," but their "true content," Tyler argued, included more than "the ostensible message of social toleration which they carry like a picket sign."[50]

The most famous was *Gentleman's Agreement*, which starred Gregory Peck as a gentile journalist researching anti-Semitism. By simply changing his name (and nothing else), Peck "passes" for Jewish. The film's deeper message, Tyler wrote, lay in its "automatically reversible logic," for it suggested that a "Jew may successfully masquerade as a Gentile just as a Gentile may successfully masquer-ade as a Jew. Isn't this the *easiest way* to deal with prejudice?" (Other evidence from the 1940s also shows this film being interpreted in just this way. "I'll never be rude to a Jew again," one stagehand apparently told the scriptwriter Moss Hart, "because he might turn out to be a Gentile.")[51] The implicit message in *Crossfire* was that Jewish soldiers "who passively and naively accept their Jewish-ness (that is, do nothing to 'improve' accent, or physiognomy or mannerism) are open to victimization." Such a film was "anti-Semitic," Tyler argued, "only in that its absolutist creed is *pro-assimilative*." "Amazingly enough," he continued, "the Negro films follow suit" in presenting racial differences as "fables of mere illusion despite the indelible sign of black skin which, in two cases, 'haunts' the protagonists." *Home of the Brave*, a film about a black soldier, was based on a play about a Jewish soldier; in both versions, the harassed protagonist, suffering psychosomatic paralysis, is cured by an "omniscient army psychiatrist." The film character is "enabled to walk again through the destruction of his delusion that a black skin is a fatal curse," Tyler wrote; "he is restored . . . by yet another delusion: that some sort of neutral skin color exists in the abstract, indeed, the very 'color' that is meant by 'equality' on the democratic politico-economic 'palette.'" *Lost Boundaries* told the true story of a black doctor who passed for white, whereas in *Pinky* a woman light enough to pass chose to remain black. In Hollywood's America, prejudiced individuals existed, but institutions—churches, the army, the police, and even Southern courts, Tyler noted cynically—were shown as "nondiscriminating toward race." "Assimilation," he explained, was thus repeatedly portrayed as "a sensational transformation act that has an excellent chance of success." Yet at the same time, these films were also exploring a deeper issue, for the "pith of the matter," Tyler argued, had largely been missed by most reviewers: "It is nothing but the problem of 'identity,'" he insisted, "of whose 'mistaken-ness' they have made such straight-faced sport with Jew and Negro."[52]

Yet if the question of racial or ethnic identity or the problems of discrimination were occasionally raised in such articles, they were rarely explored. Interest in popular culture did lead some American studies scholars to write about subcultural differences, such as the revival of "ragtime" among jazz aficionados or the use of "Yinglish" in borscht-belt comedy records with names such as *Bagels and Yox*.[53] In a few cases interest in social scientific studies of "the antagonisms between nations, between classes, and most of all between ethnic groups" might lead a scholar such as John Higham to link his own research on the history of American nativism to the broader question of "why men hate."[54] Such explorations, however, were largely exceptions to the more dominant belief that the best way to deal with difference was essentially by ignoring it or, more precisely, by assimilating it within a larger national whole.

Exemplifying this assimilationist ideal, for instance, is another *American Quarterly* article that probably surprised 1950s readers: "The Negro Cowboy." "Who knows, today, about the Negro cowboy and his contribution to the making of the West?" Philip Durham asked. Western novelists had largely assumed that "all readers are white and that only a white cowboy can be a hero"; if scholars switched their evidence to autobiographies, however, the Negro cowboy suddenly appeared, for in the real West, Durham reported, "Mexican, Negro and white 'vacqueros'" had all worked together harmoniously. Thus, while accepting uncritically the romantic characterization of the cowboy, and of Western history, Durham nonetheless insisted that the same mythic standards be applied "equally to the Negro cowboy," who also "became a part of the spirit of the West—a spirit which demanded a conscience but cared little for color."[55]

Although the power of this assimilationist ideal is evident in 1950s writings, at the same time a field explicitly concerned with linking past and present could hardly ignore the bitter conflicts being brought to public consciousness by the civil rights movement. From the mid-1950s through the 1960s an increasing number of *American Quarterly* articles focused on slavery and antislavery, segregation, and styles of black leadership. The deeper problem, however, was the impossibility of simply "assimilating" such materials into the larger narrative of the American past that still dominated "consensus" scholarship—a narrative that linked American culture and identity to the spread of democracy and belief in equality. Such questions had to await a far more profound confrontation with the history of American "democratic" institutions, and with the United States' thoroughly racialized past.

Too Much Inclusion? Battling over Chewing Gum

If early American studies scholarship strikes the modern-day reader as painfully exclusionary, a body of work that ignored most of the experiences of non-whites in analyzing "the culture of the whole," in its own day it failed to elicit such criticism. To the contrary, if American studies scholarship was criticized, it was usually for the opposite—being too inclusive.

Voicing one such complaint, for instance, was Max Beloff, an Oxford professor who spent time visiting Minnesota's American studies program. And though finding much to praise, Beloff feared that "the corollary of a democratic educational system is that all subjects of study must be treated as though they were born free and equal." American studies scholars ought to disentangle "the significant from the insignificant," he recommended. As far as he and other European scholars were concerned, it was in "the political and social sphere" that Americans had contributed something truly worth studying, and not in areas such as folk music or regional art. After all, did anyone seriously believe "that American folklore is as vital to America (still less to the rest of the world) as American social philosophy," he asked, or that "Paul Bunyan is as important as Thomas Jefferson"?[56]

Some of the sharpest criticism came from reviewers of one of the most paradigmatic projects of the early American studies movement, the massive *Literary History of the United States*, published in 1948. This three-volume work, produced under the general editorship of Robert Spiller, Willard Thorp, Thomas Johnson, and Henry Seidel Canby, editor of the *Saturday Review of Literature*, with assistance from fifty-one other contributors, surveyed "the books of the great and the near-great writers in a literature which is most revealing when studied as a byproduct of American experience." Its goal was to present "a whole view of literature" that would emphasize "the unity of art with the total sum of human experience and its moral values."[57]

The project's objective, Daniel Aaron summarized in his review, was to "weld belles-lettres, folklore, political writing, journals, orations, and travel literature 'into a single massive framework,' as the dust jacket puts it." Yet for Aaron, the fact that the chapters were "smoothly linked" and "the joints skillfully mortised and puttied" only accentuated "the elaborateness of the fabrication. The unity that results," he concluded, "is not organic; indeed, it is not really necessary."[58]

Far more critical was Leslie Fiedler's review. Such scholarship, Fiedler argued, was undermined by its assumption that "social values and critical standards are scarcely distinguishable." Fiedler resented the entire "MacLeish-inspired drive to make our literature safe for democracy," for such values contorted literary criticism. Thus, he mocked Willard Thorp's assertion that Carl Sandburg's *The People, Yes* was "one of the great American books." It was "oriented toward the common man and that is sufficient," he summarized; "the fact that it is poorly written" and "technically a mess" was "not even discussed." Even as sensitive a critic as F. O. Matthiessen, when facing the "good democratic doctrine" of Stephen Vincent Benét, had let himself be "bullied into confusion." Thus Fiedler quoted Matthiessen's assessment that " '*John Brown's Body* has kept its largest following among readers under twenty.' (Mr. Matthiessen originally wrote 'among high school students,' but the editors generously raised the limit.)" "But such an audience," Matthiessen had added, was "not to be scorned in a democracy." "Why *not*?" Fiedler insisted. "The whole problem arises if the critic abdicates his obligation to judge" and confuses "the criteria of literary excellence with the program of political liberalism." Such scholarship was the product of the "academic, middle-brow, liberal mind," a type of mind that "finds the confines of the university intolerable" and instead tries to make "knowledge available to the nonacademic, middle-brow mind, or, as it prefers to say, 'humanity.' " Such a mind, he declared, was the antitype to the artistic mind.

Most objectionable of all to Fiedler was the way this holism hid what he considered "the mid-twentieth-century climax of our art: the astonishing peak of artistic achievement and the acute shrinkage of a responsive audience."[59] Serious artists, he reported, were having a hard time making a living. Yet one would hardly know this by the way the editors had blurred the distinction between their work and the popular media. Thus, Spiller had reported that "American fiction and drama of the screen were beginning to dominate the imagination of the masses throughout the world, although of this striking fact the American intellectual was as yet scarcely aware."[60] "Betty Grable dominates the imagination of the world," Fiedler declared contemptuously. "Poor American intellectual! . . . He is cast in the role of villain throughout—the America Firster of the literary world." Yet it was precisely such an intellectual who was crying the loudest that "our culture at its most vulgar" was dominating the world, Fiedler replied, "though he does not, indeed, make this his proudest boast."[61]

As such controversies suggest, American studies, with its version of holism, was being constructed in the midst of a much larger and increasingly international mass culture debate, during a decade that witnessed both the rise of television and congressional hearings on the dangers of comic books. Deciding how, or even whether, to integrate American popular materials into a college curriculum posed problems. Social scientists had been the first to do so; much of their work, however, focused on gauging political influence rather than on assessing aesthetics. English departments dominated by New Critics had walled themselves off from such materials, as had most intellectuals across the political spectrum who were skeptical of if not hostile to the new media. Typifying this hostility was Dwight Macdonald, who rejected the very term "popular culture" and instead used "mass culture," for he saw these materials not as art but as articles produced "for mass consumption, like chewing gum."[62]

Yet while the new media were largely being attacked, several scholars associated with American studies tried to defend them. Among these was John Kouwenhoven. In an essay entitled "What's 'American' about America," presented both to the Columbia University Seminar on American Civilization and to readers of *Harper's* in 1956, he blurred the distinctions between high-, middle-, and lowbrow while once again linking all of American culture with American identity. Thus, answering his own question, Kouwenhoven analyzed a dozen "distinctively American" cultural items that had first emerged on his side of the Atlantic: the Manhattan skyline, the gridiron town plan, the skyscraper, the Model-T Ford, jazz, the Constitution, Mark Twain's writing, Whitman's *Leaves of Grass*, comic strips, soap operas, assembly-line production, and, most notably, chewing gum.[63] What they all shared, he argued, was a preference for process over final product. In fact, even with "no other visible sign of the national preoccupation with process," he continued, "it would be enough to point out that it was an American who invented chewing gum (in 1869) and that it is the Americans who have spread it—in all senses of the verb—throughout the world. A nonconsumable confection, its sole appeal is the process of chewing it." It was in just such products, Kouwenhoven wrote defiantly, that one could best locate American culture, in "so far as Americans have been 'American'" and not "mere carriers of transplanted cultural traditions."[64]

While Macdonald and Kouwenhoven disagreed over the cultural meaning of chewing gum, one could hardly deny the fact that the United States was certainly spreading something throughout the world. In fact, a number of early American studies articles documented precisely this phenomenon. Thus, one researcher analyzed responses to American drama in Occupied West Germany, where the U.S. government had translated and disseminated fifty recent plays. In postwar France, another reported, a monthly literary review regularly included the "scarifying titles of California thrillers." A Fulbright student in Japan told of tuning into a "Japanese radio quiz program (this, in itself, United States-inspired . . .)" in time to hear a housewife address "the 6,400 Yen question": "With what war was Abraham Lincoln associated?" (to which she correctly answered the "North-South War"). The 1953 film *Roman Holiday* "was, if possible, more popular in Japan than in the United States," he stated, "and the number of Japanese girls who as a result display Audrey Hepburn hairdo's must run into the millions."[65]

For the Yale literary scholar Harry Levin, the vogue of American culture in the postwar world could best be explained "by remembering three brusque words used by Thomas Hobbes to account for the authority of the classics: 'Colonies and Conquests.'" "Along with the Marshall Plan go jeeps and jukeboxes, CARE packages and foreign-language editions of the *Reader's Digest*; along with our products we export our culture—'culture' not in Matthew Arnold's terms," he carefully specified, "but in Ruth Benedict's patterns."[66]

By 1958, according to the journalist and American studies scholar Eric Larrabee, it had become impossible to discuss America "as a civilization" without "making a deferential bow to its most lowbrow arts," including jazz, the movies, and comic strips. "These indigent relatives, nurtured on crumbs from the high-culture table, have come to dinner to stay," he stated. "Indeed, they threaten to expropriate the family name." American popular materials, Larrabee reported, were playing a particular role internationally. "America not only has a popular culture," he declared, "it is *the* popular culture."[67]

Yet if some American studies scholars had come to embrace the forms of culture that Macdonald disparagingly christened "masscult" and "midcult," others would increasingly resist them. Over the next two decades, this battle would be fought within a field that was beginning to envision itself not merely as an interdisciplinary collaboration, but as a university discipline in its own right.

Methodological Criticism and Disciplinary Self-Consciousness, 1957–1975

By the late 1950s American studies seemed to be flourishing. According to a new survey, by 1958 the number of U.S. degree-granting programs in the field had risen to ninety-five, of which at least five had achieved departmental, rather than interdepartmental, status.[68] Several new publications would be started, including those later known as the British *Journal of American Studies* (begun in 1956), *American Studies* (1960), *American Studies International* (1962), *Canadian Review of American Studies* (1970), and an annual entitled *Prospects* (1975).[69]

Yet at the same time the very nature of this enterprise was changing, for if postwar American studies had suggested an exploratory openness and a desire to reach out to a broad public, scholarship in the post-Sputnik era would instead reward methodological rigor and professional specialization. In 1959 David Riesman could already speak wistfully of a past era of "methodological messiness" and "often grandiose generalizations" fading away. By 1960 he could write of "the good old days of not so long ago, when large error and large enthusiasm went hand in hand."[70] In the decades that followed, the very idea of describing American history in terms of a national "consensus" would seem increasingly absurd, particularly as conflicts over civil rights and the Vietnam War intensified. During the same years, the methods that American studies scholars most frequently used to bridge differences—between high-, middle-, and lowbrow art forms, between the humanities and the social sciences, even between history and literature—would themselves become the subject of fierce debate.[71]

The start of this debate is usually dated to a 1957 *American Quarterly* article entitled "Can 'American Studies' Develop a Method?" written by this movement's most prominent scholar, Henry Nash Smith. American studies, Smith summarized, studied "American culture, past and present, as a whole." The phrase "as a whole" did not imply "a global attack," he conceded, but an effort to view subjects "from new perspectives." Yet the very concept of culture posed problems, he noted, for it embraced "the concepts 'society' and 'art,'" which were pulling scholars in different directions. Whereas social scientists, increasingly led by quantifiers, believed that "all value is implicit in social experience, in group behavior, in institutions, in man as an average member of society," literary scholars, led by the New Critics, asserted that works of art "exist on a plane remote from the Waste Land of our actual experience." For Smith the goal of American studies should be to "resolve the dilemma posed by the dualism which separates social facts from esthetic values."[72]

While focusing on these differences between scientific and humanistic approaches, Smith's article also noted differences in types of literature. "Why is it not conceivable," he asked, "that the masterpiece . . . might turn out to be an expression of the culture in ways beyond the scope of stereotyped examples of popular art"? After all, "complex meanings" were "just as real" as popular fantasies. A "hundred years ago it might have been said that they make up the whole of culture," he declared. "I believe the social sciences have reacted too strongly against Matthew Arnold's view of culture," Smith now asserted, for a "fully adequate science of society will recognize the existence and the importance of the experiences and attitudes with which Arnold was concerned." "Contemporary American culture is no doubt frightening enough," he concluded, "but it is made unnecessarily appalling by studies of popular art which by implication define the culture without reference to any subtleties beyond the horizon of the mass media. There is more to us than that!"[73]

Increasingly problematic, others would note, was the long-standing collaboration between literary scholars and historians. If American studies researchers were using literature mainly to reveal history, Louis Rubin argued in 1957, then "the more imaginative the work of literature, the less 'accurate' it seems to be as history." Such usages, he concluded, were limiting and misguided. "Our major writers *should* be able to tell us more about our country's life than their less perceptive contemporaries," Rubin argued, "and if it seems to work out the other way," then perhaps the fault lay "in the way we try to use their work." Perhaps American studies scholars were failing to consider a novel "as a novel at all but as a document." For Rubin, it was America's greatest writers who could best "draw multitudinous experience together into one coherent artistic image, and tell us what American life means."[74]

By the 1960s several scholars associated with the University of Minnesota program had begun to explore an issue central to cultural critics since Arnold's day—the role of the artist in an age dominated by machinery. Leo Marx's seminal 1964 study, *The Machine in the Garden*, built upon Henry Nash Smith's research by showing how the introduction of technology had affected the mythic longing for an American pastoral utopia. Like many other critics of contemporary mass culture, Marx deplored the ways that this longing had led to a "mawkish taste for retreat into the primitive" as "exemplified by TV westerns and Norman Rockwell magazine covers." Yet the same impulses, he now argued, had also challenged "the imagination of our most respected writers," for their work showed evidence of a "heightened sensitivity to the onset of the new industrial power." A year later Alan Trachtenberg developed an equally original way to explore the meaning of art in a mechanical age, for he studied the Brooklyn Bridge as both technological feat and aesthetic symbol.[75]

If these myth-and-symbol studies reflected some of the cultural concerns of humanists, scholars associated with Penn's program, in particular Anthony Garvan and Murray Murphey, spoke for this field's more social scientific aspects. They agreed with Richard Sykes, whose 1963 article, "American Studies and the Concept of Culture," challenged Smith and Marx by conceptualizing American studies as "a specialized branch of cultural anthropology."[76] Strongly influenced by the Penn anthropologists J. Irving Hallowell, Ward Goodenough, and Anthony F. C. Wallace, Garvan tried to use anthropological categories to classify such diverse items from eighteenth-century Boston life as Samuel Sewall's diary and a Winslow sugar bowl, while Murphey sought more precise ways to link historical data with psychoanalytic theories in exploring changes in child rearing. Penn's American civilization program would also work closely with historical archeologists and would begin teaching its majors quantitative methods, particularly those used by social historians trying to gain a better understanding of everyday life.[77] The central question of how to use literature to understand culture, however, would continue to generate the most controversy.

A 1969 article by Leo Marx entitled "American Studies: A Defense of an Unscientific Method," published in the first issue of *New Literary History*, showed just how different the two approaches were becoming. It was the "judgment" implicit in the indispensable "concept of 'high' culture," Marx argued, that "marks a crucial distinction between the methods of the humanist and the social scientist." Such scholarship relied on "the established canon—a selection, we trust, based on the collective wisdom, which presumably includes the most fully realized, complex and powerful (hence enduring) work of American writers." By embodying "the highest development of literary consciousness," this canon offered "a major source for the humanist in his continuing effort to recover the usable past." Though previous scholars had used literature to reveal "some body of extra-literary experience," such as "the social life of a nation, or the 'spirit of the age,'" such criteria were no longer necessary, Marx stated, for they could be replaced by the criterion of "literary power," which meant the "inherent capacity of a work to generate the emotional and intellectual response of its readers." And though seemingly "ahistorical," this was actually a "more reliable and useful measure of historical significance than the older, relatively superficial test of representational value." Of course, Marx saw the irony in what he was proposing, for it meant that the "key doctrine of the generally anti-historical 'New Criticism'"—that literary works be assessed solely for their artistry—was now "being incorporated into the essentially historical enterprise of American Studies."[78]

Yet if this version of American studies seemed to be drawing closer to New Criticism, Penn's was moving in another direction. The "literary people," Murphey explained, believed that "the finer the artistry . . . the greater the weight." Social scientists believed the opposite, for though they conceded the evidentiary value of best sellers, the "highly crafted belletristic work with a small audience was highly suspect." "Over this issue," Murphey reported, "the attempt at interdisciplinary fusion foundered." The problem was institutional as well as intellectual, he believed, for English departments were "built upon the principle that the greater the aesthetic merit . . . the greater the attention." Murphey too was critical of how literature had been used in the past. "It is not necessary to assume that great writers are accurate observers of their societies or that they somehow express the dominant 'myths' (whatever they are) of a people in order to give literature a role in the culture," he argued. "The better method is to try to determine what role literature really does play." Instead of simply combining disciplines, Penn's American Civilization Department would hire its own literary scholars who could then ask new questions about "the cultural function of literature."[79] In 1974 the first product of this new approach appeared in an *American Quarterly* article pointedly entitled "Literature and the Historian," in which the Penn professor R. Gordon Kelly used anthropological and sociological theories to explore the didactic function of nineteenth-century children's literature.[80]

If the battles over what constituted American literature were just beginning by the late 1960s, a far more intense conflict over what constituted American history was already well under way. In analyzing this conflict, Jonathan Wiener has traced the crucial role played by a group of radical historians whose scholarship challenged interpretations that emphasized "consensus" by exposing structures of exploitation, domination, and oppression within American society. Included were works by William Appleman Williams on American imperial power, Gabriel Kolko on the power of corporate elites, Herbert Gutman on working-class culture, Eugene Genovese on Southern slaveholding, and Warren Susman on 1930s political culture. Though these scholars were often harassed or excluded from the profession during the McCarthy era, their ideas gradually moved from the margins to the center of historical debates in the decade following 1958. By 1968 even Richard Hofstadter, one of the historians most associated with consensus scholarship, had begun to frame questions in ways that legitimated the issues raised by radicals. "Whose participation in a consensus really counts?" Hofstadter now asked. "Who is excluded from the consensus? Who refuses to enter it? To what extent are the alleged consensual ideas of the American system . . . actually shared by the mass public?" Writing in an era marked by antiwar protests, racial violence, generational clashes, and political assassinations, Hofstadter too saw the need for new histories that would include "our slave insurrections, our mobbed abolitionists and lynched Wobblies, our sporadic, furiously militant Homesteads, Pullmans, and Patersons; our race lynchings and ghetto riots."[81]

For American studies scholars, both new histories as well as new literary theories intensified the need for new methods, for older techniques previously used to blur differences no longer seemed able to hold the field together. During the same years the two paradigms that had united this field in the past—myth-and-symbol scholarship and national character studies—would both come under concerted attack. Neither would emerge unscathed.

While the very idea of an American national character had always produced skeptics, during the 1950s and early 1960s this research had been sustained by its close ties to social science studies. In 1963, for instance, Michael McGiffert's bibliography surveying the literature on national character seemed hopeful, for he saw psychologists, anthropologists, and sociologists working to "build bridges which will join conceptually what is felt to be united in experience." Updating this survey six years later, however, McGiffert reached a different conclusion. "It is not clear in 1969, as it was thought to have been in 1963," he reported, that this field could rely any longer on social science theories. The "culture-and-personality approach has fallen on dry days," he concluded, for anthropologists had made "little headway" in working with "large, complex, modern national societies."[82] In 1971 David Stannard challenged such studies directly. Margaret Mead's writing, for example, was "filled with descriptions of the problems encountered by 'the American mother' and 'the American father,' and with explanations of what goes on, for instance, at 'the American breakfast table.'" For Stannard, such generalizations could no longer be taken seriously. "What mother? What father?" he asked. "Indeed, perhaps most telling of all—what breakfast table?"[83]

While national character studies, with their sweeping generalizations, were being seriously challenged, a similar challenge undermined myth-and-symbol studies, with their equally sweeping assumptions. The strongest blow came in a 1972 article by Bruce Kuklick. Entitled "Myth and Symbol in American Studies," it offered a devastating critique of the philosophical errors and methodological inconsistencies in the ways these authors had used the very term "myth." More broadly, while Kuklick challenged Marx's arguments about the special historical significance of "great novels," he also criticized common assumptions about "the relation of 'popular culture' to ordinary life" that had long shaped American studies scholarship. Such scholars had been "persistently eager to speak of 'the anonymous popular mind,' 'the widespread desire of Americans,' 'the imagination of the American people,' 'the majority of the people,' 'the popular conception of American life,' 'the American view of life' or 'the average American,'" Kuklick summarized. "The 'literate public' that reads popular books is much larger in number than the intellectuals," he conceded. Still, it was "by no means 'everyone,'" and "without hesitation American Studies scholarship has jumped from the 'literate public' to everyone." Thus, Kuklick quoted Smith's comment in *Virgin Land* that "most Americans would have said during the 1880's that the Homestead Act had triumphantly borne out the predictions of the 1860's [concerning the growth in numbers of yeoman farmers]." "If opinion polls today are any indication," Kuklick added, then "most Americans of the 1880's would not have heard of the Homestead Act."[84]

All these challenges illustrate the shattering of the postwar consensus long used to explain not only American culture but also American character.[85] These tensions were reflected in the contrast suggested by the title of Robert Sklar's *American Quarterly* article, "American Studies and the Realities of America." By 1969 Sklar, along with Robert Merideth, Betty Ch'maj, and several others, had formed an American studies "Radical Caucus" that would hold its own meetings, produce its own publications, and pressure the ASA and *American Quarterly* to respond more directly to social issues.[86]

For foreign scholars, these issues were equally disturbing. Allen Davis, then executive secretary of the ASA, vividly recalled the explosive atmosphere at a Bicentennial World Regional Conference of Americanists held at Schloss Leopoldskron (home to the Salzburg Seminar) in 1975, a year that "found the United States at perhaps its lowest reputation at any point in the twentieth century," for many attendees were intensely critical of the war, wary of accepting U.S. grants, and "nervous about selling out to American cultural imperialism." As Denis Donoghue, then president of the Irish American Studies Association, explained, "You think you are talking about an American novel, but before you are well begun you find yourself reflecting on the exercise of power in the world"—something that was "not an issue in, say, Irish Studies."[87]

By the 1970s many American studies scholars perceived their field to be in crisis. In the three decades since the end of World War II, American studies had been transformed from a loosely organized interdisciplinary enterprise confident of its methods and its messages to a professionalized, self-conscious, and increasingly self-doubting discipline. The decades that followed would bring even starker changes, for a broader process of transformation was already under way.

Deconstructing American Studies:
Inclusion as the "Cultures" of the Parts

If American studies as a field was in trouble, it was not reflected in enrollments. Statistically, this discipline had continued to thrive in a period that saw an enormous expansion of higher education. Between 1958 and 1973 the number of U.S. undergraduate American studies programs had grown from 95 to 243, of which 32 were independent departments, while the number of doctoral programs had tripled.[88] A similar expansion was evident abroad; in Europe, for instance, the number of Americanists had grown to about two thousand by the 1980s.[89] Even so, both the largely unfruitful "search for a method" and the gradual loss of faith in any consensus proved deeply disturbing, for they had led to the undermining of nearly all the techniques initially used to construct this field but no agreement on new ones.

Yet while many practitioners expressed frustration, others found the new situation liberating, for it allowed this discipline to be "deconstructed" and then "reconstructed" in new ways. Between the 1960s and the 1980s American studies as a discipline can be said to have been deconstructed in two broad senses. The first refers to social and political changes that gradually transformed the academic community. The second reflects theoretical changes reshaping both the social sciences and the humanities in ways that would once again move them closer to each other. Especially taken together, both radically transformed American studies.

First, American studies was in a sense deconstructed by the establishment of separate university programs exploring women's studies, African American studies, Native American studies, Chicano studies, and Asian American studies beginning in the late 1960s. Some of these programs would model their versions of interdisciplinary scholarship on American studies, or share close links, but others had their own ideas about the proper relationship between the university and the communities they saw themselves as representing and serving. In either case, their very establishment raised questions about the ability of American studies scholars to speak for any common "culture of the whole."

Equally important in deconstructing this field were new theories emanating from a range of disciplines. Especially influential was the anthropologist Clifford Geertz's *Interpretation of Cultures* (1973). Unlike Benedict and Mead, whose ethnographies strove for broad syntheses linking whole national cultures with personality patterns, Geertz presented "thick descriptions" of the local and the particular. He also offered "an alternative to the then-ascendant scientism of the social sciences," one anthropologist has noted, for Geertz saw culture as consisting of "meanings encoded in symbolic forms" that could best be understood through "acts of interpretation analogous to the work of literary critics."[90]

Even more radical were theories reshaping the humanities, including the deconstructionist arguments of Jacques Derrida, the discourse analyses of Michel Foucault, and works by a variety of structuralist, post-structuralist, postmodernist, Marxist, and feminist theorists. Largely emphasizing subjectivity and extreme relativism, such theories undermined belief in the legitimacy of any "master narrative." They also made explicit the political content hidden within many of the dichotomous terms that had once seemed so "natural"—terms such as "male" and "female," "black" and "white," and even those that the New Critics had fought so hard to uphold, "high" and "low." In the new version of cultural criticism that gradually emerged, all "texts" (including those by social scientists) were appropriate subjects for deconstruction, as were all canons.[91] Thus, ironically, under the imprimatur largely of new European theories, many American English professors finally felt free to analyze American popular culture. For these scholars, new versions of "cultural studies" led to renewed interest in American studies.[92]

The results of both movements were evident in the ways that practitioners discussed American studies, for this field would increasingly be conceptualized less as a "complex whole" than as a set of parts. For example, in writing one of the first intellectual histories of American studies in 1979 (in honor of the *American Quarterly*'s thirtieth anniversary), Gene Wise discussed the dominant ideologies evident in key texts from the 1920s through the 1950s. The late 1960s he labeled the " 'coming apart' stage." Harder to label was his own era, the late 1970s. And while he did identify several trends, including "a pluralistic rather than a holistic approach," a "rediscovery of the particular," an "emphasis on proportion rather than essence," and a "cross-cultural, comparative dimension," he also resorted frequently to describing the field in a series of lists. For instance, instead of exploring a common "American Experience," Wise wrote, "we look upon America from a variety of different, often competing perspectives—popular culture, black culture, the culture of women, youth culture, the culture of the aged, Hispanic-American culture, American Indian culture, material culture, the culture of poverty, folk culture, the culture of regionalism, the culture of academe, the culture of literature, the culture of professionalism, and so on."[93]

Yet if American studies seemed to be fragmenting, largely as the result of political, social, and methodological challenges, it was also simultaneously undergoing a process of reconstruction. In particular, new scholarship would focus new attention on how the culture itself had constructed the very categories that led to a variety of identities. The impetus for such studies would come mainly from the entrance into the academic world of large numbers of women and minorities. Works by both groups would revitalize American studies, for they too would ask questions about the relationship between American culture and American identity.

Culture, Identity, and Gender: Rethinking Women and "Midcult"

While the 1960s women's movement challenged many disciplines, it found a relatively welcoming home within American studies. The reasons for this reception were not merely political; they were also intellectual. In particular, feminist scholars asked new questions about the relationship between culture and identity in ways that resonated for scholars of American studies.

For instance, no popular book proved more important to the feminist movement than Betty Friedan's 1963 blockbuster, *The Feminine Mystique.* A former student of Erik Erikson's, Friedan followed her famous opening chapter, "The Problem That Has No Name," with two chapters whose very titles suggest their affinities for American studies scholarship: "The Happy Housewife Heroine" and "The Crisis in Woman's Identity."[94] Three years later the historian Barbara Welter published "The Cult of True Womanhood, 1820–1860" in *American Quarterly.* Explicitly seeking the historical roots of the contemporary problem Friedan had exposed, Welter explicated the nineteenth-century doctrine of "separate spheres." By carefully delineating the traits attributed to "True Womanhood," she provided a newly gendered version of historical "characterology." Somehow, this "True Woman" had "evolved into the 'New Woman,'" Welter argued. "And yet the stereotype, the 'mystique' if you will, of what woman was and ought to be persisted," she concluded, "bringing guilt and confusion in the midst of opportunity."[95] Equally important, Welter's evidence came not only from traditional historical sources such as diaries, papers, and autobiographies but also from nineteenth-century women's magazines, gift books, religious tracts, and best-selling middlebrow novels—in short, from precisely the types of cultural materials that many American studies scholars had long been interested in, and that Macdonald had disparaged as "midcult."

"The idea of separate spheres," as elaborated first by Welter and then by countless others, Linda Kerber has argued, "took on a life of its own." Whereas earlier histories had stressed the "inexorable march toward the suffrage," these studies offered new "categories, hypotheticals, and analytical devices" that allowed historians to "escape the confines of accounts of 'great ladies' or of 'the progress of women.'"[96] Other historians too would find in American studies an excellent training ground or a receptive audience for new kinds of women's history. Among these would be Kerber herself, for she had been John

Kouwenhoven's student at Barnard. "I do not believe it is an accident that the classic articles which revitalized feminist scholarship in the 1960s were written by people who thought of themselves as American Studies scholars and often appeared in American Studies journals," Kerber argued.[97]

Within literature, too, the feminist movement focused new attention on the relationship between culture and identity, and on nineteenth-century midcult materials, in ways that revitalized scholarship. Among the most stunning was Ann Douglas's 1971 article, "The 'Scribbling Women' and Fanny Fern: Why Women Wrote," which reexamined the relationships connecting female authorship, the marketplace, and personal autonomy. Even more provocative was Nina Baym's 1981 study, "Melodramas of Beset Manhood: How Theories of American Fiction Exclude Women Authors," for she took as her subject the shaping of the classic American canon.[98]

"The earliest American literary critics," Baym argued, had talked about "the 'most American' work rather than the 'best' work because they knew no way to find out the best other than by comparing American to British writing." To avoid this problem, they had created "a standard of Americanness rather than a standard of excellence. Inevitably, perhaps, it came to seem that the quality of 'Americanness,' whatever it might be, *constituted* literary excellence." This idea of the "most American" was based not on "the statistically most representative or most typical, the most read or the most sold," but on some "qualitative essence" determined by the critic. "Before he is through," Baym continued, "the critic has had to insist that some works in America are much more American than others, and he is as busy excluding certain writers as 'un-American' as he is including others." Those ultimately chosen almost all turned out to be "white, middle-class, male, of Anglo-Saxon derivation" who had expressed a slight alienation from the "so-called 'mainstream.'" And though earlier critics had seen in this modest alienation the "very essence of the culture," Baym instead classified such writing as a "consensus criticism of the consensus." Obviously excluded, she noted, were nearly all women writers as well as many others who had evidently chosen to write about the wrong themes.[99]

By 1975, a year in which only one woman (of eight) served on the editorial board of *American Literature* and one (of nine) on the board of the *Journal of American History*, the board of *American Quarterly*, under its editor, Bruce Kuklick, would be nearly half female (five of twelve).[100] By 1984 this journal would have its first woman editor, Janice Radway. Radway's own research focused on one of the "lowest" forms of literature, cheap formulaic romances. In *Reading the Romance: Women, Patriarchy, and Popular Literature*, she combined a historical analysis of the paperback marketplace, close textual readings of romances, and feminist psychoanalytic theories of personality development. Also added would be a new element that fit well with Penn's program: ethnographic interviews with the women who read them.[101]

Culture, Identity, and Race: Rethinking the "Folk" and the "Modern"

If the reexamination of the relationship between the formation of women's identities and the marketing of midcult materials would link feminist with American studies scholarship, integrating American studies with African American studies would be a more complex process. Although John Hope Franklin became ASA president in 1967 (he would become president of the OAH in 1975 and of the AHA in 1979), the organization still had few black members. "For all the rhetoric of cooperation," Allen Davis has written in exploring the history of the ASA in this era, "the Association of Negro Life and History met in the same cities and at the same time as ASA in 1971 and 1973 with little cooperation between the two groups."[102]

Yet in this field, too, a number of intellectual debates would increasingly engage a new generation of African American scholars with questions of particular concern to American studies, for much of this scholarship would also focus on the relationship between culture and identity. One of the first controversies to raise such questions was triggered by the historical debate over Stanley Elkins's work on "slave personality," which led to a broader and deeper reconsideration of the "Sambo" slave caricature. In response, historians of slavery, among them John Blassingame, addressed this issue by incorporating anthropological research on African culture into their work. This new scholarship reconsidered slave culture by documenting the powerful functioning of African folk materials—musical instruments, funeral rituals, courting rituals, conjurers—in shaping resistant and rebellious slave "identities." By the 1970s complex explorations of slave music, religion, and oral traditions in writings by Lawrence Levine, Albert Raboteau, Dickson D. Bruce, and others began to delineate the "Africanness" of African American culture and, through it, of American culture.[103]

Influential as well in demolishing older ideas about American folk traditions was a 1975 article by Alexander Saxton entitled "Blackface Minstrelsy and Jacksonian Ideology." At least since the scholarship of Constance Rourke in the 1930s, minstrel shows had been described as embodying mythic and comic folk material. Saxton's research showed minstrelsy to be less a folk tradition and more an early illustration of the mass marketing of racist images for political purposes. Like much of the best work in American studies, his essay offered a close reading of visual and verbal materials—makeup, costuming, characterization, and song lyrics—as well as a provocative exploration of covert psychological themes—the use of masks, latent sexual and homosexual content, the depiction of the South as the repository for memories of rural childhoods, the use of comedy to disguise violence and brutality.[104] Saxton's article, Eric Lott has argued, "helped close the coffin on the sort of nostalgic indulgence of blackface that ruled American scholarship on the topic into (unbelievably) the 1960s."[105] It also suggested the need to reconsider the era that had been the focus of much older American studies scholarship—the age of Jefferson and Jackson—by juxtaposing the rhetoric of white egalitarianism against the realities of black slavery.

While some scholars of African American life were exploring forms of subversion and resistance evident in folk culture, others began to take a closer look at the meanings of "modern" culture, particularly by reexamining the Great Migration and the artistry of the Harlem Renaissance. In fact, if new scholarship on the interplay between culture and identity would lead to a re-examination of the emergence of the "New Woman," the same would be true of the "New Negro," as evidenced in the writings of Nathan Huggins, David Levering Lewis, Robert Stepto, Houston Baker, and others.[106] In his *American Quarterly* article "Modernism and the Harlem Renaissance," Baker sought to describe a "constellation" that included "Afro-American literature, music, art, graphic design, and intellectual history" and that was "*not* confined to a traditionally defined belles letters." He also connected folk, popular, and elite cultural forms (e.g., blues, the rhetoric of moral and religious "uplift," modern novels) in exploring the emergence of common African American discursive traditions. "Baker's work," Robert Stepto has argued, "proves that nothing intrigues African Americanists more than seeing African America's discourse whole."[107]

By 1982, a year in which there were no African Americans on the editorial board of either the *Journal of American History* or *American Literature, American Quarterly* had added to its board both the literary scholar Kenny Jackson Williams and Henry Louis Gates Jr., then chair of African American Studies at Yale. In the years that followed, African American studies and American studies would begin to work together in ways that opened up rich new areas for reconsideration and exploration.[108]

Typifying this new relationship were the experiences of Mary Helen Washington. While intensely involved in establishing a politically engaged black studies program at the University of Detroit in the 1970s, Washington had no connections to or interest in American studies. Urged by friends to attend the ASA's San Diego convention in 1985, however, she was surprised to find that this organization might become "another home." While in San

Diego, she and others tried to establish closer contacts with Chicano and Asian American scholars. Such efforts had international repercussions, for they linked American studies more closely to the cultures of Latin America and the Pacific. Over the next decade, Washington came to view ASA conventions as "the principal gathering place where ethnic studies constituencies meet each year in our own border-crossing dialogues."[109]

By 1997 Washington had become the ASA's first black female president. The historian George Sánchez, author of *Becoming Mexican American*, would become its first Latino president in 2001. Succeeding him was Stephen Sumida, a scholar of Hawaiian literature who became the organization's first Asian American president. Members also made new efforts to reach out to Native American scholars, for included in the 2003 *American Quarterly* was a forum entitled "American (Indian) Studies: Can the ASA Be an Intellectual Home?"[110] Within American studies explorations of the interconnections linking culture, identity, and race had moved beyond black and white.

Epilogue: Inclusion and Exclusion, Wholes and Parts, Past and Present

After surveying the dynamics of inclusion within American studies, determining just what has changed—and what hasn't—is not necessarily obvious. In many ways American studies has undergone a startling transformation. Constructed in the 1940s largely as a white, male, Eurocentric quest for a holistic American cultural identity, by the century's end it had become a home to multiculturalism and new versions of "identity politics." Whereas its founders had confronted fascism by extolling American democratic ideals, many scholars of the post-Vietnam era produced increasingly sharp critiques of American racism, sexism, and imperialism—so sharp, in fact, that some critics would call such work "Anti-American Studies."[111] In a field once defined by myth-and-symbol and national character studies, more recent proponents such as John Carlos Rowe have labeled their version of American studies "post-nationalist"; in an age of globalization, cultural fusions, and increasing border-crossings, their writings emphasize the "constructedness of both national myths and national borders."[112] These forces have also transformed American studies abroad. In the 1940s American faculty took their field to Salzburg; by the 1990s Salzburg professor Reinhold Wagnleitner had produced his own interpretation of European-American cultural interaction in *Coca-Colonization and the Cold War*. Especially striking are the comments of the Japanese scholar Masako Notoji in exploring the complex functioning of cultural products internationally. "American popular culture is not the monopoly of Americans," Notoji argued; "it is a medium through which people around the world constantly reorganize their individual and collective identities."[113]

During these decades "inclusion" has become an increasingly self-conscious goal. Yet while redressing some of the most glaring and painful exclusions of the past, new versions of inclusion and interdisciplinarity have also posed challenges. For instance, as George Lipsitz has argued, though theories privileging language have led to a richness in textual interpretation, they also risk reducing all American experiences to "simply one more text." "It is one thing to say that discourse, ideology, and textualization are inevitable and necessary parts of social experience," Lipsitz warns, "but it is quite another thing to say that they are the totality of social experience. As a quip reported by Jon Wiener phrases it," Lipsitz added, " 'Tell that to the Veterans of Foreign Texts.' "[114]

Even more provocative are the challenges posed by multiculturalism. By the century's end, this concept had led to rich new interpretations of the American past. Western history, for instance, has largely been rewritten by scholars paying close attention to the interactions among Native Americans, Latinos, Asian Americans, African Americans, and various groups of "whites."[115] At the same time, however, multiculturalism has also generated a massive body of scholarship exploring its meaning and implications. And though this includes fierce attacks by critics eager to restore the traditional canon and curriculum, more intriguing are issues raised by scholars long active in and sympathetic to American studies.[116]

Among these was John Higham, who challenged his colleagues in a 1993 *American Quarterly* article, "Multiculturalism and Universalism." Ironically, it was Higham who had first used the word "consensus" in 1959 to criticize many of the histories then being written—histories, that is, largely drained of conflict.[117] Designing a new course in 1991 entitled American Identities: Belonging and Separateness in the U.S.A., he focused not only on the frequently studied categories of race, gender, ethnicity, and (less often) class, but also on other formations, including what he called "visionary identities" (e.g., socialists). It was the challenge and accomplishments of "the multicultural idea," Higham reported, that "goaded me to try to be more inclusive than multiculturalists themselves seemed to want to be." Still, this historian of immigration insisted upon conceptualizing the American nation as more than a federation of subcultures, for it included "many millions who will never conceive of themselves in those terms." "An adequate theory of American culture," Higham argued, "will have to address the reality of assimilation as well as the persistence of differences."[118] Others, too, feared that the emphasis on difference was shortchanging historical analysis of the equally complex construction of "belonging"—an idea captured in the title of a 1993 article by David Hollinger, "How Wide the Circle of the 'We'?"[119]

In more subtle ways, however, new versions of American studies bear some striking resemblances to their forebears. Especially suggestive is the analysis of multiculturalism offered by Gerald Early, director of African and Afro-American Studies at Washington University. "It is the sense of the private, the inward, the spiritual, the psychological that makes multiculturalism so curious and so curiously American," he argued in responding to Higham. Intriguingly, Early recognized in multiculturalism "a recrudescence of Puritanism: an intense therapeutic aestheticization of the anxieties of self-consciousness. The aim of multiculturalism is to make everyone in America intensely self-conscious about being *American*," Early wrote, "that is to say, self-conscious about a history of victimization and oppression . . . where everyone is entitled not simply to a room but to a culture of one's own."[120]

Equally provocative in considering past and present is the analysis offered by Michael Denning. A professor of American studies at Yale, Denning explored his field's complicated and historically ambivalent relationship to Marxist cultural theories—evident not only in 1930s works associated with what came to be called the Cultural Front, but also in 1980s studies of what scholars called the culture of consumption. Denning also compared British cultural studies of the 1950s, particularly works by Raymond Williams and Richard Hoggart, with American studies of the same era. "In 'cultural studies,'" he noted, "the central questions—'what is culture?,' 'what are its forms and how is it related to material production?'—formed a more productive theoretical agenda . . . than did the question 'What is American?'"[121]

Perhaps in response, Leo Marx recalled that as a Fulbright professor in England in 1957, he'd met Hoggart, whom he admired. Hoggart told him of an American studies scholar who, in explaining his field, had blurted out, "But you don't understand, I *believe* in America!" For Marx this comment was telling, for he too saw the study of American culture as linked to a belief in an identity connected to a set of ideals. In considering contemporary scholarship, Marx lamented the fact that many Americanists "no longer considered the United States as a whole—the nation-state, the government, national institutions generally—a worthy subject of teaching and research"; he still held to the "conviction, unpopular nowadays, that the distinctive character of American nationhood is an ineluctable premise of American studies."[122]

Marx also linked the history of his field with his own personal history. After entering Harvard in 1937, he'd become active in the idealistic leftist politics of the Popular Front. After graduating, he spent four years in the navy before reentering university life. At that time, "American Studies, by virtue of its newness and its democratic standards of equality, helped to open the doors of the sacred patriarchal grove" to "Jewish, Irish, German, Polish, and other non-WASP white males. (The turn of women and non-white people was still ahead.)" All these experiences gave his generation their "distinctive take on the subject of Americanness" as well as a "special concern with issues of American identity." It also led, in later decades, to a "willingness to open the gates of the profession to blacks, women, and other people of color."[123]

Over these decades, American studies changed from a search for a "culture of the whole" to more specialized studies of the cultures of its parts. Still, continuities as well as changes are evident—particularly in its attempts to integrate the many meanings of culture, its desire to bridge disciplinary divides, its explorations of the historical construction of what has variously been called character, personality, and identity, its awareness of the international significance of American cultural products, and its efforts to expand and to legitimate the study of new subject matter within universities. In 1954 John Everett traveled to Europe to confer with his educational counterparts; his reflections after this meeting suggested the intertwining of two issues that would shape this academic enterprise: "What is culture?" and "What is American?" Half a century later, these issues remain as contentiously intertwined as ever.

Notes

1. John R. Everett, "American Culture in the World To-Day: Reflections on a UNESCO Meeting," *American Quarterly* [hereafter *AQ*] 6 (Fall 1954): 245–252.

2. Everett is quoting E. B. Tylor's 1871 definition of culture. According to the anthropologists A. L. Kroeber and Clyde Kluckhohn, in France as of 1952 "the modern anthropological meaning of culture has not yet been generally accepted as standard, or is admitted only with reluctance, in scientific and scholarly circles." *Culture: A Critical Review of Concepts and Definitions* (New York: Vintage Books, 1952), 12–13.

3. Everett, "American Culture," 245–252.

4. Kroeber and Kluckhohn, *Culture*, 3.

5. Matthew Arnold, *Culture and Anarchy*, ed. Samuel Lipman (1869; rpt New Haven: Yale University Press, 1994).

6. E. B. Tylor, *Primitive Culture* (London: J. Murray, 1871).

7. Philip Gleason, "Identifying Identity: A Semantic History," *Journal of American History* 69 (Spring 1983): 910–931.

8. Eric Larrabee mockingly referred to "Coca-Colonization: A Cause that Refreshes?" in *Creating an Industrial Civilization: A Report on the Corning Conference*, ed. Eugene Staley (New York: Harper, 1952), 95. This idea was in use in Europe at the time, for the French feared they would be "*coca-colonisés*." See Richard Kuisel, *Seducing the French: The Dilemma of Americanization* (Berkeley: University of California Press, 1993), 37–69, and Reinhold Wagnleitner, *Coca-Colonization and the Cold War: The Cultural Mission of the United States in Austria after the Second World War* (Chapel Hill: University of North Carolina Press, 1994).

9. Philip Gleason, in "World War II and the Development of American Studies," *AQ* 36,

Bibliography Issue (1984): 343–358, makes a powerful case for the influence of the war on this field. His arguments are supported by the start of so many programs immediately following the war, as reported in Tremaine McDowell, *American Studies* (Minneapolis: University of Minnesota Press, 1948), 26. Starting dates for some programs differ among historical sources, as do the number of programs in any given year.

10. On the importance of Beard's example, see Thomas Bender, "Wholes and Parts: The Need for Synthesis in American History," *Journal of American History* 73 (June 1986): 120–136. Philip Gleason notes the popularity of Benedict's work in "Americans All: World War II and the Shaping of American Identity," *Review of Politics* 43 (1981): 483–518, esp. 487–488.

11. Joan Shelley Rubin, "'Information Please!' Culture and Expertise in the Interwar Period," *AQ* 35 (Winter 1983): 500.

12. Michael Denning, *The Cultural Front: The Laboring of American Culture in the Twentieth Century* (New York: Verso, 1997), xx. Denning notes a "distinctly plebeian accent" in both mass culture and high culture in this era. See also Joan Shelley Rubin, *The Making of Middlebrow Culture* (Chapel Hill: University of North Carolina Press, 1992); Warren Susman, "The Thirties," in *The Development of an American Culture*, ed. Stanley Coben and Lorman Ratner (Englewood Cliffs, N.J.: Prentice-Hall, 1970), 179–218; and William Stott, *Documentary Expression and Thirties America* (1973; rpt. Chicago: University of Chicago Press, 1986).

13. Gleason, "World War II" and "Americans All." On fears of fascism and MacLeish's influence, see Brett Gary, *The Nervous Liberals: Propaganda Anxieties from World War I to the Cold War* (New York: Columbia University Press, 1999). See also MacLeish's speeches collected in *A Time to Speak* (Boston: Houghton Mifflin, 1941) and *A Time to Act* (Boston: Houghton Mifflin, 1943).

14. Benjamin Fine, "U.S. History Is Made Chief Subject of Maryland University Freshmen," *New York Times*, February 7, 1945, 1, 19.

15. O. Fritiof Ander, "The New Augustana Plan and an American Studies Major," *Mississippi Valley Historical Review* 32 (June 1945): 95–100.

16. McDowell, *American Studies*, 41, 43–44.

17. Murray G. Murphey, "American Civilization at Pennsylvania," *AQ* 22 (Summer 1970): 489–502.

18. Robert Spiller, "Review of Tremaine McDowell, *American Studies*," *AQ* 1 (Summer 1949): 166–169.

19. Robert Spiller et al., *Literary History of the United States* (New York: Macmillan, 1948), 1373.

20. William Graebner, *The Age of Doubt: American Thought and Culture in the 1940s* (Boston: Twayne, 1991), 70.

21. Linda Kerber notes the connection between this early effort to link past and present and the later 1960s emphasis on "relevance" in "Diversity and Transformation in American Studies," *AQ* 41 (September 1989): 417–418.

22. McDowell, *American Studies*, 82–96.

23. William Van O'Connor, "Editorial Statement," *AQ* 1 (Spring 1949): 2.

24. Tremaine McDowell, "Review of Robert Spiller, ed., *Changing Patterns in American Civilization*," *AQ* 1 (Fall 1949): 280.

25. McDowell, *American Studies*, 79–80.

26. McDowell, "Review of Spiller," 282.

27. Max Beloff, "The Projection of America Abroad," *AQ* 1 (Fall 1949): 27.

28. Richard Pells analyzes the role of American studies in the context of a broader transatlantic relationship in *Not Like Us: How Europeans Have Loved, Hated, and Transformed American Culture since World War II* (New York: Basic Books, 1997). This first generation of Americanists "thought of themselves as pioneers," Pells reports. See 111–123.

29. Sigmund Skard, *American Studies in Europe: Their History and Present Organization*, 2

vols. (Philadelphia: University of Pennsylvania Press, 1958), 2: 641. Skard mentions that his position was created by the Norwegian Parliament, 1: 7.

30. Henry Nash Smith, "The Salzburg Seminar," *AQ* 1 (Spring 1949): 30–37; Skard, *American Studies in Europe*, 2: 635–636.

31. Carl Bode, "The Start of the ASA," *AQ* 31, Bibliography Issue (1979): 351; Charles Manning, "ASA Conference Report and Constitution," *AQ* 5 (Spring 1953): 89–91.

32. Vernon Parrington, *Main Currents in American Thought* (New York: Harcourt, Brace, 1927), iii.

33. F. O. Matthiessen, *American Renaissance* (New York: Oxford University Press, 1941), ix.

34. Wanda M. Corn, "Coming of Age: Historical Scholarship in American Art," *Art Bulletin* 70 (June 1988): 188–192.

35. John Kouwenhoven, *Made in America: The Arts in Modern Civilization* (Garden City, N.Y.: Doubleday, 1948), 1–3.

36. Murray G. Murphey, "American Civilization in Retrospect," *AQ* 31, Bibliography Issue (1979): 402; Sacvan Bercovitch, *The Puritan Origins of the American Self* (New Haven: Yale University Press, 1986). See also the essays included in "James Hoopes on Perry Miller's *The New England Mind: A Symposium*," *AQ* 34 (Spring 1982).

37. Michael Denning, "'The Special American Conditions': Marxism and American Studies," *AQ* 38, Bibliography Issue (1986): 366.

38. Carl Bode, "Lloyd Douglas: Loud Voice in the Wilderness," *AQ* 2 (Winter 1950): 340.

39. Otto Wittmann Jr., "The Italian Experience: American Artists in Italy, 1830–1875," *AQ* 4 (Spring 1952): 2–15; Charles A. Fenton, "Ambulance Drivers in France and Italy: 1914–1918," *AQ* 3 (Winter 1951): 326–343.

40. Henry Nash Smith, *Virgin Land: The American West as Symbol and Myth* (New York: Vintage, 1950).

41. On the use of the concept of myth, see also Joan Shelley Rubin, "Constance Rourke in Context: The Uses of Myth," *AQ* 28 (Winter 1976): 575–588.

42. Barry Marks, "The Concept of Myth in *Virgin Land*," *AQ* 5 (Spring 1953): 71.

43. Smith, *Virgin Land*, 253–254.

44. Ibid., 91.

45. R. W. B. Lewis, *The American Adam: Innocence, Tragedy, and Tradition in the Nineteenth Century* (Chicago: University of Chicago Press, 1955), 2.

46. Philip Gleason has traced the connections among these wartime studies, the "democratic revival," and the search for a common American identity. See Gleason, "World War II." The literature on national character studies is voluminous. See Michael McGiffert, "Selected Writings on American National Character," *AQ* 15, part 2, Supplement (Summer 1963); McGiffert, "Selected Writings on American National Character and Related Subjects to 1969," *AQ* 21, part 2 (Summer 1969).

47. George H. Knoles, "'My American Impressions': English Criticism of American Civilization since 1919," *AQ* 5 (Summer 1953): 113–120.

48. David Riesman et al., "1961 Preface," in *The Lonely Crowd* (New Haven: Yale University Press, 1989), xxvi.

49. Joseph Galbo, "From the *Lonely Crowd* to *The Cultural Contradictions of Capitalism* and Beyond: The Shifting Ground of Liberal Narratives," *Journal of the History of the Behavioral Sciences* 40 (Winter 2004): 47–76.

50. Parker Tyler, "Hollywood as a Universal Church," *AQ* 2 (Summer 1950): 165–176.

51. This conversation between a stagehand and Moss Hart is cited in Graebner, *Age of Doubt*, 93.

52. Tyler, "Hollywood as Universal Church."

53. Russell Roth, "The Ragtime Revival: A Critique," *AQ* 2 (Winter 1950): 329–339; Herbert Gans, "The 'Yinglish' of Mickey Katz," *AQ* 5 (Fall 1953): 213–218.

54. John Higham, "The Mind of a Nativist: Henry F. Bowers and the A.P.A.," *AQ* 4 (Spring 1952): 16.

55. Philip Durham, "The Negro Cowboy," *AQ* 7 (Fall 1955): 301.

56. Beloff, "The Projection of America Abroad," 23–29.

57. Spiller et al., *Literary History*, xix, 1373.

58. Daniel Aaron, "Review of Volume 1 of *Literary History of the United States*," *AQ* 1 (Summer 1949): 171.

59. Leslie Fiedler, "Review of Volume II of *Literary History of the United States*," *AQ* 1 (Summer 1949): 174–180.

60. Spiller et al., *Literary History*, xx.

61. Fiedler, "Review of Volume II."

62. Dwight Macdonald, "A Theory of Mass Culture" (1953), reprinted in *Mass Culture: The Popular Arts in America*, ed. Bernard Rosenberg and David Manning White (New York: Free Press, 1957), 59. On these debates see also Paul Gorman, *Left Intellectuals and Popular Culture in Twentieth-Century America* (Chapel Hill: University of North Carolina Press, 1996).

63. John Kouwenhoven, "What's 'American' about America," reprinted in *The Beer Can by the Highway: Essays about What's American about America* (Baltimore: Johns Hopkins University Press, 1961), 42.

64. Ibid., 69, 73.

65. Mary Gaither and Horst Frenz, "German Criticism of American Drama," *AQ* 7 (Summer 1955): 111–122; Harry Levin, "Some European Views of Contemporary American Literature," *AQ* 1 (Fall 1949): 273; Hilary Conroy, "Young Japan's Anti-Americanism," *AQ* 7 (Fall 1955): 248.

66. Levin, "Some European Views," 264.

67. Eric Larrabee, "The Popular Cult of Pop Culture," *AQ* 10 (Fall 1958): 372–374.

68. Robert H. Walker, *American Studies in the United States: A Survey of College Programs* (Baton Rouge: Louisiana State University Press, 1958).

69. These journals were originally entitled *British Association for American Studies Bulletin*, *Journal of the Central Mississippi Valley American Studies Association*, and *American News*.

70. "The State of Communication Research: Comment by David Riesman," *Public Opinion Quarterly* 23 (Spring 1959): 11; Riesman, 1961 Preface, xxvi, note 5.

71. For some of the literature of this debate, see the many anthologies that tried to encompass the many positions taken. These include Edwin T. Bowden, ed., *American Studies: Problems, Promises, and Possibilities* (1958): Joseph J. Kwiat and Mary C. Turpie, eds., *Studies in American Culture: Dominant Ideas and Images* (1960); John Hague, ed., *American Character and Culture* (1964); Ray B. Browne, Donald M. Winkelman, and Allen Hayman, *New Voices in American Studies* (1966); Robert Merideth, *American Studies: Essays on Theory and Method* (1968); and Cecil Tate, *The Search for a Method in American Studies* (1973).

72. Henry Nash Smith, "Can 'American Studies' Develop a Method?" *AQ* 9 (Summer 1957): 197–208.

73. Ibid.

74. Louis D. Rubin Jr., "Tom Sawyer and the Use of Novels," *AQ* 9 (Summer 1957): 209–216.

75. Leo Marx, *The Machine in the Garden: Technology and the Pastoral Ideal in America* (New York: Oxford University Press, 1964), 5–11; Alan Trachtenberg, *Brooklyn Bridge: Fact and Symbol* (New York: Oxford University Press, 1965).

76. Richard E. Sykes, "American Studies and the Concept of Culture: A Theory and Method," *AQ* 15 (Summer Supplement 1963): 253–270.

77. Anthony N. B. Garvan, "Historical Depth in Comparative Culture Study," *AQ* 14 (Summer Supplement 1962): 260–274; Murray G. Murphey, "An Approach to the Historical Study of National Character," in *Context and Meaning in Cultural Anthropology*, ed. Melford E. Spiro (New York: Free Press, 1965), 144–163.

78. Leo Marx, "American Studies: A Defense of an Unscientific Method," *New Literary History* 1 (October 1969): 75–90. This issue was devoted to "New and Old History."

79. Murray G. Murphey, "American Civilization at Pennsylvania," *AQ* 22 (Summer Supplement 1970): esp. 495–499.

80. R. Gordon Kelly, "Literature and the Historian," *AQ* 26 (Summer 1974): 141–159.

81. Jonathan Wiener, "Radical Historians and the Crisis in American History, 1959–1980," *Journal of American History* 76 (September 1989): 399–434. Hofstadter is quoted on p. 429. See also John Higham, "Changing Paradigms: The Collapse of Consensus History," *Journal of American History* 76 (September 1989): 460–466.

82. McGiffert, "Selected Writings on American National Character," 271–272; McGiffert, "Selected Writings on American National Character and Related Subjects to 1969," 331.

83. David Stannard, "American Historians and the Idea of National Character: Some Problems and Prospects," *AQ* 23 (Summer 1971): 202–220.

84. Bruce Kuklick, "Myth and Symbol in American Studies," *AQ* 24 (Fall 1972): 435–450.

85. Gleason, "Americans All," 511.

86. Robert Sklar, "American Studies and the Realities of America," *AQ* 22 (Summer Supplement 1970): 597–605. For these events see Allen F. Davis, "The Politics of American Studies," *AQ* 42 (September 1990): 353–374.

87. Davis, "Politics," 353–354. Donoghue is quoted on p. 354.

88. These statistics are taken from Gene Wise, "'Paradigm Dramas' in American Studies: A Cultural and Institutional History of the Movement," *AQ* 31, Bibliography Issue (1979): note 38.

89. Pells, *Not Like Us*, 124.

90. Sherry Ortner, ed., *The Fate of 'Culture': Geertz and Beyond* (Berkeley: University of California Press, 1999), 1.

91. For the impact of linguistic theories in reinterpreting anthropological texts, see, e.g., James Clifford and George Marcus, eds., *Writing Culture: The Poetics and Politics of Ethnography* (Berkeley: University of California Press, 1986), and George Marcus, ed., *Rereading Cultural Anthropology* (Durham: Duke University Press, 1992).

92. On new theories, see George Lipsitz, "Listening to Learn and Learning to Listen: Popular Culture, Cultural Theory, and American Studies," *AQ* 42 (December 1990): 615–636. For a sharp critique of the use of post-structuralist theories by the "linguistic Left," see Steven Watts, "The Idiocy of American Studies: Poststructuralism, Language, and Politics in the Age of Self-Fulfillment," *AQ* 43 (December 1991): 625–660.

93. Wise, "'Paradigm Dramas,'" 293–337. For a discussion of similar trends in history, see Bender, "Wholes and Parts."

94. Betty Friedan, *The Feminine Mystique* (New York: W. W. Norton, 1963).

95. Barbara Welter, "The Cult of True Womanhood: 1820–1860," *AQ* 18 (Summer 1966): 151–174.

96. Linda K. Kerber, "Separate Spheres, Female Worlds, Woman's Place: The Rhetoric of Women's History," *Journal of American History* 75 (June 1988): 11–14.

97. Linda K. Kerber, "Diversity and Transformation," 422.

98. Ann Douglas Wood, "The 'Scribbling Women' and Fanny Fern: Why Women Wrote," *AQ* 23 (Spring 1971): 3–24; Nina Baym, "Melodramas of Beset Manhood: How Theories of American Fiction Exclude Women Authors," *AQ* 33 (Summer 1981): 123–139.

99. Baym, "Melodramas of Beset Manhood," 125–127.

100. On the *AQ* Editorial Board in 1975 were Nina Baym, Ann Douglas, Kathryn Kish Sklar, Anne Firor Scott, and Mary Turpie.

101. Janice Radway, *Reading the Romance: Women, Patriarchy, and Popular Literature* (Chapel Hill: University of North Carolina Press, 1984).

102. Allen Davis, "Politics," 364.

103. John Blassingame, *The Slave Community* (New York: Oxford University Press, 1972);

Lawrence Levine, *Black Culture and Black Consciousness* (New York: Oxford University Press, 1977); Albert Raboteau, *Slave Religion* (New York: Oxford University Press, 1978); Dickson D. Bruce, "Religion, Society, and Culture in the Old South: A Comparative View," *AQ* (Fall 1974): 399–416.

104. Alexander Saxton, "Blackface Minstrelsy and Jacksonian Ideology," *AQ* 27 (Spring 1975): 3–28.

105. Eric Lott, Commentary on "Blackface Minstrelsy and Jacksonian Ideology," in *Locating American Studies: The Evolution of a Discipline*, ed. Lucy Maddox (Baltimore: Johns Hopkins University Press, 1999), 142.

106. Nathan Huggins, *Harlem Renaissance* (New York: Oxford, 1971); David Levering Lewis, *When Harlem Was in Vogue* (New York: Knopf, 1981); Robert Stepto, *From behind the Veil: A Study of Afro-American Narrative* (Urbana: University of Illinois Press, 1979); Houston Baker Jr., *Blues, Ideology, and Afro-American Literature: A Vernacular Theory* (Chicago: University of Chicago Press, 1984) and *Modernism and the Harlem Renaissance* (Chicago: University of Chicago Press, 1987).

107. Houston Baker, "Modernism and the Harlem Renaissance," *AQ* 39 (Spring 1987): 84–97 (part of an *AQ* Special Issue on Modernist Culture in America); Robert Stepto, "Commentary on Houston Baker," in Maddox, *Locating American Studies*, 278.

108. The African-American scholars Harry Jones of Morgan State University and George E. Kent of the University of Chicago also served as members of *American Quarterly*'s editorial board before 1982. Trying to discern the ethnicity or even the gender of scholars on editorial boards of the past is often difficult, so these lists may be incomplete.

109. Mary Helen Washington, "'Disturbing the Peace: What Happens to American Studies If You Put African American Studies at the Center?" *AQ* 50 (March 1998): 1–23. For more recent reflections on this talk, see also Washington's "Commentary" in *AQ*'s "Forum on American (Indian) Studies: Can the ASA Be an Intellectual Home?" *AQ* 55 (December 2003): 697–702.

110. "Forum on American (Indian) Studies."

111. Alan Wolfe, "Anti-American Studies," *New Republic*, February 10, 2003, 25–32.

112. John Carlos Rowe, ed., *Post-Nationalist American Studies* (Berkeley: University of California Press, 2000), 3. See also the essays in Donald E. Pease and Robyn Wiegman, eds., *The Futures of American Studies* (Durham: Duke University Press, 2002).

113. Wagnleitner, *Coca-Colonization and the Cold War*; Masako Notoji, "Cultural Transformation of John Philip Sousa and Disneyland in Japan," in *"Here, There and Everywhere": The Foreign Politics of American Popular Culture*, ed. Reinhold Wagnleitner and Elaine Tyler May (Hanover, N.H.: University Press of New England, 2000), 225.

114. Lipsitz, "Listening to Learn," 621.

115. For new multicultural versions of Western history, see, e.g., Patricia Limerick, *The Legacy of Conquest: The Unbroken Past of the American West* (New York: W. W. Norton, 1987); Neil Foley, *The White Scourge: Mexicans, Blacks, and Poor Whites in Texas Cotton Culture* (Berkeley: University of California Press, 1997); Elliott West, *The Contested Plains: Indians, Gold Seekers, and the Rush to Colorado* (Lawrence: University Press of Kansas, 1998); and Linda Gordon, *The Great Arizona Orphan Abduction* (Cambridge: Harvard University Press, 1999).

116. For a discussion of some of this literature, see Lawrence W. Levine, "Clio, Canons, and Culture," *Journal of American History* 80 (December 1993): 849–867; and David Hollinger, *Postethnic America: Beyond Multiculturalism* (New York: Basic Books, 1995).

117. See John Higham, "The Cult of the 'American Consensus': Homogenizing Our History," *Commentary* 27 (February 1959): 93–100, and Higham, "Beyond Consensus: The Historian as Moral Critic," *American Historical Review* 67 (April 1962): 609–625. See also Higham, "Changing Paradigms: The Collapse of Consensus History," *Journal of American History* 76 (September 1989): 460–466.

118. John Higham, "Multiculturalism and Universalism: A History and Critique," *AQ* 45,

Special Issue on Multiculturalism (June 1993): 195–219, and Higham, "Rejoinder," in the same issue, 249–256. See also the responses from Gerald Early, Vicki Ruiz, Nancy Hewitt, and Gary Gerstle.

119. David Hollinger, "How Wide the Circle of the 'We'? American Intellectuals and the Problem of the Ethnos since World War II," *American Historical Review* 98 (April 1993): 317–337.

120. Gerald Early, "American Education and the Postmodernist Impulse," *AQ* 45 (June 1993): 220–229.

121. Denning, "'The Special American Conditions,'" 360.

122. These comments are from two memoirs: see Leo Marx, "Reflections on American Studies, Minnesota, and the 1950s," *American Studies* 40 (1999): 47–48; and Marx, "Believing in America: An Intellectual Project and a National Ideal," *Boston Review* 28 (2003), 28–31.

123. Marx, "Reflections on American Studies."

11

THE IRONIES OF THE IRON CURTAIN
The Cold War and the Rise of Russian Studies

DAVID C. ENGERMAN

THE MANY CRITICS of American Sovietology portray it as an academic discipline with deep, even fundamental flaws. Born in "the worst years of the cold war," these critics argue, the field came into being to serve geopolitical goals. From its first days, Sovietology gave into pressures that made "usable scholarship . . . in America's national interest" more important than "detached academic pursuits." The "overconcentration on 'applied scholarship' to the detriment of straight academic topics" was "regrettable"; it led to a "neglect of social and cultural trends." A common explanatory strategy is to follow the money: critics blame support from governmental and philanthropic sources for creating a field that was "ideological" in its very structure. "Capillary lines of state power" crisscrossed Sovietology and area studies more generally. The funders called on universities to "produce a large supply of skilled specialists for public service and private business." This focus on training, in turn, limited the disciplines involved; knowledge of "the cold war enemy" required only social scientists and rendered humanistic fields "invisible." Accusations of the field's political biases are ubiquitous; scholars engaged in "self-censorship"; a "feverish atmosphere" of "anti-Communist purge" excluded unorthodox views and scholars. These factors shaped the field's output, enforcing an intellectual consensus about the "uniqueness of the Soviet regime" rooted in analogies to Russia's past.[1]

There is a strong prima facie case for the indictment of Russian studies as a creature of the cold war.[2] Few areas of American academic life experienced a more rapid and thorough transformation than Russian studies did in the two decades after World War II. Before the war only a handful of isolated scholars, many self-declared cranks and misfits, devoted themselves to the study of things Russian. Only a few works from this era were of lasting value, and those came primarily from journalists and participants in left-wing political disputes.[3] By 1965 the field was booming: more than two dozen uni-

314

versities had Soviet or East European area centers; more than three thousand scholars who identified their principal interest as Slavic or Soviet belonged to Slavic-oriented professional associations and read numerous journals devoted to Russian affairs; students of Russian language numbered in the tens of thousands. The expansion of Soviet studies in an era of heightened American-Soviet tensions has led many observers to attribute the field's primary purpose to "knowing the enemy."

Yet conceiving of Russian or Soviet studies as a cold war enterprise yields at least three important ironies. First, though the original conception of Sovietology placed political science, economics, and the emergent field of behavioral sciences at its center, humanists—scholars of history, literature, and language—benefited as much as (if not more than) their social scientific colleagues. Second, though the field may have attracted attention for its role in analyzing the actions of a cold war adversary so different from the United States, intellectual trends within the field were just as likely to promote the inclusion of Russia alongside western Europe and the United States. Finally, though critics place Soviet studies at the center of cold war conformism, its practitioners, especially in its early years, brought an impressive array of political views to the topic.

These ironies are readily explained if the field's World War II origins are considered. Important organizational work for postwar Russian studies centers took place during the war against Germany, not the cold war against the USSR. America's Soviet experts in the 1940s typically saw the Soviet Union as an unreliable ally, not an implacable foe. The dynamics of grant funding also played a role. Though foundations and government supporters may have had their own aims for the field of Sovietology, scholars molded Russian studies programs to reflect their values and institutions. For both these reasons Russian studies was never simply an extension of government, even if its agencies had their hands in the formation of the field. In identifying and explaining these ironies, I do not mean to suggest that national security concerns had no role, or that no political dissenters suffered—only that these two tropes should not be allowed to crowd out other aspects of the field's evolution.

The Cold War and the Growth of Slavic Humanities

Sovietology's critics and fans alike noted the field's contributions to national security and its emphasis on the social sciences, especially political science and economics. For instance, the presidential adviser and onetime Harvard dean McGeorge Bundy celebrated the "curious fact" that "the first great center of area studies" was in the Office of Strategic Services (OSS), the wartime predecessor to the Central Intelligence Agency.[4] Indeed, the OSS's Research and Analysis Branch housed an impressive array of scholars, divided up according to world region: Latin America, Europe and Africa, Far East, and the USSR. In analyzing each region, political scientists and economists worked alongside historians. The research aims—estimates of military and economic capabilities and predictions of political stability—placed a premium on social scientific research of current events. Researchers worked closely with each other irrespective of disciplinary training; the result was an interdisciplinary research program for the Soviet Union that one historian aptly termed "social science in one country."[5] Intelligence research had little room for the humanities; the historians there performed little work of a historical nature.

According to an oft-told tale, OSS veterans returned to their old universities and departments at the conclusion of the war and transplanted that successful experience into educational institutions.[6] Tracing the field's origins to wartime intelligence serves both to emphasize the applied nature of the work as well as the field's social scientific origins. Yet there were significant differences between the intelligence model and the university programs that soon emerged. The universities expanded the definition of area studies to include not just research, but also training a new generation of area experts.[7] Focusing on training, the university programs included the humanities in area studies programs in ways very much unlike the OSS's.

The wartime model for the training component of postwar Slavic studies came from the armed services. The Army Specialized Training Program (ASTP) sought to train personnel for wartime cooperation and possible postwar occupation. Nineteen American universities hosted ASTP Slavic programs, teaching army officers a combination of history, culture, and language of the Slavic areas. The navy's Oriental Languages School in Colorado had a Russian section as well, more focused on language than area studies.[8] Postwar university-based programs drew explicitly on both OSS and ASTP models. The "relocation" of area studies programs from the wartime intelligence agencies to cold war universities thus expanded their definition to incorporate humanities scholarship.[9] Both Harvard and Columbia universities, which housed the first two major institutes in Sovietology, expanded their offerings in Slavic humanities, especially languages and literatures, albeit in slightly different forms.

The transplantation of the OSS to Columbia's Russian Institute (RI), founded in 1946, seemed most direct—yet deceptively so. The RI's founding director was Geroid Tanquary Robinson, a historian who had run the office's USSR Division; the economist Abram Bergson (who had led Robinson's economics branch) was also on the founding staff of the RI. The other key RI faculty (the legal scholar John Hazard and the historian Philip Mosely) had served in the State Department during the war. In spite of this wealth of intelligence experience, the Columbia program from the start emphasized training over research, the reproduction of knowledge over the production of new knowledge. In 1944, while Robinson was still leading the OSS's USSR Division, he argued that Columbia could perform a useful "national service" by "doing all that an academic program can do to prepare a limited number of American specialists to understand Russia and Russians." The RI's founding document reiterated this claim. Recognizing the expansion of instruction on Soviet topics, Robinson insisted that the most urgent task was "to raise the standard of existing instruction in this field and to promote research interests among those who carry on instruction." The RI's M.A. degree, in particular, aimed to train Russia experts for work in government agencies. (In the argot of Sovietology, references to unspecified "government agencies" usually meant the CIA, though they could include the State Department.) This training regimen included significant work in the humanities. Because, as Robinson put it, the Soviet Union exhibited "an extraordinary degree of uniqueness in the major elements of its life and thought," careful analysis of Russian culture and ideas became essential. Columbia's orientation, then, called for a major augmentation of humanities offerings, including both languages and history.[10]

One of the first orders of business for the four scholars leading the RI was to bring fresh blood into the Department of Slavic Languages and Literatures. Although Columbia was one of only four universities that had graduate-level instruction in Slavic languages and literatures before World War II, its department was hardly a powerhouse. The mainstays of the department represented the prewar model of scholarly curios. One of the three tenured members was a classicist who spread his limited talents thinly across both fields; another was a linguistically gifted diplomat who published a Pequot-English dictionary; the third edited a number of undistinguished translations from Polish and Ukrainian. The department faded at the end of the war, with the death of one member and the resignation of another.[11] The RI quickly arranged for the appointment of Ernest Simmons, a Harvard-trained literary scholar who had administered an experimental Russian studies program at Cornell during the war. From this inauspicious start, Columbia's Slavic Department expanded dramatically in the postwar decade, adding faculty, courses, languages, and students.

The rise of Soviet area studies at Harvard was a more complicated affair. Harvard divided research and training between separate institutions. An interdisciplinary M.A. in Soviet regional studies emerged under the aegis of a new International and Regional Studies Program in 1945. That program, devoted exclusively to teaching, incorporated a range of disciplines; the founders hoped to "make use of the lessons learned during the war in the intensive teaching of foreign languages as well as the techniques of a joint attack on social sciences and humanities on a given civilization." Its model was as much the ASTP as the OSS, complete with the militaristic metaphor.[12]

A new organization, the Russian Research Center (RRC), soon joined the Regional Program. Established in 1948 at the behest of the Carnegie Corporation, the RRC's mission was to "develop a program of research upon those aspects of the field of Russian Studies which lie peculiarly within the professional competence of social psychologists, sociologists, and cultural anthropologists."[13] Indeed, internal Carnegie memoranda refer to the RRC as Harvard's "research on problems of Russian behavior." It was perhaps the first major venture in the emerging field of behavioral sciences.[14] This particular orientation helps explain one remarkable fact about the RRC's leadership: however expert they were in behavioral sciences, none of the four members of the founding Executive Committee had studied Russian affairs or knew the Russian language. Its first director, Clyde Kluckhohn, was a specialist in Navaho culture who had spent the war analyzing the "culture and personality" of the Japanese for the Office of War Information.[15] Returning to help the sociologist Talcott Parsons establish Harvard's new Department of Social Relations, Kluckhohn had any number of skills to contribute to the RRC—administrative, methodological, and personal (he was well-connected to the wartime and postwar intelligence community)—that, in a way, compensated for his near-total ignorance of Soviet affairs.[16]

In spite of this social scientific emphasis, the RRC soon helped support a range of scholarship outside its original fields, and in the humanities in particular. The expansion of Harvard's Slavic humanities had dual sources. On the one hand, the M.A. degree in the Soviet Regional Program required linguistic competence as well as knowledge of Russian culture. And on the other, the RRC's particular emphasis on understanding Russian behavior and national character entailed some knowledge of that nation's culture. Even if behavioral scientists defined "culture" along anthropological rather than artistic lines, they recognized the need to know something about Russian literature and the arts.

Harvard's offerings in Slavic languages and literatures, minimal before World War II, quickly expanded and improved. Samuel Hazzard Cross, whose original training was in medieval Germanic literature, was the key figure at Harvard before the war. Cross taught in the Department of Germanic Languages and Literatures—typical of the taxonomic mess of pre–World War II

Slavic studies—until his death in 1946. Two years later Harvard established its Department of Slavic Languages and Literatures, though its first chair was a historian. With the establishment of the Cross Chair in Slavic Languages and Literatures in 1948, however, the department came into its own. In the next dozen years the department produced twenty degrees in language (up from one before 1948) and eighteen in literature (compared to two before 1948).[17]

Newly minted experts in Slavic languages and literatures quickly found teaching appointments, thanks to the dramatic increases in Russian enrollments at the undergraduate level. A number of contemporary sources—on the basis of woefully inadequate data—indicate that the boom in Russian-language enrollments began in the early 1940s and then steadied by 1950 or so. One language teacher credited the initial spurt to the optimism of the wartime Grand Alliance: "Only after the Russians had proved that their resistance to the Nazis would not collapse did widespread interest in things Russian grow." Another source, entirely consistent with the first, concluded that the rate of growth for Russian enrollments was greatest between 1942 and 1950.[18] Much of this increase came by the time that the Columbia and Harvard centers were established. In 1941–42 American universities offered only 27 *courses* in Slavic languages and literatures; only six years later, 140 *institutions* employed more than 240 Russian teachers.[19] The boom in Russian language, then, predated the rise of Soviet-American hostilities in the late 1940s.

The spike in enrollments created bifurcated departments of Slavic languages and literatures. While the split between scholars with Ph.D.'s and basic language teachers (often native speakers) was not unique to Slavic studies, it was especially noticeable in that subject, thanks to a large pool of émigrés employable as language teachers. Vladimir Nabokov described the divide in typically savage terms. At the bottom were those of his compatriots—female in his recounting—engaged in language teaching: "Those stupendous Russian ladies . . . who, without having had any formal training at all, manage somehow, by dint of intuition, loquacity, and a kind of maternal bounce, to infuse a magic knowledge of their difficult and beautiful tongue into a group of innocent-eyed students in an atmosphere of Mother Volga songs, red caviar, and tea." His self-inspired narrator, though better educated, had allowed his social scientific degree to lapse into a "doctorate of desuetude" while he taught elementary Russian. Then there were those professional scholars of language, residents of "the lofty halls of modern scientific linguistics, that ascetic fraternity of phonemes wherein earnest young people are taught not the language itself but the method of teaching others to teach the method."[20]

Nabokov, however, did not discuss another crucial figure in such departments: the scholar of literature. Even while departments hired native speakers to teach basic language courses, they also sought to hire and train scholars in Slavic literatures, up-to-date in the latest techniques of literary analysis. Indeed, these new scholars not only created a full-fledged profession in about a decade; they also had significant influence far outside their own departments as they helped to remake literary studies in the postwar era.

The field of history was spared this division between what colonial officers would have called "native experts" and American scholars because Russian-born and Russian-trained scholars held some of the key positions in American universities. Indeed, the two leading U.S.–based historians of the early postwar era, Michael Karpovich (Harvard, 1927–57) and George Vernadsky (Yale, 1927–56), had both studied history in Russia, where they had been classmates. Their paths to the Ivy League differed greatly, as did their contributions to the field: Vernadsky published much and taught few students, while Karpovich did the reverse.[21]

Almost all the first postwar generation historians had studied with Karpovich. He had trained a handful of scholars before the war (including Philip Mosely at Columbia), but he literally reinvented the field in his Russian history seminar in the late 1940s and early 1950s. The contrast to Geroid Robinson at Columbia is striking; Robinson had only one Ph.D. student in the two decades after he joined the faculty in 1928. One prospective student described him as "austere . . . in both appearance and personality . . . [and] incapable of exuding warmth." When the postwar generation of students contemplated historical training, most opted for Karpovich's amiability and availability. As one Moscow-based historian put it, with a combination of delicacy and residual Soviet jargon, "subjective factors" made Harvard and not Columbia the home base for Russian history after World War II.[22]

Although history did not have quite the same "service" function that language departments did, its role in the rise of Soviet studies is even more striking. Situated between the humanities and the social sciences, historical scholarship contributed greatly to the field in both quantitative and qualitative ways. Harvard's Regional Program and Columbia's Russian Institute both required significant coursework in Russian history. Furthermore, history was the single largest discipline among American scholars of Russia.

By a variety of measures, the cold war expansion of Sovietology benefited historians and other humanists more than social scientists. (History, between the social sciences and humanities, appears separately in this chapter's tables.) The field's first decade set a pattern that would not change significantly over the course of the cold war.

TABLE 11.1. Degrees in Russian Studies by Field, 1946–1956

Field	M.A. degrees	Ph.D. degrees
Social sciences	59.4%	47.6%
History	24.3%	28.0%
Other humanities	16.3%	24.4%

SOURCE: Recalculated from data in Cyril Black and John M. Thompson, "Graduate Study of Russia," in *American Teaching about Russia*, ed. Black and Thompson (Bloomington: Indiana University Press, 1957), 63.

TABLE 11.2. Junior Scholars Selected for Exchanges to USSR, 1958–1968

Field	Percentage
Social sciences	15.6%
History	35.5%
Other humanities	35.5%
Sciences	6.3%
Professional schools	6.8%

SOURCE: Inter-University Consortium for Travel Grants (IUCTG), "Policies and Procedures of the Inter-University Consortium" (1968), in CUCF, Subject Subseries: IUCTG.

Over half the doctorates in Russian studies came in humanities disciplines (table 11.1). Master's degrees recipients, however, were more likely to study the social sciences—which is not surprising, given that most were destined for nonacademic careers. (According to the results of a survey conducted in 1956, the universities had fulfilled their plan to train experts for government careers; almost 45% of those who received graduate degrees on Russian topics went to work for Uncle Sam.)[23] Other quantitative indicators, while varying slightly in the specifics, confirm that the humanities disciplines—especially if they include history—were major beneficiaries of the flow of money into Soviet studies. This trend is visible in Soviet exchange programs, fellowships, professional associations, and publications throughout the cold war.

The emergence of scholarly exchange programs with the USSR marked a major change in Soviet studies.[24] The winds of the post-Stalin thaw led, by the late 1950s, to a bilateral exchange program administered by a consortium of major universities. In the first decade of exchanges, the social sciences got very short shrift (table 11.2). The reasons for this are many: the high level of language competence expected of participants; the social scientists' emphasis on disciplinary competence; and the expected times-to-degree in different departments. Nevertheless, the skew is striking.

A more even distribution is visible in the most important (and prestigious) program funding graduate students in area studies: the Foreign Area Fellow-

TABLE 11.3. Foreign Area Fellows by Field

Field	1952–1962	1962–1972
Social sciences	49.1%	44.6%
History	35.3%	46.3%
Other humanities	15.5%	9.1%

SOURCE: *Directory: Foreign Area Fellows,* 1962–63 (New York: Foreign Area Fellowship Program, 1963), iv; and *Directory: Foreign Area Fellows* (New York: Foreign Area Fellowship Program, 1973), iii–iv.

ship Program sponsored by the Ford Foundation. While favoring the social sciences, Ford still awarded a majority of its grants to those whose disciplines were not central to contemporary political or economic analysis (table 11.3).

These tables suggest that the development of Soviet studies was a boon to the humanities. In the course of the cold war scholars in Slavic Languages and Literatures transformed their field, in the words of one participant, from a loose agglomeration of "self-styled amateurs" into a "mature" discipline.[25] Similarly, Russian history, once the province of a few isolated scholars, became the largest discipline in the growing field of Soviet studies. At the first national meeting of the American Association for the Advancement of Slavic Studies, in 1964, for instance, historians accounted for 29.7 percent of the registrants; language and literature scholars, 17.8 percent; and political scientists, only 15.0 percent.[26] Its role in the association's leadership was even greater.[27] In short, humanistic scholars dominated the field. Though the financial supporters of Soviet studies—including both foundations and government agencies—had created the field to learn more about the Politburo, they ended up creating experts on Pushkin. Though they sought insights into Lenin, they also boosted the study of Lermontov.

Slavic Humanities and the Inclusive Impulse

Not only did specialists on the Slavic world tilt toward the humanities, but their scholarship hardly was about isolating the Russian enemy, dealing only with what one Columbia official called Russia's "extraordinary degree of uniqueness." Indeed, the universalistic impulses of the 1950s found full expression in American Slavic humanities scholarship.[28] Four of the most influential U.S.–based scholars of Russian culture each promoted a vision of Russia that stressed its similarities and connections to other nations, including the United States. That all four were born and educated in eastern Europe no doubt helps explain their fierce resistance to the exoticizing orientation that had defined earlier scholarship in their fields. The historian Michael Karpovich described

Russia as a fully European nation, not just culturally but also economically. His Harvard colleague, the economic historian Alexander Gerschenkron, similarly promoted the idea that imperial Russia was a European nation, well on its way to "normalization" when the Bolshevik revolution derailed it. As these historians situated Russia within Europe, distinguished Slavists developed more rigorously universal systems of thought that placed Russia on equal footing with the rest of the world's languages and literatures. Yale's René Wellek, a native of Czechoslovakia, joined forces with native New Critics to erase national boundaries in American literary scholarship. The linguist Roman Jakobson brought structuralism into American linguistics, arguing that scholars must develop a set of analytical techniques applicable to any language. All four scholars trained an impressive number of students, thereby helping to define their fields for generations to come. Three of them (all but Karpovich) made their own important contributions not just to the understanding of Russia, but to the direction of their disciplines. Taken together, Karpovich, Gerschenkron, Wellek, and Jakobson represent the finest contributions of an intellectual "sea change" that was, in its own area, just as dominant as the intellectual emigration from Germany.

Michael Karpovich came to the United States during World War I as a representative of Russia's short-lived Provisional Government, so called because it planned to exist only until a duly elected government could establish itself. Karpovich had already completed his historical training, having earned an advanced degree from Moscow University and undertaken additional studies at the Sorbonne. By the time he arrived in Washington, the government he represented was barely functioning. The Bolshevik takeover in November 1917 might have deprived him of a job, but the ambassador's dogged optimism, combined with the uncertain fate of the revolution, meant that the embassy continued to function for five years. His reentry into the historical profession came after an urgent plea in 1927 to teach courses in Russian history at Harvard, where he would stay for thirty years.[29] His progress through the ranks was slow; he took two decades to attain the rank of full professor. With the new attention to Russian topics in the late 1940s, though, he cut a larger profile in and beyond his own department; in 1949 he became the first chair of the newly formed Department of Slavic Languages and Literatures.

His few books were teaching-oriented overviews of Russian history. In them he outlined the case that Russia had become a part of Europe by the early nineteenth century, "the golden age of Russian civilization." This label applied to Russian cultural and intellectual history—it was the era of Pushkin, Turgenev, and Gogol—but he also extended it to show how the Russia of Alexander I (1801–25) and Nicholas I (1825–55) advanced economically and politically. The process of westernization, started by Peter the Great (1688–1725), had taken hold in the eighteenth century. Though Peter was most interested in technological innovations, "western technique and western ways of living were inevitably followed by western ideas," such as constitutional government, civil equality, and personal liberty. Belying its nickname from the period, "gendarme of Europe," Russia had become a Western-style monarchy. A similar story held economically. Far from being backward, Karpovich wrote, Russian economic development in the early nineteenth century "exhibited a more dynamic character than that of any other European country." In certain branches of industry (metallurgy, for instance), Russian industry was ahead of any nation in Europe, even England.[30]

By the mid-1930s Karpovich had taken charge of the latter half of History 1 (Europe since the fall of the Roman Empire). His lecture on Russia in that course—fortunately published in Russian for use in language classes—opens by sounding the theme of Russia as a European nation. He complained that the historical literature describes western Europe in the early nineteenth century as being in the midst of "an epoch of uninterrupted and rapid progress" while demeaning contemporaneous Russia as wallowing in "immobility" and "stagnation." Yet this could not be further from the truth: Russia was full of "dynamism"; its economic development was "gradually remaking the social structure"; it had taken on the responsibilities of a "great European power."[31]

The notion that Russia was wholly European had few adherents in the United States before the 1930s; even by the 1940s it was hardly the dominant view. Karpovich waged a public and private battle against any doubters. In 1945, for instance, he chastised the historian Hans Kohn in a letter: "I would not stress the peculiarity of Russia's development"; its future, he wrote "would not . . . [be] so different from the path of western liberalism." He later railed against the notion that Soviet institutions were "legitimate successor[s]" to elements of tsarist Russia. Karpovich bristled at those who associated Russian literature with Dostoevsky's psychological musings about the Russian soul, or with the revolutionary tendencies of later Russian thought. The best writers of his homeland, he believed, addressed universal, not national, themes.[32]

The Bolshevik revolution, in Karpovich's view, was not the result of Russian backwardness, still less of some essential Russian character. By the early twentieth century, he wrote, Russia was in the midst of its "constitutional experiment." Conceding that there was no actual constitution, and that parliamentary powers were sharply limited, Karpovich nevertheless held that Russia was "in the process of a profound internal transformation." Its economic and political opportunities had expanded greatly and its cultural scene was the sign of "a stronger and healthier soul." The eruption of World War I, however, derailed Russia at its most hopeful yet most vulnerable moment.[33] In his writings, then, Karpovich kept alive the hopes of the European-oriented intellectuals of Russia's silver age.

He also imparted this perspective to many of his students. The cohort of his postwar students both redefined the study of Russian history and trained many younger generations of historians. They studied primarily Russian history rather than the Soviet period, explored intellectual history, and examined Russian thought in relationship to European ideas. These students and protégés included a handful of young historians who, like Karpovich, were part of the Russian intellectual emigration (Marc Raeff and Nicholas Riasanovsky) as well as others such as Leopold Haimson, Martin Malia, Richard Pipes, Hans Rogger, and Donald Treadgold. With one exception, all these historians shared aspects of their adviser's historical vision and sensibility. A contemporary historian thus exaggerates only slightly when he concludes that Karpovich was the "principal 'founding father' of the American school of Russian studies."[34]

Though Karpovich himself was born in Georgia, he and most of his students rarely explored Russia's extensive (and expanding) empire. The one exception, again, was Karpovich's eventual successor at Harvard, Richard Pipes, who had termed his teacher's influence on him "more personal than intellectual." The slippage between the Russian Empire and Russia proper was a common feature of Slavic studies for many decades.[35]

Meanwhile, across Harvard Yard, Alexander Gerschenkron shared many of Karpovich's attributes and ideas. Like his colleague, he insisted on the viability of the Russian economic and political system up until World War I—when the great promises of tsarist Russia were stolen by the Bolsheviks. He was legendary around Harvard for his ability to master languages in pursuit of some passing interest; for the breadth of his knowledge; and for his passionate if painful devotion to the Red Sox. Coming to the United States in 1938, he spent the war working as an economic analyst at the Federal Reserve Board and the OSS. Harvard's Economics Department—with the enthusiastic support of Kluckhohn—offered him a permanent post in 1948. He quickly established himself as a fixture there, advising students in European economic history as well as Soviet economics and publishing on these and many other topics. His occasional forays into Russian literature led to persistent, if unconfirmed, rumors that administrators offered him the Cross Chair in Slavic Languages and Literatures.[36]

Gerschenkron's most famous article, "Economic Backwardness in Historical Perspective," contained his usual trademarks: an interweaving of intellectual and economic history; confident and sweeping characterizations of industrialization all across Europe; the frequent use of Latin phrases; and literary references ranging from Matthew Arnold to Emile Zola. It makes for an unusual form of economic analysis. Though he makes loose references to rates of industrial production and of capital accumulation, Gerschenkron does not cite a single statistic in support of his argument. In short, it was about as humanistic as any economics article could be. Though Gerschenkron's career is closely tied up with the term "economic backwardness," the title was not his own; a conference organizer vetoed his proposed title because of its wordiness.[37] The new title fit well the major themes of the article. He defined backwardness as the tension between "the actual state of economic activities in the country" and the "great promise inherent in . . . [industrial] development"—a tension, as he later put it, between "what is" and "what can be."[38] Gerschenkron described some of the key substitutions that latecomers could use to close the gap. For moderately backward economies like France's and Germany's in the mid-nineteenth century, a banking system could aid progress by facilitating capital accumulation. In nations like Russia, with a greater disparity between what was and could be, even German-style banks were insufficient to spark industrialization. Direct government investment in industry was the only solution. Ultimately, however, even the most backward economy would catch up enough to render state investment unnecessary.

Gerschenkron argued that the Russian economy on the eve of World War I had "graduated from the government-instituted . . . school of industrialization." It was undergoing "westernization"—it was becoming more European in form. The government's role in economic life, he argued, was waning, with the slack taken up by an expanding financial sector.[39] The war interrupted a particularly dynamic phase of Russian development, weakening governmental power, disrupting the economy, and rendering it incapable of rebuffing the Bolsheviks' grab for power. Like Karpovich, Gerschenkron maintained an optimistic view of Russia in the silver age. Russia had traveled a long way toward becoming a Western nation in the first years of the twentieth century, only to see World War I disturb the pattern. In this claim is a counterfactual argument, in Karpovich's case implicit, in Gerschenkron's explicit: "If not for the war . . ." For both scholars, this phrase took on a nostalgic, even longing, tone. The notion that the war diverted Russia's path toward a liberal state and an industrial economy, as future generations of scholars pointed out, must reckon with the unevenness of economic development, the rising social tensions, and the incapacity of tsarism and indeed the tsar himself. (As one of Karpovich's students reported, a joke around Nicholas II's court questioned whether a limited monarchy was necessary in Russia, which already had a limited monarch.)[40] These wistful tones suffused much American historical scholarship on Russia. They served at once to delegitimize the Bolshevik regime and to portray tsarism in the rosiest possible light.[41]

As this emphasis on "westernization" suggests, Gerschenkron assessed Russian history in a broad European context. Though not placing Russia on par with Germany, France, and England, he sought to demonstrate how it was becoming more and more like those nations. Russia's differences from Europe were in degree rather than in kind. Even economic forms that seemed specifically Russian were part of a single process of industrialization; the national particularities would fade away. Gerschenkron provided a single heuristic for the process, one that placed Russia fully within a continental context. Indeed, in the late 1960s he gave a set of lectures, "Europe in the Russian Mirror," using Russian circumstances to shed light on major questions in European history.[42] Gerschenkron's discussion of "economic backwardness," originally adumbrated to explain the evolution of Russian political economy, has found resonance and influence among economic historians of all world regions.[43] His students Joseph Berliner, Gregory Grossman, and Alexander Erlich (among others) wrote important works in the Soviet field. He taught European economic history in equally renowned undergraduate lectures and graduate seminars. He advised numerous students on European topics, spreading his influence well beyond studies of Russia. Others of his students rose to prominence for their analyses of the economic histories of China, Japan, and early modern Europe.[44]

Emigré scholars of literature and language shared the historians' impulse to understand Russian within Europe. Though both Wellek and Jakobson considered their ideas universal, they shared with virtually all their contemporaries the notion that the universe was coterminous with Europe. Both these scholars drew on the intellectual dynamism of interwar Prague, but their ideas originated farther to the east. The Prague Linguistics Circle, of which Jakobson was a major figure and Wellek an important interpreter, devoted much of its work to drawing out the implications of Russian Formalism.[45] The Russian Formalists, a group of literary scholars, poets, and writers, investigated the philosophical content of literary works, trying to disentangle those works from sociological or political arguments. Works of art, they insisted, were not merely byproducts of their own time, but efforts to transform existing artistic forms.[46]

For Wellek the Formalist project entailed recognizing the literariness of literature, as distinct from its social and political contexts. His work shared much with the American New Critics, with whom he had a long and productive relationship.[47] Wellek's encounter with these New Critics was in large part accidental. Wellek's work reflected the tensions of his upbringing; his father, an "ardent" Czech nationalist, raised him in cosmopolitan Vienna and Prague. He interrupted advanced work at Charles University in Prague to study at Princeton in 1927, where he found the courses to be "a bore." Returning to his alma mater in 1931, Wellek published his dissertation on the reception of Immanuel Kant's ideas in England. He then took a post at the School of Slavonic Studies at the University of London; funded by the Czech government, Wellek gave public lectures for the Czech cause and against Hitler in the later 1930s. With the arrival of the Nazis in Prague in 1939, Wellek's funding, not surprisingly, evaporated. He soon found a post at the University of Iowa, where he quickly made common cause with the New Critic Austin Wallace. During the war he taught Czech language in Iowa's ASTP program. The nationwide growth of interest in Russian topics soon took him to Yale, where he was the founding (and for some time the sole full-time) member of its Slavic and Comparative Literature Department. He trained a handful of important Slavic scholars, including Victor Erlich (the brother of the economist Alexander), as well as a generation of comparative literature specialists (such as A. Bartlett Giamatti, future president of Yale and the National League).[48]

Wellek contributed to a 1941 volume that helped introduce New Criticism to an academic audience; the book demanded a new approach to studying literature, one that "should, first and foremost, concentrate on the actual works of art themselves." While acknowledging that writers had concerns other than the purely artistic, he sought to "restrict attempts to account for literature in terms of something else." Wellek sought to bridge the "dangerous gulf between content and form" with reference to the Prague Circle's interpretation of Russian Formalism. He recognized the "transformation [that] every experience must undergo in the artistic process," as it yielded a literary form that was related to, but not the same as, its social or political content.[49] Wellek reiterated this point in his most widely read work, *The Theory of Literature* (cowritten with Warren, 1949). That book also proposed a distinction between "intrinsic" and "extrinsic" realms. The intrinsic consisted of the artistic elements of a work of literature, and was the proper subject of study and evaluation. Wellek and Warren relegated everything else—history, biography, psychology, politics, and sociology—to the extrinsic realm, where it should relate only minimally to literary scholarship's main concerns.[50]

Wellek demanded a restructuring of graduate education; it is in these institutional forms that the universalistic implications of his work are most visible. He predicted that the United States—wealthy, relatively untouched by war, and with potent combination of American and European critics—would lead the next generation of scholarship. Its graduate education in literature thus took on added importance. His most radical proposal here was to re-order literature departments; they should make appointments by "types of mind and method," not by nations and periods. The same techniques of criticism were of universal interest and application; the specific literatures covered were secondary to the methods employed. He brought the same approach to comparative literature, demanding that the field abandon the study of influences—which created a "strange system of cultural bookkeeping"—and turn instead to the study of literature as a whole; he envisioned a critical enterprise that was "a unified discipline unhampered by linguistic restrictions." He criticized departments set up along national traditions; they were institutional manifestations of the "romantic ideal of the study of a national spirit" and obscured the "unity of European literature." A new approach to literature would involve a "new systematic theory," capacious enough to be "applicable to any and all works of literature."[51] Wellek, trained and employed as a professor of Slavic literature, had no little ambition: the literature of the world (which he defined as European literature) was his subject. At the same time as Wellek sought to reconstitute literary criticism and reconfigure the study of literature, he also continued to work along the more conventional national lines that had previously organized the field (and some of his own work). For instance, he wrote all forty-two articles on Czech and Slovak authors for the *Columbia Dictionary of Modern European Literature*. He continued to publish on Czech topics throughout his career, especially around the time he assumed the presidency of the Czechoslovak Society of America in 1962.[52]

Wellek and the other New Critics, even if under direct challenge since the mid-1960s, left a powerful legacy in the study of literature. In Catherine Gallagher's assessment, the New Critics permanently shifted the subject and approach of literary studies. Their "cosmopolitanism," furthermore, "was largely responsible for making English departments hospitable to theoretical diversity."[53] The growing interest in Slavic topics thus helped bring new and more universal approaches to literary studies.

Even more than Wellek, linguist Roman Jakobson had an influence well beyond Slavic studies. After receiving a first degree in Oriental languages in Moscow, he moved to Prague in 1920 with the Soviet Red Cross mission. He completed his doctoral work at Charles University and stayed in Czechoslovakia. When the Nazis took control in 1939, Jakobson escaped, ending up in the United States in 1941. He held the Czech studies chair at Columbia before becoming the first occupant of the Cross Chair in Slavic Languages and Literatures at Harvard in 1949. Jakobson's work with graduate students in Slavic languages and linguistics was legendary; as one student put it, Jakobson trained "virtually all of the major Slavists in that [1950s] generation."[54]

Like the other Russian Formalists, Jakobson sought to reconsider the relationship between form and content in literary expression. Focusing on the study of language, the Formalists insisted that poetic attributes such as meter, rhyme, and alliteration were not external impositions on artistic expression, but were themselves part of that expression; the formal modes of communication, in other words, were an essential part of what made literature literary. Jakobson's linguistic innovations emerged from his study of poetry, which he called his "first passion" during his student years. He sought to understand the formal structures of poetic language—and, by extension, all language—through careful study of all the elements that made up that language. His first works explored the evolution of Slavic languages, with particular attention to how they began to differentiate from a common source. Though previous scholars had described phonemes as indivisible "atomic entities," Jakobson claimed that phonemes were themselves further divisible into "distinctive features," the most basic building blocks of speech. These distinctive features were so basic that they constitute the building blocks of all languages; by organizing them, the linguist could develop "structural laws of universal validity."[55] According to one protégé, Jakobson treated linguistics as "a science that sought to discover something fundamental, something real and invariant in the real world." Jakobson's conception of the elements of communication steered semiotic theory in a new directions; semioticians such as Umberto Eco claimed Jakobson as one of their own: "His entire scientific existence has been a living example of a Quest for Semiotics."[56] From his work on Slavic languages, then, Jakobson quickly leapt to the discussion of universal themes. His approach to linguistics, dominant for many years, still has many adherents among Slavicists as well as linguists.[57]

The career of Russian Formalism in American studies of literature and language does not properly end, as this analysis does, with René Wellek and Roman Jakobson. Since the 1970s at least two major trends in literary criticism—within and beyond the Slavic field—took their inspiration from Russian theorists and their interpreters, many of whom held positions in America's Slavic departments. Fredric Jameson, perhaps the most important American literary scholar today, reckoned with the Russian Formalists in his first Marxist works, expressing disapproval, even disgust, with American scholars who treat Formalism as "the spiritual property of the Slavicists."[58] The insights of the Formalists, he indicated, applied to all literature, not only that emanating from eastern Europe. Similarly, the present-day fascination with the notions of Mikhail Bakhtin (a Formalist who traveled in different circles than Jakobson did) dates back primarily to the reinterpretation of his ideas by Caryl Emerson, Katerina Clark, and Michael Holquist, the latter two being Wellek's successors at Yale.[59] Thus, Russian Formalism's impact on America, which émigrés such as Wellek and Jakobson brought with them via Prague, has continued to reshape literary studies. The universalist project of these Slavicists has succeeded: Bakhtin has become a social theorist, not a critic of Russian literature; linguists apply insights originally derived from analysis of Slavic tongues to all languages.

Of course, the ideas of the Russian Formalists, like Gerschenkron's notions of economic backwardness, did not require the cold war. The expansion of Slavic studies in the 1940s, though, paved the way for key scholars and their innovations. Jakobson inaugurated the chair in Slavic Languages and Literatures at Harvard—a department led by Michael Karpovich. Wellek created (indeed, for a time, *was*) Yale's department in that field. Gerschenkron entered the academy as a Russia specialist. All four, furthermore, were involved in the rise of Slavic studies in the postwar period. Wellek served as a founding member of the American Council of Learned Societies and the Social Science Research Council Joint Committee on Slavic Studies; Gerschenkron and Karpovich both served on the Russian Research Center's Executive Committee for many years; and Jakobson remained in close contact with AATSEEL, in part because so many of its leaders were his students.[60]

These four scholars helped shape American knowledge of the Slavic world in ways that promoted inclusion. Russian history was a chapter in European history, undergoing the same processes and explicable with the same categories. Slavic writers were full and equal participants in the world tradition. Slavic languages illustrated not "Balkanization" but important aspects of grammar and syntax that could shed light on other tongues and indeed on the nature of language itself. These scholars' rapid advancement was a sign of the growing importance of Slavic studies as well as an indicator of the acceptance of universalistic premises in the postwar era.

The Politics of Sovietology

The diverse national origins of the scholars in Soviet studies were matched, more surprisingly, by an impressive range of political perspectives. Both the institutions and the individuals in the field exhibited a political complexion more consistent with an attitude of wartime mobilization than with cold war conformity. The origins of Russian studies at both Harvard and Columbia date back to the last years of World War II, even if the two centers did not open until American-Soviet relations become hostile. For instance, the original plans for Columbia's Russian Institute included a permanent slot for visiting scholars from the USSR.[61] The wartime circumstances also reduced the political barriers, even for intelligence work. Scholars with left-wing connections found employment at all sorts of government agencies, including the OSS—which hired a significant percentage of the Frankfurt School émigrés for its Research and Analysis branch.[62] This acceptance of a wide range of political views—so long as scholars were anti-Stalinist—carried well into the 1950s, as non-Communist radicals found new audiences. The Frankfurt School's Herbert Marcuse, for instance, received support from both Harvard and Columbia for his work on the USSR; the two institutions competed against one another to support his work.[63] The need for scholars who could work with Russian sources seemed, at times, to outweigh the need for political conformity.

Indeed, the participants in Russian seminars at Harvard and Columbia might easily be confused with denizens in radical salons decades earlier. They all shared not just a topic—the revolution, of course—but also a range of experiences with radicalism. At Harvard participants included two Russian émigrés, one who had been jailed for his participation in the Socialist-Revolutionary Party (Karpovich) and another once active in the Austrian Social Democratic Party (Gerschenkron); an American whose enthusiasm for the Bolshevik revolution led to his membership in the Student League for Industrial Democracy (Parsons), and a onetime member of the American Labor Party who had supported Henry Wallace's 1948 campaign (the historian H. Stuart Hughes).[64] As the group looked to hire additional scholars, politics definitely came into play. The sociologist Barrington Moore was at first treated warily, out of concern that he was "not as objective as one might hope"—because he was too firmly attached to the notion of inevitable Soviet-American conflict. Meanwhile, Karpovich wanted center funding for three émigré socialists, all of whom he described as participants in the Russian "labor and socialist movement."[65]

At Columbia the political complexion was similar if somewhat less cosmopolitan; the conversations about revolution were in the bland English of small-town America. At least three of the five founding members of the Russian Institute had radical connections. Geroid Robinson had spent his twenties in Greenwich Village, writing for its small and left-leaning magazines (including the *Dial* and the *Freeman*); one 1919 essay on Russia, for example, offered an endorsement of the Bolshevik revolution from a syndicalist perspective.[66] His fellow historian Philip Mosely reported traveling to Atlanta in 1921 to celebrate the release from prison of the socialist leader Eugene Victor Debs.[67] Ernest Simmons had more extensive and recent experiences in American radicalism; he had been a member of the League of American Writers and had served as vice chair of the American Labor Party in New York.[68] Among the early postwar appointments in the Slavic department, furthermore, was a Danish linguist who was denied reentry to the United States under the terms of the McCarren Act, which excluded foreigners who had been members of any Communist party.[69]

Many of the key figures in the early years of American Sovietology, going well beyond the ones listed above, had political commitments to one or another group on the far left. The sociologist Sigmund Diamond called Harvard a front in the cold war's "hot war against dissent." Though he presents important evidence that some faculty members ran into trouble with the administration for their past radicalism, Diamond's examples—which include his own case—were not necessarily representative. One important case did involve the RRC. Under pressure from the Carnegie Corporation, Harvard relieved the historian H. Stuart Hughes (an OSS veteran) of his post as the center's associate director. Thanks to quick backroom negotiating by the RRC's director, Clyde Kluckhohn, and some ethical hairsplitting by Provost Paul Buck, Carnegie covered Hughes's salary while he taught in the History Department. The issue was not Hughes's cheerfully acknowledged lack of expertise in Russian matters, but instead his support for the Wallace campaign, which Carnegie officials considered "offensive." Hughes later presented a number of mitigating factors, including the fact that he withdrew his support for Wallace (for his own reasons) by summer 1948, but Carnegie officials were adamant that they would not support a program employing him.[70] Hughes's case, though serious, did not represent the treatment of all of those with radical beliefs in the field of Soviet studies.

In the early years of Sovietology, the World War II–era attitude held sway; those studying the USSR did not necessarily consider it a permanent foe. A number of younger scholars in the field, including Hughes, entered the field in the hopes of helping to improve international understanding. Caught up in the optimistic spirit of wartime alliance rather than the growing mistrust of the postwar years, they wanted to work toward Soviet-American rapprochement.[71] Other students, including Communist Party members, wrote to senior Sovietologists asking to get involved with the center. Harvard, for instance, received inquiries from both the labor historian Philip Taft and the future historian Staughton Lynd; Lynd wrote openly of his party membership, but he explained that he was on the right wing of the party.[72] Similarly, Columbia offered William Mandel a senior fellowship at the RI; one internal memorandum praised Mandel's "impressive" record "in spite of his lack of formal education." What it did not directly mention was that Mandel had built up his record as a member of the Communist Party.[73]

Some of the former radicals who populated early Sovietology had close ties to government agencies. The State Department appointed Abraham Brumberg as editor of its influential journal, *Problems of Communism*, without regard for what he called his "socialist values."[74] Many of these connections emerged from wartime experience; Mosely and Robinson at Columbia, for instance, remained in constant contact with CIA officials. Harvard's relationships with U.S. intelligence were more frequent and more formal. As Kluckhohn told a review committee in 1952, the RRC had "provided services to numerous Government agencies" from its very inception. Indeed, he complained privately that the center had been "swamped . . . by representatives of various government agencies."[75]

The involvement of former (or more rarely, current) radicals in intelligence work had a number of curious side effects. Take, for instance, Kluckhohn's preparations for a leave of absence in 1953–54. He had been the RRC's main contact with the CIA and needed to find a successor. The Executive Committee's first choice was the center's assistant director, a young political scientist. Even though he warned his supervisor that he might not be able to obtain the necessary security clearances, Kluckhohn was optimistic—unjustifiably so, as it turned out. Kluckhohn then turned to the political scientist Merle Fainsod, a professor who had traveled to the USSR in the 1930s. He too failed the security clearance, which "infuriated" him. Fainsod's actual involvement in radical activities was minimal; though one colleague considered Fainsod "left of center," another described his crime as simply "being interested in Russia too early."[76]

Sovietologists who performed classified work also provided evidence about their past political involvements. A group of twenty-two junior scholars working in Harvard's Refugee Interview Project, for instance, were required to obtain FBI approval to conduct their interviews of Soviet displaced persons in 1950–51. The clearance form asked all participants to list any organizations, of any sort, to which they had ever belonged. One scholar listed only his membership in the New York Yacht Club. Many of his less pedigreed colleagues, mostly graduate students at Harvard and Columbia, were involved in Popular Front organizations. About half the scholars who attended American universities had been involved with the American Student Union (ASU) in the 1930s or the American Veterans Committee during and after the war; a handful had been members of both.[77] (The ASU's history is typical of 1930s radical groups; born a joint Socialist-Communist effort, it split into factions within two years and fell under Communist control in 1939. Some of the Sovietologists involved in the ASU had left by this point, but others remained until the organization's collapse in 1941. The American Veterans Committee went through a similar process about a decade later and slightly faster, split apart by the Wallace campaign.)[78] The Sovietologists' early connections to these Popular Front organizations hardly proves that their field was rife with card-carrying Communists—but it does suggest that pioneering scholars had came from a wide range of political perspectives, including some with tendencies on the farther side of the left.

It is no coincidence that many of the first students attracted to Soviet studies had radical attachments. Many Americans interested in the USSR in the 1930s came from one or another precinct of the left. The most incisive and most vocal critics of Stalinism, in the 1930s as in the postwar period, came from the anti-Stalinist left.[79] Some of the most widely read analyses of the USSR in the 1940s came from beyond the groves of academe and often from the ranks of present or former leftists: for instance, biographical works of the former Communists Louis Fischer and Bertram Wolfe received (deservedly) both popular and scholarly acclaim. Less distinguished works by others with radical pasts flooded bookstores in the early years of the cold war. Even those who had not renounced leftist attachments earned the respect of early Sovietologists. The Briton E. H. Carr was the second speaker ever invited to Harvard's seminar and received competing offers from leading American universities; one of his compatriots, the onetime Trotskyist Isaac Deutscher, similarly received acclaim.[80] These scholars' left leanings shared one crucial trait with mainstream American opinion: an antipathy for Stalinism.

The major institutions of Sovietology were open to a wide, but not infinite, range of political affiliations. Members of a Communist Party could not gain full access to the Harvard or Columbia programs. The case of Ruth Fischer, once the leader of the German Communist Party (KPD), reveals the limits of Harvard's political openness. Even before the center opened its doors, Kluckhohn contemplated having Fischer write up her years of research on Stalin's interference in the KPD, an event that led to her own removal as party head. In internal correspondence, Kluckhohn wrote that Fischer "might be useful to us" not as a staff member but as a "consultant or informant." In its early years the center awarded her numerous grants for research assistance. After the first such grant, RRC's Executive Committee revised its treatment of Fischer and extended it into a "general policy": those with "definite political convictions" could maintain affiliations with the center as "informants," but not as "consultants," let alone staff members; the policy was necessary to "protect the Center . . . from the charge of political bias." Even while supporting her work with varying degrees of patience (for missed deadlines), the center kept Fischer, as an ex-Communist, at an arm's length.[81] The political diversity engendered by the mobilization of Russia expertise had its limits.

The Field Expands

As the intensity of anti-Communist politics receded in the mid- and late 1950s, Soviet studies began to change dramatically in both quantitative and qualitative terms. The rising generation of Russia specialists had been shaped by very different domestic and international political events. Whereas the early leaders went through their training in the radical 1930s (when support for the Soviet Union was far from uncommon among intellectuals and students) and had wartime responsibilities shaped by the Grand Alliance, the new generation had entirely different landmarks. The younger scholars who had served in the war had more typically been soldiers or sailors, not intelligence analysts. The headlines during their graduate training tracked not the Red Army defeat of Nazi advances but the Sovietization of eastern Europe, the domestic turmoil of late Stalinism, and, most important, the Korean War.

Changing political moods were only one factor, and probably not the most significant one, in the evolution of Russian studies. In the aftermath of the Soviet launch of Sputnik in 1957, American investments in teaching and training increased dramatically in two dimensions: science education and area studies. The National Defense Education Act (NDEA) transformed the financial basis of area studies, designating some existing programs "National Resource Centers" and spurring the creation of many more. It also provided for Foreign Language and Area Studies (FLAS) fellowships that became a staple for generations of graduate students, up to the present day. Before 1957 Sovietological resources were concentrated in Cambridge and Morningside Heights, with a small and relatively insignificant outcropping in the Bay Area. Federal funding accounted for the expansion of Soviet studies into a national enterprise in the early 1960s.[82]

The impetus to improve—and, even more, to expand—training in Russian and Soviet affairs goes a long way in explaining the increase in language departments, in terms of both faculty and students. Enrollments in language courses, including Russian, exploded in the late 1950s and early 1960s. Russian enrollments went from 16,300 in 1958 to 30,600 in 1960, nearly doubling in only three years. Interest in languages was hardly limited to Russian: Spanish enrollments also came close to doubling in a similar period.[83] Cold war competition—the "language gap"—sparked an increase in student demand as well as in the supply of courses and scholarship.

The NDEA–led expansion of Russian studies shaped not just language and literature, but all scholarship in the field. Early scholarship had brought together students of Russian and Soviet history, culture, politics, society, and economics. The Columbia and Harvard institutes had explicitly interdisciplinary aims for their research and training programs; while the achievements of transcending disciplinary divides fell far short of these high aims, the reigning notion for the field was one that celebrated mastery of a country or region over adherence to disciplinary standards. As the field expanded, however, historians began speaking primarily to other historians, economists to other economists, and so on. Specialized journals appeared, competing for attention with journals, like the *Slavic Review*, that reflected an area-studies orientation.

This expansion of the field in the 1960s did not change its basic distribution of disciplines. Nor did the financial crises that buffeted the field in the early 1970s, when major foundations reduced their funding for international studies. Publications by faculty at NDEA centers on the USSR and eastern Europe favored the humanities over the social sciences even into the last years of Brezhnev's rule. Between 1976 and 1981, 40.3 percent of these publications were in the social sciences, 16.6 percent in history, and 43.1 percent in other humanities disciplines.[84]

The 1970s brought a sharpened political edge to the field as the turmoil of the 1960s arrived in earnest. Numerous scandals involving scientists and social scientists on the payroll of the Pentagon or the CIA made younger scholars deeply distrustful of the ties between scholars and government that had been a hallmark of the World War II generation. A controversy involving the role of government agencies in U.S.–Soviet scholarly exchanges resulted in the end of the Inter-University Committee for Travel Grants and the formation of IREX in 1968. Critics, especially younger scholars, lambasted the founders of Soviet studies for promoting a cold war sensibility and for letting geopolitics shape scholarship. Scholars coming of age in the 1970s opened up new venues and new vistas for scholarly work: the political and cultural history of the 1920s, for instance, and the role of Soviet bureaucracies. While these scholars were hardly the first to criticize the scholarship of their elders, they did so with a particular vehemence. In so doing, they contributed to the critical vision of 1950s Soviet studies distilled at the start of this chapter. The work of the 1970s thus bequeathed both innovations for understanding the Soviet Union and obstacles to understanding the history of Soviet studies.[85]

Notes

1. The quotations' sources are, in order, Stephen F. Cohen, *Rethinking the Soviet Experience: Politics and History since 1917* (New York: Oxford University Press, 1985), 8; Alexander Dallin, "Bias and Blunders in American Studies on the USSR," *Slavic Review* 32 (September 1973): 567; Stephen White, "Political Science as Ideology: The Study of Soviet Politics," in *WJJM: Political Questions—Essays in Honour of W. J. M. MacKenzie* (Manchester: Manchester University Press, 1974), 260; Bruce Cumings, "Boundary Displacement: Area Studies and International Studies during and after the Cold War," in *Universities and Empire: Money and Politics in the Social Sciences during the Cold War*, ed. Christopher Simpson (New York: New Press, 1998), 163; Cohen, *Rethinking*, 10; Immanuel Wallerstein, "The Unintended Consequences of Cold War Area Studies," in *The Cold War and the University: Toward an Intellectual History of the Postwar Years* (New York: New Press, 1997), 210; Ron Robin, *The Making of the Cold War Enemy: Culture and*

Politics in the Military-Intellectual Complex (Princeton: Princeton University Press, 2001), 54–56; Charles Thomas O'Connell, "Social Structure and Science: Soviet Studies at Harvard" (Ph.D. diss., University of California at Los Angeles, 1990), 11; Alfred G. Meyer, "Coming to Terms with the Past . . . and with One's Older Colleagues," *Russian Review* 45 (October 1986): 402; Sigmund Diamond, *Compromised Campus: The Collaboration of Universities with the Intelligence Community, 1945–1955* (New York: Oxford University Press, 1992), 54; Dallin, "Bias and Blunders," 566, 571; Alan Wolfe, *The Rise and Fall of the Soviet Threat: Domestic Sources of the Cold War Consensus* (Washington, D.C.: Institute for Policy Studies, 1979). Most of these sources refer to Soviet studies in particular, but others speak to area studies programs more generally.

2. While the distinctions between "Russian studies" and "Soviet studies" are relevant in some contexts, I will use the terms, along with Sovietology, interchangeably in this essay. Both the Harvard and Columbia programs, of course, referred to Russia, not the Soviet Union. In the context of McCarthyism, the founders of Sovietology's major journal (and, later, professional association) banished the word Soviet and insisted that the titles begin with "American"; hence *American Slavic and Eastern European Review* (later *Slavic Review*) and the American Association for the Advancement of Slavic Studies (AAASS)—see Chauncey D. Harris, "Russian, Slavic and Soviet Studies in the United States: Some Memories and Notes," *Russian History/Histoire Russe* 24 (Winter 1997): 444–445.

3. For aspects of Russian studies before World War II, see Stephen Marshall Arum, "Early Stages of Foreign Language and Area Studies in the US, 1915–1941" (Ed.D. diss., Columbia University Teachers College, 1975); Terence Emmons, "Russia Then and Now in the Pages of the *American Historical Review* and Elsewhere: A Few Centennial Notes," *American Historical Review* 100 (October 1995): 1136–1149; and David C. Engerman, "New Society, New Scholars: Soviet Studies Programmes in Interwar America," *Minerva* 37 (Spring 1999): 25–43. Eduard Mark, "October or Thermidor? Interpretations of Stalinism and the Perception of Soviet Foreign Policy in the United States, 1927–1947," *American Historical Review* 94 (October 1989): 937–962.

4. McGeroge Bundy, "The Battlefields of Power and the Searchlights of the Academy," in *The Dimensions of Diplomacy*, ed. E. A. J. Johnson (Baltimore: Johns Hopkins University Press, 1964), 2. Cf. Diamond, *Compromised Campus*, 73.

5. Barry Katz, *Foreign Intelligence: Research and Intelligence in the OSS, 1942–1945* (Cambridge: Harvard University Press, 1989); Betty Abrahamsen Dessants, "The American Academic Community and United States–Soviet Relations: The Research and Analysis Branch and Its Legacy, 1941–1947" (Ph.D. diss., University of California at Berkeley, 1995).

6. Aside from Bundy, see, e.g., Philip E. Mosely, "The Growth of Russian Studies," in *American Research on Russia*, ed. Harold H. Fisher (Bloomington: Indiana University Press, 1959), 7–8.

7. The training imperative was, of course, not limited to area studies programs. A very suggestive article by David Kaiser argues that the intellectual content of postwar physics was shaped by the conceptualization of physics departments' "products" as physicists, not physical knowledge. See David Kaiser, "Cold War Requisitions, Scientific Manpower, and the Production of American Physicists after World War II," *Historical Studies in the Physical and Biological Sciences* 33 (2002): 131–159.

8. Oleg A. Maslenikov, "Slavic Studies in America, 1939–1946," *Slavonic and East European Studies* 25 (April 1947): 531–532. On the Navy's Oriental Languages Program, see A. E. Hindmarsh, "The Navy School of Oriental Languages: History, Organization, and Administration" (ca. May 1945), appendixes 36–37, University of Colorado Archives. See also William Nelson Fenton for the Commission on Implications of Armed Services Educational Programs, *Area Studies in American Universities* (Washington, D.C.: American Council on Education, 1947).

9. Cumings, "Boundary Displacement," 163.

10. Robinson, "The Russian Institute," appendix to "The Report of the Committee on the

Proposed Graduate School of Foreign Affairs" (November 27, 1944), Columbia University Central Files (hereafter CUCF) (Columbiana Collection), Personal Subseries: Schuyler Wallace; Robinson, "A Program of Advanced Training and Research in Russian Studies," April 24, 1947, CUCF, Personal Subseries: Philip Mosely.

11. Albert Parry, *America Learns Russian: A History of the Teaching of the Russian Language in the United States* (Syracuse: Syracuse University Press, 1967), 83–86, 124; William B. Edgerton, "The History of Slavistic Scholarship in the United States," in *Beiträge zur Geschichte der Slawistik in nichtslawischen Ländern*, ed. Josef Hamm and Günther Wytrzens (Vienna: Austrian Academy of Sciences, 1985), 494–495.

12. *Report of the President of Harvard College, 1945–46* (Cambridge: Harvard University, 1946), 37.

13. The historian Morton Keller points out that senior administrators insisted on calling the new unit a "center" rather than an "institute" because it would seem less permanent. Like predictions about the Soviet Union's imminent demise, this was an optimistic goal; the RRC's successor, the Davis Center for Russian and Eurasian Studies, is still going strong. See also Paul H. Buck Oral History, Oral History Research Office, Columbia University, 53–54.

14. [John Gardner, Carnegie Corporation,] "Russian Studies" (July 15, 1947), RRC Correspondence, Harvard University Archives, UAV 759.10, box 1; Devereux Josephs to Clyde Kluckhohn, January 20, 1948, Carnegie Corporation Records, Columbia University, box 164, folder 4. See Robin, *Making of the Cold War Enemy*.

15. Virginia Yans-McLaughlin, "Science, Democracy and Ethics: Mobilizing Culture and Personality for World War II," in *Malinowski, Rivers, Benedict, and Others: Essays on Culture and Personality*, ed. George W. Stocking Jr. (Madison: University of Wisconsin Press, 1986). For a critical view, see Christopher Simpson, "A World Made Safe for Differences: Ruth Benedict's 'The Chrysanthemum and the Sword,'" *American Quarterly* 47 (December 1995): 659–680.

16. For a more generous assessment, see Alex Inkeles, "Clyde Kluckhohn's Contribution to Studies of Russia and the Soviet Union," in *Culture and Life: Essays in Memory of Clyde Kluckhohn*, ed. Walter W. Taylor et al. (Carbondale: Southern Illinois University Press, 1973).

17. Calculated from Jesse J. Dossick, *Doctoral Research on Russia and the Soviet Union* (New York: New York University Press, 1960).

18. Maslenikov, "Slavic Studies," 530; Jacob Ornstein, "The Development and Status of Slavic and East European Studies in America since World War II," *American Slavic and East European Review* 16 (October 1957): 375. For an even more precise contemporary dating of the rise of the interest, see Maurice W. Rosenbaum, "Slavonic Studies in America," *Journal of Higher Education* 14 (January 1944): 9, 58.

19. Josef Brozek, "Slavic Studies in America," *Journal of Higher Education* 14 (June 1943): 293; J. A. Posin, "Russian Studies in American Colleges," *Russian Review* 7 (Spring 1948): 64.

20. Vladimir Nabokov, *Pnin* (Garden City, N.Y.: Doubleday, 1957), 10–11.

21. Vernadsky's own role in shaping American interpretations of Russian history is complex, but is in any case different from Karpovich's. Vernadsky borrowed a great deal from the Eurasianist movement among Russian émigrés in the interwar period, suggesting that Russia represented a distinct region with its own unique culture. For varying views, see V. N. Kozliakov, "'Eto tol'ko personifikatsiia ne nashego ponimaniia istoricheskogo protsessa': Georgii Vladimirovich Vernadskii (1887–1973)," in Vernadskii, *Russkaia istoriografiia* (Moscow: Agraf, 1998); and Charles J. Halperin, "Russia and the Steppe: George Vernadsky and Eurasianism," *Forschungen zur Osteuropäischen Geschichte* 36 (1985): 55–194.

22. Samuel H. Baron, "Recollections of a Life in Russian History," *Russian History/Histoire Russe* 17 (Spring 1990): 35; N. N. Bolkhovitinov, "Rol' russkikh istorikov v stanovlenii rusistiki SShA," *Voprosy istorii*, no. 4 (2001): 10.

23. Cyril E. Black and John M. Thompson, "Graduate Study of Russia," in *American Teaching about Russia*, ed. Black and Thompson (Bloomington: Indiana University Press, 1957), 65.

24. A useful history of the exchanges, written by a scholar active in the organization of programs, is Robert F. Byrnes, *Soviet-American Academic Exchanges, 1958–1975* (Bloomington: Indiana University Press, 1976); one recent account argues that the exchanges contributed to the end of the cold war: Yale Richmond, *Cultural Exchange and the Cold War: Raising the Iron Curtain* (State College: Pennsylvania State University Press, 2003).

25. Lauren G. Leighton, "Thirty Years of *SEEJ*," *Slavic and East European Journal* 31 (1987): 2. See also Victoria Bonnell and George W. Breslauer, "Soviet and Post-Soviet Area Studies," in *The Politics of Knowledge: Area Studies and the Disciplines*, ed. David L. Szanton (Berkeley: UCIAS Publications, 2002).

26. Harris, "Russian, Slavic and Soviet Studies," 453.

27. Almost half the presidents of the AAASS have been historians, thus continuing a long-standing trend in area studies. When the American Council of Learned Societies and the Social Science Research Council established the Joint Committee on Slavic Studies in 1948, three of the eight members (including the chair) of the committee were historians; Gordon B. Turner, "The Joint Committee on Slavic Studies, 1948–1971: A Summary View," *ACLS Newsletter* 23 (Spring 1972): 9.

28. For an overview of 1950s universalism, see David Hollinger, "How Wide the Circle of the 'We'? American Intellectuals and the Problem of Ethnos since World War II," *American Historical Review* 98 (April 1993): 317–337. For universalism in social scientific work on the USSR, see David C. Engerman, *Modernization from the Other Shore: American Intellectuals and the Romance of Russian Development* (Cambridge: Harvard University Press, 2003), epilogue.

29. Biographical details from Philip E. Mosely, "Michael Karpovich, 1888–1959," *Russian Review* 19 (January 1960): 56–60; and George Vernadsky, *Russian Historiography: A History*, ed. Sergei Pushkarev, trans. Nickolas Lupin (Belmont, Mass.: Nordland, 1978), 366–368.

30. Michael Karpovich, *Imperial Russia, 1801–1917* (New York: Henry Holt, 1932), 8, 14; Witt Bowden, Michael Karpovich, and Abbott Payson Usher, *An Economic History of Europe since 1750* (New York: American Books, 1937), 289, 301. A brief and insightful overview of Karpovich's historical thinking is provided in Martin E. Malia, "Michael Karpovich, 1888–1959," *Russian Review* 19 (January 1960): 60–71 (quote from p. 60). See also Bolkhovitinov, "Rol' russkikh istorikov," 5.

31. Michael Karpovich, *A Lesson on Russia History*, annotated by Horace G. Lunt (The Hague: Mouton, 1962), 8–10.

32. Karpovich to Hans Kohn, March 20, 1945, Michael Karpovich Papers, Bakhmeteff Archive, Columbia University, box 5; Karpovich, "The Historical Background of Soviet Thought Control," in *The Soviet Union: Background, Ideology, Reality*, ed. Waldemar Gurian (Notre Dame, Ind.: University of Notre Dame Press, 1951), 16–17; Malia, "Michael Karpovich," 63–64, 67.

33. Bowden et al., *Economic History of Europe*, 694–696; Karpovich, *Imperial Russia*, 74, 85, 94.

34. Though Riasanovsky earned his doctorate at Oxford, he relied on Karpovich (who knew his parents) as an academic mentor, sharing both intellectual and professional concerns with him; see their correspondence in Karpovich Papers, box 6. Malia's antipathy for the Soviet system is ideological rather than national; see Yanni Kotsonis's insights in "The Ideology of Martin Malia," *Russian Review* 58 (January 1999): 124–130, and Malia, *Russia under Western Eyes: From the Bronze Horseman to the Lenin Mausoleum* (Cambridge: Harvard University Press, 1999).

35. For the other students and the quotation, see Bolkhovitinov, "Rol' russkikh istorikov," 9. Richard Pipes, *Vixi: Memoirs of a Non-Belonger* (New Haven: Yale University Press, 2003), 61–62. While some of Karpovich's scholars (Treadgold and Raeff) wrote of Russian expansion in Siberia, none but Pipes wrote on the multinational nature of the Russian empire.

36. For biographical details on Gerschenkron, see Lewis A. Coser, *Refugee Scholars in America: Their Impact and Their Experiences* (New Haven: Yale University Press, 1984), 154–163, and especially a very personal biography by his grandson, Nicholas Dawidoff, *The Fly Swatter: How My Grandfather Made His Way in the World* (New York: Pantheon, 2002). On his "loan" to the

OSS, see Director, FBI, to SAC—Washington, July 13, 1946—FBI document 77-30528-4.

37. The original title was "Historical Bases for Appraising Economic Development in a Bipolar World." The conference resulted in a book edited by the organizer: Bert Hoselitz, ed., *The Progress of Underdeveloped Areas* (Chicago: University of Chicago Press, 1952); his essay reappeared as Alexander Gerschenkron, "Economic Backwardness in Historical Perspective," in *Economic Backwardness in Historical Perspective: A Book of Essays* (Cambridge: Harvard University Press, 1962). On the title, see Bert Hoselitz to Alexander Gerschenkron, March 31, 1951, Alexander Gerschenkron Papers, Harvard University Archives, HUG [FP] 45.10, box 8.

38. Gerschenkron, "Economic Backwardness," 8; Gerschenkron, "Russian Agrarian Policies and Industrialization, 1861–1914" (1965), in Gerschenkron, *Continuity in History and Other Essays* (Cambridge: Harvard University Press, 1968), 152.

39. Gerschenkron, "Reflections on Economic Aspects of Revolutions" (1964), in *Continuity in History*, 273; Gerschenkron, "Problems and Patterns of Economic Development, 1861–1958" (1960), in *Economic Backwardness*, 141–142.

40. Hans Rogger, *Russia in the Age of Modernization and Revolution, 1881–1917* (New York: Longman, 1983), 15, 22.

41. On the power and implications of this strain of argument, see George W. Breslauer, "Counterfactual Reasoning in Western Studies of Soviet Politics and Foreign Relations," in *Counterfactual Thought Experiments in World Politics: Logical, Methodological, and Psychological Perspectives*, ed. Philip E. Tetlock and Aaron Belkin (Princeton: Princeton University Press, 1996). For an influential effort to dethrone the World War I counterfactual, see Leopold Haimson's articles, "The Problem of Social Stability in Urban Russia, 1905–1917," *Slavic Review* 23 (December 1964): 419–441, and 24 (March 1965): 1–34.

42. Gerschenkron, *Europe in the Russian Mirror: Four Lectures in Economic History* (Cambridge: Cambridge University Press, 1970).

43. The effect of Gerschenkron's writings on the field of economic history is evident in Richard Sylla and Gianni Toniolo, eds., *Patterns of European Industrialization: The Nineteenth Century* (New York: Routledge, 1991), and Donald N. McCloskey, "Alexander Gerschenkron," *American Scholar* 62 (Spring 1992): 2141–2146; on banks in particular, see Douglas J. Forsyth and Daniel Verdier, eds., *The Origins of National Financial Systems: Alexander Gerschenkron Reconsidered* (New York: Routledge, 2003).

44. James R. Millar, "Where Are the Young Specialists on the Soviet Economy and What Are They Doing?" *Journal of Comparative Economics* 4 (1980): 317–329.

45. René Wellek, "Prospect and Retrospect," *Yale Review* 69 (December 1979): 311. On the Prague Circle's approach, see especially F. W. Galan, *Historic Structures: The Prague School Project, 1928–1946* (Austin: University of Texas Press, 1985).

46. Victor Erlich, *Russian Formalism: History, Doctrine* (The Hague: Mouton, 1955).

47. Gerald Graff, *Professing Literature: An Institutional History* (Chicago: University of Chicago Press, 1987). A useful antidote to Graff's skepticism about professionalizing motives—especially vis-à-vis the New Critics—is Catherine Gallagher, "The History of Literary Criticism," in *Academic Culture in Transformation: Fifty Years, Four Disciplines*, ed. Thomas Bender and Carl E. Schorske (Princeton: Princeton University Press, 1997). Ewa M. Thompson, *Russian Formalism and Anglo-American New Criticism: A Comparative Study* (The Hague: Mouton, 1971).

48. René Wellek, "My Early Life," in *Contemporary Authors: Autobiographical Series*, ed. Mark Zardzony (Detroit: Gale, 1988), 7: 205–226 (quotation from p. 217). Other details from Martin Bucco, *René Wellek* (Boston: Twayne, 1981).

49. Wellek, "Literary History," in *Literary Scholarship: Its Aims and Methods*, by Norman Foerster et al. (Chapel Hill: University of North Carolina Press, 1941), 97, 130, 103; René Wellek and Austin Warren, *The Theory of Literature* (New York: Harcourt, Brace, 1949), 285.

50. Wellek and Warren, *Theory of Literature*, parts III–IV.

51. Ibid., 288; Wellek, "The Crisis of Comparative Literature" (1959), in René Wellek, *Concepts of Criticism*, ed. Stephen G. Nichols Jr. (New Haven: Yale University Press, 1963), 289–290; Wellek, "Literary Scholarship," in *American Scholarship in the Twentieth Century*, ed. Merle Curti (New York: Russell and Russell, 1953), 115, 123.

52. Bucco, *René Wellek*, 50–51, 70; Horatio Smith, ed., *Columbia History of Modern European Literature* (New York: Columbia University Press, 1949).

53. Gallagher, "History of Literary Criticism," 151, 158.

54. Horace Lunt, in *A Tribute to Roman Jakobson* (New York: Mouton, 1983), 76–77.

55. Roman Jakobson and Krystyna Pomorska, *Dialogues* (Cambridge: Cambridge University Press, 1983), 2; Jakobson, "Phoneme and Phonology" (1932), and Jakobson and M. Halle, "Phonology and Phonetics" (1955), both in Roman Jakobson, *Selected Writings*, 2nd ed., 7 vols. (The Hague: Mouton, 1971), vol. 1. See also Hugh McLean, "A Linguist among Poets," in *Roman Jakobson: What He Taught Us*, ed. Morris Halle (Columbus, Ohio: Slavica, 1983).

56. Umberto Eco, "The Influence of Roman Jakobson on the Development of Semiotics," in *Roman Jakobson: Echoes of His Scholarship*, ed. Daniel Armstrong and C. H. van Schooneveld (Lisse: Peter de Ridder, 1977), 42.

57. Noam Chomsky, in *Tribute to Roman Jakobson*, 81–83; Barry Scherr, "Formalism, Structuralism, Semiotics, and Poetics," *Slavic and East European Journal* 31 (1987): 127–140.

58. Fredric Jameson, *The Prison-House of Language: A Critical Account of Structuralism and Russian Formalism* (Princeton: Princeton University Press, 1972), 85. Also Jameson, *Marxism and Form: Twentieth-Century Dialectical Theories of Literature* (Princeton: Princeton University Press, 1971); Sean Homer, *Fredric Jameson: Marxism, Hermeneutics, Postmodernism* (Cambridge, Eng.: Polity Press, 1998), 27.

59. Mikhail Bakhtin, *The Dialogic Imagination: Four Essays*, ed. Michael Holquist, trans. Caryl Emerson and Michael Holquist (Austin: University of Texas Press, 1981); Katerina Clark and Michael Holquist, *Mikhail Bakhtin* (Cambridge: Belknap Press of Harvard University Press, 1984).

60. Parry, *America Learns Russian*, appendix I; J. Thomas Shaw, "AATSEEL: The First Fifty Years," *Slavic and East European Journal* 35 (1991): 76.

61. See the correspondence between Abram Bergson, Geroid Robinson, and Ernest Simmons in fall 1945, Geroid Tanquary Robinson Papers, Columbia University Archives, box 50.

62. Katz, *Foreign Intelligence*, chap. 2.

63. RRC Executive Committee Minutes, April 12, 1952, Harvard University Archives, UAV 759.5.

64. On Karpovich, see Malia, "Michael Karpovich," 56; on Gerschenkron, see Dawidoff, *Fly Swatter*, 96–104; on Parsons, see Howard Brick, "The Reformist Dimension of Talcott Parsons's Early Social Theory," in *The Culture of the Market: Historical Essays*, ed. Thomas L. Haskell and Richard F. Teichgraeber III (Cambridge: Cambridge University Press, 1993), 365. On Hughes, see H. Stuart Hughes, *Gentleman Rebel: The Memoirs of H. Stuart Hughes* (New York: Ticknor and Fields, 1990), 205–210.

65. John Gardner to Clyde Kluckhohn, October 17, 1947 (reporting on a conversation with Geroid T. Robinson about Barrington Moore), RRC Correspondence, box 1; Michael Karpovich to Kluckhohn, March 4, 1948 (nominating George Denicke, Boris Nicolaevsky, and Solomon Schwartz), RRC Correspondence, box 2. Karpovich, in fact, proposed a litmus test; he wanted individuals "of Russian origin, who have been associated with the background of the present-day Russia, both as students of Russian affairs and as direct participants in Russian political and social life."

66. Geroid Robinson, "Russia Re-Examined," *Freeman* 1 (April 21, 1920): 132–133; Robinson, "Russia's Double Experiment" (May 8, [1919?]), Robinson Papers, box 16.

67. Baron, "Recollections," 37. Mosely once ran afoul of the security clearance process, in 1954, apparently on the basis of accusations of association with Popular Front organizations in the 1930s; see Philip Edward Mosely Papers, University of Illinois Archives, box 12.

68. Ernest Simmons to Provost Albert Jacobs, August 5, 1948, CUCF, Personal Subseries: Ernest Simmons; James A. Hagerty, "Hilman Is Elected State Head of ALP," *New York Times*, April 9, 1944. He faced public charges for his past in the late 1940s and again in the early 1950s; see, e.g., Philip Wittenberg, ed., *The Lamont Case: History of a Congressional Investigation* (New York: Horizon, 1957), 24, 30.

69. On Adolf Stender-Peterson, see Ernest J. Simmons to Dean John Krout, November 23, 1951, CUCF, Personal Subseries: Ernest Simmons. Also see Stender-Peterson to Roman Jakobson, July 19, 1951, and Simmons to Jakobson, October 12, 1951, both in Roman Jakobson Papers, Massachusetts Institute of Technology, box 46; and Stiven Rudi [Stephen Rudy], "Iakobson pri Makkartizme," in *Roman Iakobson: Teksty, dokumenty, issledovaniia*, ed. Kh. Baran et al. (Moscow: RGGU, 1999).

70. Diamond, *Compromised Campus*, 69–76; Seymour Martin Lipset and David Riesman, *Education and Politics at Harvard* (New York: McGraw-Hill, 1975), 184–185; Hughes, *Gentleman Rebel*, 205–209.

71. Hughes, *Gentleman Rebel*, 205; Baron, "Recollections," 46; William Edgerton, "Adventures of an Innocent American Professor with the CIA and the KGB," *Russian History/Histoire Russe* 24 (1997): 321–327; Robert F. Byrnes, *A History of Russian and East European Studies in the United States: Selected Essays* (Lanham, Md.: University Press of America, 1994), 248.

72. Walter Galenson to Clyde Kluckhohn, February 13, 1948, RRC Correspondence, box 1; Staughton Lynd to Kluckhohn, February 6, 1948, RRC Correspondence, box 1.

73. John Hazard to Geroid Robinson, September 15, 1947, Robinson Papers, box 50.

74. Abraham Brumberg, "Problems of Communism and Early Soviet Studies," unpublished paper (2000), 1.

75. "Confidential Background Material for the President's Review Committee" (January 1952), Merle Fainsod Papers, Harvard University Archives, HUG 4382.8, box 4. Clyde Kluckhohn to Provost Paul Buck, June 13, 1949, RRC Correspondence, box 3.

76. Adam B. Ulam, *Understanding the Cold War: A Historian's Personal Reflections*, 2nd ed. (New Brunswick, N.J.: Transaction, 2002), 107. Alfred Meyer correspondence, June 19, 1987, cited in O'Connell, "Social Structure and Science," 145. The story also appears, without naming names, in Alfred G. Meyer, "Coming to Terms with the Past," 403.

77. See the Personnel Security Questionnaires in Harvard Refugee Interview Program Correspondence, Harvard University Archives, UAV 759.175, box "Mo–P."

78. Robert Cohen, *When the Old Left Was Young: Student Radicals and America's First Mass Student Movement, 1929–1941* (New York: Oxford University Press, 1993); Robert C. Tyler, "The American Veterans Committee: Out of a Hot War and into the Cold," *American Quarterly* 18 (Fall 1866): 419–436.

79. See, for instance, John Patrick Diggins, *Up from Communism: Conservative Odysseys in American Intellectual History* (New York: Harper and Row, 1975), or, in a less triumphalist spirit, Judy Kutulas, *The Long War: The Intellectual People's Front and Anti-Stalinism, 1930–1940* (Durham: Duke University Press, 1995).

80. On Carr, see Minutes of the Russian Seminar, March 5, 1948, Russian Research Center Seminar Notes, Harvard University Archives, UAV 759.8, box 1; Dean Schuyler Wallace to Geroid Robinson, September 9, 1945, in Robinson Papers, box 50. Jonathan Haslam, *The Vices of Integrity: E. H. Carr, 1892–1982* (New York: Verso, 2001), 120–124.

81. Clyde Kluckhohn to Donald McKay, November 12, 1947, in RRC Correspondence, box 1; Executive Committee Minutes, February 7, 1948, in RRC Executive Committee, Harvard University Archives, UAV 759.5, box 1; Sabine Hering and Kurt Schilde, *Kampfnahme Ruth Fischer: Wandlungen einer Deutschen Kommunistin* (Frankfurt: Dipa-Verlag, 1995), chap. 4.

82. On the institutional and funding frameworks supporting Soviet studies, see Alexander Dallin, "Soviet and East European Studies in the United States," in *Soviet and East European Studies in the International Framework*, ed. Arnold Buchholz (Berlin: Berlin Verlag, 1982); and

Harris, "Russian, Slavic and Soviet Studies." The founder of the major journal in Slavic language and literature, *Slavic and East European Review,* identified World War II and Sputnik as the landmarks in his field; see Shaw, "AATSEEL: The First Fifty Years," 8.

83. Richard Lambert, *Language and Area Studies Review* (Philadelphia: American Academy of Political and Social Science, 1973), 150–154.

84. Richard Lambert et al., *Beyond Growth: The Next Stage in Language and Area Studies* (Washington, D.C.: Association of American Universities, 1984), 357–358.

85. This essay also appears in *Cahiers du Monde Russe* 45 (2004), 465–496.

12

WHAT IS JAPAN TO US?

ANDREW E. BARSHAY

I HAVE CRIBBED my title from Fyodor Dostoyevsky's short article "Geok-Tepe: What Is Asia to Us?" Written in 1881, this was a meditation on Russia's civilizing mission and destiny as a European and Asian empire. My own purpose is post-Dostoyevskian and post-imperial: to offer an analytical overview of the relationship between the humanities and social sciences in the field of Japanese studies since 1945. What has Japan been—and what is Japan now—to us? How has Japan been constituted in the professional fields of inquiry that have taken it as their chief object? Why should there be such a field as "Japanese studies" in the United States? Beyond such academic questions, what is the broader significance of "Japanese studies" in American intellectual life, that is, to "us"?[1]

For the United States 1945 marks a rise to global power, pursued and maintained over the course of a five-decades-long rivalry with a self-avowed "socialist" world that was, in its own way, also a self-denying empire. Victory over the Axis, whose constituent regimes had held power through the massive mobilization of political viciousness against naturalized ethnic "others," compelled the United States to pursue social inclusiveness with a renewed moral mandate. There was no excuse not to do so. At the same time, under the aegis of "development," liberal noblesse oblige and rivalry with socialism brought Americans into unprecedented levels of contact with "other" peoples. Insofar as the humanities represent an attempt to understand the workings of the world, its communities and conflicts, through the frame of culture and values, it was natural that they should play a significant role in promoting both social inclusion and global intercultural ties. To what extent have they done so, or—intentionally or not—worked to marginalize or exclude significant groups from American political and intellectual life? How well did the humanities assist American society in redeeming the cost of victory overseas by striving to make that society more just? As the full dimensions of that cost were revealed—not only in lives lost and peoples shattered, but in the nuclearization of imperial rivalry in full knowledge of what happens when such weapons are used against actual human beings—did the humanities rise to the occasion?

For Japan, and therefore for the study of Japan, 1945 stands first of all for the moment of defeat, total and unconditional; it stands for the experience of a country and empire laid waste and defeated by the United States and its allies, including at the last moment the Soviet Union. Defeat, loss, and occupation were the first authors of Japan's "postwar." More urgent than explaining victory, perhaps, was the task (taken up on both sides) of explaining the war that preceded and produced Japan's defeat, and on that basis (and all too teleologically) to consider the prehistory of that war in Japan's imperial society of the early twentieth century. For those who came to the professional study of Japan any time around midcentury, the perception that the recent war had *social* roots was widely shared. To explain that war and prevent the next one, it was necessary to acquire and apply a broad understanding, rather than just restricted, opportunistically gained "intelligence," to the question "What is Japan to us?"

The Prehistory of Japanese Studies: A Few Episodes

The Japanese intellectual historian Maruyama Masao (1914–96) proposed that the "history of thought" occupy itself with four "levels" of ideas: moving from "top" to "bottom," these were: (1) that of "abstract and systemized theories and doctrines" such as Thomism; (2) a broader level composed of "views and images of the world" (*Weltanschauungen*); (3) particular opinions and attitudes; and (4) "feelings, moods, and sentiments about life that lie below the surface of man's conscious awareness." The task of the intellectual historian is to show the interrelation of these levels of "ideas" in order to grasp their "value, meaning, function, or role." As a general rule, Maruyama holds, "it is the relatively high levels of thought which give orientation, that is to say, direction and goals, to ideas. . . . An awareness of goals . . . moves from the higher to the lower levels, while the energy of thought, that energy which can be said to propel ideas, rises from the lower to the higher. . . . Energy alone does not know in which direction to move, or what function to play, and . . . the establishment of goals and a sense of direction alone does not have enough energy to propel ideas without being accompanied by the real feelings and sentiments of the people."[2]

Though not a "doctrine," "Japanese studies" as an intellectual formation in the American academy does seem to correspond most closely to Maruyama's "top" level of thought. It reached that position, I argue, only after Japan was thrust "upward," first by the unparalleled energy generated through war, and then by Japan's unexpected and spectacular run of sustained economic growth after the mid-1950s. Together these "thrusts" had a transformative effect at all levels, most emphatically including the lowest. In the process of its emergence, Japanese studies also drew into itself, or subsumed, much of the intellectual material characteristic of the second and third levels.

Before World War II, though Japan was not an intellectual tabula rasa for Americans, there was no institution of "Japanese studies" in the United States. Why should there have been? American concern with Japan, in comparison with China, to say nothing of Europe, was episodic and transient, and the perception of the country imagistic. This means that rather than turning to the few individuals who *did* possess a "top level" knowledge, for a retrospective existential grasp of what Japan *meant* we would do better to "lower" our gaze.

But where to start? Regretfully, I will set aside the fascinating early decades of American-Japanese interaction. The salient period of prehistory for our subject, I think, would be the decade between 1895 and 1905. These were the years of Japan's victory in wars against China and Russia and its associated colonial *démarches* in Taiwan, Korea, and Manchuria, and of domestic political consolidation and rapid industrialization under the aegis of a neotraditional ideology that stressed the historical uniqueness of Japan as the sole non-Western society to make an independent transition to modernity. Japan, it was claimed, was a society whose very traditions, by selective preservation, provided both discipline and dynamic to that transition in a way that effected a new mode of modernity. Japan had moved from object to subject, not just made by but a maker of history, including the *right to self-interpretation*.[3] These were achievements that throughout the West, from the United States through western Europe to Russia in the "east," provoked the syndrome of combined fascination, admiration, and racist alarm, the conflicting urges to praise and denigrate, embrace and alienate. There were by this point experts on Japan, minuscule in number to be sure, working in various fields of the still-young social sciences, as well as budding comparativists and the intellectually adventurous—Thorstein Veblen, for example.[4] And there were the geopoliticians, journalists, and propagandists who foresaw that the rise of Japan would ultimately bring about war with the United States over the issue of hegemony in the Pacific: the turn-of-century "condominium" arrangement was not to last. In somewhat larger numbers, humanists—Ernest Fenellosa, William Griffis, Charles Eliot—joined with historians to produce individual works on religion and art, some of them still of considerable merit. And of real importance were Japanese, some based in Japan and others abroad, writing for foreign audiences. One thinks here of *Fifty Years of New Japan* (1909), a collection of essays in which the highest figures of state, politics, education, and cultural life (or their ghost writers) reflected on the successes of Meiji. In the same moment, Nitobe Inazô (1862–1933), a Christian, expert on colonial policy, educator, and sometime diplomat, published *Bushido: The Soul of Japan* (1899) in order to show that in its "genuine," refined form, Japan's warrior ethic could support a modern, ethical national life and imperial policy, one fully consistent with Christian belief. Taking a somewhat different approach, Okakura Kakuzô (or Tenshin, 1862–1913), the author of the *Book of Tea* (1906), *Ideals of the East* (1905, with its famous opening line, "Asia is One"), and the posthumously published *Awakening of Japan* (1921), signaled Japan's essential difference from the West in its aesthetics and philosophical attitudes. Like Nitobe, Okakura also strove to identify Japan as a functioning member of the modern fraternity of imperial powers. Indeed, Japan was more modern, Okakura held, than Russia (an attitude, by the way, that he shared with Lenin), and for this reason it deserved the support of Western opinion in its struggles with the tsar's empire. But Okakura's aestheticized politics, and politicized aesthetics, revealed a profound alienation from the Western milieu in which (as curator of Asian art at the Boston Museum of Fine Arts) he had chosen to operate.[5]

Such, in outline, were the intellectual events that constituted the "matrix" out of which Japanese studies was eventually to form: "tradition in, not versus, modernity" was the watchword. But clearly there could be no straight line in thought, any more than in the "real" world, from the turn of the twentieth century to its midpoint. Nitobe's brand of nationalism-within-internationalism, symbolized by his appointment as undersecretary of the League of Nations, along with the era's incipient democracy, foundered on the rocks of economic depression and, more directly, on Japan's hard turn toward a militarized foreign policy in the late 1920s.

The flash point was the issue of China. Here, a deep-rooted American (and, more broadly, Western) sympathy, tinged with orientalism, reacted against what seemed Japan's crudely aggressive materialism. A protean divide opened between the Japan-inclined and the China-inclined, with far-reaching consequences for American and Western perceptions and studies of Asia. Briefly stated, for the former, Japan remained an exemplar of an efficient, new-old form of modern life, progressive, enlightened, even humane in governing its ungrateful Korean colony.[6] But in comparison with China, it seemed to some foreign observers that Japan's claims to have achieved a balance between its past and future were at best overblown. Instead of balance, they saw frenetic, almost schizoid cultural oscillations that, for all the political dysfunction and backwardness of Chinese society, did not seem to plague that country or its people (as far as they knew).

The British historian Eileen Power (1889–1940, the author of *Medieval People*, among other works), for example, visited first China, then Japan, in 1921. "The place I really loved," she wrote to a friend, "& to which I shall never be happy unless I can return is Peking. I like the Chinese immensely & of all the cities I have ever seen, Peking is miles the most fascinating. Paris & Cairo are the only other that come near it." By contrast, Power found Osaka (which she visited with Bertrand Russell) "a hideous manufacturing town for all the world like Manchester. The whole thing, smoke & chimneys & canals, westernised municipal buildings, clank of machinery, dismal piece of common, were painfully familiar. . . . They make a desert & call it industry." The Japanese, Power asserted, were "an imitative race"; the people "had adopted the Western idea of civilisation as material progress while clinging to the Eastern idea of religion in the shape of a blind patriotism."[7]

Power found it annoying to be "asked to admire Japan for the things I most dislike in Europe"; medievalists do sometimes romanticize the not-yet-industrialized societies "out there," as if they could stand in for their own lost, preindustrial past. But there was also a political edge to Power's reaction against Japan. Power was a socialist by inclination—she was a close associate of R. H. Tawney at the London School of Economics—but "nearly came to blows" over the Japan versus China question with her compatriots in the cause, Sidney and Beatrice Webb. The Webbs had visited Asia a decade before Power, and they "came down on the side of the Japanese." For them, Japan was the "land of hopefulness, the land of the rising sun in Asia." To be sure, they drew attention to the plight of urban workers and the poverty and penury of the countryside; but these were "transitional developmental problems." China, however, "had no capacity for anything"—except "endurance." It would be easy to dismiss both Power's and the Webbs' cultural pronouncements, since their time on the ground was short and they had only the power of contemporary and historical analogy to guide them in organizing their impressions. But the split in perception pointed ahead, to the slow, unmistakable sharpening and hardening of intellectual attitudes toward Japan as the 1930s wore on. Power for her part was increasingly alarmed by Japanese incursions in Manchuria and Shanghai, the violent tenor of politics, and military dominance over the conduct of foreign affairs. "What do you think of the Japanese now?" she wrote to an LSE colleague in 1932. "Did I tell you my theory that it was they who stole the Lindbergh baby in order to get themselves off the front page?"[8]

The point here is that admiration for Japan—and there was once a great deal—had largely dissipated by the 1930s. Now the romanticizers of tradition could still dream their dreams, perhaps with even greater intensity than before. Arthur Waley translated the *Tale of Genji* between 1925 and 1935 without setting foot in Japan. The sophisticated, decadent world he depicted was Bloomsbury projected onto eleventh-century Japan. Waley had his Japanese counterparts: the *Genji* was translated into the modern language twice before 1945. These too were necessarily projections of their translators' immediate milieu, and each could not help highlighting the contrast between that milieu and the wider actualities of its translator's present.[9] That "present" was increasingly one of war, of militarism, of political repression, and of cultural atavism; it was a present—some said—of Japanese "fascism." The more elite admirers of the country wondered how it could have regressed so badly; their "liberal" friends there had not prepared them for the ascendancy of the generals and colonels. The humanists, the scholars of Buddhism and art, were compelled to part ways with their Japanese confrères as their countries moved toward conflict. On the left, where there can have been only despair, were exposés ("Third Degree in Japan," for example, published in the *Manchester Guardian*) of torture and surveillance of ideological offenders and the pressures put on them to "return to Japan."[10]

It is interesting in this connection to note the remarks by the sociologist Louis Wirth in his preface to Karl Mannheim's *Ideology and Utopia* (1936): "A dramatic instance of the difference between the effects of and attitude toward technological as contrasted with social knowledge is furnished by contemporary Japan." Contrasting the "enthusiasm with which the results of physical and biological science are embraced in Japan . . . with the cautious and guarded cultivation of economic, political, and social investigation," Wirth notes that the latter were "subsumed . . . under what the Japanese call *kiken-shiso* [*kiken shisô*] or 'dangerous thoughts.' The authorities regard discussion of democracy, constitutionalism, the emperor, socialism, and a host of other subjects as dangerous because knowledge on these topics might subvert the sanctioned beliefs and undermine the existing order."[11] Writing of the same phenomenon at a remove of more than sixty years, Robert Bellah put the point as follows: "Preexisting structural and cultural conditions made fascism a more likely possibility in some nations [Italy, Germany, Japan] than others." Fascism combines "an intense national mobilization with an attempt to collapse significant differentiations—between divinity and state, between state and society, and between society and self—that involves a symbolic regression not only to premodernity, but, with the collapse of the distinction between divinity and the state, even to a preaxial condition." For Bellah, Germany's regression was the more traumatic, as it required a far greater and more violent effort than occurred in Japan, where "the very differentiations that fascism collapsed were only incipient and fragile."[12]

The Wartime Transformation

Japanese studies arose from the urgent need to explain why it was that Japan went to war, at first in Asia, and then with its former allies from World War I—and, in some sense, against itself. In terms of Maruyama's schema, it was not just the strategic needs of wartime that propelled the "upthrust" of Japan from the level of discrete opinions and worldviews to that of "doctrine" or system; also at work was the heaving, overwhelmingly negative emotion of hatred. In this upthrust, the humanities were forcefully displaced by a mobilized social science as the key to opening, or perhaps reopening, the doors of Japan. But this displacement was not permanent; in each generation, and in response to the sheer contingencies of history itself, the relation between the two orientations has been renegotiated and each has in some ways been transformed.

How did that first displacement happen? First, I think, through the heightened importance of serious reportage in informing and shaping public and elite opinion. Along lines I suggested earlier, much of this opinion was strongly sympathetic to China. Though a cadre of conservative "old Japan hands" such as Joseph Grew remained, they were temporarily in eclipse, their insistence on Japan's tractability having proven false. Hints of what was happening came from poets-as-chroniclers: W. H. Auden and Christopher Isherwood wrote from occupied China of the "places/Where life is evil now:/Nanking; Dachau."[13] In *Japan's Feet of Clay* (1937), Freda Utley described Japanese right-wing leaders as a "cross between the masterless samurai of the feudal period and Chicago gangsters."[14] Enduringly, the writings of Edgar Snow helped to raise awareness of the stakes of the China conflict, generating invaluable sympathy for the Communist "peasant reformers" and damning Japan for loosing a modern pestilence on an innocent people. The few Western experts on contemporary Japan—those with language skills—who had been able to work together with Japanese colleagues under the auspices, say, of the Institute of Pacific Relations, could no longer do so.

Particularly important roles were played by two Japan-born historians, E. H. Norman (1909–57) and Edwin Reischauer (1910–90), both sons of missionary families (Canadian and American respectively), who had completed graduate studies at Harvard. Horrified though they were by Japan's conduct of the war, as the conflict deepened they faced the prospect of watching the country of their birth brought to ruin, and in the closing phase of the war saw places they knew at firsthand ravaged and scorched by bombing, acquaintances and friends lost, some forever. I would venture to guess that the visceral identification felt by these men with the country they knew had some effect—beginning in limited circles—in humanizing perceptions of Japan at a time when truly savage hatreds otherwise ruled the day.

Yet there were differences, intellectual and political, between Norman and Reischauer, that were to play out rather consequentially in later years. Norman's writings during the war portrayed a Japan betrayed by a juntalike leadership that lacked the political skills, realism, and mettle of the Meiji oligarchs. He did not begrudge that early leadership their right to drag Japan by main force through a program of modernization in which the acquisition of national strength was the paramount goal. He saw that they had an opportunity, or "breathing space" (the reasons need not detain us here), and made the most of it. What Norman did condemn was the failure of those who came later. A Japanese analyst of the early 1920s, quoted by Norman, put the matter as follows: "It is not fair to the bureaucrats to condemn them as destructive reactionaries. They did much good. In a period of transition someone must take the helm, and they were expert pilots. But the period of transition is now over." [15]

Norman, then, did not see a simple continuity from the Meiji Restoration to Pearl Harbor; what he saw was avoidable regression and decadence in place of the democratic progress that he believed to be the Japanese people's birthright. To be sure, Norman's portrayal of the "feudal" Tokugawa regime was dark, particularly in comparison with the sunnier treatments of more recent vintage. Norman drew on a wide range of scholarship, including some by participants in the so-called debate over Japanese capitalism that galvanized the Marxist left during the previous decade. Norman argued that the restoration had only incompletely liquidated the ancien régime; in search of an alliance between low-ranking warriors and urban merchants, along the lines of the English revolutionary coalition, Norman had come up short. The warriors monopolized power, subordinating the would-be bourgeoisie and creating the "Prussia of the East" that was absolutist Meiji Japan. Astutely, Norman recognized the Janus face of Japan's rural elite; he also pointed out that bureaucratic dominance acted as a brake in Japan on out-and-out fascist dictatorship. But his overall rendering of "feudal" and "absolutist" Japan was stark all the same.

In no sense, however, was Norman party to the avowedly more scientific wartime analyses of the Japanese "national character," which sought to convey to the public why an already hated enemy behaved as he did—in other words, to offer an "overdetermined" account of "why we fight" that lent support to exterminationist tendencies.[16] It is hard to imagine that Norman would have found these to be anything other than abhorrent. In terms of Japan's future, Norman pinned his hopes on the liberated people of Japan's cities and villages and on the forces of the left. I do not think he looked to bureaucracy, let alone the imperial institution, as a source of needed stability. Less such stability in the past, he suggested, might have been for the better: "If the Japanese people had struggled to win a democratic constitution, it is not impossible that incalculable misery and blood, both Japanese and Chinese, might have been spared."[17]

The theme of bureaucratic dominance and continuity provides a tie-in to the case of Edwin Reischauer. Trained by Serge Eliseeff in Harvard's trademark cultural-philological tradition, Reischauer (along with his elder brother, Robert) produced studies of Japanese Buddhism and early cultural relations with China. By 1950 he had formulated the argument for which he became widely known: that Japan "has been the country which has diverged the most consistently and markedly from Far Eastern norms, and these points have been, by and large, points of basic resemblance to the West."[18] The tie-in mentioned above lies in Reischauer's wartime work as an adviser to Washington on Japan. In a memorandum prepared for the War Department in September 1942, he proposed a two-pronged policy: first, protect the Japanese emperor (from directly negative propaganda), since it would be in American interests to use the institution as a stabilizing "puppet" in any future occupation; and second, encourage interned Japanese Americans to join the military so as to demonstrate the magnanimity of American power—presumably by allowing them to die for the country that had trampled on their citizenship. This would have the effect of countering Japanese propaganda directed at the "yellow and brown" peoples of Asia that sought their support in Japan's avowed campaign against Western imperialism.[19]

E. H. Norman was considered one of the leading Western historians of modern Japan in the early postwar years, and he had a wide readership in Japan as well. He was called to his country's diplomatic service but in 1957, under (renewed) accusations that he had lied about his early Communist Party membership, Norman committed suicide in Cairo. At the time—the height of the Suez crisis—he was Canada's ambassador to Egypt. Norman's dark views of the Tokugawa era and of the succeeding absolutism remained current, perhaps, through the end of the 1950s, but they have since gone into what seems permanent eclipse. In other respects, for example his enormous and wide-ranging learning and profound humanism, Norman did not so much go into eclipse as set an unattainable standard. He retained the affection of his Japanese readers and had many close friends among the humanist and modernist intellectuals of the early postwar years—Maruyama Masao, Watanabe Kazuo, Hani Gorô—who were shocked and aggrieved by his being "taken from them" in death. For his part, Reischauer was perhaps the first Japan expert to gain a national audience; as a member of the Harvard faculty, he trained many of the leading scholars of the first postwar generation, and he famously served as American ambassador to Japan from 1961 to 1966. More will be said about that episode, but for the moment let us hold in our minds the symbolism of the two Japan-born ambassadors and their fates.

Some comment is in order here about the other crucial development of the war years. In the wake of the attack on Pearl Harbor, there was an obvious, desperate lack of competent speakers of Japanese that had to be remedied;

both training programs in a few major universities and language schools were set up by the various armed services. Recruitment brought largely Caucasian prospects with little or no prior knowledge of Japanese, some of whom came almost casually to their new assignment; for many, however, the experience was personally life-altering.[20] Their numbers were small, and the degree of intimacy and esprit de corps very high. Collectively, these were the individuals who, out of wartime exigency, created the institution we know today as "Japanese studies"—not, to be sure, in one stroke.

As we will see shortly, Japanese studies came together over two great phases, the first more or less contemporaneous with Japan's defeat and occupation, and the second with its recovery and rehabilitation during the era of the cold war. But it seems plausible to argue that the Japan that was studied through the lens of wartime strategic anthropology was the first and paradigm case of a foreign "area" requiring an integral, holistic, social scientific approach, beginning *always* with language training.

It must be recalled here that second-generation Japanese Americans (nisei) were brought into only a supporting role in language training, with small numbers allowed to teach (alongside Japan-born officers of American missionary parents) but not to form the core cadre of language officers. The majority of nisei who joined the armed forces, many directly from so-called relocation camps, fought in Europe. As operational needs demanded, of course, some also served in units in the Pacific, as document translators, interrogators of POWs, and so on. These were roles that continued into the occupation years, but only small numbers of nisei translated their experiences into careers in academic Japanese studies. In terms of our considerations here, that policy does raise the issue of "inclusion": that institutionalized racism prevented nisei from assuming a central role in language and area training seems incontestable. Clearly the military did not wish to entrust culturally sensitive work to a group only recently suspected of disloyalty-by-race. It was content to create a functional caste, as Reischauer's memo suggests. On the other hand, we should not presume that nisei ought to have been professionally interested in Japan: was there not typically a turn away from the parental homeland in the second generation following immigration, one overdetermined in this case by hostility to Japan in the wider society? The issues surrounding dual identity, needless to say, arose with ferocity for the third generation.

Language training, in any case, could not stop with language; the issue inevitably arose as to the context in which language functions. Of his experience at the Naval Language School in Boulder (where he was trained by Japanese American instructors) and later occupation service, the historian Thomas C. Smith wrote: "I believe most of us escaped the demonization of the enemy that is the usual effect of war. This was no doubt partly because our job did not require active participation in the fighting. . . . But our generally humane view of the enemy, as compared to most of the rest of the population at the time, was partly because of our year-long study of Japanese. Successful study of a foreign language requires some sympathy for the people and culture it represents." [21] As the war drew toward its close and Allied forces drew closer to Japan, the admittedly ad hoc planning for the coming occupation was stepped up. Yet ironically, this meant that just as the concern with Japan was moving away from defeating the enemy to the more humane tasks of reforming the soon-to-be-former enemy's society, the actual level of violence deployed against that society was rising, as the strategic bombing campaign reached its ghastly apogee. In a real sense the "backwardness" of Japan that was so great a presence in the rhetoric of the early postwar years was deepened by the combined effects of material *destruction* and social scientific *construction*. In any event, Japan was to be democratized and the social roots of warmongering excised. Policies had to be set on a vast range of issues, from the very form of state to land and legal reforms, public hygiene, and "civil information"; surveys of all kinds had to be conducted, documents read and translated, reports written and digested.

Before the end of the fighting, with Japan still inaccessible, "substitute" Japanese also had to be used as sources of information about the country and its people. To a limited degree it was possible to use Japanese POWs for that purpose, but a major source of live informants was the Japanese American relocation camps. It was this incarcerated population that, along with Japanese films, famously provided data for one of the founding texts of Japanese studies, Ruth Benedict's *The Chrysanthemum and the Sword* (1946). Japanese Americans proved "useful" indeed.

Postwar: Toward Rehabilitation

With defeat and occupation, Japan was opened up to empirical research as never before; Benedict's famous dichotomy of Japan's "culture of shame" versus the West's "culture of guilt," her discussion of groupism and Japanese value orientations, and her argument that collective shame could prove a dynamic for progressive change could all be tested against the real society.[22] Just as important, albeit under conditions of occupation censorship and asymmetry of power, and under parlous material circumstances, Japanese scholars could once again resume their work, free at least of the fear of suppression and arrest by the now-abolished "thought police." Part of that work—and this was something radically new—involved sustained scholarly ties with young and eager former members of the occupation forces, many of whom went on to academic careers and sent their students (who in turn sent theirs, and so on and on) to Japan for field research. For the Japanese involved, these early interactions could not help but arouse feelings of ambivalence. Their hopes for the democratic transformation of Japan were real and passionate, but their country lay in ruins and dishonor. Three million Japanese were dead, as were many millions more in Asia at the hands of the emperor's forces. And the vanquished were hungry; the victors were not.

Among the greatest surprises for budding American scholars in these years and thereafter was the discovery of a resurgent Marxist academic culture—a legacy of interwar Japan's cultural ties to Weimar Germany—of which few of them had any presentiment.[23] In some cases it was transformative, yielding a changed conception not only of Japan but also of historical analysis—indeed, of intellectual and scholarly life as such. Also reminiscent of Japan's Weimar experience was the enormous purchasing power of foreign currency; just as Japanese at that time had been able to buy entire libraries for virtually nothing—along with private tutorials with eminent but destitute scholars—American Japan specialists could, on behalf of their universities, acquire major, even invaluable collections of books and art. It is necessary to add, of course, that Japanese scholars and collectors in the former empire had made ample use of their status as colonialists to build up Japan's own holdings of cultural treasures from Asia.

It lies far beyond the scope of this chapter to recount the twists and turns of occupation policy or of Japanese intellectual and cultural history of the period, beyond saying that Americans were now involved in making both. We can summarize the legacy of the occupation (1945–52) and the immediately succeeding period as follows: "Japanese studies" was well and truly begun, with modest but quite tangible results in social science fields that were rising in importance across the board. Japan was the paradigm of the foreign research area, a field (if no longer a laboratory) for integral study. But in important ways the widely remarked hegemony of social science over area studies was still some distance in the future. To be sure, the advent of the cold war after 1948, the founding of the People's Republic of China in 1949, and the outbreak of the Korean war in 1950 heightened the sense among policy and opinion makers that Japan was strategically important. But this did not necessarily translate to the writing of foundational texts, let alone classics of social science. Such works, as we shall shortly observe, did emerge from Japanese studies, but it was necessary first to begin to think less instrumentally.

Indeed, the really significant American writing on Japan was John Hersey's *Hiroshima* (1946)—perhaps the most important piece of humanistic reportage ever written, but not the work of a specialist on Japan. Could a specialist have written a work of such apparently artless power? One does not read *Hiroshima*; one is read by it, in the sense that it interrogates the meaning of humanness for each reader each time it is read. Perhaps that is the definition of a classic text of any kind. But Hersey's book did have great significance, I am convinced, for Japanese studies in the long run. Hersey's original account in the *New Yorker* and the book version that followed must certainly have brought home to readers that the victims of the atomic bomb were innocent human beings who were also Japanese; it was possible to be both.[24] Hersey did not argue or polemicize, but it is conceivable that his account helped to soften American attitudes toward Japan at a time when the country was suffering its period of deepest postwar privation.

There is, however, a political irony involved as well. Like Benedict's book, Hersey's appeared just as the occupation was undertaking to preserve not only the imperial institution but the very occupant of the throne in whose name the war had been launched. In his surrender rescript the emperor justified the "extraordinary measure" of "accepting the joint [Potsdam] declaration" by saying that he was doing so to save human civilization from the "cruel bomb" that the Americans had dropped on Japan. This, I think, was itself a "cruel" dissimulation. But the point for us is that Hersey's short book may have provided the means by which the Japan of the "worldview" and "opinion" levels (of Maruyama's schema) was brought to experience a sort of transubstantiation. Hiroshima stood for an innocent Japan: the city's suffering inaugurated the country's moral rehabilitation. Since then the subtext of a deservedly guilty conscience, often repressed or vociferously (and to that extent unconvincingly) denied, has never been absent from American attitudes toward Japan, or indeed from Japanese studies in the United States.

Two other early postwar legacies may be noted. Insofar as specialists on Japan contributed to the country's rehabilitation in American public life and opinion—and to the enterprise of Japanese studies—at this phase it was humanists in the person of translators who should be credited. The early appearance of translations by Donald Keene of novelists such as Dazai Osamu and Ôoka Shôhei opened up to readers a Japan in the grips of an existential crisis. Defeat, social upheaval and inversion, privation, and sexual license were its ingredients and major motifs. This was in part another form of rehabilitation through the portrayal not only of suffering (both inflicted and experienced), but of a universal, modern condition of disorientation and struggle with meaninglessness. Keene's translations were joined by those of Edward Seidensticker and others; collectively, they won readerships for novels by Tanizaki and before long Mishima and Abe Kôbô. Films (ranging from works by Ozu, Mizoguchi, and

Kurosawa to *Godzilla*) and poetry and some paintings were also introduced; but it was the novels that drew attention. It was largely as translators, rather than as expository interpreters, that Keene and Seidensticker made their contribution. The preference for the annotated translation has been a lasting legacy of the "founding years." Somewhat paradoxically, this diffidence toward assigning meaning ultimately proved to be a limitation on the intellectual openness or receptivity of the field. Later generations have had to struggle to overcome the tendency to think that translation was a neutral, innocent act of transmission, dependent only on the objective skills of the rendering scholar. In that same moment, they have also had to face their own responsibility to act openly as critics who can talk not only to the field or to the general public, but to their counterparts in other domains of literature. The aggiornamento, signaled by works such as Masao Miyoshi's *Accomplices of Silence: The Modern Japanese Novel* (1974), was slow, difficult, and resented in some quarters, but also irreversible.

Finally, there was the interest in Zen Buddhism, at once recalling the prewar humanistic representation of Japan and the overlapping postwar rise of beat culture. Here again, the academic specialists were hardly involved. D. T. Suzuki's influential *Zen and Japanese Culture* (1959) was only one among a huge variety of writings that sought to promote a serious understanding of Zen and provoke innovation in art, poetry, and cultural sensibility more generally.[25]

A full discussion of this phenomenon would take us far afield, but one point does bear emphasizing. The striking thing, in retrospect, about the surge of publications on Zen—it has hardly stopped—was its studied avoidance of contemporary historical analysis. It was often asserted, though in fact it is not entirely the case, that Zen was to be equated with the spiritual ethos of the warrior class. But what was Zen in modern Japan? What were its institutional features, its political involvements, particularly during the war years? As one who came to Japanese studies in part through an interest in Zen—my own road took me through Thomas Merton and the "Zen Catholicism" of the English Benedictine Aelred Graham—I can testify that I was utterly unaware of such matters at the time. Nothing of what I read even raised the question. It is worth speculating whether there was a politics involved in the "Zen = Japanese *culture*" campaign: to reintroduce to the world a Japan transcendent of worldly entanglements, a Japan not implicated in the horrors of modern Asian history, may have been part of the motivation for its rather energetic propagation overseas during the 1950s, once it had been discovered on this side. Was this in some way related to the impulse among thoughtful, curious, but confused Americans to assuage a collective (but individually experienced) "bad conscience" brought on by the gradual recognition of the price of our victory over Japan and scornful of the dogmatic certainties of cold war political theology?

Modernization and Its Critique

For those who came to Japanese studies any time after the mid-1950s, the daily academic bread has consisted, in an overlapping sequence, of the production and absorption and then the critique and historicizing of the literature of Japan's "modernization." It is not really necessary to put the word in quotation marks, as if to say that the changes that took place in Japan beginning in the mid-nineteenth century did not happen or did not have world-altering consequences. Yet the interpretation of that process has evolved so dramatically over the last four decades that it is hard to recall that its meaning once seemed to be a given rather than a problem. But where had that "given" meaning of Japan's experience, and of the world's experience of Japan, come from? The translators and prewar humanists were not, on the whole, powerful interpreters of Japan as a living society; the policy- and power-oriented were more prone to a colonializing, or at least strongly instrumental, viewpoint. "Modernization" as a notion was meant to bridge that gap. Did it? Could it?

Recalling (in 1985) the intellectual atmosphere surrounding the emergence of modernization theory and its application to Japan, Robert Bellah wrote:

> Modernization theory, especially in the United States, was a kind of late child of the enlightenment faith in progress. Modernization was a process that produces all the good things: democracy, abundance—in short, a good society. Like ours. I'm afraid that was a major implication of the whole idea. America and a handful of other "advanced industrial societies" were, if not already good societies, so clearly headed in that direction that they made clear the end to which all the other societies, as they modernized, were tending. It was not that evil was denied. Fascism and Communism and other assorted disasters of modernity, including some in the United States, were indeed recognized but explained as distortions or pathologies of the "normal" course of modernization. . . . It is hard for us to realize today how optimistic, how euphoric, was the atmosphere in American social science in that first decade after the end of World War II. The belief that social science was rapidly becoming scientific and the belief that its results would be socially ameliorative still held together to an extent hard to imagine today. . . . Japan was the only non-Western nation to have transformed itself into a "modern industrial nation," thus joining that small handful of exemplars of the course all would take.[26]

In 1975 John Dower published a furious critique of Japan studies in the United States, seeing in it not "euphoria" but a darker complicity. The vehicle was an anthology of E. H. Norman's writings, introduced by Dower's lengthy examination of Norman's oeuvre, his politics, his suicide, and the historical and ideological context in which his work came to superseded.[27] Dower attacked the founding generation of Japanese studies for contributing its expertise to what he saw as a corrupt, politically repressive, ideologically driven program of American empire building in the name of modernization.[28] In an atmosphere of reflexive anti-Communism, Dower held, Norman had been sacrificed rather than protected, while his peers in the field temporized or even apologized for official policy. The tone is harsh, fitting the moment of the American debacle in Vietnam, out of which the critique had emerged. The essay had a powerful compounding effect on the sense of doubt and revulsion at imperial hubris that had grown steadily across the field of Asian studies over the previous decade. Americans, Dower suggested, were now learning what Japanese of the "Co-Prosperity Sphere" generation should have known. Indeed, he notes in an aside, it would be instructive to compare the Shôwa Kenkyûkai, the brain trust that formed around Prince Konoe Fumimaro in the late 1930s, to John F. Kennedy's advisers "or even the modernization theorists themselves."[29]

The particular animus of Dower's essay was directed first at Edwin Reischauer and then at Marius Jansen, with some attention to Robert Bellah and John Whitney Hall. Of these, only Bellah, as a student of Talcott Parsons, could actually claim to be a theorist of anything—the sociology of religion. The rest were all historians to whom sociological theory as such was rather alien—indeed, they may not have seen themselves as intellectuals at all. Reischauer was the most consciously ideological; he did not pretend otherwise. Jansen's manner and style reflected more a political aesthetic: he argued for and embodied "brightness" against "gloom" and saw Tokugawa as early modern rather than feudal, and so on, but he certainly remained within the domain of academic historiography in a way Reischauer did not. Dower's subject was the ideological cooptation of scholarship by scholars themselves and by others. His essay is part polemic, part eulogy, part analysis. In some respects it is difficult to reconcile Dower's critique with a reading of the key works that emerged from Japanese studies in the late 1950s: Bellah's *Tokugawa Religion* (1957), for example, is not mentioned, let alone discussed; nor is the work of Thomas C. Smith—at all. The latter omission is peculiar, since it was Smith's *Agrarian Origins of Modern Japan* (1959), following upon a number of seminal articles, that did the real work of grounding the reinterpretation of the Tokugawa era. Reading Dower's account, one cannot understand why the applicability of "feudalism" to Tokugawa society came to be called into question, except out of an ideological will to find a "bright" past to go along with a "bright" present. As reconstructed, however, Smith's rethinking of Tokugawa began with an impression gained from actual observation:

> When I began studying Japanese history after World War II, the dark side of the Japanese past needed no elaboration and had many distinguished analysts.

What seemed to me to need study was how, in such darkness, *so much that was admirable about Japanese life, even under the most trying postwar conditions, had flourished.* No question in that connection intrigued me more than whether modern Japanese industry had strong indigenous roots or was merely a cunning transplant made possible by the combination of a talent for imitation and an absolutist government able to mobilize popular energies on behalf of national expansion. In the one case there was great hope for revival; in the other decidedly less, since at least one of the conditions of earlier success was not likely to be repeated.[30]

It seems to me that, *mutatis mutandis,* Smith's attitude has much in common with that of Albert Hirschman, who famously spoke of his "bias for hope," yet whom no one could categorize as a foot soldier in ideological combat. If, as Smith observed, there was an underlying pattern to Japanese social (and economic) life that had survived both exploitation under the imperial system and the cataclysm of war, where and how had that pattern arisen? He began, that is, with a question, not an answer.

It is true enough that modernization was *coopted* as a framework, that it emerged as a "countertheory" to Marxism—or more precisely to Leninism—in the "febrile ideological moment" of cold war rivalry over the destiny of the postcolonial world.[31] This is hardly the place to talk about the fate of Marxism in any of its functions. We simply need to bear in mind the degree to which the superpower rivalries of the cold war had been overlain onto an already highly politicized Marxism, and more fundamentally the extent to which Marxism was itself no more than an earlier version of modernization theory. Perhaps because Marxism explicitly combined canonicity with partisanship, it was more directly prone to manipulation and degradation as an orthodox science–cum–*Weltanschauung*–cum–political weapon. Modernization theory may have claimed Weber for its authority, but it never formed a Weberian party, let alone a personality cult; its pitfall was an un-Weberian and emotional disavowal of the political drives, the "erotics" of ideology, among some of its proponents. In any event, Reischauer was alarmed at the allegiance shown to Marxism by Japanese intellectuals and students, and more broadly across East Asia and the Third World. As ambassador to Japan from 1961 to 1966, he took up arms in what was known as the "Reischauer offensive." His principal target was also his principal weapon: Japan. It was a target because he had to win intellectual allegiance among what I would call the left-nationalist intelligentsia of the post-occupation period, which had been seriously disillusioned by American political regression in the so-called Reverse Course after 1948. Japan was his weapon because Reischauer had to hand, by the early 1960s, the unfolding spectacle of Japan's economic growth.[32] Far beyond the expectations, let alone the planning capacity, of economic experts, the Japanese economy had taken off, and the transformation of Japanese society in every aspect was stunning and dramatic. The intellectual demonstration effect of the Japanese "miracle" (as the *Economist* proclaimed it in 1962) would propel Japan's rise to the status of model for all developing societies. As such, it would indicate to the existing socialist bloc the path to prosperity that revolution had blocked and, for those wavering between "systems," the path that would be blocked by the wrong choice or by subversion.

It is more than forty years since the 1960 Hakone Conference on the Modernization of Japan began to codify the theory of Japanese modernization. Perhaps in the initial post–cold war years, some might have thought that its proponents were nothing less than prescient. Yet today, even with the ideal of "socialism" condemned to ideological purgatory, we cannot say that capitalism ("growth") has brought to the world a heaven of justice or equitable distribution of wealth. As a problem for historical interpretation, the Hakone conference and subsequent modernization project in Japanese studies should be seen first (though perhaps not finally) in terms of the powerful and persistent disagreements among the participants. Even among the Americans it was debated whether one could bracket the question of the *politics* or *values* of modernization: was democracy inherent to the process? Was it legitimate to advocate, or even consider, the use of open authoritarianism in the pursuit of material, infrastructural development and hope that democracy would somehow evolve later on? For many of the Japanese who were present, the question itself was virtually immoral. Modernization without democracy was not modernization; it was an ersatz with real-world consequences already proven to be tragic. Such was the testimony of the rise and fall of the Japanese empire. Not all the Japanese at Hakone were Marxist; those who were could not accept a definition of modernization that abstracted the character of the political-economic system. Capitalism had to be named as such, as the actual *subject* of the developmental history being discussed, since it was on the table as an alternative, rather than a predecessor, to socialism.[33]

In the event, the Hakone program did seek to "reduce the process of modernization to its simplest terms." As Hall recounted, the effort that proved "most congenial" in that regard sought to place Weber's notion of *rationality* at the definitional core of modernization. As proposed by Benjamin Schwartz, who introduced Weber into the mix, modernization "involves the systematic, sustained and purposeful application of human energies to the 'rational' control of man's physical and social environment for various human purposes."[34] The patent (and potent) mix of Weberian, positivist, and behaviorist elements hardly settled the question of political means; the "strong and slow boring of hard boards" of which Weber himself actually spoke (in "Politics as a Vocation") was simply ignored. The first of the projected five volumes on modernization, consisting of papers delivered at the Bermuda conference in 1962, the one closest to Hakone in its "problem consciousness," is exceedingly interesting to read now; some of the individual essays are superb, and the orienting papers are highly revealing, even if despite themselves. The very title of the volume is an exercise in ambiguity that may serve as a metaphor for the project as a whole. *Changing Japanese Attitudes toward Modernization*: was "changing" an adjective, or, as a student of mine once slyly suggested, an American verb taking a Japanese object? The Hakone record and subsequent writings by Japanese participants suggest strongly that "changing" was meant to function as a verb.[35]

At Hakone the Japanese disagreements were rooted in history and in opposition to Japan's post-occupation status as a subaltern to the United States. The succeeding decade saw, on the one hand, the continuation (with some troughs) of Japan's economic surge; the crowning symbols of that success and the country's rehabilitation were the 1964 Tokyo Olympics, the Meiji Centenary of 1968, and Expo 70. On the other, of course, came the powerful and in some ways traumatic autocritique of democratic regimes and societies represented by the "1968" movements. In certain respects Japan's entry into the period of autocritique had begun early, in 1960, with the groundswell of opposition to the continuation of a revised U.S.–Japan Security Treaty; in any case, Japan was engulfed in "1968"-style movements as fully as if not more than any industrial society. Japan an exemplar? it was asked. No, it was the most polluted industrial country in the world, housed its workers in what were called rabbit hutches, and processed its school graduates along increasingly rigid and segmented lines.

It is inconceivable that Japanese studies and the modernization approach could have gone unaffected by the combination of continued rapid growth with the emergence of serious pathologies: the argument, as Dower had framed it in connection with Norman's earlier analyses, was whether a "good" process had somehow gone bad or had been flawed from the start. In any case, ideological lines hardened, totalism mirroring totalism, violence in the name of order begetting violence in the name of its negation, and on and on. But the rhythms and patterns by which that happened were different in Japan and the United States. In Japan the "old" left of the Communist and Socialist Parties was involved in the initial critique of modernization in 1960; by 1970 the new left had risen to contest not only modernization and its apologists, but the old left in the bargain.[36]

In terms of the professional American understanding of Japan—of Japanese studies—thanks to the McCarthy "purge" that had caught figures such as Owen Lattimore, John Emmerson, and Norman himself, there was of course no "old left" critique to disturb the peace, and so the generally admiring approach of modernization theory did extend its hegemony for a longer time than it had been able to do in Japan itself—until Vietnam, that is, which prompted, or forced, the development of an "antimodernizationist" stream of Japanese studies (in Australia, for example) that for some time remained isolated and unrecognized. Even in the United States the new left critique began eventually to open fissures in what was a growing if still modest academic edifice, for example via the Concerned Asian Scholars movement and its journal.

The effects were complex. John Dower's approach was typical, perhaps, in its harsh antielitism, but despite his paean to Norman's work, he himself remained largely an antielite historian of elites. (His recent *Embracing Defeat: Japan in the Wake of World War II* goes beyond this in treating non-elites, but it does not offer any reconsideration of those elites.) In both the United States and Japan a strong stream of populism entered the scholarly mix, with studies appearing of socialist thought, protest movements, peasant unrest and uprisings, and other instances of social conflict that had now to be properly theorized: they were not to be dismissed as deviant or marginal, or merely celebrated as "resistance."[37] As I have noted, younger Japanese scholars had already turned away, not only from the modernization approach, with its insistent focus on consensus and functionality and deriving these from "good" traditional values; they also turned against the initial critics—their modernist teachers—of that approach, whom they regarded as embodying a different form of elitism. Historians of the so-called *minshûshi* or People's History school began to attract serious attention among senior American scholars (including Marius Jansen as a kind of sponsor, and Irwin Scheiner as a more engaged practitioner)—and through them a new generation of graduate students. There was an excited, collective rediscovery of "community" as a source of creative alternatives to the overdetermined forces of Tokyo-centered capitalist rationalization and official nationalism. Mobilizing the ethnographic approach of Yanagita Kunio (1875–1962) and taking it in directions he could hardly have foreseen, the proponents of cultural history from below did succeed in opening a new phase in the representation of the Japanese past. It goes without saying that this was tied in to contemporary "local residents'" and "citizens'" movements that ran throughout the 1970s in city after city, large, small, and in between, across the archipelago.[38]

Along with this trend, the gap between American and Japanese specialists began to close, to be less intellectually polarized and burdened by the need to represent a set of larger, more political relationships.[39] In a broader sense, the dissolution of modernizationist hegemony left in its wake a field that most resembled an intellectual mosaic. Perhaps its most notable feature was the emergence of humanistic approaches, mediated by the "interpretive turn" in anthropology, that in effect prepared the way for the highly contested role, assumed shortly thereafter, of literary and critical theory. To speak of humanities was no longer to speak of philology or translation, but rather of metacriticism or theory.

As the 1980s arrived, this intellectual migration by the humanities had yet to occur within Japanese studies. Yet when one thinks of Japanese studies of that period, there is a force of greater import to be considered first. Writing in 1983, John Whitney Hall predicted that Japanese studies, following a period of remarkable growth in the 1970s, would enter a phase of stasis and consolidation. He was quite mistaken.[40] The Japanese economy of the 1980s—the era of the so-called bubble—unleashed a gush of funds into Japanese studies and also came close to reorienting the field as an enterprise devoted to explaining Japan as a new kind of exemplar: of development for the already developed, a model for the most advanced economies and societies. Prefigured, interestingly enough, in the work of two sociologists—Ronald Dore and Ezra Vogel—the true landmark of this tendency was Chalmers Johnson's *MITI and the Japanese Miracle* (1982). Johnson offered an exciting historical account of the Japanese "developmental state" that took its place in venues ranging from seminar rooms and think tanks to airport book racks. The thrust of discussion was not so much that Japan, as had been said nearly a century before, was historically and institutionally unique (Johnson heatedly disavowed what he called "cultural" explanations). Rather, it was that Japan's dirigiste political economy represented a creative new phase in the history of capitalism and that the vectors of influence between Japan and the West might now be reversed. In its coarser version the "Japanese model" was held to have abolished the business cycle, its enterprises miraculously able to motivate labor without conflict and strife. The national past was doubly mobilized: as before, the preindustrial family and village provided prototypes of a modern, collective instrumental rationality. To these, by the mid-1980s and with Edo as the preferred site, was added a form of urban postmodernity *avant la lettre*, with play, consumption, high-quality goods, and rising incomes its chief features. This may be more caricature than characterization, but an excess of funds did, inevitably, lead to hubris and poor judgment on both sides. Assertions of Japanese racial superiority called up the worst of the old dispensation in response, as in Theodore White's scurrilous revival of war hysteria in his 1985 *New York Times Magazine* article, "A New Pearl Harbor." In fact, the neo-exceptionalism of the 1980s had serious adherents and serious critics both. Materials in support of many positions were ready to hand in the studies done over the previous three decades; but the evidence of the senses, the glut of new building, the sheer volume of goods produced, the conspicuous consumption, the ease of travel and of getting research funds—all were hard to ignore, and they affected everyone involved at some level of awareness, like a diminishing but persistent hangover.

But when the bubble burst in the early 1990s, what actually turned out to have happened? To speak impressionistically: first of all, the large numbers of students who thought they were interested in Japan (or in employment involving Japan) were an epiphenomenon of "excess"; and often their interest foundered on the rocks of language. Enrollments have fallen, though not nearly to the catastrophic depths as has the number of students studying Russian. On the other hand, in Japanese and related courses across the disciplines, the proportion of Asian-heritage students must be half or more, but within that number the presence of Japanese Americans is not great. In other words, students whose backgrounds are Chinese, Korean, Vietnamese, and Filipino have taken up the study of Japan as part of their higher education. How this relates to the sociology of recent immigration and its cultural trends is an issue I am not really competent to discuss. But it does seem to have a direct bearing on the "dynamics of inclusion" that is our common concern. Among other things, it suggests that the politics of inclusion is actually global in character. For such students to take courses on Japan has often required overcoming parental resistance, not so much, or not only, to the humanities, but to the study of Japan—for Koreans and many Chinese the country most responsible for the suffering visited upon their families in earlier generations. At the graduate level, too, the number of Asian and Asian American students working on Japan has increased, as has their entry into faculty ranks. A related phenomenon must certainly be the slow undermining of the walls separating Asian and Asian American studies as academic fields. But my guess would be that though the sociology of Asian studies will shift toward greater ethnic plurality within each of its constituent fields, the gap between Asian and Asian American studies will likely remain fairly wide. This is perhaps one further implication of Steinhoff's observation that while Japanese studies has gained institutional presence and meaning, its basic pattern has remained stable: of studying Japan within a *disciplinary* orientation, and secondarily affiliating with a collectivity of "Japan people." Japanese studies is a small enterprise, a *chûshô kigyô*, contrasted either with the mammoth proportions of the Japanese economy or, more locally, with other area studies groupings. Steinhoff estimates, for example, that as of 1993 there were about five times as many specialists in Latin American studies as there were in the Japan field: roughly 7,500 compared to 1,500. As she puts it, "we are truly invisible."[41]

And yet Steinhoff's title spoke of the "loss of irrelevance"—one should not speak, I suppose, of lost innocence. In what sense is Japan relevant? Its postwar history is actually just now coming to be written. The trajectory of Japan's political economy remains incontestably important, but its significance has changed with the deepening of Japan's economic interactions with China and East Asia—in other words, as that interaction has taken on greater political and social meaning. Political and policy concerns, which are ultimately also military, have also gained in salience and continue to do so every day. Ironically, what Bernard Silberman has termed an "oversocialized" social science that assimilated economy to culture and "forgot" politics has helped to make Japan more rather than less irrelevant: to the extent that its economy (and therefore its culture) has failed and fallen from the status of exemplar, Japan ceases to be of interest; it "disappears." This is cause not for despair but for hope. With the fading of an earlier model of holistic universalizing under the sign of culture, may not the "real" Japan, the Japan that failed, the Japan that has both succeeded and failed, the Japan beyond success and failure, now emerge into view? Not yet: for blocking it, from the other side, lies what Silberman terms the "undersocialized," radically individualizing approaches associated with rational choice. For him these provide nothing more than an inverse, no less false universalism. What he argues for is a social science that operates on a "concept of embeddedness in which the individual is in a constant bargaining process with the central elements of social order." To understand such modes of embeddedness, and the protocols of bargaining that have made and remade social order in Japan, would seem to me the task of a social science infused with humanistic concerns and skills. It may be that the Japan we have known, the putative whole to which our specialized training has gained us access, may be disappearing, to be replaced by many Japans. The area studies model itself, as Silberman charmingly puts it, is like a Cheshire cat, with little left but a smile formed by the memory, or trace, of what was formerly known.[42]

As with every other construct or category, "Japan" could not but change under the impact of theoretical *démarches* from "outside"—the figures of Heidegger and Bourdieu and also of American pragmatism, for example, are clearly discernible in the "embedded bargaining" approach just outlined. It is simply obscurantist to wish away the outside world, whether in everyday or in academic life. People are thinking *everywhere, all the time*, and we simply do not know from what quarter the next vital inspiration will come. We should not confine ourselves to Japan or any other territory in looking for meaning, or even lament the passing of an area studies model that has anesthetized us against theory and self-criticism.[43]

Having said that, I must end on a doubly reactionary, perhaps self-contradictory note. On the one hand, I do not think that "many Japans" is always to be preferred to a single "Japan." As is true of conceptualizations of capitalism and modernity, unchecked pointillism, endlessly placing the "nation" in quotation marks, can lead to incoherence and to a rigid, almost metaphysical refusal of synthesis, which is also, after all, a respectable operation of the intellect.

The two recent, and different, efforts to theorize "Japan"—by S. N. Eisenstadt and Johann Arnason—are worthy of note in this connection.[44] On the other hand, I worry a great deal when graduate students in Japanese history cannot read texts in Japanese with speed and accuracy and an eye—or better, an ear—for nuance. This is not just a practical concern for the work they will have to do in order to produce original research or find appropriate employment later on. It means that they (and therefore "we," their non-specialist audience) are cut off from a vast world, a sea of enriching and invigorating ideas, of tangible expressions of sensibilities and mentalities—cut off, in short, from the world of discourse whose "levels" of form and articulation Maruyama described as the proper concern of intellectual history. It takes time and patience and commitment to learn language at all these levels. By definition, such study is what specialists do to become real specialists. The Japan field needs to be made as theoretically sharp and sophisticated as it can be. But if that sophistication is not matched by the full engagement of our intellects with language in all its facets, if we are not local humanists, our new "knowledge" will become a desiccated shell and scatter at the next stirring of the wind.

Notes

1. For recent accounts of the development and standing of Japanese studies in the United States, see Japan Foundation and Association for Asian Studies, eds., *Japanese Studies in the United States: The 1980s* (Ann Arbor: Association for Asian Studies, 1984); Marius Jansen, ed., *Japanese Studies in the United States: Part I: History and Present Condition* (Ann Arbor: Association for Asian Studies, 1988); Japan Foundation and Association for Asian Studies, eds., *Japanese Studies in the United States: The 1990s* (Ann Arbor: Association for Asian Studies, 1996); and Helen Hardacre, ed., *The Postwar Developments of Japanese Studies in the United States* (Leiden: Brill, 1998). See too the illuminating article by Patricia Golden Steinhoff, the compiler of the Japan Foundation/AAS surveys, "Japanese Studies in the United States: The Loss of Irrelevance," *IHJ Bulletin* 13 (Winter 1993): 1–9. In all, there have been five self-studies of academic Japanese studies since the late 1960s (1969–70, 1974–75, 1982–83, 1988, 1996), support for which was provided variously by the Social Science Research Ccouncil (SSRC)–American Council of Learned Societies (ACLS) Joint Committee on Japanese Studies, the U.S.–Japan Conference on Cultural and Educational Interchange (CULCON), the Japan Foundation, and the Association for Asian Studies. A new one is now under way.

2. Maruyama Masao, "An Approach to the History of Thought: Its Types, Realms, and Objectives," *Asian Cultural Studies*, no. 5 (October 1966): 10–11. Maruyama goes on to

discuss how one measures the value of thought at each level, in terms of its "weight," "scale of permeation" or "sphere of circulation," "breadth," logical "density," and "generative quality" (11–12).

3. "If the identity between professional area specialists, say, Japanologists, and the field of study appears more prominent and thus overdetermined than in other area studies, it is, I believe, because of the overwhelming production of native knowledge and thus self-consciousness that has marked the path of Japan's own modernity." H. D. Harootunian, "Postcoloniality's Unconscious/Area Studies' Desire," in *Learning Places: The Afterlives of Area Studies*, ed. Masao Miyoshi and H. D. Harootunian (Durham: Duke University Press, 2002), 160.

4. See Thorstein Veblen, "The Opportunity of Japan" (1915), in his *Essays in Our Changing Order* (New York: Viking, 1934).

5. See Maruyama Masao, "Fukuzawa, Uchimura, and Okakura: Meiji Intellectuals and Westernization," in *Developing Economies* 4, no. 4 (1966): 1–18.

6. See T. Philip Terry, *Terry's Guide to the Japanese Empire*, rev. ed. (Boston: Houghton Mifflin, 1928), chap. 6.

7. See Maxine Berg, *A Woman in History: Eileen Power, 1889–1940* (Cambridge: Cambridge University Press, 1996), 104–107.

8. Ibid., 184, 237.

9. The translations were made by the poet Yosano Akiko (published 1912) and the novelist Tanizaki Jun'ichirô (published 1939–41).

10. See the dialogue between Maruyama Masao and Kozai Yoshishige, "Ichi tetsugakuto no kunan no michi," in *Shôwa shisôshi e no shôgen*, ed. Mainichi Shinbunsha (Tokyo: Mainichi Shinbunsha, 1969), 7–102. The *Guardian* exposé, which "caused a sensation," is mentioned on p. 42.

11. Louis Wirth, preface to Karl Mannheim, *Ideology and Utopia* (1936; rpt. San Diego: Harcourt, Brace, Jovanovich, 1985), xiv. Wirth continues: "But lest we think that this condition is peculiar to Japan, however, it should be emphasized that many of the topics that come under the rubric of 'dangerous thought' in Japan were until recently taboo in Western society as well."

12. Robert N. Bellah, *Imagining Japan* (Berkeley: University of California Press, 2003), 45–46.

13. W. H. Auden, "Commentary," in *Journey to a War*, by W. H. Auden and Christopher Isherwood (1939; rpt. New York: Paragon House, 1990), 274.

14. As quoted in Maruyama Masao, "The Ideology and Dynamics of Japanese Fascism" (1947) in *Thought and Behavior in Modern Japanese Politics*, by Maruyama Masao (New York: Oxford University Press, 1969), 79.

15. Iwasaki Uichi, *The Working Forces in Japanese Politics* (New York: Columbia University, 1921), 52; quoted in E. H. Norman, *Japan's Emergence as a Modern State* (1940; rpt. New York: Pantheon, 1975), 210. *Japan's Emergence* was Norman's doctoral dissertation.

16. See the extensive discussion of wartime social science in John Dower, *War without Mercy* (New York: Pantheon, 1986).

17. E. H. Norman, "Militarists in the Japanese State" (a 1943 book review), quoted in John Dower, "E. H. Norman, Japan, and the Uses of History," introduction to *The Emergence of the Modern Japanese State: Selected Writings of E. H. Norman* (New York: Pantheon, 1975), 31.

18. Edwin O. Reischauer, *The United States and Japan* (Cambridge: Harvard University Press, 1950), 184. Robert Reischauer was among the earliest Western victims of the fighting in China; he was killed in a bombing raid on Shanghai in August 1937. On Eliseeff see Kurata Yasuo, *Eriseefu no shôgai—Nihongaku no shiso* (Tokyo: Chûkô Shinsho, 1977).

19. See Takashi Fujitani, "The Reischauer Memo: Mr. Moto, Hirohito, and Japanese American Soldiers," *Critical Asian Studies* 33, no. 3 (2001): 379–402. The memorandum is reproduced on pp. 399–402.

20. See Thomas C. Smith, "The Kyoto Cyclotron," *Historia Scientiarum* 12, no. 1 (2002): 74–75; Otis Cary, ed., *Eyewitness to History: The First Americans in Postwar Asia* (New York:

Kodansha International, 1995); Center for Japanese Studies, ed., *Japan in the World, the World in Japan: Fifty Years of Japanese Studies at Michigan* (Ann Arbor: Center for Japanese Studies, University of Michigan, 2001).

21. Smith, "The Kyoto Cyclotron," 74.

22. On Benedict, see Clifford Geertz, *Works and Lives: The Anthropologist as Author* (Stanford: Stanford University Press, 1988), esp. chap. 5; Jennifer Robertson, "When and Where Japan Enters: American Anthropology since 1945," in Hardacre, *Postwar Developments*, esp. 299–306; Aoki Tamotsu, "Anthropology and Japan: Attempts at Writing Culture," *Japan Foundation Newsletter* 22 (October 1994), esp. 4–5; Alexander Stille, "Experts Can Help Rebuild a Country," *New York Times*, July 19, 2003. Aoki estimates that Benedict's book has sold 350,000 copies in the United States; Stille, quoting an Australian anthropologist, gives a figure of 2.3 million for Japan.

23. See, e.g., Delmer M. Brown, "The Social Sciences in Japan," *Far Eastern Survey* (March 9, 1949): 53–55; and the review by John Whitney Hall of *Nihon shakai no shiteki kyūmei* (1949) in *Far Eastern Quarterly* 11 (November 1951): 97–104. It is tempting to wonder how different Japanese studies in the United States would have been if a critical mass of dissident or persecuted scholars from Japan had chosen, or been able, to establish themselves in American exile. Only a tiny number did so.

24. In composing *Hiroshima*, Hersey seems to have been inspired by Thornton Wilder's *Bridge of San Luis Rey*, in which "a man tries to trace the hand of fate in the lives of victims of a terrible accident." Robert Stone, "The Survivors" (review of Steven Brill, *After: How America Confronted the September 12 Era*), *New York Times Book Review*, April 20, 2003, 10.

25. See Helen Westgeest, *Zen in the Fifties: Interaction in Art between East and West* (Zwolle: Waanders, 1996).

26. Robert Bellah, "Introduction to the Paperback Edition" of *Tokugawa Religion: The Cultural Roots of Modern Japan* (New York: Free Press, 1985), xii.

27. Dower, "E. H. Norman," 3–101.

28. I stress "contributing to": the real theorists were political scientists and policy intellectuals such as Karl Deutsch, Gabriel Almond, Sidney Verba, Cyril Black, and Walt Rostow, who ranged quite widely in intellectual caliber among themselves.

29. Dower, "E. H. Norman," 88–89. For recent critiques along the same lines, see the essays by Masao Miyoshi, Bruce Cumings, and Moss Roberts in Miyoshi and Harootunian, *Learning Places*.

30. Thomas C. Smith, *Native Sources of Japanese Industrialization, 1750–1920* (Berkeley: University of California Press, 1988), 2–3; emphasis added. See also Ôshima Mario, "Amerika no Nihonshi kenkyû to kindaikaron hihan," *Rekishi kagaku*, no. 166 (November 2001): 16–26; "The Notion of Historical Backwardness in Modern Japan: 'Invented Traditions' in Japanese Historiography and the Significance of Thomas Smith's Stance," *Osaka City University Economic Review* 35 (October 1999): 13–22.

31. See Nils Gilman, "Modernization Theory, the Highest Stage of American Intellectual History," in *Staging Growth: Modernization, Development, and the Global Cold War*, ed. David Engerman et al. (Amherst: University of Massachusetts Press, 2003), 47–80.

32. The very appointment of a Japanese-speaking ambassador was of enormous symbolic significance in its own right. Reischauer could at least read his opponents' writings and argue with them in their own language. Amid his deepening difficulties with the administration over its Vietnam policy, Reischauer seems to have been suspected of "going native," not just personally (through marriage), but politically. On the "Reischauer offensive" see Victor Koschmann, "Modernization and Democratic Values: The 'Japanese Model' in the 1960s," in Engerman et al., *Staging Growth*, esp. 237–242.

33. See the unpublished transcript of the conference proceedings of the Association for Asian Studies, "Hakone kaigi gijiroku," Tokyo, 1961.

34. See John Whitney Hall, "Changing Conceptions of the Modernization of Japan," in *Changing Japanese Attitudes toward Modernization*, ed. M. Jansen (Princeton: Princeton University Press, 1965), 7–41, esp. 21–24.

35. Koschmann, "Modernization and Democratic Values," 232–237. See also the rather tendentious discussion in Stefan Tanaka, "Objectivism and the Eradication of Critique in Japanese History," in Miyoshi and Harootunian, *Learning Places*, 80–102. Tanaka manages to accuse Maruyama Masao, who if nothing else maintained a position at Hakone that was consistently independent, of triviality and sycophancy as a "native informant" for the Americans (97).

36. For contemporary Japanese critiques of the modernization approach, see Kinbara Samon, '*Kindaika'ron no tenkai to rekishi jojutsu* (Tokyo: Chûô Daigaku Shuppanbu, 2000), and Wada Haruki, "Kindaikaron," in *Nihon shigaku ronsô*, vol. 9 of *Kôza Nihonshi*, ed. Rekishigaku Kenkyûkai and Nihonshi Kenkyûkai (Tokyo: Tokyo Daigaku Shuppankai, 1971), 255–282.

37. See for example, J. Victor Koschmann and Tetsuo Najita, eds., *Conflict in Modern Japanese History: The Neglected Tradition* (Princeton: Princeton University Press, 1982), particularly Najita's introduction. It is to be noted that scholars of the "founding generation"—Hall, Jansen, Reischauer—could be quite receptive to these new trends; the political pressures that might have made them leery a decade earlier had dissipated.

38. See J. Victor Koschmann, ed., *Authority and the Individual in Japan* (Tokyo: University of Tokyo Press, 1974).

39. On the Japanese "*minshûshi*" historians see Carol Gluck, "The People in History: Recent Trends in Japanese Historiography," *Journal of Asian Studies* 38 (November 1978): 25–50; Takashi Fujitani, "*Minshûshi* as Critique of Orientalist Knowledges," *positions* 6, no. 2 (1998): 303–322.

40. See Steinhoff, "Japanese Studies in the United States," 1.

41. Ibid., 3. On the Asian–Asian American studies issue, see the essays by Sylvia Yanagisako and Richard Okada in Miyoshi and Harootunian, *Learning Places*, 175–189, 190–205; and the comments in Fujitani, "The Reischauer Memo," 391, 397–398nn22–23.

42. See Bernard Silberman, "The Disappearance of Modern Japan: Japan and Social Science," in Harootunian and Miyoshi, *Learning Places*, 303–320.

43. In addition to the materials cited above, see the dialogue between Harry Harootunian and Naoki Sakai, "Japan Studies and Cultural Studies," *positions* 7, no. 2 (1999): 593–647; Harry Harootunian, *History's Disquiet* (New York: Columbia University Press, 2000), chap. 1; Masao Miyoshi, "Japan Is Not Interesting," in *Re-mapping Japanese Culture* (Victoria [Australia]: Monash Asia Institute, 2000), 11–24.

44. S. N. Eisenstadt, *Japanese Civilization: A Comparative View* (Chicago: University of Chicago Press, 1996); Johann P. Arnason, *Social Theory and the Japanese Experience: The Dual Civilization* (London: Kegan Paul International, 1997).

13

HAVANA AND MACONDO

The Humanities in U.S. Latin American Studies, 1940–2000

ROLENA ADORNO

SPANISH-LANGUAGE study was an essential component in the creation of U.S. Latin American area studies, and it has distant antecedents. Thomas Jefferson was one of the first American statesmen and politicians to envision the study of the Spanish language in the United States as a necessary adjunct to the education of the new country's citizens.[1] Jefferson the Francophile saw the academic value of the Spanish language for the study of hemispheric history, but most of all he foresaw its value as a vehicle for the development of hemisphere-wide commerce.[2] By the end of the nineteenth century this view had gained ground. In his 1883 Phi Beta Kappa lecture at Harvard College, Charles Francis Adams Jr. remarked, "The Spanish tongue is what the Greek is not,—a very considerable American fact."[3] It was probably Adams's involvement with the construction of the Union Pacific Railroad that accounted for his assertion, because his insight into the importance of the Spanish language was not the view generally held by academicians at the time.[4] Upon welcoming scholars to the eighth annual Modern Language Association convention in 1890, the chancellor of Vanderbilt University, Landon C. Garland, called attention to "a Spanish speaking people, over whose territory we are stretching out our railroads, and with whom we are daily enlarging our commercial relations, and over whose territory we are extending our missionary operations."[5]

Within such purviews, the teaching of the Spanish language was introduced in American universities late in the nineteenth century.[6] It arose out of a two-layered debate over the American university curriculum regarding the respective values of teaching the ancient versus the modern languages and, more broadly, the value of pursuing the natural sciences rather than classical subjects.[7] The emergence of Spanish was part of the "practical turn" in the early development of the U.S. university curriculum. Spanish-language study thus long antedates the advent of Latin American studies as such, and its support and promotion would come to constitute the earliest developments in the field.

372

The growth of Latin American studies in the United States in the second half of the twentieth century came about through a series of convergences between events external and internal to the academic disciplines that it comprises: history, political science, anthropology, economics, sociology, and language and literary studies. In addition, the period under discussion includes the emergence of U.S. Latino studies, Afro-Hispanic studies, and Latin American cultural studies. This brief overview attempts to assess how cold war initiatives fomented Latin American studies in the humanities, particularly Spanish-language and literary studies, and how, by the end of the century, the field of literary studies was complemented by new critical trends that ranged from the study of gender and sexuality to testimonial writing.[8] The rhetorical figure that best captures this era of tremendous growth and significant transformation is irony—that is, the irony of outcomes that ignored, subverted, or transcended original intentions.

The Soviet launch of Sputnik in 1957, the Cuban Revolution of 1959, the Cuban missile crisis of 1962, the Operation Camelot scandal of 1965, the Vietnam War of the late 1960s–early 1970s, and the Sandinista Revolution in Nicaragua in 1979 affected the shifting fortunes of U.S. Latin American studies in general. Yet many important developments internal to Latin American area studies predate these events, and others have been only indirectly affected by them. The core disciplines did not develop simultaneously. Language and literary studies and history are the oldest, along with anthropology, political science, economics, and sociology.[9] There is no doubt that cold war initiatives had an influence on Latin American studies, particularly the social sciences.[10] At the same time the development of area studies centers and programs made possible the exponential institutional growth of the Latin Americanist humanities, even though such programmatic initiatives did not successfully anticipate or control the paths that humanistic studies actually took.

With the important exception of the attention drawn to Latin America by the Cuban Revolution, the other influential events for the U.S. Latin Americanist humanities in the cold war era have been literary rather than political; these literary events—from Borges to the international "Boom" of the Latin American novel—have oriented the course and content of language and literary studies developments.[11] The trump card was not the federal programs that would "strengthen resistance to totalitarianism"[12] but, rather, in those same years, the Spanish-language publication, and English-language translation, of the richly imagined worlds of Latin American literature. The greatest strength of the field, which has guaranteed and renewed its vitality, is the vigorous dialogue and debate that increasingly exist (in this Internet era) between Latin Americanists in the United States and Latin American writers and critics abroad.[13]

Factors crucial to the development of Latin American literary studies in this country in the post–World War II era include the remarkable flourishing of Spanish American literary activity, especially the international recognition of Nobel Prizes for Literature awarded to Spanish-speaking writers from Latin America and Spain, in addition to the Boom.[14] These events have drawn and held the interest of new generations of U.S. academics and students, which, in turn, stimulated the institutional support necessary to sustain them with courses and professors. This growth has been owed not only to the enormous literary charisma of Gabriel García Márquez or to the indefatigable promotion of Mexican and Latin American culture in Carlos Fuentes's impeccable English, among the Boom writers, but also to the interest in the post-Boom authors, such as Manuel Puig, and the robustness of Latin American poetry, notably that of Pablo Neruda.[15] The post-Boom writers have been translated into English, and their international renown has contributed to the continued prominence of Latin American literature in the U.S. academy.[16] Above all, there is Borges, whose legacy to Latin American (and world) literature is skepticism of all the mind's certitudes that nevertheless deepens, rather than denigrates, respect for the human condition.

U.S. Foreign Policy and Academic Programs
World War II Developments

If modern area and international studies came to maturity in the context of the cold war, their intellectual and organizational roots are found in World War II.[17] A significant though not voluminous body of scholarship accompanied the rise of U.S. dominance in the region between 1898 and 1945.[18] The major areas were language and literary studies and history—with diplomatic history, which represented the dominant mode of U.S. historiographic production until that time, being particularly well represented.[19] Spanish-language study had become extremely popular, thanks to U.S. Army wartime efforts, and in literary studies a few literary historical works that attempted to "grasp the field as a whole" were particularly successful.[20] Archaeology and anthropology were also prominently represented through their study of indigenous American cultures.[21] Political science and international relations would not appear until the cold war era.[22]

In the humanities language study prevailed over literary study. In 1947 Lewis Hanke decried the "the enthusiasm of certain zealots who believe the A[rmy] S[pecialized] T[raining] P[rogram] system is the language panacea," and in 1964 the historian of Latin America Richard Morse lamented that "pedagogical and technological innovations in methods of language-teaching

have far outpaced any renovation in the understanding and teaching of literature."[23] To the disappointment of these and other academics, the U.S. Army's
Foreign Area and Language Curricula of the Army Specialized Training Program (ASTP–FALC) reflected the pragmatic concerns of its extrauniversity
sponsors and set the tone for a nonhumanistic approach to language learning.
As it turned out, language study was to become the "major justification for
postwar U.S. governmental financing of area studies."[24]

In addition to the U.S. government, private philanthropic foundations
played a role in language and area studies after the post–World War I emergence of the Carnegie Endowment for International Peace.[25] The Rockefeller
Foundation's 1930s support for Spanish-language study and the development
of Latin American studies was particularly significant.[26] The Rockefeller
Foundation designated Spanish, after English, as an important tool in facilitating international communication and supported Spanish-language study
by encouraging basic research in linguistics and the study of teaching techniques.[27] By 1941 the "unusual" languages had become "strategic" languages,
and the Rockefeller Foundation's 1942 survey of U.S. universities' training in
Latin American studies concluded that enrollment in Spanish tended "to be
greater than that of any other language."[28]

Cold War Initiatives

The greatest boost to the growth of Spanish-language study in the postwar period came from the orbiting of the Soviet satellite Sputnik in October 1957.
The ten titles of the National Defense Education Act, passed by the Eighty-fifth
Congress on September 2, 1958, and articulated by Arthur S. Flemming, secretary of the Department of Health, Education, and Welfare, aimed to motivate
talented young men and women "to devote themselves to the sciences, foreign
languages, technology, . . . [to] strengthen resistance to totalitarianism, and enhance the quality of American leadership on the international scene."[29] Title
VI authorized the U.S. commissioner of education to contract with American
universities to establish and operate foreign-language and area study centers at
the university level and to offer summer institutes for the advanced training of
modern foreign-language teachers in elementary and secondary schools.[30] Efforts were quickly mobilized, and in the summer of 1959 twelve summer language institutes of six to nine weeks' duration were held, with a total enrollment
of 1,002 public school Spanish-language teachers.[31] Latin America area studies were incorporated into the Title VI mission in 1960.[32] As amended by the
Eighty-eighth Congress and signed into law in October 1964,[33] the NDEA established more language institutes in Spanish than in any other language, and it
was estimated that during the decade of the institutes' operation approximately

11,000 public school Spanish teachers, roughly one-third of all those teaching at the time, received NDEA–sponsored summer institute training.[34] In addition, the NDEA funded research projects in language pedagogy and gave hundreds of fellowships for doctoral study in foreign languages.[35]

Castro's Consequences

"Somos todos filhos de Fidel" ("We are all the sons and daughters of Fidel") is the memorable and oft-repeated pronouncement that Thomas Skidmore made at a conference at the Universidade Federal de Pernambuco in Recife, Brazil, in November 1961,[36] eleven months after the United States severed diplomatic relations with Cuba following the revolutionary general strike on January 1, 1959, and the launch of the Cuban Revolution.[37] A decade and a half later, in 1977, the political scientist Richard R. Fagen reemphasized the point that the institutionalization of Latin American studies in U.S. universities owed much to the Cuban Revolution. He pointed out that although Latin American studies were already established in the U.S. academy, "the *institutionalization* of Latin American studies on a national scale began only in the early 1960s. Whatever embers of interest glowed before, it took a hot wind from the South to fan the flames, and large infusions of cash from the U.S. government and private foundations to fuel the conflagration."[38]

Developments in U.S. federal funding included adding to the NDEA's Title VI "a special program (Program B) of individual fellowships for advanced training in selected humanities and social sciences in Brazil and Spanish America."[39] The other congressional creation at the height of the (Castro-era) cold war was the 1961 Fulbright-Hays Act, Section 102 (b)(6) of the Mutual Educational and Cultural Exchange Act, which provided for educational exchange by sending American teachers, scholars, and students abroad and receiving foreign students and scholars in the United States. Together, Title VI and Fulbright-Hays were intended to provide "the necessary long-term investment in building the language and foreign area capacity that responds to national strategic requirements" and to constitute "a discrete area of our official foreign relations, parallel with overseas information programs, technical assistance and others."[40]

Growth across the Disciplines: Hot Winds from Havana

The "hot wind from the South" filled classrooms in Spanish language and Latin American literary studies as well as history and the social sciences. If federal legislation and the foundations provided institutional support "from above," the Cuban Revolution fomented a shock wave of student interest and demand "from below." Comparisons of Spanish-language enrollments with those in French, and literature enrollments with those in the other Latin American studies disciplines, testify to the steady growth of the humanities field.

Spanish-Language Studies

In the wake of the establishment of new federal programs to promote the study of Spanish, professional academic organizations also took new initiatives. The American Council on the Teaching of Foreign Languages (ACTFL) was founded in 1967 to take over from the Modern Language Association's initiative, begun in 1952, to promote modern language study. The American Association of Teachers of Spanish and Portuguese (AATSP), which had been founded for the study of Spanish in 1917 and which had incorporated Portuguese into its purview in 1944, also geared up.[41] An earlier preference for teaching Castilian Spanish usage and pronunciation was augmented by Latin American Spanish usage and pronunciation. This occurred in the 1960s, when Latin America exiles, often highly trained professionals from other walks of life, entered U.S. classrooms as Spanish-language instructors.[42] Membership of teachers in the AATSP grew from 3,600 in 1950 to more than 16,000 in 1970; it peaked at some 17,000 in 1974 and dropped to 12,200 in 1983.[43] Individual membership in 2004 stood at 10,850; institutional membership, at 1,192.[44]

Statistics compiled by the U.S. Department of Education for the period 1949–50 onward show that, after an initial postwar slump in the decade of the 1950s, the number of academic enrollments and degrees granted in Spanish tripled between 1960 and 1970, even before the end of the decade was reached. Part of this growth was shared by Spanish's nearest companion and competitor, that is, departments of French, which continued their traditional dominance over Spanish beyond the end of the 1960s.[45] After the national birthrate had peaked and undergraduate enrollments began to fall, the overproduction of Ph.D.'s was painfully felt, and both the Spanish and French fields experienced a period of decline. Movement was still downward by 1984–85, at which point Spanish had definitively outdistanced French in the number of academic enrollments and degrees granted.[46] If federal governmental support for Spanish-language study had been motivated by strategic political objectives, it largely fomented instead humanistic endeavors. At the same time the continued growth of the study of Spanish from the mid-1970s onward has also been due to the increasing U.S. Hispanic population and the emergence of Spanish as the second most commonly spoken language in the United States. Continuing high classroom enrollments attest to the interest in studying Spanish by monolingual English speakers and by bilingual students proficient in spoken Spanish whose formal education has been in English. In this regard, the study of Spanish today has a dual profile as a humanistic and a socially oriented endeavor.

Literature, History, and the Social Sciences

Comparative statistics on course enrollments in the fields of literature, history, political science, anthropology, geography, economics, and sociology at 149 universities for the years 1949, 1958, and 1969 reveal the prominence of Latin American literary study. Discipline by discipline, the 1958 figures were virtually identical to those for 1949, but the 1969 figures almost doubled those of 1958 and 1949.[47] Whereas in 1949 these 149 universities offered 8.8 and 8.8 courses in the respective disciplines of literature and history, these course offerings approximately doubled by 1969 to 18.5 courses in literature and 16.9 in history. The number of courses offered in political science jumped from 2 to 5 between 1949 and 1969 and, in anthropology, from 2 to 4.8 in the same period. Geography, already slightly stronger than political science and anthropology in 1949, gained further strength by 1969, moving from 2.6 to 3.6 courses. The single course offering in Latin American economics went from 1 to 2 courses. Sociology was the exception, as its offerings devoted to Latin America "prior to 1960 were so small as to be almost invisible."[48]

Latin American Exceptionalism

While the cold war generated direct support for Spanish-language study in the United States, the cold war and its antecedents were keenly if indirectly felt in Latin American literary studies in Latin America and the United States. If the social sciences and, to a lesser degree, history developed approaches to Latin American studies along the lines of economic determinism—modernization and dependency[49]—the humanities, especially literary studies, produced theories about the uniqueness or originality of Latin American culture as being determined by broader historical and cultural processes.[50]

Arguments for Latin American exceptionalism appeared in the areas of literary criticism and history in the 1940s, and they posited that the New World identity and mestizo character of Latin American culture defined its uniqueness. Mariano Picón-Salas's 1944 formulation of Latin American cultural history was one of the first to do so, and Alejo Carpentier's 1975 lecture at the Universidad Central de Venezuela exemplified the continued strength of these ideas. Carpentier set Latin America apart from the rest of the world as having had "a different history from the outset" insofar as "this American soil was the theater of the most sensational ethnic encounter registered in the annals of our planet: the encounter of the Indian, the black man, and the European of more or less light skin, destined in the future to mingle and intermingle, to establish symbioses of cultures, beliefs, popular arts, in the most tremendous racial mixing that has ever been contemplated."[51] Carpentier had first and best expressed these ideas in 1949, in his prologue to *El reino de este mundo*, wherein he narrated his discovery in Haiti of the conjugation of impossible human actions and firm collective convictions ("fe," "faith," in Spanish) that he designated as "lo real maravilloso" ("the marvelous real"). He not only attributed this to Haiti but also saw it as "the patrimony of all America" at work everywhere in the lives of those "who inscribed dates in the history of the Continent and bequeathed surnames that are still being carried," from the seekers of the Fountain of Youth to "certain modern heroes of our wars of Independence."[52]

Complementarily, Octavio Paz's 1961 essay on the foundations of Latin American literature had defined Latin America's exceptional status in its being conceptualized and named from abroad: "Before having our own historical existence, we began by being a European idea. We cannot be understood if it is forgotten that we are a chapter in the history of European utopias. In Europe, reality preceded the name. America, on the other hand, began by being an idea. A victory for nominalism: the name engendered the reality. The American continent had not yet been wholly discovered when it had already been baptized."[53] In referring to the sixteenth century Paz also could have had in mind the nineteenth, for the concept of a "Latin America" likewise had European origins. Although anticipated by Ranke, Hegel, and Tocqueville, the concept was crystallized by a young French writer, Michel Chevalier, and the explicit term was coined by South Americans living in European exile, notably the Colombian José María Torres Caicedo.[54] José Martí reclaimed Latin America for Latin Americans in the most famous of his essays, "Nuestra América" ("Our America"), which set forth the region's essential unity and its wary juxtaposition to the United States: "But our America may also face another danger, which comes not from within. . . . The disdain of the formidable neighbor who does not know her is our America's greatest danger."[55]

Chevalier had come upon his notion of a "Latin America" after visiting the "two Americas," passing through Mexico and Cuba after his 1833–35 study of communications systems in the United States, and Martí pitted "our America" against the other one in the anxious year of 1891. These pre-1898 conceptualizations anticipated the formulations that have oriented the humanistic study of Latin America since the 1940s and that Carpentier and Paz, respectively, emphasized in the post–World War II and post–Cuban revolutionary cold war eras. They named the imperial gestures—from Spain in the sixteenth and nineteenth centuries, from the United States in the nineteenth and twentieth—that provoked their expressions of Latin American uniqueness, and in 1975 Carpentier

pointedly did so by juxtaposing Martí and his notion of a mestizo America with
the triumph of the Cuban Revolution and its reaffirmation in the Bay of Pigs
(Playa Girón) victory over "the most fearsome of imperialisms."[56] "El imperi-
alismo yanqui" is one of the central factors for advocating a Latin American exceptionalism that has prevailed among Latin America's writers since the days of
José Martí and among Latin Americanist cultural historians from World War II
onward.

Literary Studies: Tropical Breezes from Macondo

Until the mid-1960s the literature of Spain, preferentially if not exclusively,
dominated the study of Spanish-language literature in the North American
academy.[57] The U.S. government and North American universities began to
invest in Latin American studies in the 1960s; given the paucity of North
American academics prepared in this field, a group of Latin American critics,
including, notably, Emir Rodríguez Monegal, became foundational figures of
the field in the United States and set a high standard of aesthetic criticism.[58]

Over the last half century and out of the cold war context there have emerged
essentially two views of Latin American literature in the North American academy. The first is that Spanish American literature differs little from European
works and that its history can be understood only in the context of European
ideas (Paz and Borges took this position). The other, which is the prevailing and
more polemical one, is that Spanish American literature has an individuality
"linked with the struggle for political and cultural independence."[59] According
to this position, if the very idea of literature as we know it has existed only since
the beginning of the nineteenth century, "then Spanish American literature
has existed since there has been literature. . . . In this sense, it is not a recent
literature, as some would suggest, but rather a literature whose foundational
peculiarities are more concrete and intense than those of European literatures,
but not necessarily different."[60] The meditation on these "foundational peculiarities" accounts for developments in literary history and criticism from the
1940s onward, the most influential of which make strong arguments for Latin
American cultural exceptionalism.[61] The pattern that emerges is the production of works of synthesis, written by Latin Americans explaining Latin America not to themselves but to others, especially to North Americans.

Syntheses of Spanish American Literature and Culture in the 1940s and 1950s

The tendency to define Spanish American literature and culture for an Anglo-
American audience is found in literary critical and literary historical works
written mostly in English that appeared, significantly, during World War II.

Arturo Torres Ríoseco's 1942 *The Epic of Latin American Literature* initiated the trend. Ríoseco, a professor at the University of California at Berkeley, argued that after the development of the regional novel of the 1920s and 1930s, Latin American literature was reaching a "golden age" insofar as its authors realized that a literary consciousness rooted in their own land could lead them away from the imitation of other literary traditions.[62] Although it would not be published in English until the early 1960s, Mariano Picón-Salas's 1944 *De la conquista a la Independencia: Tres siglos de historia cultural hispanoamericana* was another work that sought to characterize the uniqueness of Latin American cultural history.[63] Picón-Salas focused on racial and cultural factors and how they coalesced into a Spanish American culture whose European forms were modified by contact with the New World and whose "mestizo spirit," the concept of which he developed from his readings of Fernando Ortiz, provided a major constituent.[64] Pedro Henríquez Ureña rightly called the work "one of the first attempts at synthesis of new ways of considering our three centuries of colonialism," and he lauded Picón-Salas's analysis of the "fusions" (and lack of them) in Spanish American culture.[65] Of particular interest in the present context is that Picón-Salas elaborated his theory of Spanish American culture while teaching in 1942 and 1943 at Columbia University and Smith and Middlebury Colleges, where his interlocutors were not only U.S. students and professors but also major Spanish intellectual and cultural figures who were working in the United States.[66]

The writing of Spanish American literary history in English in North America, which had great influence on literary criticism produced in Latin America, began in earnest with Henríquez Ureña's *Literary Currents in Hispanic America*, originally delivered as the Charles Eliot Norton Lectures at Harvard in 1940–41 and published in 1945 by the Harvard University Press.[67] Starting with the colonial period, Henríquez Ureña grounded his study of the Spanish American literary tradition in tropes (the depiction of "natural man," the idea of utopia, the Edenic description of nature, the conciliar disputes over the treatment of native peoples) and thus created a panoramic, synthetic view over time that allowed readers to appreciate the continuities "between Columbus and Carpentier, or between Balbuena and Neruda."[68]

Two major books in English on Spanish America written by Anglo-American authors appeared in 1949 and are in print to the present day: Irving A. Leonard's *Books of the Brave* and Lewis Hanke's *The Spanish Struggle for Justice in the Conquest of America*. These two volumes were accompanied in the same year by a reprint of R. B. Cunningham Graham's *The Horses of the Conquest;* the three works together speak to a North American interest in the "romance," as Charles Bergquist characterized it, of the era of discovery, exploration, and settlement of the New World.[69] All three books were reviewed widely in the North American daily press.[70] Leonard's book, which is the only one of the three devoted specifically to literary culture, analyzes the Spanish book trade with America; he demonstrated that the first edition of *Don Quixote* (1605) arrived in the New World, and he argued for the influence of popular tales (the novels of chivalry) on the minds and imaginations of the Spanish conquistadors. Compelling but not demonstrable, his thesis continues to hold sway among readers. Leonard's signal contribution, however, was to show that Inquisitional book censorship did not curtail the development of a vigorous book trade between Spain and the Spanish Indies. By revealing Spain's exceptional promotion of book culture in the New World, Leonard countered popular British, Anglo- and Latin American arguments about the Black Legend of Spain's Inquisitional and colonial history.[71]

A centennial commemoration in English of Latin America's premier poet-patriot also appeared. In 1953, on the centenary of his birth, a selection of José Martí's works was published in English translation by Juan de Onís under the title *The America of José Martí*. Given Martí's fifteen years of residence in New York and the "thousands of dense, impassioned pages [that he wrote] about what he saw, heard, read, felt, and experienced" there, he might have been the first Latin American literary and political figure well known in the United States. Yet in contrast to the renown he enjoyed in the Spanish-speaking world for the poetry he published in New York and throughout Latin America,[72] he was virtually unknown in English-speaking North America during his lifetime and long afterward.[73] "Who was José Martí?" is as pertinent a question after the turn of the twenty-first century as it was fifty years ago, when the great Cuban poet and essayist José Lezama Lima addressed the question on the one-hundredth anniversary of Martí's birth.[74]

In 1954 Enrique Anderson Imbert's *Historia de la literatura hispanoamericana* appeared, and it was translated into English in 1963 as *Spanish American Literature: A History*.[75] This is arguably the most authoritative, inclusive, and detailed literary history of Spanish America to date. Anderson Imbert took his readers from Christopher Columbus to the latest novels and poems of the 1940s and 1950s. Unlike Henríquez Ureña, he did not seek in Spanish American literature its uniqueness but rather its aesthetic standards and values within the broader Western tradition. Like Paz and Borges, he leaned away from arguments about Latin American exceptionalism in order to give a panoramic account of "Spanish American literature as literature."[76] By the end of the 1950s, the rhythm of production of literary translations and literary criticism in English was well established. In 1959 Irving A. Leonard published his *Baroque Times in Old Mexico*, and Juan Rulfo's novel *Pedro Páramo*, which would be belatedly added to the list of requisite novels of the Latin American Boom, appeared in English translation.[77]

The Borges Phenomenon of the 1960s

In the 1960s the first works in English by and about Jorge Luis Borges appeared, introducing that writer's world to the North American public.[78] Beyond the intriguing world of ideas so captivatingly dramatized in his short stories, Borges's literary fascination with the English language further increased his appeal. About his collaborative work with Norman Thomas di Giovanni, Borges wrote: "Perhaps the chief justification of this book is the translation itself, which we have undertaken in what may be a new way. Working closely together in daily sessions, we have tried to make these stories read as though they had been written in English. We do not consider English and Spanish as compounded of sets of easily interchangeable synonyms; they are two quite different ways of looking at the world, each with a nature of its own. English, for example, is far more physical than Spanish. We have therefore shunned the dictionary as much as possible and done our best to rethink every sentence in English words."[79]

With Borges the linguistic barrier between Spanish and English dissolves; that is, the other language is not alien but simply different. Reveling in the concreteness of English, Borges gains converts to his Spanish. The legions of students today who study the Spanish language or Latin American literature because they want to read Borges provide another indemonstrable proof about the influence of books and ideas on minds and imaginations. Although the NDEA Title VI promoted the study of modern languages for "practical" and avowedly strategic purposes, outcomes have eluded such aims in ways that are peculiarly Borgesian.

The Boom and the Cultural Cold War

The Boom of the Latin American novel is a case in point.[80] Its meaning for Latin American literary studies and the humanities more generally picked up in the second half of the cold war era where Title VI legislation left off. Yet a precondition for the Latin American literary Boom was the Cuban Revolution itself, insofar as it brought writers of the continent together in a common cause. The establishment of the Casa de las Américas in 1960, "with its yearly awards and aggressive marketing of the Revolution among Spanish American intellectuals, created a shared sense of purpose. This continental cohesion was validated when Vargas Llosa received the Biblioteca Breve prize of Seix Barral in Barcelona in 1962 for *La ciudad y los perros* (*Time of the Hero*)," and the novel returned from Europe "to the readers in Bogotá, Mexico City, and Buenos Aires as a Spanish

American novel,"[81] that is, as representing all of Latin America, not merely one of its republics.

If Cuba marketed Latin American literature and culture through its cultural institutions, the same was true from the other side. The economic interests and cultural politics of the United States are often implicated in the Boom novels' 1960s–1970s promotion, described as an effort "sponsored largely by the United States' aggressive investment in Latin American culture aimed at defusing the political threat of a post-revolutionary Cuba."[82] A signal literary event in this regard was the 1960s creation of *Review*, a journal of "views/reviews/interviews on Latin American literature," published by the Center for Inter-American Relations in New York City and directed by Ronald Christ.[83] Emir Rodríguez Monegal was for several years *Review*'s literary editor.[84] The importance of *Review* in disseminating information about Latin American literature, music, and the arts cannot be overestimated.[85] In offering excerpts from new literary work and translating essays from other languages into English, *Review* followed patterns that Rodríguez Monegal had established earlier for the literary and cultural journal *Mundo Nuevo*, which he directed in Paris from 1966 to 1968.[86] During Rodríguez Monegal's editorship, and in a single issue, he published a critical review of the Operation Camelot scandal and a fragment of the soon-to-appear *Cien años de soledad* by García Márquez.[87] Rodríguez Monegal's *Mundo Nuevo* is in fact "widely regarded as the main journal that contributed to the promotion and diffusion of the Spanish American narrative *Boom*" for its publication of texts of and interviews with such writers as Borges, García Márquez, Fuentes, Neruda, Onetti, Puig, and Sarduy, among others.[88] The long-term impact of *Mundo Nuevo* and *Review* has been to bring Latin American literary culture to the attention of U.S. and European audiences, and, with a certain irony, this effect has outweighed and far outlasted the magazines' sponsors' original anti-Communist, anti-Castro ideological intentions.

The Boom had an extraordinary effect on the development of literary studies and criticism. As "a movement of continental dimensions and aspirations," González Echevarría writes, the Boom "had a tremendous impact on the criticism of Latin American literature as a whole. The most important was to endow Latin American writers, as well as those who write about Latin American literature, with a sense of the prominence and relevance of that literature. . . . In short, because of the international character of the Boom, the history of Latin American literature could no longer be conceived as a self-enclosed development, a genealogy leading from Rómulo Gallegos to Gabriel García Márquez, or from Rubén Darío to Octavio Paz. It became evident that Latin American literature was produced at the crossroads of all the major modern literary traditions."[89]

1970s and 1980s Focus on Cultural Origins and the Colonial Past

If the 1960s saw the swift translation of the Latin American novels that came to be read worldwide,[90] the 1970s produced a small "boomlet" of works explaining the Boom.[91] More important, the 1970s, catching the Boom's tailwind, registered significant efforts to theorize and present to an English-language audience the sweep of Spanish American literature from its origins to the present. The first of these was Octavio Paz's 1972 Charles Eliot Norton Lectures at Harvard, published in 1974 as *Los hijos del limo: Del romanticismo a la vanguardia* and *Children of the Mire*.[92] The second was Emir Rodríguez Monegal's 1977 two-volume *The Borzoi Anthology of Latin American Literature from the Time of Columbus to the Twentieth Century*, which, like Jean Franco's 1973 *Spanish American Literature since Independence*, was "fundamentally a pedagogical tool conceived to take advantage of the sudden popularity of Latin American literature in the English-speaking world."[93]

Paz argued that modern poetry was created against the rationalist claims of the Enlightenment, and he and other Latin American writers, including José Lezama Lima, looked back beyond Romanticism to the baroque as the point of literary historical origin. About writings of the colonial period, Rodríguez Monegal observed that "fiction thinly disguised as fact, or fact generously contaminated by fiction, was the stuff of some of the most exciting chronicles, memoirs, and documents produced in Colonial times. In truth they do belong to the domain of fiction, and have been treated as such in this anthology."[94] Historiographically, Paz's formulation of literary history and Rodríguez Monegal's anthology beginning with Columbus reflected the desire to chart Spanish American literary beginnings as far back as possible, to recover Spanish peninsular and colonial-era writings, and to reinterpret them from a contemporary perspective.[95] Early in the 1960s José Juan Arrom had taken a long view back and formulated a generational approach for organizing the history of Spanish American letters. It was particularly helpful for the early portion of the colonial era, if much less so for later centuries; Arrom's *Esquema generacional* came into its own in the 1970s, when colonial studies were on the rise.[96]

The fascination with cultural origins and the colonial past, not as history but as fiction or as textuality per se, continued to grow in the 1970s and 1980s. In contemporary literary criticism, the first book-length study of Alejo Carpentier's works in English appeared: Roberto González Echevarría's 1977 *The Pilgrim at Home*, expanded in subsequent editions to include the final works of Carpentier,[97] revealed the literary and philosophical mind of one of Latin America's deepest thinkers and greatest literary virtuosos, who captured Latin America's essences in its darkest jungles ("lo real maravilloso") and its residues in the opulent closed precincts of the Vatican. Following after a long hiatus Irving Leonard's work of the 1930s through the 1960s, colonial Spanish American literature exerted a new pull; the first book-length study in English of an indigenous Andean writer, Felipe Guaman Poma de Ayala, appeared in 1986: *Guaman Poma: Writing and Resistance in Colonial Peru.*[98] This renewed stimulus to study the Latin American past, particularly the era of Spanish colonization in the Americas, was based not on notions of the "romance" of discovery, conquest, and settlement themes, as had been the case in the 1940s; what held scholars' attention was the utterly modern and conflictual character of such writings. As González Echevarría writes:

> Until recently, colonial texts were used as sources of historical information or as objects of philological study. They were considered merely repositories of independent works that revealed the birth of a coherent, harmonious, and unique Latin American consciousness out of the fusion of European and New World cultures. If some colonial narratives were incorporated into the literary tradition, it was because of their referent, the fabulous stories that they told, not because of their formal or discursive peculiarities. Today they stand at the problematic origin of a literary tradition that does not promise such tranquilizing totalizations. . . . Only after reading [Cortázar's] *Rayuela* or [Sarduy's] *De donde son los cantantes* can one appreciate the profound beauty of Guaman Poma's apparent disregard for form and purity in language and composition.[99]

Contemporary Latin American fiction, the Boom of Latin American narrative —in Carpentier, Cortázar, García Márquez, and others—made possible and stimulated the interest in colonial-era writings.

Theoretical and Thematic Formulations in the 1990s

A select handful of major literary critical events brings the century and the millennium to a close. Written mainly by Latin American literary critics either living and working in the United States or, like Octavio Paz, teaching as visiting professors, their key integrating features are the presentation of literary and cultural perspectives on Latin America to an English-language audience. For the colonial period, the great "monographic" topic has been the literary works of the Mexican nun and poet Sor Juana Inés de la Cruz (1648–1695), whose life, literature, and world were explored by Octavio Paz in successive editions of *Sor Juana Inés de la Cruz, o Las trampas de la fe* and its English translation,[100] and in the scholarly work of Georgina Sabat de Rivers, Rosa Perelmuter, Margo Glantz, Stephanie Merrim, José Antonio Rodríguez Garrido, and Frederick Luciani.[101] Spanish-language editions coincided with or anticipated the English-language translations of Sor Juana's works that commemorated the third centenary of her death.[102] In these cases, the birth of the U.S. feminist movement and women's studies programs in the 1970s, as catalogued by Wallerstein among the "unintended consequences of area studies,"[103] converged with emergent Latin Americanist literary studies of the viceregal period to elevate the cerebral, literary Mexican nun from the village of Nepantla (meaning "in between") to the status of one of the most internationally celebrated figures of feminine aspiration and accomplishment in the late twentieth century.

It had been more than fifty years since Pedro Henríquez Ureña explained the history of Spanish American letters to a Harvard audience when Roberto González Echevarría elaborated a theory of Latin American narrative that endeavored not to catalogue by theme, as Henríquez Ureña had done, but rather to explain by disciplinary principle (law, science, anthropology) the generation of Latin American narrative writing from the colonial period to the twentieth century. *Myth and Archive: A Theory of Latin American Narrative* (1990) is the first systematic, sustained attempt in half a century to take account of Latin America's literary accomplishments, and its hallmark is the avoidance of a false developmental model as González Echevarría elaborates, post–Lévi-Strauss, post-Foucault, a theory by which distinct discursive formulations gave rise to major transformations in Latin American letters.[104] Although working within a single national literary tradition, Josefina Ludmer has also taken up the challenge of the broader formulation.[105] In the recently translated *Gaucho Genre: A Treatise on the Motherland* (2002), Ludmer identifies language as the central issue of Argentine (and Latin American) modernization inasmuch as it is the site of the clash between high and low or popular culture, and in *The Corpus Delicti: A Manual of Argentine Fictions* (2004) she posits two discourses of truth, the chronicle and the confession, as central to the narrative tendencies of Argentine and Latin American culture.[106]

The complementarity of González Echevarría's and Ludmer's works exemplifies major trends of the end of the period here examined: to see literature as a system rather than as a series of organic but separate works; to do so without losing sight of the literary and philosophical values of the text's specificity, insisting always on close textual analysis; and to articulate literary discourse with those that presumably lie outside it but in fact permeate its core. If González Echevarría emphasizes a fuller, more nuanced understanding of the literary and aesthetic values of the Latin American literary tradition, Ludmer foregrounds a more sociological orientation, focusing on the relationship of literature to the state, gender articulations, and the correlation between criminal law and the literary representation of crime. These theoretical contributions to the study of Latin American literature are worthy responses to Richard Morse's 1964 lament that the cold war, Latin

American studies emphasis on Spanish language-learning ignored the need for improvement in the understanding and teaching of literature.

Another benchmark of the post–cold war end of the millennium and a monument of Anglo–Latin American literary studies is the 1996 *Cambridge History of Latin American Literature*, edited by Roberto González Echevarría and Enrique Pupo-Walker. It was impossible, a half century after publication of Enrique Anderson Imbert's comprehensive literary history, for a single pen to encompass the entire span, from 1492 to the present—and including Brazil—or for a unifocal aesthetic approach to dominate in the selection and interpretation of texts. Hence, *The Cambridge History* follows the model not of an interpretative essay à la Anderson Imbert but rather of an encyclopedia, with essays written by specialists in various fields, each taking the approach deemed appropriate to the subject at hand by the sensibility of the contributor. If there is an overarching synthesis to be constructed, it is to be done in the minds of the readers. Such diversification was the ethos of comprehensive projects of the 1990s,[107] and it continued and renewed tendencies toward diversity in language and literary studies that had begun in the 1970s.

Alongside Literary Studies

Structuralism took hold in Latin American literary studies in the United States in the late 1960s and early 1970s. The attention to the text relatively detached from the author also gave way to Marxism and psychoanalysis in its Lacanian version.[108] The impact of structuralism and its followers has been to submit literary criticism to the social sciences, especially linguistics,[109] and to create in the 1960s and 1970s new critical trends of enduring vitality, including deconstruction, feminism and post-feminism, gender and sexuality studies, cultural studies, ethnic studies, subaltern studies, and postcolonial studies.[110] Most of these perspectives and the cultural criticism they produced appeared against a cold war frame of reference, as Wallerstein has argued, insofar as they challenged and rejected the universalizing center that ignored and excluded cultural expressions at the margins.[111]

U.S. Latino (Including Spanish-Language) and Afro-Hispanic American Studies

Hispanic ethnic studies interests emerged in the United States in the 1960s and early 1970s, thanks to the efforts of Mexican Americans in the Southwest and Puerto Rican Americans in the Northeast. For the first time the Spanish language became a proud symbol of ethnic identity vis-à-vis mainstream Anglo-American society.[112] In 1963 *Hispania,* the journal of the American Association of Teachers of Spanish and Portuguese, recognized the Spanish of the U.S. Latino population by promoting the bilingual Mexican American as a potential teacher of Spanish.[113] Soon enough, with the U.S. Congress's passage of the 1968 Bilingual Education Act and its subsequent reauthorizations (1974, 1978, 1984, and 1988), the focus shifted not to students' Spanish but to their poor command of English and "had the net effect of dramatically weakening support for native-language instruction and boosting monies for English-only programs."[114] Meanwhile, the focus on such students' Spanish shifted to higher education and resulted in the development of college-level courses in Spanish for Spanish speakers. These were in place by the end of the 1970s at the universities that were traditionally strong in Latin American studies, such as the University of California at Berkeley, the University of Texas at Austin, the University of Wisconsin at Madison, and the University of Massachusetts at Amherst. These institutions and others had heard the 1972 call of the AATSP to initiate Spanish-language classes for Spanish speakers. This development was quickly followed by the first studies, carried out by Guadalupe Valdés in 1975, on teaching Spanish to the U.S. Spanish-speaking population, and it is an avenue of inquiry that continues to be the subject of academic conferences to the present day.[115] For Afro-Hispanic (American) studies, the founding of African American studies programs, combined with the Latin American literary Boom, drew interest to African Hispanic cultural production in English and Spanish; centers of Afro-Hispanic study were created, publishing outlets and markets became available to poets and novelists of African descent, and academic research and undergraduate courses have followed.[116]

Following the 1970s creation of academic programs in ethnic studies and concurrent with the approaching end of the cold war, which signaled the demise of the "national interest" justification for funding area studies, U.S. Latino studies and Afro-Hispanic American studies became vibrant and active.[117] At some places this reconstitution of area and ethnic studies "is arguably succeeding at revitalizing and reshaping the field in the twenty-first century."[118] Others argue that such pursuits are misplaced in Latin American studies insofar as they respond to "the urgencies of U.S. culture and to the ends of Latin American immigrants to naturalize themselves as U.S. subjects."[119] To the degree that their language of cultural expression and social experience is based in the United States and on the English language, the greater potential exists for locating Hispanic-related ethnic studies in American studies programs.[120]

Latin American Cultural Studies

Latin American cultural studies, concerned with "the study of how cultural meanings and thus identities get sedimented and organized through cultural practices and relations of power," has been practiced since the 1980s, although its European antecedents, unheralded at the time, date from the mid 1960s.[121] For many Angel Rama's posthumous *La ciudad letrada* (1984), which examined the relationships among literate culture, state power, and urban life in Latin America from colonial to modern times, is considered to be "the matrix text of Latin American Cultural Studies, influencing a generation of later scholars."[122] The debate rages about the character of the field in relation to the British model of cultural studies (Latin American contestation and crisis versus British inclusion), about whether the rubric itself isn't "just another dominating Anglo-Saxon current," and about whether it is not more accurate to identify cultural studies' critical practices as the "sociology of culture and cultural analysis," as Beatriz Sarlo and Carlos Altamirano have argued.[123] Latin American cultural studies has been productive as "a new home for feminist cultural criticism"; it has also been a place for the examination of popular and mass cultures, liminal literary production such as testimonial writing, the problem of modernity, the interface between cultural studies and postmodernism, and subaltern studies.[124] Since the late 1980s there also has been considerable interest in issues of sexuality.[125] The vigor of Latin American cultural studies is attested by the international *Journal of Latin American Cultural Studies*, founded in 1992 and published twice yearly. Latin American cultural studies is clearly one of the most successful "unintended consequences" of cold war area studies.

Debates and Ironies

Perhaps one of the best ways to sum up the Latin Americanist humanities pursuits of the cold war and post–cold war eras is to briefly review a number of the significant debates that have taken place in the field.

In the mid 1970s the journal *Ideologies and Literature* was founded out of the conviction that "a reading that does not question a work's ideological consensus neglects an important aspect of art's confrontation with human experience," and it sought to remedy the critical crisis whereby "specialists and teachers have often refrained from coming to terms with cultural and political ideologies in a sociohistorical context even though the literary works themselves are products of these conditions."[126] By 1980 the Latin American literary Boom, long spent, was critically examined at a conference at the Woodrow Wilson Center in Washington, D.C., that questioned the relationship between literature and the market and the marketing of literature.[127] Gathering novels written before and after the Latin American Boom into the thematic category of the "dictator-novel," critics in the 1980s also examined the status of fictional works that focus on dictatorship in their relationship to history and debated whether a more productive critical stance is one that sees such novels as self-referential within the system of literature or one that sees them in reference to historical political processes that lie outside it.[128] Critical approaches to the ethnographies and histories written in the early Spanish colonial era became the topic for an early 1990s interdisciplinary debate on "colonial discourse"— that is, the studies that undertook "to redirect contemporary critical reflections on colonialism (and its aftermath) toward the language used by the conquerors, imperial administrators, travelers, and missionaries" and to examine the "linguistic screen through which all political language of colonialism, including reactions to it and liberations from it, need to be read."[129] Another early 1990s project chronicled the debates on poetic practice in twentieth-century Latin America and argued for the strength of the poetic tradition that sought its roots in local experience and popular culture in the face of capitalist modernization.[130] The baroque tradition in Latin America was also the object of renewed and divergent formulations in which one influential perspective argued that the baroque was a transhistorical phenomenon and a constant of the Latin American literary experience linked to its Spanish origins, while another saw it anchored in a particular historical epoch as a cultural phenomenon that produced in Latin America an aesthetic which significantly diverged from its European models.[131] Latin American cultural studies has been the producer and object of debates about the field's engagement with Latin American culture as an "armchair," abstract pursuit or a "hands-on," language-specific inquiry.[132]

Finally, in an important debate at the end of the millennium, Beatriz Sarlo and Alberto Moreiras took opposing views on the question of values in literature, with Sarlo arguing that "cultural studies do not resolve the problems that literary criticism faces" and that "literature is socially meaningful because something, difficult for us to capture, endures in texts and can be activated once more once the text's social functions have been exhausted."[133] Moreiras rejected the view that cultural studies forecloses the question of aesthetic value as "the only possible ground for determining the social significance of symbolic practices in a historical sense," and he argued that "cultural studies *does not have* to accept the presupposition that a thinking which is not based on aesthetic values is thereby barred from reflection on aesthetic values."[134]

This debate on the importance of aesthetic values puts us in a vertiginous spiral that resonates, though imperfectly, with the positions taken by Anderson Imbert and Henríquez Ureña at the beginning of the cold war era. Although it would be naïve to suggest that we have "come full circle," what has occurred (or so it appears in my version of this half-century story) is that while projecting forward in time we nevertheless return to earlier but still (or again) incandescent questions such as the transcendence of literary value. This "return" is another of the ironies (or successes) of the Latin Americanist humanities in the cold war era.

Looking back, it is clear that the impact that World War II and the cold war had in fomenting the study of the Spanish language and its literatures was manifold. Spanish-language and Latin American area studies had been targeted for support by the Rockefeller Foundation even before World War II, and during the war years that foundation's interest was accelerated. The early initiatives supported in the 1930s by the Rockefeller Foundation for the purpose of "international communication" became the target of strategic objectives through the NDEA from the late 1950s onward. It is "a very considerable American fact" that the NDEA's Spanish-language summer institutes for public school teachers were up and running within ten months of the passage of the 1958 legislation and that, during the decade of their operation, those institutes trained a third of the entire U.S. public school Spanish-teaching population. Another very "considerable American fact" is the Fulbright-Hays program, with its grants for educational exchange and research awarded to approximately 13,000 Latin American scholars and 4,500 U.S. researchers between the time of its inception in the early 1960s and 1985.[135] Yet while these major U.S. government programs and the private foundations funded humanities projects, they did not control the outcomes, which included the 1970s development of U.S. Latino studies and Afro-Hispanic studies; the broadening of literary scholarship and criticism to include marginalized or understudied areas or topics, such as colonial studies; and, in the 1980s, the full development of Latin American cultural studies.

Overall, the degree of cold war influence on U.S. Latin American studies is significant, less for its statistically traceable interventions than for its legacies, which are multiple. One of them is the mindfulness, among U.S. and Latin American academics and intellectuals, of the U.S. cold war outlook and the biases that it entrenched and that can reappear—and often do—in any one of a number of its latter-day variants. A positive aspect is that the cold war helped make Latin America a permanent area of study in the U.S. academic curriculum. A third factor, also positive, is that the cold war strategic agenda has been outreached by the generations of academics and students who, from the start, stretched and bent its objectives to their own pursuits. This applies to history and the social sciences, whose courses far exceeded any guidelines according to which their programs and centers were funded in the 1950s and 1960s, but it applies especially to language and literary studies, whose paths were charted by language classrooms at home, literary events (including literary magazines) abroad and in the United States, and collegial scholarly exchange (and often fierce debate) wherever in the world Latin Americanists gather. In the face of the ongoing debates about the meanings and agendas of humanistic study focused on Latin America, what has prevailed is the reputation of, and ongoing interest in, Latin American literature and arts and the examination of their relationship to the societies that produce them.

Spanish-language study, catapulted into prominence by World War II and its U.S. Army–inspired teaching methods as well as by cold war initiatives, has gained its proper place in the humanities enterprise as the means by which to know the Latin American literary canon and to explore the contestatory visions that have arisen around it in relation to the social realities of today. Latin Americanist literary criticism and scholarship in this country by Latin American and U.S. intellectuals have spawned many vibrant generations of teachers and interpreters of Latin American literature and culture to which now have been added U.S. Latino studies, Afro-Hispanic studies, the increasingly prominent field of Latin American cultural studies, and the newest permutation: comparative, hemispheric Anglo–Latin American literary studies.

The work begun by the private foundations and the federal government decades ago has long since been loosened from those moorings, and the humanities work that advances today is anchored in the self-sustaining dialogue and critical debates among Latin Americanists internationally. These are the unforeseen, ironic consequences of the U.S. programs that a half century ago intended to make language and area studies "a discrete area of our official foreign relations."

Notes

1. As a member of the Board of Visitors of the College of William and Mary in 1779, Jefferson had modern languages substituted for Latin and Greek, and as a member of the Board of Commissioners founding the University of Virginia in 1818, he and his colleagues incorporated Spanish into the curriculum alongside French, Italian, and German (College of William and Mary, *The History of the College of William and Mary from Its Foundation, 1693 to 1870* [Baltimore: John Murphy, 1870], 66; Lyon G. Tyler, "Early Courses and Professors at William and Mary College, " *William and Mary Quarterly* 14 [October 1905]: 76–77).

2. Jefferson wrote in the 1818 Board of Commissioners' report: "The Spanish is highly interesting to us, as the language spoken by so great a portion of the inhabitants of our continents, with whom we shall probably have great intercourse ere long, and is that also in which is written the greater part of the earlier history of America" (Nathanial Francis Cabell, ed., *Early History of the University of Virginia as Contained in the Letters of Thomas Jefferson and Joseph C. Cabell* [Richmond, Va.: J. W. Randolph, 1856], 440).

3. Charles Francis Adams Jr., *A College Fetich [sic]: An Address Delivered before the Harvard Chapter of the Fraternity of the Phi Beta Kappa, in Sanders Theatre, Cambridge, June 28, 1883* (Boston: Lea and Shepherd, 1883), 35.

4. Patrick Charles Pautz, "'Liberal' Education and Linguistic Bias: The Late Introduction of Spanish Language Instruction at the College of New Jersey," unpublished manuscript, 73.

5. Langdon C. Garland, "Address of Welcome to the Eighth Annual MLA," *PMLA* 6 (1891), 1.

6. Sturgis E. Leavitt, "The Teaching of Spanish in the United States," *Hispania* 44, no. 4 (1961), 601. Exceptionally, the first college course in Spanish had been offered at the University of Pennsylvania in 1766 (ibid., 592–593), and, as mentioned earlier, courses were instituted a dozen years later at the College of William and Mary and subsequently at the University of Virginia.

7. Pautz, "'Liberal' Education," 28–29, 78.

8. This survey is limited to Spanish-speaking Latin America and the Spanish-speaking Caribbean. For Portuguese language and Luso-Brazilian literature, see K. David Jackson, "Literature, Culture and Civilization: Studies of Brazil in the United States: An Historical Survey and Assessment," in *Envisioning Brazil: A Guide to Brazilian Studies in the United States*, ed. Marshall C. Eakin, Paulo Roberto de Almeida, and Rubens Antonio Barbosa (Madison: University of Wisconsin Press, 2005), and Roberto González Echevarría and Enrique Pupo-Walker, eds., *The Cambridge History of Latin American Literature* (Cambridge: Cambridge University Press, 1996), vol. 3.

9. Paul Drake and Lisa Hilbink, "Latin American Studies: Theory and Practice," *University of California International and Area Studies Digital Collection*, vol. 3, *The Politics of Knowledge: Area Studies and the Disciplines*, ed. David L. Szanton (Berkeley: University of California Press, 2004), 7–8. For assessments of developments in history and the social sciences by disciplinary specialists to the mid-1980s, see Christopher Mitchell, ed., *Changing Perspectives in Latin American Studies: Insights from Six Disciplines* (Stanford: Stanford University Press, 1988), and for a broad but detailed overview of U.S. Latin American studies with reference to history and the social sciences up to the present, see Drake and Hilbink, "Latin American Studies."

10. For a comprehensive, critical review of U.S. studies on Latin America in relation to U.S. foreign policy over the past century, see Mark T. Berger, *Under Northern Eyes: Latin American Studies and U.S. Hegemony in the Americas, 1898–1990* (Bloomington: Indiana University Press, 1995). For recent reflections on the cold war's impact on universities, see David Engerman, "Rethinking Cold War Universities: Some Recent Histories," *Journal of Cold War Studies* 5, no. 3 (2003): 80–95. One survey has revealed that among area studies specialists Latin Americanist social scientists authored the lowest percentage of publications with clear foreign policy relevance (Drake and Hilbink, "Latin American Studies," 24, citing Richard Lambert with Elinor G. Barber, *Beyond Growth: The Next Stage in Language and Area Studies* [Washington, D.C.: Association of American Universities, 1984], 156–157, 363–364).

11. The term "Boom" refers to the 1950s–1960s production, and especially the 1960s–1970s promotion, of Latin American novels. Whether literature and art were actually created in response to cold war pragmatics is addressed by Jean Franco, *The Decline and Fall of the Lettered City: Latin America in the Cold War* (Cambridge: Harvard University Press, 2002). On the international cold war–era promotion of Latin American literature, see "The Boom and the Cultural Cold War," below.

12. Arthur S. Flemming, "The Philosophy and Objectives of the National Defense Education Act," *Annals of the American Academy of Political and Social Science* 327 (1960): 132.

13. This characteristic has often been noted for history and the social science disciplines (Joseph S. Tulchin, "Emerging Patterns of Research in the Study of Latin America," *Latin American Research Review* 18, no. 1 [1983]: 90–91; Gilbert Merkx, "Foreword," *Latin American Research Review* 31, no. 4 [1996]: ix; Thomas E. Skidmore, "Studying the History of Latin America: A Case of Hemispheric Convergence," *Latin American Research Review* 33, no. 1 [1998]: 119–120). It is no less true, and perhaps more so, for literary and cultural studies.

14. The list includes Gabriela Mistral, Chile, 1945; Juan Ramón Jiménez, Spain, 1956; Miguel Angel Asturias, Guatemala, 1967; Pablo Neruda, Chile, 1971; Vicente Aleixandre, Spain, 1977; Gabriel García Márquez, Colombia, 1982; Camilo José Cela, Spain, 1989; and Octavio Paz, Mexico, 1990.

15. In my view Neruda's poetry has lived outside its historical moment, even in the cold

war era, but see Franco, *Decline and Fall*, 72: "It was not the realist novel but poetry that came to represent the utopian hopes of the communist Left. . . . *Countersong to Walt Whitman* by the Dominican poet Pedro Mir, published in Guatemala in 1952, and *Canto General* by Pablo Neruda, composed during the 1940s and published in 1950, brought together Marxism's utopian vision, an aesthetic manifesto, and anti-imperialist polemic with a national and continental narrative. Two decades later and in the wake of the Cuban Revolution, Ernesto Cardenal's *El estrecho dudoso (The Doubtful Strait)* and Nicolás Guillén's *El diario que a diario (The Daily Daily)*, both published in 1972, fragmented the totalizing enlightenment narrative of liberation and brought this particular corpus to a close."

16. Their narrative fiction has been characterized as "more linear, more transparent, thematically less ambitious, structurally less complex" than the Boom novels (Peter Standish, "Mexico, Central America, the Caribbean, and the Andes," in *The Companion to Hispanic Studies*, ed. Catherine Davies [New York: Oxford University Press, 2002], 125). Puig is sometimes credited with inaugurating the "post-Boom" with his 1969 *Boquitas pintadas*, which incorporated popular songs and soap operas into his narrative fiction; Isabel Allende and Antonio Skármeta, from Chile, and Luisa Valenzuela and Mempo Giardinelli, from Argentina, are also often named as exemplars of this trend (Philip Swanson, "The Southern Cone," in Davies, *Companion to Hispanic Studies*, 141).

17. Engerman, "Rethinking Cold War Universities," 88. For World War II initiatives leading to the establishment of Latin American studies, see Immanuel Wallerstein, "The Unintended Consequences of Cold War Area Studies," in *The Cold War and the University: Toward an Intellectual History of the Postwar Years*, ed. Noam Chomsky (New York: New Press, 1997), 195–231. For classic essays written between 1904 and 1965 on the development of U.S. Latin American studies from 1898 to the mid-1960s, see Howard F. Cline, ed., *Latin American History: Essays on Its Study and Teaching, 1898–1965*, 2 vols. (Austin: University of Texas Press, 1967). Illuminating 1940s assessments of U.S. universities' Latin Americanist activities and the state of the art of the disciplines are found, respectively, in Irving A. Leonard, "A Survey of Personnel and Activities in Latin American Aspects of the Humanities and Social Sciences at Twenty Universities of the United States," and Lewis Hanke, "The Development of Latin-American Studies in the United States, 1939–45," both in Cline, *Latin American History*, 1:289–316, 317–335.

18. Berger's periodization defines this era by a "Pan Americanism" emerging in the 1890s as a "set of ideas about hemispheric cooperation and the organization and infrastructure to go with it," that is, the notion of a U.S. "civilizing mission" to Latin America (Berger, *Under Northern Eyes*, 64–65).

19. Hanke, "Development of Latin-American Studies," 330–331.

20. Ibid., 333. These includes works by Arturo Torres Ríoseco and Pedro Henríquez Ureña, which will be discussed in " Literary Studies: Tropical Breezes from Macondo," below.

21. Drake and Hilbink, "Latin American Studies," 7–8; Hanke, "Development of Latin-American Studies," 323.

22. Berger, *Under Northern Eyes*, 31. In 1947 Hanke lamented the fact that "the principles and practices of politics in Latin America have not engaged the attention of U.S. specialists to any considerable extent nor have those who have interested themselves in these problems produced particularly important works" (Hanke, "Development of Latin-American Studies," 329).

23. Hanke, "Development of Latin-American Studies," 332; Richard Morse, "The Strange Career of 'Latin-American Studies,'" *Annals of the American Academy of Political and Social Science* 356 (1964): 109.

24. Wallerstein, "Unintended Consequences," 200.

25. Berger (*Under Northern Eyes*, 33) has argued that by the end of the 1920s "the philanthropic foundations had established an institutional framework for international cultural relations which, although it was still relatively fragile, complemented both US foreign policy and the consolidation of [academic] 'Latin American studies.'"

26. Joel Colton and Malcolm Richardson, "The Humanities and 'the Well-Being of Mankind': The Humanities at the Rockefeller Foundation since 1928," unpublished manuscript, 57.

27. Ibid., 49.

28. Ibid., 56–57; Leonard, "Survey of Personnel and Activities," 312.

29. Flemming, "Philosophy and Objectives," 132.

30. "The National Defense Education Act," *Journal of Higher Education* 30 (1959): 55.

31. Robert G. Mead Jr., "Second-Level Spanish Institutes in Latin America under the National Defense Education Act," *Hispania* 46 (1963): 106.

32. Drake and Hilbink, "Latin American Studies," 1n3.

33. Andrea McHenry Mildenberger, "The NDEA as Amended by the 88th Congress," *Modern Language Journal* 49, no. 5 (1965): 305–306.

34. Robert G. Mead Jr., "Progress in Hispanic Studies in the United States since World War II," *Hispania* 53, no. 3 (1970): 388.

35. Ibid.

36. Skidmore repeated the utterance at the end of his remarks upon accepting the Distinguished Service Award of the Conference on Latin American History in Washington, D.C., January 9, 2004.

37. Louis A. Pérez Jr., *Cuba and the United States: Ties of Singular Intimacy,* 2nd ed. (Athens: University of Georgia Press, 1997), 238–239, 242–243.

38. Richard R. Fagen, "Studying Latin American Politics: Some Implications of a *Dependencia* Approach," *Latin American Research Review* 12, no. 2 (1977): 4.

39. Howard F. Cline, "The Latin American Studies Association: A Summary Survey with Appendix," *Latin American Research Review* 2, no. 1 (1966): 64.

40. Testimony on Fiscal Year 2002 Appropriations for the Departments of Labor, HHS, and Education, submitted to the House Subcommittee on Labor, HHS, and Education Appropriations, U.S. House of Representatives, March 29, 2001; Demerise R. Dubois, "Responding to the Needs of Our Nation: A Look at the Fulbright and NSEP Education Acts," *Frontiers, the Interdisciplinary Journal of Study Abroad* 1 (1995): 11 (www.frontiersjournal.com/back/one/dub.htm).

41. In 1960 the AATSP published the first edition of the textbook *Modern Spanish* "in the new audio-lingual key" and followed it with *Modern Portuguese* in 1966 (Mead, "Progress," 387, 390–391; Robert G. Mead Jr., "*Hispania* and the AATSP," *Hispania* 75, no. 4 [1992]: 1084). The vogue for Spanish-language teaching using audio-visual methods peaked and declined well before the mid-1980s. Though the emphasis on verbal communication (which conformed to most students' interest) continued, methods more suitable to adult learners than the rote memorization of the audio-lingual methods were introduced.

42. Exceptionally, as Irving Leonard ("Survey of Personnel and Activities," 307, 312) remarked in 1942, Professor Frederick Bliss Luquiens at Yale University had used the "Spanish American orientation" in his "intensive and significant" Spanish language instruction for the previous quarter century.

43. Mead, "Progress," 390; Mead, "*Hispania* and the AATSP," 1085.

44. Chitra Kannan, Financial and DB Administrator, AATSP, Exton, Pa., electronic communication to the author, March 1, 2004.

45. That is, bachelor's degrees granted in Spanish numbered 2,122 in 1949–50, dropped to 1,610 in 1959–60, and grew to 6,381 in 1967–68. The production of Ph.D.'s in Spanish dropped from 34 in 1949–50 to 31 in 1959–60 and then rose to an unprecedented 123 in 1967–68. Between 1960 and 1970 the number of Ph.D.'s in French tripled (from 58 to 181), and bachelor's degrees nearly quadrupled (from 1,927 to 7,624). This parallel trend in comparative Spanish and French growth peaked in the mid-1970s, when Spanish began to pull ahead of French, reversing the traditional ranking. By 1975 bachelor's degrees produced in Spanish significantly outnumbered those granted in French (6,719 Spanish degrees to 5,745 in French), but the production of Ph.D.'s was equivalent: 202 Spanish Ph.D.'s, 200 in French ("Earned De-

grees in French, German, and Spanish Conferred by Degree-granting Institutions, by Level of Degree: 1949–50 to 1997–98," in *Digest of Educational Statistics 2000* [Washington, D.C.: Office of Educational Research and Improvement, 2001], 329, table 289).

46. In the academic year 1984–85, 3,415 bachelor's degrees were granted in Spanish, compared to 2,991 in French; 115 Ph.D.'s were awarded in Spanish, 74 in French. By the mid-1990s Spanish had resumed robust growth at the undergraduate level, with 2.5 times the number of B.A.s granted in French: in 1998, 6,595 to 2,530, respectively, and Ph.D. production in Spanish led French by 160 to 104 (ibid.). Overall, Spanish-language enrollments went from 389,200 in 1970 to 656,600 in 1998, compared to 359,300 enrollments in French in 1970 and 199,100 in 1998 ("Higher Education Registrations in Foreign Languages: 1970 to 1998," in *Statistical Abstract of the United States: 2001* [Washington, D.C.: U. S. Bureau of the Census, 2002], 169, table 271). In the year 2000, 7,031 bachelor's degrees were awarded in Spanish, 2,514 in French; there were 175 Ph.D.'s granted in Spanish, 129 in French ("Bachelor's, Master's, and Doctor's Degrees Conferred by Degree-granting Institutions . . . : 1999–2000," in *Digest of Educational Statistics 2001* [Washington, D.C.: Office of Educational Research and Improvement, 2003], 308, table 258).

47. Martin. C. Needler and Thomas W. Walker, "The Current Status of Latin American Studies Programs," *Latin American Research Review* 6, no. 1 (1971): 133.

48. Ibid.

49. See Drake and Hilbink, "Latin American Studies"; Charles Bergquist, "Recent United States Studies in Latin American History: Trends since 1965," *Latin American Research Review* 9, no. 1 (1974); Albert Fishlow, "The State of Latin American Economics," and Alejandro Portes, "Latin American Sociology in the Mid-1980's: Learning from Hard Experience," in Mitchell, *Changing Perspectives*, respectively, 87–119, 121–142.

50. For the social sciences, Drake and Hilbink, "Latin American Studies," 1–2, argue the opposite view, namely, that the New World and mestizo character of Latin American societies provided them with important commonalities that mitigated against interpreting them as exclusive or exceptional.

51. Alejo Carpentier, "Conciencia e identidad de América," in Alejo Carpentier, *Obras completas de Alejo Carpentier,* vol. 13, *Ensayos* (Mexico City: Siglo Veintiuno, 1990), 133. My translation.

52. Alejo Carpentier, *El reino de este mundo,* 3rd ed. (Mexico City: Compañía General de Ediciones, 1969), 12–14. My translation.

53. Octavio Paz, "A Literature of Foundations," in Octavio Paz, *The Siren and the Seashell,* trans. Lysander Kemp and Margaret Sayers Peden (Austin: University of Texas Press, 1976), 174–175.

54. Arturo Ardao, *Génesis de la idea y el nombre de América Latina* (Caracas: Consejo Nacional de la Cultura, Centro de Estudios Latinoamericanos Rómulo Gallegos, 1980), 43–47. In 1875 Torres Caicedo recalled: "Desde 1851 empezamos a dar a la América española el calificativo de latina. . . . Hay América anglo-sajona, dinamarquesa, holandesa, etc.; la hay española, francesa, portuguesa; y a este grupo, ¿qué denominación científica aplicarle sino el de latina?" (cited ibid., 73–74).

55. José Martí, *José Martí: Selected Writings,* ed. and trans. Esther Allen (New York: Penguin, 2002), 288, 295.

56. Carpentier, "Conciencia," 137; my translation.

57. The exceptions were Pedro Henríquez Ureña's 1940 Charles Eliot Norton Lectures at Harvard University and Enrique Anderson Imbert's history of Spanish American literature of 1954 and his 1960 anthology of Spanish American literature, coedited with Eugenio Florit. Other leaders in the field include José Juan Arrom, who studied Spanish American colonial literature, and Alfredo Roggiano, who guided the development and activities of the Instituto Internacional de Literatura Iberoamericana (Roberto González Echevarría, *Crítica práctica/práctica crítica* [Mexico City: Fondo de Cultura Económica, 2002], 15).

58. Most of these intellectuals came from journalism, often with little university training in the humanities, which meant that they practiced a type of criticism that was not academic and that they did not have the formation to take advantage of the resources for scholarship that the North American university provided. Most did not know English (ibid., 16).

59. Roberto González Echevarría, "A Brief History of the History of Spanish American Literature," in González Echevarría and Pupo-Walker, *Cambridge History*, 1:8.

60. Ibid., 8–9.

61. Like González Echevarría (ibid., 8), I consider that "literary histories are not really metadiscursive, but rather that they belong to the textual economy of the period in which they are written. Literary history, then, is a narrative form, perhaps even a minor genre."

62. Ibid., 23. Arturo Torres Ríoseco, *The Epic of Latin American Literature* (New York: Oxford University Press, 1942); the work was later published in Spanish as *La gran literatura iberoamericana* (Buenos Aires: Emecé, 1945).

63. Mariano Picón-Salas, *De la conquista a la Independencia: Tres siglos de historia cultural hispanoamericana* (Mexico City: Fondo de Cultura Económica, 1944); Picón-Salas, *A Cultural History of Spanish America: From Conquest to Independence*, trans. Irving A. Leonard (Berkeley: University of California Press, 1962).

64. Picón-Salas, *De la conquista*, 15, 49–50, 69–75. See Fernando Ortiz, *Contrapunteo cubano del tabaco y el azúcar* (Havana: J. Montero, 1940).

65. Pedro Henríquez Ureña, "Nota," in Picón-Salas, *De la conquista*, 9–12.

66. These included the Spanish academicians Tomás Navarro Tomás and Angel del Río at Columbia University, Juan A. Centeno at Middlebury, and the Spanish poets Pedro Salinas at Johns Hopkins and Jorge Guillén at Wellesley College (Picón-Salas, *De la conquista*, 15).

67. González Echevarría, "A Brief History," 23–24. In 1947 Lewis Hanke ("Development of Latin-American Studies," 333) lamented the premature death of Henríquez Ureña, "this profound and humane scholar," whom he described as a "final illustration of the inter-American nature of learning today. One of the most fruitful periods of his life was spent in Mexico with Alfonso Reyes, he obtained his doctorate at the University of Minnesota, 'death surprised him' a few months ago in Buenos Aires, and his last work [*Literary Currents*]—a truly notable contribution—was published in the United States." Henríquez Ureña's work appeared in Spanish as *Las corrientes literarias en la América Hispánica*, trans. Joaquín Díez-Canedo (Mexico City: Fondo de Cultura Económica, 1969).

68. González Echevarría, "A Brief History," 24.

69. Bergquist, "Recent United States Studies" 7–8. See Irving A. Leonard, *Books of the Brave: Being an Account of Books and Men in the Spanish Conquest and Settlement of the Sixteenth-Century New World* (1949), with a new introduction by Rolena Adorno (Berkeley: University of California Press, 1992); Lewis Hanke, *The Spanish Struggle for Justice in the Conquest of America* (Philadelphia: University of Pennsylvania Press, 1949); R. B. Cunningham Graham, *The Horses of the Conquest* (1930), ed. Robert Moorman Denhardt (Norman: University of Oklahoma Press, 1949).

70. Rolena Adorno, Introduction to Leonard, *Books of the Brave*, xxxi.

71. Ibid., xv–xxv.

72. Roberto González Echevarría, "José Martí: An Introduction," in Martí, *José Martí: Selected Writings*, xvii.

73. Allen, in Martí, *José Martí: Selected Writings*, 415–416. Allen's substantial selection and translation is the first to appear since Onís's 1953 anthology. During his years in New York Martí brought out some twenty-nine short essays in the daily *New York Sun*, only a few of which were originally written in English, and he wrote an occasional letter to the editor, such as the one published in the *New York Evening Post* in 1889 opposing the plan of the U.S. annexation of Cuba (Martí, *José Martí: Selected Writings*, 32–40, 263–267). Upon learning of Martí's death in battle in May 1895, the *Sun*'s longtime editor and owner, Charles A. Dana, published a moving

tribute to Martí as "a man of genius, of imagination, of hope and courage" (ibid., 421). Yet when in 1896 Andrew Summers Rowan and Marathon Montrose Ramsey published a lengthy and well-informed account of Cuba's history, geography, and current political upheaval in response to the need for balanced information regarding "the Cuban question," Martí appears in the briefest mentions as "chief organizer" of the "rising in Cuba" and the "acknowledged head and general-in-chief of the insurrection," who was "killed in action May 19 [1895]" (Rowan and Ramsey, *The Island of Cuba: A Descriptive and Historical Account of the "Great Antilla"* [New York: Henry Holt, 1896], 151, 153, 155). I thank Roberto González Echevarría for sharing this rare source.

74. Allen, in Martí, *José Martí: Selected Writings*, 415.

75. Enrique Anderson Imbert, *Historia de la literatura hispanoamericana*, 2 vols. (Buenos Aires: Fondo de Cultura Económica, 1954); Anderson Imbert, *Spanish American Literature: A History*, trans. John V. Falconieri, 2nd ed. revised and updated by Elaine Malley (Detroit: Wayne State University Press, 1969).

76. González Echevarría, "A Brief History," 26.

77. Irving A. Leonard, *Baroque Times in Old Mexico* (Ann Arbor: University of Michigan Press, 1959); Juan Rulfo, *Pedro Páramo*, trans. Lysander Kemp (New York: Grove Press, 1959); Randolph D. Pope, "The Spanish American Novel from 1950 to 1975," in González Echevarría and Pupo-Walker, *Cambridge History*, 2:232.

78. Anthony Kerrigan's translations of Borges's short stories appeared in 1962 and 1967: Jorge Luis Borges, *Ficciones*, ed. Anthony Kerrigan (New York: Grove Press, 1962); and Borges, *A Personal Anthology*, ed. Anthony Kerrigan (New York: Grove Press, 1967). In 1965 the English translation, by Robert Lima, of an expanded version of Ana María Barrenechea's 1957 *La expresión de la irrealidad en la obra de Jorge Luis Borges* (Mexico City: Colegio de Mexico, 1957) appeared under the title *Borges the Labyrinth Maker* (New York: New York University Press, 1965); and in 1969 Ronald Christ's *The Narrow Act: Borges' Art of Allusion* (New York: New York University Press, 1969) was published. In 1970 Norman Thomas di Giovanni's translations of Borges's stories appeared, and in 1983 James Irby and Donald Yates's translations of Borges's stories came out under the title *Labyrinths:* Jorge Luis Borges, *The Aleph and Other Stories, 1933–1969*, trans. Norman Thomas di Giovanni (New York: E. P. Dutton, 1970); Borges, *Labyrinths: Selected Stories and Other Writings*, ed. and trans. Donald A. Yates and James E. Irby (New York: Modern Library, 1983).

79. Borges, Preface to *The Aleph*, 9. Borges's paternal grandmother was English (Frances Haslam, "from Staffordshire of Northumbrian stock").

80. As different as the Boom novels were from one another—and the minimal list must include Cortázar, Fuentes, García Márquez, Rulfo, and Vargas Llosa—they shared a move away from their immediate predecessors (except for Borges) and harked back to the experimentation of the avant-garde movements of the early part of the century, such as the works of Macedonio Fernández. They employed complex points of view and made time and linear progress questionable (Pope, "Spanish American Novel," 229, 231). They were "ambitious in scope, all-embracing in their implications, and technically adventurous" (Standish, "Mexico, Central America, the Caribbean, and the Andes," 124).

81. Pope, "Spanish American Novel," 228, 230. On the Casa de las Américas cultural initiatives, see Franco, *Decline and Fall*.

82. Vera M. Kutzinski, "Afro-Hispanic American Literature," in González Echevarría and Pupo-Walker, *Cambridge History*, 2:164.

83. *Review*, which began publication in 1968, came out of efforts by David Rockefeller and other businessmen who established the Center for Inter-American Relations in 1965 for the (cold war) purpose of understanding the political, economic, and cultural issues facing the Americas. In 1985 the center and its *Review* were absorbed into the Americas Society, whose mission statement still today asserts that "innovative artistic expression is vital to free societies

and provides an invaluable window on the ever-evolving reality of our Hemisphere." For the social sciences, the coincident event was the 1965 creation of the *Latin American Research Review* and its 1967 transfer to the newly founded (1966) Latin American Studies Association (Cline, "Latin American Studies Association," 67, 69). Its cold war thrust, however, was not the promotion of Latin American culture but rather the creation of responsible social science research in the wake of the 1965 Project Camelot scandal and the ethical debate that it generated (Berger, *Under Northern Eyes*, 93). Devoted mainly (with notable exceptions) to the social sciences in the first decade and a half of its existence, *LARR* began regularly to publish review articles in literature on the 1980s (Drake and Hilbink, "Latin American Studies," 19; "Index 1965–1995," *Latin American Research Review* 31, no. 4 [1996]: 161–165).

84. Although he was designated a "Contributing Editor" on the masthead of the journal, it was clearly Rodríguez Monegal's vast range of contacts in the international literary community that brought Borges and Neruda, to name only two, to the pages of *Review*.

85. *Review* originally reprinted significant English-language reviews of Latin American literature and presented translations of interviews and longer essays; in 1971 the format was expanded to include original essays and reviews and excerpts of literary works that were about to appear (The Editors, "Foreword," *Review* 72 [1971–72]: 1).

86. *Mundo Nuevo* is widely known as an anti-Castro weapon in the cultural cold war for its indirect funding by the CIA. Most recently, Franco (*Decline and Fall*, 44, 45, 48) called the journal "another Cold War warrior," describing it and its promotion of the Boom as efforts at "weaning influential intellectuals away from Cuban influence." Citing the magazine's funding by the Instituto Latinoamericano de Relaciones Internacionales (ILARI) and the Ford Foundation, and the reported evidence of its having received CIA funds, Franco underscores the charge, noting that some authors initially refused to collaborate with the magazine and others regretted having done so. She nevertheless acknowledges the magazine's role in registering "Latin American specificity within an international culture."

87. See Gabriel García Márquez, "El insomnio en Macondo," and Robert H. Nisbet, "El Plan Camelot: Una autopsia," *Mundo Nuevo* 9 (March 1967), 9–17, 78–94, respectively. Operation Camelot (1965) had been designed to develop a general social systems model that would make it possible to predict and influence politically significant aspects of social change in the developing nations of the world. It unraveled when the noted Norwegian sociologist and peace studies specialist Johan Galtung declined the invitation to participate. When he informed his Latin American colleagues about the project, the news spread, and it ultimately prompted a protest by the president of Chile to the U.S. State Department, a debate in the U.S. Congress, and the cancellation of the project worldwide (Wallerstein, "Unintended Consequences," 220, 222–224). Engerman ("Rethinking Cold War Universities," 87–88) has observed that "for many scholars at the time and since, Project Camelot represented a high-water mark of the corruption of social science by Cold War needs," and he identified its ultimate origins in World War II, citing Ellen Herman's study of changes in intellectual life that had been brought about by the war, in which the line between military and civilian research had been blurred and behavioralist social science had arisen. Project Camelot was at least partly responsible, according to Engerman ("Rethinking Cold War Universities," 94), for "shaping later (and more critical) views of the social-scientific enterprise."

88. Aníbal González Pérez, "Literary Criticism in Spanish America" in González Echevarría and Pupo-Walker, *Cambridge History*, 2:454.

89. González Echevarría, "A Brief History," 30–31.

90. Carlos Fuentes, *The Death of Artemio Cruz*, trans. Sam Hileman (New York: Farrar, Straus and Giroux, 1964); Julio Cortázar, *Hopscotch*, trans. Gregory Rabassa (New York: Random House, 1966); Mario Vargas Llosa, *Time of the Hero*, trans. Lysander Kemp (New York: Grove Press, 1966); and Gabriel García Márquez, *One Hundred Years of Solitude*, trans. Gregory Rabassa (New York: Harper and Row, 1970). One of the first books published in English about

these writers, as well as about Rulfo, Carpentier, Asturias, Borges, and Onetti, was Luis Harss and Barbara Dohmann, eds., *Into the Mainstream: Conversations with Latin American Writers* (New York: Harper and Row, 1967); see Pope, "Spanish American Novel," 231.

91. Pope, "Spanish American Novel," 229; José Donoso, *Historia personal del "Boom"* (Barcelona: Anagrama, 1972); Donoso, *The "Boom" in Spanish American Literature: A Personal History*, trans. Gregory Kolovskos (New York: Columbia University Press, 1977); Emir Rodríguez Monegal, *El boom de la novela latinoamericana* (Caracas: Tiempo Nuevo, 1972).

92. Octavio Paz, *Los hijos del limo: Del romanticismo a la vanguardia* (Barcelona: Seix Barral, 1974); Paz, *Children of the Mire* (Cambridge: Harvard University Press, 1974).

93. González Echevarría, "A Brief History," 30; Emir Rodríguez Monegal, *The Borzoi Anthology of Latin American Literature from the Time of Columbus to the Twentieth Century*, 2 vols. (New York: Knopf, 1977); Jean Franco, *Spanish American Literature since Independence* (New York: Barnes and Noble, 1973).

94. Rodríguez Monegal, *Borzoi Anthology*, xv.

95. González Echevarría ("A Brief History," 31) suggests that Paz's formulation, perhaps merely an "enabling fiction, a literary myth," was "a very romantic kind of project, very much akin to what the European Romantics did with the Middle Ages."

96. José Juan Arrom, *Esquema generacional de las letras hispanoamericanas: Ensayo de un método* (1963), 2nd ed. (Bogotá: Instituto Caro y Cuervo, 1977).

97. Roberto González Echevarría, *The Pilgrim at Home* (Ithaca: Cornell University Press, 1977). The second English-language edition appeared in 1990 (Austin: University of Texas Press), and the second revised and enlarged Spanish-language edition has recently been published under the title *Alejo Carpentier: El peregrino en su patria* (Madrid: Gredos, 2004).

98. Rolena Adorno, *Guaman Poma: Writing and Resistance in Colonial Peru* (1986), 2nd ed. (Austin: University of Texas Press, 2000); Adorno, *Guaman Poma: Literatura de resistencia en el Perú colonial*, trans. Martín Mur U (Mexico City: Siglo Veintiuno, 1991).

99. Roberto González Echevarría, "The Criticism of Latin American Literature Today: Adorno, Molloy, Magnarelli," *Profession 87* (1987): 11–12.

100. Octavio Paz, *Sor Juana Inés de la Cruz, o Las trampas de la fe* (México City: Fondo de Cultura Económica, 1982); Paz, *Sor Juana Inés de la Cruz, o Las trampas de la fe*, 2nd ed. (Barcelona: Círculo de Lectores, 1994); Paz, *Sor Juana, or the Traps of Faith*, trans. Margaret Sayers Peden (Cambridge: Harvard University Press, 1988).

101. Georgina Sabat de Rivers, *Estudios de literatura hispanoamericana: Sor Juana Inés de la Cruz y otros poetas barrocos de la colonia* (Barcelona: Promociones y Publicaciones Universitarias, 1992); Sabat de Rivers, *En busca de Sor Juana* (Mexico City: Universidad Nacional Autónoma de México, 1998); Rosa Perelmuter, *Noche intelectual: la oscuridad idiomática en el Primero sueño* (Mexico City: Universidad Nacional Autónoma de México, 1982); Perelmuter, *Los límites de la femineidad en Sor Juana Inés de la Cruz: Estrategias retóricas y recepción literaria* (Madrid: Iberoamericana, 2004); Margo Glantz, *Sor Juana Inés de la Cruz: ¿Hagiografía o autobiografía?* (Mexico City: Grijalbo and Universidad Nacional Autónoma de México, 1995); Stephanie Merrim, ed., *Feminist Perspectives on Sor Juana Inés de la Cruz* (Detroit: Wayne State University Press, 1991); Stephanie Merrim, *Early Modern Women's Writing and Sor Juana Inés de la Cruz* (Nashville: Vanderbilt University Press, 1999); José Antonio Rodríguez Garrido, *La Carta Atenagórica de Sor Juana: Textos inéditos de una polémica* (Mexico City: Universidad Nacional Autónoma de México, 2004); Frederick Luciani, *Literary Self-Fashioning in Sor Juana Inés de la Cruz* (Lewisburg, Pa.: Bucknell University Press, 2004).

102. Sor Juana Inés de la Cruz, *A Woman of Genius: The Intellectual Autobiography of Sor Juana Inés de la Cruz*, ed. and trans. Margaret Sayers Peden, 2nd ed. (Salisbury, Conn.: Lime Rock Press, 1987); Sor Juana Inés de la Cruz, *A Sor Juana Anthology*, trans. Alan Trueblood, (Cambridge: Harvard University Press, 1988); Sor Juana Inés de la Cruz, *The Answer/La Respuesta, including a Selection of Poems*, ed. and trans. Electa Arenal and Amanda Powell (New York: Feminist Press, 1994).

103. Wallerstein, "Unintended Consequences," 195.

104. Roberto González Echevarría, *Myth and Archive: A Theory of Latin American Narrative* (1990; rpt. Durham: Duke University Press, 1998), and for the Spanish-language audience, *Mito y archivo: una teoría de la narrativa latinoamericana*, trans. Virginia Aguirre Muñoz (Mexico City: Fondo de Cultura Económica, 2000).

105. In the first thirty years of publication of *LARR*, Argentina represented the greatest number of essays devoted to the literature of a single country (fourteen entries); Mexico and Cuba followed, with seven entries each ("Index 1965–1959," 163–165).

106. Josefina Ludmer, *The Gaucho Genre: A Treatise on the Motherland*, trans. Molly Weigel (Durham: Duke University Press, 2002), originally published under the title *El género gauchesco: Un tratado sobre la patria* (Buenos Aires: Libros Perfil, 1988); Ludmer, *El cuerpo del delito: Un manual* (Buenos Aires: Libros Perfil, 1999), published in English as *The Corpus Delicti: A Manual of Argentine Fictions*, trans. Glen S. Close (Pittsburgh: University of Pittsburgh Press, 2004).

107. See also Ana Pizarro, ed., *América Latina: Palabra, literatura e cultura*, 3 vols. (São Paulo: Memorial, 1993–1995).

108. González Echevarría, *Crítica práctica*, 20.

109. Ibid., 22, 300.

110. Ibid., 23.

111. Ethnic studies and women's studies inverted the pattern of 1945–70 area studies, which had been a "top-down" enterprise, initiated by government agencies, university administrations, and large foundations. These new departures, in contrast, had "bottom-up origins," representing "the (largely post-1968) revolt of those whom the university had 'forgotten'" (Wallerstein, "Unintended Consequences," 227).

112. Ofelia García, "La enseñanza del español en las escuelas de los Estados Unidos: Pasado y presente," II Congreso Internacional de la Lengua Española, Valladolid, cvc.cervantes. es/obref/congresos/valladolid/ponencias/unidad_diversidad_del_espanol/3_el_espanol_en_ los_EEUU/garcia_o.htm. See also Ofelia García, "From Goya Portraits to Goya Beans: Elite Traditions and Popular Streams in U.S. Spanish Language Policy," *Southwest Journal of Linguistics* 12 (1993).

113. García, "La enseñanza," 5.

114. Jill Fitzgerald, "Views on Bilingualism in the United States: A Selective Historical Review," *Bilingual Research Journal* 17 (Winter–Spring 1993): 42.

115. García, "La enseñanza," 6.

116. Kutzinski, "Afro-Hispanic American Literature," 164.

117. See William Luis, "Latino US Literature," in *The Companion to Latin American Studies*, ed. Philip Swanson (New York: Oxford University Press, 2003), 122–153; Luis, "Latin American (Hispanic Caribbean) Literature Written in the United States," in González Echevarría and Pupo-Walker, *Cambridge History*, 2:526–556, 3:720–738; Luis, *Dance between Two Cultures: Latino Caribbean Literature Written in the United States* (Nashville: Vanderbilt University Press, 1997); Luis Leal and Manuel M. Martínez Rodríguez, "Chicano Literature," in González Echevarría and Pupo-Walker, *Cambridge History*, 2:557–586, 3:739–742; Vera M. Kutzinski, "Afro-Hispanic American Literature," in González Echevarría and Pupo-Walker, *Cambridge History*, 2:164–194, 3:632–642; Kutzinski, *Against the American Grain: Myth and History in William Carlos Williams, Jay Wright, and Nicolás Guillén* (Baltimore: Johns Hopkins University Press, 1987); Kutzinski, *Sugar's Secrets: Race and the Erotics of Cuban Nationalism* (Charlottesville: University Press of Virginia, 1993).

118. Drake and Hilbink, "Latin American Studies," 24.

119. John Beverly (*"Adiós:* A National Allegory [Some Reflections on Latin American Cultural Studies]," in *Contemporary Latin American Cultural Studies*, ed. Stephen Hart and Richard Young [London: Arnold, 2003], 56) cites Hugo Achugar on this point.

120. Apart from ethnic studies' location in American studies, another model for a home

base for Hispanic-related ethnic studies is Yale University's Program in Ethnicity, Race, and Migration.

121. Hart and Young, Introduction to Hart and Young, *Contemporary Latin American Cultural Studies*, 8; Beatriz Sarlo, "Cultural Studies and Literary Criticism at the Crossroads of Values," *Journal of Latin American Cultural Studies* 8, no. 1 (1999): 118, points to the pioneering work of Richard Hoggart, Stuart Hall, and Raymond Williams in the United Kingdom.

122. Hart and Young, Introduction to Hart and Young, *Contemporary Latin American Cultural Studies*, 2. See Angel Rama, *The Lettered City* (1984), ed. and trans. John Charles Chasteen (Durham: Duke University Press, 1996). For recent perspectives on Latin American cultural and subaltern studies, see the remarks by Daniel Mato, George Yúdice, Robert Carr, and Ileana Rodríguez in *LASA Forum* 33, no. 2 (2002): 8–15.

123. Hart and Young, *Contemporary Latin American Cultural Studies*, 3–4.

124. Ibid., 3–7. Walter Mignolo's *The Darker Side of the Renaissance: Literacy, Territoriality, and Colonization* (Ann Arbor: University of Michigan Press, 1995), exemplifies the recent trend. Before the current identity politics thrust of Mignolo's and others' works, in the 1970s Roberto González Echevarría (*Relecturas: Estudios de literatura cubana* [Caracas: Monte Avila, 1976], 21) had argued not only that colonialism's legacy was the destruction of dominion over territories but also that those territories' history and the mechanisms of its destruction and rewriting were visible "with a clarity that never fails to astonish" in colonial Spanish American literature. The necessary counteroffensive of decolonization signaled by González Echevarría framed my 1986 monograph on the *Nueva corónica y buen gobierno* of Felipe Guaman Poma de Ayala, which I characterized as being "engaged in a process of decolonization in which the territories to be recovered were not only geographical but also spiritual and historical" (Adorno, *Guaman Poma: Writing and Resistance*, 3).

125. Some of the key texts were published in two edited volumes: Emilie Bergmann and Paul Julian Smith's *Entiendes? Queer Readings, Hispanic Writings* (Durham: Duke University Press, 1995) and Daniel Balderston and Donna Guy's *Sex and Sexuality in Latin America* (New York: New York University Press, 1997). Key figures in this field are Sylvia Molloy, David William Foster, Oscar Montero, Daniel Balderston, Robert Irwin, Licia Fiol Matta, and José Quiroga. Quiroga's *Tropics of Desire* (New York: New York University Press, 2000) is currently the most influential book in the field. A useful bibliographic resource on sexuality studies in Latin America is housed on the Web page of the Stanford University Library.

126. "Editorial," *Ideologies and Literature: A Journal of Hispanic and Luso-Brazilian Literatures* 1, no. 1 (December 1976–January 1977), 3.

127. David Viñas et al., *Más allá del boom: Literatura y mercado* (Mexico City: Marcha Editores, 1981).

128. See Roberto González Echevarría, "The Dictatorship of Rhetoric/The Rhetoric of Dictatorship: Carpentier, García Márquez, and Roa Bastos," *Latin American Research Review* 15, no. 3 (1980): 205–228; an expanded version appears in Roberto González Echevarria, *The Voice of the Masters* (Austin: University of Texas Press, 1985), 64–85.

129. Patricia Seed, "Colonial and Postcolonial Discourse," *Latin American Research Review* 26, no. 3 (1991): 181–200, esp. 183; Hernan Vidal, "The Concept of Colonial and Postcolonial Discourse: A Perspective from Literary Criticism," *Latin American Research Review* 28, no. 3 (1993): 113–119; Walter D. Mignolo, "Colonial and Postcolonial Discourse: Cultural Critique or Academic Colonialism?" *Latin American Research Review* 28, no. 3 (1993): 120–134; Rolena Adorno, "Reconsidering Colonial Discourse for Sixteenth- and Seventeenth-Century Spanish America," *Latin American Research Review* 28, no. 3 (1993): 135–145; and Patricia Seed, "More Colonial and Postcolonial Discourses," *Latin American Research Review* 28, no. 3 (1993): 146–152.

130. Mike González and David Treece, *The Gathering of Voices: The Twentieth-Century Poetry of Latin America* (London: Verso, 1992).

131. Roberto González Echevarría, *Celestina's Brood: Continuities of the Baroque in Spanish*

and Latin American Literature (Durham: Duke University Press, 1993); Mabel Moraña, ed., *Relecturas del Barroco de Indias* (Hanover, N.H.: Ediciones del Norte, 1994). See Antony Higgins, "Dos nuevas lecturas del barroco," *Revista Iberoamericana* 61, nos. 172–173 (July–December, 1995): 685–689.

132. For example, Richard J. Kaliman ("What Is 'Interesting' in Latin American Cultural Studies," *Journal of Latin American Cultural Studies* 7, no. 2 [1998]: 267–268) engages Walter Mignolo's work and asks whether "the intellectual inertia of the field leads to the work of the cultural scholar not being led by the problems of Latin American cultural reality and, thus, to the practices falling outside the interests of the discipline."

133. Sarlo, "Cultural Studies," 118, 119.

134. Alberto Moreiras, "The Order of Order: On the Reluctant Culturalism of Anti-Subalternist Critiques," *Journal of Latin American Cultural Studies* 8, no. 1 (1999): 138, 139.

135. Drake and Hilbink ("Latin American Studies," 4) cite U.S. Board of Foreign Scholarships, *Fulbright Program Exchanges Annual Report, 1984–1985* (Washington, D.C., The Board, 1985).

Acknowledgments

This volume is part of the Humanities Initiative of the American Academy of Arts and Sciences, chaired by Denis Donoghue, Steven Marcus, Francis C. Oakley, and Patricia Meyer Spacks. The academy's chief executive officer, Leslie Berlowitz, has been an engaged supporter of this volume from its inception and continues to direct the overall initiative. Mapping the Humanities, a project of the Initiative, is a series of volumes intended to describe the evolution and changes in the humanities in recent years. It is under the leadership of Patricia Meyer Spacks, president of the academy, and Steven Marcus, editor of the academy. We are grateful to the following foundations whose funding has helped to support this series: the William and Flora Hewlett Foundation, the Rockefeller Foundation, and the Sara Lee Foundation.

As editor of this volume, I wish also to thank several other individuals for their roles in making this book a reality. Phyllis Bendell of the academy's publications office has been invaluable in overseeing the publication process. Editor Jacqueline Wehmueller of the Johns Hopkins University Press has been a joy to work with. Ann Twombly has been an exemplary copy editor. Malcolm Richardson, former program director of the Humanities Initiative, was a key advisor in the early stages of this project and capably oversaw a conference at the Academy's House in Cambridge, Massachusetts, where the contributors were able to react to each other's drafts and integrate the volume thematically. Andrew Heinze, J. B. Schneewind, and Werner Sollors were also helpful participants in this project in its early stages. The focus on the theme of "inclusion" was Schneewind's idea. I owe special thanks to Thomas Bender for a discerning critique of the volume as a whole when in draft. Bender's suggestions have made this book much better than it would have been without his advice. Finally, I want to say that my thirteen contributors have been ideal colleagues and collectively give the lie to the widespread claim that editing multi-authored volumes is a dreadful experience.

—David A. Hollinger

CONTRIBUTORS

Rolena Adorno is Reuben Post Halleck Professor of Spanish at Yale University. Her books include *Guaman Poma: Writing and Resistance in Colonial Peru* (Austin, 1986; 2nd edition 2000) and *The Polemics of Possession in Latin American Literary Narrative* (2006). She is a fellow of the American Academy of Arts and Sciences.

Andrew E. Barshay teaches modern Japanese history at the University of California at Berkeley. He has published *The Social Sciences in Modern Japan: The Marxian and Modernist Traditions* (Berkeley, 2004) and is currently writing "The Gods Left First: Imperial Collapse and the Repatriation of Japanese from Northeast Asia, 1945–1956."

David C. Engerman is an associate professor of history at Brandeis University. He is the author of *Modernization from the Other Shore* (Cambridge, Mass., 2003), as well as articles in *Diplomatic History, Modern Intellectual History*, and other journals.

Roger L. Geiger is Distinguished Professor of Higher Education at Pennsylvania State University. His recent publications include *Knowledge and Money* (Stanford, 2004), *The American College in the Nineteenth Century* (Nashville, 2000), and a reissue of *Research and Relevant Knowledge* and *To Advance Knowledge* (Somerset, N.J., 2004).

John Guillory is Silver Professor of English and chair of the Department of English at New York University. He is the author of *Cultural Capital: The Problem of Literary Canon Formation* (Chicago, 1993) and of numerous essays on the history and sociology of literary study and on Renaissance literature, including the forthcoming "The Bachelor State: Philosophy and Sovereignty in Bacon's 'New Atlantis,'" to be published by Princeton University Press in 2006.

David A. Hollinger is Preston Hotchkis Professor of History at the University of California at Berkeley. His recent publications include *Cosmopolitanism and Solidarity* (Madison, 2006) and the tenth anniversary edition of

"

Postethnic America: Beyond Multiculturalism (New York, 2006). He is a fellow of the American Academy of Arts and Sciences.

JONATHAN SCOTT HOLLOWAY is a professor of African American studies, history, and American studies at Yale University. He is the author of *Confronting the Veil: Abram Harris Jr., E. Franklin Frazier, and Ralph Bunche, 1941–2000* (Chapel Hill, 2002) and the editor of Ralph Bunche's *A Brief and Tentative Analysis of Negro Leadership* (New York, 2005).

MARTIN JAY is Sidney Hellman Ehrman Professor of History at the University of California at Berkeley. His most recent books are *Refractions of Violence* (New York, 2003) and *Songs of Experience: Modern European and American Variations on a Universal Theme* (Berkeley, 2004). He is a fellow of the American Academy of Arts and Sciences.

JAMES T. KLOPPENBERG is Harvard College Professor and David Woods Kemper '41 Professor of American History at Harvard University. He is the author of *Uncertain Victory: Social Democracy and Progressivism in European and American Thought, 1870–1920* (New York, 1986) and *The Virtues of Liberalism* (New York, 1998) and the coeditor, with Richard Wightman Fox, of *A Companion to American Thought* (Oxford, U.K., 1995).

BRUCE KUKLICK is Nichols Professor of History at the University of Pennsylvania. His most recent book is *Blind Oracles: Intellectuals and War from Kennan to Kissinger* (Princeton, 2006).

JOHN T. MCGREEVY is a professor of history at the University of Notre Dame. He is the author of *Catholicism and American Freedom: A History* (New York, 2003) and *Parish Boundaries: The Catholic Encounter with Race in the Twentieth-Century Urban North* (Chicago, 1996).

ROSALIND ROSENBERG is Anne Whitney Olin Professor of History at Barnard College, Columbia University. Her recent publications include *Changing the Subject: How the Women of Columbia Shaped the Way We Think about Sex and Politics* (New York, 2004).

JOAN SHELLEY RUBIN is a professor of history at the University of Rochester. She is the author of *The Making of Middlebrow Culture* (Chapel Hill, 1992) and a book on American readers and the uses of poetry, forthcoming from Harvard University Press in 2007.

Leila Zenderland is a professor of American studies at California State University at Fullerton. Her publications include *Measuring Minds: Henry Herbert Goddard and the Origins of American Intelligence Testing* (Cambridge, U.K., 1998).

INDEX